Herma

THE SEA WAR IN KOREA

The SEA WAR in KOREA

Malcolm W. Cagle & Frank A. Manson

Naval Institute Press
Annapolis, Maryland

Naval Institute Press
291 Wood Road
Annapolis, MD 21402

The Library of Congress has assigned catalog card number 57-11294 to this book.

Printed in the United States of America on acid-free paper ∞

07 06 05 04 03 02 01 00   9 8 7 6 5 4 3 2

Foreword:

The Navy's Role in Limited War

When the Communists invaded Korea on 25 June 1950, the United States was neither expecting nor prepared to fight in that remote area. They apparently had analyzed United States willingness, readiness, and ability to fight and concluded that we would simply watch and complain, but not fight. The Communists apparently saw an opportunity to seize some additional free world territory with little risk and at little cost.

The United States Army had no troops in Korea, the United States Air Force had only a few wings in the Far East, and the United States Navy had only one cruiser, four destroyers, and a few minesweepers in the Sea of Japan.

With so few combat forces initially available, control of the seas (taken for granted as is too often the case) was a prerequisite in implementing the United Nations decision to resist aggression against the Republic of Korea. *Without* the capability to use the seas, the decision to intervene on a rocky peninsula half-a-world away would have been meaningless and unenforceable. *With* control of the seas, the decision was sound and reasonable.

Once the decision was made, ships of the free world navies converged on Korea from every one of the seven seas—combatant ships, oilers, supply ships, ships loaded with troops, ammunition, guns, tanks, and aircraft; ships from the South China Sea, the Indian Ocean, the Pacific, the Atlantic, and from the far-away Mediterranean.

Control of the seas gave the United Nations the advantage of mobility —the opportunity to consolidate and combine the free world's economic and military strength. Seapower brought American troops, first from Japan, later from the United States. Seapower defeated the initial aggression with the classic amphibious assault at Inchon. Seapower made it possible to redeploy the U. S. forces from Hungnam. Seapower helped to limit the conflict.

Use of the seas was denied to the Communists. This placed serious limitations on their ability to build up military power in Korea. It exposed the land flanks of the North Koreans (and later the Red Chinese). It denied them easy resupply by sea.

The Communists' attempt to seize Korea by military action was a failure. But this failure does not mean an abandonment of military adventures by the Communists. They will try again whenever other means fail or when they see a weakness they can exploit or find a vacuum they can fill.

The Communists have stated repeatedly that any means may be used to attain their goal of world domination, including war. The most important tenet of Communism—the one given most stress in their doctrine—is that Communism must continuously strive to possess all power, and conversely to destroy all rival power. This proposition is basic to Communism. It must be borne in mind constantly when dealing with Communists. Their tenet and their goal do not change.

There are many other explosive areas in the world. They are explosive because of this standing threat and this goal of Communism.

While the Korean War was unusual in many respects, it nevertheless has great meaning and significance for the future. In 1957 terminology, it would be called a "limited war." In the thermonuclear age, as major nations of the world improve their capability to wreak mutual destruction upon one another, the probability of all-out nuclear war is diminished. The probability of limited war is increased. It is important that the Korean War receive careful study. It is the first limited war the United Nations have fought against Communist totalitarianism.

The naval history of the Korean War is outlined in this book in great detail. The authors have distilled from it the lessons, results, and significance of the Korean War. This effort should be of great interest and benefit to every student of international or military affairs.

Of the many lessons of the Korean War, three stand out above all others:

1. The military forces of the United States must be vigilant and ready to defeat aggression in any area and in any form, whether it be large or small, atomic or conventional. Our hope, of course, is that our visible, vigilant strength will discourage Communist aggression. To do so, we must be capable of effective counteraction, ranging from the use of a squad of Marines to the use of atomic-tipped ballistic missiles. Our Navy must have many different arrows in its quiver.
2. Control of the sea is prerequisite to victory in modern war, whatever its size, type, or scope.
3. The Korean War was a limited war. A limited war is the type of war most likely to occur in the thermonuclear age.

ARLEIGH A. BURKE
Admiral, United States Navy
Chief of Naval Operations

Washington, D.C.
1 May 1957

Preface

Four years have passed since the end of the Korean War. Other international emergencies have come and gone, and some are still with us. The period from June 1950 to the present has been one of intense pressure upon every conscientious naval officer in the Fleet. Ships have toiled long hours, days, weeks, and months, to raise and maintain the readiness of the Fleet. Only in the war colleges, and to a restricted degree there, has it been possible for even the career officer, who makes the study of war his life's work, to assimilate the many lessons and the deep significance of the Korean War.

In passing time, as the U. S. Navy moves away from the Korean War, it becomes increasingly obvious how that war wrought tremendous changes upon naval thinking, naval developments, naval strategy, and naval policy. In every field—amphibious, logistical, aviation, operational and planning— the impact was monumental. Korea was a naval proving ground. Its lessons, some still undigested, and its significance, yet largely unappreciated, are still unconsciously erupting, and disrupting the Fleet.

Yet, strangely, there is a tendency in military circles to dismiss the Korean War as one so artificial, anachronistic, unorthodox, and hedged with restrictions that any study of it is unprofitable, and more likely to impress the student with wrong conclusions than right ones. Nothing could be further from the truth. It is indeed true that the Korean War was artificial and unique in many respects. So, indeed, is every war. None is standard. To accept the Korean War as a standard pattern for future war would be as imprudent as it would be to prepare solely for an atomic-blitz type war.

The Korean War taught many lessons of the highest significance; it initiated progress in the field of amphibious warfare which had been stalled by between-the-wars events; it revitalized naval aviation; it reemphasized the importance of mine warfare.

This book is not written as history alone. The authors hope it is also, and more importantly, history *plus* significance, a form of rigorous introspection and self-analysis. Only by measuring the lessons of the past can we forge a yardstick for the future. Only by interpreting the lessons of the Korean War can we logically prepare for the future wars.

This book seeks to distill the essence of the naval portion of the Korean War in a readable, concise, and interesting manner, with three objectives in mind: First, to teach and transmit the many naval lessons of that war; second, to record and preserve the splendid accomplishments of the United States Navy in the seas surrounding that beleaguered peninsula; third, to document the conclusion that the advent of the atomic age, whether it brings large or small wars or an indefinite period of tense preparedness, has not diminished, but rather has *increased,* the need for a strong and adequate Navy.

This book is therefore dedicated to all the officers and men of the United States Navy, who, in their service in Korea, advanced the Navy's skill, and who are today maintaining the Navy strong, vigilant, and ready in the continuing task of keeping our beloved country safe and secure.

MALCOLM W. CAGLE
Commander, U. S. Navy
FRANK A. MANSON
Commander, U. S. Navy

Washington, D.C.
25 March 1957

Contents

Communist Mining Campaign——The Modern Mine——U. S.
Navy Mine Warfare Cutback, 1945-50——Shoestring Navy——
Beginning the Sweep of the Wonsan Minefield——Efforts to
Clear a Channel——The Sinking of *Pirate* and *Pledge*——The
Discovery of Magnetic Mines in Wonsan——North Korean Min-
ing Tactics——Marine Air Comes to Wonsan——Wonsan Taken
by the ROKs——Seventh Division Lands at Iwon——Wonsan
Critique

sponsibility for the Interdiction Campaign and Its Coordination
——Reasons for Failure of Interdiction——Communist Reaction
to the Interdiction Campaign——The Weapons of Interdiction
Used in Korea——The Target Systems of the Communists——
Summary

List of Illustrations

U. S. NAVAL COMMANDERS: RADM John E. Gingrich.
RADM Bernard L. Austin. CDR Gordon Gemmill. CDR Paul
N. Gray.

THE TIDE THAT TURNED: Inchon's mudflats. Destruction
of port facilities. Inchon's stone seawall. LCMs at Inchon.

INCHON BALANCING ACTS: *LST-799* high and dry. Salvaging submerged tank. LCM rides pickaback on LST.

PARTICIPANTS IN KOREAN NAVAL OPERATIONS: LT
E. F. Clark wins Navy Cross. RADM J. M. Higgins and CAPT
R. C. Williams. Marine LT John Yancey and LCDR Frank
Manson. LCDR D'Arcy Shouldice wins Navy Cross.

OCCUPATIONAL HAZARDS OFF WONSAN: *Firecrest* explodes contact floater mine. *MSB-5* tows captured mine. Communist shore batteries straddle sweepers.

MINE PLUMES: Communist influence-mines explode. *Endicott*'s rifle fire dispatches enemy mine. PBM detonates moored
mine.

MINING COUNTERMEASURES: Lowering paravanes over
the side. *Mocking Bird* lowers acoustic detonator. *Gull* streams
magnetic cable. LSD *Catamount*'s brood of LCVPs.

FROGMEN IN ACTION: APD *Diachenko*'s demolition team
embarks in rubber boat. Demolition team paddles through
mined Wonsan Harbor. Team drags 300-pound rubber boat
ashore.

DEATH AT WONSAN: Russian mine destroys ROK mine-
sweeper. Bruce Barrington, executive officer of *Partridge*, rescued
from his sunken minesweeper.

HEROIC SHIPS: *Collett, Swenson, Mansfield,* and *DeHaven*
awarded Navy Unit Citation. *Merganser, Osprey, Chatterer,* and
Mocking Bird received Presidential Unit Citation. Presidential
Unit Citation "posthumously" awarded AM *Pirate*.

NAVY ACHIEVEMENT: MinRon 3 completes successful
sweeping of Wonsan Harbor. AMS *Waxbill* lays smoke screen.

KOREAN SHORE TARGETS BLASTED: Phosphorous shell explodes over Hungnam. Shell from *St. Paul* hits Wonsan target area. Pre-invasion bombardment of Inchon.

ON THE RECEIVING END: 16-inch shell from *Missouri* blasts crater in road near Pohang. Wrecked Wonsan oil refinery. Unscathed church stands among the rubble.

MARINE AIR AND SEA MOBILITY: Marines climb aboard helicopters. Amphibious tractor heads for shore at Wonsan. Marines board transport.

MARINES IN THE FIELD: Sikorsky helicopter lowers supplies. Marines call for mortar fire. Advance toward rugged terrain.

BACKGROUND OF WAR: Religious services in the field. Engineers repair a bridge. DUKW creeps over mud shore.

COMMUNISTS UNDER THE GUN: North Korean prisoners on board a U. S. ship. Communist boatmen surrender. Enemy military dead.

MANY WOUNDED SURVIVED: Helicopter picks up injured Marine at Wonsan. 'Copter lands on deck of *Consolation*. Navy nurse feeds Thanksgiving dinner to wounded Marine.

SOME WERE LOST: Chaplain reads last rites on deck of *Toledo*. Memorial services on board *Lewis*. First Marine Division cemetery at Hamhung.

CRUISERS UNDERWAY AND AT ANCHOR: *Rochester* off east coast of Korea. *Toledo* alongside *Bremerton*. *Los Angeles,* with *Boxer* in background, steams in Korean waters.

NAVAL COMMANDERS: VADM J. J. Clark. RADM G. R. Henderson. RADM G. C. Dyer.

List of Charts

THE SEA WAR IN KOREA

1.

Gathering War Clouds

The Diplomatic Background of the Korean War

War was to erupt suddenly in the remote Land of the Morning Calm on 25 June 1950, not because of any local or long-standing differences between North and South Koreans, but as a result of an ideological struggle being waged between two global camps of adversaries, the freedom-loving nations versus the Soviet dominated countries—a struggle over which the Koreans themselves had little control. As the curtain for a fantastic tragedy was about to rise on the macabre stage of war, neither North nor South Korea was to be a major player.

After emerging from 35 years of Japanese occupation, the unfortunate people in North Korea found themselves completely engulfed beneath a Red sea of communism. The people of South Korea, on the other hand, were similarly overwhelmed by the freedom and responsibilities of a democratic system which was new and unfamiliar.

The war between North and South Korea was not merely a civil clash. On top of it was piled an international war which involved 25 nations, and which brought five million men from around the globe to a small Asian peninsula. In no sense was it a "small" war; rather, in the words of Vice Admiral Struble, "it was a major war confined to a small area." The conflict was outwardly ignited by a few North Korean political puppets whose strings were actually responsive to Soviet hands. These same hands also held numerous other strands both east and west of the Russian periphery. Thus, the Korean battlefront was but a small wedge in an arc of global conflict that had developed between the victorious allies of World War II.

To bring into focus the sea struggle as sailormen were to see it, it is first necessary to take a long-glass view of the international events which preceded the war.

The Communists of Russia are skilled in speaking from both sides of their mouths at once. From one half, they announce that their avowed purpose is

3

to dominate the world. From the other half, they contend that it is *they* who are the peace lovers, that it is *they* who are under siege, and have been for more than 250 years. The most recent example of this never-ending siege, they say, is the tide which only subsided when Hitler's armies were pushed out of Stalingrad and from the very doors of Leningrad and Moscow.

Leaders of the free world agree that a siege is on, to be sure, but that it is the *free world* which is standing on the defensive against a series of planned aggressions in the Soviet's seemingly interminable master plan for world conquest. To support this thesis, they point to a map of the world. Except for sections of Korea and Indochina, the Communists had expanded their frontiers to control the entire Pacific coastline of the Asian continent. On the other side of the world, from Stettin in the Baltic to Albania in the Adriatic, the piratical hands of Stalin and his heirs had drawn a political line that virtually isolated East from West.

Within these hemispheric arcs lay all the capitals of central and eastern Europe's states as well as the ancient cities of the Orient. Such cities as Berlin, Prague, Shanghai, Warsaw, Vienna, Peiping, Budapest, Pyongyang, Bucharest and Sofia had been enclosed within the Soviet sphere of influence, all subject to control from Moscow. Additionally, Communist fifth columns were established in every country in the world, working in complete harmony with and obedience to transmissions from the Kremlin.

Stalin, with astonishing defiance, blithely disregarded many of his Yalta promises almost before he had made them. For instance, he bluntly repudiated his pledge to permit Allied airmen the wartime use of certain airfields near Budapest; he denied free elections to the Poles. On the very day (27 February 1945) that Prime Minister Churchill told the British House of Commons that it was his Yalta impression that the Soviet leaders wanted to live in honorable friendship with the Western democracies, Stalin issued a two-hour ultimatum to Rumania's King Michael to dismiss his Prime Minister, General Radescu. Subsequently, on 3 March—the day President Roosevelt brought Congress an optimistic report on Yalta—Stalin ordered King Michael to appoint Patru Groza, the Rumanian Communist leader, as the new Prime Minister.

So flagrant were the Soviet dictator's violations of Yalta that President Roosevelt, 12 days before his death, cabled Stalin that he could no longer conceal his concern for the lack of progress being made in carrying out the Yalta decisions. He stated that even if a thinly-disguised Communist government continued in Poland, the American people would consider Yalta a failure.

Stalin, of course, ignored President Roosevelt's objections; his military-political offensive rolled on unabated. While the Western nations, spurred by Soviet-inspired propaganda, demobilized their military forces, the Soviet Union, in startling contrast, maintained her armed forces at full strength, and, in fact, began to expand her navy.

Meanwhile, the Soviet Government tightened her political web inside the Baltic and Balkan countries. In May of 1946, Stalin's forces crassly overthrew the legally constituted government of Czechoslovakia.

At this point, the Western Powers took heedful note.

In an historic step which must mark the point when the tide of international communism commenced to recede, President Truman obtained Congressional approval for the Marshall Plan to bolster the economic fronts of Western Europe. The Treaty of Rio de Janeiro was signed in 1947, committing the United States to resist any attack upon her neighboring republics to the south. European regional alliances began to take shape. Such national groupings as Benelux[1] and the Western Union[2] were born.

Stalin retaliated by blockading all highways and rails leading to Berlin from Western occupation zones. By 24 June 1948, he had blockaded every communicating link except the one corridor he could not close without gunfire: the international airways. Two days later, the Berlin airlift was organized by the United States and Great Britain. For 15 months (until 30 September 1949), the airlift operated with such psychological and military success that the Soviets reluctantly withdrew the blockade. Perhaps the most significant aspect of the Berlin blockade was the fact that it alerted the Western Powers to the aggressive and militant nature of the Soviet Government and the imminent gravity of the Soviet threat. Even before the blockade was lifted, the Western Powers had signed, on 4 April 1949, the North Atlantic Treaty (NATO)* in Washington.

In this treaty, the NATO members stated that an armed attack against any one member would be considered as an attack against all. This was followed by various military assistance bills being extended to practically all of the NATO countries, and to many countries in South America and Asia, through which medium the United States agreed to extend commercial credits, provide new military equipment, and modernize old Allied equipment in areas where it could be most profitably used.

The Mutual Defense Bill, passed by the U.S. Congress on 6 October 1949, specifically authorized that military equipment, technical and trained assistance, machine tools, and industrial equipment could be sent to Allied areas.

It was during this period of Allied build-up in Western Europe that the Soviet Union made the decision to open an active battlefront on the Korean

* The treaty was originally signed by Belgium, Canada, Denmark, France, Iceland, The Netherlands, Norway, Luxembourg, Italy, Portugal, the United Kingdom, and the United States. Later, in February 1952, Greece and Turkey signed, and Western Germany entered in May of 1955, to make a total of 15 nations.

peninsula. It seems reasonable that the Soviet shift of the scene of action from West to East was largely intended to counteract and negate the embryonic plans of the free nations of NATO.

At Potsdam, on 26 July 1945, the representatives of the United States, the United Kingdom, and the Republic of China had pledged, as they had similarly done at Cairo in 1943, that Korea would become a free and independent country, ending more than three decades of Japanese occupation.

Upon entering the war against Japan in 1945, the Soviet Government had publicly declared its intention of adhering to the Potsdam Declaration. An official USSR news release on 8 August 1945 stated: "Loyal to its Allied duty, the Soviet Government has accepted the proposal of the Allies and has joined in the declaration of the Allied Powers of 26 July."

Later, on 27 December 1945, in Moscow, the Soviet Government reaffirmed this pledge in a meeting with the Foreign Ministers of the United States and the United Kingdom. The Soviet Government agreed that a provisional democratic government should be established for all Korea until the Koreans themselves could permanently organize an independent and united country. This was yet another of those solemnly written promises made by the Soviet Government which was to be broken.

The 38th parallel*—a boundary line that was to become as famous as the Chinese Wall and the Iron Curtain—was first given official prominence on 11 August 1945, in connection with the surrender of Japan. On that day the Secretary of War of the United States submitted to the Secretary of State a draft of a surrender document that was to be known as General Order Number One. By this order General Douglas MacArthur, as Supreme Commander for the Allied Powers, would supervise the surrender of the Japanese Government to Allied forces.

Following approval by the Joint Chiefs of Staff and President Truman, General Order Number One was telegraphed to General MacArthur in Manila on 15 August 1945. Simultaneously, it was radioed to the British Government, and to Generalissimo Stalin. Stalin suggested certain amendments to the General Order, all of which were acceptable to the United States; but he made no mention of its provisions having to do with the surrender in Korea which stated that, as a matter of convenience, Japanese forces north of the 38th parallel would surrender to the Soviet Commander and forces south of that line would surrender to the American Commander.

* The 38th parallel of North Latitude measures 19,648 miles around the globe. The part that crosses Korea—196 miles—is exactly one percent of the whole. Few latitude lines span more land than 38° North; it crosses 12 countries, including the United States, China, and Russia.

General Order Number One was issued by General MacArthur on 2 September 1945, three weeks after Soviet forces had first entered North Korea.[3]

With the 20-20 hindsight that is conveniently available to historians, it is clear that the Soviet Union actually tipped its hand on its future interest in Korea at the Potsdam Conference. It was there (according to General T. S. Timberman's testimony before the House Committee on Foreign Affairs) that the Russians asked the Americans to cooperate with them in the reduction of Japanese forces in Korea.[4] General Marshall replied that this would be impossible since the United States would require its total military strength in capturing the Japanese homeland. The Russians then asked if the Americans would assist them with an amphibious operation in Korea. Again General Marshall demurred, stating that all U.S. amphibious lift would be needed in the invasion of the Japanese homeland.

Under these circumstances of demonstrated Soviet interest and actual Soviet troop deployments, Soviet forces might very well have occupied the entire Korean peninsula before the arrival of U.S. troops on 8 September 1945. The nearest U.S. military forces had been bivouacked at Okinawa, 600 miles from Korea, and in the Philippines, some 2,000 miles distant. It seems very probable, therefore, that the establishment of the 38th parallel for surrender purposes may have kept the southern half of Korea free, saving two-thirds of its population from immediate Communist domination.

In any event, the Allies neither envisaged the 38th parallel as anything more than a convenient line of surrender, nor did they foresee that it would give rise to a permanent split in the political and economic life of Korea. The 38th parallel was merely a fortuitous line brought about by the exigencies of the war.

Even though little importance was attached to the 38th parallel by United States officials, it was soon apparent that the Soviet forces occupying North Korea considered it much more than a "line of convenience." The Reds quickly hung a "no trespassing" sign on the 38th parallel and prohibited passage across it except by the express permission of the Soviet military commanders. Thus, with signs, a very complex international problem was created.

The physical division of the Korean peninsula at parallel 38 made it abundantly clear that Red Army commanders had been ordered to create a permanent delineation between the two military zones. Henceforth, the 38th parallel assumed increasingly ominous significance.

Lieutenant General John R. Hodge, the American occupation commander, fully realizing that such a physical barricade which neatly divided the industrial north from the agrarian south would eventually paralyze any future chance for uniting Korea, continued to urge his opposite number, Soviet

General Chistiakov, to remove the barrier. Unless this was accomplished, as both the United States and the Soviet Union had solemnly promised, he said, Korean unity and Korean freedom were doomed. The Reds remained synthetically sympathetic, always willing to discuss the situation but never agreeable to doing anything which might ameliorate the problem which they themselves had created.

In accordance with terms of the Moscow Agreement of 1945, the Soviet Government had agreed to establish a joint United States-Soviet commission to work out a temporary four-power trusteeship for Korea as a prelude to the development of democratic self-government and the establishment of national independence for Korea. Among the rather general instructions issued by the three ministers in Moscow to the joint commission was a provision "that the Joint US-USSR Commission consult with Korean democratic parties and social organizations in preparing their proposals to their respective governments concerned." Whether such loosely-worded instructions were deliberately written into the Commission's instructions by the Communists is not known. In any event they served the Soviet purpose of reaching an impasse.

In the joint commission the Soviet delegation took the position that the occupying powers should confine consultations to those Korean groups who had agreed fully and consistently with the Moscow declaration. This was tantamount to showing favor to the representative of the communist groups.

The Soviets took the position that before any Korean "political or social organization" could qualify and be considered acceptable for consultation with the Joint Commission, the party or organization had to be acceptable to them. Secondly, the Soviets hotly disputed the definition of what constituted "a social group." Thirdly, without bringing specific charges, the Soviets arbitrarily accused *all* non-communist Korean political parties of bad faith in that all of them were opposed to the trusteeship idea.

The United States, on the other hand, took the position that all Korean parties were innocent until indicted and proven guilty; that their present attitude was more important than their past record; furthermore, if the Joint Commission restricted its consultations to the degree insisted on by the Soviets, the Commission would never get a fair sampling of Korean opinion; it would therefore lack the rudimentary knowledge for making recommendations to the Four Powers concerned.

The difference was composed by a formula which limited consultation to those groups which were democratic in principle and which agreed to uphold the aims of the Moscow declaration and also abide by the Commission's decisions.

Then the Soviets raised a new objection: they insisted upon barring consultations with any individuals *who had expressed opposition* to the Moscow trusteeship provisos. The United States delegation said that such a restriction was at odds with the ostensible purpose of the commission to establish a democratic government.

Thus went Soviet-United States deliberations for some twenty-four months —words, words, words—*ad nauseam, ad infinitum.* Meanwhile, legal passage across the 38th parallel remained as restricted as ever.

Finally, the United States recommended in a letter of August 26, 1947, since she and the Soviet Union could not end their stalemate with regard to the functioning of the Joint Commission, that secret elections be held in both North and South Korea to form provisional legislatures in each zone. Representatives from these legislatures would constitute a national provisional legislature which in turn, would meet in Seoul to establish a provisional government for a united Korea. This recommendation might have been acceptable to the Soviets had it not included what the Reds thought was a joker; the United States proposal specifically provided that representatives of the United Nations should be invited to watch the balloting to assure the world and the Korean people "of the wholly representative and completely independent character of the action taken."

Molotov, Foreign Minister of the U.S.S.R., politely tabled the free election idea in a note signed 4 September 1947, and stepped forward with a counter-proposal. The US-USSR Joint Commission, he said, was still far from exhausting all its possibilities for working out agreed recommendations; and besides, such elections would only further divide Korea, and this would be contrary to the vital task at hand: "the establishment of a single, even though provisional, organ of authority."

On 9 October 1947, about a month after Molotov had, in effect, accused the United States of trying to further divide Korea by holding free elections, he came up with still another proposal. Since the United States delegation in Korea had made impossible the formation of a provisional Korean democratic government, Molotov suggested that both the American and the Soviet troops get out of Korea and let the Koreans organize a government for themselves. Soviet troops, he promised, would be ready to leave simultaneously with the Americans.

By now it was plain to the United States Government that further bilateral talks with the Soviets were futile. The alternatives were weighed. The United States had these choices: (1) she could apply military pressure against the Soviet Union for her refusals to carry out her diplomatic promises; (2) she could abandon all of Korea to the Soviets; (3) she could establish what might amount to a United States' protectorate over South Korea; or (4) she could provide the South Korean people with assistance and guidance so that they, through their own efforts, might progress toward their goal of freedom and independence.

After weighing the alternatives, the United States chose the last course. This course would permit the South Koreans at least to start laying the foundation for a free and independent country. At the same time it would permit the United States to reduce progressively her Korean commitments of manpower and resources in accordance with the necessities of her own contracting military strength.

Meanwhile, on 17 September 1947, the United States Government placed the Korean question before the United Nations General Assembly in order that the inability of the two powers to reach an agreement should not further delay the early establishment of an independent, united Korea.

Both the United States and the Soviet Union made their recommendations to United Nations.

The United States proposed the following: " (a) Elections in the two occupation zones of Korea by March 31, 1948, under observation of the United Nations 'as the initial step leading to the creation of a National Assembly and the establishment of a National Government of Korea'; (b) creation of a national security force by the Korean National Government immediately upon its establishment, early transfer to that Government of the governmental functions exercised by the occupying powers, and early arrangements between it and the occupying powers for the withdrawal of their forces; (c) creation of a United Nations Temporary Commission on Korea to oversee the elections and to be available for consultation on each of the steps proposed for developing self-rule in Korea and the end of occupation in that country."[5]

The Soviets opposed the United States recommendation. They reiterated the position that the United States alone had violated the Moscow agreement and had blocked the independence of Korea. They viewed the Korean question as one concerning the peace terms and, therefore, beyond the jurisdiction of the United Nations. They offered a counter proposition for mutual withdrawal of occupying troops as the first step and organization of a national government as the second.

Although it was to have little practical effect, the UN General Assembly decided—on 14 November 1947—to approve the United States' recommendation that the Korean question was a matter for the Korean people themselves to decide, that the matter could not be resolved without the full participation of representatives of the indigenous population. The UN Assembly passed a resolution that the Korean people should have the opportunity to elect representatives, draft a democratic constitution, and establish a national government. To insure that this was done properly, they decided to send a UN Temporary Commission with representatives from Australia, Canada, China, El Salvador, France, India, Philippines, Syria, and the Ukrainian Socialist Republic. The Temporary Commission, minus the Ukrainian delegate, arrived in South Korea 8 January 1948, and held its first meeting four days later. The Soviet Union protested that a matter such as the establishment of a Korean government did not fall within the jurisdiction of the United Nations. Furthermore, she would not permit the Temporary Commission to enter North Korea. The Soviet military commander even refused to receive a communication from the Commission proposing a courtesy call. After meeting numerous rebuffs from the Soviet commander, the Temporary Commission referred the matter back to the UN.

What next?

On 26 February, the United Nations instructed the Temporary Commission to proceed to carry out the UN program "in such parts of Korea as are accessible to the Commission."

As a consequence, the only free election and free government established in Korea would of necessity be confined to the southern half.

The first election was accordingly held 10 May 1948, and the government of the Republic of Korea was established 15 August 1948.

The new government of South Korea was recognized by the United States and 31 other nations. It was accepted by the UN as the legally elected and lawful government. It was *not* recognized, however, by the Soviet Union, who created in North Korea what it termed the "Democratic People's Republic of Korea." This puppet regime was proclaimed 8 September 1948. Claiming jurisdiction over the entire country, it was destined to live as it was created: in complete defiance of the United Nations.

Such is the diplomatic history of an ethical government trying to deal with distortionists on the single issue of Korea.

During the years of 1948 and 1949, the Soviet-controlled North Koreans did everything possible to promote disorder and confusion along and south of the 38th parallel. Subversives infiltrated southward in great numbers. Communist terrorists made threats, incited rebellion, and actually participated in armed raids across the border.

By the fall of 1948 the security of the Republic of Korea was endangered. A riot in the port of Yosu in October involving 3,000 people, including a regiment of the Republic of Korea Army, cost the lives of 500 loyal police and army troops and left the city in ruins.

Meanwhile, the North Koreans took the diplomatic initiative by requesting troop withdrawals by both the United States and the Soviet forces. This was agreeable to the United States; and on 1 July 1949, the Department of the Army announced that all U. S. troops had been withdrawn from Korea after nearly four years of occupation. Of the 50,000 United States troops that had originally been in Korea following VJ-Day, a scant 500 were left as a provisional military advisory group.

Following withdrawal of the U. S. troops, North Korean subversive agents stepped up their operations. In two years of guerrilla warfare the South Koreans lost an estimated 500 dead. Between 9 and 20 September 1949, intensive fighting took place near the 38th parallel, with casualties on both sides.

On 4 August, North Korean forces invaded the Ongjin peninsula but were repulsed after heavy fighting. In mid-October, a new offensive was begun by North Korean forces in the Ongjin peninsula, and severe fighting continued for several days. So violent did the raids become that, in March of 1950, the UN Secretary General ordered eight UN representatives then in Korea to observe the guerrilla actions along the 38th.

"I always believed," said Vice Admiral C. Turner Joy, Commander Naval Forces, Far East, "that the guerrilla activities and raids were deliberately planned and directed by the North Korean Government to promote unrest and disorder in South Korea with a view toward eventual Communist control of the entire peninsula through civil war."

The Evolution of U. S. Military Strategy, 1945-1950

Against this ominous diplomatic backdrop in Korea, the United States was developing a post-World War II military strategy, the validity of which was soon to be tested in the Korean War. Before any study of the naval portion of the Korean War can be made, therefore, an analysis of what this military strategy was, and how it had been reached, is necessary, so that in a final chapter a judgment of that prewar strategy can be rendered in the light of wartime experience.

After the end of World War II, the goals which the United States set for itself, while commendable, were actually beyond realization within the self-imposed limits. The United States was trying to maintain a military posture, assimilate the lessons of World War II, accommodate the facts of the atomic age and jet propulsion, and simultaneously reduce military forces to peace-time levels despite *expanding* overseas commitments.

As the national strategy took shape, some of it was old and some of it was new. It was old in the sense that it preserved the basic rights of the individual as well as the sovereignty of the United States without impinging on the rights of other nations. It was new in the sense that the Government of the United States had determined that it could no longer be insulated from

FOR GOD AND THE UNITED NATIONS. *At top,* a Sunday communion service is held aboard attack transport *Bayfield* destined for the Wonsan invasion. *Below,* the United Nations flag is unfurled to be raised for the first time aboard heavy cruiser *Helena,* after delivery by battleship *Missouri.*

LOGISTICS DOMINATE WAR. *Above,* the invasion fleet at Wonsan Harbor. *At left,* an Army boxcar is unloaded in Korea to be used in transporting supplies to frontline units. *Below,* drums of aviation gasoline at Hungnam await loading on *LST-898* during withdrawal of First Marine Division.

UNDERWAY REPLENISHMENT enabled United Nations vessels to control and use the seas around Korea. *Above,* CV *Antietam* and DD *Shelton* refuel simultaneously from fleet oiler *Tolovana,* while CV *Essex* waits her turn. *At right,* ammunition ship *Paricutin* restocks the magazine of light cruiser *Manchester* right under the noses of Communist shore batteries at Wonsan. *Below, Luzon,* a repair ship, helped keep the fleet afloat and fighting.

SHIPBOARD LIFE, ABOVE AND BELOW DECKS. *At top,* crew swabs bore of 16-inch gun on battleship *Wisconsin. Above left,* a bluejacket's thoughts turn to home. *Above right,* Machinist's Mate Christian at throttle station of DD *Taylor. At left,* mascot of CV *Bon Homme Richard* during abandon-ship drill.

world events; that by virtue of its greater moral and physical strength, it must play a strong hand in organizing, unifying, and leading the political, economic, spiritual, and military efforts of all freedom-loving nations. Only by combining the several resources of free nations could freedom be preserved and encouraged to spread and flourish among less fortunate peoples.

If the United States was ever to succeed in such a noble mission, it was patent that she herself must unify her strength in a practical plan that would accommodate her aspirations. Never again could she afford the prodigal military wastage that had characterized her World War II efforts. In the future she must carefully evaluate her preparedness for conflict and know both her assets and liabilities. She must evaluate every aspect of her national strength: her industrial productivity and potential, her access to and the availability of raw materials, her educational needs (particularly in the fields of science and engineering), and her manpower levels. The military program which resulted would have to dovetail neatly with the political and economic realities of the postwar world.

Altogether, these factors called for military unification—unification of national resources and national strengths. The trouble with unification came in the military sphere. How could it be accomplished most effectively? What military weapons and strategy would best implement the national policy? What roles and missions should be assigned to the individual military services? What type of defense organization would most likely assure the United States of a peaceful and secure future?

All military leaders initially favored unification of the Armed Services; both Army and Navy officials supported this view in the findings of a joint board headed by Admiral James Otto Richardson which had been ordered to study the problem of postwar defense.[6] Before any laws were passed, however, many outstanding naval leaders began to voice serious doubts as to the wisdom of military unification. Many thought that merger of the Armed Services would stultify competition and progress. The heart of naval doubt was found in a statement made by Fleet Admiral Ernest J. King in October 1945: "Sea power will not be accorded adequate recognition because the organization contemplated would permit reduction of the sea power by individuals who are not thoroughly familiar with its potentialities. . . ."

After considerable naval opposition and much heated Congressional debate, the National Security Act of 1947 was passed and signed by the President on 26 July of that year. This new union continued to find, in the words of a subsequent report rendered by the House Armed Services Committee, "a Navy reluctance . . . an overardent Army, a somewhat exuberant Air Force."[7]

The concept of the first unification law was federation, not merger, of the Armed Forces. It had created, in effect, a coordinator of three executive departments: a Secretary of Defense and a Defense Department.

The first Secretary of Defense, Mr. James Forrestal, stated in his first annual report to the Congress: "I would be less than candid . . . if I did not underline the fact that there are still great areas in which the viewpoints of the Services have not come together." He went on to state, "It is out of the competition inherent in the division of the total funds allocated to the National Military Establishment that the controversies arise." More specifically, Mr. Forrestal pointed out that "balancing of these two aspects of air power (Air Force and Navy), and seeing to it that adequate, but not unnecessary, funds are allocated to each, is one of the most difficult tasks of the Secretary of Defense."[8]

Meanwhile, the interservice struggle intensified—both in private and in public—principally between the Navy and the newly-created Air Force. Books and magazine articles with such provocative titles as *Disaster Through Air Power*, *The Strategic Bombing Myth*, and *The Case Against the Admirals* appeared in public print. Influential editors and publishers took sides in the highly emotional controversy. Many military officers continued to voice their convictions publicly and before Congress. It was only natural that the nation's military leaders, who had fought vastly different wars in different parts of the world, should hold basic differences on matters involving weapons systems and techniques for their employment. But as General of the Army Dwight D. Eisenhower pointed out when he was asked for his views: "We are dealing with distinguished Americans, people who have their country's good at heart, and, therefore, we should not be too critical or too ready to call names on either side; above all, we should not be too ready to question motives."[9]

By the summer of 1949 the controversy had reached a climax. Governmental leaders, both in the executive and legislative branches, were now offering opinions; industrialists, specialists, and neo-experts joined the arguments in everything from weapons design to tactics.

The fireworks actually began 23 April 1949, when the Secretary of Defense, Mr. Louis A. Johnson, announced that work on the Navy's new aircraft carrier, the USS *United States*, would be discontinued. This decision was made while the Secretary of the Navy, Mr. John L. Sullivan, was out of Washington. Three days later Mr. Sullivan resigned. He stated that he could no longer serve as Secretary in view of the manner in which the decision had been made.

By April's end, unofficial reports were circulating that the Marine Corps' integral aviation was to be transferred to the Air Force; that naval air was to be further cut and perhaps also transferred to the Air Force. Rumors that the Marine Corps was to be abolished and the Navy reduced to a convoy-and-escort force became so widespread in the spring of 1949 that Mr. Carl Vinson, Chairman of the House Armed Services Committee, queried the Secretary of Defense.[10]

Secretary Johnson replied on 28 April 1949 that these things could *not* be done under the National Security Act, that they had not been contemplated; and furthermore, before any such steps were seriously considered, he would ask permission to discuss the matter with Congress.[11]

Charges and countercharges mounted, some of them involving political matters, until eventually a full-scale Congressional investigation was ordered.[12]

In the subsequent twelve days of testimony before the House Armed Services Committee, the differing viewpoints of the postwar military strategy of the United States emerged.

As the Armed Services Committee hearings opened, Chairman Vinson stated: "These disagreements involve such basic subjects affecting the national defense that this committee could not properly ignore the situation."

What should the national defense program of the United States be? What strategy should it follow? What kind of wars would be fought in the future? Would there be global wars, peripheral wars, limited wars, atomic or non-atomic wars? What weapons would be most effective in fighting such wars?

It could scarcely be expected that dedicated professional men with varied wartime experiences, varied strategic concepts, a myriad of interests, and varied technical knowledge would agree on what they saw as they gazed into the crystal ball of future war.

The Air Force concept was expressed by Secretary of the Air Force W. Stuart Symington: ". . . the Air Force believes that the atomic bomb plus the air power necessary to deliver it represents the one most important visible deterrent to the start of any war." Mr. Symington repeated a statement once made by General Hoyt Vandenberg, Air Force Chief of Staff: "The only war you really win is the war that never starts."[13]

"Secondly," continued the Air Force Secretary, "if war comes, we believe that the atomic bomb plus the air power to deliver it represent the one means of unloosing prompt, crippling destruction upon the enemy, with absolute minimum combat exposure of American lives. If it is preferable to engage in a war of attrition, one American life for one enemy life, then we are wrong. That is not our way. That is not the way in which the mass-slaughter of American youths and invasion of Japan was avoided. . . .

"We can hope, but no one can promise, that if war comes the impact of our bombing offensive with atomic weapons can bring it about that no surface forces ever have to become engaged. Disregarding such an illusory hope, we do know that the engagement of surface forces will take place with much greater assurance of success and much fewer casualties to the United States and its allies if an immediate, full-scale atomic offensive is launched against the heart of the enemy's war-making power."[14]

Mr. Symington said that the United States should continue to "concentrate on America's greatest asset—quality of product, superior weapons capable of development, and mass production in our system of free economy —weapons like the B-36 with its intercontinental bombing range without refueling, and other modern bombers and planes with their projected intercontinental range with refueling."[15]

General Hoyt Vandenberg followed the Secretary, and his testimony included his military estimate of what types of weapons were most needed to perform such future military jobs as could be foreseen from his vantage point. The Air Force Chief of Staff said he was "in favor of the greatest possible development of carrier aviation to whatever extent carriers and their aircraft are necessary for fulfillment of a strategic plan against the one possible enemy we may have to face. Less than this would be unsound. More than this would be an unjustifiable burden upon the American taxpayer. . . ."

General Vandenberg said he was "not only willing but insistent that the types of carriers which can help meet the threat of an enemy submarine fleet shall be developed fully and kept in instant readiness. The sea lanes must be kept open. There is no dispute on this matter." He went on to say, "I do not believe there is justification for maintaining large carrier task forces during peacetime unless they are required by the strategic plans of the Joint Chiefs of Staff. In my judgment they are not required by those plans. . . .

"My opposition to building it* comes from the fact that I can see no necessity for a ship with those capabilities in any strategic plan against the one possible enemy.

"Any war we may have to fight in the future will obviously be unlike the Pacific war against Japan. It will tend to resemble the war against Germany, though with certain differences. There will be the same problem of killing submarines. . . . There will be the same problem of protecting Atlantic Ocean supply lines, although the threat to our shipping will come almost wholly from the submarine, since the potential enemy has no surface units of the character of the *Bismarck* and the *Tirpitz*. There may or may not be amphibious landings, but if there are, they will not be like the landings in

---

* General Vandenberg is referring to the CVA-58, the USS *United States,* whose construction had been cancelled by the Secretary of Defense, Louis Johnson.

North Africa and Normandy, and probably unlike most of the landings in the Pacific islands.

"Finally," said General Vandenberg, "the industrial heart of the potential enemy lies not on any seashore, not on any island, but deep inside the Eurasian land mass. It is to that type of war we must adapt all of our forces, including carrier aviation."[16]

All of the witnesses, including naval men, were agreed that air supremacy was vital to future military success, but the unity-splitting question was *how* to achieve air supremacy.

Protagonists of the Air Force felt that the B-36 (the long-range, land-based bomber) and the just-cancelled aircraft carrier *United States* were duplicative; that both of them were designed to accomplish the same purpose: strategic air warfare. They felt that United States taxpayers could not afford the heavy expenditures involved in providing two similar weapons systems.*

Since the Air Force had been assigned the mission of strategic air warfare, they felt it was the sounder procedure for most of the money to be budgeted into the Air Force's plan of accomplishment. By so doing, they claimed, the United States could assure itself of the best possible deterrent to war, and, if war came, the cheapest and the easiest victory. The Air Force backers argued for a strategy based on hitting the heartland of the most probable enemy with intercontinental land-based bombers, on the logic that this was the best possible means at this particular time of getting there "fustest with the mostest" atom bombs.

The Army position in the hearings was stated by General Omar Bradley, who spoke both from his Army background and from his position as Chairman of the Joint Chiefs of Staff. Bradley agreed with the Navy that he did not believe our country should rely solely on strategic bombing or on atomic weapons. Properly balanced land, air, and sea forces were required. However, he doubted there would ever be any campaign similar to the Pacific campaign. He also doubted that there would ever again be large-scale amphibious operations.[17] General Bradley also recalled his own participation in two of the largest amphibious landings in history—in Sicily and Normandy—and that in neither were there any U.S. Marines.

As far as national military strategy was concerned, General Bradley pointed out that "our basic concept for defense includes protection of the

---

* General Carl Spaatz, USAF, former Chief of Staff of the Air Force, had written in *Newsweek*, 17 October, 1949, that "The Navy now spends more than half its total appropriations in support of naval aviation. The result is that the nation is dissipating its wealth and wasting aviation talent in supporting two air forces.

"This is dangerous. Nothing less than United States air supremacy is at stake. This leadership can not be maintained unless the country's military air resources are pooled and placed under the control of one organization. . . ."

United States and this continent, in case we are attacked. It provides for early retaliation from bases which we hope to have ready at all times.

"This concept includes a decision that we shall have to be ready to seize other bases that we may need and hold those bases against enemy attack, so that we may attack the enemy country at shorter ranges, and, at the same time, deny him bases close to this country from which he could attack us.

"Ultimately, however, we will have to carry the war back to the enemy by all means at our disposal. I am convinced this would include strategic bombardment and large-scale land operations."

General Bradley went on to say, "In addition to the concept I have just outlined, we must go back to the realization that the first prize for any aggressor in the world today is Europe, with its industrial potential and its market for goods."[18]

Naval strategists, led by Admiral Arthur W. Radford, then Commander in Chief, Pacific, and destined to relieve General Bradley as Chairman of the Joint Chiefs of Staff, opened the Navy's case by stating that the major issue of the investigation "deals with the kind of war for which this country should be prepared."[19] He pointed out that it was difficult, in fact impossible, to predetermine a fixed concept for fighting a war. Admiral Radford testified: "An aggressor nation can set the time and place for initial military operations, and hence may strongly affect early defense measures."

Further, he pointed out: "A potential enemy can be expected to make sound estimates of our military strength. He does not depend entirely on what he reads in the papers. If the armed forces of this Nation are unsoundly organized and improperly equipped, they will not be fully effective as a deterrent to aggression. They even invite it."[20]

Radford went on to say that the issues were much broader and much more important than the B-36 program, that a strategy—atomic retaliation—was being overemphasized, a strategy which most military men did not accept as sound.

In discussing future war, Radford stated that "at some critical phase of future war—and that phase may come early—the security of our country may substantially depend on a mobile air power required to insure control of the air in vital areas.

"We have in the United States developed mobile air power to such an extent that we can project it anywhere in the world where there is enough water—and that is quite a large part of the world—and no other country can do that. As I told you, air power is the key to victory in any military operation from now on—all kinds of air power. The United States has the unique capability to project air power to get control of the air in vital areas of operation. No one else has it. The Navy today must be built not to meet an enemy navy but with the idea, after evaluation, of the need for air power in theaters of war and parts of the world where we can't get air power any other way."[21]

The testimony of another Navy witness, Captain "31-Knot" Arleigh A. Burke, whose future seemed foreordained to be as exciting and challenging as his past, had strong appeal to the nations of such coalitions as NATO, whose bonds were no stronger than the sea catalyst which brought them all together.

"If war develops," said Captain Burke, "one of the first duties of our maritime country will be to gain and hold command of the sea. We must do that before we can send assistance to our allies and our overseas forces and bases. If we fail to command the seas, we cannot support our war effort overseas. In such a case, all forces operating from bases which must be supplied by sea would be cut off from adequate support." In other words, every U.S. airfield and U.S. division stationed overseas was a vote of confidence in the U.S. Navy's ability to supply and maintain it.

"The United States needs a navy which can prevent the enemy from denying us the oceans in which we want to operate."

If the Navy could not assure the safe arrival of raw materials from overseas, the U.S. economy, both civilian and military, would quickly perish. Specifically, Burke testified, "Whatever it takes to exercise that command of the sea, I think that this country must have it because we are a maritime nation. We must import materials, we must get our forces overseas. If we can't do that, we will fight our wars in this country. . . ."[22]

General Clifton B. Cates, Commandant of the Marine Corps, reinforced the Navy's position in forceful language.

". . . Without a well-trained landing force, the Fleet is not a balanced implement of warfare," said the Commandant. Marine forces, he said, "are possessed of great utility in augmenting the national defense—if they are permitted to do so."

Discussing future war, the Commandant said: "In view of the enormously increased scope of this Nation's international responsibilities, I am convinced there is even greater likelihood of a recurrence of need for such emergency forces (the Marines) poised and ready to proceed in company with the Fleet, to the scene of crisis. . . . We are confronted with the possibility of a war in which our opponent would hold the initiative. We must prepare to meet his moves with promptness and with whatever force we can muster."

The Chief of Naval Operations, Admiral Louis E. Denfeld, pointed out that naval forces could help discourage aggression either on a large or a small scale: ". . . The presence of our Fleet in the eastern Mediterranean has effectively contributed to keeping local conflicts from degenerating into global war."[23]

He pointed out further that "operations of carrier task forces, through application of the principle of mobility and surprise, have repeatedly demonstrated the ability to concentrate aircraft strength at any desired point in such numbers as to overwhelm the defense. No other force and no other nation possesses this capability to a like degree.

"We have a lead of more than a quarter of a century over any probable enemy. Let us not squander it for any false doctrines—any unsound concept of war. That would be the real extravagance.

". . . The Navy's ultimate function in war is to exert the steady, unrelenting pressure of our Nation's military might against the homeland of an enemy." He went on to say, "The Navy must be organized in peacetime as a balanced force capable of . . . underseas warfare . . . amphibious warfare . . . including many highly specialized groups . . . underwater demolition teams, high-speed minesweeping groups, teams to control air and gunfire support, joint communications and many others.

". . . The properly balanced Fleet must have as a major component a Fleet Marine Force of combined arms, including its close-support tactical aviation. The inclusion of such a force permits a fleet commander a degree of initiative and flexibility in his operations not otherwise obtainable. He can seize advanced bases as required by the development of the campaign, or, if the situation dictates, be assured of adequate defenses for those bases already in his possession."

Little did Admiral Denfeld, who was soon to be relieved as Chief of Naval Operations, realize that within less than a year his words would read like prophecy.

Another Navy witness to put his finger on the core of the problem was Vice Admiral Robert B. Carney, at that time head of naval logistics, and later to become Chief of Naval Operations.

Admiral Carney pointed out that "To settle on a concept of sustained intercontinental bombing or a program of procuring costly intercontinental bomber types could only be justified by overriding considerations of the greatest urgency, because, logistically, in terms of treasure and effort, there are better ways of conducting strategic bombing."[24]

He stated that the only basis for the country's relying on intercontinental bombing would be "absolute assurance of its decisive character," and he cautioned that it should not be pursued to the point that other elements of the military machine were starved into impotence.

The issue, concluded Admiral Carney, is for the nation to decide "whether the American Air Force power in its present form is needed to the extent of accepting deterioration and inadequacy of other essential components of the military team. I believe that is today's Number One military problem."

The naval concept of future war thus boiled down to this: The United States could not anticipate *what* kind of a war would be fought or *where,* or *when,* nor could she safely predict *what weapons* would prove most effective. These matters were of necessity to be determined by time, the enemy and by circumstance. Naval leaders thought that the national strategy should avoid a fixed concept of future war; that the country should be prepared to fight in many differing areas, with many types of weapons. They thought it folly for this nation to arbitrarily restrict itself either in concept or in method. Fleet Admiral Halsey summarized the Navy's views about a future war when he said: "It will be started by a foreign aggressor—at the time, at the place, and in the manner he desires."[25]

The United States, argued the Navy, should retain flexibility and balance in her armed forces; she should retain the mobility, versatility, built-in defenses, the concealment, and the qualities of concentration, dispersion, and surprise inherent in the Navy's floating airfields; for the Navy held that no single Service or no single weapon would ever win the war.

Naval officers contended that "the Nation's long-range objective is a stable world society—and that this objective must underlie the Nation's preparations for war and govern the methods by which it wages war; otherwise, according to the testimony, the Nation may thwart its objectives, although winning the war waged to achieve those objectives."[26]

As the Congressional hearings progressed, there was much heated debate. At times the hearings were less strategic in nature than technical and tactical. At times tempers flared. One distinguished soldier suggested that "this is no time for 'fancy-dans' who won't hit the line with all they have on every play, unless they can call the signals."[27] One Congressman told a witness that he had been "farther back under my barn hunting for eggs than some generals have been away from home."[28]

The Chairman of the Committee, Mr. Carl Vinson, said at one point in the hearings that one of the troubles had been that the Army, the Navy, and the Air Force had not been around Congress very much recently. "We hardly know what is going on," said the Chairman, "and it is not often that we and the country have the benefits of such statements as are being made right now. . . . I think these hearings are going to help the Services. I think they are going to let the country know something about what the Services stand for and what the Services represent." The Chairman voiced a popular sentiment among the Congressional committee when he stated that he "did not want any strategy drafted . . . which is going to deny to the country an efficient and effective arm to play its proper role in the defense of the country. We don't want to keep one strong member of the team sitting on the bench too long."[29]

To summarize the two viewpoints, the Air Force held the view that warfare in the atomic age gave overriding importance to air power. The missions of ground and naval forces, in their view, had been relegated to collateral tasks. The safest way to prevent a future war was to concentrate preponderant strength in atomic weapons and superlative aircraft to deliver them.

The Navy, on the other hand, held the view that while it was indeed true that air power held the key to victory, our potential enemy held the power of initiative and could choose the time, the place, the size, and the scope of a future war. Our national military forces, therefore, should be mobile, balanced, and flexible, capable of handling a variety of military contingencies. Ground and naval forces were quite as vital in the age of the atom as they had ever been in the past.

These conflicting views which emerged in the House Armed Services Committee hearings were in only nine months to be tested by the war in Korea.

The Military Background of the Korean War

Why Soviet leaders ordered the commencement of a war in Korea is a mystery still locked inside the walls of the Kremlin.* The most logical explanation, perhaps, is that Soviet leaders miscalculated the American reaction. Any analysis or poll of our national attitude toward the Far East during 1948-49 would have reached the same conclusion that the Soviets must have made: America would stand idly by as Korea was invaded. This estimate was fortified by such public announcements as the one that our defensive perimeter no longer included Korea. On 12 January 1950, the United States Secretary of State, Mr. Dean Acheson, speaking before the National Press Club in Washington, D. C., defined a United States defensive perimeter in the Far East which did not include either South Korea or Formosa.

The defensive perimeter, said Secretary Acheson, "runs along the Aleutians to Japan and then goes to the Ryukyus . . . from the Ryukyus to the

---

* On 10 June 1956, the Italian Catholic Action newspaper, *Il Quotidiano,* published what is said were missing portions of Nikita Khrushchev's now famous speech attacking Stalin which were not included in the version released by the U.S. State Department. Herein, the newspaper stated that Khrushchev recognized Soviet responsibility for the Korean War. The theory advanced is that Stalin's jealousy of Red China's dictator, Mao Tzetung, caused him to embroil Red China and the U.S. in Korea so that he might emerge the undisputed dictator. According to the Roman newspaper, these were Khrushchev's words:

"His (Stalin's) anti-realistic consideration of the attitude of the Western Nations in the face of developments in Asia has contributed to the risky situation for the entire socialist cause such as developed around the war in Korea."

Philippine Islands. . . . So far as the military security of other areas in the Pacific is concerned, it must be clear that no person can guarantee these areas against military attack. But it must also be clear that such a guarantee is hardly sensible or necessary within the realm of practical relationship."[30]

Secondly, Soviet strategists certainly noted that the U.S. Government had not only removed occupation troops from Korea, but had earlier removed its U.S. Marines from the Shantung peninsula in China. U.S. military forces were obviously withdrawing from the Asian mainland. Any military move by the Communists into South Korea would probably be unopposed.

Thirdly, any military men, including the Soviets, could deduce from the just-completed Navy-Air Force debate before a Congressional committee that the U.S. military strategy was drifting toward preparation for only one kind of war—a global atomic one. The constant reduction being made in both the U.S. Army and Navy made it a calculated and acceptable risk to the Soviet leaders that the U.S. would not—or could not in time—interfere in a local, ground-type war in Korea.

In a speech before the American Legion convention at St. Louis on 2 September 1953, the United States Secretary of State, John Foster Dulles, gave his opinion of why the Korean War started:

"The Korean War began in a way in which wars often begin," Secretary Dulles said, "—a potential aggressor miscalculated. From that we learn a lesson which we expect to apply in the interests of future peace.

"The lesson is this: If events are likely which will in fact lead us to fight, let us make clear our intention in advance; then we shall probably not have to fight.

"Big wars usually come about by mistakes, not by design. . . . It is . . . probable that the Korean War would not have occurred if the aggressor had known what the United States would do.

"The Communists thought, and had reason to think, that they would not be opposed, except by the then small and ill-equipped forces of the Republic of Korea. They did not expect what actually happened."

At a press conference on 2 February 1955, President Eisenhower stated that the Korean conflict started because we failed to make clear to the Soviets that we would defend South Korea.

That a military invasion of South Korea by the North Korean puppet government was possible or even imminent was evident in the intelligence despatches coming into Washington:[31]

8 December 1949: North Korean government and their Chinese allies are under complete domination of Russia. Soviets will not permit the indefinite existence of a noncommunist state in the Korean peninsula. . . . Patterned

on the master plan, the North Korean government is merely a puppet of Soviet Russia. Acting as an overseer is a Soviet mission of 300 persons in Pyongyang. . . . The army is composed of four to eight divisions and Inf. Brigades and possesses normal infantry weapons, howitzers of 76-mm. and 122-mm. calibers, 30 to 40 tanks, model T-34, and 36 to 70 aircraft. All equipment is of Soviet origin. Recent influx of Chinese communist troops makes up an (unidentified) divisional unit. . . . Capitalizing upon (the) weakness of the democratic system, the Communist-dominated South Korean Labor Party is the instigator of practically all civil disturbances (in South Korea). . . . North Korean sponsored guerrilla forces are creating fear and unrest in the South Korean populace. . . . To the Communist, an armed invasion of South Korea is probably considered as the final resort to gain control of the peninsula. . . . With the conclusion of the Chinese Communist campaign in China, more troops and supplies may be channeled into North Korea. (The) danger to the Southern Republic will mount at that time. . . . Climatic conditions have passed (December). (The) next favorable period for (any such) action will occur in April and May 1950.

5 January 1950: North Korea has set March and April 1950 as the time to invade South Korea. Such threats should be viewed in relation to military activities. By this criterion, the movement of the 3rd North Korean Division into the western 38th parallel, the arrival of Chinese Communist personnel, the southward displacement of the North Korean 2nd Division and expansion of Border Constabulary seem significant in terms of military action in the spring.

10 March 1950: North Korean People's Army will be prepared to invade South Korea by fall or possibly by spring of this year (1950) as indicated by armed forces expansion and major troop movements. . . . Soviet intentions in Korea believed closely related to the Communist program in Southeast Asia. If checked in their operations in these countries, Soviets may divert their efforts to Korea. . . . Latest reports received that the North Korean People's Army will invade South Korea in June.*

15 April 1950: In mid-March, the Communist government ordered evacuation of all civilians residing in an area within three miles of the 38th parallel. Vacated housing in latter area then occupied by troops and guerrillas. Purpose reported as "preparation for war and to interfere with South Korean Intelligence operations."

25 May 1950: National Inspection teams have completed field inspections

---

* To this particular dispatch, the G-2 section of the Commander in Chief, Far East (CINCFE) headquarters attached the following comment:

"Comment: The People's Army will be prepared to invade South Korea by fall and possibly by spring of this year indicated in the current report of armed force expansion and major troop movements at critical 38th parallel areas. Even if future reports bear out the present indication, it is believed civil war will not necessarily be precipitated. . . ." Secretary Acheson also called attention to a G-2 CINCFE comment made 25 March 1950 on their estimate of the probability of civil war in Korea:

"It is believed there will be no civil war in Korea this spring or summer. The most probable course of North Korean action this spring or summer is furtherance of its attempt to overthrow the South Korean government by the creation of chaotic conditions in the Republic through guerilla activities and psychological warfare."

of all units of the armed forces in North Korea (as preparatory war measures). Positive identification of seven Army divisions. . . . Note the existence of several regular Army divisions, located roughly in a cross-country belt between the 38th and 39th parallels. . . . Previous evidence of the entry from Manchuria of trained Communists of Korean ethnic origin would furnish the necessary manpower (for additional divisions). In addition, there is continuous compulsory recruitment; estimates indicate as many as 100,000 to 150,000 of North Korean youths.[32]

Despite such despatches, coming in from various intelligence agencies throughout 1949 and the first half of 1950, there was, in Secretary Acheson's words, agreement that the outbreak of war "did not appear imminent."

The Korean War actually commenced without warning at 0400 of 25 June 1950. A 45-minute artillery bombardment by North Korean batteries across the 38th parallel was followed by rapid assaults of Communist infantry and armor, composed of six North Korean divisions of infantry, three Border Constabulary Brigades, supported by approximately one hundred Soviet-made T-34 and T-70 tanks, ample heavy artillery, and the North Korean Air Force. The total strength of the attacking units was later estimated at 100,000. The North Korean Army rapidly advanced against light forces of the Republic of Korea which were unprepared and ill-equipped for any such assault.* Along the east coast, a Border Constabulary Brigade, numbering 10,000 troops, carried out two amphibious landings at Kangnung and Samchok.

On 26 June, two more North Korean divisions moved south across the parallel, and on 28 June the enemy entered Seoul, the capital of the Republic of Korea, without effort. In four full days of almost unimpeded Communist success, the Republic's forces were driven steadily down the peninsula without being able to rally even for temporary resistance along the Han River, 32 miles from the 38th parallel.

First official word of the assault, a report from Ambassador Muccio in Seoul made at 11:25 a.m. of 25 June in Korea, reached Washington at 9:26 p.m. on 24 June.

According to Korean Army reports which are partly confirmed by Korean Military Advisory Group field adviser reports, North Korean forces invaded Republic of Korea territory at several points this morning. Action was in-

---

* An observation team of the UN commission on Korea forwarded a report of an inspection trip dated 24 June 1950 which said that they "had, in the course of a two-weeks inspection trip, been left with the impression that the Republican Army was organized entirely for defense and (was) in no condition to carry out a large scale attack against the forces in the north." The observers found that the ROK forces were disposed in depth all along the 38th parallel with no concentration of troops at any point, that a large number of ROK forces were actively engaged in rounding up guerrillas, and were, in any case, entirely lacking in the armor, heavy artillery, and air support necessary to carry off an invasion of North Korea.

itiated about 4 a.m. Ongjin was blasted by North Korean artillery fire. About 6 a.m. North Korean infantry commenced crossing the (38th) parallel in the Ongjin area, Kaesong area, and Chunchon area, and an amphibious landing was reportedly made south of Kangnung on the east coast. Kaesong was reportedly captured at 9 a.m., with some ten North Korean tanks participating in the operation. North Korean forces, spearheaded by tanks, are reportedly closing in on Chunchon. Details of the fighting in the Kangnung area are unclear, although it seems that North Korean forces have cut the highway. I am conferring with Korean Military Advisory Group advisers and Korean officials this morning concerning the situation.

It would appear from the nature of the attack and the manner it was launched that it constitutes an all-out offensive against the Republic of Korea.

Muccio

The war was now seven hours old. The United Nations was informed immediately. At 3 a.m., 25 June, Washington time, the United States Government requested a meeting of the United Nations Security Council in the following words:

Dear Mr. Secretary-General: I have the honour to transmit herewith the text of the message which I read to you on the telephone at three o'clock this morning, June 25, 1950.

Will you be good enough to bring the message to the immediate attention of the President of the United Nations Security Council.

Faithfully yours,

Ernest A. Gross
(Deputy Representative of the United States
to the United Nations)

When this meeting took place at 2 p.m. that day, a report of the invasion sent in by the United Nations Commission in Korea was at hand.

Government of Republic of Korea states that about 04:00 hours 25 June attacks were launched in strength by North Korean forces all along the 38th parallel. Major points of attack have included Ongjin Peninsula, Kaesong area and Chunchon, and east coast where seaborne landings have been reported north and south of Kangnung. Another seaborne landing reported imminent under air cover in Pohang area on southeast coast. . . .

At 17:15 hrs. four Yak-type aircraft strafed civilian and military air fields outside Seoul, destroying planes, firing gas tanks and attacking jeeps. Yong-dung-po railroad station on outskirts also strafed.

Commission wishes to draw attention of Secretary-General to serious situation developing which is assuming character of full-scale war and may endanger the maintenance of international peace and security. It suggests that he consider possibility of bringing matter to notice of Security Council. Commission will communicate more fully considered recommendation later.

(The United Nations Commission to Korea to the Secretary-General.)

By a vote of 9 to 0—with one abstention, and with the Soviet representative absent, as he had been since January 1950—the Security Council took action by resolution, as follows:

The Security Council,

Noting with grave concern the armed attack upon the Republic of Korea by forces from North Korea,

Determines that this action constitutes a breach of the peace,

I. Calls for the immediate cessation of hostilities, and

Calls upon the authorities of North Korea to withdraw forthwith their armed forces to the thirty-eighth parallel;

II. Requests the United Nations Commission on Korea

(a) To communicate its fully considered recommendations on the situation with the least possible delay;

(b) To observe the withdrawal of the North Korean forces to the thirty-eighth parallel; and

(c) To keep the Security Council informed on the execution of this resolution;

III. Calls upon all Members to render every assistance to the United Nations in the execution of this resolution and to refrain from giving assistance to the North Korean authorities.

(Resolution Adopted by the Security Council, June 25, 1950.)

On the evening of the same day, as a result of a Blair House* meeting of the President with representatives from the State and Defense Departments, the Joint Chiefs of Staff notified General MacArthur: "Assist in evacuating United States dependents and noncombatants (names to be furnished by the United States Ambassador in Korea). MacArthur authorized to take action by Air and Navy to prevent the Inchon-Kimpo-Seoul area from falling into unfriendly hands."

General MacArthur was also told to furnish to the Korean Government additional military supplies under the Mutual Defense Assistance Program, and to dispatch a military survey group to Korea to obtain first-hand information on the assistance required by the Republic of Korea to meet the Communist attack.

By 26 June it was apparent that the North Koreans had the capability of taking Seoul within a short time and that their advance might interfere with the completion of the evacuation task. Another conference of representatives of the State and Defense Departments was held at Blair House with the President presiding. Following this conference, the Joint Chiefs of Staff advised General MacArthur: ". . . at the direction of the President, the Commander in Chief, Far East (CINCFE) is authorized to utilize Navy and Air Force elements of the Far East Command to attack all North Korean

---

* Blair House, in Washington, was being used as the temporary Executive Mansion pending repairs to the White House itself.

military targets (troop columns, guns, tanks) south of the 38th parallel in order to clear South Korea of North Korean military forces. . . . he is authorized to use naval forces of the Far East Command in the coastal waters and sea approaches of Korea without restriction. . . ."[33]

The following day, 27 June, the United Nations Security Council adopted a second resolution:

The Security Council,
Having determined that the armed attack upon the Republic of Korea by forces from North Korea constitutes a breach of the peace,
Having called for an immediate cessation of hostilities, and
Having called upon the authorities of North Korea to withdraw forthwith their armed forces to the 38th parallel, and
Having noted from the report of the United Nations Commission for Korea that the authorities in North Korea have neither ceased hostilities nor withdrawn their armed forces to the 38th parallel and that urgent military measures are required to restore international peace and security, and
Having noted the appeal from the Republic of Korea to the United Nations for immediate and effective steps to secure peace and security,
Recommends that the Members of the United Nations furnish such assistance to the Republic of Korea as may be necessary to repel the armed attack and to restore international peace and security in the area.[34]

On this same day, President Truman issued a statement:

In Korea the Government forces, which were armed to prevent border raids and to preserve internal security, were attacked by invading forces from North Korea. The Security Council of the United Nations called upon the invading troops to cease hostilities and to withdraw to the 38th parallel. This they have not done but on the contrary have pressed the attack. The Security Council called upon all members of the United Nations to render every assistance to the United Nations in the execution of this resolution. In these circumstances I have ordered United States air and sea forces to give the Korean Government troops cover and support.
The attack upon Korea makes it plain beyond all doubt that Communism has passed beyond the use of subversion to conquer independent nations and will now use armed invasion and war. It has defied the orders of the Security Council of the United Nations issued to preserve international peace and security. In these circumstances the occupation of Formosa by Communist forces would be a direct threat to the security of the Pacific area and to United States forces performing their lawful and necessary functions in that area.
Accordingly I have ordered the Seventh Fleet to prevent any attack on Formosa. . . .

On 7 July, the United Nations Security Council adopted a third resolution:

The Security Council, having determined that the armed attack upon the

Republic of Korea by forces from North Korea constitutes a breach of the peace, having recommended that members of the United Nations furnish such assistance to the Republic of Korea as may be necessary to repel the armed attack and to restore international peace and security in the area,

(1) Welcomes the prompt and vigorous support which governments and peoples of the United Nations have given to its resolutions of 25 and 27 June 1950 to assist the Republic of Korea in defending itself against armed attack and thus to restore international peace and security in the area;

(2) Notes that members of the United Nations have transmitted to the United Nations offers of assistance for the Republic of Korea;

(3) Recommends that all members providing military forces and other assistance pursuant to the aforesaid Security Council resolutions make such forces and other assistance available to a unified command under the United States;

(4) Requests the United States to designate the commander of such forces;

(5) Authorizes the unified command at its discretion to use the United Nations flag in the course of operations against North Korean forces concurrently with the flags of the various nations participating.

(6) Requests the United States to provide the Security Council with reports, as appropriate on the course of action taken under the unified command.[35]

Seven countries voted for the resolution: the United States, the United Kingdom, France, China, Cuba, Ecuador and Norway.

Three countries abstained: Egypt, India and Yugoslavia.

One country was absent: the Soviet Union.

2.

Retreat to Pusan

Holding the Bridgehead

The war which neither the American people nor the United States Navy expected to fight—and, for that matter, the war which neither the Russians, Chinese Communists, nor the North Koreans expected us to fight—found the following ships of the United States Navy in the waters around Japan on 25 June 1950:

AMPHIBIOUS FORCE
(RADM J. H. Doyle)

USS *Mt. McKinley* (AGC-7)
(CAPT C. A. Printup)

USS *Cavalier* (APA-37)
(CAPT S. S. Bowling)

USS *Union* (AKA-106)
(CAPT G. D. Zurmuhlen)

USS *LST 611*
(LT J. C. Wilson)

USS *Arikara* (ATF-98)
(LCDR K. A. Mundy)

SUPPORT FORCE
(RADM J. M. Higgins, ComCruDiv 5)

1 CL—*Juneau*
(CAPT J. C. Sowell)

DesDiv 91 (CAPT H. C. Allan)
4 DDs—*Mansfield*
(CDR E. H. Headland)

De Haven
(CDR O. B. Lundgren)

Collett
(CDR R. H. Close)

Swenson
(CDR R. A. Schilling)

Minron 3
6 AMs—*Redhead*
(LTJG T. R. Howard)

Mocking Bird
(LTJG S. P. Gary)

Osprey
(LTJG P. Levin)

> *Partridge*
> (LTJG R. C. Fuller, Jr.)
>
> *Chatterer*
> (LTJG J. P. McMahon)
>
> *Kite*
> (LTJG N. Grkovic)

In Tokyo, the staff of Commander Naval Forces, Far East, Vice Admiral C. Turner Joy, numbered 29 officers.

In an interview at Tokyo in October 1950, Admiral Joy said:

"My main peacetime mission had been largely one of promoting the recovery and rehabilitation of Japan. Operations involving the U.S. Navy were relatively minor. Instead, my staff supervised the mine clearance work and the Japanese merchant marine and shipbuilding program. My staff also supervised the naval stations at Yokosuka and Sasebo.

"The one cruiser, four destroyers, and six minesweepers assigned to me had a variety of peacetime tasks: patrolling the Tsushima Straits to prevent smuggling between Korea and Japan; periodic patrols around Hokkaido; the showing of our flag in the various Japanese ports; various training operations; and patrols along the Ryukyus to prevent smuggling by the Chinese pirates.

"When the word of the invasion of South Korea reached me, I felt that we should oppose the aggression, but I didn't think we would. Consequently, when the United Nations took action, and American forces were ordered into Korea, I was quite surprised. This was the general impression among all of us in Japan.

"General MacArthur was likewise surprised, and commented that this action was a complete reversal of our Far East policy. He and I agreed that opposing the invasion was the correct action, but we were surprised that it happened. As a consequence, we had no plans for this type of war.

"At first, the Army estimated that Korea would be overrun within six weeks. Also, there was great concern lest the civil war in Korea prove to be merely the starting point for World War III.

"For this reason, I ordered the Seventh Fleet into Okinawa rather than Sasebo. Sasebo was too near Russian airbases."

General MacArthur told the authors that the United States-United Nations decision to intervene in the Korean conflict was a surprise, and added: "The military policy of the United States as communicated to me up to that time was to avoid action on the Korean Peninsula—and I was not consulted with regard to the decision to intervene before it was taken."

The units of the Seventh Fleet were divided among Sangley Point, Subic Bay, and Hong Kong. Vice Admiral Arthur D. Struble, the Seventh Fleet

Commander, was in Washington, and Rear Admiral J. M. Hoskins, Commander Carrier Division Three, was acting.

SEVENTH FLEET (VADM A. D. Struble)
ComCarDiv 3 (RADM J. M. Hoskins)

1 CV —*Valley Forge* (CAPT L. K. Rice)
1 CA —*Rochester* (CAPT E. L. Woodyard)
8 DDs—*Shelton* (CDR C. B. Jackson, Jr.)
      Eversole (CDR C. E. Phillips)
      Fletcher (CDR W. M. Lowry)
      Radford (CDR E. C. Ogle)
      Maddox (CDR P. B. Hines, Jr.)
      S. N. Moore (CDR R. H. Wanless)
      Brush (CDR F. L. Sheffield, Jr.)
      Taussig (CDR W. C. Meyer)

The Fleet's peacetime mission had largely been that of showing the flag around the Orient; in fact, the planes of Air Group Five had flown in parade over Inchon and Seoul on 5 April from the decks of the *Valley Forge*. A few days later they had appeared over Hong Kong.

"At the end of May, the Seventh Fleet had held large scale exercises between China and the Philippines," said Admiral Struble later.[1] "These Fleet exercises had taken place during the turn-over period when a greater number of ships were present, and when Admiral Joy's forces could be present. For the rest of the summer, I planned to have the Fleet pay a visit to Manila on 4 July, then a visit to Hong Kong, and a summer trip to Japan.

"In mid-June, I flew up to Manila to confer with the Secretary of Defense, Mr. Louis Johnson, and the Chairman of the Joint Chiefs of Staff, General Bradley. We talked about many problems: the Huk problem in the Philippines, and the many probabilities of what might happen in other areas— Formosa, Indo-China, and Japan. Although Korea was in the Seventh Fleet area of responsibility, the subject of that country was not brought up.

"On 18 June I left Manila for Pearl Harbor and Washington for talks with Admiral Radford and Admiral Sherman, and to attend the wedding of my daughter.

"Therefore, I was in Washington on Sunday, 25 June, when the Korean War started. I raised the question of my departure time, and Sherman told me to wait until the next day after conclusion of the talks he was having with the President and other senior officials.

"I did so, and upon my departure Admiral Sherman assured me that U.S. forces would definitely be committed in Korea."

The free world could consider itself fortunate that the Seventh Fleet and the NavFE (Naval Forces, Far East) ships were within fast cruising distance of Korea, and that they were well prepared and in a high state of readiness.

The *Valley Forge,* with Air Group Five aboard, was the number one carrier and jet-trained air group of the Pacific Fleet. Cruisers *Rochester* and *Juneau* were likewise well trained. The ships of the Destroyer squadron and division were old hands in the Orient.

Two other circumstances proved fortunate as the war intensified. First, Amphibious Group One (RADM James H. Doyle, USN, aboard the *Mount McKinley*) was in the area conducting amphibious training exercises in Japanese waters. It was, perhaps, the most seasoned group of amphibious experts in the Pacific Fleet. Second, Mobile Training Team Able of the Troop Training Unit, Amphibious Force, Pacific (Officer in Charge Colonel Edward H. Forney, USMC) was engaged in indoctrinating the U.S. Eighth Army in Japan.

The presence of these naval ships, the amphibious group, and the Marine training team were of critical importance to the maintenance of a toehold in Korea. The first eighty-two days of the Korean War—from 25 June until the Inchon landing on 15 September 1950—were a retreat to a defensible perimeter and a desperate holding action. All military efforts—Army, Navy, Air Force—in these critical days were devoted to a single objective: maintaining a Korean bridgehead around the port of Pusan and preventing South Korean and American soldiers from being overrun, outflanked, cut off, captured, or eventually thrown into the sea.

With this perspective, the naval history of the early days of the Korean War can be divided into four principal efforts: the flights of the carrier aircraft of Task Forces 77 and 96 on close air support, armed reconnaissance, and interdiction missions; the naval gunfire support and bombardment efforts of the cruisers and destroyers along the east coast; the timely amphibious landing at Pohang, and the amphibious evacuation of the Third ROK division in July and August, respectively; and the timely arrival of the U.S. Marines.

None of these efforts can lay exclusive claim to the salvation of the peninsular toehold by the UN forces. In combination, however, these several naval events powerfully contributed to holding the Pusan perimeter. Had these naval events *not* been successfully executed, Korea could certainly *not* have been held.

Initial Orders to an Assembling Fleet

On Sunday, 26 June, Washington time,* in a teletype conference between

---

* A time difference of fourteen hours exists between Korea and Washington. For example, Sunday noon in Washington is two o'clock Monday morning in Korea. Crossing the international dateline westward in mid-Pacific at the 180th degree of longitude, the calendar is moved forward one day. The time used hereafter in this book will be that of the place in which the event occurred.

the principal military figures in Tokyo and Washington, the following orders regarding U. S. naval forces were issued:

> . . . CINCFE is authorized to take such action by air and Navy to insure safe evacuation U.S. dependents and noncombatants. . . . Seventh Fleet is ordered to proceed immediately to Sasebo and report to ComNavFE for operational control. . . . While the foregoing decisions are geared to the protection of dependents and noncombatants, further high-level decisions may be expected as military and political situations develop. . . .

Simultaneously, in a despatch from the Chief of Naval Operations, Admiral Forrest P. Sherman, to Admiral Arthur W. Radford, Commander in Chief, U.S. Pacific Fleet, the order to ready other ships for duty in the western Pacific was issued:

> . . . In an orderly manner and as soon as practicable organize another task group plus appropriate support for the western Pacific. . . .

At 0800, 27 June, Rear Admiral J. M. Hoskins sortied the Seventh Fleet from Subic Bay and Hong Kong, and headed for Sasebo. En route north in the vicinity of Formosa, *Valley Forge* planes (which had departed Hong Kong 24 June) flew through the Straits of Formosa and over the city of Taipei on 29 June. For the first few days of the Korean War, the sole task of the Seventh Fleet was the neutralization of Formosa in accordance with the Presidential order.

As the Seventh Fleet steamed northward at high speed, Vice Admiral C. T. Joy, Commander Naval Forces, Far East, ordered Hoskins to pull into Buckner Bay, Okinawa, rather than Sasebo, Japan. Here the Fleet would be close to Formosa, it would be close to Korea, and yet not too close to either Soviet or Chinese air bases. In the hectic initial days of the Korean War, no one knew whether or not the eruption was the first evidence of a local war or a global one. The news of the "incident" in Korea was only hours old when Secretary of State Dean Acheson alerted both diplomatic and military circles in Washington with the following despatch:

> Possible that Korea is only first of series of coordinated actions on part of Soviets. Maintain utmost vigilance and report immediately any positive or negative information. . . .[2]

No orders to the Fleet had yet been received from General MacArthur's headquarters, and no authority to attack *north* of parallel 38 had been issued from Washington. At this early stage, there was even some hope that the mere prospect of involvement of American airplanes and ships in accordance with the UN resolutions might cause the North Korean People's Army to cease and desist.

Meanwhile, on 27 June, Vice Admiral Joy ordered Rear Admiral Higgins to take his flagship *Juneau* and the destroyer *De Haven,* and patrol the coastal waters south of the 38th parallel and oppose any hostile landings. *De Haven* and *Mansfield* had just completed the Navy's first task, the evacuation of American nationals from Inchon and Pusan. *Juneau* and *De Haven* had also escorted the ammunition ship *Sergeant Keathley* from Tokyo to Pusan, while *Collett* and *Mansfield* were escorting the *Cardinal O'Connell.* Both the *Keathley* and the *O'Connell* were carrying badly needed ammunition and military supplies to Korea.

With so many tasks to perform, and so few ships with which to accomplish them, the receipt of a message from Admiral Sir Patrick Brind, RN (Commander in Chief, Far East Station, Hong Kong) on 28 June was most heartening and welcome to Admiral Joy:

"I shall be very glad to know of any operations in which my ships could help," Brind radioed. "Present dispositions are Task Group 96.8 in South Japan under Rear Admiral Andrewes consisting of *Triumph, Belfast, Jamaica,* two destroyers and three frigates. . . ."*

The Australians and New Zealanders were equally prompt:

"Her majesty's Australian ships in Japanese waters are placed unreservedly at your disposal as you wish."

"Two New Zealand frigates will be ready to leave Auckland 3 July. Further ships later."

Joy replied that these ships were needed very badly indeed. The carrier, cruiser, and two destroyers could join the American Striking Force, the other ships the escort and blockade force.

The naval preliminaries were thus completed. American nationals and noncombatants had been evacuated from Korea. Urgently needed military supplies requested by the South Koreans had been delivered. Fighting ships had assembled. The ships of the blockade force were joined by British and Australian ships. The Seventh Fleet in Okinawa's Buckner Bay was joined by the British cruiser *Belfast* (flagship of Rear Admiral W. G. Andrewes, RN), carrier *Triumph,* and destroyers *Cossack* and *Consort.*

"Upon my arrival in Okinawa from my conference in Tokyo," said Admiral Struble subsequently, "RADM Andrewes reported to me, saying that he was very anxious to have his ships join the first expedition into the Yellow Sea. Although the *Triumph* was slower than the *Valley Forge,* and there were other operating difficulties, these were successfully solved. I decided to include them in the Task Force 77 organization."

And lastly, orders for the offensive employment of the assembling fleet

---

* Destroyers were HMS *Cossack* (CAPT R. T. White, DSO) and HMS *Consort* (CDR J. R. Carr); frigates were HMS *Black Swan* (CAPT A. D. H. Jay, DSO, DSC), *Alacrity* (CDR H. S. Barber) and HMS *Hart* (CDR N. H. H. Mulleneux, DSC).

north of the 38th parallel were received by General MacArthur from the Joint Chiefs of Staff in Washington:

> The Seventh Fleet is assigned to your operational control. You are authorized to extend your military operation into North Korea against . . . purely military targets if and when in your judgment this becomes necessary.*

The Pyongyang Strikes (3–4 July 1950)

Upon his arrival in Tokyo on 29 June, Vice Admiral Struble immediately conferred with Admiral Joy and Generals MacArthur and Stratemeyer. Where could the striking power of the carrier *Valley Forge* best be utilized? After consultation and study, the military targets in the North Korean capital of Pyongyang were selected: principally, the airfield and aircraft upon them; secondly, the Pyongyang railroad yards and bridges, over which a major portion of the enemy's munitions were being transported into South Korea.

Task Force 77 sortied on the evening of 1 July for the west coast of Korea with Pyongyang as its objective. As the combined British-American fleet steamed northward, the benefits of previous combined US-UK (United States-United Kingdom) training were noted by RADM Andrewes.[3]

"During the passage of Okinawa," recorded the British Admiral, "United States tactical signals were brought into force on 30 June. A large proportion of our commanding officers and communication personnel had, of course, had previous experience of United States procedures during World War II, but the combined exercises with the United States Fleet in March 1950 proved of value. As a result of these exercises, we were already in possession of the United States books and many of us had had recent experience with their use. . . . It all seemed familiar, joining up in Formation Four Roger, as it was just what we had done so often during the exercises in March with very similar forces. We didn't feel out of things. . . ."

Task Force 77 Tactical Organization

TF77 Striking Force† (VADM A. D. Struble, USN)

---

* Thus, for the first time, General MacArthur received operational (but not tactical) control over large carriers. This operational control was exercised through COMNAVFE and ComSeventhFleet:

"Never once throughout the course of the Pacific war did that Headquarters (MacArthur's) exercise direct tactical command of a single fast carrier. . . . Both King and Nimitz feared the consequences of placing fast carriers under the supervision of a headquarters (MacArthur's) which so evidently looked upon them as expendable. Marines and escort carriers were later assigned to the Southwest Pacific area." (*The U. S. Marines and Amphibious War*, Isley and Crowl, p. 92.)

† The term "Striking Force" was retained until 25 August 1950 when, by Commander Seventh Fleet Operation Order #14-50, the term "Fast Carrier Force" was used.

TG77.1 Support Force (RADM W. G. Andrewes, RN)
  HMS *Belfast* (CAPT Sir Aubrey St. Clair-Fox, Bt, RN, DSO)
  USS *Rochester*
TG77.2 Screening Group (CAPT C. W. Parker, USN)
  Shelton
  Eversole
  Fletcher
  Radford
  Maddox
  S. N. Moore
  Brush
  Taussig
  HMS *Cossack*
  HMS *Consort*
TG77.4 Carrier Group (RADM J. M. Hoskins, USN)
  Valley Forge (CAPT L. K. Rice, USN)
  HMS *Triumph* (CAPT A. D. Torless, DSO)

As the task force steamed northward, a series of messages from Commander Naval Forces, Far East, was received:

> CINCFE authorizes you to continue strikes past the first day in view of the rapidly deteriorating Korean situation. Highest priority to be given to rail facilities in vicinity of Kumchon, Sariwon, and Sinanju. . . .

In the pre-dawn of 3 July, commencing at 0545, the *Triumph* launched twelve Fireflies and nine rocket-loaded Seafires for attacks upon hangars and installations at the Haeju airfield with railway traffic and bridges as secondary targets. The flight returned at 0815 without casualty except minor flak damage.

Valley Forge's attack group—sixteen F4U Corsairs from VF-54, led by Lieutenant Commander D. K. English, and twelve AD Skyraiders from VA-55, led by Lieutenant Commander N. D. Hodson—were off at 0600. The Corsairs were loaded with eight 5-inch rockets, the Skyraiders with two 500-pound bombs and six 100-pounders.

Shortly thereafter, eight F9F2 Panthers were catapulted from *Valley Forge* led by air group commander Commander Harvey P. Lanham. Although the jets (being used in combat for the first time by the U. S. Navy) departed behind the propeller-driven strike group, they would overtake and climb above them, and arrive just ahead in order to catch North Korean planes on the ground.

While the en route weather was poor, the weather over Pyongyang was good. The jet sweep's first pass across the Pyongyang field accounted for three planes: Commander Lanham's guns fired a transport plane on the ground, Lieutenant (Junior Grade) Leonard Plog and Ensign E. W. Brown,

Jr., each destroyed an airborne YAK fighter.[4] The second pass accounted for two more aircraft on the ground—one by Lieutenant (junior grade) Donald L. Christianson, the other by the U. S. Air Force exchange officer, Major Edward F. Connor, USAF.

Concurrently, while the jets were igniting the hangars, ammunition dumps, and revetments, the propeller strike group arrived overhead. The twelve ADs made a high-speed approach, and a final pushover from 7,000 feet, closely followed by the Corsairs.

The pattern of the bombs and rockets was excellent, and little of the Pyongyang airfield's installations escaped damage. One bomb was a direct hit on the field's fuel storage farm; all three of the hangars were demolished; the runways were liberally cratered.

The enemy antiaircraft fire was meager and inaccurate, and no hits on the naval aircraft were reported.

The afternoon flights were similar, with the Pyongyang railyard and rail and road bridges across the Taedong River as primary targets. Rockets and bombs exploded in the roundhouse, the repair sheds, the station house, and the tracks; fifteen locomotives were destroyed, ten others damaged; many boxcars were bombed, strafed, and set afire. Although several bombs were close enough to qualify as "hits," the bridge was left standing.

However, Hodson's VA-55 pilots destroyed a span on the 4 July Independence Day attacks, as well as destroying ten locomotives. Small ships in the nearby river (thought to be gunboats because of their return fire) were also attacked and put out of action. Four aircraft, all Skyraiders, were struck by antiaircraft fire during these attacks but all succeeded in returning safely to the "Happy Valley." One of the damaged ADs, unable to reduce speed by lowering its flaps, made a high and fast approach, took a cut, landed wheels first and bounced over the protecting barriers into the planes parked forward. One AD and two F4Us were totally destroyed while three ADs, one F4U, and two F9Fs were damaged.

The initial two days of carrier strikes on the airfields and rail facilities of North Korea's capital city had been highly successful. The American-British fleet had worked together with the greatest harmony, and Struble congratulated Andrewes' ships. In addition to wrecking the city's rail center, dropping a span of the key Pyongyang bridge, and demolishing the airfield and its installations, the Seventh Fleet aircraft had destroyed eleven enemy aircraft and had damaged one.

In the month of July, as a matter of fact, *Valley Forge* pilots claimed thirty-eight aircraft destroyed and twenty-seven damaged, all except two on the ground. This performance was undoubtedly a major reason for the failure of the North Korean air force* to play an important role in the subsequent fighting.

As Rear Admiral E. C. Ewen recorded later:

"It is quite possible that the early appearance of the Panthers (the F9F-2 jet aircraft) over northern Korea on 3 July had a quieting effect on Russian and Chinese plans to provide North Korea with large numbers of obsolescent propeller-type aircraft."

The Landing at Pohang

To appreciate the contribution and timeliness of the Pohang landing in holding the Pusan perimeter, a brief résumé of the ground fighting is needed. The map on page 40 illustrates the rapidity of the North Korean drive southward.

On 7 July, only seven hundred-odd men of the U.S. 24th Division were in action. These had been hastily flown from Japan to Korea. General MacArthur summarized the desperate situation thus:

"The immediate problem presented is that of blocking the advance of enemy ground and flanking units now advancing on every highway and trail in Korea from coast to coast. Our estimates continue that the North Koreans are employing a total force of nine divisions supported by attached armor. The morale of their forces is extremely high and is being spurred by a continuous advance southward. Nothing that we have been able to do currently has sufficed to take the edge from the victorious ardor of the North Koreans."

On 10 July, the badly-outnumbered American and Korean troops in Korea took up defensive positions in front of Taejon, a city of 37,000 and an important communications center. Four enemy divisions, supported by heavy artillery and tanks, waded the Kum River on 14 July, attacked advanced elements of the U.S. 24th Division[5] (commanded by Major General William F. Dean), and drove toward Taejon from several directions.

The thin ranks of the 24th Division, committed piecemeal into action, were shredded by the heavy pressure. Each of the 24th's three infantry regiments had only two battalions instead of the standard three, making the defense of so wide a front impossible. The 24th was also short of artillery, having only two instead of three batteries in each artillery battalion. And the few American tanks which were available were light ones, badly outnumbered, and no match for the Soviet T-34s. In addition, the American 2.36-inch bazookas proved ineffective against the Soviet tank armor.

---

* The North Korean Air Force before the war had been estimated at 54 aircraft—33 YAK-type fighters and 21 IL-type attack bombers. Their primary operating fields were Pyongyang, Wonsan, Sinanju, and Sinuiju.

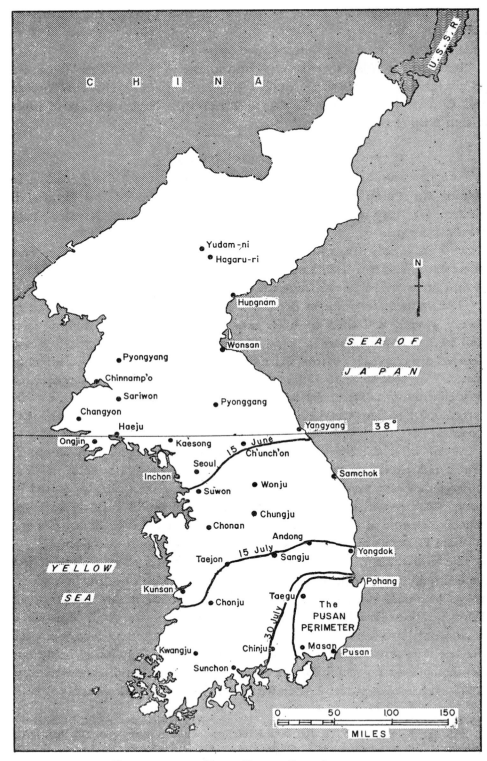

RAPIDITY OF THE NORTH KOREAN DRIVE SOUTHWARD

The enemy, moreover, refused to attack in conventional patterns. His high state of training was demonstrated on the night of 16 July when a coordinated night attack struck the 24th. The attack was four-pronged— a strong frontal attack and an enveloping attack on each flank, plus infiltrating attacks from the rear. Large numbers of Red troops, disguised as refugees and with disassembled weapons hidden in innocent-looking bundles, passed through the UN lines, assembled in the rear areas, and began to harass the 24th Division from the rear.

With the ROK (Republic of Korea) forces all but collapsed, the salvation of Korea depended on getting the maximum number of American troops into action in the shortest possible time. However, getting troops from Japan to Korea was no easily-solved problem. Only limited amphibious lift was available, the main port of Pusan was already congested and confused, and the roads from Pusan to the front lines were horribly jammed by traffic and refugees, mostly southbound.

On 18 July, the prospects for holding the peninsula were ominously poor. Despite a series of brilliant rear-guard actions, the 24th Division could not hope to check the coordinated attacks of four enemy divisions in its front. Fortunately, the 25th Division was arriving, having been sea-lifted by a Military Sea Transportation Service shuttle from Kyushu to Pusan, and was getting into action. But even its hastily-arriving strength was insufficient.

The swollen, refugee-jammed dirt roads from Pusan to Taejon could accommodate no more troops or trucks. If Korea was to be saved, other reinforcements had to come by sea—and quickly.

In retrospect, it is clear that the unspectacular and unpublicized amphibious landing at Pohang-dong on 18 July did as much to preserve the perilous Korean toehold as any single event.

The Selection of Pohang

By good fortune, on the day the North Koreans smashed across the 38th parallel, Rear Admiral James H. Doyle, USN, was ordering his Amphibious Group One ships to get under way from Yokosuka, Japan, to conduct amphibious training exercises with the embarked troops of the 35th Regimental Combat Team (25th Infantry Division) on Chigasaki Beach, Sagami-Wan.

Thus, a program of amphibious familiarization for the Eighth Army troops had been begun in May. While the Army units were not thereby prepared or well trained, certain rudiments of the amphibious art had been transmitted. The brief training given to the Army units would be of later value in the several amphibious landings in the next six months of the Korean war: Pohang, Inchon, Wonsan, Iwon, and Hungnam.

More important, however, was the on-the-spot availability and know-how of Amphibious Group One's amphibious shipping for rushing Army troops to Korea.

The selection of Pohang was one of simple expediency. In early July, Doyle and seven selected members of his staff had been ordered to Tokyo for consultation with Joy and MacArthur's staffs in connection with the planning of an offensive amphibious operation with the First Cavalry Division. Following these conferences, MacArthur had directed that plans be made to land the division at Inchon, or, alternatively, at Kunsan on the west coast. Planning to do so went forward until 9 July. In the words of Doyle's planning officer, CDR John V. Noel, Jr., USN: "The nine days between 4 July and 13 July were controlled pandemonium. The expression used at the time was that Inchon would be the 'anvil' upon which the First Cavalry Division would land, hammer, and destroy the North Koreans. These rosy dreams were quickly shattered by the rout of the South Koreans. . . ."

The rapid deterioration of the ground fighting in Korea made it apparent that another landing site, one on the *east* coast, had to be found for the defense of the Pusan perimeter. Doyle suggested Pohang as the most likely objective. This was accepted on 10 July.

The village of Pohang, 15,000 inhabitants, lay 70 miles north of Pusan. On 10 July it was still a safe distance from the advancing front, thanks in great measure to the sharp-shooting efforts of Rear Admiral Higgins' cruiser and destroyer naval gunfire support. The city had a useable airfield, fair anchorages, and a thousand-yard strip of sandy beach which would facilitate an amphibious landing. Better still, a single track railroad ran westward into Taegu, thence northwestward to Taejon; this could rapidly transport the First Cavalry to the central front.

While Pohang looked ideal, much vital data was needed before a landing there could be sensibly planned. Accordingly, a reconnaissance group flew into Pohang on 11 July. The party consisted of three men from Amphibious Group One staff (LCDR Jack Lowentrout, CAPT Vincent J. Robinson, USMC, and LTJG George Atcheson, III), plus members from Major General Hobart Gay's First Cavalry Division staff. This reconnaissance party returned on 13 July with valuable information on the conditions of the proposed beaches, depths of water, unloading facilities, and general capabilities of the port.

The urgent need to deposit the First Cavalry Division in Korea at the earliest moment disclosed other problems. The first of these was the shortage of suitable amphibious assault shipping. Two former Military Sea Transportation Service ships, *Oglethorpe* (AKA-100, Captain Paul D. Heerbrandt) and *Titania* (AKA-13, Captain Frank D. Giambattista) were rushed into Yokosuka and fitted with hastily pre-fabricated boat skids. Other needed equipment, such as boat servicing gear, towing bridles, and boat and vehicle slings, was quickly manufactured.

In addition to getting the so-called AKAs ready, six LSUs were reactivated at Yokosuka. These six ex-Japanese vessels, under the command of Doyle's Chief of Staff, Captain Norman W. Sears, would perform the lion's share of the unloading work at Pohang.

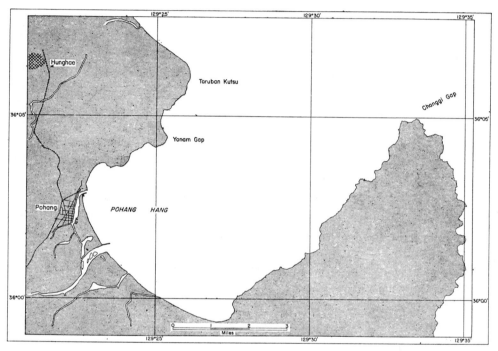

TOE HOLD AT POHANG

The final shortage was personnel; boat crews, hatch crews, and communication personnel were particularly short. This problem was solved by the Amphibious Base at Coronado, California, which rushed additional personnel westward by the first available air transportation.

The assault forces for Pohang were underway from the Tokyo-Yokosuka area on 15 July to the strains of an Army band playing "Anchors Aweigh." As the Fleet sailed, no one was certain whether the fighting front would be *north* or *south* of Pohang upon their arrival. The troops might have to fight their way ashore, or they might be able to debark unopposed. Situation reports coming into the *Mount McKinley* told of a battle along the coastal road only seven miles north of Pohang. Could the Third ROK Division hold the town until the First Cavalry got there? One hopeful harbinger came from the ships of Mine Squadron Three (LCDR D. V. Shouldice) which had swept the approaches and harbor on 15-17 July. No mines were present.

With the departure of the ships, an advance party from the staffs of Admiral Doyle and General Hobart Gay, commanding the First Cavalry, flew to Pohang in order to furnish last-minute intelligence on the enemy situation and to make all possible preparations for the landing.

The naval forces arrived in Pohang's harbor at 0500 on 18 July after dodging a capricious typhoon called "Grace." All was well. The battleline was still *north* of Pohang.

Accordingly, at 0558, Doyle hoisted the signal, "Land The Landing Force," and executed his alternate "No Opposition" landing plan. Ships anchored in the inner transport area, and began landing men and equipment at the docks in the inner harbor. "This was very fortunate," said CDR Noel, "because the beaches we had planned to land on were not at all satisfactory."

Troops and vehicles unloaded as rapidly as possible. As the first soldiers stepped ashore, they were heartily welcomed by Lieutenant General Walton H. Walker, Commanding General, Eighth Army. Trains were standing by to rush them and their equipment to the front.

By midnight the same evening, 10,027 troops, 2,027 vehicles and 2,729 tons of bulk cargo had been unloaded. At noon the next day, General Gay had his command ashore and had assumed responsibility for them.

Less than forty-eight hours later, the first units of the First Cavalry Division had joined the landing force; and a week later, this Division was blunting the enemy's drive down the Taegu-Pusan highway.

"I do not believe the perimeter could have been held without the timely reinforcement of our forces by the First Cavalry Division," said VADM Joy.

The Wonsan Oil Refinery Strikes

By the early morning of the 18th, it was apparent that the amphibious landing at Pohang would be administrative (i.e., unopposed). Accordingly, shortly before H-hour, Admiral Doyle released the Seventh Fleet aircraft from their support role.

Admiral Struble ordered the Seventh Fleet northward into the Sea of Japan.

"While I was in Tokyo discussing the Pohang operation," said Admiral Struble later,[6] "I had several long conferences with General Stratemeyer and his FEAF staff.

"It was understood that the Seventh Fleet would cover the Pohang landing. That was our job. Even though the Air Force had planes operating from

NOT A WINTER WONDERLAND. Ice, snow, and the cold of the Korean winter hamper naval operations. *Above,* the gun captain of mount on CVA *Oriskany* surveys the de-icing job before him. *Center,* Seamen Dokken and Mockbee man 40-mm. battery aboard AGC *Eldorado.* *Below,* CVE *Badoeng Strait*'s snow sweepers work to permit flight operations.

KOREAN PRESIDENT SYNGMAN RHEE BOARDS U. S. WARSHIPS. *At top,* Marine battleship detachment provides an honor guard. *Below,* crew of heavy cruiser *Toledo,* flagship of Task Force 95, mans the rail in salute to President Rhee, who awarded them the Korean Presidential Unit Citation.

KOREANS AT WAR. *At top,* ROK marines make unopposed landing on Sin-do Island. *Center,* South Korean civilians form volunteer supply train, carrying ammunition on their backs for miles across country to aid American fighting units. *Lower left,* Korean nuns at Pusan port patiently await transportation to a coastal island. *Lower right,* CAPT Daniel Carlson and two Maryknoll Clinic sisters inspect relief supplies.

MASTERMIND OF THE INCHON ASSAULT. General of the Army Douglas MacArthur is piped aboard battleship *Missouri*. Confident of the capabilities of the Navy and Marine Corps to carry out this operation, General MacArthur saw his expectations fulfilled. He continued to emphasize the vitally important functions of both services.

northern Kyushu, it was recognized that they didn't have the communications.

"During the course of our discussions, I told General Stratemeyer that after the landing I was going to take the Fleet and conduct air strikes north of the 38th parallel, striking targets of opportunity. If we found anything appropriate, we'd hit it. There was no objection and no mention made of what we should or shouldn't hit."

The *Valley Forge,* therefore, launched planes to strike targets in North Korea. A morning flight of seven Panthers, led by Commander A. D. Pollock, commanding officer of VF-51,[7] swept up the northeast coast past the harbor of Wonsan. Prominent along the curving shoreline on the south side of the city was an oil refinery which looked untouched and in operation.

At 1700, twenty-one planes from the *Valley Forge* were launched. The eleven AD Skyraiders, each carrying one 1,000-pound bomb, one 500-pound bomb, and two HVAR* rockets were led by LCDR N. D. Hodson (Commanding Officer, VA-55). The ten F4U Corsairs, each carrying two rockets and full belts of 20-mm. ammunition, were led by LCDR W. R. Pittman (Commanding Officer, VF-53).

"The oil refinery," recorded LCDR Pittman, "stood out like a sore thumb. It was a tremendous installation, and we all recognized it immediately. My Corsairs started firing their rockets in pairs from 4,000 feet, with LT Carl E. Smith's team taking the southeast side and my four the northeast side. . . .

"Hodson followed us down and spaced his planes so as to cover the whole refinery. His squadron's bomb pattern was excellent. . . .

"When the attack was finished, it was difficult to see the target or to distinguish portions of the plant that were not destroyed due to the tremendous clouds of belching smoke from the refinery. . . . There were constant explosions as the fires steadily spread to the unbombed areas. The entire coast appeared to be on fire.

"As we went back to the 'Happy Valley,' from an altitude of 3,000 feet we could still see the smoke of that attack 60 miles away. In fact, it was still burning the next day (Note: It actually burned for four days, and it gave all our pilots an excellent navigation aid.)."[8]

After the capture of Wonsan in October 1950, the president of the Wonsan Oil Refinery Factory, Mr. Cho Byung Kwi, his chief accountant, and four of his engineers were interviewed. The six North Koreans told how the refinery had been attacked by aircraft five times *prior* to the *Valley Forge's* strike on the 18th of July. On these attacks, only three bombs had

* High velocity aircraft rocket.

fallen inside the refinery in a storage area. The remainder had dropped without damage in nearby fields. No bombs had hit any vital area, and production had not been affected.

Regarding the naval air strike of July 18th, however, the group told how this attack had started fires which covered the entire area, both factory and storage. Direct hits and near misses saturated every vital area. The refinery engineers stated that further operation of the plant after July 18th was impossible, that it was turned into a mass of twisted steel and rubble. Twelve thousand tons of refined products had gone up in smoke. Not one building was fit for occupancy. Streets throughout the plant were running six inches to two feet deep in oil following the attack; many roads were impassable because of rubble. The main power plant, the water tanks, the storage building, the cracking plants, the boilers, air compressors, and coke furnaces were virtually all destroyed.

In retrospect, the attack on the Chosin oil refinery (the biggest in Korea, having an estimated annual production of 1,700,000 barrels) was a target for "strategic warfare," according to the roles and missions which had been given the Armed Services in 1948 by the Key West Agreement.*

However, in the tension and confusion of the Korean fighting, when American lives were at stake and everything possible was being done to halt and hurt the Communists, the academic question of *who* was supposed to do *what* received scant consideration. On many occasions during the war, in fact, the Navy was asked to perform tasks which, according to the Key West Agreement, were not among its primary responsibilities. General MacArthur's request that the Navy strike the Yalu River bridges (November 1950), the request that the Navy assume the responsibility for the interdiction of northeast Korea (January 1951), the several emergency requests for "close air support" by Task Force 77 (July-August 1950), the destruction of the Yalu River hydroelectric plants (23-24 June 1952), and the Aoji oil refinery strike (1 September 1952) are cases in point.

The destruction of the Wonsan Oil Refinery was the first instance which

* The Key West Agreement resulted from a conference in Key West, Florida, 11-14 March 1948, between the Secretary of Defense and the Joint Chiefs of Staff. Following this conference, the Secretary of Defense issued a statement which, in seven parts, laid down the common functions of the Armed Forces and the specific functions of the JCS, the Army, Navy, Air Force, and Marines. The second listed primary function of the Air Force was "To be responsible for strategic air warfare." This is defined as: "Air combat and supporting operations designed to effect, through the systematic application of force to a selected series of vital targets, the progressive destruction and disintegration of the enemy's warmaking capacity to a point where he no longer retains the ability or the will to wage war. Vital targets may include key manufacturing systems, sources of raw material, critical material, stockpiles, power systems, transportation systems, communication facilities, concentrations of uncommitted elements of enemy armed forces, key agricultural areas, and other such target systems."

illustrated the inherent flexibility displayed by the Navy during the Korean War.

"Close Air Support" at the Pusan Perimeter

On 23 July 1950, as the heavily-outnumbered UN forces were pushed slowly and steadily backward toward Pusan by the savage and cunning attacks of the Communists, an urgent plea for close support help from the carriers was received.

Eighth Army's dispatch, tagged with that awful precedence prefix "emergency," was multiple-addressed to every major commander in the Far East theater: MacArthur, Joy, Struble, and Stratemeyer.

> Request information as to possible naval air employment in close and general support role in Korea . . . urgent requirement exists west coast Korea commencing 23 July. . . .[9]

This sudden request for naval air assistance commenced a two-month period of participation by Task Force 77 in a "close air support" effort which, until the Inchon landing, would occupy the major portion of the aircraft carriers' time and energy.

This period would also highlight a fundamental difference of opinion and disparity in doctrine regarding close air support between the Navy and Marines on the one hand, and the Air Force and Army on the other.

But most important, the air support rendered by the Task Force 77 carriers would prove a major factor in the salvation of the Pusan perimeter.

Before commencing the narrative of this effort in behalf of the Pusan perimeter, however, it is first necessary to define and describe "close air support," for this term had a different meaning for each of the main parties in Korea.

In the military lexicon, "close air support" is defined as "air action against hostile surface targets which are so close to friendly targets as to require detailed integration of each air mission with the fire and movement of those forces."[10]

In laymen's language, close air support is simply the use of the armament of an airplane in behalf of, and near to, the soldier on the ground.

Simple definitions notwithstanding, the concepts and technique of providing close air support can be exceedingly complex and difficult, as will be seen. The close air support system developed and perfected by the Navy and Marines (the system least used in Korea) was substantially different from the system developed by the Air Force and the Army (the system most used in Korea).

To achieve a better understanding of how close air support influenced the course of the Korean war, and particularly the outcome of the battle to save Pusan, it is helpful to know how, why, and under what conditions the two differing systems were developed.

Navy-Marine System of Close Air Support

The seed of close air support, as practiced by the Navy and Marine Corps, was planted in the 1920's during Marine Corps action in Nicaragua, Haiti, and Santo Domingo. In these Caribbean countries, airplanes and infantry functioned as a team for the first time in military history.

As an outgrowth of these primitive efforts, serious consideration was first given by Marine and naval planners in the mid-thirties for using the airplane in conjunction with the then-developing art of amphibious warfare to strengthen a weak link in the amphibious assault chain. At the vital moment when the first wave of Marines was charging across a hostile beach, naval gunfire had ceased and artillery was not yet ashore. Could not the firepower of the airplane strengthen this critical period when an amphibious assault was at its most delicate stage? Might not the guns and bombs of the airplane take the place of artillery during the initial landing?

This simple need—to contribute to the success of an amphibious assault—was the genesis of the Navy-Marine system of close air support.

The actual Navy-Marine system of close air support was perfected during World War II. In the early days of the Pacific campaign, it was recognized that properly controlled air attacks would be a major asset, even a necessity, in the successful prosecution of an amphibious advance across the Pacific. Navy and Marine officials believed that airplanes could be a valuable "supporting weapon" to help ground troops advance against the Japanese.

The Navy-Marine doctrine of close air support had its battle test during the Tarawa campaign in November 1943. For the first time in combat, front-line units were accompanied by air-liaison parties whose main duty was to assist unit ground commanders in selecting suitable targets and in transmitting this target information and instructions for attack to the airplanes overhead. At Tarawa, also, liaison aircraft were flown by senior experienced aviators who were conversant with the ground plan, and who were in radio contact with the close air support airplanes.

Following Tarawa, the Navy-Marine system was further improved under fire at Iwo Jima. The final innovation, however—the direction of attack aircraft by frontline ground units—was not extensively used until the Battle of Okinawa, at which time sufficient portable radio communication equipment made air-ground communications reliable.

Thus, by the end of World War II, the Navy-Marine system of close air support had been fully developed and battle-tested. The Navy-Marine system had proved itself time and time again—at Guam, in the Philippines, at Iwo Jima, and especially in Okinawa. Naval and Marine aircraft, under the control of foot soldiers, had learned to quickly and effectively deliver their bullets and bombs upon "close" targets (50 to 200 yards distant) directed by trained parties in the front lines.

This system was available and ready for use at the outbreak of the Korean war.

Air Force Close Air Support

The system of close air support developed by the Army-Air Force and used in Korea was engendered against a different background and under a different set of conditions.

Before the European war began, the Army Air Corps, struggling even then for independence, was reluctant to embrace any concept which would tie them closer to the parent organization. The suggestion that their airplanes be used to supplement or increase the firepower of *ground arms,* or to support ground forces, was, if not anathema, very unpopular. Even the word "support" was displeasing since it had a subservient connotation. "Coordination" was a much preferred word since it implied equality.

Furthermore, the airmen strongly felt that any organization or employment wherein foot-soldiers exercised command over airplanes was "an attempt to shackle the air to the ground, and therefore, a failure to realize the full capabilities of air attack."[11]

In the mid-1930's, therefore, "close air support" in any size, shape, or form was an unpalatable concept to the embryonic Army Air Corps.

As the European war unfolded, the Army Air Corps watched Hitler's armies stab across Poland and speed across the Lowlands and France, spearheaded by the famed dive-bombing Stukas of the German Luftwaffe. Here, airplanes were coordinated with tanks and infantry under the Luftwaffe doctrine of allowing planes to be placed under the operational control of ground commanders.

Studying the German technique, U. S. Air Force planners quite accurately saw a serious fault. The Luftwaffe was tied *too* closely to the ground forces as a supporting weapon. As a consequence, the Luftwaffe's ground support aircraft had not been designed to *live in the air,* as well as to assist the ground fighting. To avoid this fatal error, the U. S. Air Force—and Britain's Royal Air Force as well—concluded that tactical airplanes must *not* be given to ground forces. Instead, tactical air power should be *centrally* controlled and applied en masse for the over-all objective of gaining control of the air. Only after the air had been swept clear of the enemy's planes and "interdiction of the battlefield" commenced, should tactical air be permitted to perform the secondary role of close air support.[12]

As for the mechanics of providing close air support, the Air Force system depended on *airborne* controllers. A light liaison-type plane would circle the frontlines area to spot enemy targets and to direct the bombs and gunfire of other planes upon them.

Two other factors were present in World War II which had their effect upon the differing systems of close air support that were developed.

The first of these was the differences in geography and terrain. The war in Europe was fought across a continent where rapid movement was common and, except in Italy, where battlelines were fluid. In contrast, the Pacific war was fought across an ocean, from one island group to another. The terrain of these islands was rugged and limited and made large movements of ground forces unnecessary.

The second influence which contributed to two different systems was the difference in the enemy. In the European war, the enemy was the German soldier, fighting a Western-style war. In the Pacific, however, a fatalistic, even suicidal enemy had to be blasted from his defending positions, foxhole by foxhole, cave by cave, and from one line of resistance to the next line of resistance. Such a war demanded "close" air support at its best.

When the Korean War began, the Air Force system of close air support was not immediately ready, for two reasons. The first and fundamental reason was that an earlier high-level decision reached in Washington (discussed in Chapter I, "Gathering War Clouds") had given far greater importance and priority to Strategic Air than to Tactical Air. The second reason was the fact that the mission to train for close air support types of operations was not included in either Far Eastern Air Force or Eighth Army missions. The Fifth Air Force in Japan had as its primary mission the *air* defense of Japan, while the Eighth Army's primary responsibility was the *ground* defense of Japan.

For these reasons, prior to the start of the Korean War, there had been no effort made in Japan to erect a tactical air control system, to train ground liaison officers, to stockpile equipment, or to conduct training operations in which air-ground operations were stressed or employed.

One of the early naval missions, in fact, was a special trip by the USS *Boxer* to Japan on 23 July to bring 145 F-51 prop-type aircraft for the Far Eastern Air Force. *Boxer* made the transpacific run in eight days and seven hours.

Thus, the start of the Korean War saw two different systems of close air support in being.

The Air Force system had largely been developed in the European theater. There, the exercise of command over aircraft was not given to frontline units; employment of aircraft was jointly coordinated at the Army level by two officers—one air, one ground. Strike planes did not orbit the battlefront, but were assigned to a particular mission as approved by the joint operations center (JOC). Upon arrival at the scene of conflict, planes would be directed and controlled by airborne, liaison-type aircraft, not by ground parties. Close air support targets were considered to be those within the immediate battle zone, as much as ten miles away.

At the time of the outbreak of the Korean war, this system was not immediately ready.

The Navy-Marine system, on the other hand, had largely been developed in the Pacific war as an indivisible part of an amphibious assault. A certain number of aircraft were committed for use and control by the ground commander, who could use their services as and where he saw fit. A few planes constantly orbited the battlefield, ready to strike "close air support" targets that were within 50 to 200 yards of the immediate front lines. The pilots received guidance and information for their attacks from a trained crew directly in the front lines.

At the outbreak of the Korean war, this system was ready.[13]

Eighth Army Endangered

The shrinking perimeter around Pusan was threatened with encirclement and collapse in late July as the first elements of the Sixth North Korean Division swept into Mokpo, the South Korean naval base at the southwestern tip of the Korean peninsula. Travelling mostly at night, enemy troops had rapidly infiltrated south. So skillfully was this flanking movement conducted that Republic of Korea police reported the movement merely as a movement of guerrilla forces. On 24 July, U.S. naval air reconnaissance reported large movements of unidentified troops to southwest Korea.

The Eighth Army now realized that regular North Korean army units were involved and that it was in danger of encirclement and isolation. Between the enemy and Pusan, a scant 150 miles, there were few United Nations ground forces to stop the encirclement.

It was this situation which compelled General Walker to query Tokyo about close air support from the Seventh Fleet.

"The first word of the encirclement reached me at my desk . . . ," reported Rear Admiral A. K. Morehouse, Chief of Staff to Admiral Joy. "The call came from Brigadier General Jarred V. Crabbe of the Air Force. He told me that the ground situation was desperate, and that the Navy's help was needed at once. . . . It was obvious we had to help, even though I had a lot of personal misgivings. In the first place, I knew there were too few trained ground control parties available at the front. Air-ground communications were bound to be crowded. Numerous details essential to a job like that just had to be forgotten—things like arrangements for marking our front lines, and using the same maps with identical co-ordinates. But our forces were in such a desperately bad way that naval air had to come to their rescue the best way they could."[14]

Admiral Struble answered the Eighth Army's emergency message for help in fifty-one minutes flat. The Seventh Fleet commander replied that his naval aircraft, as soon as refueling and replenishment of ammunition was completed, would be available. However, Struble cautioned that the successful use of the carrier planes for close air support missions was predicated on the establishment of "satisfactory communications and control." As a minimum requirement for any successful air-ground support, Struble suggested that either Commander Amphibious Group One's Tactical Control Squadron be despatched to Korea immediately with their equipment,* or that a small seven-man party from the Fleet experienced in ground control operations be sent ashore.

Admiral Joy, in answering the EUSAK (Eighth U.S. Army in Korea) emergency despatch, sounded the same note:

> In the coordination of naval air with the Fifth Air Force, no great difficulty is anticipated. However, coordination, which has been delegated to CG, Fareast Air Force, depends absolutely on successful joint communications. . . .[15]

Joy also despatched Struble that the dangerous and desperate situation on the ground in Korea demanded that the fast carriers participate at the earliest possible time:

> ". . . The calculated risk of damage to friendly forces must be accepted," he told Struble. "The ground situation is so critical that commencement of operations on 25th is highly desirable. . . ."

At midnight 24 July, the Seventh Fleet weighed anchor and headed for the east coast of Korea to participate in the first close air support strikes of the Korean War.

Planes from the *Valley Forge* were launched at 0800 the next morning, with orders to report to the U.S. Fifth Air Force's advanced headquarters, Joint Operation Center (JOC), Taegu.† The British carrier *Triumph* supplied the majority of the combat air patrol in order that every available *Valley Forge* plane could be sent over the battle zone. In twenty minutes the naval planes were over the frontlines.

---

* This suggestion was vetoed in Tokyo because of TacRonOne's participation in the preliminary planning for Inchon landing, already then underway.

† JOC, Taegu was a joint Army-Air Force center located at Taegu, although it temporarily retreated to Pusan when the perimeter shrank. Still later, the JOC moved to Seoul where it remained for the duration.

The pilots, having been briefed that the Eighth Army was in desperate straits and in sore need of every bullet and bomb which could be delivered to their defense, circled the JOC, trying to report their presence.

However, the too-few communication channels were jammed, and the too-few "Mosquito" plane controllers were overloaded.* Proper maps were lacking, and circuit discipline was non-existent.† In some instances, while Skyraiders and Corsairs circled the frontlines trying to establish communications with the liaison aircraft, F-80 jets from Japanese bases, some carrying two rockets, others only machine gun ammunition, were called in for strikes. After varying periods of trying to contact the "Mosquito" controllers, the naval pilots flew westward searching the roads and trails for military targets of opportunity. Some aircraft found targets; others did not; a few pilots jettisoned their loads in the sea before returning to the carrier.

Struble's early afternoon despatch reported this first close air effort:

> The results of the morning sweeps and strikes were very minor due to a dearth of targets. No rolling stock seen, only a few donkey carts plus men in rice paddies. On the whole, the area is one of peaceful agriculture. Seven trucks strafed did not burn. Four trucks strafed and burned. Will continue afternoon strikes, but under above conditions, the prospects appear poor. Consider it mandatory that proper communications be arranged. . . .

The *Valley Forge* planes flew close support on the 26th of July, again with limited success. Few of their heavy loads could be delivered, and none of it in the Naval-Marine technique of close air support. However, several flights found enemy targets. Pittman, leading ten VF-53 F4Us, got five trucks; Hodson, leading six VA-55 ADs, got two more; Barker, leading seven VF-53 F4Us, got two more; Ramsey, leading four VA-55 ADs, got another, damaged a railroad bridge, and fired a village concealing troops.

Because of deteriorating weather conditions, the Fleet moved during the evening of the 26th to the west coast of Korea, refueling en route.

Admiral Joy summarized the initial efforts in a despatch to Admiral Sherman:

> Even though MacArthur and Walker express enthusiasm over the effect of carrier air assigned to close and general support missions, the results were

---

* With the arrival in Korea on 3 July of the one under-strength battalion of the 21st Infantry, 24th Division, were two TACPs (Tactical Air Patrol Parties) and one L-5 VHF-equipped flivver airplane known as "Mosquito." One of the two TACPs was assigned to the 24th Division, one to the ROK forces. The L-5 airplane was put to use as an independent observation and spotting plane. As additional units of the 24th Division arrived, other TACPs and "Mosquito" aircraft arrived. But it was with these first TACPs and airplanes that the Task Force 77 airplanes were trying to perform close air support.

† In addition to the communication trouble, there was the practical difficulty of Korean names. They were difficult to pronounce and understand over the radio, and many names were similar.

disappointing. . . . Investigation of Army and Air Force tactical air in Korea indicates need for reorganization and training before minimum Navy standards can be attained. Air Force appears receptive to Navy's suggestions, but training will take time. The critical situation continues at front and overrides any consideration of whether the missions given our naval forces are optimum. In view of the situation, we must do everything within our capabilities. . . .

In Tokyo, meanwhile, an effort was made to alleviate the air-ground communication problem. Admiral Joy had attached to his command part of an ANGLICO* Company, OinC LT E. B. Williams, a unit specifically trained in the control of both naval gunfire and naval aircraft on shore targets. If Army-Air Force personnel could be provided and radio equipment assembled, this ANGLICO might quickly train frontline teams for controlling the attacks of the Air Force and naval aircraft. Joy sent the following proposal to the headquarters of MacArthur and Stratemeyer:

> . . . Suggest the most profitable use of the ANGLICO detachment is to conduct training in the Tokyo area, preferably at Johnson Air Force Base. Admiral Doyle will assume responsibility for the training. In three days time, the ANGLICO can train six tactical air control parties, each party consisting of one officer and five enlisted, including one technician. Please advise me if this training is desired. I am ready to begin now. . . .[16]

The Fleet, meanwhile, was also considering remedies. Successful close air support hinged on air-ground communications. Without a good link between ground and air, the full power of the naval aircraft could not be exploited.

First, Admiral Hoskins called a three-way huddle: his own staff, the *Valley Forge,* and the Britishers from HMS *Triumph.* What could be done? Well, the Royal Navy officers replied, they had a radio jeep, and one army major and one captain trained in the close support control of airplanes; could *they* be used?

They certainly could. *Valley Forge* offered to supply the technicians and other personnel to form a complete tactical air control party. Even *one* more experienced ground control party in Korea would be a big help.

Admirable as was the intent of this suggestion, it never came to pass. On the 29th of July the *Valley Forge* returned to the battleline, the British carrier was detached from the American task force to join the British task group and never returned.

The second thing Hoskins thought of to increase the Navy's contribution to holding the Pusan perimeter was to send a personal representative to the Joint Operation Center, Korea. He discussed the problem with Vice Admiral

---

* ANGLICO is an abbreviation for "Air Naval Gunfire Liaison Company."

Struble on the TBS radio. The task force commander authorized Hoskins to send a representative to JOC, Korea. On 27 July, therefore, LCDR C. H. Gates of CAG-5 was catapulted off *Valley Forge.*

Gates' visit to the JOC proved valuable. He arranged for the establishment of a direct communication channel between the JOC and the Fleet. He briefed the JOC personnel on the capabilities and limitations of a carrier and its airplanes. He explained the disparity in maps.

The naval aviators were using World Aeronautical Charts (WAC), whereas the Air Force pilots were using coded and gridded charts.* To give directions to naval pilots meant that the Air Force controller flying in his Mosquito airplane would have to locate the target on his gridded chart, convert the target's co-ordinates to latitude and longitude, and pass these to the naval pilot. This laborious conversion, while adding to the already-strained communication channels, had to be accepted. Gates also arranged an armament loading code, and was able to induce the JOC to divide the burden of control among the controllers and to reduce the orbit time of the naval airplanes.[17]

Gates also brought back to the Fleet the first accurate description of the desperate ground situation.

The next effort to improve the Fleet's close air support contributions took place on 3 August while ships replenished at Sasebo. At a conference in Tokyo between FEAF and COMNAVFE officers (VADM Struble, the Fleet Commander, was not present, then being in Formosa with General MacArthur), a memorandum of agreement was prepared which made close support the first priority task for the Seventh Fleet carriers "under direct control of the Fifth Air Force."† (However, close air support was provided only upon request of FAFIK (Fifth Air Force in Korea) and *after* approval by COMNAVFE; at other times, the carriers were free to operate in other areas of Korea.) Second priority targets were interdiction targets south of the 38th parallel; and third priority targets were the B-29 targets. This memorandum allowed little leeway for the avoidance of bad weather. This informal memorandum, which Struble had not concurred in, was later abrogated in part by Admiral Joy on 24 August.

Philippine Sea (CAPT W. K. Goodney) arrived on the first of August.‡

---

* Use of the WAC charts meant that pin-pointing a target was impossible. Only a general area, such as a village or stream, could be indicated.

† At this conference, FEAF was represented by four generals and one colonel; the Navy, by one captain from COMNAVFE, two commanders and two lieutenant commanders representing ComCarDiv-3.

‡ For the *Philippine Sea,* her appearance in the Korean theater culminated two months

At long last, the "Happy Valley" had a teammate. On the 5th, the two carriers headed for Korean waters to perform close support over the front lines. Once again an attempt was made by the Navy to reduce the control and communications bottleneck. Liaison pilots from both *Valley Forge* and *Philippine Sea* were despatched ashore to Taegu to perform the dual role of liaison and to control the attacks of naval planes. The plan was for one pilot to return to the Fleet daily so that he could present the existing ground and intelligence picture. The other planes would supplement the too-few Mosquito aircraft. Five such liaison planes were sent in on the 5th and 6th, six planes on the 7th, and one plane on the 8th.

As a result of these visits, the frontlines were divided into four sectors, each one having an airborne Air Force controller, plus a naval aircraft controller. The naval planes were supposed to control only naval strikes—but it became quickly apparent that the naval planes would have to control anything and everything that came into their area.

This temporary expedient helped to reduce the confusion and resulted in diminishment of the communication snafus. Controlled by the Mosquitos, LCDR Hodson, CO, VA-55, led 5 ADs from *Valley Forge* to attack and kill many enemy troops near Korysong; the next day, Hodson did a repeat, bombing, rocketing, and napalming more troops and destroying a supply dump. LTJG Billy Glen Jackson, leading four *Valley Forge* Skyraiders, destroyed two trucks, one jeep, and one tank in an attack near Kumchon.

Notwithstanding these successes, close air support was still not what it might have been. Many of the naval aircraft assigned for close support could not be directed and were diverted to armed reconnaissance missions along the roads approaching the battlefront. Lightly-loaded flights of F-80 Shooting Star jets from their Japanese bases arrived over the battle zone, and because of their short endurance, had to be used immediately. As they were sent in by the Air Force Mosquitos to make attacks, the naval aircraft were often ordered to "stand by" or to "stand clear." To the naval pilots circling with their heavy loads,* it was disappointing to be told to wait while a succes-

---

of intense effort. An Atlantic Fleet carrier, the *Philippine Sea* had arrived in San Diego on 10 June 1950. She was originally scheduled to relieve *Valley Forge* on 1 October 1950. Upon outbreak of the Korean war, *Philippine Sea* was ordered forward. CAG-11 (CDR R. C. Vogel, USN) received emergency orders to embark prior to sailing 5 July. This air group had not finished its training cycle, and its jet squadrons had only recently received new aircraft. An intensive ten days' training was accomplished in the Hawaiian area enroute to the Far East.

It is a high compliment to both ship and air group that despite these handicaps, their performance in Korea was outstanding.

* Typical load for close air support: (a) F4U: 800 rounds ammunition; one 1,000-pound bomb; eight 5-inch rockets; four hours' endurance; (b) AD: 400 rounds ammunition; three 500-pound bombs; twelve 5-inch rockets; four hours' endurance.

sion of lightly-loaded jets, some with only five minutes to spend over the target, were called in for strikes.

Moreover, in the minds of the naval pilots, the circuit discipline of some of the Air Force aviators was poor. There were many long-winded discussions between them and the Mosquito pilots about the targets, their location, the terrain, the mission, the weather, and the ordnance—and the results. In a few isolated occasions, as naval aircraft orbited, F-51 aircraft from other areas were ordered to strike the same sectors that naval aircraft had been circling.

The ground situation worsened during the 7th and 8th of August. General MacArthur, fearful lest the Eighth Army be overwhelmed, directed that during the period 8-17 August *all* of the air effort, including that from the carriers of Task Force 77, be devoted to close air support and interdiction. *Valley Forge* and *Philippine Sea* were directed to stagger their withdrawals for resupply in order to maintain continuous pressure on the frontlines.*

"Immediately after my trip to Formosa with General MacArthur," said Vice Admiral Struble, "I commenced Seventh Fleet operations on as intensive a schedule as possible, in order to apply a steady and unremitting pressure upon the the North Korean ground forces. I ordered the support force of the Seventh Fleet to transfer its base of operations from Okinawa to Sasebo in order to increase the amount of time that the carriers could spend on the line."[18]

Reports from leaders of the carrier strikes indicated considerable results:

10 Aug: LT S. Dalzell, Jr., leading two F4Us and two ADs from *Philippine Sea*: "Incendiary and GP bombs were used against barracks—results good, although attacks were not controlled."

16 Aug: LT M. D. Gallagher, leading 5 ADs from *Valley Forge:* "Destroyed 8 trucks, one jeep. Damaged 3 trucks, one village. Mosquito controller appeared inexperienced. We assisted in spotting targets and frontlines."

16 Aug: LCDR L. W. Chick, leading 8 ADs and 8 F4Us from *Philippine Sea:* "Enemy troops were hit in 9 villages by bombs and strafing, and in 3 orchards by rockets and strafing. 2 trucks strafed."

16 Aug: LT C. E. Smith, leading 4 F4Us from *Valley Forge:* "Burned supply and gasoline dump and 4 villages near Taegu."

19 Aug: LCDR E. T. Deacon, leading 10 F4Us and 8 ADs from *Philippine Sea:* "The Mosquito controller was contacted on the assigned channel, and although all channels were very crowded, it was possible to maintain good contact . . . Troop concentrations and supply dumps east of Hypochan were bombed with depth bombs and frags. Large fires resulted in five separate areas. The burned area was between Hypochan and the frontlines along the Naktong river. When these concentration areas were set on fire, personnel

---

* During this period, the two carriers operated for two days, replenishing each third day.

ran out into the fields where they were strafed. Two trucks were blown up and three others possibly destroyed. Approximately 30 troops were killed and a like number were probably wounded by the frags and 20-mm. shells. Two command cars were caught driving into a warehouse to hide. The warehouse was set on fire and the vehicles destroyed."

"As the Fleet retired to Sasebo following this considerable series of operations," said VADM Struble, "a temporary lull in the ground fighting had been reached. It was at this time that I was informed that I was to command the Inchon invasion. I immediately assembled a few staff officers and departed for Tokyo in order to commence the top command planning for Inchon."

Commenting on the close air support, Rear Admiral E. C. Ewen, who had taken command of Task Force 77, evaluated the carriers' efforts:

"A continuation of the present method of providing close air support," he recorded, "is both wasteful and ineffective. It is my opinion that less than 30 percent of this Fleet's potential close air support air power has been used in 'Taegu-type' close air support operations."[19]

Admiral Hoskins commented that better results would have been obtained if the Fleet had only been asked to provide four to eight planes on station continually over the battleline instead of a "maximum all-out effort."

The simple fact was that there were too few trained control parties on the ground, too few "Mosquito" planes in the air, and too little equipment to handle the numbers of aircraft over the battleline.

While it was irritating to some and regretful to all that the full striking power and the precision skill of the naval planes in the close air support mission could not be delivered in behalf of the Pusan perimeter, the contributions of the carriers were nonetheless substantial.

A close air support flight flown by *Valley Forge* aircraft on 10 August will illustrate the frequent daily accomplishments made during this period. By comparing this strike with a Marine strike on page 64, the reader will note the differences of the two close air support systems in actual practice.

Four F4Us from *Valley Forge* (VF-53), led by Lieutenant Clarence E. Smith, reported to the JOC at Taegu and were ordered to contact the U. S. Air Force liaison airplane "Mosquito Wildwest 7," airborne over Chinju.

Smith did so and reported his loading: four aircraft, each with one 500-lb VT-fuzed bomb, eight 5-inch rockets, and full machine gun ammunition.

"Mosquito Wildwest 7" directed the naval fliers to destroy a small bridge west of the village. The pilots circled the bridge, noted the wind, and climbed for altitude. The dive-bombing was precise: two direct hits, two near misses from four bombs. The bridge was demolished.

"Mosquito Wildwest 7" then directed that the planes follow the road northward. About a mile from the city of Chinju, he said, troops and vehicles were reported. The pilots were ordered to find and destroy them if they could.

At flat-hat level, the four Corsair pilots combed the road. A mile or so away, hidden in the trees, a wooden house was discovered, with vehicles concealed nearby, and an oil dump. These were destroyed with rocket and machine gun fire.

Such damage by a single flight of four planes, multiplied hundreds of times, had heavy attrition effect upon the fighting. But to the naval pilots it was armed reconnaissance or "deep support," not "close air support."

The hard, bloody, and bitter ground fighting to hold the Pusan perimeter had already produced two emergency requests for all-out close air support assistance from the carriers. These requests from Fifth Air Force headquarters in Pusan had been transmitted directly to the Seventh Fleet, bypassing the COMNAVFE headquarters in Tokyo.

On 19 August, to allay any possible misunderstanding regarding the employment of Task Force 77's services in support of the Fifth Air Force mission to furnish close air support, Admiral Joy sent a despatch to General MacArthur, with copies to Generals Walker, Stratemeyer, and Partridge (CG 5th Air Force Korea):

> All requests regarding employment or modification of schedules involving naval forces should be addressed to either CINCFE or COMNAVFE X CINCFE indicates the general type, time, and area where naval air effort is desired X His decision may be influenced from recommendations or requests from other activities X COMNAVFE implements CINCFE's desires, or if not expressed, determines the what, when, and where instructions. . . .[20]

In late August also, Joy sent the following message to General MacArthur in an effort to have the primary mission of the carriers changed to strikes on lucrative enemy targets in North Korea:

> . . . North Korea contains a multiplicity of very lucrative and profitable targets which are well suited to carrier strikes, whereas, in the south, targets are few and well hidden. After 25 August I strongly recommend that Task Force 77 be employed north of the 38th parallel. . . .[21]

On the 25th, however, in a direct "flash" message to the Seventh Fleet, the Fifth Air Force again requested further Navy close air support strikes. The Communists were preparing to launch an all-out attack across the Naktong River, and "close air support" was the most urgent role the carriers could perform.*

---

* A few days before this major attack, a novel effort was made to use B-29s in a "close air support" role. On the 16th of August, 98 Superfortress B-29s made a "carpet bombing" attack on the enemy build-up northwest of Waegwan. Some 40,000 troops were reported in

At 1101 on 31 August, still another emergency call came from JOC Pusan: ". . . all available effort for close support." The North Korean Army's full-scale and long-awaited attack upon the Naktong defense line had commenced, and the situation was described as "critical."

Upon receiving this despatch, Ewen recalled his airborne planes (then attacking targets in the Seoul-Inchon area), and turned the task force southeast at high speed. Planes on deck were hastily respotted and armed for a close air support strike.

The on-rushing Fleet flashed a message to JOC at Pusan:

The Fleet's close air support strikes will start at 1430. First strike will be 12 Skyraiders each with three 1000-pound bombs. Also, 16 Corsairs, each with one 1000-pound bomb plus four rockets and full cannon ammo. Second similar flight follows at 1530. More coming.[22]

The first close air support launch from *Valley Forge* and *Philippine Sea* left the decks at 1315 on 1 September.

The following excerpts are taken from action reports of the *Valley Forge* and the *Philippine Sea* for that afternoon:

Valley Forge: . . . At 1315, fourteen planes flew across Korea on close support missions. Armed to the teeth with 1000-pound bombs, contact-fuzed, they were told to orbit by the controller as he had no targets for such bombs. During the 45 minutes in which they orbited, the controller called in a flight of F-51s to strafe and rocket an enemy troop concentration. . . . The Corsairs were finally directed to bomb five villages near Kaepyodong which they destroyed. They also damaged a supply dump by strafing. . . .

. . . The six ADs were directed to hit three villages . . . which they destroyed. . . . These villages were reported to be military concentrations. Nearby, three trucks were also burned. . . .

. . . At 1430, eleven more planes went into the battle area for close support. The six F4Us completely destroyed one third of Haman after TAC (the Mosquito controller) had directed them to do it. They were told that the town was loaded with troops. On the road running west from town they burned eight trucks and damaged twelve more. . . .

. . . The five ADs were directed to bomb a ridge just west of Haman where their fourteen 1000-pound bombs leveled the entire ridge. . . . At Chugam-Ni, they destroyed three buildings supposed to contain vehicles with 100-pound bombs. . . .

. . . Eight jets were launched at 1615 for close support. Due to the number of planes over the area, they could not raise any controller. Four planes circled the two TAC (Mosquito) aircraft but still could not raise one of them due to cluttered circuits. These same four planes exploded one locomotive and damaged another. Vehicles with white stars on the top were seen. . . .

. . . At 1745, a final launch of eight jets went in on close support. The con-

---

this area. Eight hundred fifty tons of bombs were dropped in an area 7,000 yards wide by 13,000 yards long, one bomb to each five acres. The next day, the Communists launched one of the heaviest attacks of the war through this area.

troller was too busy to control the flight so they split into two four-plane divisions. The first division damaged about ten small boats which were on the east bank of the Naktong River. . . . The other division, an artillery emplacement. . . .[23]

The *Philippine Sea's* action report for that same afternoon commences:

This was to be a hectic day. . . .

. . . The event at 1312 sent out a four-plane CAP plus a standard offensive strike group (8 F4Us and 6 ADs) whose mission was close support. The launch was made 200 miles from our frontlines. The group proceeded in to the bombline but was unable to get an air controller to work them. They did receive orders to make one attack on a tank concentration located well to the east of the bombline. Fortunately the flight leader from VF-113 (LT Donald G. Patterson) made a low pass first to identify the target which turned out to be U.S. equipment. The group had to find their own targets. Troop concentrations were attacked . . . a bridge was bombed and one span knocked out. . . . The last attack was on twelve rafts south of the bridge which were strafed . . . three were sunk. . . ."

. . . The next event at 1430 sent out a standard offensive launch plus two additional F4Us, one of which aborted the flight. This flight had no more success than the earlier close support group. They, too, were unable to get a controller. They, too, attacked troops concentrations and warehouses. . . . The result of this attack was the destruction of one warehouse and one small fuel dump and considerable damage to two villages in which troops were concentrated. The effectiveness of this flight was curtailed due to lack of controlled support. . . ."

. . . The next event was a jet sweep. . . . They were unable to get contact with a controller. They did not fire a shot."

. . . The next event was another jet sweep; again, the jets were unable to get a controller. The flight also did not fire a shot. . . .

. . . The last event of the day was a launch of one AD4N (with CAG-11 as a passenger) and one F4U5N which proceeded into Pusan for the purpose of establishing better working liaison in the matter of close support. . . .[24]

These action reports are from the total 263 sorties which Task Force 77 delivered to help stop the enemy's full-scale attack.

While the Fast Carriers of Task Force 77 were flying close air support as practiced by the Air Force, the escort carriers *Sicily* and *Badoeng Strait* (TF 96.8, RADM R. W. Ruble, Commander Carrier Division 15) with Marine Squadrons VMF-323 and 214 aboard, were demonstrating the Navy and Marine doctrine of close air support in behalf of the First Provisional Marine Brigade, the 24th and 25th Infantry Divisions, the First Cavalry Division, the ROK First and Second ROK Corps, and the ROK Marines.

"During the early days of the war," said Lieutenant General Shepherd, "I spoke to General MacArthur and General Stratemeyer about the Marine Wing. I explained to them that Marine Air was an integral part of the Marine team, that they were trained to function as a unit, and that they should be permitted to function as they had trained. General MacArthur agreed."

No other naval staff saw such varied duty in such a short time as Carrier Division 15. The war was only a week old when Admiral Ruble's escort carrier division (based at San Diego with the peacetime role of carrying out antisubmarine warfare Hunter-Killer operations) was given air-priority-one orders to report to COMNAVFE for temporary additional duty. The presence of Ruble's staff would provide Admiral Joy with an advisory group familiar with aircraft operations, particularly with close air support and antisubmarine warfare, as well as provide additional and sorely-needed communication personnel.

Ruble and his staff arrived in Tokyo by air and reported to Joy on 10 July. On 12 July Ruble was given the title "Commander Naval Air Japan," with the duty of providing logistic support to all naval aircraft in the theater, plus getting the groundwork laid for the arrival of the two Marine fighter squadrons then enroute aboard his jeep carriers.

Badoeng Strait (Captain Arnold W. McKechnie), with VMF-214 and VMF-323 embarked, arrived at Kobe, Japan, on 31 July. The small carrier was chock-a-block with personnel, equipment, and planes—70 F4Us, 8 OY observation planes, and 6 HO3S helicopters. *Sicily* (Captain J. S. Thach), in the meantime, had arrived on 27 July after disembarking AntiSubmarine Squadron 21 at Agaña airfield, Guam. On the 31st, *Sicily* embarked the remainder of Ruble's staff, less the admiral himself, and joined the *Badoeng Strait* at Kobe, where ground elements and equipment of VMF-214 were hurriedly loaded aboard. Thach was designated as CTE 96.23, comprising the *Sicily*, *Kyes* (DD-787), and *Doyle* (DMS-34); he was given hurry-up orders to provide close air support to the beleaguered Pusan perimeter. Thach had *Sicily* underway for the battlefront next day, recovering aircraft of VMF-214 (Lieutenant Colonel Walter E. Lischeid, USMC) on the afternoon of the 3rd of August, and launching an eight-plane strike at 1638 the same afternoon.

Upon reporting to JOC, the Marine fliers were ordered to shoot at anything west of the Naktong River, and to pay particular attention to the recently captured city of Chinju.

Badoeng Strait, meanwhile, completed replenishment, took aboard Admiral Ruble (who had now been relieved as Commander Naval Air Japan), and Marine Squadron VMF-323. *Endicott* (DMS-35) and *Taussig* (DD-746) were designated as escorts. By breeches buoy, Ruble's staff transferred from *Sicily* to *Badoeng Strait*.

The little task group was again together and operating, a scant month after leaving San Diego.

TASK GROUP 96.8

Carrier Division 15 (RADM R. W. Ruble)
  Badoeng Strait (CAPT Arnold W. McKechnie)
    VMF-323 (MAJ Arnold Lund, USMC)
  Sicily (CAPT John S. Thach)
    VMF-214 (LTCOL Walter E. Lischeid, USMC)
  Endicott (CDR John C. Jolly)
  Doyle (CDR Charles H. Momsen, Jr.)
  Kyes (CDR Fran M. Christiansen)
  Taussig (CDR Wm. C. Meyer)

Although the Marine airmen aboard *Sicily* and *Badoeng Strait* flew several interdiction hops prior to 8 August, including some preparatory strikes in the Inchon area, and furnished a few days' close air support as practiced by the Air Force, the task group's primary duty during this period was the furnishing of close air support to the First Provisional Marine Brigade.*

On 7 August, the just-arrived First Provisional Marine Brigade was committed to action in the Pusan perimeter, first in the area southeast of Chinju as part of Task Force Kean.† VMF-214 and 323 were ordered to furnish close air support for the Task Force. The personnel in the Marine ground tactical air control parties were the same people with whom the Marine fliers had been rehearsing close air support at Camp Pendleton a few weeks earlier.

For the next six days, the Marine brigade attacked to the westward, covered by the Corsairs of VMF-323 and 212, demonstrating the intricate teamwork of the Navy-Marine system of close air support. Approximately six aircraft were kept over the Brigade during daylight hours. The Corsairs' average load consisted of either a 500-pound bomb or a napalm tank, eight rockets, and a full load of machine gun ammunition.

10 Aug *Badoeng Strait:* Strike George attacked a large roadblock three miles north of Kaesong at 1500. Steep dive bombing rocket and strafing runs were made on enemy troops on the hillsides, destroying 75% of the enemy position. After these attacks, Marines of the First Marine Brigade were able to stand up and walk through the roadblock, continuing their advance on Kaesong.

11 Aug *Badoeng Strait:* Third Battalion standing by to attack Kaesong. Preparatory Marine artillery fire landed in the town. Suddenly, as the Marine artillerymen watched through their binoculars, a column of enemy vehicles, numbering almost a hundred, were observed, preparing to make a dash for safety. Circling overhead was a VMF-323 flight of four F4U4B aircraft (led by

---

* The First Provisional Marine Brigade was basically a reinforced Marine regiment. The infantry element thereof was three battalions, but each with only two instead of the regular three companies. This meant approximately 1,500 men were available for front-line engagement. Subtracting a reserve, company clerks, etc., the First Provisional Marine Brigade did its job with less than 1,000 riflemen in the frontline.

† Army Task Forces take the name of the senior commander.

their commanding officer, Major Lund). The ground controllers immediately directed Lund's attention to the column of motorcycles, jeeps, and troop-filled trucks.

The Corsairs made an immediate low-level strafing run in an effort to bring the column to a halt. The Marine airmen spewed rockets and bullets into the column. Vehicles crashed into one another or piled up in the ditch while enemy troops scrambled for cover. Soviet-made jeeps and motorcycles were stopped or abandoned by the rockets and 20-mm. fire. Return fire from enemy's guns on the low-flying aircraft seriously damaged two Corsairs; LT Doyle Cole ditched in a nearby bay to be rescued by the helicopter carrying the Brigade Commander, BGEN Edward A. Craig; Captain Vivian Moses crashlanded in a rice paddy and was killed. Four additional Corsairs of VMF-323 relieved Lund's flight to continue the destruction of the column.

The second task given the Marine Brigade was to help eliminate an enemy-held bridge in the Pusan perimeter near Yongsan.

The Communist main line of resistance lay to the west of Yongsan along a rugged ridge, Obong-ni (also nicknamed "No-Name" Ridge). The ridge consisted of six knolls; the Marine Brigade was ordered to take them. Six Corsairs were kept on station during daylight hours.

The Marines attacked during the morning and afternoon but were repulsed. In the late evening, after bloody fighting, the Marines succeeded in capturing two hills of the ridge. Throughout the night, despite enemy attacks using automatic fire and hand grenades, the Marines grimly held their positions.

By the early morning of 18 August, the enemy had infiltrated additional strength onto the ridge to the south of the Marines and were making preparations to recapture the two knolls they had lost.

But the 3rd Platoon, Able Company, Fifth Marines, led by LT George C. Fox, attacked first at 0700. As Fox's platoon, reduced to 20 effective men by the previous day's fighting, moved forward, a nest of four Red machine guns opened up on them and pinned them to the ground. Captain John R. Stevens, Company A commander, spotted the nest and asked for an air strike.

Strike planes were already circling overhead, having flown in from *Badoeng Strait.* The tactical air coordinator was LTCOL Norman W. Anderson, and the four Corsairs were led by Major Arnold A. Lund from VMF-323. The Corsairs were briefed on the situation by LT James W. Smith, the forward tactical air controller. The enemy gun nest was only 50 yards in front of the attacking Marines. After receiving the description of the target, LTCOL Anderson decided to use a single plane and to use a 500-pound bomb. Lund designated his section leader, Captain John P. Kelley, to make the attack.

First, however, Anderson himself made certain of the target's location, and then fired a smoke rocket at it to mark it for Kelley. Kelley observed the rocket, spotted the nest, and climbed for dive-bombing altitude. Carefully noting the wind, Kelley made his attack. His markmanship was precise: the 500-lb bomb fell squarely into the four machine guns. The entire area was completely obliterated, and the shock to the nearby Marines was intense.

The attack had taken less than five minutes. With the sound of the bomb blast still reverberating from the rocky hills, the Marines rushed forward and with gathering momentum swept the enemy from the main line of resistance.

"From that moment," General Craig reported in his special action report, "the issue west of Yongsan was no longer in doubt. A routed enemy fled westward, racing desperately from the continuing combined ground and air assault of the Marines, who, before the day was over, accounted for the destruction of more than 4,000 enemy troops."

The rout was continued on 18 August, as the Leathernecks dissolved the Naktong bulge and hurled hundreds of the fleeing Reds into the river.

18 Aug *Sicily:* The first flight attacked the ridge ahead of the advancing Marines near a bend in the Naktong river at Sinnam-ni. Two tanks and a fieldpiece were attacked; one tank was dismantled by a 500-pound bomb, another destroyed with rockets. The fieldpiece was obliterated with rockets. At this time, Marine ground forces, aided by our close-air support, drove the retreating enemy into the Naktong river. While several thousands of these were attempting to swim across, this flight commenced to attack, strafing with 20 mm. explosives and incendiaries. The enemy was killed in such numbers that the river was definitely discolored by blood.

There can be little doubt of the terrible efficiency displayed by the Marine aviators in support of the Pusan perimeter. Pound for pound of TNT, and hour for hour of effort, their destructive efficiency left little to be desired.

The box score for TG 96.8 for the period ending 14 September 1950 was as follows:

Sicily: 688 sorties
Badoeng Strait: 671 sorties

Flying 24 planes from each jeep carrier, averaging a splendid aircraft availability of 92 percent, the Marine pilots achieved the following damage on behalf of the troops of the Pusan perimeter:

Target	Destroyed	Damaged
Tanks	13	7
Boxcars	35	121
Vehicles	197	11
Buildings	73	13
Guns	72	10
Bridges	23	15
Fuel dumps	10	—
Supply dumps	1	—
Ammo dumps	5	1

Despite the difficulties and shortages, the contributions of the naval **and** Marine aircraft to holding the Pusan perimeter cannot be minimized.

From 5 August until 3 September 1950, Task Force 77 launched 2,481 strikes against the enemy under the control of the JOC and in the close air support style practiced by the Air Force. Of these, 583 were actually

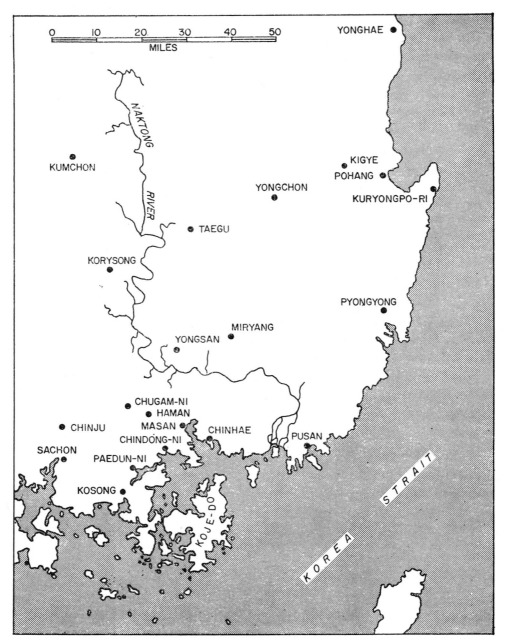

THE PUSAN PERIMETER

controlled by the Mosquito liaison planes; the remaining 1,888 missions were flown in the immediate battle zone against Communist troops, tanks, and supplies in "armed reconnaissance" missions.

These 2,481 strikes by naval aircraft and the 1,359 sorties of the Marines resulted in great damage to enemy personnel and equipment at and near the frontlines, and in decelerating the enemy's advance toward Pusan. The enemy was forced almost totally to abandon daylight attacks and daylight work of all kinds.

The Air Group Commander of Air Group FIVE recorded the effective support rendered by the naval aircraft:

". . . The heavy ordnance loads carried by the Corsairs and Skyraiders were always welcomed heartily," wrote Commander Harvey P. Lanham. "As one air controller put it to his counterpart in the frontlines, 'I'm coming over with a bunch of Navy planes, and brother, they're really loaded.' On another occasion, the Navy liaison pilots at Taegu heard glowing praise of the Navy pilot who had wiped out a complete company of enemy troops by tossing a napalm bomb into the mouth of the tunnel in which they had sought refuge. Navy liaison officers in Taegu in August, heard the results of Prisoner-of-War (POW) interrogation at the JOC. To the question 'Which U.S. weapon do you fear the most?', the answer was 'the blue airplanes.' "[25]

Marine Line Backers

As mentioned in the opening lines of this chapter, the retention of a Pusan beachhead was in large measure due to several naval events—the timely Pohang landing, the air support and interdiction efforts of the naval aircraft of Task Force 77 and Marine aircraft of Task Group 96.8 (just described), the naval gunfire suport supplied by the ships of Task Force 96 on the eastern terminus of the battlefront (see Chapter IX "The Seaborne Artillery," page 281), and finally, the back-stopping efforts of the First Provisional Marine Brigade.

Early in July, before the loss of the entire Korean peninsula became a distinct probability, it was General MacArthur's intention to disembark the First Provisional Marine Brigade at Kobe, Japan, and have it prepare to make an amphibious assault in the enemy's rear as soon as the position of the Eighth Army could be stabilized. However, the rapidly deteriorating situation in the Pusan bridgehead made it imperative that the Brigade be committed in that area at once.

Accordingly, on 2 August, the Brigade sailed directly into Pusan and commenced unloading. Five days later, on 7 August, the Brigade was ordered to attack to the westward and seize Chinju in order to relieve pressure on the Eighth Army lines along the Naktong River. In this first operation lasting six days, the Marine Brigade made a 20-mile advance, the first successful counter-attack by American troops since the Korean War began. During this period the Marines routed an enemy force estimated as a motorized regiment, captured or destroyed the complete armament and vehicles of at least one battalion, and destroyed 1,900 enemy troops. Even more important than this military contribution to the holding of the Pusan bridgehead, perhaps, was the spiritual uplift in morale which the Leathernecks gave to all the forces in Korea.

Twice more, in August and early September, the U.S. Marines played a vital role in the defense of the perimeter.

After the enemy's flanking movement had been squelched in the south by the Marines as part of Task Force Kean, the North Koreans increased their pressure in the central area of the perimeter in the vicinity of Yongsan. Elements of the North Korean Fourth Division forded the Naktong River on the 5th of August. By 6 August one battalion of the enemy's 4th Division was across the river. A major effort to force the river at this point was obviously coming. Any major penetration in this area would seriously endanger the security of the bulk of the Eighth Army and its supply line to Pusan. Despite heavy and effective opposition by U.S. and ROK forces, the North Koreans succeeded in ferrying two regiments across the Naktong and held a bridgehead area measuring six by eight miles.

The First Provisional Marine Brigade and two regiments of the 24th Division were given the task of eliminating this dangerous bulge and driving the enemy back across the river.

After a fast march northward the Brigade led the coordinated attack on 17 August. Objectives were captured in 48 hours. The crack North Korean 4th Division (which had captured Seoul early in the war) was destroyed or driven back across the river, and large amounts of enemy material captured. Enemy casualties were estimated to be 2,500. (A typical close air support strike of this action has been described on page 64.)

On 3 September, the Brigade performed its third mission in holding the perimeter. As part of a coordinated attack, the First Provisional Marine Brigade again made a deep penetration of the enemy's defensive position along the central front. A great amount of enemy ordnance, engineer, signal, and other equipment was captured. Vast numbers of enemy dead were observed in this area, and after the engagement it was estimated that enemy casualties were at least 4,500.[26]

The initial preparations for the amphibious assault at Inchon were now being made. Doyle's operation order called for the First Provisional Marine Brigade to lead the way. Accordingly, a despatch was sent to General Walker advising him that "future operations require withdrawal of Marine Brigade from Korea in September, date to be determined. Brigade will be combat-loaded for amphibious landing."

In view of the still delicate situation at the front lines, General Walker was reluctant to release the Marines unless suitable reserve forces were given to him.

"At our meeting with General Almond relative to the release of the Marines," said Vice Admiral Struble, "the issue boiled down to the need for an Eighth Army reserve. I suggested that a regiment of the Seventh Infantry be embarked and moved to Pusan as a reserve to be landed in an emergency as a substitute for the Marines. This solution was accepted."

"We had considerable difficulty in breaking the Brigade loose," said Major General Oliver P. Smith. "Along with Admirals Struble, Joy, and Doyle, I finally called on General Almond on the afternoon of 5 September, to ask him to spring the Brigade. Joy said that unless they were made available, he would be impelled to despatch Washington. Struble told Almond that if the Fifth Marines weren't made available, Inchon *would* be impossible. Whereupon, Almond went in to see General MacArthur, and when he came back, the Brigade was released."[27]

The same evening, in a heavy rainstorm, the Marines left the front lines and marched back to Pusan.

The final naval contribution to the salvation of the Pusan perimeter occurred on 16 August 1950. This was the unpublicized rescue of the 3rd ROK Division by sea after it had been surrounded and cut off by enemy forces near Yonghae.

For five days, ably supported by Rear Admiral Hartman's Task Group 96.51, this division had blocked the enemy's advance down the coastal road while a new defense line north of Pusan was being readied.

The Third ROK Division had held fast while inland units were withdrawn. As a result, this division was isolated and in danger of annihilation. General Walker requested the Navy to evacuate the Third ROKs.

On the night of August 16th, the cruiser *Helena,* with escorting destroyers and four landing ships, took station off-shore.

Covered by naval gunfire from *Helena* and the destroyers, Captain J. R. Clark, Commander Destroyer Squadron Eleven aboard *Wiltsie,* ordered the four LSTs into the pre-arranged beach, guided by the lights of jeep headlights ashore. The LSTs beached, and the ROK division began an orderly embarkation. Before daylight broke, the LSTs had loaded six officers and seventeen men of the Korean Military Advisory Group, 327 officers and 5,480 troops of the ROK Third Division, 1,260 civilian evacuees, and 100 vehicles without loss of personnel or equipment.

The next day, the Third ROK Division was re-landed at Kuryongpo-ri, and was back in action.

To these troops, "control of the sea" assumed a fresh, new meaning.

Significance of Initial Operations

Two general results are perceivable from a study of the early period of the Korean war from 25 July 1950 to the invasion of Inchon on 15 September 1950.

The paramount result was to demonstrate the fact that *without* the American Navy, the bridgehead in Korea could never have been held. The gunfire support supplied at the eastern anchor of the battlefront, the timely landing of the First Cavalry at Pohang, the rescue of the Third ROKs, the air strikes of Task Force 77 and Task Group 96.8, and the three counterattacks by the First Provisional Marine Brigade, were of decisive importance in holding Pusan. In addition, the logistic link connecting Korea to Japan and the United States was a bridge of ships bringing personnel and munitions of war.

"It is not an exaggeration to say that without the Navy the Pusan perimeter could never have been held," said Vice Admiral Joy. "The unspectacular role of carrying personnel and supplies to Korea was perhaps the Navy's greatest contribution. Next in importance was the Navy's support of the 8th Army by bombardment, interdiction and close air support missions, as well as the timely landing of the 1st Cavalry Division at Pohang. The vital role played by our carriers in this connection cannot be overemphasized. As

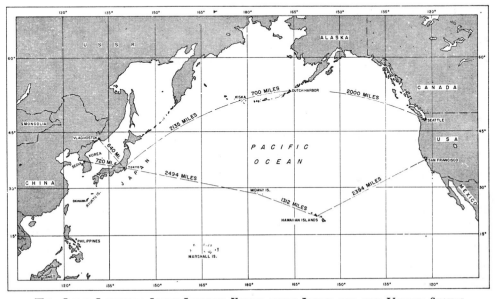

THE LONG LOGISTICS LINES LINKING KOREA WITH JAPAN AND THE UNITED STATES

General MacArthur said to me at the time: "Had you not employed the carriers as you did in sustained support of the 8th Army, Congress would think twice about further appropriations for the construction of aircraft carriers."

The commanding general personally acknowledged the vital role played by the Navy. Asked by the authors if he considered the naval assistance vital to holding the Pusan perimeter, General MacArthur replied: "Naval forces in a peninsula campaign, such as Korea, are always a vital factor, for they alone can effectively interdict enemy coastal movement and amphibious operations. Furthermore, in Korea I knew that if our meager forces were impelled to fall back to Pusan proper, the Navy could hold open our lines of supply, and under its guns we could hold a beachhead indefinitely."

Regarding the services rendered by the four carriers in holding the perimeter, General MacArthur wrote: "The Navy carriers were a vital factor in holding the Pusan perimeter, especially until our land bases were developed effectively to handle the air phase of the campaign. Even then they provided a powerful adjunct to the land-based aircraft supporting our ground operations."

The second result of the battle to save Pusan was to spotlight a Navy-Air Force disparity in the doctrine and technique of close air support.

The dissection of this disparity is extremely difficult, technical and involved, but nonetheless a meaningful and necessary study for the student of naval warfare.

The Battle of Pusan revealed three fundamental differences between the Air Force system and the Navy-Marine system of close air support:

1. A difference in philosophy over use of air power.
2. A difference in techniques.
3. A difference in semantics.

The root of the disparity is one of concept. First of all, the Air Force believes the proper place to apply air power is first and foremost upon the sources of the enemy's war-making potential, and second, in the immediate battle area. *Isolation of* the battlefield, in their view, takes precedence over air strikes *in the battlefield.* And control of aircraft, they believe, must never degenerate to individual ground commanders whose limiting perspective cannot result in the most effective theater-wide use of the airplanes' potential.

As for the Navy, the validity of the strategic bombing concept has never been fully accepted, in the sense that it is the sole and only arbiter of modern warfare. Neither is there any firm belief that "strategic" targets can be neatly separated from "tactical" targets. In the accomplishment of any given military objective, it is the Navy's view that sufficient force of the proper type should be applied to the enemy to attain any given objective. Close air support is regarded as a vital and indispensable tool for defeating an enemy's ground forces.

The second major difference is one of technique. The Navy-Marine system of close air support requires that pilots be trained to recognize terrain features and to appreciate the capabilities and limitations of ground arms in order that strikes can be performed very close to friendly forces. Marine pilots are especially well trained in this respect, naval pilots less so. Air Force pilots do not receive the same degree of training.

In the matter of control, the crux of the difference of the two systems, the Marines have thirteen Tactical Air Control Parties in a division: one for each battalion (total of nine), one with each regiment (total of three), and one for the division itself. Any or all of these control parties are capable of requesting and directing the delivery of "close" air support.

In contrast, the Air Force system only provides one Tactical Air Control Party per regiment, or a total of *four* for a division, as compared with thirteen in the Marine division. The greater number of control parties for a Marine division is to provide for the anticipated *critical* situation during the amphibious operation, a contingency that the Army division in the field need not anticipate.

But the difference in numbers of TACPs is only a reflection of the real difference in the concept of control. The Marines admit that wartime manpower restrictions would make it impractical for an Army division to have the same number of TACPs as is required for their division in an amphibious assault. However, even if the Marines had fewer TACPs, their *method of control* would be no different; for it is the Marine Corps' view that the frontline commander should be able to make his request direct to the supplying agencies, with no interference or delay from intervening agencies. One of the basic presumptions is that unless close air support is immediately available (within 10 to 15 minutes), its value to the frontline commander is questionable or considerably reduced. The Marine system places the controller *in the frontlines with the troops,* while the Air Force-Army doctrine places the air controller of the Tactical Air Control Party aloft in a liaison-type aircraft. By so doing, the close personal contact with the ground commander is lost, and the centralization of authority in Air Force commands is emphasized.

The final difference is semantical: the definition of "close air support." Each Service believes itself to be providing close air support; yet, each Service defines close air support differently. This misunderstanding is compounded by the vague definition of "close air support": "Air action against hostile ground or naval targets which are so close to friendly forces as to require detailed integration of each air mission with the fire and movement of those forces."[28]

What is meant by "close"? To the Navy-Marines, "close" is considered to be that area *immediately* in front of friendly troops—50 to 200 yards. The Air Force on the other hand, considers "close" to mean within several thousand yards of the front line . . . the distance to which field artillery pieces would effectively reach.[29]

Thus, what the Army-Air Force defines as "close" air support is given another description by the Navy and Marines: "deep support." Generally speaking, the Air Force did not and does not perform what the Navy calls "close" air support.[30]

All these differences were later succinctly summarized by Lt. General Lemuel C. Shepherd, Commanding General, Fleet Marine Force, Pacific, as a result of his visit to Korea in 1951:

"We believe in providing for a small number of on-station planes; the Air Force does not. We believe in continuous direct communication between the frontline battalion and the controlling air agency; the Air Force does not. We believe that close air support of the frontline troops should take precedence over routine interdiction missions; the Air Force does not."

In appraising and studying close air support in Korea, the naval student must recognize the special, unusual and favorable circumstances which prevailed. First of all, there was no effort made by the North Koreans to contest UN control of the air. Had they done so, the propeller-driven close air support aircraft of both Navy and Air Force certainly would have had greater difficulty in giving close air support. Not having to fight for control of the air over the battlefield freed a great many more UN planes for close air support missions which otherwise would have been impossible.

Secondly, the uncontested control of the seas meant that carrier task forces could move in closely to shore, almost becoming immobile. Never again, perhaps, will these two special circumstances be duplicated.

The Marines, whose close air support doctrine requires a minimum of one aircraft squadron for each Marine battalion, had available, at times, almost *double* that amount of close air support in Korea. During the battle for the Pusan perimeter, for example, with only one battalion in assault, the Marines often had *two* squadrons of close support aircraft (averaging 40 effective airplanes) supporting them.* This abundance of close air support, while seldom in excess,† must not leave the impression that such abun-

* In comparison, the 12th Army in Europe during World War II had only 35 close support aircraft per division.

† Records indicate that 80 percent of the Marine strikes were *directed* by Tactical Air Control Parties.

dance is necessary or will always be available. When other supporting weapons such as artillery, tanks and mortars are available and effective, the more expensive airpower weapon must take a lower priority. In Korea, however, there were many times when more economical means were either unavailable or unable to handle the support task. In these cases, the abundance of effective close air support was able to meet the need.

In other wars in other places, against air and sea opposition, and under poorer weather conditions, it must be recognized that the rather luxurious condition of close air support which existed in Korea—no air opposition and extremely close carriers—will probably never happen again.

Results

The Battle of Pusan spotlighted but did not resolve the close air support problem. Two major campaigns which followed—Inchon and Hungnam—amply demonstrated the merits of the Navy-Marine system. After Hungnam, however, the Navy did not again raise the close air support question. Not so the Marines, whose First Marine Air Wing was thereafter detached from the Marine Division.

Neither the Air Force nor the Navy-Marine Corps changed their systems. Both the Navy and the Air Force considered their own system adequate and effective, and that of the other not wholly suitable to its respective needs.

The Army made an investigation of the merits of the two systems in the combat zone and concluded:

> . . . it would be illogical if not dangerous in the long run to substitute the Marine system for the Ground Forces-Air Forces system.[31]

The Navy also made a study and concluded:

> The Marines and Navy should continue to adhere to their system until a better system can be developed. Under no circumstances should the present system employed by the Air Force be adopted by the Navy and the Marines.[32]

There was one other result. The controversy brought about the reestablishment of the Tactical Air Command in the U. S. Air Force and its restoration to a position of importance if not equality. The tactical airplane saw a rebirth. On 1 December 1950, the U. S. Air Force established the Tactical Air Command under the command of Lieutenant General John K. Cannon, with the basic mission of training and developing tactical aviation "in cooperation with Army Field Forces."

Thus, the dispute over close air support leveled the heavy unbalance of pre-Korean days when the preponderance of our nation's air power was being devoted to the strategic bombing role.

3.

The Magnificent Gamble: The Amphibious Assault at Inchon

Introduction

As far as the U.S. Navy is concerned, the one single operation of the Korean war which in history must receive transcendent importance is the Inchon assault.

For eighty-two days, the UN ground forces had been constantly on the defensive and often at the brink of disaster. Ridge by ridge, and mile by mile, the U.S. and ROK armies had retreated from the 38th parallel to a tiny perimeter around the port of Pusan, bloodily punishing the Communists with every backward step. The issue in the perimeter hung in balance for almost a month.

On 15 September 1950, with the shattering suddenness of a bursting shell, the course of the Korean war was reversed by the Inchon landing. In ten swift days the North Korean People's Army, which had been hammering at the threshold of victory, was broken and beaten. The landing at Inchon and the capture of the capital city of Seoul had won the war.

History records no more striking example of the effectiveness of an amphibious operation.

Conception

The credit for the conception of making an amphibious assault at Inchon can only be given to one man: General Douglas MacArthur. It was he who conceived it, who fought for it over the intense but unpublicized opposition of many and the reluctance of most military leaders in the Far East and the Joint Chiefs of Staff.[1] The heaviest opposition came from the Chairman of the Joint Chiefs, General Omar Bradley, and from Army Chief of Staff J. Lawton Collins.[2] Lesser objection was raised by the Chief of Naval Operations, Admiral Forrest P. Sherman. Collins and Sherman had flown to Tokyo in mid-August to confer with MacArthur about the forthcoming operation.

Of Generals Bradley's and Collins' objections, General MacArthur wrote the authors: ". . . I believe that Generals Bradley and, probably, Collins were fundamentally opposed to amphibious operations as an acceptable technique to modern war. General Bradley some time before publicly had so expressed his professional judgment. General Collins based his objection more upon the depth of the turning movement which, of course, was essential if the operation was to be effective."[3]

According to Vice Admiral Joy, Admiral Sherman initially objected to the site of Inchon because of its hydrographic hazards. "At no time did I hear any naval officer tell the General that Inchon was impossible," said Vice Admiral Joy, "but we were all anxious to point out the obvious dangers."

"Not impossible" was the general attitude of the Navy in the Far East. Rear Admiral James H. Doyle's concluding remarks at the 23 August briefing for the benefit of General MacArthur: "General, I have not been asked nor have I volunteered my opinion about this landing. If I were asked, however, the best I can say is that Inchon is not impossible."[4]

Vice Admiral Joy has described General MacArthur's 45-minute talk at this final briefing, wherein General MacArthur gave a glowing testimonial of his confidence that the Navy would make Inchon a success. The Navy had never let him down, he said. He recognized the undertaking as a gamble, quoting its odds at 5,000-to-1, but said he was accustomed to taking such odds.

Vice Admiral Joy said that after listening to the General's eloquent and passionate soliloquy, "My own personal misgivings about Inchon were erased. I believe that the General had persuaded me, and all others in the room—with the possible exception of Admiral Sherman—that Inchon could be successful. Admiral Sherman was almost persuaded. Nevertheless, he retained some slight misgivings. In fact, the next day he spent one and one-half hours alone with General MacArthur, and upon coming out of this conference, was won over to the General's position. He said to me, 'I wish I had that man's confidence.' "[5]

Of Admiral Sherman's objections, General MacArthur wrote the authors: "During his discussions on the matter I sensed that Admiral Sherman's objections to the Inchon movement were largely animated by a sense of duty which necessitated the presentation in their most naked form of all professional difficulties and objections which could be foreseen."

After the return of Sherman and Collins to Washington, the Inchon

STRATEGY AND PLANNING. Naval and military officers pore over charts and maps during Korean operations. *At top,* VADM Arthur D. Struble points out a Wonsan target area to VADM William Andrewes, Royal Navy, and RADM Allan E. Smith. *Below,* MAJGEN Edward M. Almond, USA, with Vice Admiral A. D. Struble and RADM James H. Doyle, aboard battleship *Missouri.*

RADM JOHN E. GINGRICH, Commander, Task Force 95, the Blockade and Escort Force.

RADM BERNARD L. AUSTIN, Logistic Support Force Commander, Inchon, Wonsan and Hungnam.

CDR GORDON GEMMILL, Commanding Officer of DD *Brinkley Bass,* holding the "Key to the City of Wonsan."

CDR PAUL N. GRAY, the Navy's "Bald Eagle," three times fished out of Wonsan Harbor, the Navy's most rescued aviator.

THE TIDE THAT TURNED. *Top,* Inchon's Red Beach mudflats extend three miles seaward at low tide. *Center,* destruction of port facilities at time of final U. S. evacuation. *Lower left,* Inchon's stone seawall rises 15 feet above rocky beach. *Lower right,* LCMs crowd the restricted port area of Inchon after the invasion, bringing ashore necessary supplies for troop operations.

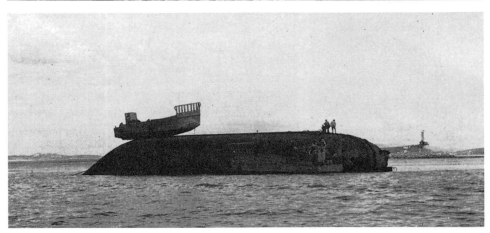

INCHON BALANCING ACTS. *At top, LST 799,* undamaged, but obviously out of her element for the moment. Later she became the first U. S. vessel to be used as a wartime helicopter carrier, rescuing 22 ditched fliers off Wonsan. *Center,* troops recover a tank that slipped off seawall during unloading at Inchon. *Below,* a thirty-foot receding tide left this LCM perched atop a sunken LST.

operation was approved by the then-Secretary of Defense, Louis A. Johnson.

". . . General Collins—maybe the censor will want to strike this out—did not favor Inchon and went over to argue General MacArthur out of it," Secretary Johnson testified. "General MacArthur stood pat. I backed Mac-Arthur."[6]

General MacArthur credits Admiral Sherman for final approval of the decision.

"I am sure he must have been largely instrumental in influencing the ultimate solution to accept my own point of view and approve the project," he wrote.

MacArthur's Choice of Inchon

MacArthur's selection of Inchon as the point of assault was a blend of his strategic, psychological, political, and military reasoning. As the Reds drove the UN forces southward, he made frequent reference to their over-extended supply lines, most of which passed through Seoul. If Inchon, only fifteen miles away, could be seized by sea assault, the enemy's supply lines would be quickly severed. "The history of war," he said, "proves that nine times out of ten, an army has been destroyed because its supply lines have been severed." A successful landing at Inchon would shorten the war, save unnumbered casualties, and possibly obviate a winter campaign.

Psychologically, the General felt that a successful landing at Inchon would not only reverse the course of the war but would rescue the Western world's falling prestige throughout the Orient. In addition to checking the aggression of the North Koreans, it would capture the imagination of the Far East and halt the expanding course of Communism.

Strategically, MacArthur insisted that an amphibious landing should be made deep into enemy-held territory. "The amphibious landing is the most powerful tool we have," he said, "To employ it properly, we must strike hard and deeply into enemy territory."[7] Inchon, he added, would be the anvil on which the UN forces would drive northward out of the Pusan perimeter to crush the North Korean enemy. The other recommended points, near Pyongyang, Posung-Myon, and Kunsan, were too far and too close to the battlefront, he said. The beaches opposite Pyongyang, the North Korean capital, were well above the 38th parallel and therefore too distant, while those near Kunsan were too close to the Pusan perimeter. A landing at Kunsan, he thought, would not succeed in trapping the North Korean People's Army. The Reds would merely retreat a few miles to negate and contain the landing.

General MacArthur's Inchon strategy is revealed in his own words: "The deep envelopment, based upon surprise, which severs the enemy's supply lines," he wrote, "is and always has been the most decisive maneuver of war. A short envelopment, which fails to envelop and leaves the enemy's supply system intact, merely divides your own forces and can lead to heavy loss and even jeopardy."

Politically, MacArthur felt that a successful landing at Inchon and the capture of Seoul would reap gains equal to the military one. On the first meeting of Major General Oliver P. Smith, USMC, and General MacArthur, the latter stated: "The landing of the Marines at Inchon will be decisive. It will win the war, and the status of the Marine Corps will never again be in doubt."[8]

Also motivating MacArthur's selection of Inchon was his confidence that it would not be strongly defended. This was merely the extension of his South Pacific World War II experience and military philosophy to "hit 'em where they ain't."[9] The North Koreans, he said, would consider a landing at Inchon impossible and insane, and would be taken by surprise.

Again, MacArthur was right, for enemy opposition to the landing was only nominal. On the first two days of the Inchon landing (15-16 September) the First Marine Division had the following battle casualties: 22 KIA, 2 DOW, 2 MIA, 196 WIA;* total 222.

(Subsequent to the landing, however, several events proved that the race to invade at Inchon had been a photo-finish, for a mine-laying effort to seal Inchon had commenced a few days before the actual landing took place.)

The Objectives and Hazards of Inchon

Perhaps the principal and most sobering hazard which every naval and Marine planner who examined the charts of the Inchon area found was the miserable geography. The tides of Inchon (33 feet at their maximum; 23 feet at average spring tide) were among the greatest in the world, and certainly the worst in the Orient. Moreover, these extreme tides reached their peaks in approximately six hours, producing a five-knot current.

The tidal approach to Inchon channel was generally eastward. Over the centuries, the tides had deposited vast mudbanks near Inchon which at low water extended some 6,000 yards to seaward.

The approach channel to Inchon, poetically called "Flying Fish Channel," was narrow, tortuous, and difficult even for a daylight passage. With the absence of navigation lights and the possibility of enemy gunfire and mines, the navigation of an invasion fleet through such a channel was made extremely dangerous. So narrow was the channel that, if a ship foundered in the final approach to Inchon, the vessels ahead of it would be trapped, par-

* KIA—"Killed in Action"; DOW—"Died of Wounds"; MIA—"Missing in Action"; WIA—"Wounded in Action."

ticularly at low tide. By chance, the destroyer *Collett* had been in Inchon harbor just before the war started; Commander Robert H. Close was one of many who knew from recent and firsthand experience the difficult navigation of Flying Fish Channel.

The final effect of the tides was that they controlled the invasion date. To make a large scale amphibious assault at Inchon demanded at least 29 feet of water to insure that the LSTs would have sufficient water beneath their keels to reach the selected landing beaches. On only four days a month were such high tides available. The date for any landing in the fall of 1950,

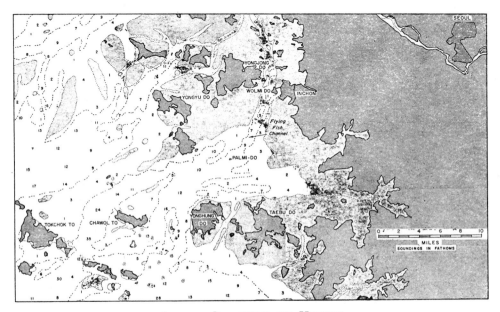

INCHON: OBJECTIVES AND HAZARDS

therefore, had to be September 15, October 11, or November 3, give or take a day or two. Obviously the enemy could punch tide tables with as much accuracy and ease as we ourselves could. Moreover, the tides not only dictated the day but even the hour—the time of high water. Thus, there was little leeway in the selection of an assault date. The tides predetermined both day and hour to the detriment of those elements so essential to the success of an amphibious assault—surprise and flexibility.

The next hazard was the strategic location of the city, with its protecting seawalls, and the related island of Wolmi-do. Never before had U. S. Marines made an amphibious assault into the heart of a large city, or across a so-called "beach" protected by stone seawalls. The oriental city would give excellent cover to enemy troops and defense forces, and there would be little room for the Marines to maneuver, once they were ashore. Moreover, there was only limited space for beaching the vital LSTs which had to accompany the troops, bringing in the necessary supplies, food, and ammunition. Inchon, while South Korea's best west coast harbor, was only mediocre. It had, for example, only ten per cent of Pusan's capacity. Its inner harbor had a single dredged channel, twelve to thirteen feet deep. Its pier space was restricted; its unloading areas were several miles apart, and its cargo-handling facilities were inadequate.

The island of Wolmi-do was yet another geographic handicap. This oyster-shaped, pyramidal island lay in the channel off Inchon and only 800 yards distant, and was connected to it by a narrow causeway. The island's topography and location gave it excellent command over the sea approaches in every direction. Wolmi was suspected to be heavily armed, although a great deal of intelligence of its exact defenses and their locations was not known.

The potentially impregnable location of Wolmi demanded that it be neutralized before any attempt to capture Inchon was made; otherwise, it would stand in a flanking position to thwart the Marine assault upon the Inchon beaches. This necessity for neutralization meant that some of the element of surprise had to be sacrificed. For when the two-day bombardment effort necessary to neutralize Wolmi was made, the enemy might logically conclude that UN forces planned to land at Inchon.

The necessity for reducing Wolmi-do and other Inchon strong points commencing two days before the assault further highlighted a serious and oft expressed objection to Inchon: surprise, that most valuable ingredient of an amphibious assault, might thereby be lost.

In addition, however, there were other factors related to the element of surprise. The principal one was that the U. S. Navy would be building up and loading out from an insecure base. In every landing of the Pacific war, the U. S. forces had operated from a secure base where the knowledge of a forthcoming landing could be rigidly controlled. In the case of Inchon, however, the operating and assembly area was Japan; and Japan was known to be alive with spies and Communist sympathizers. It was unlikely that the assembly of a huge fleet, the gathering of supplies, and the loading of two divisions of troops, could be concealed from the enemy.* The only hope of success was to keep the point of landing a secret from the enemy.

In Tokyo, the imminent invasion was referred to as "Operation Common

---

* Nine months after Inchon, on 15 May 1951 in Tokyo, the U. S. Army opened the prosecution of the cases of 18 spy suspects. According to the prosecutor, Major Robert M. Murray, USA, the ringleader of a North Korean-Japanese spy ring was one Yoshimatsu Iwamura, aged 38, who had been captured with the top secret plans of the Inchon operation in his possession only one week before the landing. (United Press 15 May 1951, reported in the *Washington Post*.)

Knowledge." Official statements hinted of something afoot. Syngman Rhee said, "We are about ready to go." General Walton H. Walker, when asked when UN forces would take the offensive, replied, "In a very short time."

As has been stated, Army leaders objected to the Inchon operation because, as General MacArthur stated, they believed the depth of the turning movement was too great; also because it would denude the Eighth Army of all its reserves. In the unhappy event that the Inchon landing miscarried, no reserve troops could be sent to Korea for at least four months. General Walker, it must be recalled, had vigorously opposed releasing the Marine Brigade for this very reason.

The senior naval and Marine officers who objected to an amphibious assault at Inchon did so solely because of the amphibious obstacles of Inchon itself.

No naval or Marine officer who had studied the military problem had any quarrel with the need for an amphibious assault. Nor did any naval or Marine officer question the strategic logic, the psychological wisdom, or the political promise of an amphibious landing at Inchon. Most of the naval and Marine experts who examined the problem of a west coast amphibious assault held the view that *all* of General MacArthur's objectives could be achieved by landing at *other* places which offered *fewer* natural hazards than Inchon. MacArthur listened, but firmly rejected the alternative locations. It had to be Inchon.

"We drew up a list of every conceivable and natural handicap—and Inchon had 'em all," said LCDR Arlie G. Capps, the gunfire support officer of Task Force 90.

"Make up a list of amphibious 'don'ts,'" said CDR Monroe Kelly, Doyle's communication officer, "and you have an exact description of the Inchon operation. A lot of us planners felt that if the Inchon operation worked, we'd have to rewrite the textbook."

In summary, therefore, General MacArthur's choice of Inchon, in spite of the physical hazards, the organized resistance, and the well-founded doubts which had been expressed, was one of military genius and calculated daring. The choice was his alone, and to him full and unfettered credit must be given.

The naval officer who would command the Joint Task Force Seven—Vice Admiral Arthur D. Struble—had this to say, "General MacArthur deserves full and complete credit for three things: his conception of the operation; his determination to carry through with the operation; and his full, personal acceptance of the many hazards in the operation."

Major General Oliver P. Smith, USMC, commented as follows regarding the concept of Inchon: "There is no doubt but that the concept was Mac-

Arthur's, but the concept of a water-borne envelopment is inherent in amphibious operations. The Navy made many water-borne envelopments during World War II. What the general public is left unaware of is that the concept would have been valueless if the execution had been faulty."

Planning

After the final briefing of General Collins and Admiral Sherman in Tokyo on 23 August, the decision to land at Inchon was firm, except for the formal approval of the Joint Chiefs of Staff, which arrived a few days after the two JCS members had returned to Washington. The three officers who would be responsible for formulating the plans for the operation, and executing them, were Commander Seventh Fleet, Vice Admiral Arthur D. Struble; Commander Amphibious Group One, Rear Admiral James H. Doyle; and Major General Oliver P. Smith, USMC, Commanding General First Marine Division. Struble would determine the broad plans; Doyle would handle the amphibious planning; Smith the landing force plans. For the Inchon assault, Struble would have an additional title: Commander Joint Task Force Seven.

The presence of Struble, Doyle and Smith in the Far East for the forthcoming Inchon operation was fortuitous. Struble had participated in or had supervised twenty-two amphibious operations, including Normandy, Leyte, Ormoc Bay, Mindoro, and Corregidor, during World War II. Moreover, he had worked closely with MacArthur in the latter's South Pacific campaign, and Struble's experience and reputation were well known to the General. Doyle had had experience in amphibious warfare during World War II on the staff of Commander Amphibious Forces South Pacific, seeing action at Guadalcanal and Tulagi during the Solomon Islands campaign and later as commanding officer of the cruiser *Pasadena*. He had been Commander Amphibious Group One since January 1950. Smith, one of the Marines' top amphibious experts, had commanded a regiment at Cape Gloucester, and had participated in the Peleliu and Okinawa operations.

No more experienced senior officers in the field of amphibious warfare could have been found in the American Navy.

It was also fortunate that Doyle's staff had commenced their study of a landing at Inchon in early July.

"On 4 July," said Doyle, "I received orders to bring a number of my staff to Tokyo by air for temporary additional duty in connection with the planning of amphibious operations in loading the First Cavalry Division for an amphibious landing somewhere in Korea. Inchon on the west coast was tentatively selected. At this time, only an administrative landing at Inchon was planned for the purpose of bolstering the retreating and sorely-pressed ROKs. This was then changed to Pohang. The studies we did of Inchon in July, however, were the basis of amphibious planning which followed two months later."[10]

Struble was at sea with the Seventh Fleet during the several conferences which discussed the point of landing, including the final briefing of 23 August. "Upon returning to Sasebo on August 25th," said Vice Admiral Struble, "I received word that I was to command the Inchon invasion. I immediately assembled a few staff officers and departed for Tokyo to commence the top planning for Inchon.

"On my arrival in Tokyo, I was apprised of the decision to land at Inchon on 15 September—less than three weeks away. After a personal study of the problem, I could appreciate why General MacArthur had chosen Inchon: it was the prize gem if we could take it. After a careful study, and after the plans had been completed, I was convinced we *could* take it. I also formed the impression that our chances for a fair amount of surprise at Inchon were good. It was my job to organize the operation so that it *would* be a success.

"The next few days saw a number of conferences between my small staff, Admiral Doyle and his planners, and General Smith and his planners. On 30 August, I had a conference with Admirals Andrewes, Ruble, and Higgins, and Captain Austin, who flew up from Sasebo; Admiral Doyle and Admiral Henderson also attended.

"On 7 September, I flew to Sasebo for another conference with Andrewes, Ewen, Higgins, and Austin. After that one, I flew to Kobe for another one with Almond and Smith.

"These conferences served to rapidly coordinate the final planning of the various forces and greatly facilitated the coordination of later operations. Many of my decisions had to be transmitted orally to Admiral Doyle and General Smith and others in order to expedite the writing of their detailed amphibious and landing force plans."

The plan of operations was soon promulgated and contained the following concept:

(1). An initial landing will be made on Wolmi-do to secure the island prior to the major landing. This step is essential because of the commanding position of the island in relation to the Inchon shoreline. On D-day at L-hour, one battalion of Marines will land in assault on Wolmi-do to seize the island prior to additional landings. L-hour will be on the early morning tide about 0630.

(2). After the Wolmi-do landings, the principal landings will be made on RED, YELLOW, and BLUE beaches at Inchon by the First Marine Division (less one RCT) (Reinforced) landing in amphibious assault. H-hour for these landings will be on the afternoon high tide about 1700. This division will then seize a beachhead in the Inchon area.

(3). The beachhead will be expanded rapidly to seize Kimpo airfield and the Han River line west of Seoul. The advance will be continued to seize and secure the city of Seoul, the terrain commanding Seoul, and an area to the south. The Seventh Infantry Division reinforced plus Tenth Corps troops will land administratively from second and third echelon convoys in the city of Inchon at a time to be designated after D-day and then carry on combat operations as directed by the Commanding General Tenth Corps.

(4). Bombardment and fire support in connection with all these operations will be provided by cruisers and destroyers. Air cover, strikes, and close support will be provided by fast carrier and escort carrier aircraft within the objective area.

/s/ *A. D. Struble*
Vice Admiral
Commander Joint Task Force SEVEN
and Commander Seventh Fleet

There was the basic plan: neutralize Wolmi, invade Inchon, seize the major airfield at Kimpo, and capture Seoul.

As the concept of the operation was finalized in 'round-the-clock conferences, the details of the amphibious force and landing force plans were determined and written down.

The dovetailing of the fleet, amphibious and landing force plans was accelerated by the close proximity of the naval and Marine staffs.

Major General Smith's command group and advance planning staff (23 officers and 12 enlisted men) had arrived in Tokyo from Camp Pendleton, California on 22 August and had established an advance command post aboard USS *Mt. McKinley*. The remainder of the Marines moved into General MacArthur's headquarters in the *Dai Ichi* building in downtown Tokyo. It was an ideal situation in view of the extreme urgency. "It was possible to employ the quickest and most informal method of doing business," reads Doyle's operational report. "Telephone conversations and oral directives were used in place of despatches, letters, and formal directives."

In a matter of days the detailed plans were ready.

Thus, the planning of this vast and complex operation was completed in only 23 days*—a record which seems likely to stand in military history. This speed is a tribute to the ability and skill of the planners and to the soundness and solidity of the amphibious doctrine.

The principal forces for the Inchon assault were:

Attack Force (RADM J. H. Doyle)
Landing Force (10th Corps) (MAJGEN E. A. Almond)
Patrol & Reconnaissance Force (RADM G. H. Henderson)

* In actual fact, less than 23 days were available, as a large number of vessels had to be moving by 10 September.

Blockade & Covering Force (RADM W. G. Andrewes, Royal Navy)
Fast Carrier Force (RADM E. C. Ewen)
Logistic Support Force (CAPT B. L. Austin)
Advance Group (added after original plan was put out) (RADM J. M. Higgins)
Flagship Group (CAPT E. L. Woodyard)

The principal duties of these forces were as follows:

(a) The *Advance Group,* including the Flagship of 7th Fleet, would conduct a reconnaissance in force of the Inchon Area on 13 September. The primary purpose would be to locate and silence gun positions on both Wolmi-do and the adjacent Inchon area which might threaten the success of the landing. Six destroyers would be sent up the channel to anchor in a fan-shaped ring around Wolmi-do Island to draw its fire and to silence its gun positions. At the same time, two American and two British cruisers would conduct a long range bombardment of the Inchon area with air spot, to reduce strong points and positions. Coordinated with the cruiser-destroyer fire would be heavy air attacks from the carriers. This neutralization operation by the advance group would be repeated on 14 September.

(b) The *Attack Force* under RADM Doyle would make the assault landing and control the close air support and the naval gunfire support for the assault troops. The attack force would continue to provide support of the landing force after they had accomplished their landing.

(c) The *Landing Force* (10th Corps) would land on the designated beaches in the Inchon area and carry out the ground plan. Smith's Marine division would carry the assault and seize the beachhead. The Seventh Division, inexperienced in amphibious warfare, would follow Smith's Marines ashore administratively.

(d) The *Patrol and Reconnaissance Force* under RADM Henderson would provide long range reconnaissance and other aircraft patrols covering the whole area of operation.

(e) The *Blockade and Covering Force* under RADM Andrewes, Royal Navy, would conduct special reconnaissance missions and provide for covering of units of Attack Force en route to the objective area. Andrewes was also assigned specific interdiction missions and was to maintain a naval blockade of the west coast of Korea.

(f) The *Fast Carrier Force* would conduct air operations to maintain air supremacy in the objective area and for the isolation of the objective area. The carriers would also provide air cover and support for the actual attack landing operations.

(g) The *Logistic Support Force* would provide refueling and reammunitioning facilities in the objective area.

Preparation

Preparation by the U. S. Marines for the Inchon landing unknowingly began the day the war started in Korea. For the first few days, the Marines had no specific orders—only precedent. But 177 years of precedent was good enough, and was to prove consistent in this case. The first order directing the First Marine Division to prepare to embark a reinforced regimental combat team came on 2 July. Five days later, the First Provisional Marine Brigade was activated, and between 12 and 14 July this brigade sailed.

While this Marine Brigade was fitting out, it became obvious that it was only a matter of time before every available marine would be en route to Korea. General MacArthur, in the first thirty days of the war, sent a total of six despatches to the Joint Chiefs of Staff requesting the Marines. But large scale participation by the Marines was not possible with the reduced peacetime size of the active forces. Accordingly, Marine Reserves were recalled on 19 July and replacements were ordered to the First Marine Division from the Second Marine Division.

From posts and stations all over the world, Marines charged into Camp Pendleton. From the desert supply depot at Barstow, California, came the jeeps, the DUKWs, and the amphibian tractors to complement the rapid build-up.

"The magnitude of the task accomplished by the Marine Corps in the first ten weeks of the conflict may be judged by the fact that on 30 June, the First Marine Division (Reinforced) at Camp Pendleton had an active strength of 641 officers and 7,148 enlisted," reads General Shepherd's report on the activities of Fleet Marine Force, Pacific. "From this initial strength, the First Provisional Brigade (266 officers and 4,503 men) was taken. Yet, by 15 September, the First Marine Division had been expanded to 26,000—an expansion, augmentation, and movement without parallel in American military history."

An amphibious assault is often compared to a chain—a series of interlocking operations, each one dependent on the others. One link breaks and the whole chain fails.

The Inchon operation placed exceedingly difficult stresses on the amphibious assault chain. The shortage of time, the lack of rehearsal, the shortage of trained personnel complicated the always-difficult problem.

"So many times during an amphibious attack, the little guys in the little boats need more knowledge of the big picture," said Admiral Doyle. "This was especially true at Inchon. I considered it vital that every key man be given the most recent data available. As there was no time prior to Inchon for a rehearsal, I held a briefing on board the flagship for all commanding officers, loading officers, control officers, and all those actually concerned with making the assault. I told them that since there was no time for rehearsal, I wished all CO's to personally instruct boat crews and coxswains what they were to do, why they were to do it, and how their individual tasks fitted into the overall picture. I wanted the cox'ns to have all this background information so that they could react in the event of unforeseen developments. We have such high-type enlisted men in the Navy that I knew with proper instructions, they would prove resourceful in the event of trouble."

One of the urgent needs prior to the Inchon landing was intelligence. Despite the fact that South Korea had been occupied by American forces for more than two years, and that Inchon had been one of the main harbors in use, there was an incredible lack of information regarding the harbor.

Pictures were poor. Maps were wholly inadequate. The close air support charts used at Inchon were hastily made into books by the U. S. Army's 64th Engineer's Base Topographic Battalion. The charts were mostly monochrome, and in some cases reproductions of World War II Japanese maps. "Considering the extremely short time allowed," reported CDR J. T. Moynahan, after a special inspection for the Hydrographic Office, "it is a miracle that the books were produced at all." There was little late information on the condition of the mudflats, the height of the seawalls, the tractional qualities and the gradient of the mudflats.

One of the most helpful sources of information on Inchon was Captain Thomas F. Brittain's World War II report of the landing of American occupation forces in Korea in 1945.

From unusual sources and by unorthodox methods, frantic efforts were initiated to obtain the needed intelligence.

These methods and efforts took three forms. First of all, an Army officer, Warrant W. R. Miller, was loaned by the Second Transportation Medium, Yokohama, to ComPhibGruONE. Miller had spent more than a year handling LSUs and LCMs in Inchon, and he had had recent and firsthand experience with Inchon's tidal conditions and unloading problems. "His knowledge and advice was accurate and invaluable," said CDR H. W. McElwain, the intelligence officer of Task Force 90.

To determine the seawall heights which the attacking Marines would be forced to scale, a special team of one officer and two civilians who were in the area from the U.S. Air Force's Wright Field in Dayton, Ohio, were made available to PhibGruONE; Colonel Richard W. Philbrick, USAF, and Mr. Amrom H. Katz and Mr. Donald J. Graves. From aerial photographs taken by RF-80 jet aircraft flying at 200 feet, these gentlemen determined the heights of the seawalls at various tidal stages within a few inches of their actual height, corroborating the information available from other sources.

The third source of information would come from a small behind-the-lines intelligence party led by Lieutenant Eugene F. Clark, USN. Clark, an ex-chief yeoman, had fought through the Pacific war, including duty on Okinawa with the Army's Military Government Group. After the war he served aboard an AKA, had commanded an LST running the China coast, and had also commanded the USS *Errol*, an attack transport which received the Battle Efficiency Pennant under his command.

At the outbreak of the Korean War Clark was assigned to MacArthur's headquarters GHQ staff. His previous experience ideally fitted him for the most unusual of missions for a naval officer. Clark's party, consisting of himself and two specially picked South Koreans, was to land on one of the small harbor islands near Inchon, and to send back to Tokyo the missing details of the needed intelligence.

On 31 August, Clark and his two interpreters sailed from Sasebo aboard the British destroyer HMS *Charity*, and transferred the next morning to the South Korean frigate *PC-703*. By nightfall that evening, Clark's party was ensconced on Yong-hong-do island, a scant 13.8 miles from Inchon itself. The island, six miles long and three miles wide, was typical of the hundreds of small islands dotting the west coast. The Yong-hong-do islanders were friendly and helpful. Clark commandeered the only motorized sampan on the island; he also organized the teen-aged boys of the three-hundred-odd inhabitants into coast-watching parties. Two machine guns were set up facing the nearby island of Taebu-do, which was occupied by enemy troops.

For two weeks Clark clung to his perilous roost, fighting sampan battles with North Korean vessels from the adjacent islands, and capturing infiltrators who crossed from Taebu-do at low tide to dislodge him from his stronghold. Nightly, Clark sent into Inchon missions composed of young loyal South Korean boys who were instructed to measure the mudflats and the heights of the seawall, to count the defending troops, and to chart the positions of the hostile guns, observation posts, and trench implacements. Clark personally rowed into Inchon harbor one moonless night and wallowed about on the mudflats to prove that not even an amphibious Marine, much less a tank, could negotiate the spongy gumbo.

In his nocturnal prowling in the waters south of Inchon itself, Clark succeeded in capturing some 30 small vessels, most of them carrying civilians in transit between Inchon and the harbor islands. Occasionally, however, Clark captured a sampan with policemen or soldiers who were able to contribute to the over-all intelligence picture.

His most valuable contribution to the Inchon landing, Clark thought, was his discovery that one of the main navigation lights of the difficult Flying Fish Channel, located on Palmi-do, could be lit. The Reds had not entirely destroyed it, merely damaging the rotation mechanism and extinguishing the wick; otherwise it was intact. Clark reported these facts to Tokyo by radio and was instructed to light this important navigational light at midnight on 14 of September. This aid made the invasion fleet's passage up Flying Fish Channel a great deal faster and easier on the morning of 15 September 1950.[11]

It was an exceedingly dangerous mission exceedingly well accomplished. For his bravery and accomplishment Lieutenant Clark was awarded the Navy Cross.

Wolmi—The Cork in the Bottle

As stated previously, a successful landing at Inchon demanded that the island of Wolmi-do be captured first. In the planning stages there was much discussion on how best to do this. Could the island be sufficiently neutralized by a bombardment on the morning of the invasion? If so, the critical element of surprise might be preserved until the very moment of landing. The experts who examined the island's position and studied its defenses thought not. The lessons of other Pacific island pre-invasion bombardments were too plentiful and too recent. To assume that Wolmi might be neutralized in a single morning would be dangerously optimistic.

"A series of balanced operations were planned for the neutralization of Wolmi-do commencing 10 September," said Vice Admiral Struble. "First, Admiral Ruble's Marine airmen of Task Group 96.8 would burn the island with napalm. The Advance Force attacks on 13 and 14 September would follow. Finally, there would be another bombardment on the morning of the assault.

"In all the planning, it was my intention to so balance the air operation on the west coast that the finger of suspicion would not be heavily pointed at Inchon. To accomplish this, I had the carriers not only strike Wolmi and the Inchon area, but also the Kunsan area to the south* and the Pyongyang area to the north. I also ordered an amphibious feint in the Kunsan area on 7 September.

"I felt that if we could keep the point of our landing concealed until the first bombardment of 13 September the enemy would not reach the conclusion that Inchon was to be invaded until it was too late."

---

* The diversionary landing at Kunsan was carried out by the British frigate *Whitesand Bay* supporting American U. S. Army commandoes and the Royal Marine commandoes.

In planning the destroyer bombardments of Wolmi, the question of whether or not to bombard at night was raised.

"One thing we all agreed on," reported Rear Admiral John M. Higgins, commanding the Gunfire Support Group, "was the desirability of making the attack on Wolmi in broad daylight despite the fact that this forced us to give up the surprise element and made us better targets. But if we went up there at night and hit heavy opposition, there'd be a lot of confusion in that narrow channel."[12] Making the attacks in daylight would also diminish any danger of collision, and in case one or more ships became immobile from enemy fire, the towing task would be less difficult.

It was planned that the destroyers would operate close enough to Wolmi to tempt the hidden guns to open fire.

"The 'sitting duck' concept was carefully discussed and agreed upon in advance," said Vice Admiral Struble, "as a means of drawing enemy fire and thereby revealing the locations of their gun positions."

Finally, the decision was made to anchor near Wolmi in order to counteract the five-knot current; further, the destroyers' time of anchoring would be adjusted so that they would ride the *flooding* tide, and thereby *face* the incoming tide. By keeping their anchors underfoot to steady ships' head and position, the destroyers would be headed out of the channel and ready for a fast exit in case the return fire from the island was too heavy. Riding the flood tide would also place the destroyers broadside to the island, thus allowing all guns to bear.

The destroyers, meanwhile, were making preparations for the bombardment. In his action report, the skipper of the *Gurke*, CDR Frederick M. Radel, described his crew's efforts to repel boarders—a rare precaution in the age of atom bombs, supersonic airplanes, and guided missiles:

"About the only preparations we made," said Radel, "were to prepare ship for towing, to rig fenders for going alongside a damaged or stranded vessel, and to brief and arm repair parties to repel possible boarders." The destroyers, if disabled, would be so close to the enemy island that boarding across the mudflats became a distinct possibility.

De Haven took a bizarre step to invite the enemy's attention. Since the destroyers would be as close as 800 yards to Wolmi, where individuals on deck would clearly be visible, might not *De Haven* attract Wolmi's fire by setting dummies on the open deck? CDR Oscar B. Lundgren thought it worth the effort and approved his crew's plan of placing several straw and rag-filled dummies on the forecastle.

Extra 40 mm. ammunition was stacked on deck, for the ship's magazines were already full.

The Neutralization of Wolmi-do

The neutralization of Wolmi-do was commenced on 10 September by Rear Admiral Richard W. Ruble's Carrier Division 15 aircraft. The Marine aircraft of VMF-212 and 323 dropped 95 tanks of napalm in a systematic pattern all over Wolmi. Photo reconnaissance the next day showed 39 out of 44 buildings in the warehouse area destroyed, the entire dwelling area burned out, and buildings on the north peninsula 80 per cent destroyed. Periodically, over the next two days, a pattern of air strikes to soften the island's defenses was delivered.

The pre-invasion bombardments of Wolmi-do commenced at 0700 on 13 September.

Gunfire Support Group Six—cruisers *Toledo, Rochester,* HMS *Kenya,* HMS *Jamaica,* and destroyers *Mansfield, De Haven, Lyman K. Swenson, Gollett, Gurke,* and *Henderson*—started up Flying Fish Channel. The weather was clear, the sea calm.

A few miles south of Inchon, as the channel narrowed, the cruisers dropped out of the column and anchored in their bombardment stations.

The destroyers continued northward.

Shortly before 1145, *Mansfield,* the leading destroyer, reported what appeared to be a string of mines. *De Haven's* skipper, CDR Lundgren, confirmed the sighting. The order for open fire was given and both cruisers and destroyers opened fire on the enemy mines. The first mine was hit by *Gurke* at 1146.

"The mine menace was in the general vicinity of Palmi-do," said Vice Admiral Struble, "and had apparently been placed in this location because of a bombardment fired at Inchon about a month earlier by two British cruisers and two destroyers.[13]

"Fortunately, due to our decision to come in at low tide, the mines were uncovered, discovered, and generally destroyed by gunfire."

Destroyer Squadron Nine's commander, Captain Halle C. Allan, detached *Henderson* to remain behind temporarily to destroy as many of the mines as possible, and then when the rising incoming tide hid them from view, to rejoin at high speed. Except for a few mines, most of this minefield was destroyed by the cruiser-destroyer fire.

The destroyers boldly sailed past the doomed island, then under heavy air attack from Task Force 77 carrier aircraft. *Gurke* anchored first at 1242, only 800 yards from Wolmi. Behind her, the other destroyers halted in their assigned positions.

Hundreds of eyes aboard the American destroyers scanned Wolmi-do's surface trying to detect the telltale humps of concealed gun positions. For several minutes nothing happened, and the destroyers rode to their anchors in the terrible silence.

Captain Allan two-blocked his signal: "Execute assigned mission."

De Haven opened fire first, shortly before 1300, followed by *Collett*. Not until 1303 was there any fire returned from Wolmi, and it was concentrated on the three destroyers nearest the island: *Gurke, Swenson,* and *Collett*. The first enemy shots were over, then short; at 1306, *Collett* took her first hit. She was struck again at 1310, again at 1320, and again at 1329. The last shell was a 75 mm. armor-piercing shell which broke into two pieces, one piece going into the engineroom and fracturing a low-pressure steam line, the larger half plowing into the plot room, where it broke the firing selector switch and wounded five men. *Collett* shifted to individual control and shifted her anchorage on which at least one enemy gun had found the range.

Gurke was hit next in two places, neither seriously. The *Swenson* took a near miss which instantly killed LTJG David H. Swenson and wounded ENS John N. Noonan.

"As the first hits were reported to me," said Vice Admiral Struble, "I directed Captain Woodyard to heave short and have the *Rochester* stand by to enter the narrow channel to Inchon in order to support the destroyers if it developed that they would be unable to handle the problem themselves." But the bombardment proceeded without further casualty, the *Mansfield* being narrowly missed during the retirement.

The destroyers steamed out of the anchorage at 1400, having blasted the island for more than an hour, supported by shellfire from the cruisers in the lower bay. As the destroyers steamed clear, the planes from Task Force 77 resumed the air attacks.

"After the bombardment," said Vice Admiral Struble, "the entire advance force departed from the area off Inchon and proceeded down Flying Fish Channel to produce the illusion, if possible, that we were retiring.

"After we were well clear, I ordered the task force to stop for a conference aboard the *Rochester*. Admiral Higgins and his staff officers and Captain Allan of the destroyers were present.

"After a discussion of the first bombardment, I decided to re-orient the carrier attack from south to west, and to accept the attendant risk of bombs dropping on the causeway between Wolmi and Inchon. At the request of the Marines, I had previously ordered this causeway spared so that the Marines who captured Wolmi on the morning of the 15th could use it to cross to Inchon and join the main assault.

"I also took action to improve the next day's air spotting for the cruiser fire, which had not been satisfactory."

The reduction of Wolmi was resumed in similar fashion the following day. Prior to standing up Flying Fish Channel, the advance force hove to, half-masted flags, and conducted burial-at-sea ceremonies aboard the *Toledo* for the late LTJG David H. Swenson.

Only five destroyers (*Collett* having been detached) entered the channel. As *Henderson*, *Mansfield*, *De Haven*, *Swenson*, and *Gurke* steamed northward, a small portion of the previous day's minefield was seen and again taken under fire.

The remaining five destroyers resumed their positions around Wolmi and commenced fire. Wolmi's batteries were slow to answer, and indeed, for the first forty minutes, not a shot from the island splashed around the destroyers. For seventy-five minutes the bombardment group earthquaked the tiny island. As the ships retired, this time unharmed, not a shot was heard in retaliation from the wounded island.

In retrospect, the bombardment of Wolmi in such a manner and under such circumstances was extremely audacious. That it was so successful is a tribute to the aggressive spirit of the U.S. Navy, which has always accepted great risks where there is great promise. History must record this bombardment as a heroic and daring action.[14]

Silenced and shrouded in smoke, Wolmi was now ready for capture. The Marines made last-minute preparations to remove the Wolmi cork from the Inchon bottle.

The advance attack force, Captain N. W. Sears, consisting of three APDs and one LSD[15] steamed up Flying Fish Channel in the darkness on the early morning of the 15th, guided by the flames of still-burning Wolmi-do and the light from Palmi-do island, atop of which sat LT Eugene Clark, shivering inside his blanket, watching the invasion fleet steam past in the darkness. Ahead of these ships were the destroyers *Mansfield*, *De Haven*, *Swenson*; and, following them, the LSMR division of three rocket ships (*401*, *403*, and *404*), plus the *Southerland*, *Gurke*, *Henderson*, *Toledo*, *Rochester*, *Kenya*, *Jamaica*, *Collett*, and *Mataco*.

At 0545, the bombarding ship opened fire on Wolmi, and again the F4U Corsairs from Carrier Division 15, ten of them, sprayed the landing beaches. At 0633, LTCOL R. D. Taplett's Third Battalion (Fifth Regiment) landed from seventeen LCVPs and three LSUs on the shattered isle.

There were two waves of LCVPs of eight boats, each carrying troops, and one wave of three LSUs carrying a total of nine tanks. The first wave of LCVPs was re-employed as Wave Four. The resistance was generally light, for many of the 500-odd enemy troops defending the island had been reduced to dazed inaction by the three days of air and surface bombardment. Some of the defending troops—elements of an artillery regiment and an independent marine regiment—had slipped back across the causeway to Inchon during the night. The U.S. Marines stormed up the hilly slopes, and in forty-two minutes the American flag was flying from Wolmi-do. However, for several hours more, the Marines rooted the defenders out of their holes. The enemy suffered 120 dead and 190 captured, to the 20 wounded of the U.S. Marines. The rest of the day was spent by these Marines getting emplacements ready for two battalions of light artillery which would be landed on Wolmi with the main attack, to support the Inchon invasion. The tanks were also made ready to cross the causeway to join the attack upon Inchon.

Inchon Invasion: Across the Seawalls

The actual invasion of Inchon commenced at 1730 on the evening of 15 September. There were three unusual features of the assault. First of all, the U. S. Marine Corps had never before made an assault into the heart of a large city, against the prospect of heavy opposition from warehouses, buildings, and other cover. Nor had they ever landed on seawalls.

After observing the Reds' response to the Wolmi bombardment, General Lemuel C. Shepherd, Commanding General, Fleet Marine Force, Pacific, said: "There clearly remained little further justification for anticipating an unopposed or lightly opposed landing. . . . The size of the task force, clearly visible to the Communists," continues Shepherd's report, "left no doubt that the Wolmi-do landing must be only a preliminary, and evidence of hurried enemy preparations to move into the Inchon area were detected by our aircraft and appropriate attacks launched. Nevertheless, the initial shock and surprise which forms a valuable part of most amphibious attacks was largely anticipated, and the enemy was alert for the evening landings."[16]

The second undesirable feature was the fact that the landing had to take place just prior to darkness, which meant that the Marines did not have a daylight period in which to get set for the night.

A third undesirable feature of the landing across the Inchon seawalls was the necessity of having LSTs right behind the assaulting Marines: because of the tides and the late hour of the landing, sufficient supplies—3,000 tons—had to be beached simultaneously with the invading Marines in order to guarantee logistic support during the night and until the next high tide would permit replenishment.

"One of the toughest decisions I had to make during the planning for Inchon," said Admiral Doyle, "was the decision to leave the LSTs on the beach during that first night of the landing. It is easy to imagine what would have happened to me if something had gone wrong; I especially worried about the possibility of having a United States Navy ship captured.

"However, the Marines asked that the LSTs be left on the beach for their support; they said they'd protect them. I had complete reliance and confidence that they could do it. Once the decision was made, I worried no more about it."

Doyle and his planners were well aware of the risks—and were frank to admit that these LSTs, as never before, would be "large slow targets" and fortunate if half survived. The Pacific Fleet evaluation group summarized this dilemma in their report:

"The possible sacrifice and loss of eight LSTs had to be accepted in order to insure logistic support to troops ashore at Inchon during the night. . . . Dried out on the mudflats by the receding tide, these eight LSTs were helplessly vulnerable to enemy fire, and with their explosive inflammable cargo were subject to loss."[17]

Perhaps it was the high expectancy of loss which necessitated the choice of the eight LSTs for this hazardous but necessary phase of the assault. At any rate, the eight LSTs which made the assault landings were amongst those that had been turned over to the Army and SCAJAP* after World War II. For five years they had been used, misused, unused, and abused for cargo work around the Japanese harbors. When recommissioned into the U.S. Navy, it was found that much of their original equipment had been altered, stripped, or damaged. Their overhaul and upkeep during the five years had almost been nil. As a result, Commander Tractor Squadron Three (CAPT R. C. Peden) estimated that each of these LSTs would ordinarily have required at least four months of refitting and overhaul in a U.S. shipyard to bring them up to a minimum condition for operations. Another of the SCAJAP LSTs, in fact, was in such uncertain material condition that it was towed to Inchon.

Almost as bad was the lack of experienced people to man these vital LSTs. To take an LST into Inchon harbor, against its fast-flowing current, gunfire, mudflats, and in darkness, ordinarily would have demanded handpicked skippers with special training. Instead, LT R. M. Beckley, skipper of *LST-898*, who had made two previous landings in an LST, and LT Trumond E. Houston, skipper of *LST-799*, who had made none, were typical of the commanding officers.

"On 13 July 1950," wrote Houston, "I received immediate detachment orders from my duty station at the U.S. Naval Training Center, Recruit Training Command, San Diego, California, to report to Commandant,

* Supreme Commander Allies, Japan.

Twelfth Naval District, for air priority class one to Japan to take command of an undesignated LST.

"Upon arrival in Japan, I found I was one of ten prospective commanding officers of LSTs which had been operating with Japanese civilian crews since 1946 and were at that time being assembled at the U.S. Naval Repair Facility, Yokosuka, Japan, for repair, fitting out, and recommissioning in the U.S. Navy. My ship, the *LST-799*, arrived about the same time in Yokosuka as I did. What a revelation! It was stripped, dirty, stinking, and generally in a horrible operating condition (all LSTs were the same).

"My crew and officers arrived piecemeal. Some came by surface, some by air, some were from local commands. The crew, numbering sixty men and five officers, could be broken down roughly in three parts. One third was regular Navy, one third was recruits from training centers, and one third was recalled reservists, most of whom had been at home only ten or twelve days before.

"We were a motley, ragtag crew. Three days before commissioning, we descended on the *799*, directed the Japanese crew to retreat within a half hour, and took over.

"We were commissioned on 28 August, about 0930. At 1000, we had orders to get under way for a berth shift. I had never handled an LST before.

"During the ensuing few days, all hands did everything possible to make our ship ready for sea. Material needs were the most critical. Even a day prior to getting under way, we had no sextants, bearing circles, special signal flags, and many other very necessary items of equipment. We had no wardroom equipment: linen, silver, dishes, and blankets. We used Japanese equipment wherever it was available.

"On the third day after commissioning, we were on our way to Kobe, Japan, where Marine elements were deployed for loading for the assault at Inchon, Korea. We arrived in Kobe, rode out a typhoon there where the eye of the storm passed directly overhead; eventually we were re-routed to Pusan, Korea, for loading of Marine units and equipment.

"We picked up the convoy from Japan off southern Korea and continued together for Inchon. On the evening of 15 September 1950, *LST-799* was the last of eight LSTs to land on Red Beach, landing on the extreme left flank.

"This was my own and my crew's first beaching. We had had no training or practice time. I shudder as I remember how green and inexperienced the entire ship was. Only the basic knowledge of mechanics so many of our young Americans acquire, their inquisitive and exploring minds, their 'can-do' attitude can explain how we ever arrived at the beach at all."

Upon such vessels and such men did the success of the landing at Inchon depend.

"My orders were to get as many of the eight ships into the Red area and unloaded as was humanly possible, no matter what the cost," said LCDR James C. Wilson who commanded the LSTs.[18]

The final afternoon bombardment of the Inchon beaches lasted for forty-five minutes, with rocket ships, destroyers, cruisers and airplanes all joining in the large and tremendously powerful bombardment.

Vice Admiral Struble's orders to the bombardment forces clearly specified that there should be no promiscuous firing at the city itself or at civilian installations. To achieve this, the entire objective area had been divided into 60 sub-areas. Known military targets had been previously assigned, and those which offered the greatest potential hazard to our landing troops were circled in red. It had been agreed that any ship could fire into a red-circle area with or without a "spot." In the uncircled areas, however, firing was permitted only if definite targets were found and an air spot was available. This differentiation between types of areas was adopted to reduce destruction of nonmilitary targets to a minimum, to save the city of Inchon for occupation forces, and to avoid injury to civilian personnel. "The Seoul-Inchon area is inhabited by our South Korean Allies," said Struble in an order to his forces, "and our forces plan to utilize facilities in this area. Unnecessary destruction will impede our progress. Bombing and gunfire will be confined to targets whose destruction will contribute to the conduct of operations—accurate gunfire and pinpoint bombing against specific targets, rather than area destruction, is contemplated."

Belting Inchon's harbor area was a large, grey, heavy stone seawall. Four lengths of this harbor wall had been selected as the landing "beaches," though certainly the word "beach" was a misnomer in every case. "Red" beach was to the north, 1,000 feet long, with a 15-foot seawall. It lay beneath a protecting hill atop of which was a Korean cemetery. It was to prove a troublesome spot. The other main beach, "Blue," lay to the south of the city, relatively clear of the urban area, and in such a position that the Marines could sever the city's communications from the rear. Green beach and Yellow beach (not used until D+1) were on Wolmi and the tidal basin of the inner harbor, respectively. The latter two were logistic beaches only, Red and Blue being the assault beaches.

The assaults on Red and Blue beaches were simultaneous, roughly an hour before sunset and high tide. Twenty-three waves of LVTs made the Red beach assault with the eight LSTs. In each LVT was a pair of scaling ladders—some metal, some wooden—with hooked ends designed to catch the seawalls. As the first wave of boats touched the seawall, the tops of these seawalls were still four feet above the boats' bows. In some cases the ladder hooks were too small to fit the wall, and the Marines leap-frogged over one another. The first wave tumbled ashore with relatively little opposition, but the enemy fire picked up as Waves Two and Three approached.

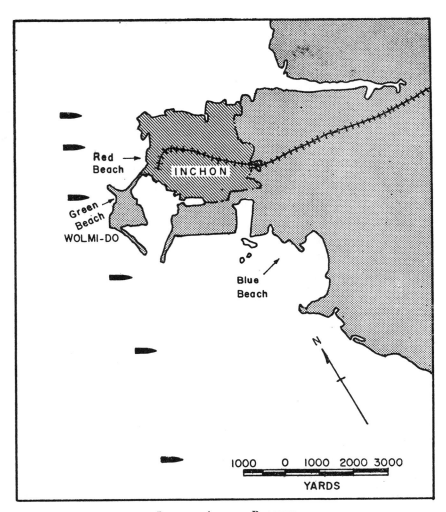

INCHON: ASSAULT BEACHES

The LSTs, led by *859*, started in one by one at five-minute intervals at 1830, one hour after the first Marine wave. These vessels seemed to draw the fire of the defending Reds, enabling the Marines ashore to move forward. Despite the smoke, dust, haze, and the approach of sunset, the eight LSTs succeeded in making the beach, although not in the order originally planned.

Just as *LST-973* (LT R. I. Trapp) beached, it was hit by a mortar shell that could have meant disaster. The shell struck among gasoline drums parked topside; raw gasoline gushed down the deck, into the ventilator and crew compartments. Quick work on the part of the damage control party prevented a fire which, spreading to the abundant ammunition nearby, might have caused a major accident. *LST-914,* fourth in line, was struck by enemy gunfire and set afire, but the blaze was soon under control. LSTs *857* and *859* were also hit.

The seawall proved troublesome. Some LSTs bounced off it, others found the wall too high to lower their ramps.

"It was almost dark as we headed for the beach," said Lieutenant Houston. "Due to heavy sky, light rain, and smoke from burning buildings ashore, visibility was extremely poor. Sporadic mortar and small arms gunfire was being received from ashore. While this was our first beaching, it was going to be a good one. We hit the seawall at about six knots. The ship shuddered and bounced for several minutes before hanging onto the quay. It was well that we had hit hard, for we shattered the quay wall, enabling us to commence immediate unloading of heavy equipment.

"Bulldozers went out first and immediately commenced covering the slit trenches along the waterfront from which enemy small arms were being received. Additionally, they helped break up the quay in order that other LSTs could get their bows in a position to commence unloading.

"Two Marines seriously wounded by mortar fire at the bow door entrance were brought aboard. Both died on board and were transferred to an adjacent hospital LST.

"Unloading continued throughout the night as ships remained dried out on the mudflats."

The Marines continued to press forward, and in about one hour and a half had secured the hill near Red beach.

On Blue beach, 15 waves of LVT(A)s and LVTs and 6 waves of LCVPs took the Marines ashore. Again, the seawall was a problem. Dynamite was used to blast openings, and one charge almost blew up Vice Admiral Struble and General Almond.

In the afternoon Vice Admiral Struble went past the *Mount McKinley* and picked up General Almond of the Tenth Corps to observe the afternoon landing. Struble had recognized that the approach in connection with Blue beach was very difficult, and that the conduct of the ship-to-shore movement here might well have difficulty; he also thought it desirable for General Almond, who had little or no previous amphibious experience, to actually observe the conduct of a difficult ship-to-shore problem.

Struble and Almond approached the seawall in the barge, with about the second or third wave, to the left of the landing area. As the two officers approached the seawall, a sergeant of the Marines hollered out in an irate fashion, "Boat there! Get the hell out of here!" Recognizing the urgency of his voice, Struble ordered the coxswain to get out in a hurry. After the barge turned, a large explosive charge blew up and destroyed the nearby seawall. The sergeant was making a breach in the seawall in order that the boats in following waves could go into the breach and the men could get across the top of the wall quicker and better.

The pre-bombardment smoke, combined with the dust and haze, lowered the visibility to less than 100 yards. A 24-inch searchlight was trained on the desired beach to assist the boatmen taking the Marines ashore, and this was a great help. Nevertheless, part of Wave Sixteen became lost and was deposited to the north of Blue beach on the salt beds. (Later, these troops were reembarked and relanded on Blue beach.) Fortunately, resistance was light in this area, and the Marines pressed inland in the fast-falling darkness.

On 16 September, the ground forces advanced against light resistance on an arc radiating five miles from Red beach. The Korean Marines mopped up resistance in the town of Inchon. Air interdiction in the vicinity north and south of the objective area was successful in preventing effective enemy reinforcement. The waterfront unloading, which was very slow at first, improved on D+1 Day, and henceforth unloading proceeded on schedule. Many enemy tanks, vehicles, and mortars were strafed and rocketed on the Seoul-Inchon road. General unloading commenced at 1030 as transport types were moved to berths close off the harbor entrance. Development of unloading facilities commenced in the inner harbor. A causeway on the west side of Wolmi-do was completed, but because of the tidal current, only one LST could be berthed alongside. Commander Amphibious Group Three (RADM L. A. Thackrey, USN) arrived in *Eldorado* and was placed in charge of unloading operations ashore. *Consolation* arrived and commenced embarking casualties. At 1800, Commanding General, First Marine Division, assumed command of the landing force elements ashore. The Gunfire Support Group continued deep and close support fire missions with good results.

At 0550, 17 September, two enemy aircraft, believed to be YAK-3s, made bombing runs on *Rochester*. The first drop of four bombs missed astern, except for one which ricocheted off the airplane crane without exploding. The second drop missed close aboard on the port bow and shrapnel did minor damage to electrical equipment. There were no casualties. The first plane to make a bombing run also strafed the *Jamaica* and was shot down by that ship. *Jamaica* suffered three casualties.

The First Marine Division continued to advance against light resistance, although the enemy resistance stiffened on the flanks. During the morning, two hundred enemy troops and five tanks attacked the Fifth Marine Regiment six miles southeast of Inchon. Results: all tanks destroyed and enemy troops annihilated. Kimpo airfield was secured by 2005.

Much traffic was observed moving into Seoul from the east and north. From 500 to 1,000 enemy troops were observed 12 miles south of Munsan, moving toward Seoul. These troops were wearing white clothing over dark; they turned and walked in the opposite direction when U.S. aircraft approached.

U. S. 7th Infantry Division commenced administrative landing at 1400.

The Inchon assault must be recorded as an audacious gamble. That it succeeded so notably and brilliantly enhanced the military reputation of the one man who said it could be done—Douglas MacArthur. It also reflects great credit on the three principal naval and Marine officers—Struble, Doyle and Smith—who planned and carried it off.

Admiral W. F. Halsey's telegram to the General said as much: "It was," said Halsey, "the most masterly and audacious strategic stroke in all history."

Rear Admiral Arleigh A. Burke, the Deputy Chief of Staff to Commander Naval Forces Far East, footnoted the operation: "This operation really shows the greatness of that man."

General MacArthur saluted the Navy and Marines on the morning of the 15th, in a message to Vice Admiral Struble: "The Navy and the Marines have never shone more brightly than this morning. MacArthur."

Significance of the Inchon Landing

That Inchon was a magnificent gamble grandly taken by General MacArthur, and that it also was brilliantly conducted by the U. S. Navy and Marine Corps, there can be no doubt.

In researching the multitudinous reports of the Inchon campaign, frequently found are such words as "fortunately," "phenomenal," "in spite of," "unique," "unorthodox," and "improvised." It was "fortunate," says an Amphibious Group One report, "that the staff of ComPhibGruONE had commenced its research on an Inchon landing in July." "It was fortunate," says the First Marine Division report, "that a Marine Mobile training team was in the Far East when the war began," "It is phenomenal," says the *Pacific Fleet Interim Evaluation Report,* "that the LSTs were able to perform their assigned missions only fifteen days after commissioning." "It was fortunate that the typhoons Kezia and Jane didn't interfere," said Admiral Albert K. Morehouse, Chief of Staff to Commander Naval Forces, Far East.

It should not be inferred, however, that the planning or the execution of the Inchon landing was haphazard or that its success was due solely to good fortune. Quite the contrary is true. The planning and execution of the Inchon landing in record time, and with a minimum of casualties, despite the considerable hazards, is a tribute to the skill, training, readiness, and courage of the men of the U. S. Navy and Marine Corps who made it possible.

The results of the Inchon operation were notable in many fields: the effect it had on the war; the effect it had upon the Chinese; the effect it had upon the Navy and the Marine Corps; and the effect it had upon our national military policies and programs.

The immediate military effect upon the Korean War was instantaneous and decisive. The Commanding General himself had a brief but erroneous moment of doubt that the intended purpose of the landing had not been realized. On the 17th of September, with the Marines plunging toward Seoul, there was still no evidence that the landing had resulted in any relaxation upon the Pusan perimeter. General Walton H. Walker's U. S. Eighth Army was still in its positions.

On the *Mount McKinley,* General MacArthur sent for Rear Admiral Doyle, and expressed his fear that the landing had not achieved the results he had hoped for; and thereupon, he directed Doyle to commence planning another amphibious landing, this time at the point the Navy had originally chosen, near Kunsan. When Doyle asked what troops he should plan on using for the new assault, MacArthur suggested the First Cavalry Division.

In a few hours, however, a despatch from General Walker reported that resistance in his front had weakened, and by that evening it was apparent to all that the great gamble had paid off.

The Inchon landing can be credited with ending the North Korean aggression, for in a matter of days the entire half of the peninsula below the 38th parallel had been recaptured by the UN forces, and the North Korean Army was a beaten and broken army.

Admiral Doyle credits one fortuitous circumstance with having a direct bearing on the success of the 8th Army breakout from the Pusan perimeter as a result of the Inchon operation: the death of their number one general, General Kang Kun. "The death of their number one general," said Doyle, "greatly influenced the deterioration of the North Korean Army in the Pusan perimeter. He was a very good general and even General MacArthur conceded his ability. His successor did not have the ability to hold the North Korean Army together."

To the naval student, the results of the Inchon landing are many and varied. The immediate lesson is that Inchon demonstrated afresh the incalculable value of amphibious operations. Completely contravened was such a statement as the one made only nine months earlier, in Ocober 1949, by the Chairman of the Joint Chiefs of Staff, General Omar S. Bradley: "I predict," said the General, "that large scale amphibious operations will never occur again."

An excellent condensation of the results of Inchon are found in Admiral Doyle's action report:

The target date which was designated, 15 September 1950, did not give adequate time by normal standards for joint planning between the Commander, Attack Force and the Commander, Landing Force. There was no time available for the joint training of the landing forces involved, or for holding rehearsals for the Marines, ships, planes and landing craft which participated in the operation. Many naval and Marine units arrived in Japan with barely sufficient time to combat load in accordance with loading plans.

The successful accomplishment of the assault on Inchon demanded that an incredible number of individual and coordinated tasks be performed precisely as planned in the face of almost insuperable difficulties. The fact that the assault was successful is a matter of history.

Under the circumstances I have briefly mentioned above, it is my conviction that the successful assault on Inchon could have been accomplished only by United States Marines. This conviction, I am certain, is shared by everyone who planned, executed or witnessed the assault. My statement is not to be construed as a comparison of the fighting qualities of various units of our armed forces. It simply means that because of their many years of specialized training in amphibious warfare, in conjunction with the Navy, only the United States Marines had the requisite know-how to formulate these plans within the limited time available and to execute these plans flawlessly without additional training or rehearsal. To put it another way, I know that if any other unit of our armed forces had been designated as the landing force for the assault on Inchon, that unit would have required many, many months of the specialized training, including joint training with the Navy, which is a regular part of the Marines' everyday life.

All these facts emphasize the soundness of our national policy in entrusting to the Navy and Marine Corps the specialization in, and the development of, amphibious warfare. Conceivably, in the future, we may be required to execute many amphibious landings on many fronts.

Vice Admiral Struble subsequently made the following observations:

"General MacArthur's choice of Inchon for the landing demonstrates his great military sagacity. Inchon-Seoul was a strategic target of the greatest value, and his decision as Commander-in-Chief to face the many amphibious difficulties was indeed courageous.

"The critical ground situation in the Pusan perimeter, and the necessity for a landing with the higher high tides on September 15th, or waiting until October 13th, made action by the earlier date of vital importance. Hence the time available to prepare and issue the instructions to seven major forces and arrange for the coordination between them was very limited. That the many varied operations went off like clockwork, despite a typhoon, indicates the high intelligence of the commanders concerned.

"Their names should be mentioned: Rear Admiral Higgins and the Sitting Duck Destroyers under Captain Allan for their mighty bombardment of Wolmi and Inchon. Rear Admiral Ewen and Rear Admiral Ruble for their powerful, accurate air attacks, which stunned the North Korean defenders of Inchon and harassed the supporting forces trying to reinforce the city. Rear Admiral Doyle and Major General Smith, USMC, who successfully landed the First Marine Division in the courageous assault that captured Wolmi-do and Inchon. Major General Almond, U. S. Army, whose Tenth Corps captured Seoul in short order. Rear Admiral Andrewes, Royal Navy, Rear Admiral Henderson, and Captain Austin, whose forces strongly supported the assault.

"Their aggressive action and splendid teamwork carried out the operation with a precision and effectiveness which were wonderful to behold and which are now a matter of record.

"The landing demonstrates the great power of an assault from the sea. Such an operation requires the maximum of coordination to attain that great power. Naval training after World War II, despite great budget difficulties, had prepared naval amphibious forces and Fleet Marine Forces that could produce the precise coordination required for an amphibious assault. The Navy and the Marines were ready for the call.

"The continued development of amphibious warfare by the Navy and Marines will make this powerful tool in modern clothing available to the next American commander who needs another Inchon on short notice to defeat the forces of aggression."

The landing at Inchon also had significance and bearing upon the continuing dispute over effective close air support. As related in an earlier chapter, the Navy felt its efforts to assist the hard-pressed UN troops holding the Pusan perimeter had been "woefully ineffective," with a wastage of 70 per cent of the close air support sorties. The largest part of this difficulty was traceable to the lack of proper communication facilities, air-to-air and air-to-ground; to the lack of maps common to all; and to the lack of cross-education, common doctrine, and training in the close support of troops.

The logic and proof of the Navy's arguments regarding close air support of troops was beautifully demonstrated during the Inchon assault and the capture of Seoul. So effective and so smoothly did the close air support go that it, in the words of Admiral Ewen's report, "left little to be desired."

The Tenth Corps commander, General Almond, sent warm praise to Admiral Struble on 27 September:

Air support by your command for the 10th Corps attack on Seoul 25 September was outstandingly effective, comprehensive, and timely. Please pass to Admiral Ewen and his men my congratulations and appreciation for this splendid effort which markedly furthered the capture of Seoul.[19]

Congratulatory messages and letters also were received from other commands: Brigadier General H. W. Kiefer and Major General D. G. Barr of the Seventh Infantry Division, as well as General MacArthur himself.

The Inchon landing taught no new lessons about amphibious techniques. None were used, and none were needed. What was demonstrated was that for traditional warfare the doctrine and command relationships and tactics of World War II were still effective and still decisive.

General MacArthur was lavish in his praise of the naval and Marine officers who had planned and executed Inchon. In a letter to the authors, the General stated: "Admirals Struble and Doyle and General Smith delivered a performance in planning and execution which not only sustained our country's great naval tradition, but which in ultimate effect is probably unexcelled in the history of warfare."

One of the most important, delayed-action lessons of Inchon was the realization that the shipping and troop concentrations of the traditional amphibious landing had to be modified to obviate the danger of the atomic bomb. The Inchon assault spurred future thinking and planning for the use of assault helicopters instead of landing craft, and for the need of new amphibious-type vessels which would have greater speed, not only for avoiding submarines en route but for greater, faster, and more automatic unloading capabilities at the beachhead. Inchon demonstrated that our APA and AKA types were obsolescent; that the threat of the atomic bomb would no longer permit the slow discharge of cargo in a confined harbor.

As General MacArthur had indicated to General Smith, the result of the Inchon landing was to make certain the permanence of the Marine Corps in the United States military establishment. The incomparable achievement of the Marines at Inchon demonstrated in clearest terms the need of an adequate and ever-ready Corps.

Another result of Inchon was the demonstration of our appallingly poor tactical intelligence. Why maps were inadequate, photography nonexistent, and intelligence sources undeveloped is beyond comprehension. The Navy would do well to learn that no matter what the announced national policy objectives, intelligence collection by the Navy regarding areas of potential amphibious, or other, operations should be worldwide.

Any analysis of Inchon, like any judgment of the naval aspects of the Korean War, must recognize the unique and peculiar circumstances which obtained. First of all, there was no submarine opposition—indeed, with the exception of a few mines, no naval opposition of any kind. Secondly, there was no air opposition. Thirdly, the actual opposition of the landing was light.

These three factors, had any or all been introduced, would have made the assault more difficult and costly; but, in the opinion of VADM Struble, would not have altered the successful outcome. Any future amphibious campaign, however, must reckon with these three missing components. Even when measured in terms of traditional warfare, and omitting the atomic bomb, the success at Inchon, therefore, cannot blindly be accepted as a standard for any future amphibious venture. Inchon must be a guide, not a criterion.

The effects of the Inchon landing on our national military planning were immense. First of all, the U. S. Marine Corps, which in the eyes of many had been largely relegated to garrison tasks, was revitalized. MacArthur's prediction to Smith, "the future of the Marine Corps will never again be in doubt," was accurate. Secondly, the adaptation of doctrine and technique of amphibious warfare to the atomic age, which had largely stagnated between the wars, was resumed. The assault at Inchon had been a textbook repetition of the Pacific war. The experience and cogitation of first five years of the atomic era, 1945-1950, convinced the naval and Marine experts who witnessed the Inchon assault that never again could the concentration of troops, ships, and munitions be permitted in amphibious warfare. New methods, new doctrines, new techniques, and new equipment had to be developed. Inchon provided the spark which revitalized the art of amphibious warfare, and gave birth to the technique of "vertical envelopment."

Finally, far from being *passé*, as many post World War II amateur and professional strategists had predicted, naval forces, including Fleet Marine Forces, were a solid and practicable means for implementing the national strategy of the United States.

4.

The Battle of the Mines
(Part I—Wonsan)

The Mopup of the North Korean Army

By September's end, the shattered North Korean Army was in full retreat. Entire Communist divisions had completely disintegrated and were spread over the Korean countryside in disorganized units. Enemy lines of communication and supply had been completely severed, and escape routes, except for the mountainous areas, were in United Nations hands. Many enemy troops were trapped in the peninsula's southwest corner. In their haste to escape, the enemy had abandoned both arms and equipment; tanks, mortars, artillery, and small arms littered the roads, rice paddies, and ditches of South Korea.

Without hope of replenishment or reinforcement, unable to travel or communicate with impunity, and completely blockaded at sea, the remaining Communist soldiers who had not been captured or who had not surrendered were forced to hide, to organize guerrilla bands, or to sneak over the mountainous areas toward their homeland.

Within a matter of days following the Inchon landing, the North Korean military effort that had reached the very doorstep of Pusan was now struggling frantically to reassemble and redeploy for defense of the territory north of the 38th parallel.

The United Nations ground forces, meanwhile, advanced rapidly on all fronts. On the east coast, the Republic of Korea First Corps, four divisions strong, lined up near the 38th parallel, awaiting orders to drive toward the ports of Wonsan and Hungnam. The South Korean Third, Sixth, Eighth, and Capital Divisions were poised and eager to capitalize on the enemy's desultory status.

West of the First Corps, the forces of the U. S. Tenth Corps fanned out of the Seoul area in hot pursuit of enemy stragglers. The First Marine

Division, supported by the Marine Corsair pilots of Task Group 96.8, pushed northward to take Uijongbu, a vital road hub twelve miles north of Seoul, which had briefly served as temporary headquarters for the retreating North Korean Army. Simultaneously, the 187th Airborne Regimental Combat Team commenced a mopup of the Inchon peninsula.

Eastward from Seoul, the U. S. Seventh Division pushed 25 miles to capture the important rail junction of Osan and to close other retreat avenues for the Reds.

In South Korea, the Eighth Army reoccupied territory held captive since the war's beginning. The U. S. 25th Division entered Kunsan, a west coast port; the U. S. 24th Division and the South Korean First Division mopped up South Central Korea, clearing out enemy pockets around Taejon, Yongdong, and Kumchon. Before these Eighth Army divisions could actually renew the offensive, however, they would have to transit the lines of the Tenth Corps.

As the complexion of the war on the peninsula shifted from the defense to the offense, from positional warfare to pursuit, UN naval forces kept the enemy under constant blockade, surveillance, and bombardment whenever possible. However, only a few of the ships were fortunate enough to have shooting assignments. Canada's destroyer *Athabaskan* and Australia's destroyer *Bataan* took potshots at enemy hideouts in the Kunsan area. *Missouri* anchored in Inchon channel south of Wolmi-do and fired missions against enemy troop concentrations on the road leading north from Suwon. The cruisers *Toledo* and *Rochester,* from a position in the Inchon channel north of Wolmi do, heavily shelled troop concentrations and strong points in the Seoul-Kimpo area.

Early in the morning of 27 September, a particularly heavy bombardment was commenced by the cruiser *Manchester* and destroyers *Ozbourn, Hollister, McKean* and *Frank Knox.* Five thousand enemy troops had been reported bivouacked on Fankochi Point. At eleven minutes past seven, the five-ship armada opened fire and shelled the area continuously for forty-nine minutes with five- and six-inch fire. Following this bombardment, thirty-three rocket- and bomb-loaded Corsairs and Skyraiders roared in from *Boxer's* Air Group Two (CDR Donald M. White, USN) to attack the Communist defenders.

For four days, the pilots of Task Force 77 contributed to the reduction of enemy forces and military targets on Fankochi Point.

The only incident of the entire bombardment happened to Ensign Claude E. Dorris of Fighting Squadron 23, who was hit by antiaircraft fire during a bombing run. Dorris crash-landed ten miles south of the North Korean capital city of Pyongyang. It was a 60-mile flight for a Kimpo-based Marine

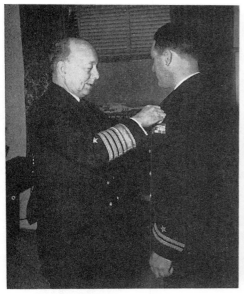

LT Eugene F. Clark wins Navy Cross. ADM Donald B. Duncan makes award for Clark's preinvasion reconnaissance of Inchon.

RADM John M. Higgins, ComMinPac, inspecting minesweeping operations of MinRon 3, poses with CAPT Richard C. Williams.

The Fight Out of Chosin Reservoir is related by Marine LT John Yancey to LCDR Frank A. Manson, one of the authors of this book.

Navy Cross Recipient LCDR D'Arcy Shouldice is congratulated by LTJG Robert Fuller and CAPT Richard T. Spofford, Commanding Officer, MinRon 3.

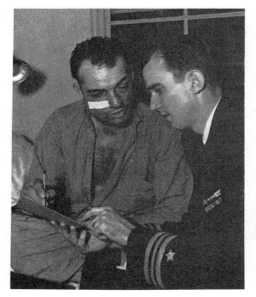

OCCUPATIONAL HAZARDS OFF WONSAN. *Top,* AMS *Firecrest* explodes a contact type floater mine on harbor surface. *Inset,* crew of disposal boat *MSB 5* carefully tows a captured mine. *Below,* sweepers straddled by splashing salvos from Communist shore batteries continue their operation undeterred.

MINE PLUMES. *At top,* explosion to the right has just triggered explosion on left in first Communist use of influence mines. *Center,* small arms fire from DMS *Endicott* dispatches another. *Below,* a PBM detonates a moored mine near Chinnampo.

MINING COUNTERMEASURES. *Top left,* crewmen put a paravane over the side in sweeping operations. *Top right,* AMS *Mocking Bird* lowers an acoustic detonator. *Center,* AMS *Gull's* crew stream a magnetic cable over ship's fantail. *Below,* part of LSD *Catamount's* brood of LCVP's in the well deck between shallow-water mining operations.

helicopter (from VMO 6). In an adventurous flight by helicopter (flown by Captain Victor A. Armstrong, USMC), a successful pickup of Dorris was made in about two hours, but the 'copter ran out of gasoline in the vicinity of the Han River. Fortunately, the emergency landing occurred in friendly-held territory.

In the post-Seoul mopup, Task Force 77 lost six aircraft and suffered damage to twenty. One man had been killed in action. The Seventh Fleet carriers struck eight railway bridges, destroying five. Twenty-four highway bridges were attacked and eight destroyed. Also reported destroyed in the free-swinging offensive were three aircraft, two hundred and three trucks and vehicles, twenty warehouses, nine locomotives, ten gun emplacements, fifty-two railroad cars, four tanks, and one hundred and forty-three oxcarts.

After operating in the Yellow Sea from 21 September through 3 October, Task Force 77 departed for Sasebo, Japan. Rear Admiral Edward C. Ewen stated that the carriers had supported the UN forces with both close- and deep-support air strikes and by serving as target air coordinators and by spotting for naval gunfire. Ewen reported that targets below the 38th parallel had been reduced so effectively and rapidly after the recapture of Seoul that carrier aircraft were out of targets.

The American Navy was now ready and eager to carry the war back into the territory of the North Koreans who had initiated it.

The UN Debates the Decision to Cross Parallel 38

As the North Korean People's Army scurried back across the 38th parallel, Communist diplomats in the UN now sought to win with words what they had failed to win by arms.

Obviously, the North Korean forces were hopelessly defeated. The only chance of salvaging the situation for the hard-pressed North Koreans was to forestall the victorious UN armies from pursuing the North Korean People's Army across the border until the forces of Red China were ready to intervene.

Most UN members felt that the 38th parallel, always unrealistic, had ceased to exist the moment the North Koreans violated it on 25 June. UN naval and air elements had fought north of the 38th from the war's beginning. President Truman personally felt that the UN forces had every legal basis for engaging the North Korean People's Army north of the 38th parallel. President Syngman Rhee of the Korean Republic had strongly held this opinion from the very beginning. Nothing less than full sovereignty and capitulation was acceptable to him.

Communist delegates in the General Assembly of the United Nations at Lake Success, New York, led by President Andrei Vishinsky, took violent exception. If UN troops crossed the 38th, thundered Vishinsky, the United Nations Forces would become aggressors.

Surprisingly, the Soviet delegate's argument found one sympathetic ear in the person of India's Jawaharlal Nehru, a man whose political philosophy for peace was scarcely in consonance with that of Vishinsky and his Communist supporters.

Although the debate at Lake Success was to last less than a week, every day the military movement north of the 38th parallel could be delayed by the Communist verbal barrage would be critically important to the rescue of North Korea.

Much of the Soviet harangue fell on deaf ears. The majority of the non-Soviet delegates felt that General MacArthur's original authority was sufficient to bring peace and security to all of Korea. No orders to march across the parallel were needed.

Sensing that his verbal battle was being lost, Vishinsky tried still another stall; he recommended that both North and South Koreans be invited to the UN headquarters to tell their story to the General Assembly.

To those experienced in the devious doubletalk of the Reds, this proposal was pathetically flimsy. Vishinsky was stalling, grasping for time— time for the North Koreans to rest, regroup, replenish; and, more than anything else, time for Chinese Communist troops to reach the front so that the fighting could be resumed.

The U.S. delegate to the UN, Ambassador Warren R. Austin, recommended that if the Soviets were sincerely interested in halting the conflict, they accept his eight-point proposal:

1. Establishment of a free, independent, and united country.
2. Creation of a United Nations Commission empowered to devise and recommend the unification process.
3. Free elections under the auspices of the United Nations Commission.
4. Consultation with the thus-established government of Korea in all matters pertaining to the united republic's future.
5. The United Nations to assist in Korea's reconstruction and development.
6. Retention of United Nations forces in Korea only as long as necessary to achieve these objectives.
7. Elimination of special privileges for any nation and the development of friendly relations with all.
8. Admission of Korea to the United Nations and assumption by her of the obligations, duties, and privileges of membership.

Vishinsky promptly countered with a seven-point proposal:

1. That the belligerents cease hostilities. (The UN had voted a cease fire on June 25, but Communist Korea had refused.)

2. That United Nations troops be withdrawn to permit the Korean people the sovereign right to settle "freely" their internal affairs. (The UN had already voted against return to the pre-June 25 status.)

3. That all-Korean elections be held to establish a unified, independent government. (The Soviet had refused to permit such elections in 1948.)

4. That the North Korea Assembly and the National Assembly of South Korea elect a commission of delegates from each to organize and conduct free elections. (This required recognition first of the North Korean puppet government.)

5. That Red China and Russia be members of UN committee observing the election. (Russia had consistently refused to participate in any previous UN commission on Korea. The price now was recognition of Communist China.)

6. That a unified and independent Korea be given economic aid through the UN. (All agreed.)

7. That after the establishment of the all-Korean government, the Security Council consider admitting Korea to the UN. (The records to date: Russia vetoed admitting South Korea to the UN and the United Nations had voted against admitting North Korea.)

In essence, Vishinsky wanted the UN to surrender and to apologize for starting the war.

On 4 October, the UN General Assembly's Political Committee passed the following resolution:

. . . That all appropriate steps be taken to ensure conditions of stability throughout Korea;

That all constituent acts be taken, including the holding of elections under the auspices of the United Nations, for the establishment of a unified, independent, and democratic government in the sovereign state of Korea;

That all sections and representative bodies of the population of Korea, south and north, be invited to cooperate with the organs of the UN in the restoration of peace, in the holding of elections, and in the establishment of a unified government;

That United Nations forces should not remain in any part of Korea otherwise than so far as necessary for achieving the objectives specified;

That all necessary measures be taken to accomplish the economic rehabilitation of Korea; and,

That a commission drawn from Australia, Chile, the Netherlands, Pakistan, the Philippines, Turkey, and one other nation be established to achieve the listed objectives.

Noble ideas all—but unfortunately none of them would resolve the problems existing on the battlefield.

The Decision to Land at Wonsan

In the Far East, meanwhile, General MacArthur was making his own tentative plans to cross the parallel.

Two members of the U. S. Joint Chiefs of Staff, Admiral Forrest P. Sherman, USN, and General J. Lawton Collins, USA, while in Tokyo in late August to discuss the Inchon landing, had agreed that the ultimate military objective was the destruction of the North Korean military forces. They also agreed that ground operations would be extended beyond the 38th parallel as necessary to achieve that goal. This Tokyo agreement took the form of a recommendation that was placed before the U.S. Secretary of Defense George C. Marshall on 7 September.[1] A week later, while en route to the Inchon beaches, MacArthur received a JCS despatch stating that while President Truman had approved certain conclusions relating to the Korean conflict, these early "conclusions" were not yet to be construed as final. Although President Truman approved the plan to push north of the 38th, MacArthur was told to make plans, but to take no implementing actions without explicit permission.[2]

That General MacArthur anticipated authority to cross the 38th parallel was evident on 26 September. On this day the General directed his Joint Special Plans and Operations Group (JSPOG) to develop a plan for operations north of the parallel. MacArthur stated his belief then that the Eighth Army should make the main effort either on the west or the east coast. Once this matter was resolved, he felt there should be an amphibious envelopment on the opposite coast—either at Chinnampo or Wonsan, or elsewhere.[3]

The next day, 27 September, General MacArthur received from his G-3 (operations officer), Brigadier General Edwin K. Wright, Operations Plan 9-50. This plan made two assumptions: first, that the bulk of the organized North Korean People's Army had already been destroyed; and secondly, that neither the USSR nor Red China would enter the conflict. This plan provided that General Walker's Eighth Army should attack across the 38th parallel directing its main effort along the Kaesong-Sariwon-Pyongyang axis, this drive to be undertaken in mid-October; and that General Almond's Tenth Corps should concomitantly land amphibiously at Wonsan, on the east coast. Almond's Corps, after landing, would continue westward through the Pyongyang-Wonsan corridor and link up with General Walker's Army in North Korea, thereby trapping the remainder of the North Korean People's Army. The plan further envisioned that these two commands, after uniting, should advance north to the Chongju-Kunuri-Wongwon-Hamhung-Hungnam line, a line measuring fifty to one hundred miles *south* of the Yalu River marking the border between Korea and Red China. Only ROK troops would be allowed to proceed *north* of this line.

Although the plan to make an amphibious landing at Wonsan was first proposed to COMNAVFE in Tokyo shortly after the Inchon landing, it was not until 29 September that General MacArthur himself outlined the plan to subordinate commanders. This was done on the second floor of Seoul's capitol building, following the ceremonies in which he gave Seoul back to the government of the Republic of Korea. General MacArthur described

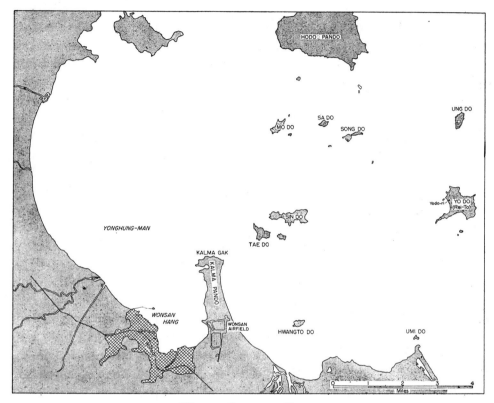

WONSAN LOCATION CHART

to those present, including Vice Admiral Joy, Lieutenant Generals Walker and Stratemeyer, and Major General Almond (plus representatives from the Eighth Air Force and Tenth Corps), how he planned to end the war with another amphibious envelopment.

On 20 October, he said, the Tenth Corps would land at Wonsan. The Marines would be outloaded at Inchon, and, because of Inchon's limited port facilities, the Seventh Division would be embarked at Pusan. While the Tenth Corps made a seaborne run-around-end, the Eighth Army would push directly toward the North Korean capital of Pyongyang.

After landing at Wonsan, he continued, the Tenth Corps was to move northward between the sea of Japan and the Taebek Mountain Range, turning westward through passes in the mountains to link up with the Eighth Army.

The reasons motivating a seaborne landing at Wonsan were later explained by General MacArthur. "The Eighth Army's lines of supply were already taxed to their maximum capacity to sustain the day-to-day minimum requirements of its troops in the line," he said. "Furthermore, the dispatch of Tenth Corps by sea was intended as a flanking movement against enemy remnants still trying to escape from the south to the north, and as an envelopment to bring pressure upon Pyongyang should the attack upon that enemy capital result in a long drawn-out siege."[4]

General Almond started to implement the Wonsan plan immediately following the MacArthur conference in the Seoul capitol building on the 29th. Almond called his Tenth Corps commanders together that same afternoon for a second conference at Ascom City, near Inchon.

There, Almond stated that he hoped it would be possible to land at Wonsan by 15 October, advancing by five days the D-day deadline set by MacArthur.* Almond believed that the Eighth Army should be able to pass through and relieve Tenth Corps by 3 October, on which date the shipping would start arriving in Inchon for loading.

To the naval planners 15 October seemed extremely optimistic. As late as 29 September, the First Marine Division was still fighting north of Seoul; on 2 October, in fact, the Marines had 16 killed and 81 wounded in heavy fighting at the front. Moreover, should the first vessels not arrive at Inchon until 3 October, and if five days were required to load, as had been estimated by JSPOG, plus four more days to steam from Inchon to Wonsan, then only two of the original six days would be left for unloading the landing force in the objective area.

In early October the Marines did not know how many ships or what type would be made available for transporting the division. Moreover, they had no maps of the Wonsan area, and there was little intelligence.

As events unfolded, Almond's desire that Tenth Corps should be relieved by 3 October was accurate as far as the Seventh Division was concerned.

As a matter of fact, elements of the Eighth Army began relieving the Seventh Infantry Division on 2 October, and General Almond ordered this division to begin moving toward Pusan by motor and rail.[5]

Despite his lack of planning information, Major General Oliver P. Smith, the Marine Commander, established a tentative task organization composed of three regimental combat teams (RCT) and issued his operation order.

---

* At no time, however, did General MacArthur advance D-day.

In it he earmarked the First and Seventh Marines to launch the Wonsan amphibious attack. Each regiment would employ two battalions in assault. All Marine units would combat-load out of Inchon. General Smith did not welcome the probability of splitting his division, once ashore, in mopping-up operations.

Next day, 4 October, General Almond issued Tenth Corps Operation Order No. 4. This ordered the Seventh Infantry Division to outload at Pusan for the landing at Wonsan and the First Marine Division to report to the Attack Force Commander of the Seventh Fleet as a landing force for the Wonsan amphibious assault. The Marines were to seize the Tenth Corps' base of operations at Wonsan, to secure the Wonsan airfield, and to furnish logistic support until relieved by the shore party.

On 5 October the Fifth Marines were relieved. On the 6th and 7th, the First and Seventh Marines were relieved. On 7 October, the First Marine Division command post at Inchon was transferred aboard Admiral Doyle's flagship, the USS *Mount McKinley*. Marine outloading at Inchon began 8 October.

For the first several days, an amphibious landing at Wonsan was not questioned by the Navy. Both Admiral Joy and Admiral Struble recognized the military need for an assault, as well as the logistic urgency for capturing an additional logistic port.

The naval planning for an amphibious assault at Wonsan was a near duplication of the preparation for Inchon. Admiral Struble issued his preliminary plan on 5 October and his final plan on 9 October. The tasks given by Admiral Struble to his forces were several: (1) To maintain an effective naval blockade of the east coast; (2) to furnish naval gunfire and air support to any east coast Army units in addition to those to be landed at Wonsan; (3) to conduct pre-D-Day bombardments; (4) to load and transport the Tenth Corps to Wonsan; (5) to seize Wonsan by amphibious assault; (6) to occupy and defend a beachhead; and following the successful accomplishment of all this, (7) to provide naval gunfire, air, and initial logistic support to the Tenth Corps.

The major elements of Admiral Struble's task organization included:

CTF 90 Attack Force (RADM James H. Doyle)
CTF 92 Tenth Corps (MAJGEN Edward M. Almond)
CTF 95 Advance Force (RADM Allan E. Smith)
CTG 96.2 Patrol and Reconnaissance Group (RADM George R. Henderson)
CTG 96.8 Escort Carriers (RADM Richard W. Ruble)
CTF 77 Fast Carriers (RADM Edward C. Ewen)
CTF 79 Logistics Support (CAPT Bernard L. Austin)

Advance into North Korea Approved

As the planning and preparation to invade Wonsan went forward, a message was received from the Joint Chiefs of Staff authorizing General MacArthur to proceed north of the 38th parallel:

> Your military objective is the destruction of the North Korean armed forces. In attaining this objective you are authorized to conduct military operations, including amphibious and airborne landings or ground operations, north of the 38th parallel in Korea, provided that at the time of such operations there has been no entry into North Korea by major Soviet or Chinese Communist forces, no announcement of intended entry, nor a threat to counter our operations militarily in North Korea. . . .[6]

From this despatch it was apparent that although the U. S. Joint Chiefs of Staff did not want to expand the war, they did not discount the possibility that the Soviet Union and Red China *might* intervene.

The JCS despatch further instructed MacArthur:

> . . . under no circumstances will your forces cross the Manchurian or USSR borders of Korea and, as a matter of policy, no non-Korean ground forces will be used in the northeast provinces bordering the Soviet Union or in the area along the Manchurian border. Furthermore, support of your operations north or south of the 38th parallel will not include air or naval action against Manchuria or against USSR territory. . . .

Two days later, 29 September, General MacArthur was further instructed in a despatch from Secretary of Defense Marshall ". . . to feel unhampered tactically and strategically"[7] in proceeding north of the 38th parallel.

Thus General MacArthur now had sufficient latitude to carry out his Wonsan plan which he had submitted to the JCS for final approval on 28 September. Additionally, he told the JCS:

"There is no indication at present of entry into North Korea by major Soviet or Chinese Communist forces."[8]

JCS approved the MacArthur plan three days later.

On 9 October, the JCS amplified its instructions to the Commander in Chief as follows:

> Hereafter, in the event of open or covert employment anywhere in Korea of major Chinese Communist units, without prior announcement, you should continue the action as long as, in your judgment, action by forces now under your control offers a reasonable chance of success. In any case you will obtain authorization from Washington prior to taking any military actions against objectives in Chinese territory.[9]

Red China Replies to MacArthur Call for Surrender

During the preparations for the Wonsan landing, General MacArthur twice called on the enemy to surrender.

His first appeal, issued on 1 October, was addressed to the North Korean commander in chief, Kim Il Sung, who was also the Premier of North Korea. The appeal was broadcast by radio and showered from aircraft in leaflet form:

> The early and total defeat and complete destruction of your armed forces and war-making potentials is now inevitable.
>
> In order that the decision of the United Nations may be carried out with a minimum of further loss of life and destruction of property, I, as the United Nations Commander in Chief, call upon you and the forces under your command, in whatever part of Korea situated, forthwith to lay down your arms and cease hostilities under such military supervision as I may direct and I call upon you at once to liberate all United Nations prisoners of war and civilian internees under your control and to make adequate provision for their protection, care, maintenance, and immediate transportation to such places as I indicate.
>
> North Korean forces, including prisoners of war in the hands of the United Nations command, will continue to be given the care dictated by civilized custom and practice and permitted to return to their homes as soon as practicable. I shall anticipate your early decision upon this opportunity to avoid the further useless shedding of blood and destruction of property.[10]

Kim Il Sung made no direct response to the surrender request. Instead, a reply in the form of a warning came indirectly from another source two days later. Red China's foreign minister, Chou En-lai, informed K. M. Pannikar, the Indian ambassador at Peiping, that China would intervene in the event United Nations forces crossed the 38th parallel. Chou En-lai stated further that China would *not* intervene if only *ROK troops* entered North Korea.[11]

On the same day, in an 11,000-word speech, Chou En-lai also warned that Red China would not "supinely tolerate seeing our neighbors being savagely invaded by 'imperialists.' "

General MacArthur issued his second surrender ultimatum on 9 October, less in the expectation of a response than as a forewarning to the North Koreans that further military action was contemplated. The second surrender message was again addressed to the Premier and government of North Korea:

> In order that the decisions of the United Nations may be carried out with a minimum of further loss of life and destruction of property, I, as the United Nations Commander in Chief, for the last time call upon you and the forces under your command in whatever part of Korea situated to lay down your arms and cease hostilities.

MacArthur added:

> And I call upon all North Koreans to co-operate fully with the United Nations in establishing a unified independent and democratic government

of Korea, assured that they will be treated justly and that the United Nations will act to relieve and rehabilitate all parts of a unified Korea. . . .

Unless immediate response is made by you in the name of the North Korean government, I shall at once proceed to take such military action as may be necessary to endorse the decrees of the United Nations.

The second surrender request also met with silence.

The Wonsan Landing Decision Debated

As North Korean defenses on the east coast collapsed and the ROK Army's northward advance accelerated, the question arose in early October if it would not now be wise to take Wonsan's harbor by an overland drive, rather than by an amphibious landing. Most military and naval commanders in the Far East were in solid agreement that in order to destroy all the North Korean forces in North Korea, the remarkable victory at Inchon had to be followed quickly with a prompt and vigorous pursuit. As the ROK's rapid advance up the east coast proceeded, the question of whether to travel by *land* or by *sea* was debated on the Service command levels and in the press.

Most Army men favored a sea assault on Wonsan, although there were Army dissenters even among MacArthur's staff. Generals Doyle O. Hickey and Edwin K. Wright felt that Tenth Corps could best be incorporated into Eighth Army at the close of the Inchon-Seoul phase of the operation. Brigadier General George L. Ebberly, MacArthur's G-4 (Logistics Officer), thought Tenth Corps could be more easily supplied if it was made a part of the Eighth Army.

As the situation ashore was changing, the original reasons which motivated a sea-borne landing at Wonsan were still compelling. First, by landing the Tenth Corps at Wonsan, the heavy supply load on the port of Inchon would be relieved, as an additional harbor would thus be opened for the direct supply of the Tenth Corps. Secondly, the Tenth Corps would be strategically located to operate as an enveloping force against the enervated North Korean People's Army as it opposed the U.S. Eighth Army's drive toward Pyongyang.

The Army's arguments for a sealift to Wonsan were well stated by the Tenth Corps commander, Major General Edward M. Almond. On 17 October 1950, aboard *Mount McKinley,* he told the author that "from a tactical point of view, it's cheaper to go to Wonsan by sea." Going overland, he said, was simply out of the question. "Half of our heavy equipment— bulldozers, big guns, and heavy trucks—would have been left in ditches by the side of the road." Almond said that the terrain in North Korea made an overland movement inadvisable. Moreover, there was poor lateral communication between east and west above the 38th parallel.

Paradoxically, while recognizing the urgency for having the Tenth Corps on the eastern half of the peninsula, most Navy men looked with disfavor on a sea movement to Wonsan.

"None of us at COMNAVFE could see the necessity for such an operation," said Admiral Joy, "since the 10th Corps could have marched overland to Wonsan in a much shorter time and with much less effort than it would take to get the Corps around to Wonsan by sea."

Naval preference for an overland movement stemmed from several reasons. First, if the entire Tenth Corps outloaded at Inchon, the use of the comparatively small port with its swift tides would seriously interfere with the offloading of *incoming* supplies for the Eighth Army. If more than half of Inchon's facilities were used for outloading Tenth Corps, Eighth Army was certain to be in short supply and its forward advance hobbled. Second, shipping and amphibious craft were in limited supply. To assemble all the sealift for a major invasion would seriously restrict the support that could be given to UN forces operating in other areas. Third, commencing 10 October, reports were received from the minesweepers that they were encountering more mine interference than expected. A landing delay at Wonsan might happen.

The Marines, after hearing about the rapidly advancing ROKs, did not anticipate with avidity the prospects of invading a beach likely to be in friendly hands in a matter of days or even hours. As reports came into the headquarters in October, they progressively indicated that the First ROK Corps, spearheaded by the naval gunfire support of Admiral Smith's ships, would soon hold Wonsan before any amphibious seizure could be affected. The "Rambling ROKs" were averaging about 14 miles per day from their jumpoff on 1 October.

The naval preference for an overland movement to Wonsan was succinctly stated by Rear Admiral Arleigh A. Burke, Deputy Chief of Staff to Commander Naval Forces Far East: "As events had developed, we objected to an amphibious assault as being unnecessary," said Burke.[12] "It would take a lot of troops out of action for a long time when the enemy was already on the run. We felt that the same objective—to seize the port of Wonsan—could be achieved by marching the Tenth Corps up the road leading from Seoul to Wonsan."

One other Army officer who agreed with the Navy was Major General David G. Barr, Commander of the Seventh Division. Barr told Admiral Doyle that it was his preference "to take the high road" from Seoul to Wonsan.

Despite the debate and discussion the original MacArthur decision to land from the sea in Wonsan, was never reopened with the General himself. "I was never apprised of any Navy objection to the seaborne landing at Wonsan," he later told the authors.[13]

COMNAVFE made his objections known to MacArthur's chief of staff, General Hickey, shortly after the operation was proposed. The advantages of going overland were all brought out. The Chief of Staff was sympathetic but said that the General had made up his mind about the landing and there was no use trying to talk him out of it.

"In retrospect," said Admiral Joy, "it must be said that the landing was to pay dividends for the Navy. Had it not been undertaken we might never have become fully alerted to the menace of mine warfare nor profited from the lessons we learned about mine sweeping."

MacArthur Considers a Landing at Hungnam Instead of Wonsan

While the decision to make an amphibious landing at Wonsan was never changed, General MacArthur *did* consider a plan to invade at Hungnam rather than at Wonsan. On 8 October, he confided to Admiral Joy that if the First ROK Corps took Wonsan prior to D-day, he was considering landing the Seventh Division administratively at Iwon. In this case the Seventh Division could drive west-southwest to join the Eighth Army on the west coast. At the same time, said the General, the First Marine Division could make an assault landing at Hungnam, instead of Wonsan, to cut the enemy's lines of communications through Hamhung. Vice Admiral Struble told Joy that a landing on Iwon could probably be made on short notice "because of the limited mine problem and the satisfactory landing beaches in that area." He added "Iwon was an open beach. We could have taken chances at Iwon and made an assault there."

Landing the Marines at Hungnam, however, was a more complicated problem, and Joy pointed out to General MacArthur that because of mines, early and easy entry might be impossible; that there were insufficient landing craft to land simultaneously at *two* places; that the timetable for the operation was already critically tight; there was no time to shift ships, rewrite plans, and all the rest. But the most important deterrent, he reminded MacArthur, was there were far too few minesweepers to clear even one area, let alone *two*.

On 9 October, Admiral Joy informed Admiral Struble by dispatch that he was trying to prevent a change in plans, but that because the General was personally sponsoring the Hungnam assault, his efforts might prove unsuccessful. Joy said it appeared probable that unless the ROK Army soon captured Hungnam, MacArthur might order the Marines and the Seventh

Division to land at Hungnam, or the Marines to land at Hungnam and the Seventh at Wonsan.

Admiral Struble was in full agreement with Joy that no Hungnam change should be tried. "If anything," he told the authors after the war, "Hungnam represented a potentially longer minesweeping problem than Wonsan. Because of the very considerable lack of minesweeping forces and experienced personnel available, only one mined area could be cleared at a time."

With the support of Struble and Doyle, and in view of all factors, Joy persuaded MacArthur to continue the original Wonsan plan.

Historical Background of the Communist Mining Campaign

Before commencing the narrative of the problems encountered by the U.S. Navy's minesweepers at Wonsan, it will help the reader's understanding if the Russian interest in mine warfare is documented and a brief description is given of the hydrography of Korea, which in many ways was an ideal location for the use of mines.

Historically, Russia has long been noted for her interest and success in mining—more so perhaps than with any other naval weapon in modern times. Russia used the mine effectively in the Crimean War, in the Russo-Turkish War of 1877 and '78, and in the Russo-Japanese War of 1904 and 1905. In the latter conflict, for example, the Russian Navy sank two Japanese battleships off Port Arthur, in southern Manchuria, with moored contact-type mines of a type very similar to those that were to be used at Wonsan nearly a half century later.*

Initially the Soviet mining effort in North Korea was probably undertaken to keep UN ships out of North Korean harbors and to limit UN naval offensive capabilities. As it turned out, Korea provided the Soviet Navy an ideal opportunity to test the United States Navy's ability to cope with mines in the western Pacific as of 1950. At the same time Soviet Russia could help her North Korean satellite delay the advance of the UN ground forces.

Actually, the Korean peninsula was almost ideally suited for an experiment in defensive mine warfare. After the UN's entry into the war, the Communists could foresee that U.S. naval forces would take every advantage of their amphibious warfare specialty to move northward. The landings at Pohang and Inchon were eloquent testimony of this special skill. Moreover, the Communists recognized the vulnerability of Korea's eastern coast to amphibious assault, and also to bombardment from the sea. The waters

---

* This Russian predilection for mines is very evident in the Soviet Navy today. Nearly every Soviet combatant ship—cruiser, destroyer, escort vessel, and submarine—is fitted for minelaying. Russian aircraft can lay mines as well.

off the east coast were deep and the coastal plains narrow. The coastline was reasonably straight, and the 100-fathom curve lay fairly closely to shore. Off the good harbors of Wonsan and Hungnam, there was a large shelf of shallow water which made mine planting exceptionally effective.

On the opposite shore, Korea's western coastline was a honeycomb of shallows, with the Korean rivers emptying into the Yellow Sea. Nowhere in the Yellow Sea was the water more than sixty fathoms deep; mean tidal range was twenty-one feet. While not ideal, the west coast was certainly mineable.

Thus, the Soviets could once again make full use of mines—to forestall further amphibious assaults by planting minefields off every suitable beach area, and to make coastal bombardments hazardous by the use of offshore moored minefields.

The Modern Mine

To properly understand the complexity and severity of the mine problem faced in Korea by U.S. naval forces, a brief description of the modern mine is necessary.

Mines have been employed in naval warfare for more than 350 years. Until about 1880, sea mines were known as "torpedoes." Admiral Farragut's famous order at Mobile Bay, "Damn the torpedoes, Four bells!" was made in regard to the crude sea mines built and used by Confederate forces during the Civil War.

Until the advent of World War I, the sea mine was a simple but effective weapon. A large charge of gunpowder or TNT, encased in a suitable container, was chained to the floor of the ocean by an anchor so that the mine itself bobbed beneath the surface some 10 to 20 feet. Several triggering "horns" protruded from the mine container. If a passing ship made contact with one of these horns, the mine's firing circuit was closed and the mine exploded—usually with fatal consequences to the contacting ship.

In sweeping such a minefield, these mines are cut by streaming sweep cables from the stern of the small sweeper with "depressors" and "otters" to hold the cable—with cutting gear attached—at proper depth as well as to force the cutting cable to plane *outboard* of the sweep vessel. Floats or "pigs" keep the cable from running too deep.

Commencing with World War I, however, this simple type of contact mine was joined by the first of several other types of mines. During World War I, mines were developed that could be controlled by an electrical circuit from the beach. The British also developed and used the first *magnetic* mine.

In World War II, still more treacherous mines were developed—ones that would lie on the ocean floor and wait to be exploded by the noise of a ship's propellers, by the reduction of water pressure caused by a passing ship's hull, or by the shifting of the lines of force of the earth's magnetic field as a ship's steel hull passed by—or by a combination of these influences.

The first of the modern mines is the *magnetic* mine, first used by the British but perfected by the Germans in World War II. Unlike the contact mine, the magnetic mine does not have to be chained to an anchor, but can be sown freely on the ocean floor.

When the Nazis first began use of the magnetic type mine in 1939, they made two mistakes. Instead of waiting until enough of them were ready so that all British ports could be mined simultaneously, the Nazis employed them in driblets. The second Nazi mistake was inadvertent. A Luftwaffe pilot dropped one of the new magnetic mines on a mudbank in the Thames estuary instead of in the ocean, and the Royal Navy promptly disassembled it and discovered its secret.

"The Nazis were able to employ these mines in limited quantities and only in a relatively few ports," said Captain N. B. Atkins, officer in charge of the U.S. Navy's mine warfare section in the Office of the Chief of Naval Operations when the Korean war started. "Had larger quantities of German magnetics been available to permit a more widespread and continuing use, the employment of this weapon might have forced the capitulation of England. This was a serious German blunder and leads to one of the major considerations in the introduction of new types of mines in modern war. New mines should never be introduced until sufficient stocks are on hand to insure full exploitation of the new mines' effectiveness. If this is not done, the expense and effort devoted to the mine's development may be wasted."

Another reason for the failure of the German magnetic mine effort was Great Britain's success in the field of countermeasures. "Great Britain had countermeasures to the magnetic mine largely worked out and 'on the shelf' in advance of its use by the Germans," said Atkins. "They had developed a system of degaussing ships (neutralizing the ship's magnetic field) and had built crude magnetic sweeps. Neither of these countermeasures had been placed in service by the Royal Navy because of the cost and copper involved."[14]

To sweep the magnetic mine, minesweepers must duplicate the influence to which the mine itself responds. The magnetic sweep gear consists of two large cables—a short "leg" and a long "leg"; these cables are lowered into the sea from the minesweeper's stern. Floats known as "pigs" keep the cables buoyant. The long leg is allowed to drift astern of the sweeping vessel for some 1,200 feet. At the end of each leg is a copper electrode.

When the electrical cables are in position, a powerful generator aboard the sweeping vessel is turned on. This transmits a powerfully pulsed current which passes through either a closed loop of cable or through the cables and a water path between their electrodes kept safely astern of the sweeper. Thus, a strong magnetic field is created, capable of detonating any mines within the cables' influence.

As will be seen, magnetic mines were present in the Wonsan minefield.

The second type of modern mine is the *acoustic* mine, which can be detonated by the machinery or propeller noise of a passing ship. Like the magnetic mine, it can also be planted on the floor of the sea. The acoustic mine utilizes a simple hydrophone or "artificial ear" that is set to "hear" a ship's engines or propellers. When it does, its diaphragm vibrates and closes the fatal switch. Acoustic mines are destroyed by duplicating the noise of a ship's propeller. The equipment for doing so is called a "hammer" or a "bumblebee" that rumbles as it is dragged through the water.

The third type of modern mine is the *pressure* mine. In the evil lexicon of mine warfare, pressure mines are even more unsweepable and diabolical than either acoustic or magnetic mines. In a pressure mine, the negative pressure of a passing ship sucks a diaphragm upward, closing the firing switch. Consequently, to sweep pressure mines, the minesweeper must endeavor to duplicate the change in water pressure produced by a passing ship. This requires that either an underwater hull like that of a ship, in both size and shape (called a "guinea pig" ship), be pulled through the minefield, or some other means be found to induce the same kind of pressure change in the water. The pressure mine is generally used in combination with a magnetic or an acoustic mechanism.

Fourthly, the toughest type of modern mine is the *combination* mine— one that combines one or more of the above types in the same carcass: a magnetic-acoustic, or a pressure-magnetic mine. This combination type mine will explode only when the sweepers employ two or more of the disturbing forces.

To make the problem even more complicated, "ship counters" can be built into the firing circuit of nearly any type mine. These counters can be pre-set so they will explode only after five, ten, or more ships have passed safely by. Thus, a minesweeper can sweep a channel a predetermined number of times, declare the channel "clear," and still have the mine explode beneath the next passing ship.

Finally, there is the deadly, but rarely used, electrically-controlled mine that is wired to and activated by a switch on the beach.

These are the modern types of mines which naval science had devised at the time of the Wonsan landing. They are passive weapons which complement other naval weapons in controlling the seas. They can deny access to harbors, approaches, and ocean areas (where the water depth will permit), to friend and foe alike.

The United States Navy would have found command of harbors and minable waters in the Korean theater much easier to maintain if adequate mine sweeping forces and experienced people had been ready before the war commenced.

U. S. Navy Mine Warfare Retrenchment, 1945-1950

The job of the minesweeper is specialized, dangerous, and difficult. There is little glamor and less publicity accompanying the task.

The attitude in the U.S. Navy toward mine warfare—general until October 1950, and occasional since—has not been unlike the bitter sentiment against mines expressed in 1806 by the British Admiral, Earl of St. Vincent, to Prime Minister Lord Grenville. The British Ministry had given encouragement to Robert Fulton to build a mine from a gunpowder keg.

"Why should we who depend utterly on command of the sea," asked the British Admiral, "seek to develop a weapon which we do not need, and which, if perfected, would deprive us of that command?"

During World War II, the U.S. Navy's Pacific minesweeping fleet had varied between 525 and 550 ships. When the Korean War began, the U.S. minesweeping force in Far Eastern waters consisted of only four 180-foot, steel-hull, fleet minesweepers (three of them in a caretaker status), and six wooden auxiliary minesweepers.

Ninety-nine per cent of the U.S. Navy's mine personnel during the Pacific war were Reserves. Between 1945 and 1950, this reservoir of trained officers and men had dwindled to the vanishing point due to budgetary cuts and a lack of naval interest and emphasis on mine warfare. There was little effort made toward improving minesweeping gear or toward developing new minesweeping techniques. The excellent minesweeping forces of World War II had literally dissolved.

To trace the cause of the U.S. Navy's minesweeping inadequacies in Korea, which the five-day delay off Wonsan brought into sharp focus, it is helpful to review a series of the historical events between the end of World War II and the opening of Korean hostilities.

In March of 1946, the headquarters of Mine Force, Pacific Fleet was transferred from the command ship in Japanese waters to Treasure Island, San Francisco. The allocation of minesweepers was largely placed in the hands of the Chief of Naval Operations. All minelayers (as distinguished from minesweepers), except for four which were transferred to the Atlantic Fleet

Mine Force, were put in mothballs. All mine locator ships, except for three transferred to the Atlantic Fleet Mine Force, were scrapped. All minesweep tenders were inactivated and later sold or scrapped.

The heaviest blow to the Navy's mine warfare readiness came in January 1947, at which time the Chief of Naval Operations, Fleet Admiral Chester Nimitz, dissolved the mine warfare command in the Pacific and further reduced the Atlantic and Pacific mine warfare forces, in order to meet further 1948 budgetary limitations imposed on the Fleet forces.

Minesweeper strength in the Pacific Fleet was further reduced in subsequent months, and what was left was divided up between two type commanders: Commander Service Force, Pacific Fleet, and Commander Cruisers-Destroyers Force, Pacific Fleet. Only three officers from the original Mine Force, Pacific Fleet staff with its wealth of operating experience were left to perpetuate the continuity of mine warfare in the Pacific Fleet. Commander Donald N. Clay was given over-all responsibility as CINCPACFLT's Operations and Readiness officer. Clay had two key assistants. One was the Readiness Training officer (CDR George C. Ellerton, USN), who reported to Commander Service Force with logistical responsibility to maintain minesweeping gear. The other was the Readiness Plans officer (CDR Richard D. Hugg), who reported to CINCPACFLT staff to maintain a continuity of policy and plans. "This was the best possible solution at the time," said CDR Clay.

The Navy Department directed that the mineman rating be abolished in 1948, but rescinded the order prior to its effective date.

These severe reductions were inevitably accompanied by a de-emphasis of training and a diminishment of the importance given to mine warfare. It became increasingly difficult to keep qualified personnel to promote mine research or to maintain any kind of a training program. Because of the concurrent severe destroyer and high-speed tug shortage, the destroyer-type minesweepers were employed more and more as antisubmarine warfare and towing ships. Those of AMS* type (except for the six stationed in Japan) were distributed at Pearl Harbor, Guam, and San Diego for protection of strategic ports. Meanwhile, Commander Service Force was conducting an orderly rollback of minesweeping equipment to Pearl Harbor and to the continental United States.

As far as the general service attitude in the Navy was concerned, mine warfare was regarded as a task which virtually any line officer could perform when the time came. Numerous papers and strategic studies by the too few younger experts were written on the subject, but at command levels, mine

---

* AMS is hereafter used to designate the small 136-foot wooden-hulled minesweeper to help distinguish it from the steel-hulled AM.

warfare was not generally appreciated to be the kind of warfare that required a lot of training, experience, or research. Consequently, the mine as a modern naval weapon became more and more neglected as a serious threat to control of the seas.

Paravanes were no longer installed on naval vessels as protection against the moored contact-type mine. Degaussing test facilities were limited in the Pacific. Although the discovery had been made near the end of World War II that destroyers' sonars could be modified to detect moored mines, the possibility had not been implemented. Ships actually designated for minesweeping were limited in their training by the lack of realistic drill mines. Minesweeping training had been sacrificed to make time for more antisubmarine work and target-towing services.

On 25 June 1950, there were two divisions of destroyer minesweepers (DMSs), two divisions of fleet minesweepers (AMs), twenty-one minesweepers (AMSs), and two new minesweeping boats (MSBs) in active service in the U.S. Navy. However, there was no mine type commander in the Pacific. Minesweeping types and responsibilities had been split between Commander Service Force Pacific, who had the AMs and AMSs, and Commander Cruisers-Destroyers Force, Pacific, who had the DMSs. CINCPACFLT had twelve minesweeper type ships under his command: four DMSs in West Coast yards for overhaul and refresher training, and three AMSs for port protection; three AMSs at Pearl Harbor for port protection; and two AMSs for port protection at Guam.*

Preparations in the Far East

When the Korean War began, COMNAVFE had six AMSs and one AM in active commission, three AMs in a caretaker status, and twelve Japanese minesweepers under contract, making a total of twenty-two ships available in Far Eastern waters. These vessels were charged with the task of check-sweeping Japanese harbors and channels in which bottom-influence mines had been planted by the U.S. Navy and the U.S. Army Air Corps during World War II.

Directing Far Eastern minesweeper operations at the outbreak of hostilities was Commander Mine Squadron Three (LCDR D'Arcy V. Shouldice), whose flagship, the *Pledge* (LT Richard O. Young), served also as tender and logistics supply ship.

---

* Throughout the Korean War, the minesweepers were designated as follows: The destroyer minesweeper was designated DMS; the steel-hulled fleet minesweeper was designated AM; the wooden-hulled sweeper, AMS and the converted small boat (LCVP) designated MSB. Throughout this book, these designations will be used. Subsequently, the designations have been changed.

In addition to his flagship, Shouldice's force included the following ships:

Partridge (AM-31) (LTJG Robert Fuller) (CoMinDiv-31)
Kite (AM-22) (LTJG Nick Grkovic)
Osprey (AM-28) (LTJG Philip Levin)
Redhead (AM-32) (LTJG T. R. Howard)
Chatterer (AM-40) (LTJG James Patrick McMahon)
Mocking Bird (AM-27) (LTJG Stanley P. Gary)

"These ships had been engaged in check-sweeping operations since the termination of World War II," said Shouldice. "This meant that by 1950, they had five years of active minesweeping behind them—and five years of age.

"We were operating on a shoestring," Shouldice continued. "Our type commander was COMSERVPAC, and our operational commander was COMNAVFE.

"The NAVFE staff was itself a very small organization at the time. They too were operating on a shoestring. We worked directly under NAVFE's operations officer, Commander E. S. Burns, who gave us our broad directives and left the minesweeping details up to us.

"Our most recent directive before the Korean War was to check-sweep the Inland Sea of Japan from Kobe to Kure for influence mines. We had hoped to finish this by early December 1950, before winter weather set in.

"The organization to support us was the most elementary and primitive of any I have ever known. 'Pitiful' is the word. It was a hand-to-mouth proposition. This is not intended as criticism of anybody. It's just the way it was.

"Our biggest prewar bugaboo was water in the fuel oil. It was not uncommon to see a minesweeper belch a puff of white smoke and stop dead in the water. This meant that water had been injected into the engines and probably had damaged them.

"Consequently, our usual request when we went alongside a tug or a SCAJAP LST to refuel was 'Give it to us from the top of the tank.' This helped to limit the amount of water and residue piped into the sweepers' tanks."

Shouldice said that his sweepers' communication gear was obsolescent and needed standardization so that all the minesweepers could talk to each other on the same radio circuit.

"Instant communications are a 'must' in the minesweeping game," said Shouldice. "If you can't warn the ship astern, or if you can't change your tactics immediately as required by unforeseen developments, it may be fatal."

Despite material and logistic deficiencies, the minesweepers in Japanese waters were in a good state of training; however, their training had not included the sweeping of live-contact or drill mines.

"Each ship had a minimum requirement of forty hours' sweeping a week," said Shouldice. "I left it up to my skippers when they got their forty hours in. If they preferred to sweep by moonlight, it was okay by me.

"The ships were able to get under way in a minimum period of time. They steamed smartly in and out of harbors in perfect formation, at a 10-knot clip. Off Hokkaido, they swept through blizzards, snowstorms, and rough water. They continuously encountered such items as fish nets and uncharted rocks to foul their sweep gear. Yet, none of the sweepers ever failed their commitments by reason of material failure or breakdown."

As the war on the Korean peninsula intensified in July-August 1950, the mine warfare problem which was to arise in late September and October could not be foreseen. First priority for the reactivation of ships, therefore, had been given to amphibious types, carriers, and escort ships. Rear Admiral F. C. Denebrink, Commander Service Force, Pacific (COMSERVPAC), ordered the three AMs in caretaker status at Yokosuka reactivated. On 14 August, *Pirate* and *Incredible* were placed on the active list. The third ship, *Mainstay*, remained inactive for a time because of material shortage. COMSERVPAC also sent the AMSs *Merganser* and *Magpie*, then at Guam, and the AMSs *Pelican, Gull* and *Swallow*, then at Pearl Harbor, to the Korean theatre.

Just before the minesweeping problem became first priority, Captain Richard T. Spofford was ordered to duty as Commander Mine Squadron Three. Spofford had had much experience in the mineplanting side of mine warfare.

"I assumed command on 3 August," said Spofford, "and immediately told LCDR Shouldice, who took Commander Mine Division 31, to take our sweepers over to Pusan and keep that port open. Shortly thereafter, I reported to Admiral Joy that my squadron was not adequate to conduct assault sweeping operations against a major combatant power. I emphasized to Admiral Joy that there was negligible intelligence on enemy mines and mine-laying vessels; that I had insufficient ships to carry out an assault sweep against a well-planned minefield, particularly a mixed-type of minefield.

"Also, there were shortages of all types of materials, including training materials, as well as shortages of personnel."[15]

In late August, Joy relayed Spofford's comments to Admiral Sherman, who was in the Far East at the time, and asked him about the possibility of increasing minesweeping types. The Chief of Naval Operations said that because of the higher priority of other type vessels, minesweepers could not be activated for the time being.

Sherman's views were concurred in by Admiral Radford.

Beginning the Minesweep at Wonsan

On 2 October, Vice Admiral Struble, riding at anchor at Inchon aboard his flagship *Rochester,* ordered Joint Task Force Seven reformed for the Wonsan amphibious assault. Simultaneously, he ordered all Seventh Fleet minesweepers under way for the Wonsan area as soon as possible. An experienced mine warfare officer,* Vice Admiral Struble had very little to warn him of the impending enemy mining effort other than isolated bits of evidence which, when added to intuition, provided less than an optimistic picture. Admiral Struble viewed the possibility of mines in Wonsan as a calculated risk. He thought that the sea approaches to Wonsan were mined; that the minefields might consist of moored mines of Russian type, probably of magnetic and controlled mines; that acoustic and pressure mines might be found in the area; and that, in addition to the mines, opposition could be expected from emplaced artillery in the Wonsan approaches.

Vice Admiral Struble was reasonably certain that if there was to be any future naval threat from the Communists, it must come from their use of sea mines. The North Koreans still retained the capability to plant mines and to launch "drifters" from the many junks and sampans. This fact had been early recognized by Joy as well as Struble long before Inchon. First of all, much of the Korean coastal area was shallow—ideal for minefields. Secondly, the muddy waters offered near-perfect concealment. Thirdly, ocean currents in both the Sea of Japan and the Yellow Sea were of such a nature that floating mines launched at any North Korean port would traverse the entire length of the peninsula within 15 days. Thus, the drifter mine itself presented a constant danger to surface vessels.

Vice Admiral Struble had recently received several reports of mines sighted and mines destroyed. Altogether, more than 300 mines had been sighted around the Korean coastline. Enemy sea mines had been reported by the U. S. destroyer *McKean* (CDR Harry L. Reiter, Jr.) at the entrance to the North Korean harbor of Chinnampo on 4 September, 11 days before the Inchon landing. On 7 September, HMS *Jamaica* sighted and sank a floating mine 25 miles north of the Changsangot area, in the sea area off Chinnampo. Another was almost immediately seen and exploded by HMS

---

* Admiral Struble had been Commander Mine Force Pacific at the end of World War II. He had participated in 22 amphibious operations and had commanded several. Many of these involved minesweeping.

Charity. There was some doubt at first whether the mines were moored or drifting, but the Britishers concluded that the mines were drifters, having been set loose in the hope of catching some of the blockade ships. At Inchon, on the morning of 13 September, destroyers *DeHaven* and *Mansfield* of DesDiv 91 had spotted a minefield in Flying Fish Channel.[16]

Altogether, from the period of 4 September to 30 September, UN ships and aircraft sighted mines on 54 separate occasions, most of them in the shallow Yellow Sea, between Chinnampo and Inchon.

To make matters even worse for the Seventh Fleet Commander, more than 25 floater contact-type mines had been sighted *on the surface* in the high seas around Korea. It was assumed that these drifter mines were contact-type mines which had become detached from their moorings and were floating on the surface. Whether the fact that these mines lacked self-scuttling devices* was intentional or whether the devices were merely omitted for reasons of simplicity and economy was not known.

Obviously such a mine situation would be a considerable threat to ships engaged in fire-support missions. Support ships would either be confined to operating in swept channels or they would have to remain outside the 100-fathom curve.

Brush (CDR Fletcher L. Sheffield, Jr.) was the first U.S. Navy ship to be mined. On 26 September 1950, while steaming 1,000 yards astern of the destroyer *Maddox* (CDR Preston B. Haines) as the two ships prowled along Korea's northeast coast in search of enemy shore batteries, *Brush* struck a mine.

The destroyer was instantly rendered helpless. Thirteen men were killed and thirty-four others were seriously wounded. One of *Brush's* firerooms, the messing compartments, and the Chiefs' living quarters were open to the sea. Her bow rode a full fathom low; her plotting room was completely demolished and flooded. A flash fire which was described by one of the officers, Ensign Charles Cole, as being bright red, had swept through three deck levels. The forward steering gears were destroyed, forcing the skipper to conn his ship by telephone relay to the helmsman in the steering engine-room aft.

To make the situation even more critical, the nearest safe port was in Sasebo, Japan, about 470 miles distant. During World War II, the destroyer *Meredith* had been similarly damaged during the invasion of Normandy

---

* At The Hague Convention of 1907, it was agreed that all contact mines should be moored and so constructed as to *destroy* themselves if they should break loose. This law was written to protect neutrals and non-combatants, but it was never signed by the USSR or North Korea. Article I of The Hague Convention specifically provided that it was forbidden "to lay anchored automatic contact mines which do not become harmless as soon as they have broken loose from their moorings."

and had sunk before she could negotiate the short but choppy English Channel.

The salvation of *Brush* was a ticklish undertaking for Commander Sheffield, but it was a success. Escorted by the cruiser *Worcester* (Captain Harry H. Henderson), the destroyer *DeHaven* (CDR Oscar B. Lundgren) and soon augmented by the salvage tug *Bolster,* the *Brush* limped into a Sasebo drydock on 30 September. On that same day the destroyer *Mansfield* (CDR Edwin H. Headland) struck a contact mine while searching inside the North Korean harbor of Chosen, 60 miles north of the 38th parallel, for a downed Air Force B-26 pilot.

Mansfield was hit in the bow. Her damage, less severe than that to *Brush,* would still require stateside repairs. The explosion occurred just beneath the hull number on the bow, 728. Numbers "2" and "8" had been blasted away, leaving number "7," which could hardly be considered as lucky. However, of 28 casualties aboard the *Mansfield,* none were killed; and besides that, the crew was now due to get stateside pre-Christmas leave.

A third U.S. warship, the 136-foot, wooden-hulled minesweeper *Magpie* had no luck at all when a mine escaped her sweeps on 1 October. While she and a sister ship, *Merganser* (LTJG Alvin L. Short), both recently arrived from Guam, were sweeping a channel two miles off Chuksan, 30 miles north of Pohang, her starboard bow nudged the horn of a floating mine. Of her 33-man crew, only 12 survived, every one of them injured. They were picked up by *Merganser* and taken to Pusan for treatment. Among the 21 lost with the *Magpie* was the captain, Lieutenant (jg) Warren Roy Person.

And on the same day, approaching Mokpo on Korea's southwestern tip, a fourth ship, the South Korean *YMS-504,* was severely damaged when her starboard propeller whirled into a moored mine, causing sympathetic explosions from two other nearby mines. Although only five men were hurt in the explosions, *504's* engines were wrecked and her hull was sprung and taking water.[17] Her skipper, whose name unfortunately was not attached to his blithe reply to offers of assistance, signaled that *YMS-504* would "soon be ready again to kill more Reds." Another ROK ship, *YMS-509,* had struck a mine on 28 September that knocked off her bow but left her engines operating. Chinhae Naval Base reported that one small commercial vessel had blown up in the area after striking a mine.

On 27 September, a normal contact mine* was sunk a few miles directly

---

* COMNAVFE despatched CINCFE on 28 Sep 1950 that this mine, which was sighted and sunk by the destroyers *Maddox* and *Thomas,* was either of Soviet manufacture or a type that had been built by the Japanese during World War II and kept in good stowage by the North Koreans.

east of Wonsan. The mine was unblemished, shiny with new paint, and from all appearances had been in the water a very short time.

Mine sightings, although plentiful, had not yet revealed any concentration on the east coast near Wonsan or Hungnam. However, as Admiral Struble pointed out, "this could not be construed as indicating a lack of concentration of moored minefields in either the Hungnam or Wonsan area." Except for one prisoner-of-war report which stated that mines had been laid around the Chongjin lighthouse in North Korea, and ten unassembled influence mines* found in oxcarts on Wolmi-do shortly afterward, the Navy's mine intelligence was based on what friendly forces had seen for themselves in the water.

"When they said 'go' on the Wonsan operation, mines were our biggest headache," said CDR Harry W. McElwain, Intelligence Officer for Task Force 90.

Hoping for the best, the little ships of Mine Squadron Three began departing Sasebo for Wonsan on 6 October 1950. Lt. C. E. McMullen's ill-fated *Pirate* (AM-275) was first to leave. Rear Admiral Smith gave orders for *Pirate* to rendezvous with CTG 95.2 (RADM Hartman) in *Worcester;* McMullen[18] was underway three hours later. McMullen said he left Sasebo without an OpOrder and, as far as he knew, the remaining sweepers were still in Sasebo making preparations to get underway as quickly as possible.

When Captain Richard T. Spofford and his small flotilla arrived off Wonsan in the chilling gray-green dawn of 10 October to commence sweeping operations, he knew little about Wonsan's harbor except its geography and bathymetry. Only three fragments of mine intelligence were available. First, the location of the normal navigation channel published by the Soviets was known. Second, a report had been received from the cruiser *Worcester* concerning the location of an offshore minefield near Wonsan, which had been spotted by the ship's helicopter on 9 October. And third, the earlier discovery of minefields in both Inchon and Chinnampo was indicative that Wonsan too was mined. How extensive, and what type of "cabbage patch" the Communists had planted in the harbor of Wonsan itself, was largely conjecture.

Nor did Spofford have information concerning the military status of the numerous islands in the harbor. Were they occupied by North Korean troops? Did the islands have artillery to oppose minesweeping efforts? Had the city yet been captured by friendly troops? As for the minefields them-

---

* CDR H. W. McElwain, TF 90's Intelligence Officer, stated in an interview 3 May 1956 that he had personally inspected the Soviet-built mines found at Wolmi-do before they were flown to Tokyo and to Washington for analysis.

selves, Spofford lacked even fragmentary information of how many mines had been planted in the harbor, what types they were, or where they might be located.

Had someone gratuitously handed Captain Spofford the information that the Wonsan minefield covered 400 square miles, that it numbered more than 3,000 mines, and that it was a "mixed bag" of magnetic as well as contact mines, his task of sweeping the expansive Wonsan minefield would still have been an exceedingly hazardous one.

The biggest handicap was a shortage of minesweepers. During World War II, the amphibious assaults against Okinawa had been preceded by more than 100 sweepers; at the invasion of Normandy by 300. At Wonsan, Spofford's Mine Squadron Three commenced its work on 10 October with only *six* minesweepers.

"My first inclination," said Captain Spofford, "was to start work in the regular navigation channel which the Soviet naval forces had been using, on the assumption that it would have been subjected to a faster and more careless mining effort because of the hasty retreat of the Soviet satellite forces."

After careful consideration, with the 20 October landing date in mind, Spofford decided to risk a direct-approach sweep, sending his ships, led by the two "big steel jobs,"* *Pledge* and *Incredible,* on an exploratory run straight from the 100-fathom curve to the landing beaches by the shortest and most direct route. "If it worked," said Spofford, "there was a chance we could meet the D-Day deadline."

Shortly after sunrise on the morning of 10 October, the minesweeping task got underway. The officer in tactical command, LCDR Bruce Hyatt, was riding the *Pledge,* since his flagship *Pirate* had not yet rejoined from conducting exploratory minesweeping chores in behalf of the gunfire support ships south of Wonsan.

The *Pledge* began the sweep directly from the westward tongue of the 100-fathom curve in a direct line for the landing beaches where the troops were scheduled to go ashore in only 10 days. Astern of *Pledge* steamed the *Incredible, Osprey* and *Mocking Bird,* each ship streaming its sweep gear. Two additional minesweepers followed the formation—the *Chatterer,* dropping orange-colored conical "Dan buoys"† and *Partridge,* "riding shotgun," to destroy by gunfire any mines brought to the surface by the other minesweepers.

To assist and expedite the sweeping, a helicopter from the USS *Worcester*

---

* Name given to the 1,200-ton, 180-foot steel-hulled minesweepers by men serving aboard the much smaller wooden YMSs.

† Dan buoys are used to mark the edge of a swept channel.

hovered to shoreward of the minesweepers, attempting to spot mines beneath the surface of the water. This would be the first instance in naval warfare of an organized and combined effort between surface ships and a helicopter to locate a minefield. Patrol aircraft and lighter-than-air ships were used in some instances and with varying degrees of success during World War II.

The helicopter had only recently entered the mine-hunting business, and this quite by happenstance. In September, the USS *Helena's* helicopter, flown by LT Harry W. Swinburne, while searching in the vicinity of Kokoko for survivors from the sunken *Magpie,* had discovered two moored mines. Swinburne took photographs of the mines and submitted them to the Board investigating the sinking. Soon after, helicopters were used on regular dawn-to-dusk mine search patrols around their own ships of Cruiser Divisions Three and Five.

On 3 October, *Worcester's* "copter" pilot, Chief Aviation Pilot B. D. Pennington, sighted several moored mines in the Wonsan area. From that day onward the helicopter had a welcome place on the mine warfare team.

"It didn't take long to discover the value of the helicopter as a mine-hunting platform," said LCDR J. R. Beardall, Jr., *Worcester's* gunnery officer. "If the sea was not rough, if the direction of the sun rays was right, and if the water was clear, you could see the mines very easily."

By late afternoon of the first day's sweeping on 10 October, a 3,000 yard wide channel had been swept from the 100-fathom curve to the 30-fathom curve, a distance of about 12 miles. Twenty-one contact mines had been cut and destroyed without casualty.

"We were pleased and optimistic as the first day's effort was about to end," said Captain Spofford. "If the combination of Mine Squadron Three's skillful seamanship and good luck held, I felt that we might not even need the entire time that had been allotted to clear the channel."

But good luck did not hold.

In the late afternoon of the 10th, the *Worcester* helicopter suddenly dipped, lifted slightly, dipped again and again. The voice of Chief Aviation Pilot B. D. Pennington rang out the bad news: "One mine line directly ahead of *Pledge* . . . Another line just beyond that . . . Another. . . ."

Altogether, Pennington could see five distinct lines of mines inside the 30-fathom curve, directly in the assault path to the beach. Within a few moments all the minesweeps had verified the presence of dozens of mines from sonar echoes.

As dusk fell, when the sweepers filed out of the channel and anchored in swept waters near the 30-fathom curves, every officer and man was weary and somewhat taken aback by the discovery.

In a summary despatch to Admirals Struble and Smith, Captain Spofford was most gratified in our sweepers' ability to come through the first day unscathed, "assisted by adroit handling and highly effective use of sonar—and God's blessings."

Efforts to Clear a Channel

"After receiving the information about the extensive minefield," said Captain Spofford, "I decided to shift our sweeping effort to the Russian navigation channel. It could not be much worse and the numbers of mines *might* be fewer than we had found on the 10th."

By this time Spofford had the advice and assistance of two mine experts from Mine Forces, Atlantic, CDR S. M. Archer and LCDR Don DeForest, and Mr. Howard Naeseth from the Mine Countermeasures Station, Panama City, Florida. They had been hastily flown to the Korean theater from the east coast of the United States.[19]

During the morning of 11 October, Spofford augmented the examination of the minefield by the use of "frogmen"* from the destroyer transport *Diachenko*. The "Ute's" were ordered to skim along the surface of the harbor looking for mines—or their absence—from their shallow-draft LCPRs. Spofford also requested and received help from Commander Fleet Air Wing One in the form of patrol planes to augment the air search. Patrol Squadron 47 (CDR J. H. Arnold) was directed to assign a PBM for daytime search. Rear Admiral A. E. Smith, CTF 95, sent a message to his naval beach group ashore (CTE 95.22):

> If there is a small naval craft in Wonsan harbor, it may have a chart of the swept channel and the minefield. Encourage KMAG† and others ashore to make thorough search in order to get in their logistics and ice cream.

During the previous afternoon of 10 October, the minesweeping force had been augmented by the arrival of the *Pirate, Redhead,* and *Chatterer*. These three were despatched to the Russian navigation channel. Here, sweeping went so smoothly that at a midnight conference, 11-12 October, attended by his staff and all commanding officers, Captain Spofford determined to make an all-out effort the next day in the Soviet navigation channel with the hope of beating the landing date deadline now only eight days away.

The frogmen, under the command of LCDR William R. McKinney, were ordered to reconnoiter the two outlying islands of Ung-do and Yo-do in search of any mine cables which would indicate the presence of electrically

* Underwater Demolition Team—nicknamed "Utes."
† Korean Military Advisory Group.

controlled mines. McKinney later reported "no control mine cables present."

Spofford also decided to try a rarely used technique to clear the minefield: a countermining aerial strike by Task Force 77. Could carrier aircraft carrying regular bombs drop them into the minefield?*

The Task Force 77 operators studied the problem. If the mine experts felt that such an effort might help, certainly the Seventh Fleet planes could drop the bombs. Upon hearing of the plan, Admiral Struble approved the attempt, but with little hope of its success.

During the early morning of 12 October, minefield-strike aircraft from *Philippine Sea* and the *Leyte* arrived over Wonsan harbor. AD "Skyraider" aircraft were scheduled to perform the major portion of the effort. Each AD carried three 1,000-pound general purpose bombs. F4U Corsair fighters each carried one 1,000-pound general-purpose bomb. The bombs were all fuzed hydrostatically to detonate at 25 feet.

The carriers' pilots planned to drop two 5-mile lanes of bombs 200 yards apart, with a 200-yard distance between bombs in the lanes. To solve the problem of making a bombline on the open sea, one AD under radar control flew directly above another AD loaded with smoke floats. Upon signal from the control aircraft, the smoke floats were dropped at half-mile intervals.

The strike group itself was composed of two columns of aircraft. The right-hand column consisted of fourteen AD aircraft and eight F4U aircraft; the left-hand column consisted of seventeen AD aircraft.

After both columns of aircraft had cleared the target area, eight additional Corsairs with similar loading were called in by the air coordinator to fill obvious "holidays" in the bombline.

Execution of the aerial countermining strike revealed numerous problem areas. For one thing, not one of the smoke floats functioned. Channel buoys and visual reference on two islands in close proximity had to be used instead. It was extremely difficult for the pilots to maintain an accurate distance between aircraft. They used their gun sights to check distances on the planes ahead. But the fact that a slipstream was present and that aircraft were strung out in a column five miles long was to cause unavoidable gaps in the bomb pattern. This problem was further aggravated by the fact that drops were made on voice signal.

The time interval between the air coordinator's transmissions and the individual pilot's reception and execution produced further irregularities in the pattern.

---

* Countermining by aerial strike had been attempted at the end of World War II when Admiral Struble's Mine Force Pacific Fleet was engaged in clearing the various harbors of Japan. Despite the use of heavy planes and large bombs, the attempts were unsuccessful.

Results of the countermining effort are unknown. Next day, as *Pirate* swept through a line that had been bombed, she swept only one mine in her port gear and five in her starboard gear, which indicates the bombing may have made a gap in the line. Since two ships, *Pirate* and *Pledge,* were sunk the same afternoon in the nearby vicinity, it appears doubtful that the counter-mining effort was a success.

It was an admirable innovation and effort, but it is not definitely known that mines were destroyed. Later, FEAF's General Stratemeyer offered to lend his B-29's in a countermining effort. In view of the carrier aircraft experience, and because of his own World War II aerial countermining experience, Admiral Struble rejected any further bombing of the minefield as impractical. Captain Spofford had calculated that, to be successful, each bomb had to explode within thirty feet of a mine itself. Such accuracy could scarcely be expected.

If there was any better way to sweep mines than the minesweeper, it had not been found. The conventional bombing of a minefield was not the answer. Nor did Spofford or Shouldice think in retrospect that an under-water atomic charge would have done the job. Both felt it would only have contaminated the entire area without solving the problem.

The Sinking of *Pirate* and *Pledge*

Because of the novel air strike of Task Force 77 aircraft, the minesweepers did not get underway at their usual hour—sunrise—on 12 October.

Following the air attack, the minesweepers proceeded on a westerly course toward the harbor at a speed of six knots. Ahead of them were three islands: Yo-do on the left; Ung-do on the right; and Sin-do, where the former Japanese fortress had been located, almost dead ahead. Protecting the sweepers and ready to give them gunfire support were *Diachenko, Doyle* and *Endicott.*

As in previous occasions, the "big steel jobs" were in the van on the fateful October 12th. LCDR Bruce Hyatt led the formation in his flagship *Pirate,* with *Pledge* and *Incredible* following astern. Laying Dan buoys astern of the *Pirate* was the *Redhead,* with *Kite* on shotgun duty astern of the *Incredible;* her 3-inch muzzle bared, *Endicott* steamed close astern of the sweep formation.

After passing through the Russian navigation channel, the sweepers altered course to port in order to pass between the two islands of Yo-do and Ung-do.

At 1112, the minesweeping fleet entered unswept waters.

Three minutes later, *Pirate's* ready boxes were undogged and her 3-inch gun manned as a precaution against possible enemy shore battery fire.

Then, as quickly as it is written here, things began to happen. Two mines, their cables severed by *Pirate's* sweeping gear, popped to the surface. Four more followed. The mines were 50 yards apart, and lay on a north-south line between Yo-do and Ung-do islands. Three minutes later, *Pledge*, maneuvering astern through the mines already cut by *Pirate,* swept three more with her port gear. *Incredible,* still in formation, got herself into the thick of things by cutting still another four.

"Just about this time," said LCDR Hyatt, "I received information from the helicopter pilot that a large 'cabbage patch' lay dead ahead, and that at least three more lines of mines were in the vicinity of my sweepers. The pilot told me that the lines were bounded by the islands of Ung-do, Yo-do, Mo-do, and Sin-do. The exact position of the mine lines was not indicated, nor the angles at which they lay.

"I made a quick decision to abandon the original plan to turn south, and to continue in the reported Russian-swept channel instead."

Both Hyatt and *Pirate's* commanding officer, LT C. E. McMullen, considered a turn at this critical point more dangerous than continuation on course. Any turn now would in all likelihood expose the *Pirate* to a mine while in the turn.*

Pirate's first definite sonar report came a moment later—when the range was only 100 yards. Within seconds the *Pirate's* starboard bow lookout reported a shallow mine close aboard the starboard bow. McMullen threaded his way gingerly through the treacherous field.

A few seconds later, *Pirate's* stern rose from the water, exposing her propellers, then fell back into a boiling sea of muddy spray. The explosion of a mine directly underneath had broken *Pirate's* main deck into two parts. The ship lurched to starboard, then back to port, quickly taking a list. Within four minutes the *Pirate* had capsized.

Pledge, commanded by LT Richard O. Young, immediately cut her sweep gear, hove to, and put her motor whaleboat in the water. To add to the confusion, as *Pledge's* whaleboat was being launched, previously undetected shore batteries on the island of Sin-do opened fire on the sinking *Pirate* and those of her crew already in the water. *Pledge* responded with her single 3-inch gun, whereupon the enemy fire shifted to *Pledge.* While this was happening, 13 loose mines lay floating on the surface, and nearby, countless others lay undetected beneath the surface.

"My first thought," said LT Young, "was to rescue the *Pirate's* survivors and continue to sweep."

He was soon to decide otherwise, however, in view of the concentration

---

* A thumb rule in minesweeping is to avoid turns once atop the mine lines, but, if required, to turn toward swept waters.

of shore battery fire, plus the fact that he could not pass through *Pirate's* minesweeping gear without enmeshing his own vessel. Young ordered all battle stations manned as quickly as possible to counter not only the concentration of fire that was coming from Sin-do but additionally small caliber fire from Rei-to island as well. Young made a quick radio call for air support, and ordered his minesweeping gear cut.

For a moment the *Pledge* lay to and continued to fire until all her ready 3-inch ammunition had been expended.

By now, Sin-do's shore battery had bracketted *Pledge;* and although *Pledge's* gunners had knocked out at least one enemy gun,* Young knew his position was fast becoming untenable. Enemy shells had now begun to find their target on *Pledge,* which was being slowly set to seaward toward the *Pirate.*

With the hope he might make a turn back into waters that had already been swept, Young ordered "Left full rudder; starboard engine, ahead two-thirds." The ship had turned approximately thirty degrees when she struck a mine. The time was 1220.

Pledge had been mined amidships on the starboard side near the forward engineroom. Damage throughout the ship was extensive. Decks and bulkheads were ruptured from the keel to the open bridge. The starboard side of the hull was split beneath the waterline, and water was rushing into the rupture.

When Young, who had been temporarily knocked out by the blast, regained his senses and saw the status of ship and crew (all persons in his view were seriously injured), he gave the order to abandon ship.

The mine-hunting patrol plane overhead, a PBM Mariner flown by LCDR Randall Boyd, executive officer of VP-47, had discontinued its search the moment the *Pirate* commenced to receive surface fire.

"I noticed gun flashes from the beach," said LCDR Boyd, "and splashes around the *Pirate.* I radioed the *Endicott* and told them I would spot their fire onto the enemy guns. For the next several minutes I acted as communication observer and spotter, and also kept the *Endicott* informed of the location of survivors. The *Endicott* directed her boats into the area to pick the survivors as we coached her fire on the northern coast of Cho-do island.

"As I made circle after circle over the enemy territory, I noticed several slit trenches running parallel to the beach, and also several small blockhouses. My gunners were able to keep these trenches unoccupied while the *Endicott* was doing a nice job of demolishing the blockhouses and tunnels.

---

* *Pledge's* Fire Controlman Third Class, Carleton A. Pollock, saw one 3-inch shell score a direct hit on an enemy gun emplacement on Sin-do.

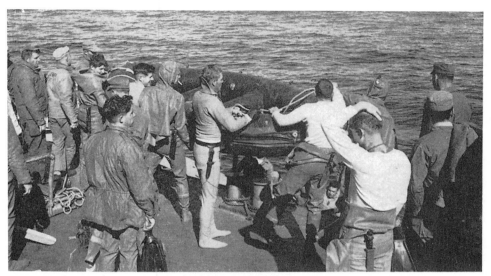

FROGMEN IN ACTION. *At top,* an underwater demolition team aboard APD *Diachenko* about to disembark in rubber boat. *Center,* they paddle through heavily-mined Wonsan Harbor on a mine-clearing mission. *Below,* the team drags the 300-pound rubber boat ashore after traversing minefield which they later destroyed.

DEATH AT WONSAN. ROK minesweeper *YMS 516* struck a Russian contact mine and blew up with heavy losses in October, 1950. Photo below shows her sinking, as other vessels stand by to rescue survivors. Anti-mine operations had to continue without letup to keep the harbor clear. *In the inset,* Bruce Barrington, executive officer of the sunken minesweeper *Partridge,* is rescued amid floating debris. Eight died when the gallant ship struck a mine off Wonsan.

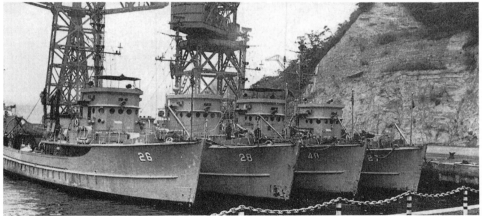

HEROIC SHIPS. *At top,* Navy Unit Citation for pre-invasion bombardment of Wolmi-do is awarded destroyers *Collett, Swenson, Mansfield,* and *DeHaven. Center,* the minesweepers *Merganser, Osprey, Chatterer,* and *Mocking Bird* received the Presidential Unit Citation. *Below,* AM *Pirate,* sunk by a mine at Wonsan, received her Presidential Unit Citation "posthumously."

MAJOR NAVY ACHIEVEMENT. MinRon 3, victorious in the battle of the mines, extends full beach rights, privileges, and courtesies to those who might follow safely after Wonsan's approaches were swept. *Below,* AMS *Waxbill* lays a smoke screen as shore batteries splash the area.

We also flew over Sin-do, and were able to distinguish reinforced concrete gun emplacements on it. Although our strafing would accomplish little, I ordered all guns that could bear to strafe them.

"Meanwhile, I had relayed the word back to the carriers of the mining of the two sweeps and of the enemy gunfire, and had requested an aircraft strike. I suggested the planes carry 500-pound bombs, rockets, and napalm.

"We continued strafing each enemy-held island and spotting survivors for the *Endicott* boats as well as spotting her surface fire until the F4Us and ADs from the *Leyte* arrived overhead.

"On our way home the tail gunner of my plane came forward and asked if I had heard him report over the intercom that we were being shot at by AA fire while we were circling Sin-do. I told him yes, but since all the tracers were being sucked aft, I hadn't worried about the small stuff. Whereupon he told me that he wasn't talking about the *small stuff* but about those big black bursts of AA directly astern of our plane and at the same altitude. Apparently, each time we circled Cho-do island, we received about twenty rounds of big stuff which I hadn't noticed at all. I suppose the 'Commie' gunners thought I was nuts, coming by again and again. At any rate, we didn't get a scratch."

With *Pirate* down, and *Pledge* sinking, *Incredible's* radio suddenly blared forth: "Dusty, Dusty, my engines are dead." At the worst possible moment *Incredible* had experienced complete engine failure. This meant that all the "big steel jobs" were out of action. The only ships left to do the sweeping were LCDR D'Arcy Shouldice's "chicks."*

Ordering his ships to the rescue, and using enemy gun flashes as point of aim, Shouldice's small wooden minesweepers were joined by the *Endicott's* gunners in taking the enemy batteries under fire with their single 40-mm. and their two 20-mm. guns.

All *Pledge's* officers, with the exception of her engineering officer, LTJG E. A. Miller, Jr., had been seriously wounded by the mine blast, but all were rescued. Miraculously, Miller had only been slightly wounded as he was tossed over the side by a geyser of oil and water.

Altogether, there were 92 casualties from the two sunken vessels; of these 12 were missing in action and one died from wounds after his rescue. Hyatt, McMullen, and Young were among those rescued.

Two attempts to open a path through the minefield had failed—a direct sweeping run to the beaches where the landing was to be made had encoun-

---

* "Chick" was an affectionate label given to the wooden-hulled bird-class fleet, which also were referred to as the "Splinter Fleet" or the "Mighty Mites."

tered heavy and well-laid minelines. Had this plan not failed, it would have been the best solution. Nor could the attempt to open the Soviet navigation channel be considered a successful experiment. And the deadline for landing the Marines was now only seven days away.

"I was aboard the *Missouri* with the heavy bombardment forces off Songjin, North Korea, when news came about the sinking of the *Pirate* and the *Pledge*," said Admiral Struble. "I jumped in a destroyer, picked up Admiral Smith, and headed south at best speed where I could take direct charge."

Even worse news was soon to be discovered—the presence of *magnetic* mines as well as the contact type.

Discovery of Magnetic Mines at Wonsan

The message that rocked the Pentagon came from Rear Admiral Allan E. "Hoke" Smith, who, as Advance Force Commander, was the officer directly over Spofford, responsible for conducting the minesweeping operations. His message, addressed to the Chief of Naval Operations opened with words the U.S. Navy never hoped to read: "The U.S. Navy has lost command of the sea in Korean waters. . . ."

The Navy that was prepared to defeat a Communist air or submarine attack, to sink an enemy's fleet of ships, to do precision bombing, rocketing and gunnery, to support troops ashore, and to blockade a hostile shore, had encountered a massive field of more than 3,000 mines laid off Wonsan under the direction of Soviet naval experts.

As a result, the strongest Navy in the world was to steam about in the Sea of Japan while a few minesweepers struggled to clear a channel into Wonsan.

Two men to agree with Smith's estimate of the situation were Admiral Joy, and the Navy's Chief of Naval Operations, the late Admiral Forrest P. Sherman. "Let's admit it," he said in conversation with his columnist friend, George Fielding Eliot. "They caught us with our pants down. Those damn mines cost us eight days' delay in getting the troops ashore and more than two hundred casualties. That's bad enough. But I can all-too-easy think of circumstances when eight days' delay offshore could mean losing a war.

"Hoke's right; when you can't go *where* you want to, *when* you want to, you haven't got command of the sea. And command of the sea is a rock-bottom foundation of all our war plans. We've been plenty submarine-conscious and air-conscious. Now we're going to start getting mine-conscious—beginning last week."[20]

With the three AMs out, two permanently and one temporarily for engine repairs, safe sweeping practice assumed paramount importance.

After reviewing with his predicament, Captain Spofford made the decision to marshal as many small boats and frogmen as he could, and they, with helicopters and PBMs spotting from above, would undertake the tedious search. Under personal supervision of LCDR DeForest, the small boat crews took to the mine field like children at an Easter-egg hunt.

A few sympathetic North Korean fishermen joined the hunt.

After two days searching, the channel had been sufficiently explored and marked that sweepers could enter it with relative safety.

Additionally, Captain Spofford ordered the destroyer transport *Diachenko* to cautiously probe her way down the channel, using the long fingers of her antisubmarine sonar in search of any additional underwater charges.

Finally it appeared that the Wonsan channel was all but swept; the sweepers *Mocking Bird, Chatterer, Redhead,* and *Kite* were making their last few penmanship ovals near the beaches, when *Redhead's* skipper, LTJG T. R. Howard,[21] reported that "the whole ocean started to erupt amidst the sweepers."

The first 250-foot geyser about 400 yards astern of *Redhead* had not subsided when a second blast occurred six seconds later, very similar to the first and not more than 100 yards away from the first. So far no damage had been done, except to the jangled and exhausted nerves of the sweep force themselves. But the third explosion, under the keel of ROK *YMS-516,* blasted that small ship into bits and pieces.

In all probability, these new-found mines were the same influence type that had been found unassembled on ox-carts at Wolmi-do one month earlier.

At this point "Dusty" Shouldice admitted that he was frightened, "plain scared, and disappointed, too. It was the disappointment of a lifetime to be within an hour of a completed mission, and then find influence mines. Everything went into a tailspin—all our plans—we didn't know what type mine we had triggered—we didn't know where—we didn't know how many. We were back where we started."

Commander Task Force 95, Rear Admiral Smith, summed it up in a despatch to Admiral Joy, thusly:

> . . . Army is calling for support by sea through Chinnampo, Kunsan, Haeju on the west coast, . . . Hungyong, Wonsan, and several other spots on the east coast. All these harbors are mined and many more smaller ones. There is adequate proof of the quantity of mines. Two thousand to four thousand in the Wonsan approaches, fifty to one hundred magnetic in Wonsan alone. Task Group 95.6, after fighting and cutting its way through for 25 miles, and within an arm's length of Blue-Yellow beaches, had three ground mine explosions.

This meant that now the AMSs must methodically form a line parallel to the landing beaches about three miles out and edge toward the landing beach by making pass after pass over virtually the same track. It was to be a very slow and nervewracking business.

Not until the following morning, 19 October, were Shouldice and his frightened "chicks" to learn what type of mines they had triggered the night before. Then, during one of the most dramatic conferences, Captain Spofford announced that the cloud of influence mines hanging over Wonsan had been dissipated.

"We know that there are magnetic mines," said Spofford. "We know at least one magnetic line has been planted, and we know their position quite well, thanks to the work of DeForest."

DeForest, after completing his supervisory task of buoying those contact mines that could be seen from the surface, had set out to the beach in search of some of the mine intelligence that was sorely needed when the operation started.

After much searching, sniper fire, and hairbreadth escapes, DeForest was led to an old strawstack under which he found a new Soviet-built search coil—the "eyes and ears" of a magnetic mine. Additionally, DeForest had found North Korean personnel who had helped to assemble and lay the mines, so that when he returned to Captain Spofford, he had much of the vital information that would be needed in order to finish the sweeping job.

Although Captain Spofford now held the combination to the Wonsan minefield, it still would require seven more days of arduous sweeping before he would have it open.

On the evening of 25 October, Shouldice reported to Captain Spofford that Wonsan had a swept channel "clear of mines." A total of 15 days had been required to complete what was supposed to have been a five-day sweep. Of approximately 3,000 mines which had originally been planted in Wonsan, only 225 had been swept and destroyed. Probably that many or more had broken their moorings and had become floaters. But the majority of the mines, probably 2,000 or more, were still anchored in place in the minefields. "These 2,000 were no longer dangerous to our operations," said Struble, "as we knew where they were, and cleared channels to the Wonsan beach had been swept."

North Korean Mining Tactics

From an examination of the available records, it is concluded that the Communist mining campaign in Korea commenced no earlier than 10 July. There is no evidence of any mine shipments or minelaying prior to that date. It is Admiral Struble's view that the decision to commence mining was not made prior to North Korean's initiating the war. His belief is further supported by the fact that North Korean forces were initially supplied with other types of weapons and war materials, not mines. Moreover, it is concluded that had the Communists anticipated U.S. naval opposition, undoubtedly the mining campaign would have commenced immediately on outbreak of war in order to deny as much water as possible to our naval forces.

Post-Wonsan assault intelligence reports indicated that the mining of Wonsan and Chinnampo began around August 1. This program was intensified after the fall of Inchon.

It is further concluded, based on an examination of recovered shipping labels and an examination of captured mines, that all the mines used in the Korean campaign originated from Soviet stockpiles. Most of them arrived in Korea during the period 10-20 July 1950 by rail, although there is evidence to indicate that a few were shipped by sea. Interrogation of railroad personnel at Wonsan after its capture verified the fact that about 4,000 mines passed through their hands, mainly for use in Wonsan itself but also for use at points further south. At Chinnampo, it was learned from the interrogation of prisoners that mines were shipped to Haeju by truck, and that other mines were shipped to Inchon and Kunsan by rail.

It was to be later discovered that the Soviet Union had not only provided the North Koreans with mines, but with torpedoes and depth charges as well. On 16 October, fourteen Soviet-built 21-inch torpedoes were found in a tunnel near the Wonsan airstrip. With warheads attached, the torpedoes were about 24 feet long, and similar to the type used by the Germans in World War II. Twenty-nine depth charges weighing 300 pounds each, and 40 depth charges weighing 50 pounds each were found. In addition 167 contact-type mines were found.[22] More than 600 sea mines were later discovered ashore in the Wonsan area.[23]

North Korean prisoners stated that in some instances Russian naval officers operated as far south as Inchon; that Soviet naval instructors gave mine technical training and supervised assembly of the mines in both Wonsan and Chinnampo between 16 July and 17 August; that they made the adjustments on the magnetic mines that were laid in the Wonsan minefield; and that Soviet military personnel actually participated in the laying of magnetic mines. Later, at Pyongyang, one officer and three men—all North Koreans—were given training in magnetic mines.[24]

Because of the excellent mine patterns laid and their close integration with the North Korean coastal defenses, it is also concluded that Soviet personnel supervised the preparation of the Wonsan minefield.

As far as the contact mines were concerned, the evidence indicates that

North Koreans did most of this work. The minelaying procedure and equipment was very simple, even primitive, in sharp contrast to U.S. Navy equipment and doctrine. Wooden barges, of a type normally used in river and coastal traffic, were equipped with iron or wooden tracks and fitted to carry ten to fifteen mines. The mines were man-loaded on the barges and towed by tugboats into pre-determined areas where, on signal, the mines were rolled off the stern of the barges at intervals of one to one-and-one-half minutes.

In this manner, about 3,000 mines were laid off the city of Wonsan in a period of three weeks.

Marine Air Comes to Wonsan

The initial planning for Wonsan had assumed a similar operation to the Inchon assault: the landing was to be followed by capture and rapid exploitation of a nearby airfield. During the assault phase, two Marine fighter squadrons would participate—VMF-214 and VMF-323, aboard CVEs *Sicily* and *Badoeng Strait*—to furnish close air support. As soon as the Wonsan airfield was seized, Marine Air Group 12 would land and operate therefrom. MAG-12's headquarters, service squadrons, and heavy equipment were to be surface-lifted from Japan. Two other fighter squadrons, VMF-312 and VMF(N)-513, were to come in by air. The other night fighter squadron of the group, VMF(N)-542, was to remain at Kimpo.

But the rapid advance of the "Rambling" ROKs negated all these plans. Major General Field Harris, Commanding General, First Marine Air Wing, and Tactical Air Controller for the Tenth Corps, flew to Wonsan on the 13th, two days after the ROKs had captured the city. After inspecting the airfield, he determined that flight operations could be initiated immediately. He ordered VMF-312 to leave Kimpo the next day. To facilitate flight operations, the Far East Air Force Combat Cargo Command started to bring in aviation gasoline in 55-gallon drums. Bombs and rockets were loaded on Corsairs of VMF(N)-513 at Kimpo and air transported to Wonsan.

According to original plans, VMF-312 was to be supported by airlift for only three days, pending the opening of the Wonsan port, when the surface echelon was due to arrive. But because the harbor was not cleared of mines until 25 October, flight operations had to be supported entirely by airlift for twelve days. The arrival of VMF(N)-513 on 17 October added to the logistical burdens.

For twelve days, two Marine air squadrons were entirely dependent on airlift for all their supply. Fuel in 55-gallon drums was rolled along the ground a distance of one mile from the supply dump to the flight line, and then pumped by hand from the containers into the aircraft. Operating with one jeep and eight bomb-trailers, the ordnance sections unloaded the transports, assembled the bombs and rockets, and reloaded them on planes. With muscle substituting for machines, flight operations were maintained.

In this manner Marine airmen gave direct support to the First ROK Corps advancing northward to Hamhung. As an example of their effectiveness, a flight from VMF-312 attacked 500 enemy troops near Yangdok on 19 October and killed approximately 100 of them. This same squadron caught a body of 800 men on the road near Kansong on the 24th and caused about 200 casualties.

Wonsan Taken—By the ROKs

Except for a few hot and hectic hours in the city's southern suburbs, the capture of Wonsan by the First ROK Corps on 10 October was a routine operation. As ROKs met stubborn resistance that morning, Admiral Ewen's Task Force 77 aircraft fortuitously appeared overhead to begin routine pre-invasion aerial bombing. The ROKs radioed an urgent call for help, and planes from *Leyte's* Air Group 3 went to work, striking gun positions, slit trenches, and tanks as directed by ground controllers.

By mid-afternoon, the South Korean troops had swept into Wonsan and out again, continuing their trek northward. Only security troops remained behind to establish local order.

With Wonsan in friendly hands, General Almond's problem was no longer one of assaulting a hostile beach and fighting in the streets. The remaining problem was simply to land his Tenth Corps as quickly as possible and to join the offensive.

The jam-packed amphibious shipping carrying the First Marine Division had Indian-filed out of Inchon's Flying Fish Channel between 15 and 17 October. In Admiral Doyle's troop-crowded flagship, USS *Mount McKinley,* were the staffs of both Generals Almond and Smith.

Upon arrival at Wonsan, 19 October, General Almond and Admiral Doyle immediately proceeded to Admiral Struble's flagship, the battleship *Missouri,* anchored in Wonsan's outer harbor.

"The purpose of the conference," said Admiral Struble recently, "was to acquaint General Almond and other commanders with the actual situation existing at Wonsan, and to give them my best estimate of when the troops would probably be landed. The decision had been reached by that time that the tactical situation ashore did not require early landing of the forces."

Vice Admiral Struble stated that Captain Richard T. Spofford's minesweeping Task Group 95.6 had started sweeping 10 October. They originally had expected to finish the sweeping within five days, but due to the presence of influence mines, the sweeping would not be finished for a landing on 20 October. Struble estimated that at least three more days would be needed to clear a path through the influence minefield.

General Almond was disturbed by the prospect of delay. He was anxious to get ashore in order to direct operations of the fast-moving First ROK Corps, which had been placed under his command. He therefore decided to proceed ashore by *Missouri's* helicopter, taking part of his staff with him. The remainder of his staff (plus a liaison group from Amphibious Group One) were ordered to come ashore in small boats the same afternoon.

As a result of the 19 October Commander's conference aboard *Missouri,* and in view of the minefield, Admiral Struble directed Admiral Doyle to issue retirement orders to the tractor and transport groups.* They were to retire along their routes of advance beginning at 1700 on the 19th. The convoys were to reverse course again in time to arrive off the channel entrance by Wonsan by the 21st of October.

Thus began what the Marines called "Operation Yo-Yo"—steam northward twelve hours, steam southward twelve hours.

Actually this process of march and countermarch was to last until 25 October, when the troop ships were finally ordered to enter the swept channel of Wonsan. Leathernecks and GI's were so sardined into the amphibious shipping during their five-day parade up and down the Korean coast that some of them contracted severe cases of gastroenteritis and dysentery. Aboard one merchant ship, the *Marine Phoenix,* 750 men were stricken.

With Wonsan in friendly hands, Admiral Doyle issued instructions on 18 October for a non-assault landing. He directed that the LVTs and LCVPs be despatched to the beach when loaded. Time schedules were to be disregarded. All ships were directed to familiarize themselves with the procedure for transiting a minefield, and to remain outside the 10-fathom curve until it was safe for them to enter the swept channel. As they entered, the tractor group, loaded with cargo and vehicles, was to proceed in two columns, with an interval of 750 yards between ships and at a distance of 600 yards between columns. The personnel-carrying transports were instructed to enter in a single column, with 1,000 yards between ships, and at speed of not over ten knots.

Jeering placards of welcome greeted the Marines as they stepped ashore at Wonsan—one from the First Marine Air Wing, and another from the

---

* The tractor group included the landing ship-type vessels: LSTs, LSMs, LSDs, LSUs, etc. The transport group included cargo- and transport-type ships.

enthusiastic ROKs. All such greetings struck the Marines as being somewhat excessive. But Major General Oliver P. Smith summed up the Wonsan landing very philosophically: "History just got ahead of us for once."

Once ashore, the Marines—22,000 strong—started moving north in strength, and they fanned out with rather formidable patrols to the south. Marine trucks and tanks started rolling northward toward the twin cities of Hamhung and Hungnam. From this area the Marines would strike northwestward toward the northern border. This trek would take the Marines through some of Korea's highest mountains, where the Communists were reported to be preparing a "national redoubt" for a winter guerrilla campaign.

Seventh Division Lands at Iwon

On 29 October, the Seventh Division was landed at Iwon administratively after the fast minesweepers *Doyle* and *Endicott* had found no traces of mines in that harbor. Nor was there any trace of the enemy since the ROK Capital Division had moved through the city four days before.

When the first troop-laden LCVPs from the Seventh Division reached Iwon's shore at 1120 on 29 October, they were greeted by the outstretched hands of their commanding officer, General Barr, and by Admiral Thackrey.

General Barr said at the time that his division would go to the Manchurian border, destroying any enemy it found in its path. Manchuria was only 75 miles away.

By nightfall of the first day, more than 27,000 Seventh Division troops had dug in for the night in the frostbitten hills and rice fields around Iwon. Supplies came ashore during the night as jeep and truck lights illuminated the beach area. Sherman tanks rolled ashore as nonchalantly as if on Fourth of July parade. Carrier planes droned overhead in constant patrol, and the destroyer *Borie* (CDR Merle F. Bowman) cruised offshore ready to open fire at moment's notice.

By the night of 31 October 1950, most of the Tenth Corps was once again on Korean soil. Some units had been at sea for nearly three weeks.

Wonsan Critique

Any attempt to "Monday morning quarterback" what happened at Wonsan is rank speculation—"What might have happened if the Marines had been landed at Hungnam and had made a deeper penetration into enemy territory?" and "What might have happened if the landing had been cancelled altogether?"

Had it been possible for the UN commanders to predict the rapidity of the ROK advance or to divine the extensive use of sea mines at Wonsan, the plans for that operation would, in all probability, have been cancelled altogether.

As a result of the minesweeping experience at Wonsan, Captain Spofford concluded that small boat sweepers are an essential component of any assault sweeping operation. If small boats had been available for Wonsan, the clearance problem might have been easier. Spofford also thought that at least one and preferably two ships with locator equipment should be available in the sweep area. With this equipment, and with small boats, Spofford believed a direct path could have been rapidly cleared to the Wonsan landing beaches.

Nor did Spofford desire to write off entirely the possibility of future countermine bombing. As long as there was some evidence to indicate that a gap had been bombed in even one mine line, MinRon Three's commander recommended that it was a tactic that deserved further experimentation.

The landing of the Seventh Infantry Division at Iwon on 29 October illustrated the Navy's flexibility to adjust an amphibious operation during a rapidly changing tactical situation ashore.

Admiral Struble saw the following lessons in the Wonsan operation: "We learned certain communications problems from Wonsan . . . also certain map problems of the three Services . . . and the need for adequate intelligence teams operated on the theatre level. We learned that a suitably equipped vessel with helicopters would be of great value for minesweeping operations. We learned that adequate mine countermeasure forces with trained personnel and equipment should be provided in each fleet and should be ready for service.

"In September, shortly after Inchon, when preliminary consideration was given to a landing at Wonsan, it was expected that heavy North Korean opposition to overland movement up the East Coast would be encountered. With United Nations ground operations contemplated in northeast Korea, the opening of either Wonsan or Hungnam harbors as a logistic port was essential. Whether the movement was conducted overland or by sea, the Naval operations necessary for the opening of one or both of these ports, including the necessary mine sweeping of a swept channel, would have to be accomplished. The original concept of the operation was based on these considerations, and was sound."

It was also Struble's view that the loss of control of the seas at Wonsan was exaggerated; that had the *need* existed to assault Wonsan, it could have been done despite the mines. "Had the assault operations against Wonsan been of great tactical and military value on 20 October 1950," he said, "the landing would have been conducted on schedule. I had determined in my own mind the method of landing at Wonsan on 20 October if military requirement had made it highly desirable. Under all of the existing conditions, particularly the rapid advance of the ROK forces past Wonsan and up the east coast, the acceptance of a very large mining risk against our heavily loaded transports would have been 'bad judgment' without military necessity. Admiral Joy and General MacArthur had been kept informed; I had sent a specific message to them indicating the situation, and had received a prompt approval from Tokyo to delay the landing."

"The main lesson of the Wonsan operation," said Admiral Joy, "is that no so-called subsidiary branch of the naval service, such as mine warfare, should ever be neglected or relegated to a minor role in the future. Wonsan also taught us that we can be denied freedom of movement to an enemy objective through the intelligent use of mines by an alert foe."

5.

The Battle of the Mines (Part II—Chinnampo)

The Need for Chinnampo

While the Marines were being landed administratively at Wonsan, the ROKs, against practically no opposition, were speeding toward the Yalu. Hamhung and its port city of Hungnam were captured on the 18th of October. By 24 November, the ROK Capital Division, supported by the interdiction fire and gunfire support of Task Group 95.2, was approaching Songjin, nearly 100 miles north of Wonsan.

In the western half of Korea, meanwhile, against stiffer resistance, the U.S. Eighth Army had occupied the North Korean capital of Pyongyang on 19 October, and General Walker was busily consolidating his positions for a push toward the North Korean boundary marked by the Yalu and Tumen rivers. On 20 October, 110 FEAF cargo aircraft airdropped the 187th Airborne Regiment—2,800 paratroops—thirty miles north of the enemy capital, near the road junctions of Sukchon and Sunchon, to add to the rout of the broken North Korean People's Army.

The progress in the west made mandatory and urgent the opening of Pyongyang's port city of Chinnampo for Eighth Army's logistic support. But Chinnampo, like Wonsan, was known to be heavily mined. General Walton H. Walker made an urgent call for minesweeping help at Chinnampo. Winter was coming soon, he said, and his entire Eighth Army, both its men and its motors, required winterization. The Army was already in short supply of fuel.

Approach of winter, shortage of fuel, and the poor condition of the much-bombed road and rail communications leading northward from South Korea —these factors made the job of opening the port of Chinnampo one of top military priority.

The urgency of Chinnampo sweeping operations was fully understood and appreciated by the Navy. General Walker's plaintive messages that his motor vehicles were being held up and that his troops were reduced to two rations per day underlined the Eighth Army's crucial need of supplies. On 21 October, therefore, Admiral Joy radioed General Walker the following message:

> Navy recognizes serious supply difficulties and extensive logistics support for your hard-fighting Eighth Army. Difficulties overland and desirability of supply from sea are known. I am doing everything possible to alleviate this situation. Haeju harbor being swept at maximum rate possible. Sweeping slow due to few minesweepers, high tides, and well-laid minefields. Wonsan is also critical, and all U. S. sweeps have been committed there since October 7. U. S. sweeps cannot be diverted from that port until it is safe for ships' entry. Sweepers are en route from States but will require instructions and training. Cannot estimate time for clearance of Chinnampo. If it is as well mined as Wonsan, it will require more than three weeks from the time we start.

The minefield problem at Chinnampo differed from the one at Wonsan largely because of the wholly different hydrographic conditions. The direct seaward approach to the port of Chinnampo, unlike the deep-water channels at Wonsan, was blocked by islands and delta-like areas formed over the years by heavy deposits of silt carried down the swift-currented Taedong River into the Daido-Ko estuary.

In further contrast to Wonsan's clear, almost tideless, and currentless harbor, Chinnampo's muddy tide rose a minimum of twelve feet and the current moved as fast as five knots. Two navigation channels approached the harbor.

The southernmost channel was extremely shallow—only 15 feet at high tide. The northern channel was almost twice as deep. Both were mineable. To further complicate the problem, according to Rear Admiral Allan E. Smith,[1] the latest charts held by UN forces were dated 1922-24. Many changes could take place in 26 years. The sweeping would have to start 69 miles from Chinnampo and proceed through a delta which was still about 33 miles from the dock.

"With three days to go before the channel was put through to the beaches of Wonsan, came a call from the Army and a command from Joy," said Admiral Smith. "I was to sweep into Chinnampo, the port of Pyongyang. The Army said they could no longer supply their advance by land and had to supply by sea.

"Sweep Chinnampo? Sweep with what?" Smith continued. "No organization, no personnel, no plans, and no ships at the moment. Three small wooden minesweepers were scheduled to arrive in Sasebo within a few days.

All the available minesweepers in Korea and most of the minesweeping gear in the Western Pacific were already committed to the east coast sweeping operations at Wonsan and Iwon.

"I scratched my head all right! I sent a despatch to COMNAVFE asking if an intelligence team could head for Chinnampo and obtain any information on mining there. Then I remembered that two mine observers had recently called on me—one from CINCPACFLT and one from Mine Forces, Atlantic Fleet. I sent the CINCPACFLT officer, Commander Donald N. Clay, to Chinnampo in search of advance mine intelligence and placed the Atlantic observer, Commander Stephen Morris Archer, in charge of Chinnampo sweep operations."

In brief summary, Smith's orders to Archer were to sweep Chinnampo "soonest-safest." Archer was to concentrate first on opening the southern shallow-water channel to permit the early entry of LSTs and other shallow-draft types. After this channel had been opened, the northern deep water channel was to be cleared to permit the passage of large cargo and troop transport-type ships.

Assembling the Sweep Force

Commander Archer was observing Wonsan sweep operations aboard the U.S. destroyer transport *Diachenko* (APD 123) when he received Smith's radio messages to clear the Chinnampo channels.

"What forces are available to me?" Archer asked by return despatch.

"None at the moment," said Smith, whose flagship, the destroyer tender *Dixie* (AD 14), was riding at anchor in the Sasebo channel. "Suggest you come to Sasebo where you are free to commandeer any suitable ships you can find."

Recruiting the Chinnampo sweep forces was that informal. Archer's first recruit was his colleague, the mine warfare expert from Atlantic Fleet Mine Headquarters, LCDR Donald C. DeForest, who likewise had been flown out to the far east with Archer to observe, and if possible, to assist combat sweeping operations.

Archer and DeForest went quickly to Sasebo where they began a recruiting drive from Smith's flagship. With binoculars from *Dixie's* navigating bridge, the two officers watched the channel traffic for any type of ship with minesweeping potential.

Two 40-foot motor launches that had been left by the recently-departed *Boxer* were the first self-propelled units to pass in front of the two channel cops. It was DeForest's suggestion that these launches be taken with the hope that they could pull light sweep gear in shallow water. Later, the USS *Carmick* (DMS 33) (LCDR R. K. Margetts) and USS *Thompson* (DMS 38)

(LCDR W. H. Barckmann) steamed past and were "designated" volunteers. Neither of these ships had previously participated in Korean minesweeping duty. Next came three small AMSs* (MinDiv-51) just arrived from Honolulu: USS *Pelican* (AMS 32) (LTJG H. V. Cronk) (ComMinDiv-51), USS *Swallow* (AMS 36) (LTJG J. Roberts), and USS *Gull* (AMS 16) (LTJG C. E. Nimitz). Next to join the force was an LST which would serve as a logistics base as well as a helicopter platform. Finally, the destroyer *Forrest Royal* would serve as flagship.†

While the ship and officer larceny was in progress, Archer was also assembling his staff. DeForest would be operations officer and troubleshooter; CDR William H. Shea, borrowed from the staff of Commander Service Division 31, would be his planning officer. From the Royal Navy's *Theseus* came LCDR W. E. H. Rodwell, RN; from Australia's destroyer *Warramunga* came LCDR G. H. Gladstone, HMAN; and from CINCPACFLT'S staff came CDR Donald N. Clay, the intelligence officer.

Sweeping Chinnampo

Intelligence was the key to success at Chinnampo—good intelligence, prompt intelligence. Long before the sweeping operations began, Admiral

---

* An AMS carries a normal complement of 3 officers and 29 men.

† When finally constituted, CDR Archer's Chinnampo Task Element 95.69 included, in addition to his flagship *Forrest Royal* (CDR O. O. Liebschner), the following:

Task Unit 95.69.1		CDR Oscar B. Lundgren
Minesweeping Unit 1	2DMS	
Thompson		
Carmick		
Task Unit 95.69.2		LTJG Henry V. Cronk
Minesweeping Unit 2		
Gull		
Pelican		
Swallow	3 AMS	
YMS-502, 306, 513, 503	4 ROK YMS	
Task Unit 95.69.3		
Helicopter Unit	1 Helicopter	LT Robert D. Romer
Task Unit 95.69.4		LCDR Alan Ray
Minesweeping Unit 3		
Horace A. Bass	1 APD	
TU 95.69.41 UDT One	1 UDT	
Task Unit 95.69.5		
Minesweeping Unit 4		
Catamount	1 LSD	
MSBs	12 LCVP	
Work Boats	2 46-foot ML	
LST-Q007	1 LST	
Task Unit 95.69.7		
Buoy Ship Unit		
Bolster	1 ARS	
Intelligence Unit		CDR Donald N. Clay

Smith had sent Commander Clay to Pyongyang to seek advance mine intelligence. Smith had also requested the Eighth Army to seize and retain all Chinnampo boat captains, river pilots, and captured minelaying personnel as well as mine plans, ships' logs, and hydrographic notes.

By the time actual channel sweeping commenced on 2 November, CDR Clay's intelligence mission had paid rich dividends. Clay had located North Koreans who had personally sailed on the North Korean minelaying ships. He now knew that North Koreans had planted both moored and ground magnetic-type mines at Chinnampo. Although swift currents and extreme tides might have caused some movement, Clay knew approximately where each line had been planted; and the general areas that had to be swept were laid out and charted.

It is certain that this intelligence, more than any other single factor, reduced the duration of the Chinnampo sweeping operation and undoubtedly was responsible for the total lack of casualties from mines, either to personnel or to ships employed in the operation.

This fact underlines and re-emphasizes the great value of naval intelligence and the reason why naval intelligence must always work closely with the other intelligence agencies. A fragment of intelligence which might seem insignificant to one Service or agency often proves vital to another.

Chinnampo sweeping operations, although jury-rigged until the last moment, included practically every weapon in the naval arsenal: surface sweeps, aircraft, and helicopters.

A component of naval air began the mine clearance task on 28 October when PBMs from FAirWing Six, tendered by the USS *Gardiners Bay* (AVP-39) anchored at Inchon, began daily mine search patrols in the Chinnampo area. PBM "Mariners" from Patrol Squadrons 42 and 47 and "Sunderland" flying boats from RAF Squadrons 88 and 209 were continuously engaged in anti-mine operations from 29 September through 15 November. During this period, the aircraft sighted 340 mines in the Yellow Sea area; 44 were exploded and 9 were sunk by machine gun fire.

In late November, patrol planes were utilized to drop depth bombs on magnetic mines off Chinnampo. On the 28th, thirty-two 325-pound depth bombs were dropped. Only one mine was exploded. Operations the next day were slightly more successful. P2V "Neptunes" dropped sixteen bombs and destroyed three mines. The patrol planes had one distinct advantage over the small minesweepers: they could operate without regard to rough seas.

Helicopters, flying from the Royal Navy aircraft carrier *Theseus*, were a vital adjunct to the Chinnampo operation. *Theseus* provided an early base for HutRonTwoDet.* The *Theseus'* "egg-beater" flew a daily search of the

_____
* Helicopter Utility Squadron Two Detachment borrowed from USS *Worcester*.

minefield; the remainder of the British carrier aircraft provided a daily combat air patrol to protect the minesweeping force from either enemy air interference or shore batteries. The damage or possible loss of minesweepers to enemy gunfire was thus forestalled.

To insure maximum safety and to prevent the loss of any of the all too few minesweepers, the utmost use of all intelligence, knowledge, and experience had to be made. Archer and his staff sat down to second-guess where the enemy minefields might be. Next, they worked out a plan to circumvent and/or sweep those fields blocking entrance to the port. The aim, in view of the shortage of ships, was to *go around* minefields wherever possible. "Sweeping *through* was to be a last resort and for final clearance," wrote Archer. "No losses were acceptable."[2]

As it worked out, subsequent intelligence confirmed on the spot by helicopter observations, proved the mining guesstimate substantially correct. It was necessary to sweep *through* only one minefield in clearing the initial channel to the docks.

Sweeping at Chinnampo began at an arbitrary point in the Yellow Sea, thirty-nine miles west of the line where mines were actually suspected. In actual fact, any starting point in the Yellow Sea outside the probable minefields was as good as another as all of it was shallow and mineable.

Two DMSs, the *Carmick* and *Thompson*, started the sweep of the so-called "end run" channel the morning of 29 October. This type could only be used in such a limited manner. "The DMS is neither fish nor fowl. It is neither a good destroyer nor a good minesweeper—too large, too costly, and too hard to maneuver as a minesweeper, too little fire power as a destroyer."[3]

Before beginning surface sweep operations in the channel itself, Archer called all his skippers together, brought them up to date on intelligence and plans, and issued final instructions.

The plan for the first afternoon, 2 November, he said, would put all ships into action except the two DMSs. The three AMSs—*Pelican, Swallow,* and *Gull*—were to start the initial sweep two hours after their arrival in Chinnampo. Ahead of the AMSs would go the helicopter and the frogmen. The ROK vessels and the *Bolster* would follow astern, performing shotgun and danning duties.

One of the young AMS skippers, LTJG C. E. Nimitz, nephew of Fleet Admiral Chester W. Nimitz, described the Chinnampo sweep thus:

"It was good duty, but uneasy duty, especially those first few days when our intelligence hadn't been authenticated. The uncertainty was bad enough, but that swift current compounded the problem. Sometimes, in turning, we found ourselves 1,000 yards out of position.

"We discovered something else on the morning of November 4: that a Chinnampo cyclone came up faster than a 'Texas Twister.' When the wind whipped up, it really whipped. Reveille had sounded only a few minutes before and most of us were sitting down to breakfast when suddenly we heard our ship banging against the steel hull of *Bolster* tied up alongside.

"Before I could make it to the bridge, two of our lines had parted and slight damage had been done to our rail. The seas were running high. Seventy-knot gusts sent gray murky water splashing against our pilothouse. We had learned our first lesson at Chinnampo—never to nest alongside another ship even in a dead calm, for ten minutes later the entire Yellow Sea might be standing on end."[4]

The storm lasted almost twenty-four hours—abating as quickly as it came. With all it wrath and fury, the storm had its blessings. Four enemy contact mines had broken their moorings and surfaced, and were later destroyed by air and surface gunfire. At the storm's height, the *Catamount* (LSD-17) (CDR Kenneth Loveland) steamed into Chinnampo. As the last unit to join Archer's force, *Catamount's* arrival was a historic event in naval warfare. She was the first LSD to participate in minesweeping operations.

Compared to the pint-sized and bobbing AMSs, the 4,960-ton *Catamount* with 458-foot keel and her 72-foot beam rode the heavy seas gracefully. She was an odd-looking mine ship with her blunt, stubby bow and high freeboard. She had a massive bridge and a squared stern that opened to the sea as her bowels flooded to take aboard and disgorge baby minesweepers. Altogether *Catamount* had brought with her 12 LCVPs, plus all the spare minesweeping gear available in Yokosuka and Sasebo.

In performing duties as an LCVP mothership, an LSD's boat operations are somewhat similar to an aircraft carrier's flight operations. Launching and recovery of the small boats, as with aircraft, must be carefully timed and supervised. As the aircraft carrier must be brought into the wind preparatory to takeoffs and landings, so must the LSD head into the sea prior to flooding the well deck for boat operations. The LSD's boat control officer is required to perform duties comparable to those of the carrier's landing signal officer.

The arrival of the *Catamount* with her LCVP sweepers strengthened Archer's minesweeping force. The tiny boats were capable of both moored and magnetic sweeping; they could sweep very shallow areas beyond the reach of larger minesweepers; and, in deeper waters, they could open shallow paths for the larger minesweepers to follow.

According to Archer, the intelligence mission of CDR Clay to discover the location of the Chinnampo minefields made the sweeping task much easier and less dangerous. Moreover, the staff's "guesstimates" of the location of the enemy minefields were confirmed by Clay's reports.

"By November 6," said Archer, "most of our guesses had been confirmed. With Commander Clay embarked in a North Korean tug, he and his North Korean pilots threaded their way from the Chinnampo dock to the open sea, checking the location of each mine line."

Once the tug had been safely navigated to the open sea, it was decided to make a return trip for the purpose of precisely plotting the minefield. The ROK *YMS-503* became the first UN ship to enter Chinnampo. Aboard her

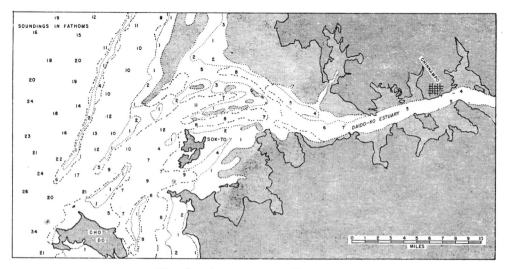

THE SEA APPROACHES TO CHINNAMPO

was *Forrest Royal's* navigator, Ensign Robert R. Munroe, who had volunteered to do the piloting. The safe passage of this ship was again confirmation of the valuable intelligence that had been obtained.

Altogether, 212 enemy mines had been planted in the harbor. The main entrance channel was thoroughly blocked by five moored lines and one magnetic line.

"In addition," said Archer, "the approach to Chinnampo from the north was blocked by three lines of moored mines. But the southern channel, the one where we thought for certain that the enemy *would* have mines, was apparently open. Actually, we think the enemy had intended to mine it, but planes from the British aircraft carrier *Theseus*, by sinking what they believed to be a mine-carrying barge, had interrupted the enemy's plan. Later on we found a sunken enemy barge where the British said it should be in the southern approaches. Fifteen mines were still aboard it.

"Once all the mine intelligence had been compiled," stated Archer, "we were able to plot a channel which permitted our initial sweep to avoid all but one minefield. That was why it was possible for us to sweep seventy miles in ten days without a casualty of any kind."

Otherwise, sweeping operations at Chinnampo were quite similar to those at Wonsan. A night conference always preceded the issuance of the next day's sweep plan. "Minesweeping would run a punctual guy nuts," said Archer. "You can't figure out what you will do tomorrow until you find out what you have done today." Archer, Shea, and DeForest listened to each skipper's progress report—Archer thinking in terms of over-all accomplishment, Shea of tomorrow's plan, and DeForest in his role as chairman of the ways and means committee.

A typical sweep day at Chinnampo read as follows:

Pelican and *Swallow* under way by 0500. Proceed to Item line, stream gear, and make moored sweep along swept channel to Chinnampo. On arrival reverse course and return to Item line. UDT team and helicopter reconnoiter Item and Jig lines. Locate and buoy. Investigate mines on north beach of Soku-to. Render safe any located. Two LCVPs recheck swept areas. Four LCVPs follow with magnetic sweep. Under way approximately 0600.

In these few words was a full, hard day's work for all hands. No more detailed instructions were necessary, so well did every man know his own specialty.

"Because of Chinnampo's swift tidal currents," said Archer, "all the mines had to be cleared out in order to render the area fully safe. There was always the possibility that the swift current would cause the mines to 'walk' out into the swept channel.

"But the sweepers were given maximum protection at all times. By using the helicopter and small boats at low tide, we double-checked our intelligence and we double-checked the possibility of tide and current moving the mines into a swept area. As an additional precaution, after we located a minefield, underwater demolition teams in LCPRs used empty 5-inch powder cans to buoy the mines at low tide. Moreover, the AMSs always swept at high tide; and, weather permitting, they were preceded by the helicopter."

With the danger factor considerably reduced, sweeping became a dull and monotonous procedure.

"To give you some idea of the monotony," said Lieutenant Nimitz, "we always passed about a half dozen bodies floating with the tide—always the same bodies, for before they could get out to sea, the tide reversed itself, bringing them in again. We named one of the bodies 'Herman' because he was so easily identified. His hands had been tied behind his back. Herman was the main topic of conversation. Where would Herman be the next morning?"

In addition to an occasional storm, the coming of cold weather to Chinnampo brought added burden to all the minesweepers, but particularly to *Catamount* and her small boats. On icy mornings, steam was used to unfreeze the big ship's ballast valves in order to flood the well-deck and lower the stern gate. Steam also had to be applied to the LCVP boat engines after a freezing night. Despite the ice, there were some compensations which accrued to *Catamount's* crew—compensations that could not be matched by any other ship in the Navy. After she had deballasted, it was a rare occasion if the crew did not find some choice fish flopping around in the docking well. Fresh fish cooked to taste was a welcome reward to the sweep crews in payment for their long hours of cold, rough-water sweeping in an open boat.

Before the Chinnampo sweeping effort was finished, thirteen Japanese contract sweepers, including one mother ship and one "guinea pig" ship with padded decks and remote controls, had joined the sweep force. The Japanese sweepers, while not permitted to operate in unswept waters, did relieve United States sweeps from the monotonous duty of check-sweeping.

As early as 7 November, after ten days' sweeping, shallow-draft vessels began to enter the port of Chinnampo. The first ship to enter was *LSU-1402*. Word that one ship had safely entered Chinnampo caused others to arrive, all bringing much-needed supplies to the Eighth Army.

Archer's message to Admiral Smith as the first line from the LST hit the dock was in the clear: "Mission accomplished."

Only shallow-draft vessels were initially permitted to enter the swept channel, and then only when they were conned by a member of the Chinnampo's Pilot's Association. This was a newly formed group of all available UN navigators and quartermasters, under the supervision of LCDR G. H. Gladstone, RAN.

"After the minesweeping chores are finished," said Archer, "the most worrisome duty is harbor control and pilotage. In spite of the fact that others may be given port and pilotage authority, everyone feels, and I guess naturally, that the minesweep commander really knows the harbor best. Consequently, the conscientious commander feels personally responsible for all the ships going in or out. He will feel the necessity for supplying pilots and, in general, for being guardian angel of the port. This, when combined with language difficulties and the Oriental philosophy, was the most nerve-wracking of all my Korean experiences."

The first LST was piloted into Chinnampo on 10 November by CDR Clay. "It seemed appropriate," said Archer, "that this event should occur on the eve of the ROK Navy's fifth anniversary. I therefore despatched all

ROK ships present that it was a pleasure to present the open port of Chinnampo to the Navy of the Republic of Korea on its birthday."

Archer ordered all U. S. Navy men-of-war to dress ship in honor of the occasion.

The deep water channel was declared open on 20 November, and Captain Charles H. Perdue's hospital ship *Repose* was the first deep draft vessel to enter. In fact, she was three times larger than any ship which had previously entered the channel. *Warramunga's* LCDR Gladstone piloted the big white mercy ship with less than a foot of water under her keel. Archer, who was more worried about the ship grounding than being mined, sent a note of congratulations to Gladstone on the successful passage, and regretted that Gladstone would have to stay aboard the *Repose* overnight. The wisecracking Australian radioed back that he could stand fifty nurses for one night!

In summary, Archer stated that Chinnampo would have been a much tougher job both for the sweeping operation and later for the redeployment if there had been enemy resistance. "We would have required constant air cover, and we could have expected losses.

"As it was, our greatest danger was the navigation hazards. We constantly took advantage of all available breaks to protect ourselves from mines. But we had to worry constantly about tides and uncharted shoals.

"It was fortunate, also, that the Commander Seventh Fleet, Admiral Struble, had once been Commander Mine Force, Pacific. He understood the mine problem. There was no breathing down the neck of the minesweep commander."

Ship performance, with exception of *Boxer's* two 40-foot motor launches, whose engines were inadequate, was excellent. The LCVPs, used for the first time in Korea, worked fine and were credited with sweeping five moored mines. The LST provided an ideal base for the helicopter. "Two helicopters can base on an LST easily," said Archer. "She makes an ideal tender and supply ship for small sweepers. She carries a large quantity of diesel oil; she can carry provisions and spare sweep gear. Her tank deck is ideal for laying out replacement sweep gear."

The LSD provided the only means for attending small boat sweeps. She was excellent in heavy weather, as well as being a good supply ship and a black oil tanker. At Chinnampo, for instance, the *Catamount* carried sufficient oil to fuel the DMSs, the APD, and the destroyer. When the fleet tankers came, the LSD and the LST made it possible to effect a quick turnaround. Had there been enemy opposition, this would have been a great advantage.

Additionally, the LSD had served as a schoolship for ROK naval personnel, both officers and men, who were the first to train for minesweeping operations and to actually see the work done. This contingent was a part of the ROK sailors from six Korean YMSs being converted for minesweeping at Sasebo. During the evening, after a full day in the boats or on AMSs, these ROK naval men studied USN minesweeping manuals and discussed their project with great enthusiasm. On their return to Sasebo, they would man their own ships and be trained in minesweeping work at sea.

By November's end, 200 miles of channel had been swept at Chinnampo, and 80 mines* had been destroyed.

Still the Chinnampo sweep force was not finished. United Nations ground forces had continued to advance northward. They might need fire support or an amphibious lift along the flanks. Accordingly, on Thanksgiving Day, 1950, Archer's force started sweeping north toward the Chongchon River.

"We felt there would be no mines," said Archer, "but we wanted to make sure that fire support ships and LSTs could get in if needed. The AMSs made the sweep to Yongmi Dong on Thanksgiving Day. The DMSs and the destroyer were used as navigational guides, and the APD was used to carry the sweeping boats.

"We swept to within three miles of the beaches that were in Communist hands and far beyond the frontlines of UN ground forces. From our sweeps, we could see B-29s bombing Chonju, which was the far point of our advance to the northwest.

"After we had completed this sweep, we withdrew to our shelter area in Chinnampo and awaited further developments. When the Chinese attack came, we didn't know whether there would be a Dunkirk at Yongmi Dong or whether the UN ground forces would be able to successfully withdraw south of the Chongchon River and perhaps reach Chinnampo. As soon as the APAs and AKAs started arriving at Chinnampo, our final chore developed.

"The entry of UN transports and covering destroyers had to be made at night. I stationed an AMS, a ROK frigate and my flagship at the critical turning point in the channel to serve as radar markings.

"During the night, one transport went aground and one destroyer caught a buoy in one of her screws. But the transport was refloated at next high tide and the destroyer cleared her screw next day.

"The Chinnampo evacuation was a complete success; the entire port logistic command as well as many civilians were safely evacuated. The deep channel surely paid for itself in this operation. Again there were no

---

* Of 80 mines destroyed, PBMs got the largest share, 36; Frogmen, 27; *Gull,* 2; *Pelican,* 1; *Bass,* 1; and Japanese minesweepers, 1. Storms accounted for twelve.

casualties. This is perhaps the most remarkable aspect of the Chinnampo operation. The job was completed without the loss of a single life or a single ship.

"Many things contributed to this record, but the outstanding source of satisfaction to me," Archer concluded, "was the complete and thoroughly enthusiastic teamwork of all hands—Americans, British, ROKs (and Japanese)—in our Task Element. Vice Admiral Andrewes and his *Theseus,* Rear Admiral Allan E. Smith and his staff, the logistic and moral support we received from Sasebo—everyone worked together with a will and enthusiasm to get this difficult task completed in spite of weather, few ships, language problems and a random assortment of ships, personnel and equipment."[5]

After five years of obscurity, the October-November minesweeping operations in Korea dramatized once again the fact that minesweeping demands a tremendous expenditure of logistic support. It requires painstaking coordination and much training; it requires a variety of equipment: tenders, motherships, flagships, buoy ships,* small-boat facilities, helicopter bases, mine disposal units and underwater demolition teams. In Korea, fire support ships were also needed.

By the end of November 1950, minesweeping had become a problem of major significance to the United States Navy.

Rear Admiral Allan E. Smith summed it up this way:[6] "The Russians apparently have everything we have and everything the Germans had in mining techniques. . . . The United States must put minesweeping on the same priority level as antisubmarine and carrier warfare."

---

* The USS *Bolster* laid all of the 3,000 pound channel marker buoys in addition to planting three moorings off Pyongyang in the Daida-Ko estuary. At least one hundred channel buoys were required to mark Chinnampo approaches.

6.

The Hungnam Redeployment

Triumph and Tragedy

By October's end, a total United Nations victory over the North Korean aggressors seemed assured and imminent. General MacArthur stated that United States troops might be home by Christmas. The North Korean Army was crushed; their divisions were in complete rout. Thousands of enemy troops had surrendered and hundreds more were deserting their arms.

On Korea's west coast, elements of the Eighth Army were nearing the Yalu River. On the east coast, likewise, elements of the Tenth Corps were sweeping to the Manchurian border.

Unlike the Eighth Army, which attacked frontally all along the western perimeter, General Almond's Tenth Corps, consisting of five divisions (First Marine Division, Seventh Infantry Division, Third Infantry Division, and the two ROK divisions—Third and Capitol), attacked northward in four columns with the exception of the U.S. Third Division, whose last elements were offlanding in Wonsan on 20 November. The First Marine Division was sent northwest, the U.S. Seventh Division went north. Third and Capitol Divisions of the ROK First Corps were advancing far up the eastern shoreline. General Almond's plan was to dominate all the main arteries of transport and communication in northeast Korea as quickly as possible.

The optimistic horizon in late October was clouded by only one storm, but one which in less than a month was to grow to hurricane proportions. Would the Red Chinese intervene? The Peking radio had said they would. On 16 October, in fact, intelligence revealed that Chinese Army units had crossed the Yalu River. Were they only, as the Peking radio had said, "volunteer forces"?

On the western front, toward the end of October, the Eighth Army was advancing toward the Manchurian border against spotty resistance, reaching Chongju on 30 October. Elements of the 24th Division fought their way into Kusong.

In the eastern half of Korea, the Seventh Regiment of the ROK Sixth Division, after reaching Chosan on the Yalu River on 26 October, found itself surrounded by enemy forces and its line of communication severed. Relief elements of the ROK Second Corps also suffered strong attacks by Chinese troops in the vicinity of Ongjon and Usan.

To make the future more ominous, units of the First Cavalry Division were surprised and suffered severe casualties during the night of 1-2 November when a strong contingent of Chinese horsemen attacked their positions.

From captured prisoners, four Red Chinese armies could be identified.

The sudden appearance of Chinese units in Korea momentarily halted the advance in the west, while the Tenth Corps in the east proceeded more cautiously.

On 5 November, General MacArthur informed the UN of the presence of organized Chinese units in Korea. It was still not clear whether the Chinese troops had joined the North Korean People's Army to prevent its annihilation and to prolong its resistance, or whether a large-scale intervention by Red Chinese was forthcoming.

It was at this point that the carriers of Task Force 77 were asked to destroy the Korean side of the Yalu River bridges across which Chinese troops, supplies, and equipment were seen and known to be streaming.[1]

As Task Force 77 commenced its work on the Yalu bridges and as General MacArthur's announcement was recorded at UN headquarters at Lake Success, the entire battlefront in North Korea became ominously quiet. Little action was seen in the Eighth Army sector.

On the east coast U.S. Marines pushed northwestward up a winding dirt road toward the Chosin reservoir area. From there, it was planned that they would attack northwestward to link up with elements of the Eighth Army.

The Chinese Challenge

In their advance to the Chosin reservoir area, the Marines had thus far met little opposition. The worst pocket of resistance had been encountered on 2 November when the 124th Chinese Communist Division challenged Colonel Homer L. Litzenberg's Seventh Marine Regiment south of Chinhung-ni. Fighting between this Marine regiment and the Chinese Division continued for five days.

On the night of 7 November, the Seventh's 3rd Battalion commander, Major Maurice E. Roach, sent word to Colonel Litzenberg that he was meeting very heavy opposition and requested artillery fire.

"That night," said Colonel Litzenberg, "we fired artillery into forty-five concentration areas, points we thought the enemy most likely to hold.

That night, also, the Chinese General threw a fresh new regiment against the Marines; but by 0400 he was forced to withdraw his division in such a crippled state that it would not fight again for five months."[2]

Aside from the Seventh Marine Regiment's initial encounter with the Chinese, the primary source of Marine concern came from reports of pilots ranging north and west of the column that numerous small groups of Chinese soldiers were spread throughout the North Korean countryside. Many of these groups were in the open; others, when observed, took refuge in houses and huts. In addition to actual troop sightings, pilots saw thousands of footprints in the snow. Were enemy forces encircling the First Marine Division?

On 15 November, the Seventh Marines arrived at Hagaru-ri, the village at the southern tip of their first objective, the Chosin Reservoir. The Fifth Marines followed closely behind. Pilots and North Korean civilians continued to report Chinese enemy troop activity to the north and west of the Marines.

To strengthen their position, the Marines decided to move the tactical air direction center (TADC) to Hagaru-ri, where it would be in a centralized position for the close support control of Marine and naval aircraft. At the same time, construction of an air strip at Hagaru-ri was begun, big enough to accommodate C-47 type aircraft. The Marines' foresight in both these decisions was to prove extremely beneficial in the fighting that lay ahead.

On 21 November, Colonel Herbert B. Powell's 17th Regimental Combat Team of the Seventh Army Division reached the Manchurian border at Hyesanjin, a deserted village known as the "ghost city of broken bridges."

So far as the occupation of enemy territory was concerned, this was the highwater mark of the Korean war.

On orders from U.S. Tenth Corps, Major General Oliver P. Smith, Commanding General First Marine Division, resumed the Marines' advance on 22 November towards Yudam-ni, a village and road center on the west-central shore of the Chosin reservoir. From there, the Leathernecks would push north and then west toward the Communist stronghold of Kanggye for the link-up with the Eighth Army and the final advance to the Yalu.

The Red Chinese Army Strikes

Late in the morning of 24 November, the Eighth Army in the east began an offensive. The enemy defenses were a series of roadblocks and obstacles to hold up the advance of wheeled vehicles and tanks. During the first few hours, enemy opposition was light. Enemy positions were not strongly defended, and gains from two to twelve miles were made.

By sunset, 25 November, however, the Red Chinese had commenced a strong counterattack which penetrated the positions of the ROK First Division in the Taechon area, forcing some of its units to withdraw several miles and exposing the 24th Division's right flank.

Night infiltrations by the enemy followed the strong daytime counterattacks.

The most powerful blow fell on the right flank of Eighth Army in the mountainous area northeast of Tokchon. The Communists struck the ROK 7th and 8th Divisions in regimental strength, infiltrating between UN positions during the night. Organized withdrawal became impossible.

The first tip-off of the impending Chinese attack against the Marines came on 25 November from a Chinese private who was captured by the 7th Marines' 1st Battalion.

The private said that as soon as the two Marine regiments arrived at Yudam-ni, two Chinese corps (six divisions) would begin the attack. Three divisions would attack and surround the two Yudam-ni regiments, one from the north, one from the west, and one cutting the road to the south behind the Marines. A fourth Communist Division would attack Hagaru-ri and would sever the road between that village and Koto-ri; a fifth division would attack Koto-ri, surround it, and break the road between Koto-ri and Chinhung-ni.[3]

That a Chinese peasant private would know the maneuver plans of two Chinese Army corps hardly seems plausible. Yet, his incredible story was to be verified during the next few days of actual battle.

As the Red Chinese attacked in the north central Korean mountains, splitting the Eighth Corps and Tenth Army, thousands upon thousands of Red Chinese soldiers poured through the open lines.

On 27 November the Fifth and Seventh Marines were in Yudam-ni. The First Marines had been left behind to protect the main supply route, which was some 60 miles long. Single battalions guarded the villages of Hagaru-ri at the southern tip of the reservoir, Chinhung-ni, at the base of the 3,400-foot plateau, and Koto-ri midway between the two.

On the night of 27 November, the Chinese armies struck, hurling at least 60,000 and possibly as many as 100,000 troops against the First Marine Division in the vicinity of the Chosin Reservoir. Although not ideally positioned by any means, the Marines' defensive posture was better than other units of the Tenth Corps, who were stretched out from Wonsan all the way to the Manchurian border, a distance of some 100 miles.

At 2200 the night of 27 November, wave after wave of Chinese attacked the Marines' Yudam-ni defense perimeter.

For some reason, unknown to the Marines, the Chinese elected to hit the 2nd Battalion of Lieutenant Colonel Raymond L. Murray's Fifth Marines first.

"This particular battalion, under command of Lieutenant Colonel Harold S. Roise, had gained about 3,000 yards during the day," said Colonel Murray, "and was in a good position to defend itself. The Fifth Regiment's other two battalions were in assembly areas and outposted for local defense. Under the circumstances the Second Battalion was better able to receive the shock of the first massed attack."[4]

Massed attack is correct phraseology. At first the Chinese attacked by squads. As these small groups were chopped down, the attacks were stepped up. Enemy platoons, and, in some instances, companies, charged the Marine lines. Soon the entire front blazed with shellfire. Coordinated with the frontal assault, the Chinese also attempted to encircle the Marines at Yudam-ni by cutting the main supply route southward to Hagaru-ri.

Although the Chinese succeeded in establishing a roadblock south of Yudam-ni, their effort proved to be a costly one. They encountered Seventh Regiment's Fox Company, which Colonel Litzenberg had outposted behind the advance atop a mountain pass to guard the supply route from Hagaru-ri.

Since the heroic attack by the U.S. Marines "in the opposite direction" has been fully covered by official Marine historians in *U.S. Marine Operations in Korea*,[5] no attempt will be made herein to chronicle the First Marine Division's fighting withdrawal from Yudam-ni to Hagaru-ri, to Koto-ri, to Chinhung-ni, and to Hungnam, where U.S. Navy transports and combatant vessels awaited their arrival. Only the highlights of the close air support rendered by naval and Marine aircraft will be recorded.

Courageous and tough fighting men that they are, it is certain that the First Marine Division could not have extricated itself as a unit from the clutches of six Chinese divisions without the close air support which was to come from Navy and Marine pilots. Nor would the job have been as easy nor as many of the injured saved without the air logistics and rescue support that was to come from the U.S. Air Force.

When morning came on 28 November, Marine pilots from the escort carrier *Badoeng Strait* and from Yonpo airfield at Hungnam, arrived over Yudam-ni expecting to support their comrades on their scheduled push toward Kanggye, had no inkling of the savage and sanguinary battles which had been fought during the night.

By radio, now, they were briefed on what had happened.

Three of Seventh Regiment's companies had been heavily hit. Easy Company had been completely overrun; a platoon commander, First Lieutenant Robert Bye, was now in charge of the company. Dog Company had been driven from the crest of the terrain it was holding three times; and three times it had returned. Dog Company's commander, Captain Milton Hull, and fourteen men were all that remained of the original company, 200 strong. Captain Hull had fourteen wounds. Fox company had been completely cut off. Reports funneled through to regiment that Fox's commander, Captain William E. Barber, had been seriously wounded and was directing his defense from a stretcher.

The Fifth Regiment, still in comparatively good shape, had been damaged as much by the severe cold and frostbite as by enemy gunfire and hand grenades.

Marine tactical air controllers on the ground instructed all pilots that the contemplated push northward on 28 November had been cancelled; instead, would the airmen survey the Yudam-ni area for Chinese troop concentrations and take appropriate action?

If Marines were shocked and stunned by the night action of 27 November, no less so were the Chinese. They were unable to concentrate for a second assault until two days later, 30 November, when aerial observers from the First Marine Air Wing reported that at noon an estimated 2,000 enemy troops were cautiously grouping north of the Marines' perimeter.

Marine aircraft immediately began to blanket the area with rockets, bombs, and napalm. By the time the enemy jumped off at 1500, his estimated 2,000 strong had been slashed to an estimated five hundred.

What had promised to be a fullscale attack was now a piecemeal venture. Nevertheless, to the accompaniment of the usual cacophony of bugles, whistles, and shouts, the Reds swept down the slope of the ridge facing the Marines. Pilots in their cockpits overhead could not hear the noise made by the enemy troops as they approached the Marine perimeter, but they needed little coaching from the forward air controller on the ground.

Peeling off at 5,000 feet, four napalm-loaded Corsairs howled down to make "on-the-deck" runs. All four napalm tanks struck the first attacking wave, scoring direct hits which tore large holes in the enemy forward wall. As the last plane dropped its ordnance, the first was back, tailed by others, to attack the faltering enemy with strafing runs. The enemy's assault lost momentum and the Reds soon had enough. They broke into disorganized flight to escape the rain of 20-mm. shells. Marine aircraft had broken the back of this enemy assault. Of the 500 enemy who initiated the attack, Marine Corsairs were credited with killing approximately three hundred.

Elsewhere on the Marine defense perimeter, planes from Task Force 77 appeared and rendered similar support. Skyraider and Corsair pilots from the USS *Philippine Sea* were told by the Marine Tactical Air Controller that their attacks for that day had been "very good. The enemy has been stopped."

Full participation by Task Force 77 in support of the embattled Marines was urgently requested 29 November in a "flash" message from Commanding General First Marine Air Wing to COMNAVFE. Major General Field Harris strongly recommended "a sustained effort by Task Force 77 in the Tenth Corps zone of action."

On this same day, carrier pilots from the USS *Leyte* (CV-32) reported their inability to contact tactical air controllers in the Eighth Army area because of the heavy traffic. However, they reported excellent results from the flights that had been flown in support of Tenth Corps.

Philippine Sea's pilots had similar experiences. Of ten flights flown in support of Eighth Army, only three were able to contact tactical air controllers and these pilots had been instructed to jettison their napalm alongside the road. The same troubles which had been so evident during the battle for Pusan had reappeared.

On the other hand, all three flights in support of the Tenth Corps had been directed upon lucrative targets, mostly enemy troop concentrations.

Following the results of the 29th, Commander Task Force 77, Rear Admiral E. C. Ewen, in a despatch to Admiral Struble, estimated that 60 per cent of Task Force 77's aircraft had not been profitably employed in the Eighth Army area due to the saturation of the area by friendly aircraft and due to communications difficulty with the tactical air controllers. He reported 100 per cent effectiveness in the Tenth Corps area.

Admiral Struble therefore notified Fifth Air Force Headquarters that because of the stack-up of UN aircraft and unsatisfactory communications in the Eighth Army area reported by Task Force 77 pilots, he was directing Admiral Ewen to adjust the percentage of air effort directed between east and west as control capabilities appeared to warrant.

In reply, General Timberlake said that:

> . . . due to the fluid ground situation, it is impossible to determine the exact status of tactical air control parties in the Eighth Army area. Many of them may have been lost or made inoperative due to enemy action. Every effort is being made to determine status of TACPs and to make replacements.[6]

Meanwhile, Fifth Air Force issued instructions giving naval flights priority of employment as soon as they reached the target area. Fifth Air Force further stated that due to critical condition in EUSAK area, the "effort of CTF-77 should be divided during the next few days."

Admiral Struble answered that in view of the cut-off position of the First Marine Division and their urgent need for air assistance, *all* fast carrier flights for the following day, 3 December, would report initially to the Tenth Corps. Thereafter, some flights would be directed to proceed on to the Eighth Army area if they were not urgently required by Tenth Corps.

On 3 December, Major General Harris again sent a despatch to Admiral Joy urgently recommending that the "main fast carrier effort be made in support of First Marine Division. Navy aircraft particularly desired by First Marine Division, because of familiarity with their report system. Desire Marine shore-based air and ship squadrons operating continuously this area."

Admiral Joy was kept informed of developments and concurred with Struble and Harris as did Lieutenant General Timberlake, who on 4 December in reply to General Harris' request sent the following despatch:

> Concur main effort fast carriers in support First Marine Division during critical period of withdrawal.

Once again, as during the Inchon assault, Marine and naval airmen would perform close air support for the First Marine Division, using Navy-Marine doctrine.

The Breakout Begins

At 0705, on 2 December, convoys of the trapped Fifth and Seventh Marines, loaded with their wounded and their equipment, prepared to move out from Yudam-ni. Before them and their immediate destination of Hagaru-ri lay fifteen miles of tortuous, icy roads, through mountains literally swarming with Chinese Red troops. Flights of close support aircraft from *Philippine Sea, Leyte, Badoeng Strait,* and Marine flights from Yonpo headed toward the cut-off Marines to spearhead the breakout.

As soon as the planes of Task Force 77 appeared over Yudam-ni, the Marines commenced their long march to the sea—distance, sixty miles.

Marine rifle units flushed enemy snipers from the nearby hills and seized the high ground on the flanks of the long column. Supporting weapons and vehicles formed the center of a moving perimeter. Overhead, 20 to 50 aircraft circled the long column, ready on a second's notice to deliver rockets, napalm, 20-mm. shells, or 500-pound bombs. Indeed, during daylight operations, the Chinese divisions who were embarked on an offensive mission were forced to take the defensive.

For instance, when the Marines encountered their first heavily-defended roadblock in the late afternoon of 2 December, 22 Navy and Marine aircraft, following an artillery barrage, pounded the enemy position with bombs and napalm tanks.

REDEPLOYMENT FROM HUNGNAM BY SEA. *At top,* North Korean refugees leaving Hungnam. *Center,* high speed transport *Begor* awaits last cargo as explosion rips harbor. *Below,* Navy landing ships wait on beach to evacuate Tenth Corps troops and supplies.

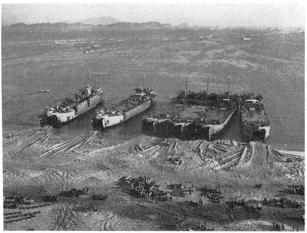

WONSAN WATERFRONT. *At top,* pre-invasion view of the city shows damage which, by war's end, would multiply many fold. *Center,* beached LST's unload men and equipment at Wonsan. *Below,* a General Sherman tank with dozer blade rumbles down the ramp of *LST 914.*

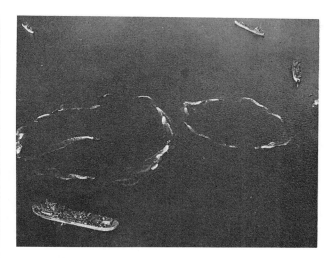

BLOODLESS INVASION OF WONSAN. *At top,* LCVPs circle in transport area awaiting signal to proceed to line of departure. *Center,* landing craft laden with Marines approach the beach. *Below,* Marines wade ashore in unopposed landing. Possession of Wonsan was a logistics prerequisite to operations in northeast Korea.

FLEET STALWARTS. *At top,* LSD *Comstock,* flagship for U N forces at Chinnampo and Wonsan, also repair vessel and mother ship for MSB's of MinRon 3. *Center,* AM *Murrelet* received Navy Unit Citation for 1952 achievements. In one day she captured six sampans and 26 prisoners. *Below,* AGC *Mount McKinley* was in Japanese waters at war's beginning, later served as flagship at Wonsan and Hungnam.

Close on the heels of the air strike, the Leathernecks jumped off in assault. The Chinese who survived the aerial attack were quickly despatched and set running by bayonet-wielding Marines in hand-to-hand fighting.

Throughout the day of 2 December, as many as 40 to 60 tactical aircraft constantly circled the Fifth and Seventh Marines.

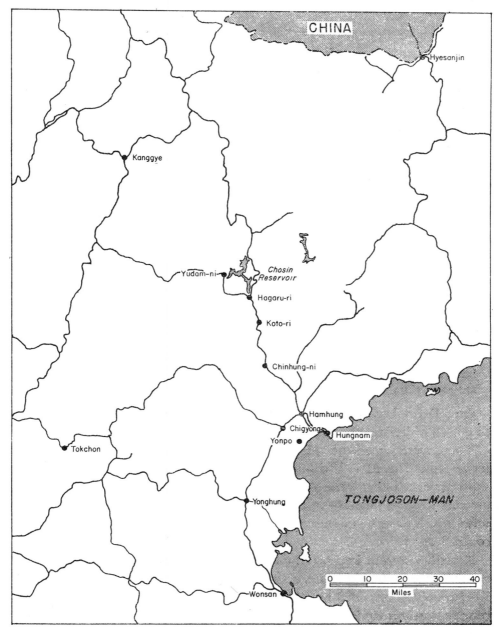

THE BREAKOUT AT HUNGNAM

Planes from *Leyte* and *Philippine Sea* spent most of their time blasting small buildings around Hagaru-ri that housed enemy troops.

"Occasionally we caught the white-uniformed Chinese troops in the open," said the commanding officer of *Leyte's* VF-33, Commander Horace H. Epes. "I vividly recall catching a couple of Red soldiers hotfooting it down the road carrying a long pole with a big kettle of what looked like soup—that no one ever drank."

At the same time, heavily-laden Air Force C-119s dropped cargoes of ammunition, medical supplies, water, food, gasoline, and C-rations in multi-colored parachutes; observation aircraft cork-screwed through the falling chutes; helicopters fluttered down to pick up the seriously wounded.

When darkness came, however, and the planes went back to their bases, the Marines were left to their own resources. As a result of the 2 December fighting, however, the enemy had been so badly mangled that he was unable to seriously threaten the Marine column during the night.

On 3 December, the pattern of the previous day was repeated. The Marines continued their advance, employing the deadly combination of air and ground attack. By 1900 on 3 December, the head of the Marine column had reached Hagaru-ri. The rear elements of the column did not arrive in the village until mid-afternoon of the next day.

On 4 December, the commanding general of the First Marine Aircraft Wing sent the following despatch to Commander Task Force 77:

> I was up on the hill today (at Hagaru-ri) and saw the Fifth and Seventh Marines return. They thanked God for air. I don't think they could have made it as units without air support. The next job is to get them off this hill. I want to be able to cover their flanks and rear one hundred per cent, and to blast any major resistance to their front. Can use all the help you can give me until they get down. Tell your pilots they are doing a magnificent job.

On 6 December, the First Marine Division departed Hagaru with 45 miles to go. Its objective—the next way station, Koto-ri.

There were some innovations in the close air support procedure for this movement. The Marine column moved out three battalions abreast. Forward air controllers were placed with each flanking battalion, and tactical air coordinators flew ahead of the columns' flanks. The air coordinators' mission was to seek out enemy forces beyond the visual range of forward air controllers.

A further step to improve the control of close air support was the use of an airborne tactical air direction center. For this purpose a four-engined R5D transport provided by VMR-152 was hastily equipped with additional communications equipment.

By 6 December, the "Flying TADC" was ready for flight operations. From its orbiting station directly above the Marine column, this novel control agency was able to communicate to all flight leaders and ground units simultaneously. In mountainous terrain, where some types of radios were limited in range, this new airborne link made a significant contribution to the air support effort.

The column had advanced only 2,000 yards when it was suddenly stopped by a concentration of enemy fire coming from a ravine 100 yards east of the road.

Friendly troops were pinned down within 75 yards of the enemy gun positions. One of the Marine forward air controllers, who was riding in a jeep immediately behind the lead tank of the column, contacted an airborne tactical air coordinator, briefed him on the enemy concentration, and directed him in on a dummy run. When the tactical air coordinator had definitely located the target, the forward air controller ordered a live run with 20-mm. fire and napalm.

Meanwhile, other Navy and Marine aircraft monitored the radio net to familiarize themselves with the target. At this time, *Leyte* had eight planes and VMF-214 had eighteen Corsairs on station. These planes were divided into three flights of eight aircraft orbiting at eight thousand, nine thousand, and ten thousand feet respectively.

A flight of eight planes from VMF-214 attacked first with rockets and proximity-fuzed 500-pound bombs. The second flight from VMF-214 was then called in and asked to use a new technique. In an effort to conserve ammunition and to keep armed aircraft on station as long as possible, every other plane was asked to make a dummy run. The second VMF-214 flight did so, but this plan worked no better than the first; pilots were thereupon asked to resume firing on every run.

An hour went by, and still the column was pinned down. Koto-ri was eight miles away and the precious daylight hours were dwindling. After a hurried conference with one of his forward air controllers, Colonel Litzenberg directed his three battalion front to move forward as the aircraft made firing runs perpendicular to the line of advance. The enemy guns were only 100 yards from the Marines.

Pilots of the next flight were the planes from the *Leyte*. They were informed of Colonel Litzenberg's decision and ordered to attack.

"My F4Us were fully loaded," said CDR Epes, "and at 5,000 feet there wasn't much margin of power. It was cold as hell in the airplane, but it was colder on the ground—25 degrees below zero, with one foot of snow. The long Marine column was preparing to attack when we arrived.

"A ground controller called me by voice radio.

" 'I'm in the lead jeep; I have a fluorescent panel marker on my hood. Fly over me and rock your wings. I see you,' he said. 'Now come over me on a heading of 180 degrees. Now push over; now commence firing.'

"Our empty cases fell among the Marines, our bullets and light bombs landed on the Chinese 50 yards ahead of them.

"Then the ground controller said, 'Come back with napalm.' That really worried us. Sometimes napalm spreads for a block. We were afraid we would burn up our own troops, but we complied. After the first Corsair's napalm dropped, the ground controller snapped, 'Move it closer.'

"We dropped napalm bombs on the sides of the hills, with Marines all along the road directly beneath. If the temperature hadn't been 25 degrees below, I don't believe the Marines could have stood the heat. Maybe it felt good.

"That sort of bombing spelled out close air support for the Marines. They pinpointed the target, told us exactly where to drop."

While planes from *Leyte's* VF-33 made firing runs, ground troops commenced firing. Eighty-one millimeter mortar shell trajectories arced higher than the low-flying attack planes. As an attacking plane would pass, Marine mortarmen aimed at the plane's tails, and by this improvised rule-of-thumb they effectively lobbed in their shells before the next airplane made its run.

Under this cloud burst of shellfire, enemy gunners at last took cover and the column's point again moved southward. New flights of close support aircraft from the carriers reported and took up the attack; aircraft control was passed rearward along the column from one forward air controller to another. By this continuous aerial bombardment, the Marines were able to neutralize and pass the enemy batteries south of Hagaru-ri.

Throughout the Marines' withdrawal to Hungnam, Chinese troops were never able to effectively counter the Navy-Marine system of close air support. The communists' best defensive weapons were their rifles and light machine guns.

Two carrier pilots were lost due to enemy action—*Leyte's* Ensign Jesse L. Brown, while flying a close support mission near Hagaru-ri on 4 December; and LCDR Ralph Maxwell Bagwell, commanding officer of Attack Squadron 35, on 12 December. Squadron pilots saw Bagwell crawl free of his inverted aircraft and take refuge beneath a nearby railroad bridge. But before a friendly helicopter could reach Bagwell, *Leyte* pilots witnessed his capture by a group of 20 enemy soldiers.*

Ensign Brown, the first Negro pilot to fly for the Navy, had been forced to make an emergency landing in a mountainous area northwest of Chosin

* Bagwell survived and was repatriated 5 September 1953 after the end of the Korean hostilities.

Reservoir. Pilots circling overhead observed that Brown was alive but apparently unable to free himself from the wreckage. They observed also that his plane was beginning to burn slowly. The temperature was below freezing, darkness was approaching, the terrain was unfamiliar, and Brown was down five miles behind enemy lines. With complete disregard for such hazards and without hesitation, LTJG Thomas J. Hudner decided to go to Brown's assistance. After making a successful wheels-up crash landing, Hudner found that Brown's leg was caught in the buckled fuselage and it was impossible to extricate the injured man from his cockpit. Hudner packed snow around Brown's fuselage in an attempt to extinguish the fire. Returning to his own plane, whose radio was still operative, Hudner requested cutting tools, along with a rescue helicopter. The helicopter, flown by LT Charles Ware, arrived shortly, but even with the cutting equipment provided, Brown could not be rescued from the wreckage before he died. Hudner was returned to safety by the helicopter.

For his selfless efforts in behalf of his friend and fellow pilot, President Truman later presented LTJG Hudner with the nation's highest military honor, the Congressional Medal of Honor.

It took twenty-two hours for the Marine column to cover the nine-and-one-half-mile road from Hagaru-ri to Koto-ri. The trip had cost the Marines 600 wounded, all of whom were deposited in Koto-ri's hospital tents for air evacuation.

The temporary airstrips at Hagaru-ri and Koto-ri proved invaluable for the air evacuation of wounded and frostbite cases. Marine engineers had bulldozed the airstrip at Hagaru-ri during late November in anticipation of a sharp increase in supply requirements for Tenth Corps elements in this sector. When the Red Chinese attacked, the airfield was usable by C-47 type aircraft. The shorter Koto-ri strip was improved solely for the air evacuation of wounded.

Casualties had also been air evacuated from Yudam-ni by helicopter and light aircraft to Hagaru-ri. A low, solid overcast usually hid the peaks rising above the Chosin plateau. At all of these improvised fields, aircraft operated under the most hazardous of flying conditions. From the short air strips hacked from the frozen and rocky terrain by Marine bulldozers, 21 Air Force C-47s from FEAF combat cargo command operated. The Koto-ri strip was so short, in fact, that one of the forward air controllers, who was also a qualified carrier landing signal officer, guided the planes in much the same manner as if they were landing aboard an aircraft carrier. From these strips Air Force C-47s and Marine R4Ds airlifted a total of 4,675 Marine and

Army wounded to safety. Light observation planes, helicopters, and three TBM aircraft contributed, flying out 163 casualties during the first ten days of December.

Breakout Completed

On the morning of 8 December the withdrawing Marine column departed Koto-ri, moving down the slippery, ice-covered mountain road toward Chinhung-ni. Chinese troops were still resisting every foot of the way. Thirty-six miles to go.

One third of the distance had been covered when the column encountered a blown bridge. Only a new bridge could prevent the abandonment of all the Marines' heavy equipment, much of which had been protected at great human sacrifice. Because of the steep cliffs rising on either side of the road, no vehicles, tanks, or artillery could bypass the gorge.

Eight Air Force C-119s were immediately despatched to Koto-ri, where each "flying boxcar" dropped a two-ton span. While under intense fire, Marine engineers built two treadway bridges which enabled the Leathernecks to cross the abyss on 9 December and thus avoid what might have been one of the most serious setbacks to the withdrawal.

At dusk on 9 December, lead elements of the Seventh Regiment attacking south joined elements of the 1st Battalion, 1st Marines, attacking north from Chinhung-ni. The men of the two Marine Regiments joined hands on a nameless ridge.

The breakout had been achieved. And in that achievement one thing stood out clearly: air-ground cooperation had reached a degree of perfection that would stand as a classic in the history of close air support.

During the Marines' withdrawal, more than 200 aircraft were frequently employed daily to attack enemy troops and installations blocking the southward march to the sea.

The amount of close air support furnished the Marines reached a pinnacle on 4 December when 239 individual close support sorties were controlled by the air support section of Marine Air Tactical Control Squadron Two. Of these flights, 128 were flown from the fast carriers, 34 by the escort carriers, and 77 were flown by the Yonpo-based Marines.

The effectiveness of the air contribution given the First Marine Division is best summarized by the report of General Oliver P. Smith, Commanding General First Marine Division:

> . . . During this phase, reliance upon support by Marine and naval tactical aircraft was stressed more than ever before. This fact was largely the result of the over-all nature of the operation which, in the final analysis, was characterized by its being beyond the range of naval gunfire support. As a result,

during daylight hours, air was the predominant supporting arm throughout the period. . . . As a result of utilizing the same aircraft day after day, and committing them to support of front-line units during their time on station, the majority of pilots in the First Marine Aircraft Wing had the qualifications desired of an airborne tactical air coordinator. These pilots knew the tactical situation through daily contact with it; they knew the position of each unit and could accurately judge those localities where targets were most likely to appear and what type of target it would be. This unity between ground and air elements became nearly ideal during the advance from Yudam-ni to the south, and it is no exaggeration to state that the successful conclusion of this operation would have been nearly impossible without the amount and quality of close air support that was provided. It was an ideal combat example of the ultimate perfection of the air-ground team needed to defeat an aggressive determined enemy.[7]

Tenth Corps' Seventh Division Commander, Brigadier General Homer W. Kiefer, tried to parallel as nearly as possible the Marine's system of controlling close air support. Kiefer stated that this system permitted him to place tactical air control parties within each infantry battalion. Such placement proved to be the ideal and gave the battalion commander a means of controlling and coordinating the close air support he received. General Kiefer considered it worthy of note that "in 57 days of combat, 1,024 sorties were flown by Marine Corsair aircraft in close support of the division, without a single casualty among our own troops due to friendly air action.

"This record I attribute to the fact that adequate control was available with frontline units," wrote General Kiefer. "In many instances, Marine planes were bombing and strafing within two hundred yards of our frontlines. . . . The Marine system of control, in my estimation, approaches the ideal, and I firmly believe that a similar system should be adopted as standard for Army divisions."[8]

Credit for the Marines' successful withdrawal from the Chosin trap might be attributed to many interlocking factors—the Marines' discipline, fighting spirit, and firepower, the close air support rendered by Navy and Marine aircraft, the air logistics and rescue support by the United States Air Force.

Once again, the mobility, flexibility, and firepower of the mobile air base had been demonstrated. The carriers of Task Forces 77 and 95 had been able to move quickly to the danger area, and to supply the abundant and accurate close air support which, as General Smith stated, was vital in extricating the First Marine Division from North Korea.

Preparations for the Pull-Out

In early November, a vague premonition that all was not well in North Korea had begun to disturb several of the senior naval officers in the Far

East theater. The isolated reports of the presence of Red Chinese forces, the absence of serious enemy resistance, the gap between Eighth Army and Tenth Corps, the threats of impending action by the Peking radio, presaged trouble to some.

Following the Wonsan landing, Admiral Joy invited Admiral Doyle to return to Tokyo, but, said Doyle, "I did not go because I was uneasy. A short time later Joy came out to visit me, bringing with him the Secretary of the Navy, Mr. Francis P. Matthews, and Senator Claude Pepper."

The visitors lunched aboard Doyle's flagship *Mount McKinley*, and afterwards they were taken into the chart room to look at a map of Korea.

"We pin-pointed our own forces ashore," said Doyle, "and explained as much as we knew about the location of enemy forces. At this time, I pointed out that we were uneasy about the division between the Eighth Army and the Tenth Corps. We didn't know what lay between them. There had been no link-up."[9]

The first precautions were taken on 28 November. Admiral Joy alerted Admiral Doyle to be prepared for redeployment of UN forces out of North Korea. Doyle was instructed to prepare either for an administrative operation or for emergency measures, and told that he would exercise over-all control of any redeployment. He was also informed that he would direct any amphibious efforts on either the west or the east coast. Doyle in turn asked Rear Admiral Lyman A. Thackrey, CTG 90.1, to direct any west coast redeployment.

The following day, Admiral Joy again despatched Doyle advising him that the military situation in North Korea was deteriorating rapidly. Joy considered it desirable that all ships of Task Force 90 be placed on six hours' notice. This alert was applicable to all ships, both in Korean and Japanese waters, for at this time much of Task Force 90's amphibious shipping was in Japan for upkeep and replenishment.

Admiral Joy also requested the recall of the *Boxer* (CVA-21) and other ships because of, as Admiral Joy put it, "the critical and rapidly deteriorating situation of the Eighth Army and the desperate situation of the Tenth Corps. I felt the ground forces needed all the help the Navy could give them in the way of air and gunfire support."

Although some objected to returning the *Boxer* immediately to Korea, CNO Sherman, when acquainted with Joy's request, directed their return.

"The uncertainty of the future and the possibility of Soviet intervention were factors in Sherman's decision," said Joy.

The military situation continued to worsen. On 30 November, accordingly, all Task Force 90 ships were ordered underway for Korea.

From early despatches, it appeared that Eighth Army was in the most critical condition. Because of the limited port facilities on the west coast, Doyle considered that the Army would have to be under extreme hardship before it would call for a sealift from the small harbors that were available on North Korea's west coast.

"At the most, they might redeploy a few remnants by sea," said Doyle, "but not the entire Eighth Army with all its supplies and equipment. I therefore sent mostly small, shallow draft ships to the west coast and made preparations to conduct large-scale redeployment operations in the Hungnam area." The anchorage area of the Hungnam harbor needed to be expanded and the minesweepers had to clear gunfire support channels. "When this was accomplished," said Doyle, "Hungnam was an ideal port for redeployment."

In a conference on 8 December aboard the *Mount McKinley,* Joy told Struble and Doyle that in view of Eighth Army's fast movement south, no major sealift effort was now needed on the west coast. Instead, the major effort would be made on the east coast at Hungnam.

The selection of Hungnam as the port of embarkation and evacuation was logical for several reasons. It was only four miles away from General Almond's Tenth Corps headquarters at Hamhung; it was approximately the same distance from Yonpo airfield which could serve as the air control center until operations were transferred to the Fleet after the airfield was abandoned. Hungnam was tactically feasible as an assembly and loading point for the Tenth Corps units which had fanned northward out of Wonsan and Iwon. And lastly, Hungnam was ideal because of its port facilities. Although small, the port was excellent and well protected. The tidal range was less than a foot and berthing space was available alongside the docks for seven ships. By double-banking ships, four additional ships could be simultaneously loaded. Other beach areas of the port were suitable for LST operations.

Hungnam Redeployment Orders Issued

On 9 December, General MacArthur issued orders specifying General Almond's mission for withdrawal: Almond was to be lifted from North Korea as he had come—by sea. After his arrival in South Korea he was to assemble his units in the Pusan-Usan-Masan area in South Korea and report to the Commanding General Eighth Army. The First ROK Corps was excepted from this order and it was to be released upon arrival at Samchok to report to the ROK Army.

COMNAVFE now assigned complete responsibility for the east coast redeployment operation to Commander Task Force 90, Admiral Doyle. He was given control of all air and naval gunfire support. He was made responsible for the protection of shipping en route to the debarkation ports and for coordinating all withdrawal movements with the Commanding General Tenth Corps, General Almond.

In contrast to the command arrangement for Inchon and Wonsan, Hungnam had no joint task force commander assigned.

Commander Seventh Fleet would provide Commander Task Force 90 with aircraft support and gunfire support ships on a "when and if they could be spared from carrier task forces" basis. The responsibility for coordinating naval air operations with the Air Force remained with Commander Seventh Fleet.

The decision for this arrangement was Admiral Joy's and it was based on the overall threat confronting Naval Forces Far East.

"It must be remembered," said Admiral Joy, "that the Chinese intervention put a new aspect on the Korean war as well as the global situation. The future was cloudy to say the least. Some sources of information even felt that it marked the beginning of World War III with Soviet participation. A Chinese attempt to capture Formosa was another possibility. I therefore felt that the 7th Fleet should be free to leave the confined waters of the Sea of Japan at a moment's notice to proceed to any more seriously threatened area in the Far East.

"It was also felt that the Hungnam evacuation could be handled satisfactorily if necessary without the support of the 7th Fleet since heavy enemy opposition was not a probability."

The Navy's Three-Ring Circus (Inchon—Wonsan—Hungnam)

As Admiral Doyle completed plans to redeploy Tenth Corps from Wonsan and Hungnam on Korea's east coast, Rear Admiral Lyman A. Thackrey, Commander Amphibious Group Three, began to redeploy elements of the Eighth Army at Chinnampo and Inchon. Redeployment of 1,800 Army and Navy port personnel and 5,900 ROK troops was completed at Chinnampo on 5 December.

The Chinnampo evacuation was carried out by five British Commonwealth destroyers (three Canadian and two Australian) and one U.S. destroyer when, in darkness and through the swept channel of a minefield, they navigated 30 miles of the shallow water of the Daido Ko estuary to cover the withdrawal of civilians, non-essential military personnel, and wounded from the Pyongyang area.

The evacuation force was led by HMCS *Cayuga* (CAPT J. V. Brock, D.S.C., RCN) with HMCS *Athabaskan*, HMCS *Sioux*, HMAS *Warramunga*, (CAPT O. H. Becher, D.S.C., RAN) HMAS *Bataan** (CDR W. B. M. Marks, RAN) and the USS *Forrest Royal* (CDR O. O. Liebschner). The five ships

* HMAS *Bataan* operated for 12 days (13-25 March 1951) with the USS *Bataan*.

plowed through heavy seas and snowstorms to the mouth of the Taedong River, with orders to provide necessary gunfire support and anti-aircraft fire during the loading of casualties and port personnel.

During the operation, Sea Furies and Fireflies from the British light fleet carrier HMS *Theseus*, flag of Vice Admiral W. G. Andrewes (who had just been promoted), flew air patrols over the flotilla.

It had been Captain Brock's intention to transit the estuary in daylight rather than face a night passage of the area with its treacherous shoals and minefields. However, on receiving a despatch that the withdrawal program at Chinnampo was ahead of schedule, Brock decided to risk a night voyage up river.

Slowly, the six ships began the passage of the twisting swept channel through the minefield which in many places was only 500 yards wide. Visibility was almost nil, and it was three o'clock in the morning before lookouts of the four ships that completed the journey (*Cayuga, Bataan, Forrest Royal, Sioux*) could make out dock buildings dimly in the darkness. Captain Brock took up position, and his ships were at action stations waiting for dawn and possible enemy air attack.

"Everything was quiet," said CDR Marks, "with members of ships loading under the full brilliancy of the arc lights."

That day the transports were loaded with wounded Republic of Korea civilian refugees, and military personnel. Altogether about 7,700 personnel were evacuated from Chinnampo without interference by the enemy.

When the last transport had left the port, Captain Brock decided to remain at anchor for another night in the dock area, and next morning, after ordering the remaining civilian population out of the military area, his ships shelled oil storage tanks, dock and harbor installations, and supply dumps. The commercial and civilian parts of the town were left untouched.

On 7 December, the outloading of all Army stores at Inchon began. By 31 December, 32,428 personnel, 1,103 vehicles, and 54,741 tons of cargo had been outloaded.[10]

Inchon's port was not to be closed until 5 January. As at Hungnam, important port facilities were then destroyed to prevent their use by the enemy. By this time a grand total of 68,913 personnel, 1,404 vehicles, and 62,144 tons of cargo were redeployed from Inchon to Taechon and Pusan.[11]

At Wonsan, outloading of UN personnel and material at the port area began on 3 December 1950.

Covering fire was furnished by the cruiser *St. Paul* (CAPT Chester C. Smith) and the destroyers *Charles S. Sperry* (DD 697) (CDR Robert M. Brownlie) and *Zellars* (DD 777) (CDR Fred D. Michael). Shellfire from these three ships effectively isolated the city from enemy attack during the day, and at night they fired star shells to illuminate suspicious areas. Their effectiveness is testified to by the fact that no enemy attack developed either during the day or the night.

The methodical and unhurried loading at Wonsan is well described in the action report of Commander Transport Division Eleven (CAPT Albert E. Jarrell):

"We commenced loading Korean civilians aboard the SS *Lane Victory* at anchor at 0500 on December 7. We had previously made arrangements with the local police to screen the civilians to be evacuated. Specifically, only those persons whom the North Koreans might classify as "enemy"—with all the finality which that word implies—were to be taken out. Originally, we'd expected about 1,000 civilians, but it became quickly apparent that this number would be greatly exceeded.

"That excess produced another neuralgic pain—if we refused asylum to any of those selected, our refusal would be two strikes against them after we left. I therefore gave orders to continue loading to capacity. By midnight, 7,009 people—many of them women and children—were embarked. There were many more than that still left. I estimated that the entire population of Wonsan (75,000) plus an equal number from outlying towns, wanted desperately to leave. About 20,000 were still clambering about the barbed wire and tank barriers long after we were chockablock with passengers."[12]

In addition to the 7,009 Korean civilians, the outloading at Wonsan included 3,834 military personnel, 1,146 vehicles and 10,013 bulk tons of cargo.

The Wonsan operation, in addition to clearing UN forces out of the Wonsan area, had another beneficial effect. It had produced a miniature dress rehearsal for the Hungnam show soon to follow.

At Wonsan, naval gunfire had held the North Korean forces at such a respectable distance from the UN perimeter that UN troops were never seriously threatened. The entire operation was completed without either the loss of a single life or the necessity to sacrifice any of UN's valuable equipment.

In the Hungnam operation Rear Admiral Doyle exercised control through various control stations: an operations unit aboard his flagship, *Mount McKinley;* a control vessel, a beachmaster, a port director, an embarkation control liaison officer, and an MSTS control board.

The flagship's operations officer coordinated all shipments, assigned anchorages, issued docking instructions, prepared and issued sailing orders for all Navy and SCAJAP vessels, and supervised the operations of all the other control stations. The beachmaster controlled LST operations, the port director berthed the ship, and the embarkation control liaison officer linked the staffs of Doyle and Almond. MSTS office handled MSTS shipping. It was a well-coordinated team of experts who knew their amphibious doctrine backward as well as forward.

These control stations went into action the moment an arriving ship entered the outer harbor. The several control stations were interconnected by radio and could speak to one another. The operations officer told the port director what berth the incoming ship was to occupy. The ship was then ordered to proceed from its anchorage and await the harbor pilot near the breakwater. The harbor pilot, with the assistance of tugs, then docked the ship. Whereupon, Task Force 90 and Tenth Corps officers went to work to load the ship and assign it a "chop" time for departure from the dock.

Ships arriving in Hungnam were directed to be ready for immediate movement on sudden notice, and to maintain a 24-hour visual watch for sailing signals. Each commanding officer or master was supplied the latest hydrographic information.[13]

The control officer in charge of redeployment operations ashore, representing General Almond, was Marine Colonel E. H. Forney, whose headquarters was a shed near the dock area. Forney was responsible for continuous operation of the Hungnam port; for the withdrawal to staging areas of Tenth Corps elements; for the loading of troops on assigned shipping; and for the evacuation of refugees and the removal of all material.

Practically all cargo, with the exception of ammunition, was loaded alongside the dock on the LST beaches. Personnel were loaded into the APAs and AKAs at anchorages as close to the beach as possible. To assist the loading operation, the USS *Foss* (DE 59) was placed alongside the dock to supply electrical power. The *Shimano Maru* served as mothership for 1,200 Japanese stevedores, who helped with the outloading of supplies and equipment.

As a unit ashore became alerted for embarkation, Forney's loading section issued instructions; the movement section directed traffic to the assigned area for staging out; and the rations section supplied the needs of the troops awaiting their turn in the tent city which had sprung up near the dock area.

General Almond's operation order called for the First Marine Division and the ROK regiments to embark first. They would be followed by the Seventh and Third Infantry Divisions in that order. Thus, Third Infantry would have final responsibility for the Hungnam defense perimeter.

Marines started to load aboard waiting transports as soon as they arrived in the Hungnam area on 10 December. It was their fourth embarkation within five months. Marine embarkation officers could load now by sight without the aid of stowage diagrams.

Marine drivers were embarked with their vehicles; troops were billeted in the cargo spaces of commercial ships. Between 4,500 and 5,500 Leathernecks were embarked on each of the three APs. Seven commercial cargo vessels, thirteen LSTs, three LSDs, an APA, and an AKA were also assigned as lift for the First Marine Division.

The task of loading the Marines was completed by the evening of 14 December, and on the morning of the 15th the last ships with elements of the First Marine Division sailed for Pusan.

The ROK regiments departed Hungnam on 17 December, the U.S. Seventh Division on 21 December, and the U.S. Third Division on 24 December.

Wall of Fire Around Hungnam

On 11 December, the Navy made final plans to lay down an aerial canopy and a curtain of steel around the Hungnam perimeter—a canopy of naval aircraft from seven carriers, plus a steel curtain of shellfire from thirteen ships.

Rear Admiral E. C. Ewen's Task Force 77 had grown from two to four fast carrier by early December: *Philippine Sea* and *Leyte* (both of which had been supporting the troops ashore from the Sea of Japan since early November); and now *Valley Forge* (hastily recalled from the United States with Air Group Two embarked) and *Princeton* (with Air Group 19, CDR Richard C. Merrick, aboard). CVG-19 first saw action on 5 December.

In accordance with Commander Seventh Fleet's operation plan of 12 December, the fast carriers were given the task during daylight hours of flying close air support and air cover for forces inside the embarkation areas. Outside the embarkation area, Task Force 77 aircraft were ordered to interdict enemy supply lines, support friendly ground operations, and provide air cover for the escort carriers and the shipping to and from the embarkation area. In company with aircraft from Fifth Air Force, they were also to provide heckling missions at night.

Rear Admiral Richard W. Ruble's escort carrier group (TG 96.8), originally composed of *Sicily* and *Badoeng Strait*, was now augmented by the light carrier *Bataan*. This force added additional air cover for the ground forces and the armada of ships in the Hungnam port area.

In charge of providing gunfire support was Rear Admiral Roscoe H. Hillenkoetter, USN. Before the evacuation task was finished on 24 December, Hillenkoetter's force included the battleship *Missouri*, the heavy cruisers *St. Paul* and *Rochester;* the destroyers *Forrest Royal, Norris, Borie, English, Lind, Hank* and *Massey;* and the rocket ships, LSMRs *401, 403,* and *404.* The ships of this Hungnam gunfire support group were stationed where they could deliver emergency support to the Tenth Corps, and at the same time provide protection in the event of enemy air attack.

No naval gunfire was requested until 15 December. On that date Hillenkoetter's gunfire support group commenced "deep" support fire at ranges up to ten miles delivering both 8-inch interdiction and harassing gunfire as well as 5-inch illumination at night. For this gunfire the ships were deployed to preselected stations at sea and in the swept channel. The recently swept fishing areas allowed the bombarding ships to maneuver in an area ten miles to the north and ten miles to the south of Hungnam.

As the operation progressed and the perimeter contracted, fire support ships were moved closer ashore to obtain better firing positions. LSMRs blasted the reverse slopes near Hungnam. On two occasions the three rocket ships were used to fire barrages on the right flank, onto the high ground overlooking Hungnam where enemy troops were reportedly concentrating.

Missouri began main battery fire on 23 December at road targets between Ori-ri and Hungnam. "Though we didn't really need her firepower," said Doyle, "General Almond kept suggesting that we call in the *Missouri*. So I called for her and gave her a target selection. She quickly got a hit on an enemy troop shelter, and the air spotter reported that the Chinese Communists were running out of it in all directions."

In addition to her main battery fire, *Missouri's* 5-inch batteries contributed harassing and illumination fire in covering the withdrawal of the last ground elements.

As Tenth Corps artillery was loaded aboard ships and withdrawn between 22 and 24 December, naval gunfire took over observed firing and close support. The shore fire control parties reported the naval gunfire as "very effective" and credited it with "destroying large numbers of enemy troops." In at least one instance, naval gunfire was reported to have broken up an enemy attack of larger than company size.

"Gunfire support was an around-the-clock daylight activity," said Captain Bruce C. Wiggin of CTF 90's staff, "and a precautionary measure at night. Illumination was vital and necessary beyond the defensive perimeter, especially during the darkness.

"Ships received their target instructions from specific requests ashore and from the flagship. We were never sure of the amount of opposition that might develop, although we never expected an all-out Chinese attack on the perimeter. After all, the enemy was not stupid. Nevertheless, we made preparations for the Dunkirk-sort of thing.

"In retrospect, it seems probable that the Chinese knew they could not interfere with the redeployment. Their losses would certainly have been greater than those they could have hoped to inflict. Fire power from the sea would have dwarfed what they had already absorbed during their attack on the Marines at Chosin."[14]

Doyle was quite disturbed about the North Korean civilians pouring into Hungnam. "If the Chinese had ever made a severe attack—and they might have," said Doyle, "there could have been mass slaughter of many of the civilians in the area. Military men very often have to make tough military decisions of this nature, and I am very happy that I did not have to make that one."

For the final D-day of withdrawal, 24 December, a concentrated naval gunfire barrage was maintained in a strip approximately 2,500 yards wide and 3,000 yards from the beaches and harbor. The only enemy troop movement to be observed on the final day was seen by Admiral Doyle and General Almond from the flagship *Mount McKinley* at the final withdrawal. "As we pulled out with all friendly troops embarked," said Doyle, "Almond and I, through our binoculars, saw Chinese Communist troops coming over the ridge behind Hungnam, only three or four miles away. I asked my gunfire support officer CDR Arlie Capps to direct some gunfire in the direction of the approaching troops."

Destructive bombardment of the port area itself was also begun. Ships' gunnery officers concentrated on the destruction of railroad cars and locomotives. Demolition crews ashore blasted everything of military value.

At no time did the enemy attempt to interfere with the Hungnam evacuation either from the air or from the sea.

"It is a mistake, however, to say there was *no* opposition at Hungnam on the ground," said Admiral Doyle. "Although the First Marine Division had rendered seven Chinese Communist Divisions ineffective, attacks were made on our perimeter every night during the period of withdrawal. Our ships were constantly called on for gunfire, rockets and star shells."

The gunfire support ships' only casualty occurred at 0645 on 24 December aboard USS *St. Paul* (CA-73) when a projectile from one of her 5-inch twin mounts hit one of her identical mounts, making it inoperative. Shell fragments ripped off one foot of a gun barrel, punctured numerous small holes in *St. Paul's* superstructure, severed one of the radars, and slightly injured four members of the crew.

From 7 to 24 December, the gunfire support ships of Task Force 90 fired a grand total of 162 rounds of 16-inch; 2,932 rounds of 8-inch; 18,637 rounds of 5-inch; 71 rounds of 3-inch; 185 rounds of 40-mm. and 1,462 rockets.

By way of comparison, approximately 800 more rounds of 8-inch, and 12,800 more rounds of 5-inch were expended in defensive fire support at Hungnam than had been expended in support of the Inchon amphibious assault.

"It should be borne in mind," said Doyle, "that Inchon only lasted a couple of days while our fire support effort at Hungnam lasted from the 15th to the 24th of December. All of it was 'call-fire' as requested by the troops. Our logistic forces deserve great credit for doing a magnificent job keeping us supplied with ammunition."

On 15 December, Admiral Doyle assumed control of all air support operations within a 35 mile radius of Hungnam. This included both the close and deep support efforts of the carriers of Task Force 77 and Task Group 96.8, the night hecklers from both FAFIK and Task Force 77, and all reconnaissance and transient aircraft flying over the area. In conjunction with the naval gunfire, the mission of the aircraft was to prevent interference with the evacuation.

The contribution rendered by air is typified by such reports as that of CDR W. F. Madden on 10 December: his flight of seven Corsairs had "strafed, rocketed, and napalmed enemy troops . . . ;" by CDR Epes whose four Corsairs strafed and bombed one hundred horses and unnumbered enemy troops; by LCDR H. H. Osborne's three Skyraiders and four Corsairs, who reported destruction of stacks of fuel drums and a supply dump.

Philippine Sea's CDR E. T. Deacon reported that on the early morning of 15 December his flight of six Corsairs attacked troop concentrations. LT Krause's six Corsairs had attacked troops concentrated in a small valley near Hungnam. *Princeton's* pilots reported the destruction of oxcarts, trucks, gasoline drums, warehouses, and railroad tunnels.

From 15 to 24 December, a total of 1,700 sorties were flown inside the Hungnam perimeter. Many additional missions were flown outside the area.

The last pilot to fly over Hungnam was *Princeton's* LT R. B. Mack, who described the night as ". . . cloudless, cold, and unfriendly. Haze was everywhere," said Mack. "The artificial haze of war—one part hate, one part frustration, stirred to an even pall by high explosives.

"I was flying the last launch of the day as one of two F4U-5Ns, Detachment Fox of VC-3 from *Princeton*.

"After a dusk launch, I received orders to proceed to Hungnam as target combat air patrol for the withdrawal of our forces from that port. After a very lonely trip, I arrived about 1900 and reported to *Mount McKinley*. The fighter director stationed me over Hungnam at 15,000 feet altitude. I had a grandstand seat for the most dismal and distressing sight I had ever witnessed.

"Below, the last of the troops and supplies had been loaded on board the LSTs and other evacuation craft and were pulling away from the dock areas. There were fires everywhere throughout the area, and, as I watched, flames broke out around the docks, growing and spreading until the whole water-front seemed ablaze. Whatever had been left behind was being made useless for the Reds.

"As the LSTs cleared the beaches, several of our destroyers moved in and did their bit to ruin the real estate for future Communist use. I circled Hungnam until 2045. The ships below formed up single file, nose-and-tail like circus elephants, and headed seaward and then south to Pusan.

"As I took departure for *Princeton*, I called for the *Mount McKinley* and we exchanged greetings. 'Merry Christmas,' we said, for it was Christmas Eve 1950. . . ."

The Lesson of Hungnam

Hungnam was a brilliantly executed maneuver. The time was short, and putting all the parts together and making them work was extremely complicated. However, the Hungnam evacuation was not opposed either by air or by submarines or by armor and artillery equipped ground forces. Had such opposition occurred, Hungnam would not have been so successful, and there would have been losses.

Undoubtedly, under the existing conditions, the Hungnam area could have been held indefinitely, had there been a strategic need to do so. While no one in Korea believed a line across Korea ending near Hungnam was either feasible or practicable, many felt a new line across the narrow neck of Korea (ending in the vicinity of Wonsan on the east coast) could and should have been held. General Van Fleet thought so, as did Admiral Doyle.

"U.N. forces could have held Hungnam for a long period of time," said Doyle, "but I felt then and I still feel that with the Navy's surface and air power available we should have held the Wonsan area indefinitely."

The significance of the Hungnam operation was that it was an amphibious operation in the reverse. No corresponding operation in military history exists. It was different from Dunkirk and it was different from Gallipoli, for both of those operations were carried out under enemy pressure.

The value of UN firepower from the aircraft carriers and surface ships contributed to the high morale of troops ashore. As far as killing the enemy is concerned, it was of questionable value.

The value of rail transport was dramatically demonstrated at Hungnam. The rail line between Wonsan and Hungnam was kept open with the help of Korean laborers; and on the four or five hundred freight cars assembled by the Tenth Corps control organization, some 8,900 tons of Class "V" ammunition were among the supplies moved to Hungnam by rail to be loaded aboard ships.[15]

Air transport also played a vital role. One hundred twelve Air Force planes and ten Marine planes airlifted 3,600 men, 196 vehicles, 1,300 tons of cargo and hundreds of Korean refugees from the Yonpo airfield. In spite of bad weather, the Flying Boxcars sometimes took off at three-minute intervals. The field was used as long as it could be defended within the receding perimeter.[16]

The importance of sea transport was never more self-evident as the statistics will verify. When the operation was finally concluded, 105,000 U.S. and ROK military personnel and 91,000 civilian refugees—nearly 200,000 in all—had been embarked. Refugees were loaded in incredible numbers: 12,000 in one APA and 8,400 in one LST were the records.

It was Admiral Doyle's opinion that if UN forces had had the shipping, every person in the Hungnam area of North Korea could have been evacuated. "We could have completely evacuated the entire area," said Doyle, "for they all wanted to leave. As we left, in fact, refugees with bundles under their arms were still pouring in for a sealift south. The Army did a magnificent job ashore with the refugees. Since Hungnam was wrecked and there was little shelter and it was terribly cold, I ordered all ships with baking capacity to bake extra bread and cook rice. Every ship with a bake shop baked to capacity. We distributed rice to all the ships to help keep the people alive."*

The statistics of supplies and equipment removed from Hungnam were equally impressive. 17,500 vehicles, 350,000 measurement tons of cargo had loaded out on 6 APAs, 6 AKAs, 12 TAPs, 76 time-charter ships, 81 LSTs and 11 LSDs.

Although there was no opposition, the command relationships worked well. In his action report Admiral Struble made the following comment:

> During the Hungnam operation, Commander Seventh Fleet was in a supporting role to Commander Task Force 90 who retained responsibility for redeployment operations. Based on my experience in the Inchon, Wonsan, and Hungnam operations, I consider that the formation of a joint task force under the fleet commander is a better solution to the command problem involved. Such a solution provides a unified command afloat for the thorough coordination of the various task forces engaged in related operations.[17]

* Following the Hungnam redeployment, Joy messaged Doyle to come to Tokyo for a press conference. "While in Joy's office," said Doyle, "two civilian representatives from the Republic of Korea Government came to thank Admiral Joy and me with tears in their eyes for our compassion toward their fellow countrymen during the Hungnam withdrawal."

Admiral Doyle disagreed. "The command relationship was a deviation from previous ones," he said, "but circumstances warranted it. The Hungnam redeployment was conducted in a very small area. It involved only one amphibious group. If, for example, there had been two amphibious groups—one at Wonsan and one at Hungnam—there would have been definite need for a joint commander to coordinate the two."

Under the circumstances, however, the command arrangement at Hungnam worked smoothly. Had serious difficulties arisen or had the withdrawal been heavily opposed, one must conclude that there might have been greater need of a joint task force commander.

The major lesson of the Hungnam redeployment was that all the basic principles of U. S. Navy and Marine Corps amphibious doctrine were sound, and that they worked in reverse as well as they worked forward.

Admiral Joy summarized Hungnam thus: "The Hungnam evacuation showed that a well-trained and well-led amphibious force can carry out an amphibious operation in reverse as effectively as the conventional type. It again emphasized the importance of having adequate amphibious forces in being and in a state of full combat readiness."

7.

The Battle of the Mines
(Part III—1951-1953)

A New Look at the Mine Problem

The defeat and collapse of the North Korean Army did not end the battle of the mines in the fall of 1950. Rather than ending the mine struggle, the entry of the Chinese and the southward shift of the frontlines marked the beginning of a new phase of the UN countermine effort.

From the war's beginning, in contrast to action in the air and on the ground, no self-imposed restrictions had been placed on UN naval operations other than to observe the blockade limits.

However, as 1951 commenced, the Chinese Communist enemy was again in complete possession of the entire North Korean coastline. His opportunities for improving defenses against UN naval bombardment forces were considerably increased. Now he could re-mine his harbors and his coastal areas. He could emplace his coastal guns.

As a consequence, minesweeping problems for 1951, in addition to being magnified, were considerably different from those encountered during 1950.

First of all, *time* was less critical in 1951 than it had been in 1950. Throughout the fall of 1950, sweep missions were usually urgent—a few hours to clear Inchon; a few days to open Wonsan, Chinnampo, Iwon, and Hungnam. Either troops or supplies, and sometimes both, were urgently needed ashore. By 1951, in contrast, amphibious operations had been curtailed, and fewer deadlines faced the sweepers.

Second, whereas in the fall of 1950 sweep crews were relatively inexperienced, by 1951 they had become old hands at the trade.

Third, in 1950 the sweepers lacked repair facilities; they lacked spare parts; and they were few in number. By early 1951, many of these difficulties had been overcome.

Finally, the policy in 1950 had been to sweep where the mines *weren't*.

In the spring of 1951, the sweepers were ordered to sweep where the mines *were*.

"This change in policy was necessary to gain more maneuvering room for the fire support ships when under attack by shore batteries," said Rear Admiral George C. Dyer, then CTF 95. "Also, the closer the ships could get to the beach, the better their gunnery."

To illustrate the results of Dyer's new policy, 186 mines were swept at Hungnam in early 1951. In preparation for the siege of Wonsan, initiated 16 February, 325 mines were swept.

From 1 May 1951 to 31 December 1951, the minesweeping task group swept a total of 683 enemy mines. Included in this number were nine Soviet ground magnetic types, five of which were detonated by *Merganser* (AMS-26) (LTJG Einer May, USN).

As has been stated, by the spring of 1951 the mine problem had lost much of its urgency and deadliness. There was now sufficient time to care for mine ships and to provide some recreation for their crews. Repair ships *Luzon* (ARG-2) and *Kermit Roosevelt* (ARG-16) were alternately available to provide routine upkeep at Sasebo.

The 1951 Mine Mission Defined

Despite ominous whispers of re-mining and of long range coastal guns being brought into North Korea from Manchuria, Captain Richard C. Williams, who had relieved Captain Spofford in March 1951, had cause for optimism. He had inherited a going concern to carry out his new mine-sweeping mission which he visualized as follows:

"First, the primary purpose of minesweeping in 1951 was to permit United Nations gunfire support to get close inshore along the North Korean coast and interdict communications; to destroy troop concentrations, gun emplacements, and supply dumps.

"The second purpose of our minesweeping was to provide tactical deception; to force the enemy to redeploy troops and equipment to counter the threat of invasion. By so doing, we would relieve enemy pressure against UN ground forces.

"Third, the minesweepers would increase the effectiveness of UN naval blockade and bombardment forces operating in the Wonsan-Hungnam-Songjin areas by providing more direct mine-free routes between these ports. This would permit more flexible fire support in the event of emergency.

"Fourth, the minesweepers would reduce, by sweeping and disposing of moored mines, the threat of floating mines to UN ships.

"Finally, the minesweepers would open new 'targets of opportunity,' particularly around the rail hub of Hamhung through which a large percentage of supplies flowed to the enemy."

Minesweeping 1951 Style as Seen from *LST-799*

One officer who was a continuous participant in Korean minesweeping operations during 1951 was *LST-799*'s commanding officer, LT T. E. Houston.[1] His observations for that period contribute to a better understanding of actual operations.

"We had ComMinRon-3 aboard in early 1951," said Houston, "having taken him and staff aboard in Sasebo.

"At this time, the minesweeping family was a heterogeneous but closely knit group. It consisted of my LST carrying one or more mine-hunting helicopters, a steel hulled sweeper, several 'chicks' or AMSs, occasionally South Korean AMSs, and often a tug that anchored out at the 100-fathom line for geographical reference purposes.

"My LST generally proceded with our sweepers during the day, staying a few hundred yards in the 'safe' area from the sweep line. From this position, we ran a sweep plot, controlled sweep movements, assisted in picking up lost minesweeping gear—pigs, dan buoys, etc.—and helped to destroy swept mines by gunfire.

"All ships recovered sweep gear and moored each night prior to darkness, usually alongside the LST.

"At first, we swept only during daylight. Later on, as we cleared the whole bay of Hungnam and both coasts, we were forced to sweep at night and to stay farther and farther offshore because of enemy gunfire.

"Moored mines were cut almost every day. The sailors of *799* engaged in their destruction whenever possible. Approximately one out of every seven mines destroyed by gunfire 'blew.' Others filled with water and sank after the mine cases were holed. This destruction livened the daily humdrum existence of a support ship, and boosted morale of the men.

"The enemy's minelaying patterns were peculiar. Some mines seemed to have been laid like the spokes of a wagon wheel, all mine lines radiating out from the hub. Other lines were at random locations. None of the patterns resembled U. S. minelaying doctrine.

"There was little pattern to the movements of our group. The amphibious force made a few dummy landings, and our sweeps always preceded them. The helicopter went first, then the small boat sweeps, followed by the AMSs and AMs. We also swept areas off the bombline and in Wonsan harbor before large ships were brought in for gunfire support and bombardment. And we moved to any area where minelaying activities were reported.

"In some places, such as the Wonsan approaches ('Tin Pan Alley' and 'Muffler') off Songjin, and over on the west coast, north of Inchon (in the area called 'Cigarette') we made daily check sweeps.

"To assist the sweeping, my LST carried on the tank deck four small LCVP-type sweep boats (MSBs). This arrangement, while novel in concept,

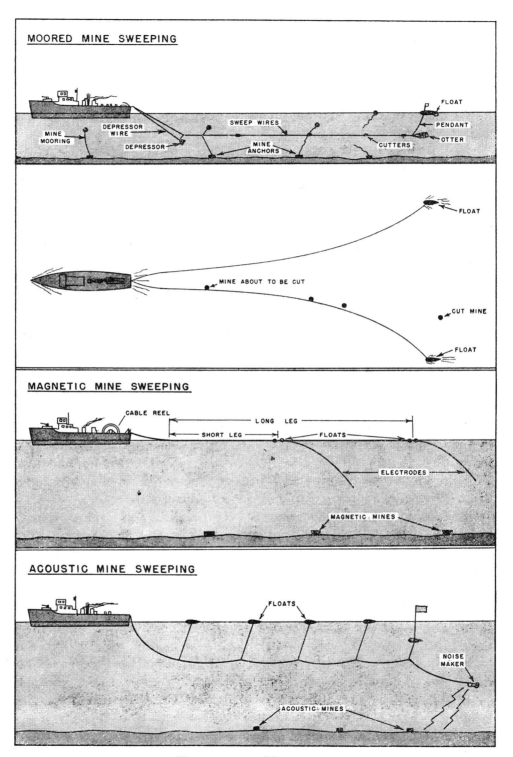

TECHNIQUES OF MINESWEEPING

did not prove practical. The LST's bow yawed too much, making it difficult to re-embark the LCVPs. The system was too complex and dangerous to use except in the mildest of weather. After a trial, we went back to housing all the MSBs aboard *Comstock* (LSD-19).

"The 'copters' aboard *LST-799* were initially mine spotters. Rescue work was a secondary mission, and done only on request. This 'copter mine spotting was fairly simple. The 'egg-beaters' hovered ahead of the lead sweep ship and radioed the word on any mines that were spotted in the sweep path.

"On a few occasions, 'copters destroyed floating mines by rifle fire from the plane, but this practice was stopped after one helicopter made a bull's eye on a floating mine, which, by sympathetic explosion, caused the detonation of four other mines. Needless to say, the 'copter was almost lost."

Sweep commanders confirmed the helicopter's usefulness.

"In good weather, the helicopter proved an invaluable aid to the minesweeper," said LT C. W. Coe, whose *Redstart* (AM-378) swept eighty large mines, captured five enemy sampans, and destroyed two self-propelled guns and one light tank during the Korean War. "The helicopter pilot was, in effect, the long range eyes of the *Redstart*."

Helicopters were also effectively used to reconnoiter areas in advance of actual minesweeping. They assisted the sweep commanders to predetermine the presence and the type of mines, the direction of the mine lines, the existence of shore batteries, and the availability of prominent land marks for navigational purposes.

"Because of the 'copters," said Coe, "it was possible for sweep operations to be more intelligently and safely planned in advance."[2]

In some cases helicopters actually led trapped sweepers out of a minefield, according to LCDR I. M. Laird, *Dextrous'* commanding officer.[3]

"From the air, they could see them when we couldn't," said Laird. "A 'copter hovered over *Dextrous'* bow when she was caught in a minefield, and the ship was conned by radio throughout the minefield and into clear water.

"The helicopters had many friends in the minesweeps."

Clearing the Coast for Bombardment Ships

Orders to start sweeping north of Wonsan were received on 30 March 1951.

"All the minesweeping forces at Wonsan sortied for Songjin at that time," said Captain Richard C. Williams, ComMinRonThree.

Williams' force included his flagship, *Comstock* (LSD-19) (CAPT E. T. Goyette), with LTJG Walter P. Sheppard's minesweeping boats embarked. It also included ComMinDiv-32 (LCDR T. L. Cleaver) in *Incredible* (LT

E. F. Flinn), *Osprey* (LTJG P. Levin), *Merganser* (LTJG D. J. O'Neill), *Chatterer* (LTJG J. P. McMahon), *Pelican* (LT Richard Cross), *Mocking Bird* (LTJG Stanley Gary) and the salvage vessel *Grasp* (ARS-24) (LT S. J. Brown).

This sweeping force, under the over-all tactical command of Rear Admiral R. H. Hillenkoetter in *St. Paul* (CA-73) (CAPT Chester C. Smith), had orders to clear a stretch of presumably safe water extending from Songjin about 20 miles to southward so that ships could get closer to the coast to bombard and blast targets of opportunity.

"On the first day of sweeping," said Captain Williams, "about fifteen moored mines were 'cut' near Songjin's harbor entrance. The sweeping operations brought the Communist defenders out of their surrounding hill positions, apparently to defend their coastline against amphibious attack. Many of them were observed and blasted as they converged on Songjin.

"Later the LSD, *Fort Marion,* was moved near the point of shore about 15 miles south of Songjin, and her embarked Royal Marines went ashore to dynamite a strategic rail line and tunnel. The British commandoes met negligible resistance and accomplished their mission.*

"The night the sweepers returned to Wonsan, *Comstock's* radar operator reported an unidentified and mysterious 'pip' moving near the island of Yo-do. The 'pip' was confirmed by the destroyer patrol. Although subsequent starshell and searchlight illumination failed to reveal the target, I ordered *Osprey, Chatterer, Pelican* and *Merganser* to sweep the suspicious area at first light. They did so, and by 0630 the following morning, 15 mines had been swept and destroyed.

"Had these mines remained unswept, *St. Paul* would have passed dangerously close to them when she stood in at about 1100 that same morning."

In a further effort to confuse the Communist coast defenders and sweep mines at the same time, the minesweepers were ordered to conduct a tactical feint at Kojo during mid-April 1951. Starting at the 100-fathom curve, the shallow-draft minesweep boats cut a channel to within 5-inch gun range of the beach which was later expanded by the larger sweepers.

"Although the minesweepers swept and sank only about a dozen mines," Captain Williams said, "they encountered the most menacing shore fire with which the sweepers had then been confronted."

Check-Sweeping Korea's West Coast

While east coast clearance and channel-widening operations to join the Kojo and Wonsan sweep areas were in progress, another operation was suddenly made necessary in early May 1951. The British forces operating on Korea's west coast requested that a check sweep be conducted in the

---

* See Chapter 9, "The Seaborne Artillery."

Chinnampo area along Chinnampo's "Cigarette" route that had been originally cleared by Commander S. M. Archer's force in November 1950.

"Check-sweeping increased in importance," said Captain Williams, "because a swept area stayed safe only so long as it was watched. Because of
the distances involved, it was impossible to watch everywhere at once, and
therefore we had to conduct monthly check-sweeping off both coasts."

Usually, a *check-sweep* involved as much effort as a *clearance* sweep. The
check-sweep of "Cigarette" in May of 1951, for instance, involved the use
of the minesweepers *Curlew, Gull, Swallow* and *Mocking Bird,* and the
fire support ships HMS *Concord,* HMCS *Sioux,* and HMS *Amethyst.* It
also required the use of an LST, six MSBs, one LSD (the *Comstock,* whose
crew replaced center-line gas buoys in the channel) and two YMSs from the
Republic of Korean Navy: *YMS-501* and *YMS-515.* The sweepers checked
both for magnetic and moored mines, but found nothing along the entire
20-mile trek.

The May 1951 re-sweep of "Cigarette" reemphasized the growing usefulness of the helicopter.[4] The helicopter was valuable not only for reconnoitering the area ahead of the sweepers, but also to drop hand grenades along each
section of the channel in the hope of neutralizing any acoustic mines present.

(The necessity of constant check-sweeping underlines the fact that actual
mines need not *exist* in order to provoke a great minesweeping effort. The
mere *threat* of the mine is sufficient.)

The check-sweeping effort in Korea was reduced by a tactic described
by the operations officer of MinRon 3.

"The sweepers developed a faster method of check-sweeping the coastal
areas," said CDR Emory B. Myers. "Two, three, or even more ships ran
abreast through an area. If no mines were cut, we assumed that the area
had not been re-mined.

"This method proved much faster than sweeping the entire area. But it
was not foolproof. If current or tide walked a mine into a swept area, the
entire area still had to be swept as a precaution against the possibility of
re-mining."

Sweepers Add New "Salt-Water" Real Estate

"Upon completion of the Chinnampo check-sweeping operation," said
Captain Williams, "work on the east coast commenced in earnest. The
coastal area from Suwan-dan to Wonsan yielded almost 200 mines during
the quarter ending 30 June."

During this period, the sweep forces were re-enforced by two AMs—
Redstart (LT Carl W. Coe) and *Dextrous* (LCDR I. M. Laird)—and two
AMSs—*Condor* (LT G. D. Morin) and *Waxbill* (LT F. J. Crozier).

Meanwhile shore battery fire was becoming considerably more of a problem. Everywhere the sweeps went, enemy artillery followed. More and more artillery pieces appeared on hills, in valleys, and in caves overlooking the areas where the sweepers were working.* Although the accuracy of these guns left much to be desired, the density of their fire made occasional hits inevitable.

"Throughout the summer of 1951," continued Williams, "the sweepers gradually cleared the coastline as far north as Hungnam.

"At the same time, the MSBs widened the sea room in Wonsan harbor, permitting our ships to come closer and closer to the enemy guns on Hodo Pando and Kalma Gak. They accounted for 138 mines there during the summer months—more than any other three divisions had swept in any comparable period of time. Their crews, led by such fearless men as LT Walter P. Sheppard, LT Allen L. Peek, LT Louis J. Compomenosi, and LT George R. Smith, were ably conned by Desnoyers, Beaver, Schultz, Polackowitz, Lunemen, and others."

By 10 September 1951, the MSBs had completed their job at Wonsan. All that remained was a check-sweep by the AMSs. Accordingly five AMSs were readied: *Mocking Bird* (LT Sidney Smith), *Kite* (LT Lee Hadaway), *Redhead* (LT Kevah Kirshenbaum), *Gull* (LT Douglas Tuel), and *Heron* (LT E. S. Roth). LT Dale Schemerhorn in *Mocking Bird* was OTC.

The AMS sweep was commenced at first light and resulted in checking a path over 1,000 yards in width from the western tip of Sin-do, three miles farther west. This sweep was greeted by a thunderous bombardment from Communist shore batteries to the north, west, and south. The only damage during this foray came when *Redhead* struck the submerged mast of a lugger which had been sunk earlier northwest of Sin-do. *Redhead*'s starboard propeller was damaged. Fortunately she was able to recover gear and to limp out of the harbor.

The four undamaged sweepers turned for another pass. The Reds held their fire, allowing the small ships to come closer and closer. Not until the four reached the western end of their run, three miles from the nearest lee, did the Communists open fire. Sea water from the splashes drenched the sweepers. Turning eastward, the skippers "chased" the splashes to avoid hits, and escaped damage until near the sheltering lee of Sin-do Island.

Suddenly the voice radio of *Heron* called, "Starboard side hit."

Still the thunderous bombardment continued. *Mocking Bird* at last had the western end of Sin-do abeam, and the other ships followed her to comparative safety.

The ordeal had ended. Four mines had been swept. *Heron* had been hit on the starboard side of her bulwark by a 75-mm. point-detonating, fuzed

* See Chapter 9, "The Seaborne Artillery."

projectile. It had showered the overhead, bulkhead, and deck with shrapnel. A few feet higher, and the 40-mm. gun crew on the forecastle might have suffered heavily. As it was, damage was insignificant.

(Later, it was learned that the Communists had thought the intensive sweeping into Wonsan was a prelude to another amphibious attack, and, as a result, had reinforced their gun batteries, evacuated civilians from areas near likely landing beaches, and redeployed some troops to meet the attack.)

Sweeping continued northward in the fall of 1951 to the relatively heavily mined harbor of Hungnam. More and more mines were swept and destroyed. And more and more enemy artillery appeared on the shore to interfere with the sweeping. Despite the heavy shore fire, as many mines were swept from 1 July to 30 September 1951 as had been swept in the whole Korean War up to that time.

"Luck, experience, and planning all played an important role," said Captain Williams.

Sweeping Close to the Bear's Tail

One of the most difficult clearance sweeps of 1951 was conducted from 3 November to 10 November 1951, at Chongjin, on North Korea's eastern coast, 75 miles south of Vladivostok.

"Our primary mission at Chongjin," said Captain Williams, "was to remove the mine danger inside the 50-fathom curve in order to permit bombardment ships to operate in that area at closer ranges.

"Intelligence reports concerning Chongjin painted a grim picture of the area. Beach-controlled mines were reported to be in the area, and radar contacts of high-speed patrol boats had been reported. Furthermore, the operating area was within range of enemy air—and against aircraft, the sweepers lacked adequate armament, fire control, and speed. In addition, to complicate this problem, winter with its high winds, its severe cold, its ice, and its rough seas was fast approaching."

The Chongjin sweeping operation commenced on 3 November. Twenty-three contact mines were swept, eighteen of them sunk by rifle fire. One detonated as it was swept, and the remaining four were probably destroyed by 40-mm. fire, as the helicopter could find no trace of them.

"On 6 November," continued Captain Williams, "*Heron*'s sonar operator discovered a new mine line in an area that had been cleared only three days before. Eight mines were swept from previously swept waters. This was a surprise. It meant that re-mining was being done right under our very noses.

"After sweeping three days inside the 50-fathom curve and then discovering that the enemy had very recently re-mined areas previously swept, we decided to concentrate farther to seaward between the 50- and the 100-fathom curve.

"At Chongjin, the LSD *Comstock* (CDR William Winter) and the helicopter again proved indispensable; but the helicopter's effectiveness was greatly reduced by mist and sleet. It failed to spot the newly laid minefield on 6 November. The MSBs also had trouble due to rough weather. In the higher latitudes their sweeping operations should be conducted only when periods of good weather can be expected. The two DMSs—*Doyle* (DMS-34) and *Endicott* (DMS-35)—proved valuable as supporting ships at Chongjin, both because they could help to guard against re-mining and because they could make a rapid check-sweep of the area."

Despite all the hazards and difficulties encountered at Chongjin, that area was cleared of mines from the 50-fathom curve to seaward—at least temporarily.

The most significant aspect of the Chongjin sweep, however, was the clear indication that North Korean mine*layers* were endeavoring to keep pace with the UN mine*sweepers*.

Mine Intelligence (1951-1953)

Concrete evidence of enemy mine replanting in the Hungnam-Songjin area came on 19 November 1951 when *Ptarmigan* (LCDR Harold Durham) swept two new contact-type mines near Hungnam. Later, on 3 December 1951, *Pelican* sank a shiny new mine in the same area. Because of the newness of these mines, it was self-evident to Captain Williams that they were recent re-plants.

Such sporadic finds gave UN commanders their most dependable clues regarding enemy mining activities. Never during the course of the war was it possible to make or keep an up-to-date chart of the enemy's mining and re-mining operations. Ships were too few, intelligence too sketchy; coastlines were too extensive, the nights too black; the enemy's mining campaign was too local. Nor did the mine experts of the U. S. Navy have more than "guesstimates" of the Communist mine stockpile.

However, it was believed that the enemy had sufficient mines "to mine extensively all the ports and harbors of Korea," and that he had "built depots at Chinnampo, Chongjin, Songjin, and Hungnam."[5] It was also generally believed that his mining campaign had a two-fold purpose: first, to deter UN forces from making another amphibious landing; and second, to hamstring the operations of UN naval bombardment forces.

Intelligence reports from North Korean guerrillas, escapees, defectors, and captured fishermen were usually skimpy and had to be verified. All of the reports, however, indicated that enemy mining was being done at night, utilizing such craft as sailing junks, fishing sampans, power junks, and MTBs. One ex-Soviet minelayer was reportedly in use, but this was never verified.

Captured sampans, which had been used as minelayers, revealed that special racks constructed of heavy timbers were placed athwartship so that mines could be housed and manually rolled over the side with ease. Despite the primitive design and small payload of the sampans (even a small sampan, however, could carry two to four mines), it was possible for the enemy to pose a mining threat against a composite of the most powerful and up-to-date navies in the world.

Typical intelligence reports received by UN commanders in the spring of 1951 are reproduced from CINCFE's intelligence summaries:

3 January: Extensive mining operations reported in Taedong channel and along shore vicinity of Chinnampo.[6]

1 March: Enemy reported unloading Soviet sea mines from freight cars vicinity Kalma railroad station. . . .

7 March: Kalma Railroad station reported effectively hit by fire from U.S. cruiser *Manchester*. One boxcar loaded with sea mines exploded.

28 March: Motor boat planting mines vicinity of Wonsan. Mines planted in north-south line.

31 March: UN naval units fired on possible mining boats in vicinity of Wonsan. COMNAVFE reports strong evidence exists that the enemy is making a determined effort to re-mine areas that have been previously swept.

10 April: One black MTB, 13 meters long, observed in the vicinity of Chinnampo. Boat believed to be laying mines during darkness. Enemy ships reported to be laying mines vicinity 38-45N, 125-29E.

Prisoners captured by the *Douglas H. Fox* (DD-779) told a typically confusing and contradictory story of enemy minelaying activities.[7]

Information from prisoners captured on 2 May 1952 was the occasion of a report: "Mines were being laid in April 1951 from Sinch'ang-ni to the southwest for a distance of about 2,000 yards. Prisoners rather indefinite about the number of mines, using the word 'many'."

Four days later, on 6 May 1952, prisoners captured by *Fox* stated, "There are no mines in the Sinch'ang-ni area."[8]

On 7 May, captured prisoners told *Fox*'s skipper, Commander James A. Dare, that mines were planted in Hamhung harbor. Three days later, 9 May, captured prisoners stated, "No minelaying noticed in Hungnam harbor."

Few such reports were confirmed or confirmable, but they typify the fragmentary intelligence that filtered in from South Korean guerrillas, civilian refugees, prisoners-of-war, fishermen, and defectors throughout 1951-1953.

Occasionally an intelligence report proved accurate. A North Korean Navy defector from Kojo stated: "Most mines now being laid are said to be of the anti-landing craft type. It is said that these mines are being laid in a section of the east coast where invasion is possible."

This fragment of intelligence was verified on 2 March 1952 when a new type of enemy anti-boat mine was discovered at Wonsan. Moored to explode from 18 inches to 8 feet beneath the surface, and containing 44 pounds of TNT, this comparatively small contact-type mine (only 21 inches in diameter) created the necessity for additional helicopter searching and underwater reconnaissance in suspected areas.

Positive evidence of an east coast mining effort was discovered on 18 June 1952 when *Curlew* (AMS-8) (LT R. O. Snure) recovered a mine with self-planting mechanism in Wonsan harbor. With this device the enemy apparently was using the river current to float mines into the harbor buoyed by oil drums, logs, and kegs. The mine release was a pelican-hook type mechanism that was released by a soluble washer. This discovery caused Commander Task Force 95 to declare the area near the river mouth unsafe for navigation.*

The North Korean prisoners volunteered a sad story about their own navy. They said it had dwindled to nothing more than a token force, with virtually no duties to perform. In fact, large numbers of naval personnel had been transferred to the Army. None of the prisoners knew of the existence of any North Korean naval craft.

The *Nootka* Incident

In late September, 1952, HMCS *Nootka* (CDR Richard M. Steele, RCN), a Canadian *Tribal* class destroyer, was to have the signal honor of capturing a North Korean minelayer, the only enemy ship captured at sea during the war. On the night of 22 September, *Nootka* was southeast of Cho-do island near the Chinnampo approaches, making a patrol known as "Blackburn."

At 0223, *Nootka's* radar detected an unidentified vessel on a northerly course close inshore near Chin'-gang'-po. When off the headland to the north of this, the vessel turned and set course for the southeast tip of Cho-do. Although suspicious and worth watching closely, the radar blip was thought probably that of a friendly reconnaissance ship returning to anchorage from a nocturnal patrol.

When the unidentified vessel reached the swept channel, it changed its heading toward a customary anchorage for the "Blackburn" patrol destroyers. But its action now appeared strongly to be that of searching, and Captain Steele ordered his ship to close the suspicious craft. *Nootka* turned to give chase, and the blip on the radar screen immediately showed a new course toward the mainland. A direct chase would take *Nootka* over the area re-

* See Chapter 12, "The Siege of Wonsan."

MOBILE AIR POWER. *At top, Philippine Sea,* second U. S. carrier in Korea, fighting with the "Happy Valley" in the major campaigns of the next critical months. *Center,* CV *Valley Forge,* first in the fray, brought striking power to bear in timely fashion. *Below,* LT John D. Ely and LTJG John G. Stranlund pilot Corsairs over CV *Boxer.*

AIR GROUP THREE ACHIEVEMENTS. *At top, Leyte's* scoreboard posts the fourteen-target record. On the bridge are CAPT Thomas U. Sisson and officers of the group which won the Navy Unit Citation. *Center,* CV *Bon Homme Richard's* wardroom plaque. Her Air Group 7 also won the Navy citation. *Below,* LT Guy Bordelon on the flight deck of CV *Princeton* amid signs of glory.

THREE TYPES OF NAVAL AIRCRAFT. *At top,* ENS Buffkin pilots Banshee jet over Wonsan. *Center,* an F4U Corsair, flown by LT Robert Pitner on mission from CV *Boxer,* levels out for observation of damage to a bridge. *Below,* an F9F-2 Panther jet during a strike on shore installations near Wonsan.

FROM BELOW DECK TO TOPSIDE. *At top,* first step in delivering this 1,000-pound bomb to enemy is performed in magazine by Seaman Donald L. Smith and Seaman Apprentice William J. Scott. *Center,* a "Korean Cruncher" in the bomb rack of an AD Skyraider, armed with new ram-type wing rockets. *Below,* three "Big Boys" (2,000-pound bombs), about to be dispatched from CV *Princeton.*

cently traversed and possibly mined by this craft, and as this seemed most unwise to Steele, *Nootka* was put on course to pass to southward and round up to intercept her.

Nootka's 29 knots did not permit interception, however, before the enemy craft had reached the protection of waters too shallow for the destroyer.

"A fruitless attempt was made to drive the vessel to seaward by firing with *Nootka*'s main armament at the cliffs over their heads," said Steele. "This vessel was now fully considered to be enemy, but it was felt that its crew were much more valuable as captives than as corpses floating in the sea.

"An attempt was next made to try and capture them by armed boats, but the enemy travelled too fast and made their escape.

"By this vessel's actions and the tracks of its courses, we concluded that it was engaged in mining operations, and that the area it had worked probably contained mines.

"In reply to my signal requesting that this area be check-swept, a U. S. minesweeper (USS *Defense*) (AM-317) arrived and did a magnetic check-sweep of the area, commencing at dusk on the 27th. At midnight she messaged 'negative results' and departed for Wonsan."

Forty-six minutes later *Nootka* established contact a second time well up in the Nam-chon River. Captain Steele moved her south quietly and slowly around the end of the suspect area and closed the coast to seek any deeper darkness that the loom of the land might offer and thus prevent, as long as posible, the enemy vessel's seeing her.

When the enemy craft was well out into route "Cigarette" in the position Steele felt was the farthest she would venture, *Nootka* closed at over 30 knots and succeeded in cutting off a good-sized vessel which was frantically attempting to reach the land.

"We closed right in with a rush to try to psychologically dominate the situation in order to prevent the enemy's fighting," said Steele. "We spoke to them in Korean, informing them that any move on their part would result in their being blown to bits.

"As we drew near, we couldn't decide what we had found. It looked like a junk, but it was different. Its silhouette was low, it was whistling along at a pretty good clip, and it was making very little if any noise.

"*Nootka* was then stopped about a half cable from the enemy, and in the darkness large black objects could just be made out dropping from her stern and floating towards us. These were assumed to be floating mines, so we backed up and put several Bofors shells into her waterline, and we then sent away our boats with assault parties. They reported the vessel deserted, and turned toward the floating objects which were then realized to be small craft containing the absconding crew.

"When close in on the first of these, *Nootka's* number one boat, using a tactic which had previously proved very successful, shone a high-powered narrow-beamed light immediately in the enemy's eyes. It disclosed a North Korean naval officer lying on a raft made of large black rubber truck tubes, with his machine gun trained on *Nootka*. Both parties opened fire together; however, with the advantage of light, number one boat had no casualties, and the Korean retreated *downward*."

The *Nootka's* boats were recalled, and the remaining enemy rafts watched on radar.

Nootka went alongside the enemy minelayer, and rather than risk sending men below in the darkness, secured several wires to a section of the vessel's deck. Then, using her 44,000-horsepower, *Nootka* ripped this section adrift to ascertain if further mines or men remained. The ship was empty. *Nootka* secured lines to her and towed her off to the westward clear of the mined area so that she might be examined at daylight.

Nootka maintained watch on the remaining crew members, and at daylight, steamed in and picked them up.

When *Nootka* closed to pick up the prisoners, they broke up their rafts and sank the tubes, and some of them tried to drown themselves. Each had been armed with a machinegun, a pistol, and a dozen grenades, which they discarded at *Nootka's* approach. Among the prisoners were two lieutenants and three chief petty officers of the North Korean Navy.

"An interesting sidelight," said Steele, "was that the first grapple we threw into the minelayer didn't hold and skidded back over the side of her bulwark. When hauled back on board *Nootka*, it was found to be hooked into a bag full of very shaky-looking hand grenades; these were very gently dropped over the side."

Later, a considerable amount of information was obtained from one of the prisoners concerning not only this minefield but also another field located considerably to the southward.

"In this instance and others where prisoners were taken by *Nootka*," said Captain Steele, "it was interesting to note the psychological reaction brought about in these men by good and kind treatment, when they expected torture. A bath, hot coffee, hot food, and other refreshment resulted, in each case, in at least one of the men becoming very talkative.

"It was noted, however, that in almost every case their first hours of evidence proved much more reliable than the stilted, revised version given by them later and which always reverted to the theme, 'I am not really a Communist. The circumstances and my environment forced me to accept the part.'"

The enemy prisoners volunteered the information that they had renewed their mining efforts on a small scale on the night of 13 September 1952, after they reactivated the mine and torpedo section at the Chinnampo Naval Base.

The torpedo section consisted of four officers and twenty enlisted men. The North Korean naval officers had received about one month's training in mine warfare at Rashin. The training syllabus consisted largely of lectures by Korean naval officers based on Korean translations of a Soviet mine manual.

The mining crew used at Chinnampo consisted of a senior lieutenant, as political officer-in-charge, plus a navigator, a junior grade lieutenant mining officer, and a half-dozen enlisted men selected for their ability to row a boat. This crew had set out from Chinnampo to the coastal port of Mongumpo, not far away, to repair a badly damaged 25-foot junk (the one *Nootka* captured) to use as a minelayer.

Nootka's prisoners stated that they had tried to build a minelaying craft that could not be heard nor seen, even by radar. Therefore, they had decided to substitute cracking good oarsmen for the junk's engine, and to reduce the junk's freeboard to within eighteen inches of the waterline, in the hope this would reduce both visual and radar detection. Wooden longitudinal supports were installed as minelaying rails.

Actual mining operations had begun six nights later, on the night of 19 September, when two magnetic mines were laid. On the nights of the 20th, 26th, and 27th, six additional magnetic mines were planted, without benefit of navigational instruments. The navigator had taken "seaman's eye" bearings on shore promontories by moonlight, and had assumed the speed of his craft to be about one knot.

This episode was fair proof that the Communists recognized that the west coast's tidal range and swift currents were better suited for magnetic mines than for contact types.

A few days later USS *Chatterer* arrived in the Chinnampo area and commenced sweeping the northern mine area on 2 October.

The first mine was exploded with a great geyser of water at eight minutes past noon on that day.

The field was swept not without difficulty, for the enemy wheeled in artillery batteries and took the sweepers under heavy fire on a number of occasions.

"To watch the little sweepers lumbering out of the welter of fire at six or seven knots, retaining their invaluable sweep gear instead of slipping it," said Captain Steele, "was inspiring to us Canadians, and built a deep respect for the tenacity and ability of the U. S. Navy's fighting men that will long remain.

"Some of the American leaders in these sweeps were Reserves called back from comfortable, safe jobs where they had been attempting to build homes and catch up on some of the time lost in World War II—men past the age where fighting is exciting adventure.

"The vigorous actions of these men must be counted among the finest examples of leadership and patriotism, and I hope that their civilian associates have a full appreciation of how much such men contributed."

UN Ships Suffer Mine Damage

Despite the enemy's constant mining and re-mining, mines caused comparatively little damage to UN naval forces from the spring of 1951 until the armistice in 1953.

On 2 February 1951 while sweeping near Yong-yang southeast of Wonsan, *Partridge* (AMS-31) (LTJG B. M. Clark) struck a floating mine and sank in less than ten minutes. Two officers and six enlisted men were killed, one officer and five enlisted men were seriously injured. *Partridge* was the fourth and last United States sweeper to be lost in the Korean War.

Sarsi (ATF-111) was sunk by a mine while on patrol off Hungnam the night of 30 August 1952. Two men were lost.

Two destroyers struck mines near Hungnam: the *Walke* (DD-723) (CDR M. F. Thompson) on 12 June 1951 and the *Small* (DD-838) (CDR F. C. Snow) on 7 October 1951. Both ships suffered extensive damage. *Walke* suffered 26 deaths; *Small* had 9 killed.

Another destroyer, the USS *Barton* (DD-722), struck a mine on 16 September 1952 approximately 90 miles east of Wonsan, while serving in the screen of Task Force 77.

Barton's skipper, Commander H. B. Seim, believed that this mine had broken loose from the Wonsan minefield when Typhoon "Karen" had blown past that area on 18 August. Vice Admiral Clark, Commander Seventh Fleet, reported 40 mines around his ships in the next several weeks. Other mines had also appeared on the surface in Wonsan harbor, and some had even washed up on the beaches.

"There were some peculiar aspects to the *Barton* mining," said CDR Seim.[9] "*Barton* was the northernmost ship of the task force, which was southbound. It was necessary for both the carriers and the destroyers directly ahead of us to steam close aboard that mine before we hit it. When the explosion came, I had just finished reading a report on a ship's vulnerability to floating mines. The report concluded that a ship making ten or more knots was safe, since the bow waves would push a floating mine aside. However, the bow wave failed to protect *Barton,* for the task force was steaming at fifteen knots!"

"The mine hit at 2115," continued Seim. "It fractured the shell plating from keel to the main deck. The forward fireroom was completely gutted and flooded. A hole 40 feet long was opened to the sea. All five men in the forward fireroom were lost. Engineroom personnel working next to the destroyed fireroom were seriously burned."

Two ROK ships were mined during this period: *JMS-306** on 6 May off Chinnampo, and *PC-704* off Yo-do island, Wonsan harbor, on the night of 26 December 1951. Twenty bodies were later recovered in the vicinity of Yo-do. ROK naval records positively state that "*PC-704* hit a mine and sank while conducting operations on east coast inside Wonsan harbor area."[10]

In company with *JMS-302*, *YMS-502*, and *PF-61*, ROK *JMS-306* was sent to Chinnampo to investigate enemy minelaying activities. On the morning of 6 May 1951, as soon as the thick morning fog cleared away, *JMS-306* began her reconnaissance patrol. Twenty minutes later, at 0920, she struck a mine. The blast flooded her engineroom, killed 6 of her 36-man crew, and wounded 18.

For 72 minutes, the 12 uninjured crew members fought to control the ship's flooding. Meantime, two friendly sailing vessels were called alongside for salvage of everything portable, including, said a ROK report,[11] "a considerable amount of office paper." The ship sank at 1032. Surviving crew members were transferred to *PF-61* for return to Pusan.

Red Artillery Versus Minesweepers

Beginning in the fall of 1951 and continuing throughout the remainder of the Korean War, more UN minesweeps were damaged by shore batteries than by mines.

"Many times," said CDR Emory E. Myers, "enemy batteries would fire at a sweep until it looked like they could not miss getting a hit with the next shell—and then for no apparent reason they would stop. This 'stop' and 'go' firing might last all day. When Red gunners got too hot, our sweepers simply cleared the area and waited for them to cool off. As a result of being frequently under fire, hardly a sweeper in Korea avoided getting hit, or having a near miss and flying shrapnel."[12]

One of the most frequently hit minesweepers was *Osprey* (AMS-28) (LT D. T. Wieland, Jr.). She caught two shells on 29 October 1951, one puncturing the top of her stack, the second striking the hull above the waterline. Only one man was seriously wounded.

Again on 23 April 1952, *Osprey* was hit by a Songjin shore battery while she and *Swallow* (AMS-36) (LTJG D. A. Rostan, USNR) spotted trains for

---

* A Japanese-built minesweeper slightly smaller than our AMS-type sweep.

their big steel sister, *Murrelet* (AM-372). "Night train busting, as well as being destructive, grew to be quite a sport for the little sweepers," said CDR Myers. "At night they would move in close to the beach and relay information to the larger ships as enemy trains came out of tunnels and ran along the beach. Minecraft helped knock off a number of trains in this manner."

Osprey was hit on a third occasion on 13 October 1952 as she participated in Kojo amphibious demonstrations,* taking numerous fragment hits and a near miss which wounded the executive officer and three enlisted men.

The only other minesweeper to be hit as often as *Osprey* was the destroyer minesweeper *Thompson* (DMS-38). She too was hit on three separate occasions.†

Other sweepers damaged were *Heron* (AMS-18) (LTJG E. S. Roth), which took one hit about six feet above her waterline on 8 September 1951, and *Competent* (AM-316) (LCDR E. A. Grant), which received near misses from an estimated 100 rounds of 122-mm. shells from a 4-gun battery on 27 August 1952. Only superficial damage was done to the latter ship and no crew members were hit.

Kite (AMS-22) (LT R. G. Zimmerman) was the target for 47 rounds of 76-mm. fire while sweeping at Wonsan on 19 November 1952. Shell fragments wounded one officer and four enlisted personnel—none seriously.

During March of 1953, three UN minesweepers were slightly damaged by enemy shore batteries near Songjin: USS *Gull* and USS *Swift* and ROK *YMS-510*.

Despite the excitement of being frequently under fire, the minesweepers logged the duels with Communist shore batteries with brevity and nonchalance. LT A. C. Sharp made the following entries in *Firecrest's* (AMS-10) log:

> 1445: Ship under fire from shore battery. All engines ahead full.
> 1504: Received hit on starboard side . . . shell entered messhall . . . tore up part of the deck . . . passed through lower part of refrigerator . . . glanced off ship's ventilation system . . . passed through port bulkhead into the sea.
> 1505: Shell did not explode and no casualties resulted.

Firecrest's damage was subsequently repaired by the *Gunston Hall* (LSD-5) (CAPT G. T. Baker). The meddlesome enemy shore batteries were later blasted by battleship *New Jersey* (CAPT David M. Tyree) and the destroyer *Epperson* (DDE-719) (CDR C. H. Mead).

LCDR I. M. Laird, the *Dextrous'* commanding officer, made the following entries in his log:

> 1243: Manned the 3-inch gun.

---

* The Kojo amphibious demonstration is fully described in Chapter 11, "The Amphibious Threat."

† *Thompson's* damage is reported in Chapter 9, "The Seaborne Artillery."

1309: Ship taken under fire from shore batteries. All hands to General Quarters. Captain took the conn.

1310: Commenced evasive zig-zag courses at flank speed, 16 knots. Took direct hit on starboard bow.

1312: Took direct hit on top of mast.

1314: Numerous air bursts and near misses. Commenced dropping smoke pots (to camouflage position).

1318: Cut loose minesweeping gear. Casualties one dead and two wounded. Two holes in ship—one about 12 inches in diameter and another about 6 inches in diameter. Much damage to electrical gear, radio antennas, radar, signal halyards, and the port truck light missing.

LCDR Laird's defensive maneuver was basic doctrine for minesweepers. When possible, they opened fire on enemy shore batteries, calling for fire support when this was available. They cranked on flank speed; they cut their sweep gear, zig-zagged, and used smoke to complicate the enemy's target solution.

"One more maneuver might be added," said Laird. "When a flash from a shore battery showed us that one was on the way, we changed course immediately—and then spent 20 or 30 seconds, depending on the range, hoping we hadn't zigged when we should have zagged."

Smoke was particularly effective when produced in sufficient quantity to conceal completely the minesweeper's evasive maneuvering.

Merganser's skipper, LT E. A. May, developed a smokemaking experiment that was promptly adopted by all the sweep skippers. May inducted diesel oil directly into the main engine muffler, which caused heavy white smoke to pour out of the stack. "The beauty of making smoke in this manner," said LT May, "was that it involved only one motion to open one valve in the engineroom, and smoke poured out when it was needed."

While this procedure was never approved by the Bureau of Ships, Captain Williams recommended that it be allowed as an emergency measure. Sweepers continued to use the "May method" when in desperate circumstances, concluding that the oil would do less damage to their engines than might be done by the shore batteries. Actually, no ship ever had a fire or damage to its engines, even though the method was used many times.

BuShips prescribed a smoke-making procedure for minesweepers involving the use of small smoke pots that could be quickly lit off and either carried on the stern or dumped over the side. The sweepers, however, found the pots too slow in producing smoke. By the time the smoke became effective, the ship was either out of danger or had been hit.

The accuracy of enemy shore batteries highlighted the importance of counterbattery gunfire support. Few destroyer skippers had experienced minesweeper support duty prior to their Korean assignment, and no prescribed method for gunfire support of sweepers existed at the outbreak of the Korean war.

Zeal's commanding officer (LT F. H. Sonntag) stated the problem succinctly in his action report.[13] "There is no basic doctrine in regard to gunfire support by destroyer types when supporting minesweepers in areas where there are known shore batteries. The decision at present seems to rest with the commanding officer of the ship providing support. This officer has seen support ships follow the inshore minesweep float . . . and thus be closer to the beach than the minesweeper. Other vessels remain . . . to seaward of the sweeper. It is recommended that a study be made of the best support positions when various combinations of vessels are involved. Fire support ships should also be apprised of the fact that in an emergency they can pass between the minesweeper and its float without fouling."*

Each fire support skipper positioned his ship in accordance with his best judgment. Some ships gave excellent fire support by following in the wake of the minesweep and then positioning themselves between the enemy shore batteries and the friendly minesweep. Other fire support ships kept well out to sea beyond the minesweepers, and in some instances the minesweepers were caught between the fire support ships and the shore batteries. Understandably, the minesweepers preferred to have the fire support ships as close as possible to the target.

One destroyer skipper whose ship supported the minesweepers for 33 days inside Wonsan harbor was *Barton's* CDR H. B. Seim.

Seim believed it was a sounder policy for the destroyers to steam abreast but *outboard* of the minesweepers rather than try to trail them. "This was particularly true inside Wonsan," said Seim, "where maneuvering room was restricted both for the minesweeper and for the destroyer. All we could do was 'figure-eight'. We wound up our batteries on one loop and unwound them on the next."

A similar fire support plan was used by the skipper of USS *Douglas H. Fox* (DD-779) (Commander James A. Dare), whose results were enthusiastically endorsed both by the minesweeper *Murrelet* and by Commander Mine Forces Pacific.

Following *Fox's* smothering fire[14] in support of *Swallow* (AMS-36) and *Murrelet* (AM-372) northeast of Lighthouse point at Hungnam, *Murrelet* sent the following message:

> "From USS *Murrelet:* Action USS *D. H. Fox:* 13/0542Z: All gunfire support ships could take lessons from you X It has been a real pleasure to work with you BT."

* The moored sweep must be of sufficient depth to permit passage.

Fox answered: "From USS *D. H. Fox:* Action USS *Murrelet:* 13/0555Z: Thank you X Your three-inch gunner is the sharpest I have seen X Will swap you even for one gun department BT."

Fox's skipper, Commander Dare, explained that "this burst of mutual admiration followed several days of sweeping the area from Cha-ho to Hungnam in which we had a few altercations with shore guns. Our sweep support plan went like this: First, the senior sweep would deliver his overlay of the swept area so we would both be using the same ground rules. I would then put the *Fox* in a position about 400 yards ahead and 10° relative to seaward of the leading sweep. *Fox* probed ahead with 5-inch and inshore with three barrels of single shot 40-mm. (or one 5-inch when ranges were over 3,000 yards). The sweeps would each take inshore targets with 3-inch and 20-mm. This worked well inasmuch as the *Fox* always drew any fire received, and the sweeps could turn across our wake to get sea room.

"When we operated this way, steaming along the coast, I always felt like one of the bad guys in a western movie riding into town with pistols banging in all directions. By looking ahead with the 20-power binoculars you could actually see North Koreans running for the hills and tunnels."

Dare's support plan had the hearty endorsement of Commander Mine Forces Pacific, Rear Admiral J. A. Snackenberg. In a dispatch to *Douglas H. Fox* on 14 May 1952, ComMinPac stated, "I have been informed by my ships that you have consistently supported them with extremely close and effective gunfire. I would like to extend to the officers and men of the *Douglas H. Fox* the appreciation of both myself and Mine Forces Pacific."

Despite the harassing effect and threat of enemy shore guns, all the sweepers continued to do their work cheerfully and aggressively, nor did they lose their sense of humor.

For example, when Mine Squadron Three's flagship, the USS *Cabildo* (LSD-16), was hit inside Wonsan harbor while recovering her small sweep boats, Captain Herald F. Stout issued a purple heart to the ship. In the citation, Captain Stout stated:

> While recovering minesweep boats with her back flap down, the enemy directed approximately ten rounds at her middle body in a most unsporting and ungentlemanly manner, scoring one direct hit which penetrated her number two deck level causing unauthorized ventilation of decks, stacks, living spaces and personal effects. Coolly disregarding this affront to the dignity and personal privacy, by an unseen but not unfelt foe, *Cabildo* went through in good order and with excellent speed.

Captain Stout postscripted the citation by stating that "the facts set forth in the enclosed citation are personally known to me and only too well."

The enemy shell had landed above the well deck within a few feet of Commander Mine Squadron Three.

Minesweeping by Moonlight

The importance of night minesweeping was greatly increased in Korea on 15 October 1952 during the amphibious feint at Kojo, an east coast city 25 miles southeast of Wonsan and 35 miles north of the battlefront.

The minesweepers arrived off Kojo on D-minus-three Day, but due to high winds and heavy seas they were unable to commence operations until morning twilight of 13 October.

Five shallow-sweep boats made the initial run. As they closed to within 1,500 yards of the beach, heavy shore battery fire was received. So intense and accurate was the enemy's artillery and machinegun fire that only the three leading sweeps were able to complete the first pass. The two boats bringing up the rear cut their sweep gear and scampered for the open sea.

Later in the day, the three AMSs, with the direct gunfire support of two U. S. destroyers, tried to sweep the area once again.

Although the destroyer gunfire support was reported as "excellent", it was not sufficient to silence the enemy guns. Both minesweeper *Osprey* and destroyer *Perkins* were lightly damaged. *Perkins,* in fact, suffered one killed and 17 wounded from two near misses which sprayed the destroyer with shrapnel.

At sunrise the next day, 14 October, the three AMSs once more tried to clear a channel. Once again heavy gunfire drove them away, this time before they could reach the sweeping area. So concentrated and accurate was the enemy gunfire that on 15 October daytime sweeping was declared a failure. If any further sweeping was done at Kojo it would have to be accomplished under the cover of darkness.

Only one more night—14-15 October—remained, but the sweep was finished that night. Fortunately, no mines were found.

The daytime failure at Kojo, and the ever increasing enemy gunfire along the northeast coast, pointed up the need for night minesweeping. Henceforth much, if not all, minesweeping in Korean waters would have to be done at night. Night sweeping had been done during World War II, but the technique had not been practiced since. There was urgent need, therefore, to become familiar again with the doctrine of night sweeping—particularly for formation sweeping prior to amphibious assaults.

The skipper of the minesweeper *Shoveler* (AM-382) (LT C. J. Casserly) recommended: (1) that night minesweeping doctrines be restudied and more fully developed; (2) that a positive means of determining mine contact with sweep wire be investigated; and (3) that methods of illumination or marking location of mines swept at night be investigated.

He further suggested that such things as underwater pyrotechnics, night-visible dye and grapnels might help in locating mines, once they had been swept.

But night minesweeping, although in less danger from enemy guns, was more difficult than day operations for numerous reasons:

First, navigation at night was more difficult, as was accurate charting of areas swept. Tide and current might cause either sweeping holidays or duplication of sweeping.

Second, mine destruction and mine buoying were more difficult at night.

Third, minesweeping at night increased the hazard to all ships following astern the lead sweepers.

Fourth, dozens of fishing sampans frequented the Korean coasts at night. There was always the danger that one of them might be involved in more than fishing.

"As the Korean war drew to a close, the AMs were doing all of their inshore sweeping at night,"[15] said LCDR E. E. Hollyfield, Jr., commanding officer of the USS *Symbol* (AM-123). "On the east coast the AMs were responsible for check sweeping the coast from the bombline to just north of Yang-do, a distance of approximately 227 miles. We streamed our gear out of shore battery range at dusk and then just at good dark we closed the beach and commenced sweeping. We swept parallel to the coast in one direction as far as we could get before daybreak the following morning, usually a distance of about sixty to seventy miles. Sometimes during the night our tracks would come within five hundred yards of the beach. Just prior to daybreak we would proceed to seaward to recover our gear out of shore battery range. With any sea at all, we never knew what, if anything, we had swept during the night. Therefore, after daybreak, we would run a fast surveillance patrol back through the area we had swept. Floaters were found from time to time in the swept areas indicating either that we had cut mines or that some had broken their moorings during the night.

"The worst night minesweeping problem north of the 38th parallel was the sampans always ahead of us," continued Hollyfield. "We knew the North Koreans were starving and needed to fish; yet, we never knew whether the blacked-out sampans ahead were loaded with fishing gear or with mines."

On such check-sweeps, Hollyfield strongly recommended against sweepers making reverse passes at night for fear of running into mines that might have been cut.

"Not only did the AMSs sweep closer inshore," said Hollyfield, "but often they reversed course at night and that is a tricky business even for experts."

Another AM skipper, LCDR A. G. Russillo, commanding officer of USS *Toucan* (AM-387), said, "The difficulty with night sweeping was that we never really knew how well we were doing. After we cut them, we had a destruction problem. In rough water our radar couldn't find them. A swept mine on the surface that can't be seen is as dangerous as a mine that still holds its moorings. We didn't know if we were endangering and complicating the problems of the sweeper following us. It was really a tough proposition on the west coast, with all its navigational hazards. The 'J' factor increased terrifically at night. Yet, as far as we know, night sweeping *was* effective."

"But Korean night sweeping with all its headaches was never as bad as night sweeping at Anzio," said CDR Myers, who had skippered minesweeper *YMS-13* during that World War II operation. "At Anzio," said Myers, "we were opposed both by accurate shore batteries and constant aerial attack. Had we confronted the Anzio type of opposition in Korea, both our sweeping problems and our support problems would have been multiplied."

Minesweepers Prove Versatile

In addition to their Korean minesweeping chores, which by the end of hostilities had accounted for a grand total of 1,088 mines swept, mine craft made other significant contributions to the over-all military effort.

By May of 1952 the minesweepers had been given duties other than sweeping port approaches, harbors, channels and island defense areas, gunfire support areas, coastal patrol and gun interdiction areas. They had been directed to perform such varied tasks as providing "flycatchers"* to safeguard swept areas, making continuous studies of enemy mining methods, gathering and disseminating mine intelligence, training Republic of Korea naval minesweeping forces, and training Republic of Korea naval liaison officers how to render sea-air rescue assistance.

As their sweeping ended, mine craft performed pilot rescue missions comparable to those performed by U. S. submarines during the late phases of World War II. *Symbol* rescued a friendly pilot near Hungnam on 19 June 1953, and *Dextrous* picked one up in the same area on 23 May 1953. *Ruddy* rescued three airmen from a ditched B-26 near the west coast island of Chodo on 1 July.

Capturing enemy sampans and prisoners also provided minesweepers a welcome break in the sweeping routine. On 7 May 1952, the *Ptarmigan*

---

* Ships assigned to catch ships fishing in blockaded waters.

(AM-376) reported the capture of five sampans and twenty-five prisoners between Hungnam and Mayang-do.

On 10 May 1952, *Murrelet* (AM-372) reported the capture of a total of six sampans and twenty-six North Korean prisoners. The "prisoner" ages ranged from 41 to 57. All were fishermen from the village of Kwandong-ni and reported they had very little food and that influenza, for which there was no medicine, existed among the children. The prisoners also stated that civilians were not permitted to travel between towns, and that no trains had been heard on the coastal line for some months.

The destroyer minesweeper *Endicott* (DMS-35) achieved distinction by scoring heavy damage against several trains during the train interdiction operation. This performance elevated *Endicott* into the distinguished membership of the "Trainbuster's Club."*

Check-Sweeping Replaces Clearance Sweeping

In June 1952 the decision was made by Admiral Gingrich to limit antimine operations to check-sweeping areas already cleared, and to discontinue clearance sweeping of new areas. Hereafter, minesweeping oprations became stable and routine.

Minesweepers continued to move up and down both Korean coasts, checking anchorages, bombardment areas, and channels for renewed mining efforts.

On the east coast, the anti-mine ships regularly swept the bombardment area from Suwon-dan, near the southern tip of Korea, to Musu-dan, near the Manchurian border. East coast minesweepers kept an estimated 270 square miles of harbor and anchorage areas mine-free, and swept all mineable waters to seaward of a coastal sweep line about 300 miles in length.

On the west coast, the Chinnampo channel was one-and-a-half miles wide and an estimated 70 miles long. The Haeju estuary channel was 73 miles long. Inchon's Flying Fish Channel was 61 miles in length, Mokpo nearly 73 miles. Counting channels, anchorages, and ports, west coast sweepers had to continuously check-sweep more than 337 square miles of water.

The decision to discontinue clearance sweeps and henceforth to limit the antimine effort to check-sweeping, diminished the mine menace during the remainder of the war.

Post-Armistice Minesweeping

After the armistice on 27 July 1953, minesweeping on the east coast was discontinued. On the west coast, however, minesweeping continued on a

---

* See section "Train Busting" in Chapter 9, "The Seaborne Artillery."

routine basis in the areas around Inchon, Haeju, and Gazan until 10 September 1953.

In place of sweeping, the minesweepers served as patrol ships on both coasts in order to survey enemy coastal traffic, to maintain surveillance over the large POW camps on Cheju-do, and to protect friendly shipping and fishing from piracy south of the demarcation line.

Commander Task Force 95 (Rear Admiral C. E. Olsen) took stringent precautions against any possible enemy allegations that UN ships were violating the truce terms. He directed that:

(1) All ROK naval vessels remain south of the demarcation line; and after 15 August 1953, all UN ships remain south of the demarcation line;

(2) No suspicious looking craft be visited or searched;

(3) All UN ships take evasive action rather than return the fire of enemy guns.

At the time of the armistice, it was not known whether the Communists planned to clear the minefields they had planted or not. On 9 October 1953, however, a Joint Armistice Team reported that North Koreans had started to sweep north of the demarcation line. Even so, the danger of Soviet-built mines in Korean waters was destined to remain for some time. In August of 1953, Vice Admiral Robert P. Briscoe, COMNAVFE, issued a mine warning in the form of a Hydropac* that waters north of the demarcation line had not been swept since 27 July. Ships entering this area would do so at their own risk. Briscoe also stated that moored mines had a pronounced tendency to walk seaward, and that heavy weather caused mines to part their moorings and become "floaters." Furthermore, he pointed out that there was always the possibility that the enemy would decide to re-mine some of the swept areas north of the demarcation line.

From 27 July 1953 until 1 January 1954, only one mine was encountered —an old floater estimated to have been in the water for about two years.

The sudden absence of floating mines following the armistice seemed to indicate that some of the floating mines encountered during hostilities actually were "drifters"—drifting by *design* rather than by *accident*.

Significance

The mine war in Korea is rich with significance and lessons.

One of the most important results of the three-year anti-mine war was to highlight the importance of intelligence.

The relation and importance of good intelligence to effective mine

---

* Bulletin giving hydrographic information on Pacific waters.

countermeasures is, as demonstrated in Korea, of immeasurable value. Mines that can be located and destroyed *prior* to planting do not require sweeping. Similarly, the destruction of minelaying facilities limits the number of mines that can be planted. Accurate intelligence as to location and composition of minefields makes the mine countermeasures problem relatively simple. It may permit avoidance of the minefield if conditions are not favorable for minesweeping.

Prompt intelligence and *accurate* intelligence are prerequisites of successful mine warfare operations.

The Korean war taught much with regard to U. S. Navy minesweeping *ships* and minesweeping equipment. All types of minesweepers were employed in Korea. The DMS proved useful in waters along the northeast coast, but remained of dubious value as a versatile minesweeper. The most capable all-around sweeper, despite her limited cruising radius, inadequate communication, and critical stability, was the 136-foot wooden AMS. She could sweep both in deep and shallow areas, and she offered a small target to the enemy; she was durable and economical to operate. The 220-foot AM proved invaluable for off-shore sweeping. She was fast. She provided a stable gunnery platform and carried good navigational equipment; she had ample space accommodations to function as a lead ship and flagship. Since only two such vessels, the *Redstart* and *Dextrous,* were in the Far East in the spring of 1951, their schedules were arranged so that one of them could be in the combat area at all times.[16]

The use of an LST as a logistics support ship, helicopter platform and mining headquarters greatly enhanced the mobility of the minesweeping task group. However, the LST did not make as good a mothership as the LSD. Launching and recovery of boats via the LST's ramp were extremely slow and, except under the most favorable weather conditions, hazardous both to crews and boats. In its place, the LSD proved to be ideal both as a mothership for small boat sweeps and as a means of supplying and supporting the larger sweepers.

Innovations to countermine warfare developed during Korean operations were the minehunting helicopters and patrol squadrons (PBMs) and the aerial bombing of the minefield.

In regard to *equipment,* the same underwater object-locator gear and the same type of sonar used in World War II to detect moored mines were used again during the Korean war. The equipment for sweeping moored mines and detonating magnetic and acoustic mines had not been improved.

Regarding the U. S. Navy mine *operations* in the Korean war, there was no significant change in technique from World War II methods. The mine countermeasures we used in Korean waters in 1953 were of 1943 vintage.

The virtually unsweepable pressure, pressure-magnetic, and pressure-acoustic mines remained the same serious threat as in World War II. Therefore, it is concluded that UN forces were fortunate in that, except for the use of the magnetic mine, the enemy employed only World War I and World War II type mines, and these were mainly simple contact types. Had they used even combination magnetic-acoustic mines, the task of minesweeping would have been increased one hundred fold.

It must be concluded, therefore, that in the perpetual race between the development of mines and mine countermeasures, the mine has maintained the commanding lead that it gained during World War II.

The Korean War also gave new insight into the capability of the Communists in the mine warfare field of naval operations. The Soviet-sponsored minelaying in Korea alerted the U. S. Navy to the need of research, development, and production of adequate countermeasures. In recognition of this fact, the mine type command was reestablished at Pearl Harbor under Rear Admiral John M. Higgins on 3 January 1951.

Shortly after taking command, Admiral Higgins made a statement with regard to the Korean mine operations that should be read frequently by the officers and men of the U. S. Navy.

"It is obvious from the mine warfare we have been engaged in during the Korean action," said Higgins, "that these deadly weapons can and will be effectively employed by any enemy we may face in the future.

"It is a basic fact that any small maritime nation, with only elementary transportation facilities, little technical experience, and a minimum of improvised equipment, can deny the use of its ports and the shallow waters along its coast to a large, modern naval force at little cost to itself, simply by the extensive laying of even elementary types of mines."[17]

By 22 August 1953, the United States Navy had ordered 125 new minesweepers of various sizes, shapes, and descriptions. Many were wooden-hulled to minimize their magnetic field. It may seem curious that the nation then in the process of building the world's first nuclear-powered submarine was at the same time building wooden fighting ships of laminated white oak—but such is the nature of modern naval warfare.

There was one residual result of the mine war in Korea. It was to make mine warfare a more dependable career specialty in the United States Navy. For, as Rear Admiral Charles B. Momsen stated: "Of one point we can be sure; if war comes, the enemy will use mines on us on a big scale. No nation in history has ever used enough mines of the right kind."

A most significant conclusion about mine warfare in the Korean war is the fact that the Communist enemy, by the use of obsolescent moored mines and magnetic mines laid by primitive means, was able to cause considerable damage to UN ships and interference to UN operations. The enemy's mining effort was entirely defensive in character, limited and local. Even so, the danger of mines kept UN vessels outside the 100-fathom curve "except in swept areas." Had a full-scale enemy offensive and defensive mining effort, using the latest type mines and the most modern methods of planting mines, been made, the task of prosecuting the war in Korea would have been vastly more costly and difficult.

The transcendent mine warfare lesson to be learned in Korea was the continuing need for battle readiness. The U. S. Navy lacked readiness on 25 June 1950. As the war progressed, readiness improved.

Prior to May 1951, about 200 mines were swept at a cost of 5 sweepers sunk. From May to December 1951, 700 were swept with no loss of sweepers. This proves that with more equipment and increasing experience, the U. S. Navy developed better techniques, effectiveness, and safety. At the same time the enemy got a good look at U. S. countermeasures. His successful use of mines in Korea portends use elsewhere.

The U. S. Navy must prepare itself for future mine threats.

8.

The Struggle to Strangle

Introduction

In early November 1950, as the Chinese entered the war in force, the aircraft carriers of Task Force 77 were given a unique and unfamiliar role: to participate in a campaign to isolate a battlefield. Specifically, the Navy was given two initial tasks: (1) to destroy the six major Yalu River bridges of the seventeen which linked Manchuria and North Korea; and (2) to perform armed reconnaissance* in the eastern half of northeast Korea (specifically, east of 127° E).

This was the beginning of twenty months of effort by the aircraft carriers of Task Force 77 to strangle the supply lines of the enemy. Throughout this campaign, the striking power of carriers supplemented that of the surface ships and escort carriers of the blockade force, the aircraft of the U. S. Fifth Air Force in Korea, the First Marine Air Wing, and the other segments of the UN air forces in Korea. In effect, the task of air power—both land and sea-based—during these twenty months was to sever the Korean peninsula at the Yalu and Tumen rivers, to undercut the peninsula, and to float the entire land mass out into mid-ocean where interdiction,† in concert with a naval blockade, could strangle the supply lines of the Communists and thereby force their retreat and defeat.

The problem for the carriers of Task Force 77 was simply this: How could they, operating an average of 150 naval aircraft in the northeast area of Korea three days out of four, hinder (and if possible prevent) the movement of enemy supplies through an area the size of the state of Minnesota, opposed by an energetic and ingenious enemy operating some 6,000 to

---

* "Armed Reconnaissance" is defined as an air reconnaissance mission which has the additional mission of searching for and attacking targets of opportunity within a specified area.

† In the JCS *Dictionary of Military Terms,* the word "interdict" means "to prevent or hinder, by any means, enemy use of an area or route."

8,000 trucks and hundreds of trains, dispersing and camouflaging his supplies, working only at night and opposing our air attacks with the ever-increasing antiaircraft fire?

The account of this heruclean effort, the successes attained by the Navy, and the ingenuity and energy which our aviators displayed, plus an analysis of why air power failed to isolate the battlefield, are profitable studies for every student of naval warfare and military operations.

The Naval Air Attacks Upon the Yalu River Bridges (8-30 November 1950)

During the month of October 1950, disturbing and increasingly frequent reports were received at UN headquarters in Tokyo regarding the entry of Chinese Communist forces into Korea. More than 400,000 Red Chinese troops were reported to be on the Manchurian side of the Yalu River; some Chinese Army units were known to have crossed the international boundary as early as 16 October, although how many and for what purpose was not known. Some thought the Communists were only sending enough "volunteer" troops into North Korea to permit the retreat and rescue of the badly-shattered remnants of the North Korean Army, or perhaps to protect the Yalu hydroelectric plants. Others believed that full-scale Chinese Communist intervention was imminent. The Chinese radio in Peking had said as much, warning that their forces would enter Korea if UN forces crossed the 38th parallel.

The northward advance of UN forces across the 38th parallel began on 7-8 October. Enemy resistance at first was light and sporadic. By 24 October, however, determined resistance was encountered all along the front, especially by ROK units in the east. The Seventh Regiment of the ROK Sixth Division, after reaching the Yalu River at Chosan, suddenly found itself surrounded and cut off on 26 October. Relief elements of the ROK II Corps met strong attacks near Onjong and Usan by forces including Chinese troops. If further evidence of the intervention of Chinese forces was needed, the First Cavalry Division was surprised and suffered severe casualties on the night of 1-2 November when a strong contingent of Chinese horsemen* attacked its position. From captured prisoners, four Red Chinese armies were identified.

In the air, meanwhile, reconnaissance revealed that Communist reinforcements and supplies were steadily streaming across the Yalu River bridges into North Korea. On five occasions, antiaircraft guns on the Manchurian side of the river fired at UN aircraft. Russian-built MIG-15 air-

---

* Horses were not the only four-footed animals used by the Communists in Korea. During the Hungnam redeployment, naval airmen reported double-humped, long-haired Bactrian camels. Also sighted were shaggy, sure-footed Mongolian ponies.

craft appeared over the Yalu for the first time on 1 November and fired at UN aircraft.

In the face of this evidence of Chinese Communist intervention and intent, an earlier JCS directive which had forbidden air attacks within five miles of the international boundary was rescinded. Attacks on the temporary North Korean capital, Sinuiju, and on the Korean terminals of the Yalu River bridges were now authorized.[1]

Vice Admiral Struble received the following despatch from Vice Admiral Joy in the early hours of 8 November:

> General MacArthur considers it urgent that the first overwater span on the Korean side of all international bridges along the Yalu and Tumen Rivers be destroyed because of the heavy use by the enemy to supply their forces in Korea. The Manchurian territory and air space under no circumstances must not, repeat *not,* be violated. You have been assigned the mission of attacking the two bridges near Chongsongjin. The Air Force is fully committed in the area of Sinuiju.

Had there been time for reflection, the assignment given the carrier task force on 8 November 1950 to destroy the Yalu River bridges would have given satisfaction to those naval aviators who had long contended that the United States had vital need of the inherent precision of the fast carrier task force. Here was a request from an Air Force command asking for assistance in destroying strategic-type targets which required the delivery of large bombs with low-level, pinpoint accuracy. General MacArthur's orders to VADM Joy had been limited. He was not to attack the bridges, but only the first overwater *span* of the bridges *on the Korean side.* Many of the Yalu bridges, therefore, could not be attacked by B-29s; to do so would force the high-flying planes to violate the Manchurian sanctuary. Moreover, high-level bombing required a "run-in" of sufficient distance to obtain a bombsight solution. In obtaining it, the B-29s would have to fly across some of the loops and bends in the winding Yalu, part of each bend and loop being Chinese territory. For the same reason, fighter protection could not be given to the B-29s even by day; and night-bombing attacks against such precise targets were out of the question. It was too much to expect that some of their bombs might not accidentally fall on the wrong side of the river.

The imposed restrictions did not increase the effectiveness of the naval aircraft attacks, either. Each pilot was personally read Admiral Joy's despatch which ordered that "zeal in prosecuting these attacks shall not result in border or air space violations." The naval pilots were ordered *not to fly over Manchuria;* furthermore, they were ordered *not to fire upon or bomb the antiaircraft guns on the Chinese side of the river.* And most certainly they could *not pursue an attacking MIG* back over Chinese territory ("hot pursuit").

The effect of these restrictions was to require that the naval aircraft make their dive-bombing runs *perpendicular* to the bridges rather than *parallel* to them as good tactics would require. The prospect of a hit was thereby greatly reduced. Psychologically, too, the condition of being under fire and unable to fire back was not conducive to the best marksmanship. To many of the airmen, attacks on the Yalu bridges were closely akin to running a gauntlet.

Admiral Joy summarized the problem in a despatch to all the aviators:

"The hazards involved in employing aircraft in precision attacks on small targets protected by intense, well-directed antiaircraft fire which cannot be attacked, as well as by enemy planes flying in the haven of neutral territory, except when the enemy chooses to attack, are tremendous. These factors were gravely considered by General MacArthur before he requested the Navy to take out the bridges. We all recognize that enemy reinforcements and supplies are coming over those bridges now, and will continue to pour into North Korea until the bridges are down. Carrier aircraft alone can make these precision air attacks. Our Government has decided that we cannot violate the air space over Manchuria or attack on Manchurian territory regardless of the provocation. If such attacks were made, the world might be thrown into the holocaust of a third world war. Our naval pilots have been given a most difficult task. May God be with them as they accomplish it."

Despite all the restrictions and hazards, the attacks of the naval aircraft were to prove effective—as will be seen.

The winding Yalu River (not to be confused with China's Yellow River), forms three-fifths of the boundary between Korea and Manchuria. It has its origin in the Chang Pai Mountains in Manchuria. From its source the Yalu runs 30 miles southward to the vicinity of Hyesanjin, thence southwestward for 450 miles through heavily forested hills to the Yellow Sea.

At its mouth, the river is more than 3,000 feet wide, and at average low tide its channel is 12 feet deep. In spring, summer, and early fall, the river is navigable by ships of under 1,000 tons as far as the Sinuiju-Antung area; but in wintertime, from late November to early April, the entire river freezes solid, except its salt water mouth.

Along both banks of the Yalu River in prewar days were lumber, paper, and iron mills, in addition to the large hydroelectric plant near Antung and other industries.

But the key military targets of the Yalu were the 17 bridges crossing the river, 6 of them major ones. The most important two were the twin 3,098-

foot long railroad and highway bridges connecting Antung and Sinuiju. The highway bridge, a structure built by the American Bridge Company in 1910, consisted of 12 spans set on stone piers. The double-tracked rail bridge, only 1,000 feet to the north, was built by the Tokyo Yokogawa Bridge Company and the Osaka Train Manufacturing Company. Other important bridges were located at Manpojin, Hyesanjin, Chongsongjin, and Kanggu.

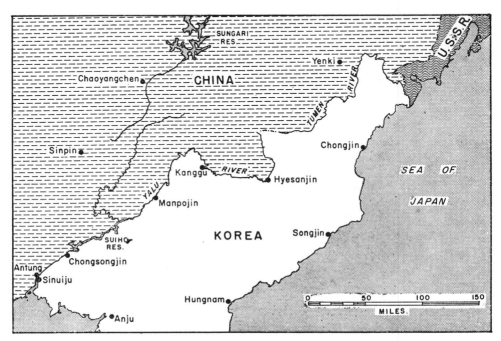

LOCATION OF MAJOR BRIDGES OVER THE YALU

For carrier aircraft operating from Korea's *east coast* to strike the main bridges at Sinuiju on the *west coast* would require an overland, long-range flight (225 miles) above treacherous mountains, with the additional handicap of the oncoming bad weather of winter.

These were the Navy's targets.

Three carriers were available to make the Yalu bridge attacks: *Valley Forge, Philippine Sea,* and *Leyte;* the latter lately arrived from the Sixth Fleet in the Mediterranean on 3 October 1950, after an 18,500 mile journey at an average speed of 22 knots to demonstrate afresh the mobility of the carrier base and the rapid concentration of naval power.

The strike group of each carrier for these bridge attacks would be a basic element of 8 AD Skyraiders, each of them carrying two 1,000-pound bombs (although occasionally one 2,000-pound bomb), plus full belts of 20-mm. ammunition. The F4U Corsair fighter-bombers would carry various loads: eight 5-inch rockets or eight 100-pound bombs (for flak-suppression of the enemy guns on the Korean side of the river); or a 500-pound bomb and six 5-inch rockets (a few carried the large 11-inch Tiny Tim rocket). As few as 8 or as many as 16 Corsairs would be scheduled for each ship's strike group.

As for the F9F2 Panther jets, there would be at least 8 of them, and frequently as many as 16 per strike group, to give high cover protection above the bombers and fighter-bombers.

Thus, each strike group from the carrier consisted of at least 24 aircraft, although many consisted of 40 aircraft.

Because of their faster speed, the jets would take off separately and later. The jets would depart the carriers in three flights—the first flight 50 minutes after the "props,"* the second and third at subsequent 15-minute intervals. Well before the bridges were reached, the first relay of jets would overtake and accompany the props in; the second flight would give protection while over the target; the third would escort the strike group out.

Between the 9th and 21st of November, naval aircraft made a total of 593 sorties on the Yalu River bridges, dropping 232 tons of 500-pound, 1,000-pound, and 2,000-pound bombs.

For the purposes of description, the comments of the commanding officer, VF-53, *Valley Forge* (LCDR W. R. Pittman) are recorded for one of the first strikes on the Sinuiju bridges, on 12 November 1950:

> The *Valley Forge* attack group was composed of 16 F4U-4Bs, 12 ADs, and 8 F9Fs. I was strike leader, and had been ordered to follow the attack of *Philippine Sea's* strike group. The *Leyte's* group would follow us.
>
> As we neared Sinuiju, our F9Fs, led by LCDR H. J. Boydstun (VF-52) reported by radio that he would be overhead in five minutes. LT M. R. Gallaher, of VA-55, led the Skyraiders.
>
> Our target was the southern Sinuiju bridge, Korean side. The weather was poor, visibility low, and overcast conditions prevailed along our entire route from the east coast to the target. Fortunately, over Sinuiju itself it began to clear.
>
> Since the *Valley Forge* group arrived prior to the two other carrier groups, I was ordered by the target coordinator to continue in first. Our jets took a position ahead and well above us. At this stage of the war, we propeller pilots were increasingly thankful (and not a little envious) of the jets. They were our only protection against the MIGs.
>
> The coordination proceeded smoothly. We reached our pushover point, which had been selected so as not to cross the border. During the entry into the dive, I saw four MIGs take off from the nearby field of Antung, which was clearly visible.

---

* "Props"—propeller-driven aircraft.

The plan was for the first eight Corsairs to strike the Korean AA positions, followed by eight additional F4Us dropping 500-pound VT-fuzed bombs. Then the Skyraiders were to drop their loads of bombs on the bridge. We had always been very successful in knocking out the AA mission by this method (by this time every pilot in my squadron had fifty missions over Korea).

Our entire group went through this plan, and good hits were observed.[2]

The three carriers sent off attacks on the Yalu bridges on 9, 10, 12, 14, 15, 16, 18, and 21 November, with a few additional flights until the end of November. The pilots began to notice that the antiaircraft fire from the Manchurian side of the river was increasing, while that on the Korean side was diminishing.

"With no elation," said LCDR H. M. Sisk, executive officer of VF-33, "our photo intelligence revealed that the enemy guns were being moved from the *south* side of the Yalu River, where we *could* hit them, to the north side, where we *couldn't.* The Reds were alert to recognize and take advantage of our self-imposed restriction. We even noticed that while the guns on the Korean side of the river were well camouflaged, the ones on the Chinese side were not.

"The *Leyte's* attack aircraft achieved several hits," said Sisk, "but I believe we might have done even better if we had used more of the larger bombs. As it was, it was frustrating to penetrate the flak, get a direct hit—and then discover your bomb had knocked out only a few supporting bridge members."[3]

It was during the Yalu bridge attacks that naval pilots first succeeded in downing MIGs.* On the initial attack on 9 November, a pilot from the *Philippine Sea,* LCDR W. T. Amen, commanding officer of VF-112, was credited with the destruction of the first MIG. The second kill was credited to a pilot from *Valley Forge,* LCDR William E. Lamb, commanding officer, VF-52; and the third to Ensign F. C. Weber, VF-31 of the *Leyte.* Not a single naval jet was lost or damaged.

The initial engagement with the MIGs produced one of the best stories of the war. Commander A. D. Pollock, Commanding Officer of VF-51, a *Valley Forge* Panther squadron, was surrounded by his pilots upon his return to the ready room.

"Were you nervous about those MIGs, Dave?" his pilots queried.

"No, I was just keeping an eye on them," replied Pollock.

"Then why did you report *20,000* MIGs coming in at *five* feet?" his pilots asked him.

---

* See Chapter 13, "On The Line," for a complete list of enemy planes destroyed by naval and marine pilots.

The Panther pilots reported that the MIGs had a better rate of climb, greater speed, a shorter turning radius, and better maneuverability than our own planes—but the superior training, teamwork, and marksmanship of the naval airmen more than eradicated these enemy advantages.

While the attacks of the carriers upon the Yalu bridges were considered successful, especially so in the face of the imposed restrictions (the highway bridge at Sinuiju and the two bridges at Hyesanjin were dropped and four others were damaged), and undoubtedly slowed the enemy's advance, the subsequent heavy attacks by the Chinese armies upon the UN forces, commencing on 24 November 1950, made it obvious that the Chinese, with ample forces, equipment, and supplies had been able to enter North Korea.*

On 29 November, therefore, the primary mission of the carriers was changed to close air support. The preliminaries for the Hungnam evacuation were on, and the First Marine Division, deep in North Korea, was in need of the aid of the firepower of every airplane that could be brought to its support.

And by now the Yalu River was beginning to freeze. Even if the carriers had been able to continue the bridge attacks, the Chinese would soon be able to cross the river at any point on the heavy ice.

East Coast Bridge Busting

On Christmas Day 1950, as the UN forces departed Hungnam, Vice Admiral Struble dispatched Major General E. E. Partridge, Commanding General, Far Eastern Air Force, to propose that the services of the fast carriers be utilized in close air support missions on the eastern flank of the Eighth Army.

Partridge replied on the 29th of December that General Ridgway desired the Navy to interdict the "east coastal road from the bombline as far north as practicable."

This role of interdiction for the carriers was further spelled out on 15 January 1951 when General Partridge requested that naval aircraft undertake the cutting of rail lines and recommended "attacks on key bridges and destruction rolling stock currently reported scattered along route between Hamhung and Susong."

Vice Admiral Struble tried to convince his superiors that close air support, of the type just performed during the Hungnam evacuation, and not

---

* It was later estimated that the Chinese in North Korea by late October numbered 275,000 troops in organized units. The 66th, 42nd, 40th, 39th, and 38th Chinese Armies had been identified.

interdiction, was the Navy's most profitable employment. On 23 January 1951 he despatched Generals Ridgway and Partridge as follows:

Without detracting from the value of armed reconnaissance and interdiction in some measure to prevent the transportation of troops, equipment and supplies to the enemy front lines, previous experience here in Korea has demonstrated that under the conditions existing, the results to be obtained from such operations are only partial. In my opinion, strong close air support . . . will do more to hurt the enemy potential than any other type of operation in which we can participate at this time.[4]

But these appeals did not succeed. Intelligence reports had been received which indicated that the enemy planned to make heavy use of the eastern rail net. It was known that at least one division of North Korean troops would be moving down that route.

Accordingly, on 29 January 1951, the carriers of Task Force 77 commenced the interdiction of the east coast bridges. The bitter Korean winter weather, with its low temperatures, snow, sleet, and ice, became a major problem for both ships and aircraft.

Admiral Joy's description of the task ahead in a despatch to Admiral Struble epitomized the resolution and purpose with which the naval forces of the Far East turned to in their efforts to obliterate the rail lines of northeast Korea:

Rail route northeast coast between Wonsan and Chongjin is of continuing value to enemy as a major route over which supplies, equipment, and troops are being transported to immediate battle areas. The enemy's known capability for quickly effecting temporary repairs to the damaged portions of this route can be seriously impaired by *deliberate, methodical, total* destruction of all piers, spans, approaches and embarkments of each vital bridge in each critical area. The enemy cannot accomplish makeshift repairs when nothing remains upon which to make them. Naval air and naval gunfire are good weapons to accomplish this job. . . .[5]

Before beginning the story of Task Force 77's lengthy and concentrated efforts to eradicate the rail system of northeast Korea, an explanation and description of the Communists' supply networks and their logistic problems is required in order that the reader may appreciate the immensity of the unique task which had been assigned to the carriers.

First of all, the logistics of the Korean War favored the Oriental soldier, who needed far less in the way of supply than did our own. The Chinese and North Korean soldier was inured to simple diet, to a bare minimum of necessities, and was independent of such Western delicacies as hot food, showers, movies, PX supplies, and twice-weekly mail from home. The production centers supplying him with food and munitions were but a few *hundreds* of miles distant *overland*.

In contrast, the UN's production centers were *thousands* of miles distant *overseas*.

Thus, the enemy's supply problem was much more manageable than our own. The average Chinese soldier required only 10 pounds of supplies per day, in contrast to our own soldier's requirement of some 60 pounds per day. A Chinese division of 10,000 men needed only 50 tons of supplies per day to keep it in action.* With never more than 90 divisions in Korea, and approximately 58 divisions in the frontlines, only some 3,000 tons of supplies had to get through from Manchuria to the battlefront every day.

How could this relatively small tonnage be moved? The Communists had four general transportation systems: rail, road, footpath, and sea. (See endsheet maps.)

The rail system in North Korea was divided naturally by the mountainous backbone of Korea into two principal zones: the eastern and the western networks. A total of six rail lines crossed the Yalu and Tumen Rivers southward from Manchuria—three on each side of the peninsula.

On the western side of Korea, the three lines from Manchuria led single-track to Sinuiju, where double-tracking commenced, thence southward to the capital of Pyongyang and the battlefront. The peacetime capacity of the double-tracked portion below Sinuiju had been estimated to be 9,000 tons per day, while the three single-tracked lines from the border to the rail junction at Sinuiju could handle a total of 6,000 tons. Later, as a result of damaged tunnels, bridges, roadbed, and track, and with Communist logistical operations confined to nighttime or inclement weather, it was conservatively estimated that the Communists could deliver approximately 500 to 1,500 tons per day to the battle area on the western rail net.

The eastern rail network of North Korea also originated in Manchuria, where three lines crossed to join in the vicinity of Kilchu, thereafter becoming a single line southward to Kowon. Here the rail line split, one line running westward to Pyongyang; the other continuing south to Wonsan. Below Wonsan, the rail net split again, one branch following the east coast, the other line continuing southward toward Seoul and in effect bisecting the peninsula.

This eastern network (to be the scene of the Navy's long interdiction effort) included 1,140 miles of track, 956 bridges and causeways, and 231 tunnels. This very large number of bridges and tunnels (one bridge for every 1.2 miles of track and one tunnel for every 5 miles of track) was required by the mountainous terrain of North Korea. The average tunnel length was 1,200 feet.

---

* A rough breakdown of this amount was as follows: 48 per cent food; 22 per cent clothing, weapons, equipage; 10 per cent petroleum products; 20 per cent ammunition.

The peacetime capacity of the eastern rail net had been calculated to be some 5,000 tons per day. Later, as a result of the Navy's interdiction efforts, the capacity of this eastern net was reduced to less than 500 tons per day—and in certain periods, to almost nothing.

Thus, even during the period of heaviest attack upon the North Korean rail network by the several UN air forces, the Reds by the regimentation of mass labor to repair bridges and breaks, by shuttling trains between breaks, and by use of the system only at night or in inclement weather, could still transport between 1,000 to 2,000 tons over the entire east and west rail systems every day. In other words, despite an all-out UN air effort by the U. S. Navy, the U. S. Air Force, and the U. S. Marines, and by various UN air units, the Communists could supply approximately half their needs by rail alone.

The second supply network available to the Communists was the highway system. While none of the Korean roads could have been rated good by Western standards (none being hard-surfaced, and all being either rough gravel or dirt), the network was to prove an even more difficult target system than the rail network. In fact, the very primitiveness of the roads was an advantage to the enemy and made them unprofitable targets to air assault.

North Korea's road network, generally speaking, paralleled the rail net, but as can be seen in the endsheet diagram, the entire area was criss-crossed with roads wherever the mountains permitted. Two thousand miles of road were estimated to be in each half of North Korea. With the fighting front at the narrow waist of Korea, the logistical capacity of this network had been estimated by road engineers to be more than 1,500 tons nightly, and probably a great deal more.

The third supply system was the animal and manpower system. With horses, mules, and even camels available, plus unlimited coolie-manpower using A-frames,* uncounted additional tons of equipment could reach the front, using trails and paths instead of the highways and rail lines. The ubiquitous A-frame on the back of a sturdy Oriental peasant was to be the one logistic system that modern air power could not effectively counter.

The fourth system—the sea—had long since been securely closed by the blockade efforts of Task Force 95.

Thus, the UN faced an almost impossible task of isolating the battlefield by air. But, as will be seen, the assignment of the interdiction task to Task Force 77 was either the most profitable employment which could be found or else was justified on the basis of urgency.

* A-frame—a wooden frame used by coolies in the Orient to facilitate the carrying of heavy back loads.

The Battle of Carlson's Canyon (The "Bridge of Toko-Ri")

The vigor, tenacity, and ingenuity displayed by Task Force 77 against the coastal rail lines of northeast Korea during the period from January to June 1951 can best be described in an account of the destruction of a single bridge over "Carlson's Canyon," near Kilchu, and the subsequent efforts of Task Force 77 to maintain cuts along this coastal railroad. The repeated attacks on this bridge, and the enemy's repair efforts, became the repetitious story of similar and simultaneous attacks on dozens of other bridges throughout the year of 1951.

After the decision had been reached that the primary mission of the carriers was to be interdiction, Rear Admiral Ralph A. Ofstie, then Commander Task Force 77, ordered his reconnaissance aircraft in February to make a complete photographic survey of the east coast rail system in order to find the most profitable targets along it. Photographs of the entire east coast rail net were taken. The intelligence officers of *Princeton* and of Commander Carrier Division Five—LCDR G. M. Douglass and LCDR B. H. Fisher—made flak analyses, terrain studies, and target selections based on this photography in order to determine the targets most likely to interdict the rail traffic and to hurt the enemy the most.

On the morning of 2 March 1951, a perfect target was discovered by the commanding officer of Fighting Squadron 193, LCDR Clement M. Craig. Craig was returning from a strike on the Kilchu bridges when he spotted *the* bridge.

"We had just been bombing other bridges along the route, and were heading south when I saw this one," said Craig.[6] "The bridge was long and high, measuring 600 feet in length and having a maximum height above the terrain of 60 feet. Five concrete piers supported six steel spans across the canyon. Adjacent to this operable bridge were an additional five piers of a companion but incomplete bridge."

Craig also noted tunnels at each end of the bridge—*two* tunnels, in fact, to eventually allow through traffic in both directions. Best of all, the target was *south* of Kilchu, at which point three rail lines from Manchuria joined. Thus, if this bridge could be interdicted—and *kept* interdicted—the flow of southward traffic over the eastern net from China could be seriously impeded.

Craig, upon landing aboard *Princeton,* personally reported this bridge to Admiral Ofstie. Craig's description impressed the admiral that a vital target had been found—one which the Communists would find exceedingly difficult to either bypass or repair.

Not a moment was lost. On the afternoon of 2 March the bridge was taken under attack, but only minor damage to the bridge approaches resulted.

The following morning, however, the bridge was demolished by *Princeton's* aircraft. Leading eight Skyraiders from his squadron, VA-195, LCDR Harold G. ("Swede") Carlson's pilots dropped one span of the bridge, damaged a second, and twisted two others out of horizontal alignment.

The bridge spanned what became known, in his honor, as "Carlson's Canyon."

The bridge was attacked again on 7 March 1951, and this time another span was dropped.

Promptly, the Communists commenced their repair campaign, working mostly at night. Using interlocking wooden beams, called "cribbing," temporary piers were quickly constructed to replace the two missing spans and to support the damaged one. The askew sections were straightened.

On 14 March, the systematic reconnaissance taken by *Princeton's* photo pilots, led by LT C. A. Hooper, revealed the status of the reconstruction progress. The frantic efforts of the Communists to get the bridge back in operation were apparent, and it was obvious that the bridge would be in commission again in a few days—unless something were done about it.

On the next day, therefore, a carrier group again struck Carlson's Canyon, this time with napalm. In this attack, not only were the new wooden cribbing structures beneath the originally damaged spans obliterated, but, in addition, a third orginal span was destroyed and a fourth seriously damaged. Of the original six spans, only two now remained standing.

During the month of March, meanwhile, the carrier aviators were blasting on both sides of the railroad north and south of Carlson's Canyon to cut the track at as many other points along the route as possible. Similar havoc was being made in the other portions of the rail network.

March 1951 saw "tunnel-busting" added to "bridge-busting." "Tunnel-busting" was a misnomer, for the carrier airmen had learned from previous experience that collapsing a tunnel, even with a big bomb, was highly improbable. Even Army demolition teams, during the evacuation at Hungnam, had failed to destroy a tunnel. Hence the approved tactic was for time-delay fuzed bombs to be thrown into the ubiquitous tunnels to destroy trains, personnel, and supplies stored therein, not the tunnel itself.

"We considered many different plans to get the key tunnels," said VADM J. J. Clark, later Commander Seventh Fleet. "One suggestion was to put raiding parties ashore and capture a tunnel long enough to drill a hole down from the top of the tunnel, set charges, and blast the roof in. But the railroad experts said it wouldn't do much good—that the damage would only cause the Communists a few hours' work. Since most of the tunnels were dug out of solid rock, detonating charges inside them only had a shotgun effect out of each end of the tunnel."

The more numerous the bridge breaks and tunnel damage, the more frequent would be the enemy's shuttle efforts to use the coastal line, and the more interdicted the network would be. Of this period, LCDR Carlson recorded: "Bridges were hit and destroyed from one end of North Korea to the other. Successful bridge strikes were the rule, and missed or just-damaged bridges were the exception."

Meanwhile, too, the Communists were concentrating upon repairs at Carlson's Canyon. Rear Admiral Ofstie's reconnaissance aircraft made careful and frequent checks of the repair activity, and night-heckling aircraft from the carriers did their best to harass and hamper the nocturnal labor. Ofstie suggested to Admiral Joy that the Communists' repair work would be further delayed if Far East Air Force aircraft would sprinkle long-delayed-action bombs on this target. A B-29 did so on 27 March.

Despite delay-action bombs and nocturnal harassment, however, the serious damage caused at Carlson's Canyon by the attacks of 15 March was almost fully repaired in two weeks by the patient and steady efforts of the Communists. Accordingly, on 2 April, Task Force 77 struck the bridge again in two lethal raids. So severe were the attacks and so concentrated the damage on these occasions that *none* of the original spans remained standing.

To the Communists, who must have looked in dismal disappointment at the naked and blackened bridge abutments standing in the pock-marked canyon, it was clear they were on the end of a losing battle. The bridge could *never* be kept open against such determined attacks. The only solution for the Communists was to build a bypass *around* the bridge on low ground which could be easily repaired by them and which would be profitless for the blue airplanes of the American Navy to attack. If traffic were to move again, a bypass of Carlson's Canyon *had* to be built.

The results of the savage attacks of the Task Force 77 aircraft on the northeastern Korean rail systems began to be visible in early April 1951.* Rear Admiral Ofstie reported that initial gaps in all major sections of the northeast coastal rail net had now been made, and that, as a result, enemy trains were operating in only a few short sections of track, supplies were moving only by laborious and frequent shuttling, and troops were moving only on foot.

The night-flying reconnaissance aircraft of FEAF corroborated the growing stricture that naval aircraft had placed on the east coast rail system. Nightly sightings of the B-26s showed that the percentage of rail traffic in

---

* From 24 February 1951 to 13 June 1951, the naval airmen, in 1,223 sorties, had made 150 initial breaks and re-breaks in the rail line, and 109 initial breaks and re-breaks in the highways.

this sector fell from 65 per cent in February 1951 to only 32 per cent in April of 1951. Reports from POWs and raiding parties added further evidence of the disruption caused by the air attacks. When the amphibious raid at Sorye-dong below Songjin took place on 7 April,* the British commandoes interrogated civilians in a nearby village. The North Korean civilians reported that not a single train had passed through their area in *forty days.*

However, two events that now transpired were to negate these splendid results.

The first was an alert in the Formosa Straits (for which the Seventh Fleet still held basic responsibility). From 2 April until 15 April, the carriers of Task Force 77 were not available to operate in northeast Korea because of some possibility that the Red Chinese might assault Formosa during this period.

The second event was the two-phase spring offensive of the Chinese armies. The first phase started at 2000 on the night of 22 April. The frontlines suddenly became alive with activity and action as the ROK 6th Division was routed. The First Marine Division stemmed, then smashed the Chinese attack, which was attempting to turn the left flank. By early May, however, UN forces had counterattacked to stabilize the battlefield.

A second enemy attack was obviously being readied. Air reconnaissance and other intelligence reported intense enemy activity and preparation. Thousands of vehicles were reported moving south as fresh Communist divisions were apparently relieving those which had been decimated in the first-phase attack.

The result of the first Chinese offensive was to divert the striking power of Task Force 77 from interdiction to close support efforts in behalf of the endangered Eighth Army.

As a consequence, there was a lapse in Task Force 77's interdiction effort upon the northeast coast rail net. For a period of almost a month, the Communists took advantage of the lull to repair a large part of the damage which their eastern rail net had suffered in February and March.

The carrier planes returned to the interdiction campaign on 1 May, and for the next thirteen days the bridges again received full attention. Thirty-one bridges and all bypasses were knocked out by the *Boxer,*† *Princeton* and

---

* See Chapter 9, "The Seaborne Artillery," for an account of this raid.

† *Boxer* had returned to the fighting on 30 March (having relieved "Old Faithful" *Valley Forge* on 27 March) with the first reserve carrier air group (CVG-101) aboard. This group, and CVG-102, were composed of the organized Naval Air Reserve Squadrons which had been recalled to active duty.

From Mothballs to Firing Line. *Above,* tugs move battleship *Iowa* from the reserve fleet for reactivation at San Francisco. *Center,* FADM Chester W. Nimitz, Mrs. William R. Smedberg, Mrs. William S. Beardsley, and Captain Smedberg with Iowa state flag in wardroom. *Below,* ADM William M. Fechteler, Chief of Naval Operations, observes *Iowa's* main battery during Wonsan bombardment.

VERSATILE HELICOPTER. The "whirlybird," about to land on heavy cruiser *St. Paul* after spotting naval gunfire, provides eyes for the fleet, as well as being a lifesaver for downed aviators and Marines wounded in the fighting ashore. *Center,* empty shell cases litter *Missouri*'s deck after shore bombardment. *Below,* a KD 2R-3 drone prepared for launching in 20 mm. target practice.

NAVAL GUNFIRE SMOKE AND FLAME. *At top,* a salvo from the *Missouri* wings toward Chongjin near Communist border. *Center left, Iowa's* number two turret produces powderpuff flash. *Center right,* a smoke ring in the wake of a five-inch round from heavy cruiser *Toledo. Below,* heavy cruiser *Helena* lobs a salvo into Chongjin.

NAVY GUNNERS LAMBASTE KOREAN SHORE TARGETS. *At top,* an exploding phosphorous shell from *New Jersey* leaves a fiery trail over Hungnam. *Center,* a shell from cruiser *St. Paul* explodes in the target area at Wonsan. *Below,* smoke rises from beach at Inchon during pre-invasion bombardment.

Philippine Sea aircraft. Eleven highway bridges and bypasses were also demolished.

During this period Rear Admiral G. R. Henderson (who had relieved Rear Admiral Ofstie on 6 May) received a request from CDR A. L. Downing, the senior naval representative on duty at the JOC at Taegu. Downing said that the Fifth Air Force had asked informally if the carrier aircraft could help them interdict the *west coast* rail lines from Pyongyang northward.

Rear Admiral Henderson directed his staff to make a study of the area and to determine what assistance his carrier forces could give. Only three carriers were available to Admiral Henderson, and in effect, with replenishment every third or fourth day, only *two* operating carriers. And two carriers, with only 150 aircraft, were not even sufficient to interdict adequately the eastern rail net, much less interdict the west coast lines.

Anxious to lend a hand, however, Rear Admiral Henderson's staff selected four rail bridges in the western net; and on 11 May 1951, 32 Skyraiders (each carrying two 2,000-lb. bombs) and 32 Corsairs (each carrying eight 100-lb. or 250-lb. flak-suppression bombs), plus 16 Panther jets, struck the selected four bridges.

Three of the four were knocked out, and the fourth damaged.

Rear Admiral Henderson informed CDR Downing at Fifth Air Force headquarters that his own commitments in the east coast area precluded any permanent assistance to the FAFIK (Fifth Air Force in Korea) campaign on the west coast. RADM Henderson said he would be glad to help them in attacks such as the one of the 11th on an assistance basis only. The Navy simply did not have enough aircraft carriers to attempt interdiction of both east and west coast rail nets.

The expected second-phase Communist attack began on 16 May under a blanket of fog and rain which hampered United Nations defensive action. Task Force 77 assistance was again needed for close air support strikes at the battleline.

After four days of bitter fighting all along the front, pressure by the attacking Chinese slackened. Despite fog and rain which turned streams into torrents and which kept most airplanes grounded, a UN counteroffensive was started in the west on 19 May and in the central sector on 21 May. This counterattack slowly ground northward until 2 June. In this fighting the Chinese losses were estimated to be 40,000 men. Fifty-five artillery pieces, 900 automatic weapons, and 22,400 artillery shells were captured.

But with the Navy's carrier planes being thus diverted to support the ground forces, another breathing spell was granted to the Communists in

North Korea to repair the heavily damaged rail network in the Navy's area of responsibility.

On 2 June, the carriers were able once again to concentrate on their interdiction targets. In the following 9 days, 24 rail bridges and bypasses and 6 highway bridges and bypasses were completely destroyed.

After the Communists succeeded in building the bypass around Carlson's Canyon in June, making further carrier attacks there unprofitable, the carrier airmen turned their interdiction attention to other key targets along the Kilchu-Hungnam rail net.

A railroad bridge north of Songjin was chosen, and repeated strikes were made on it. This bridge was low, and while repeatedly destroyed by the naval air strikes, the damage was quickly repairable by the Communists. On one occasion after it had been demolished, the bridge was again in operation in only 42 hours. And, as at Carlson's Canyon, the Communists built an even easier-to-repair bypass adjacent to the original bridge.

Next, the aviators turned to a series of three coastal bridges south of Songjin. These bridges were high, hence difficult to repair, and could also be taken under fire by the ships of Task Force 95. (The northernmost bridge of the three was later to be known as "Package 1.") In the target complex were six tunnels (useful to the Communists for hiding shuttle trains during the daylight hours, and for serving as storage centers for the bridge and track repair efforts).

The northernmost bridge, while small, stretched across a 25-foot embankment. Almost the length of 1,000 feet of open track between the tunnels, the embankment, and the bridge were exposed to observation from seaward, and to carrier attacks. The original bridge and the bypass then under construction had been damaged in mid-February.

While Carlson's Canyon was still out of action, Ofstie's railbusters commenced work at this Songjin bridge. Two attacks by jet aircraft struck on 1 April 1951. Four direct hits with 250-lb. bombs, by LCDR G. B. Riley, Commanding Officer, VF-191 and LT Arthur R. Hawkins (*Princeton*), demolished the repair effort on the latter date.*

As at Carlson's Canyon and elsewhere, the Communists promptly commenced repair work, despite the irritating and destructive harassing fire of the surface ships of Task Force 95. Stacks of material, rails, and equipment were concealed in the nearby tunnels. Antiaircraft guns and coastal guns were emplaced around the site.

Twice again in the next month the bridge at Songjin was destroyed. Twice again it was repaired.

---

* This was the first bombing attack of the Korean War by naval jets.

The destroyers of Task Force 95 lobbed shells into the area every night and every day that the weather was unflyable or when the carriers were engaged in replenishment.

Similar destructive attacks were simultaneously being made at many other bridges and tunnels in the area; the bridge and its bypass at Pukch'ong, 45 miles south of Songjin, were taken out on 25 June and again on 28 June. The bridge at Ori-ri, on the rail line north of Hungnam, was destroyed on 21 June 1951. Several bridges at Kowon, on the western line connecting Wonsan and T'yong'yong, were demolished in the period 20-25 June. The rail line south of Wonsan was broken in two places.

The carrier airmen of Task Force 77 literally combed the east coast rail lines, wrecking every bridge a bomb or rocket could possibly reach.

Throughout this period, the Task Force 95 ships added their weight to the destruction. In addition to the nightly harassing fire of the destroyers at many of the exposed coastal bridges (see Chapter 9, "The Seaborne Artillery"), the cruisers and battleships contributed to the havoc.

Between 14 and 19 March, the *Missouri* was credited with the destruction of eight railroad bridges and seven highway bridges in northeast Korea.

Helena's gunfire collapsed a span on the rail bridge below Songjin on the night of 27 July.

Thus did the traffic and rail net of northeast Korea feel the lethal lash of the U. S. Navy's striking power.

By June 1951, however, it was apparent that in spite of the destructive and widespread attacks of the carrier aircraft in the Navy's northeastern area, the battlefield was *not* being interdicted. If the enemy had been able to mount two large-scale offensives within a month, it was obvious that supplies, troops, and equipment were getting through from China to the frontlines in North Korea in abundance. The naval airmen knew that they had choked off a great part of the flow over the *east coast* rail net. Rail traffic along this line had been brought to a virtual halt through the systematic destruction of key bridges and track breaking.

How, then, were the Chinese getting their supplies through?

The answers were plain. First, the bulk of the enemy rail traffic had simply been shifted from the *eastern* to the *western* networks. Unfortunately, the Fifth Air Force in Korea lacked aircraft which could deliver a 2,000-pound bomb—the best weapon for attacking bridges—with pinpoint accuracy. Second, the western network was larger. Third, the Chinese were placing more and more dependence on truck transport. The vehicle count of enemy trucks had jumped from 7,300 in January 1951 to 54,000 in May 1951. Fourth, practically everything was travelling at night; and fifth, the skillful and highly-organized repair efforts of the enemy were matching the rate of destruction.

The Attack on the Hwachon Dam

The only time that torpedoes were used during the Korean War was on 1 May 1951, at the Hwachon reservoir.

Early in April the Communists had tried without success to block the path of the then-advancing UN forces by opening the gates of the 250-foot high dam of the reservoir. Their intention then was to flood portions of the Han and Pukhan rivers and thereby make the northward progress of UN forces more difficult.

In late April, the enemy again seemed ready to use the waters of the Hwachon reservoir to his advantage. If another advance of his own was planned, he could *close* the sluice gates of the dam and thereby *lower* the water level in the Pukhan and Han rivers to fording depth. In the event of a *UN* attack, on the other hand, he could *open* the *sluice* gates and impede the UN advance across the Pukhan and Han rivers.

To forestall either possiblity, the U. S. Eighth Army in Korea requested the carriers to destroy the sluice gates. Earlier high-level bombing attacks by B-29s on the 20-foot high, 40-foot wide, and 2½-foot thick gates had not been effective.

The EUSAK (Eighth U. S. Army in Korea) message was received aboard Task Force 77 at 1440. The dam-busting task was given by Admiral Henderson to *Princeton*—specifically to VA-195, LCDR Harold G. Carlson, USN. Torpedoes were obviously called for, but it would take a few hours to get them ready. In the meantime the Skyraiders could have a go at the dam by a dive-bombing attack.

Attack Squadron 195's first attack was launched in less than three hours from the receipt of the EUSAK message. At 1600, 30 April, six ADs, each carrying two 2,000-pound bombs and accompanied by five Corsairs from VF-193 led by LCDR E. A. Parker for flak-suppression, struck the dam. Although one hole was punched in the dam, the sluice gates were unscathed.

The next day, the torpedo attack was delivered. The terrain made a torpedo attack difficult and hazardous. The reservoir was surrounded by high hills limiting the attack to a two-plane section run-in, while the remainder of the strike orbited overhead. The straightaway was very short, and the problem of controlling the airspeed for the torpedo drop was acute, requiring extremely precise flying. The run-in was made over the high hills into the water area, where the point of torpedo drop had to be accurate, in order that the "fish" would not strike bottom; moreover, the point of drop had to be precise to insure a sufficient arming run. Added to these difficulties were the enemy aircraft batteries surrounding the dam.

Eight ADs led by CDR R. C. Merrick, CVG-19 and LCDR Carlson, each carrying a torpedo set to run at surface level, and accompanied by twelve *Princeton* fighters from VF-192 and VF-193 carrying 100-pound and 500-pound VT-fuzed bombs for flak-suppression, struck the dam shortly after 1130 on 1 May. Merrick weaved his attack group through the antiaircraft fire to pushover point, and the Skyraiders dived in for the torpedo run.

The desired results were achieved. Six of the eight fish ran true. One flood gate in the center was knocked completely out and a ten-foot hole punched in the second flood gate. The impounded waters of the reservoir were released.

Operation Strangle

During the last days of May 1951, General Ridgway's headquarters proposed a scheme by which the battlefield might be interdicted. Why not draw a line across Korea behind the Chinese lines, assign portions of it to the various air forces, and ask them to destroy every vehicle, every bridge, and every target in their section?

This was the genesis of "Operation Strangle" under which the Navy would operate from 5 June until 20 September 1951.

The "belt" interdiction idea had appeal and logic on paper, although there was now great skepticism that *any* interdiction effort could be made effective *within* the Korean peninsula. But since the system in use had achieved only limited success, why not try one which was primarily concerned with the *highways*? The highways, not the railroads, were now carrying the vast preponderance of supplies.

Accordingly, a one-degree strip of latitude across the narrow neck of North Korea—from 38°-15′ N to 39°-15′ N—just above the battleline was selected. The traffic networks within this belt were studied and divided into eight routes: the Fifth Air Force in Korea would take the three westernmost routes; the carriers of Task Force 77 would take the two central routes; and the First Marine Air Wing would take the three eastern routes. (See diagram on page 242.)

In each zone, at selected defiles and passes along the important highway routes, certain areas were designated as "strangle areas" or "choke points." In addition any bridge, embankment, tunnel, or other construction within the zone would be considered a target.

Special efforts would be made to impede enemy movement at night. Aircraft would use searchlight and flares.* Night-heckling aircraft were to in-

---

* See Chapter 10, "The PatRons," page 374.

crease their activity. Delayed-action bombs, set to explode in periods from six to seventy-two hours, would be dropped at every important choke point to impede progress and to delay repair work. Task Force 77 aircraft made an air drop of a half-million leaflets on 20 June along the route between Chongjin and Songjin. The illustrated leaflets warned that unexploded bombs were in the ground.

Certainly, it was worth a try.

For the first several weeks, in addition to their work on the northeast rail net, the carrier airmen tackled the highway routes in the mountains of central Korea, plowing craters in roadbeds, knocking out highway bridges

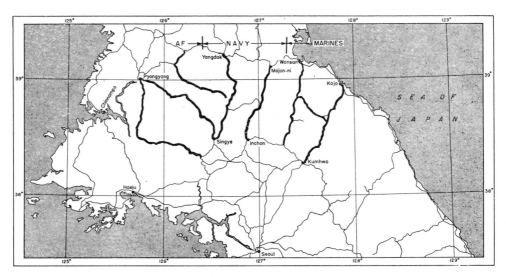

"STRANGLE": ZONES OF RESPONSIBILITY

and passes, firing rockets into tunnels, sowing delayed action and "butterfly" bombs in every choke area, and searching for the hundreds of trucks which, like ubiquitous kitchen cockroaches, were hiding by day in order to perform at night. The turbulent mountain winds complicated bombing accuracy.

Night-heckling activity also increased, and a greater number of enemy trains and trucks were frequently caught and destroyed at daybreak. Night reconnaissance efforts of "Operation Strangle" also increased, and a close watch was kept of the results. Marine Fighter Squadron 513, operating from Pusan's airfield, was credited with the nighttime destruction of 420 vehicles in a 30-day period.

At the end of two weeks, however, the total results were disappointing. Reconnaissance B-26s reported that the number of enemy trucks moving at night in each direction was unchanged. Some of the main roads had been blocked with delayed-action bombs, and several bridges had been knocked out; but these achievements had only caused the trucks to detour the main routes and to use other less-important and more difficult-to-hit secondary roads.

Nevertheless, "Strangle" went on, with the Air Force, Navy, and Marines working as an integrated team in closest harmony.

The Communists' resistance also intensified. At important points along the key roads, flak increased until the risk of making attacks often exceeded the expectation of gain. The cross-Korea highway west of Wonsan became so infested with antiaircraft guns that it was given the title "Death Valley." Enemy road repair activity also increased, and gave evidence of efficient organization. Communist crews hunted out the butterfly bombs with detectors and destroyed them with rifle fire. On other occasions the buried delayed-action bombs were simply ignored with oriental fatalism.

By late summer it was apparent that "Operation Strangle" had failed. The reasons were simple: a bomb crater on an unpaved road could not stop a truck. The hole could be too quickly filled in or bypassed. Even a damaged highway bridge was no impediment. A simple bypass could be built, or a ford made across the usually summer-dry streams. And in comparison to the rail networks, there was greater flexibility and greater area in the highway networks to make air attack more difficult.

The carriers intensified their work on the railroads.

The Raid on Rashin

From time to time in the interdiction effort, the carrier airmen had an opportunity to perform other missions. One of these was the attack on Rashin* in August of 1951.

The Korean peninsula stretches a long finger northeastward toward the Asian mainland, forming a neck of land which is separated from both Manchuria and Russia by the Tumen River. Along this narrow neck of North Korea and only 17 miles from the Soviet frontier lay the port city of Rashin. In fact, Rashin was less than 110 miles from the Russian city of Vladivostok. The two cities were connected by rail, road, and sea.

Rashin having been bombed once by B-29s in August 1950, the wisdom of making other attacks upon it was raised by the U. S. State Department in a letter from the Acting Secretary, Mr. James Webb, to the Secretary of Defense, Louis A. Johnson. Because of its nearness to Chinese and Rus-

---

* On pages 1063, 1064 and 2591, *Hearings before House Armed Services Committee and Senate Foreign Relations Committee on "Military Situation in Far East,"* General Bradley testified that General MacArthur previously had been denied permission to attack Rashin because of the risk involved in an operation so close to the Soviet frontier. "Rashin" is Japanese; "Wojin" is the Korean name of the city.

sian territory, Rashin was ordered spared from attack by the Joint Chiefs of Staff on 8 September 1950 at the insistence of the Department of State. The danger of an incident with Russian aircraft or a possible error in navigation which might cause UN aircraft to fly *over* or UN bombs to fall *on* the Russian side of the Tumen River were the main reasons for the decision to declare Rashin out of bounds.*

As a result of this ruling, the Communists had taken advantage of Rashin's sanctuary status and had increased its use as a rail hub and stock point for the transhipment of supplies.†

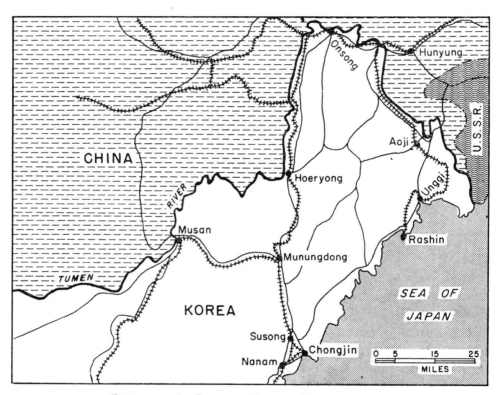

RASHIN AND ITS RAIL AND HIGHWAY COMMUNICATIONS

During February 1951, noting the continuing logistic build-up and heavy rail traffic in Rashin, MacArthur's headquarters again requested permission to resume bombing Rashin but this was again denied on 21 February. MacArthur, before a Joint Congressional Committee in May 1951, described the importance of Rashin in these words: "I was very anxious to bomb Rashin.

* See Chapter 9, "The Seaborne Artillery," for discussion of the naval blockade of Korea which affected Rashin.

† It should be pointed out, however, that no rail line ran *south* out of Rashin. Shipments further southward had to go by road.

. . . It is a great distributing point from Manchuria down the east coast of Korea. Its usefulness to the enemy is self-evident. Great accumulations, depot accumulations were made there. It was a great distributing center. . . . The Soviets could run stuff from Vladivostok right down there. We asked to bomb that and we were forbidden."

By August of 1951, the immunity granted Rashin had enabled the Communists to build that port city into the most important supply point in northeast Korea. The concentration of rail traffic was particularly heavy. Passing this intelligence to Washington, CINCFE made a further request to strike the city's warehouses, railroads, and marshalling yards. The Far East Air Force insisted that it could destroy Rashin's legitimate targets without violating either the Manchurian border or the Soviet frontier.

This time, the request was approved.* However, certain restrictions were tied to the approval of the Joint Chiefs of Staff. The Superforts must bomb on a southeasterly heading, passing over Rashin from northwest to southeast. (This stipulation was designed to prevent any violation of Russian territory.)

Second, the bombing attack should take place only in clear weather, in order to minimize any possible error in navigation or bombing.

Third, the bombers should take care to avoid any damage on a known POW camp less than a mile from the Rashin railroad station.

And, of course, at no time should any plane pass *north* of the Tumen River.

The restriction regarding the direction of bombing, and the admonition not to fly across the Tumen River, complicated the bombing mission. From Rashin northwestward to the frontier was only 34 miles. Subtracting a few miles in order to insure no violation of the border, and a few more miles to complete the high altitude turn onto bombing course, plus the distance from the Rashin targets to the bomb release point, left barely sufficient air room for the bombers to steady down and get a bombsight solution. Moreover, the specification that bombing should take place on a southeasterly heading forced the B-29s to make their *inbound* flight over the North Korean coastline far south of Rashin, and thereby give ample alert to the radar defenses of the area. The MIGs from either or both Russian and Chinese territory would certainly be alerted, and it was reasonable to expect that their opposition to an attack upon Rashin would be intense.

* The public hearings by the Joint Congressional Committee regarding the dismissal of General MacArthur dwelt at great length on Rashin. Pages 1063, 1331, 1640, 2260, 2276, 2591, 3067, *Hearings before the House Armed Services Committee and Senate Foreign Relations Committee regarding "Military Situations in Far East."* These discussions in May and June 1951 undoubtedly played a part in the approval given to bomb Rashin in August 1951.

Obviously, then, the B-29s would need heavy fighter escort. But where would it come from? The F-86 Sabres, even flying from the most northerly fighter bases in South Korea and carrying detachable fuel tanks, lacked the endurance to escort the B-29s at this range.

Far East Air Force planners turned for help to the Navy. Could the jets aboard the carriers of Task Force 77 escort the B-29s on the Rashin attack?

The request was passed through JOC to Commander Seventh Fleet and thence to RADM John Perry, Commander Task Force 77.

Certainly, replied Perry by despatch. How many jets, what time, and where?

For the next three days the details of rendezvous, altitude, radio frequencies, and escort pattern were exchanged between Navy and JOC. The Navy jets would meet the B-29s at a point 80 miles south of Rashin at 25,000 feet, take them in, over the target, and out again.

On 25 August, in CAVU* weather, the mission was launched from *Essex.* Commander M. U. Beebe, CVG-5, leading 11 F9Fs from VF-51 (LCDR E. Beauchamp) and 12 Banshee F2H2s from VF-172 (CDR M. E. Barnett), catapulted off.

"We climbed out together," recorded CDR Beebe,[7] "and met the 29 B-29s at the designated rendezvous point. It was perfect coordination, for my planes didn't even have to make a circle. We took escort stations promptly, the Banshees taking high cover and the Panthers low cover. Base altitude was 25,000 feet on the way in. Of course we weaved back and forth on top of the Superforts in order to keep all sectors covered and to maintain a combat speed.

"After passing the coastline, we were all set for the MIGs. But none interfered. As planned, we made the turn toward Rashin. The B-29s bombed in three waves, each plane dropping ten tons of bombs.

"All the while we kept rubbernecking for the MIGs, but we never saw a single one. And there was no antiaircraft fire, either.

"The B-29s did a beautiful job of bombing, making the final run in at about 19,000 feet. It was a fine, clear day, and their bomb pattern was clearly visible. I don't remember seeing a single bomb off-target.†

"The homeward flight was very routine. We peeled off and left them after we got close to *Essex.*

"Afterwards, CTF 77 received several despatches from the Air Force telling us what a fine escort job we did."

---

* CAVU—"Ceiling and visibility unlimited."

† A few minutes later, however, one B-29 jettisoned a string of bombs only 2,000 yards from the cruiser *Helena* (flag of ComCruDiv-5, RADM R. E. Libby) and destroyers *Harry E. Hubbard* (DD-748) and USS *Roger* (DDR-876), which had earlier bombarded Rashin and which were standing by to act as lifeguards if needed.

The photo aircraft which followed the strike took pictures which revealed that 97 per cent of the bombs had fallen on the Rashin marshalling yards. A turntable, a roundhouse, a railroad bridge, and approximately 75 of the 136 freight cars present were destroyed.

(Rashin's munitions factories and transportation facilities were struck a third time on 10 December 1952 in an all-Navy attack by Task Force 77 aircraft from *Bon Homme Richard* and *Oriskany*. On this occasion, twelve buildings were destroyed [including two railroad repair shops, the round-house and turntable] and five others damaged. While the Skyraiders and Corsairs were dropping their bombs, the protecting jet fighters spotted several MIGs just north of the border. The *Bon Homme Richard*'s action report reads: "The MIGs made threatening maneuvers in an apparent but unsuccessful effort to draw the target CAP across the border. Neither side violated the frontier.")

For both the B-29s and the Navy fighters, the attack on Rashin had gone without a hitch. The naval action reports, histories, and war diaries of the period mention this mission in the most routine fashion, with the single elaboration that "it is believed this is the first instance in the Korean War when Navy carrier fighters have escorted Air Force bombers."*

The significance of this mission far exceeded its bombing accomplishments. Here was yet another instance of closely integrated air effort by Air Force and Navy; second, it was an instance where naval airmen demonstrated the validity of their oft-repeated statement that many times, in many places, the mobile air power of the aircraft carrier might be essential, necessary, and helpful to the Air Force itself. In fact there might be times when naval air power would be the *only way* of accomplishing a task.

Track Busting

The interdiction effort of the carrier task force was now to enter its third phase. The first phase (breaking the Yalu bridges and the bridges of the northeast rail net) had achieved success within the northeast net. The second one (breaking the highways) had not. An effort would now be undertaken to destroy railroad *tracks* as well as the bridges themselves.

To give the carriers greater interdiction freedom, TF-77 was relieved of all responsibility for frontlines close air support missions on 20 September 1951.

The change of emphasis from bridge-breaking to track-busting had occurred for a very simple reason: increasing evidence of re-use by the enemy of the northeast coastal railroads. Moreover, American railroad engineers

* For the second time the Navy escorted B-29s, see "The Raid on Kowon," in Chapter 13, "On the Line."

estimated that it would be harder for the Communists to repair multiple rail cuts than to repair certain key bridges.

While the carriers had been employed during the summer months in either giving close air support to the frontlines or participating in "Operation Strangle," the Reds had taken advantage of the respite—first, to repair a great part of their fractured rail system; and second, to make ever-increasing use of "shuttle" trains between the broken bridges.

U. S. reconnaissance aircraft photographed or reported on several occasions as many as 300 railroad cars in the various marshalling yards. Naval aircraft themselves reported attacking and destroying or damaging 1,900 boxcars and 17 locomotives in a 30-day period between mid-August and mid-September.

Rear Admiral W. G. Tomlinson, ComCarDivTHREE and now CTF-77, following a coordinating conference aboard the *Bon Homme Richard* on 30 September 1951, with Major General Frank F. Everest (Commanding General FAFIK), made the decision to alter once again the pattern of the carriers' attacks. Hereafter, attacks would be conducted over as wide an area as possible, striking isolated rail areas at about one mile intervals in order to force the enemy to disperse his repair crews and to reduce the effectiveness of his constantly-growing antiaircraft defenses.

A list of key highway and rail bridges was prepared which reduced the number to twenty-seven: ten rail bridges and seventeen highway bridges. In addition to striking these bridges on a systematic basis, a concentrated effort would be made to cut the tracks in as wide an area as possible.

The Kapsan Strike

Information on potential Communist targets in North Korea occasionally came from bizarre sources. Escapees often volunteered information; fishermen captured or defecting from North Korea added to the total information picture; and South Koreans who penetrated into enemy territory were still another source.

One of the Navy's most spectacular air attacks—the Kapsan Strike—was based on such intelligence.

"Upon my arrival in Korea in the fall of 1951," said VADM J. J. Clark, "carrier planes were ranging the eastern half of Korea, searching for interdiction targets. While we were concentrating on bridges, trains, and the rails, we willingly accepted any worthwhile target.

"My flag lieutenant, LCDR J. A. Scholes, happened to be a graduate of the Army Parachute School at Fort Benning, Georgia, and, while there, had met a number of trainees in undercover warfare. Some of his friends were on duty at Army headquarters at Pusan. LCDR Scholes and his Army friends arranged a system of target information which we immediately put to good use.

"Groups of guerrilla bands, mostly South Koreans, were operating in certain areas of North Korea, supplying intelligence information by portable radio to their headquarters in South Korea. This information, giving the location and the nature of worthwhile targets for Navy carrier planes, was then relayed to the flagship. The selected targets were attacked at opportune times and the results of the naval air attacks reported by on-the-scene guerrillas.

"This arrangement was most beneficial, and through it many excellent targets were destroyed. Among these were the mines at Komdok, which produced lead and silver, and which were supervised by Russian technicians. On that attack the guerrillas reported that the naval air strike destroyed many installations and killed 116 men, including one of the Russian engineers.

"Another of these raids was at Pukchong, where the undercover agents had discovered an automobile shop and ammunition factory. In a series of strikes both of these targets were demolished and 100 North Korean Army personnel were reported killed.

"At Hong-gun ni, which was an electric power supply, a surprise raid caught three North Korean Army battalions at breakfast and obtained direct hits on the building housing them. Heavy casualties were reported by ground observers."

But the most successful raid based on information supplied by guerrillas was the 29 October raid on a concentration of Communist commissars and party officials in the city of Kapsan which resulted in the death of more than 500 Red personnel.

"On 29 October 1951," said CDR Paul N. Gray, Commanding Officer, VF-54, "Admiral John Perry received a request from the Eighth Army to make a raid on the headquarters of the Chinese Communist Party at Kapsan, in North Korea. Guerrillas had reported there was to be a meeting of all high-level party members of the North Korean and Chinese Communist forces at Kapsan at 0900. This city was located about 60 miles northwest of Songjin, in very mountainous terrain.

"On receiving this request, Admiral Perry ordered photos made from a high altitude by our photo reconnaissance planes. The photography was done at high altitude in order that the enemy would not become aware of our intentions.

"The target itself was a compound slightly east of the city of Kapsan. In this compound was a records section which contained all Chinese and North Korean Communist party records, a security police headquarters, and a barracks. The meeting of high-level Communists was scheduled at nine o'clock. We were ordered to strike between nine-fifteen and nine-twenty to be sure that all members had reached their seats.

"The armament carried on the flight was as follows: two 1,000-lb. bombs, of which one had a proximity fuze and the other an instantaneous fuze. Each plane carried one napalm bomb and eight 250-lb. general purpose bombs. The 20-mm. machinegun ammunition was half incendiary and half high explosive.

"The pilots were myself, LTJG Shugart, ENS Aillaud, ENS Masson. The second division was led by LT Evans, with LTJG Gollner, ENS Strickland, and ENS Kelly. (LTJG Gollner and ENS Kelly were both killed on later strikes.) We requested no fighter escort because we felt the fewer number of planes involved would give us the maximum possibility of surprise.

"On the morning of the strike the weather was clear and cold.

"We were launched about 100 miles east of Wonsan, at 0730. After rendezvous, we proceeded to the coast, staying as low as possible all the way. From a study of the maps we found valleys available all the way to Kapsan in which we could fly and thereby avoid radar detection.

"As we flew farther and farther north, the height of the mountains increased and the terrain became extremely rugged. Directly east of Kapsan was a 6,000-foot range of mountains. We approached from behind this range, made a rapid climb to 8,000 feet, crossed over the top of the mountains, and commenced our attack.

"At approximately 0913, eight proximity-fuzed 1,000-lb. bombs exploded above the compound of Kapsan. We rendezvoused in a climbing turn, made another attack and dropped the 1,000-lb. instantaneous fuzed bombs. All eight of these again landed within the compound. On our next run half the planes dropped napalm and the other half strafed. Most of the compound was set aflame by the napalm bombs, and those portions that were not ignited were set afire on the next run when the remaining four napalm bombs were dropped.

"The remainder of the attack consisted of strafing the compound and pinpointing the 250s on those sections that had not been completely destroyed. The final runs were made by our camera planes at treetop level to bring back post-strike pictures.

"When we left the target, there was nothing left but a smoking mass of rubble. Pictures showed every bomb except one inside the compound, and there was only one wall left standing.

"Any antiaircraft located at Kapsan evidently was destroyed on the first attack by the proximity fuzed 1,000-lb. bombs, because no reports of accurate antiaircraft fire were received and no planes received damage. We returned to the ship without incident, although extremely low on fuel due to the long hop and the long time spent on the target.

"Within two days an Army report was received from one of the guerrillas, who had been posted on the side of the hill overlooking Kapsan and who had watched the whole attack. He reported 509 high-level Communist party members were killed in the raid, and that all records of the Communist party in North Korea had been reported destroyed.

"The remarkable thing which the post-strike pictures showed was that no part of the city had been damaged, except the compound itself.

"This raid must have really hurt the Chinese and the North Koreans, because the next week the North Korean radio put a price on the heads of all the members of the strike and called us 'The Butchers of Kapsan'."

By mid-October 1951, the three aircraft carriers (*Bon Homme Richard, Essex* and *Antietam*) were emphasizing rail cutting. In the first three days of October, 131 track breaks were made. Between 18 to 31 October, the rail-lines were cut in a total of 490 places.

Within a month, over 1,000 individual breaks had been made in the rail tracks. The steady attrition of this naval air effort became apparent as new enemy car sightings decreased. Further evidence of the campaign's effectiveness was seen in the enemy's cannibalization of rails. Photographs revealed that a great part of all double-tracking, spurs, and marshalling yard rails had been removed for use at more essential places. Also, the pattern of antiaircraft opposition changed, increasing along the routes and becoming less intense at the bridges.

In November 1951, 922 track cuts were claimed and 44 rail bridges reported destroyed, despite increasingly difficult flying weather.

Jet aircraft of Task Force 77 proved to be ideal vehicles for the track-busting task. Their speed, silent approach, and bombing steadiness made them ideal for such precision work.

Also by now strike groups had learned to make more efficient use of their bombs. Big ones were used for bridges; small ones were saved for the tracks.

Track-breaking, however, was not as simple as it first appeared. In the first place, the width of the track—only 56 inches—made a small target indeed. Only a hit *directly* on the tracks was effective. Second, pilots had to compensate carefully for the effect of any cross wind. Third, the pilots soon found that a "seaman's eye" correction had to be made for the offset distance from the cockpit of the plane to the bombrack itself. Otherwise, the bomb would explode harmlessly on either side of the rail-bed.

In the first nine days of December, 937 track cuts were made. Between

29 December and 9 January 1952, Task Force 77 averaged 116 track cuts per day. And in the 24 operating days between 28 December and 1 February 1952, the fast carrier pilots claimed 2,782 cuts in the track.

In this same period, 141 bridge or bridge bypasses were also destroyed.

Admiral John Perry's action report for this period concludes: "An almost complete interruption of eastern rail line movement was accomplished by this effort."

Although rarely mentioned in war diaries and action reports, one of the most difficult tasks of the interdiction campaign to carrier division commanders, air group, and squadron commanders was the maintenance of high pilot morale. The unchanging routine of the interdiction missions, the

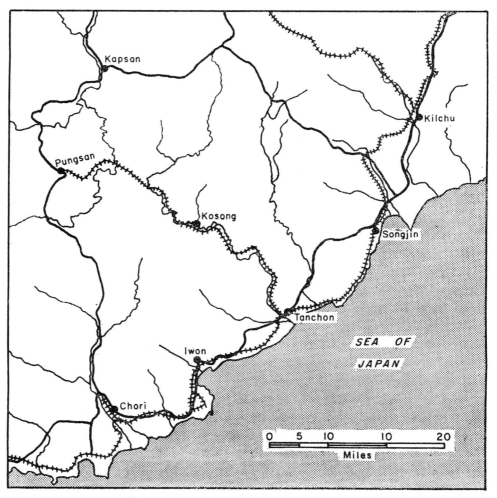

KAPSAN AND THE EAST COAST RAIL NETWORK

increasing danger of being shot down by enemy gunfire, and the often invisible results of the effort, all tended to lower the level of pilot morale.

"One of my toughest jobs," recorded CDR M. U. Beebe, Air Group commander of *Essex*'s Air Group Five, "was the constant battle to keep pilots' morale up.[8] Day after day, for weeks on end, pilots had to fly over the same area of Korea, bombing bridges or punching holes in railbeds. The antiaircraft fire over Korea grew steadily heavier, more accurate, and more intense. In comparison to what Air Group Five's experience had been during its first Korean tour in the fall of 1950, my second-tour pilots estimated that the enemy's antiaircraft fire had increased on the order of ten times. In fact, by the time we left the area, we estimated that the concentration of antiaircraft guns in certain target areas of Korea was *double* the number the Japanese had at specific targets in Japan at the end of World War II. As an indication of this, Air Group Five went through *two* sets of airplanes because of the heavy operating schedule and damage received from antiaircraft fire which was not repairable on board. From 22 August until 30 November 1951, Air Group Five's aircraft were struck 318 times, resulting in 27 aircraft losses and the loss of 11 pilots.

"A pilot would go out one day, do a first-rate bombing job on a bridge or leave several craters in a railbed, and come back the next day and find that all the damage had been repaired overnight. It was hard for him to see how his efforts were having any effect on the course of the fighting.

"For the second-tour pilots, the situation had drastically changed between November 1950 and mid-1951. The lucrative rail, supply, and individual targets had generally been destroyed. The grubby stacks of supplies, the trucks, and the bridges no longer piqued the pilots' interest. We found then what every naval aviator discovered during the last two years of the war: that any pilot could bomb a factory, but that it took an expert to knock out a truck speeding down a road or to drop a rail span supported by ties and cribbing timbers. The Reds were adroit at rapid concealment. It took a keen and skilled eye to spot the vehicles and supplies beneath the straw, vegetation, foilage, or even refuse. By the time a pilot spotted something, made a turn and armed his guns, rockets, or bombs, the target would ofttimes have been concealed.

"Any pilot could scour an undefended section of the countryside, avoiding the flak areas. But in places like 'Death Valley', west of Wonsan, it required a skillful and courageous pilot to weave his way through a maze of well-defended antiaircraft positions and still get a hit. This type of war was a new challenge.

"Generally speaking, the war in Korea demanded more competence, courage, and skill from the naval aviator than did World War II. The flying hours were longer, the days on the firing line more, the antiaircraft hazards greater, the weather worse. There was less tangible evidence of results for a pilot to see. The public appreciation and understanding of the pilot's work was less. On top of this, pilots had to know more than they did in World War II: their search and rescue points, panel marker codes, recognition signals, and their primary and secondary targets.

"The combination of these factors—the routine, the danger, the lack of visible results—made it difficult to convince the pilots that results being achieved were worth the risk. This was increasingly true after four or five months on the firing line.

"As a result, Admiral Perry and his staff tried very hard to work the air group into as many different missions as possible—such hops as strikes on Rashin, a hop into MIG Alley, or 'close air support' at the frontlines, and special targets such as the raid on Kapsan and Pukchong."

The anniversary of the first year of the naval interdiction program gave opportunity to assess the damage. In 12 months the combined attacks of the naval air and surface forces had accounted for the destruction or damage of 2,379 bridges, 4,519 vehicles, 7,028 boxcars, and 4,674 rail cuts.

Commenting on this impressive record, Rear Admiral Ofstie (now Deputy ComNavFE) said:

> These one-year figures clearly show that our naval assaults have cost the Communists heavily in vehicles, rail lines, bridges, and munitions. The enemy has had to double and triple his efforts to get supplies through to the frontlines. In addition, he has been forced to divert a considerable amount of his effort and materials toward large-scale counter-interdiction effort of his own. Historically, it is significant to note that this has been the first employment of sustained ground interdiction by naval forces.[9]

Said Vice Admiral J. J. Clark: "I don't know how we could have done any better on the east coast."

As 1952 was ushered in, it was nonetheless obvious from pilots' observations, photographic intelligence, and reports received from ashore, that the enemy's highly integrated and carefully dispersed repair organization had succeeded in matching the UN's interdiction efforts over the whole of North Korea. Individual rail cuts were quickly and simply repairable, and there were ample supplies of lumber, unused rails, and, of course, manpower.

Accordingly, carrier tactics were altered once again. Instead of scattering rail and road cuts over *wide* areas, a plan to concentrate them at selected points was adopted. Rather than crater a roadbed with one bomb for every mile of track, entire stretches of railbed were torn up. At these points crater overlapped crater, totally destroying the roadbed for distances of one-half to two miles.

In 24 days of air operations in the period of 28 December 1951 to 1 February 1952, some 2,782 cuts were made and 79 railroad bridges and 50 bridge bypasses were destroyed. Temporarily, at least, the new attack plan proved too much for the enemy's repair organization; in some places damage remained untouched for eight to ten days.

Still closer integration of naval air and surface effort against the northeast coastal routes was commenced in January 1952 in order to achieve semipermanent interdiction, regardless of weather and visibility conditions. Attack points along the northeast coast—known by the code names of "Package" and "Derail"—were selected by photographic reconnaissance. These targets were chosen so that breaks could be made and maintained by either air or surface bombardment. Against the five "Package" targets, aircraft established the initial break and planted radar buoys by which surface forces could locate, identify, and hit the target regardless of visibility conditions. At the eleven "Derail" points, responsibility for breaking the lines was assigned to the surface forces. These points would be bombarded with the aid of air spot by carrier aircraft.

As time went on, the success of both "Package" and "Derail" operations was minimized by the lack of sufficient surface bombardment units for continuous surveillance of the chosen points.*

The concentration of air attack on selected areas of track continued through February 1952, when 1,037 cuts were made in the first twenty days. The major effort was applied to the main north-south and east-west rail-lines in and around the junction point at Kowon, 22 miles northwest of Wonsan. So successful were the carriers' effort that the line from Kowon to Wonsan was kept inoperable for the entire period of 1 February to 5 March. The line linking Kowon, Hamhung, and Hungnam was cut often enough to prevent through traffic. At the same time, the rail and highway bridges west of Yangdok were under periodic attack.

In March 1952, there was another welcome break in the monotony of the rail and bridge strikes which did much to boost pilot morale. An enemy attempt to re-take the UN-held island of Yang-do, off Songjin, on 20 February met retaliation in the form of carrier aircraft attacks on small boat concentrations all along the nearby coast.† Carrier sweeps from Wonsan to Songjin destroyed 300 small boats and damaged another 500—sampans and junks which might be used in another invasion attempt. The tedium of

---

* For a description of the surface aspects of this interdiction effort, see the section, "Packages and Derails," in Chapter 9, "The Seaborne Artillery."

† Yang-do was one of three islands three miles off the Songjin mainland, and had been captured in March 1951. On 20 February 1952, a determined attempt was made by the Communists to recapture the island. Although enemy troops succeeded in making a landing, the naval element—USS *Shelton* (DD-790, CDR Stephen Carpenter), USS *Endicott* (DMS-35), and HMNZS *Taupo*—assisted in driving off the attack with gunfire.

interdiction was further relieved on 13 April when the first of many combined air strikes and surface bombardments hit Chongjin.*

To reduce the threat of invasion of Yo-do, the UN-held island in the besieged harbor of Wonsan, carrier aircraft made regular strikes on the enemy guns on Hodo Pando peninsula and also furnished periodic spotting services to the bombarding ships.†

Everywhere the railbusting campaign continued with unabated fury. During April, May, and June 1952, over 7,000 sorties were flown, achieving in the first month-and-a-half another 3,000 rail cuts and the destruction of 80 bridges and 100 bypasses.‡

Once again the enemy responded to the naval air attack by modifying his repair pattern and intensifying his antiaircraft fire. And once again Task Force 77 changed its tactics. The number of aircraft in each group was increased, flak-suppression fighters attacked the enemy guns prior to the appearance of the bombing planes, and repeated passes were avoided. Pull-outs were higher. The inherent ability of the carrier to make sudden, heavy attacks on widespread targets was fully utilized.

But whatever the pattern of attacks, the purpose of the naval airmen was the same—to maintain a stranglehold on the east coast rail system.

One night-heckler pilot waxed poetical in his assessment of the interdiction effort:

> It weren't no fun in 51
> Tried and True in 52
> Still out to sea in 53
> Don't want no more in 54
> Still alive in 55
> Amidst the blitz in 56
> Almost to Heaven in 57
> No homecoming date in 58
> Remain on the line in 59
> Pack up your ditty in 1960
> To hell with this poem
> We want to come home.

While interdiction missions were flown for the remainder of the war, the month of June 1952 saw the interdiction campaign de-emphasized. Hereafter, interdiction would take the form of massed attacks on rail and transportation centers, manufacturing areas, and supply centers, with the

---

* See "Air Gun Strikes," in Chapter 9, "The Seaborne Artillery."
† See Chapter 12, "The Siege of Wonsan."
‡ Fishermen captured by the destroyer *Fox* (DD-779) in May 1952 from the coastal area between Hungnam and Songjin reported that trains had not passed "Package 5" in a month.

hope that the enemy would thereby be forced to make concessions at the truce table.

In this 20-month naval effort to strangle the supply lines of the enemy by air, fast carrier aircraft had made more than 13,000 cuts in the rail lines and had destroyed 500 bridges and 300 bridge bypasses in northeastern Korea. The destruction and damage to hundreds of locomotives, railroad cars, trucks, and motor vehicles, and to the supplies and munitions being carried, added to the effectiveness of the damage inflicted on the rail route itself. This destruction had undoubtedly slowed the movement of goods and forced the enemy to organize a tremendous resistance. It had forced him to divert a large share of his manpower and to expend large quantities of repair materials.

But the struggle to strangle the enemy's supply lines throughout Korea, by all air forces, including Navy, did *not* isolate the battlefield. The volume of supplies reaching the static front seemed adequate for the enemy's needs. There was a growing conviction that aerial interdiction of the land lines of communication could not be entirely effective over an extended period of time unless there was coordinated *ground* action to force the enemy to increase his rate of supply expenditure.

Admiral John Perry's action report summarized the interdiction effort in one pithy sentence:

> Operations resolved themselves into a day-to-day routine where stamina replaced glamor and persistence was pitted against oriental perseverance.

Air Interdiction at Night

By their effective and incessant daytime attacks upon the bridges, tunnels, and tracking of the northeastern rail net, the carrier aviators of Task Force 77 were able to restrict its use severely. While the sun was up, the Communists were unable and unwilling to move. The flow of supplies by daylight was choked off to a thin trickle, and Chinese and North Korean trains and trucks operated at almost suicidal peril.

But at night, and in bad flying weather, the enemy desperately repaired his bridges, filled in the hundreds of holes punched in his roads and railbeds, and straightened or replaced his bent tracking; and by laborious but plentiful hand labor, he shuttled from train to train and truck to truck the munitions of war across the dozens of broken bridges and tracks. Nighttime and inclement weather brought a measure of immunity to the harassed Communists.

Concurrent with their day labors, the hardworking carriers of Task Force 77 also toiled at night throughout the entire interdiction campaign, and did their limited best to staunch the flow of supplies and to delay the repair effort. With no night carrier available, the need for the day carriers to work 'round the clock proved a heavy burden on the flight deck crews; but the burden was willingly accepted in order to increase pressure on the enemy.

The task of flying interdiction missions over Korea at night was both difficult and hazardous, although most of the night pilots felt that the danger of flying over Korea at night was considerably less than by day. In many ways, flying at night was easier. There was much less flak. Targets were much more numerous and easier to find. On dark nights, moving traffic could be identified by headlights. In bright moonlight, the enemy could move trucks and trains successfully without lights. This forced the hecklers to concentrate on the stationary interdiction targets.

However, the mountainous terrain of Korea was more of a hindrance by night than by day. Making an attack upon a bridge or a train compressed between the steep Korean hills, or on a truck concealed beside a forested road, required first-rate airmanship even in broad daylight; to perform the same job at night was even more difficult and demanding.

Despite their limited numbers, and despite the difficulties of weather, darkness, and terrain, the night flyers of Task Force 77 inflicted a great amount of damage and did much to slow down the enemy's nocturnal movement of supplies.

The typical hop for the hecklers was for each pair to be assigned to one route or road so as to cover a distance of about 150 miles. The routes were generally through the mountains or along the coastal road. On arrival in the target area, one pilot would descend to low-altitude searching of the road, looking for headlights or blacked out traffic. The other pilot remained high. When a target was spotted, the high plane initiated the attack, dropping flares as necessary. The low plane, meanwhile, climbed and made his attack.

Early Night Operations

As the interdiction campaign by the carriers in northeast Korea commenced in early 1951, the night flyers aboard *Princeton* (VC-35 Night Team 3, LT Franklin Metzner, OinC) made contact with the enemy's transport system with pleasing and pyrotechnic results:

1 Feb 1951: ". . . LT Atlee F. Clapp and LTJG Lawrence G. Rodgers destroyed the first of seventeen locomotives destroyed by this team. . . ."

22 Apr 1951: ". . . LT Franklin Metzner and ENS John D. Ness destroyed one locomotive and severely damaged five others in a marshalling yard west of Kowon. Other flights from the carriers and the Air Force later the next morning bombed and napalmed the yard—one locomotive escaped into a tunnel, but a special strike that afternoon exploded him out of the tunnel.

The engine proceeded out of control down the track into the marshalling yard where it ran into the wreckage of the destroyed train, exploded and overturned—seven locomotives were definitely destroyed in this day's operation. . . ."

18 July 1951: ". . . LT Wickenheiser and LTJG Oliver disrupted enemy traffic by attacking a convoy of vehicles in the vicinity of Kowon—4 vehicles were set ablaze. . . ."

22 July 1951: ". . . LT A. F. Borysiewicz and ENS Colvin interrupted the advance of light enemy vehicles as they were moving through a precipitous pass twenty miles south of Songjin. From the blast of the 260-pound frag bombs, it was observed that approximately two trucks were destroyed. . . ."

16 Oct 1951: ". . . One train composed of one locomotive and fifteen boxcars was sighted and severely damaged by LCDR Callis of VC-3 (aboard *Antietam*) with the assistance of LT Stixrud. . . ."

8 Nov 1951: ". . . LTJG Warfield of VC-3 destroyed two enemy trucks while LTJG Donahoe and ENS Sybeldon of VC-35 each destroyed one truck. . . ."

During this period of operations, the night hecklers developed a few practical thumb rules for their work. The darker the night and the colder the night, the better the night pilot's chances of finding and destroying trucks. The darkness forced the enemy drivers to use lights in order to remain on the twisting highways, while the cold weather usually forced them to close their windows to keep warm. In so doing, the drivers could not hear the approaching aircraft or the warning shots fired by the road sentries stationed along the highways at short intervals.

On moonlit nights, some of the pilots found the use of binoculars helpful. But whatever the degree of darkness, once a truck convoy was located, pilots found it essential to make their initial attacks with engines throttled back in order to keep the noise level low and to avoid alerting the vehicles.

"Strange as it may seem," said LCDR F. E. Ward, Officer in Charge of Night Attack Team Mike, "the night pilots dreaded the bright moonlight nights for it made them excellent targets for antiaircraft guns, and forced them to fly closer to the ground in order to locate targets."[10]

As for weapons, a great many pilots preferred their 20-mm. cannons. Others preferred the napalm tanks. Whereas a bomb could be counted on to destroy only one or two trucks, a well-placed napalm tank could do away with as many as ten trucks, besides furnishing excellent illumination for subsequent attacks. Later in the war, the 2.75-inch folding fin rocket, normally an air-to-air weapon, was tried and proved successful.

The night pilots were quick to observe the enemy's typical reaction to nighttime attacks. Trucks in a few observed convoys were equipped with bright headlights on the rear of the trucks shining backward, and only dim lights pointing forward. By this stratagem the Reds hoped to delude the hecklers into believing that *this* convoy was an "empty" moving north, rather than a "full" one heading toward the battlefront.

On occasion the pilots also observed a flashing-light warning system in certain sectors along the coastal road. On approach of a plane these mountaintop lights would blink a warning for all trucks to take cover. Trains on the exposed tracks would head for the nearest tunnel.

Pilots also noted, especially on very dark nights, that strings of simulated headlights would be placed in certain very mountainous terrain. The line of lights would be so placed that if a pilot was deceived and made a low level attack on them, he would crash his airplane into a steep, nearby hillside. None of the hecklers took the bait.

Despite the various systems used by the enemy to warn of approaching airplanes, the mere presence of the heckling aircraft achieved the desired psychological result. Communist trucks and trains scampered for concealment whenever an aircraft engine was heard. The hecklers forced the trains and truck convoys to scatter and stop, thereby halting and slowing the nighttime traffic.

"Moonlight Sonata" and "Insomnia"

In early 1952 a night heckling operation against railroads having the lyrical code-name "Moonlight Sonata" was begun. The purpose of this operation was to take advantage of the winter snowfall and moonlight, at which time the Korean hills, valleys, and rail lines stood out in bold relief.

The operation commenced on 15 January 1952, and continued through mid-March, at which time the snows began to melt. On each flyable night during the winter period, five 2-plane sections were predawn launched at 0300 each morning. Each section of aircraft was assigned a 50-mile stretch of track; pilots were briefed in advance on the locations of the best targets within that area. At the least, the presence of the hecklers would halt traffic and disrupt the rail-repair activity. If the hunting was good and trains were found, the night flyers were ordered to decommission the locomotive and then to cut the track on each side of the train so that the day flight, standing by in alert status on the carrier decks, could come in at the first light to finish the destruction of the stranded trains.

"Sonata" was partly successful, resulting in five locomotives being found, two destroyed, and three damaged. However, the periods of night which combined moonlight, good weather, and snow on the ground, plus targets, were rare.

The next special night operation was code-named "Insomnia" and commenced on 13 May 1952. This operation had one feature which some of the earlier night missions had lacked. On several occasions in the past, pilots flying the first night hops had reported that trains and trucks could not be found during the early hours of their patrols; however, just as they were *leaving* the area, the trucks and trains began to appear. Obviously, the Communists had noted the time pattern of the night aerial patrols and were withholding train and truck movements until the naval planes were homeward bound.

Accordingly, "Insomnia" launching schedules were re-shuffled and planes left the carriers at midnight and 0200.

During the spring period, 16 locomotives were sighted, and 11 of them were trapped by cutting the rail lines ahead and behind. Of the trapped 11, nine were destroyed at first light the next morning and the other two heavily damaged. Additionally, night pilots found good shooting on such occasions as:

18 April 1952: "... LT A. R. Kreutz and ENS P. J. Weiland (VC-35 Team Able—*Boxer*) had extremely good luck on a night heckler hop, destroying 8 trucks, 2 warehouses plus one ammunition dump, and damaging 12 more trucks and numerous troops with 20-mm. strafing attacks...."

23 April 1952: "... LT C. H. Hutchins and LT D. G. Creeden destroyed a railroad bridge and four trucks, damaged six others with 20-mm. fire and left one warehouse burning. LT Creeden was hit by small arms fire, returning unharmed but with a shattered canopy...."

12 May 1952: "... LT R. L. Bothwell, LT H. D. Knosp and LTJG M. D. Avery were launched from *Valley Forge*. They scored direct hits on two rail road bridges, destroyed a truck convoy, bombed a train, cutting the rail lines fore and aft. This all-night operation was extremely successful in disrupting the transportation schedules, as the early morning strikes destroyed the trains that were isolated at daybreak...."

9 June 1952: "... Two night hecklers were launched. LT Bothwell and LT Knosp destroyed a locomotive and three cars south of Songjin and completely burned a fully loaded train in the yards at Kilchu with a half hour bombing and napalm attack...."

The Use of Night Carriers in Korea

During the latter part of World War II in the Pacific, the U. S. Navy had developed special air groups and carriers (*Enterprise* and *Saratoga*) to operate exclusively at night. From the military and operational standpoint, this development was one of the major innovations and accomplishments of that war. The results achieved by the night carriers against the Japanese in both attack and defense were generally agreed to have been effective and successful.

During the Korean War, however, no night carriers were used, although a plan to do so (Operation "No Doze") was formulated and briefly placed in effect during the last few days of the war. *Princeton* was now designated for operation "No Doze"; she was given three destroyers for plane guard, and all night fighter and night attack aircraft of TF-77 were to be transferred to her. It was planned for the night hecklers to strike important junctions with both regular and delay-fuzed bombs, so that TF-77's morning flights might have lucrative targets. However, "No Doze" was postponed when *Princeton* went to Yokosuka for boiler repairs; upon her return to the fleet, the final days of the war were under way, requiring the all-out close air support of all carriers.

The proposal to employ night carriers was first raised during the early phases of the interdiction campaign in Korea. There were many persuasive reasons for doing so. First of all, a regular day carrier could not operate continuously both by day and by night. Even the task of operating eight night fighter and attack aircraft from a day carrier was an extra heavy burden on the carrier's flight deck, hangar deck, and ordnance crews. The use of a night carrier would certainly diminish the day carrier's burdens.

Second, those naval airmen who analyzed the interdiction campaign in Korea realized that its primary weakness was the lapse of effort during the night and the respite thus given the enemy. Operating approximately eight night aircraft from the day carriers could do little more than harass, heckle, and hamper, much less halt the Chinese nocturnal traffic to a significant point. Admittedly, a single night carrier could do a great deal more, although there was substantial doubt that *one* night carrier could slow down the enemy's traffic to any vital degree. Those in favor of a night carrier also believed that fliers could tighten the *surface* blockade by detecting the movement of small craft operating close inshore.

Third, the equipment for night flying, both aboard carrier and airplans, was much better than during World War II—radar, night lighting, control procedures for the ship, all-weather equipment, electronic equipment, and automatic pilots for the planes. Korea, said the night flyers, was a golden chance to learn more and to further perfect the all-weather art.

The pilots who had flown over Korea both by day and by night were convinced that the task at night was easier, less dangerous, and more productive. Little or nothing moved by day. But at night, North Korea crawled with activity. The night pilots were certain that the same number of trained pilots by night could accomplish much more than the same pilots by day—and at less risk of damage or loss to themselves.

The other side of the problem contained compelling evidence. One night carrier would be helpful but certainly not decisive. To bottle up northeast Korea by night would require *many* carriers and hundreds of planes. And for each night carrier on the line in Korea, there had to be at least one other carrier and air group training on the West Coast. The time to fully train a night pilot was 50 per cent greater. There was also the Navy-wide limitation of funds, of personnel, and the problem of priorities. Would a night carrier be more damaging to the enemy than a battleship or a squadron of destroyers?

In the operational sense, too, there was no reason to suspect that the normal enthusiasm and elation which were inherent in every returning strike pilot's report were not equally applicable to night pilots. Often there was no way of judging, measuring, or photographing the claims of the night pilots. Under the stalemated conditions in Korea, many naval airmen felt that a carrier operating by day would hurt the enemy more than a carrier by night. Moreover, a survey made early in the war showed that the night pilots were expending 67 per cent of the ordnance in twilight and daylight periods; on the other hand, the usual time of launching hecklers during these early months—near dawn and dusk—contributed to this high percentage.

The use of a night carrier was thus debated and re-debated. But the night carrier was destined not to appear during the Korean War.

Night Heckling (1952-1953)

The night heckling by the day carriers, contributing to the over-all damage to the enemy in Korea, went steadily on. By now the airmen had developed the night attack work into an art. The flight over a 40-mile stretch of track or road might consume an hour's zigzagging back and forth, as each curve and embankment was observed for traffic. Locomotives were hardest to see, as they rarely used headlights or made smoke. But careful, tedious searching paid off:

15 July 1952: ". . . night heckling aircraft from *Princeton* stopped a train near Tanchon and eighteen propeller planes were launched by the *Bon Homme Richard* at 0915 to finish it off. . . ."

22 July 1952: ". . . the night hecklers destroyed three trucks and damaged thirteen north of Wonsan. . . ."

23 July 1952: ". . . the night hecklers, surprising a convoy of trucks, damaged fifteen, leaving a path of flame and rubble. . . ."

24 July 1952: ". . . the hecklers as usual had their choice of targets, sighting at least two hundred trucks within a thirty mile radius of Wonsan . . . at least three definitely destroyed and 21 damaged. . . ."

27 July 1952: ". . . at 0330 dawn hecklers left to attack rails northwest of Tanchon. VC-4 detachment (LCDR E. S. Ogle) found a moving train, cut the rails in front and behind, and damaged the locomotive before expending all the ammunition and bombs. A destroyer later destroyed the train by shelling. . . ."

28 July 1952: ". . . again the hecklers trapped a locomotive and three cars.

Following the prescribed doctrine, the rails were cut and the trains attacked. Direct attacks on the boiler stopped the engine, leaving it stalled for a later *Princeton* flight to destroy. . . ."

1 Aug 1952: ". . . the night hecklers reported the destruction of eleven and damage to fifteen trucks in the Wonsan area. . . ."

3 Aug 1952: ". . . the hecklers found choice targets in trucks in the Wonsan area. Bombing and strafing vehicles pinpointed by flames, the night flyers destroyed at least nine and damaged 25 trucks. . . ."

As the daytime interdiction effort was de-emphasized, beginning in June, the enemy made increasingly bold use of his highways. The night flyers of TF-77, in the month of November, were credited with the destruction of 206 trucks and damage to 274.

Types of Night Heckling Aircraft

Throughout the Korean War there were two airplanes exclusively used for night work: the F4U5N Corsair and the AD4N Skyraider. Each carrier had four of each type assigned to its air group, these units being attached to the appropriate attack and fighter squadron.

The Corsair fighter aircraft were night defense aircraft charged with the protection of the task force at night. Since there was no enemy aerial opposition, these aircraft were released for attacks in Korea. The parent squadron of the F4U5N pilots and aircraft was VC-3, located at Naval Air Station, Moffett Field.*

The Skyraider aircraft came from VC-35, located at Naval Air Station, San Diego. The pilots and planes from this squadron were assigned to and especially trained in the night attack role. For this mission the Skyraider was an ideal vehicle. The usual load for a night heckling AD Skyraider was one 500-pound bomb, six 250-pound bombs, six flares, and full ammunition for their four 20-mm. cannon.

"The combat aircrewmen of VC-35 had to be the best trained and the most courageous type of men," said LCDR Ward. "It takes a particular brand of courage to participate in protracted night operations, sitting in the back end of a plane, unable to see either ship or target."

"The AD4N planes were ideally suited for the night interdiction mission," said LCDR W. C. Griese, Officer in Charge of *Valley Forge's* VC-35s Baker team. "The provision of extensive electronic equipment and stations for two crewmen to operate the gear made this aircraft approach a true all-weather airplane and allowed us to effectively complete many missions which would otherwise have been impossible. The ability of this airplane to carry a sizable ordnance load with a good endurance factor also endeared it to the hearts of the night people.

* VC-4, the Atlantic Fleet Squadron, also supplied a few night fighter teams to Korea.

"When we first arrived on the line aboard *Valley Forge* in January 1953, our job after locating enemy locomotives was to cut the tracks ahead of and behind the locomotives and let the day boys knock it off the next morning. . . . We conscientiously did as we were told until discovering that the locomotives that we stranded at night often weren't there the next morning due to the Commies' amazing ability to fill bomb craters and repair rails within an hour or two. We then decided among ourselves that the best place to cut the tracks was directly *beneath* the locomotive—and then we started to do some good.

"Although we evaluated many types of ordnance for our missions, we finally concluded that the best weapon we had was the 20-mm. gun. One round of 20-mm. high explosive incendiary in the gas tank or engine of a truck would completely and permanently knock it out, and a few rounds through the boiler of a locomotive could stop it very effectively. Also, with this weapon, we didn't have to worry about minimum safe altitudes in the run, and each shell hitting at night gave a good flash which made for very easy correcting, and our accuracy became very good.

"Our most effective single mission," continued LCDR Griese, "was on the night of 13 February 1953. It was a pretty miserable night, with ceilings at about 700 feet and a light freezing rain falling. Apparently the enemy didn't think we'd be out in weather like this, and they were moving gasoline tankers in convoy on the coastal highway about 20 miles south of Hamhung. Of course, we didn't know for sure what we were attacking, since all we could see when we began our run were the headlights; but after the first round of incendiary found the gasoline there was no doubt about it! We burned *seven* of the tankers (and damaged three others) and we had no further use for flares in that area for the rest of the night! It was quite a sight to see a large tanker truck scream down the highway, trailing burning gas for a mile or more, and finally erupting in a big column of flame.

"This particular incident pointed out the fact that, in general, the worse the weather was, the better the hunting!"

Imaginative planning and persistence by *Valley Forge's* night hecklers paid off on a mission flown the night of 3 May 1953 against the Chosin reservoir hydroelectric plant.

"Chosin No. 1 power plant had been attacked several times by large groups of our aircraft during daylight hours," stated LCDR Griese, "despite the extreme concentration of enemy antiaircraft of all types. Since this target was right on one of our night recco* routes, we were flying directly over it almost every night, at low altitude, practically on a schedule, and we never got a buzz out of any protective AA. It occurred to us, of course,

* "Recco"—Reconnaissance.

that we could attack this target, and we so proposed to the planners. We were initially refused, however, on the basis that it would be too dangerous. (The intelligence people had told us that there were probably a dozen or more heavies and thirty to forty 37-mm. automatic weapons around that power plant.) We persisted, however, and finally got a crack at it in the early morning hours of 3 May. We had three of our ADs loaded with one 1,000-pound GP* and one 1,000-pound SAP* bomb apiece. We briefed carefully and were catapulted at 0300. The lead plane made a landfall on radar and hit the enemy beach just south of Hungnam. We had no difficulty locating the target even though it was in a deep valley and completely blacked out. The lead plane immediately pulled up and dropped a flare which illuminated the target beautifully and allowed the following planes to commence immediate glide bombing attacks. As each flare approached the ground, it was replaced by another; thus a blinding light was kept continually between the attacking planes and the enemy gunners, who, after about four minutes, finally got the word and commenced shooting wildly with everything they had. Despite this fire we stayed over the target for a total of seven minutes, and each pilot made two deliberate bombing runs plus additional flare runs. No plane suffered damage from the enemy's intensive fire. Of the six bombs carried, one GP (general purpose bomb) hung up, one hit right alongside the plant, setting off great electrical fire-balls, and one landed fifty feet beyond the target. All three SAPs (semi armor-piercing bombs) released, but since they penetrated deeply before exploding, no results could be observed.

"The lesson from this incident lies in the fact that night pilots in night airplanes successfully navigated inland, found, illuminated, and attacked a heavily defended enemy target with comparatively little risk. It was an optimum military situation."

The "Mighty Mouse" Rocket Used at Night

During the night interdiction campaign, one new type of ordnance was tried in Korea which proved highly successful: the 2.75-inch folding-fin aircraft rocket, which had the nickname "Mighty Mouse." Developed initially as an air-to-air weapon, this small rocket found peculiar but suitable use as a night interdiction weapon late in the Korean war.

The "Mighty Mouse" rockets were carried in packages of seven; and six pods or packages were carried on each AD Skyraider, with flares and 250- or 500-pound bombs on the remaining stations. Each package of seven was fired in a ripple, with a split second between each rocket.

* "GP"—general purpose; "SAP"—semi-armor piercing.

The initial fleet testing and evaluation of the 2.75-inch folding-fin aircraft rocket on ground targets had been accomplished at Inyokern, California, in early December 1952, by the executive officer of VC-35, CDR Frank G. Edwards. So pleased was Commander Edwards with the test results that he convinced his superiors that a war trial over Korea was in order. In April 1953, therefore, Night Attack Team Mike aboard the *Philippine Sea* (CAPT Paul H. Ramsey) conducted "Mighty Mouse" rocket attacks on interdiction targets:

7 April: "CDR Edwards and LCDR Ward were launched as late evening hecklers. Edwards broke the ice when he made a fine run on a truck and burned it with seven rounds. . . ."

8 April: "LT Harmon nailed four trucks on one run with two packages, burning all four, with secondary explosions observed."

13 April: "Encountering what appeared to be lights on a road, Ward made several passes at the head of the column without firing. During each pass the lights went out until finally, on the last pass, the truck lights were left burning and Ward continued the attack, firing all six packages (42 rockets) down the length of the column of approximately twenty trucks from a quartering direction. Several secondary explosions resulted and at least four large fires were left burning down the length of the column. The local 'hero' medal was transferred to Felix upon his return to the ship. . . ."

26 April: "The hecklers had their best night—Sullivan got at least five trucks with two rocket packages; fires in supply buildups in two villages; Ward burned half the village of Soho-ri with a four package attack; DeSmet burned at least four trucks and damaged two with three packages, silenced an automatic weapon near Wonsan, burned three or four buildings in a village; Erickson burned two buildings and silenced an AA position. . . ."

The destructive ability, the accuracy, the ease of handling and using the rockets was proved. Captain Ramsey reported that "the rockets were extremely effective weapons against trucks or similar targets." Rear Admiral R. E. Blick, ComCarDiv-3, recommended a rapid increase in output, so that general Fleet usage in Korea could be accomplished.

"The use of the 'Mighty Mouse' rockets against ground targets was very successful," said CDR F. G. Edwards. "Using them was like going after a bug with a flyswatter instead of trying to stab him with a pencil."

Significance

Despite unusually favorable conditions, and despite the costly, vigorous, and prolonged effort just described, UN air power failed to isolate the Korean battlefield. Perhaps only the use of the atomic bomb against sources of supply and against the stockpiles in Manchuria could have accomplished this isolation; but this effort was never made.

Air power was denied the attempt to isolate the peninsula from the mainland by making attacks upon the Manchurian sanctuary. Thus, the air interdiction of the Korean battlefield took the only course which remained —that of attacking the supply system *in Korea*—the rail lines and highways (and the traffic upon them) which carried the enemy's strength into his frontlines.

Responsibility for the Interdiction Campaign and Its Coordination

In analyzing the Navy's role in the interdiction campaign in Korea, it must be remembered that the conduct of interdiction upon land was the primary responsibility of the U. S. Air Force as laid down in the Functions Paper.* The Navy's responsibility for interdiction on land was purely collateral. Throughout the Korean war, therefore, the general supervision of the interdiction campaign was exercised by the U. S. Air Force, through the Joint Operation Center at Taegu, under the command of the Fifth Air Force in Korea.

At no time during the Korean War were the interdiction efforts of the U. S. Navy and the U. S. Air Force upon the Korean peninsula coordinated at the theater level.† For the first six months of the war, coordination was not necessary, because of the fluid state of the ground fighting. After the evacuation of Hungnam, and especially after the ground fighting became positioned, there still was no coordinated plan for the centralization of interdiction effort, the priority of targets, or the choice of best available weapons. This lack showed up in such variances as in bridge reconnaissance by Air Force and Naval aircraft in a certain east coast area. Based on their reconnaissance pictures, the Air Force reported 36 rail and highway bridges out of commission. The Navy's report, for the same day and for the same area, reported only six bridges out.

Lack of theater coordination also showed up in varying criteria used by Air Force and Navy. In the first months of the war, the Air Force considered that a successfully attacked bridge would normally be out of action for 30 days. The Navy's experience showed that a bridge successfully attacked might only be out of action for two days—or even a matter of hours.

Further evidence of the lack of coordination was indicated by the fact that there was no written or formal assignment of areas of effort between the Air Force and the Navy. In the absence of such an agreement, one grew to be understood and accepted: the Navy had primary (but not exclusive)

---

* Functions Paper of the Armed Forces and the Joint Chiefs of Staff—The agreement established shortly after the unification of the Armed Forces whereby the particular responsibilities and type of operations of each of the three Services were established.

† The Navy coordinated its own surface and air interdiction efforts, commencing in April of 1951, at which time Admiral Ofstie received approval of his proposal that Task Force 77 coordinate its interdiction contributions with those of Task Force 95.

ON THE RECEIVING END OF NAVAL GUNFIRE. *At top,* crater excavated in a road near Pohang by a 16-inch shell from *Missouri. Center,* a wrecked Wonsan oil refinery. *Below,* an unscathed church remains amidst target rubble, illustrating pinpoint accuracy of naval gunfire.

MARINE AIR AND SEA MOBILITY. *At top,* men from "C" Company, Seventh Marines, climb aboard helicopters for first ship-to-shore assault by air in Far East. *Center,* Leathernecks in an amphibious tractor head ashore in Wonsan invasion. *Below,* the Seventh Marines board transport for redeployment after 13-day fight out of Chosin Reservoir.

MARINES IN THE FIELD. *At top,* a huge Sikorsky helicopter lowers supplies to assault troops in rough mountain area. The Leathernecks were first to exploit helicopters in combat. *Center,* Marines call for mortar fire during bitter cold withdrawal from Koto-ri. *Below,* Fifth Marines advance toward rugged terrain.

BACKGROUND OF WAR. *At top,* priest celebrates mass in tne field for combat troops. *Center,* Marine engineers repair a bridge as truck pulls mount across shallow river bed detour. *Below,* DUKW's crew keeps the vehicle out of the mud on flexible metal mesh.

responsibility for the east coast rail and highway systems of North Korea, while the Air Force had primary (but again not exclusive) control over the western rail and highway networks. This division of effort grew and came to be understood and accepted.

The division of responsibility for interdiction was first provided on 7 July 1950 after the naval air attacks on Pyongyang. General Stratemeyer told Admiral Struble in a dispatch that "if you participate in further air strikes, request you confine activities to area north of 38° and east of 127°."[11] The east coast assignment was further spelled out on 5 November 1950 when Task Force 77 was assigned the area *north* of the immediate battlefront, and *east* of the line of longitude of 126°-40′E, but remaining five miles *south* of all Manchurian territory.

These assignments, plus the subsequent long days of effort by Task Force 77 in the immediate area of the Hungnam redeployment, the shortage of U. S. Air Force bases in South Korea, and the fact that the Air Force could effectively reach the upper parts of northeast Korea only with B-29s, were the several factors which resulted in the allocation of the east coast area to the Navy.

Several months later, on 15 February 1951, the division of North Korea was further solidified when FEAF headquarters informed COMNAVFE that interdiction of the northeast coastal area was difficult for them because of the distance from their bases. FEAF requested that the Navy cover the northeast coastal route until 25 February. On the latter date Admiral Joy ordered TF-77 to continue the interdiction campaign until further notice.

Certainly, one of the lessons of the prolonged interdiction campaign in Korea was that theater control and coordination of such a costly and major effort must be effected if success is to be achieved.

Reasons for Failure of Interdiction

Notwithstanding the heavy damage inflicted by naval air, the over-all air interdiction campaign in Korea had only partial success. Even when the attacks of Task Force 77 were added to those of the Marine Air Wing and the Fifth Air Force, the combined destruction did not succeed in restricting the flow of the enemy's supplies to the frontlines, or in achieving "interdiction of the battlefield." The attrition caused the enemy to triple and re-triple his efforts to supply the frontlines; it laid a terrible and costly burden upon his supply organization; it caused him the most widespread damage and loss. But no vital or decisive effect could be observed at the fighting front. Throughout the campaign, the enemy seemed to have ample strength to launch an attack if he wished. His frequent heavy artillery barrages upon our frontlines were evidence that he did not suffer from a shortage of ammunition.* Captured prisoners said they had plenty of food, clothing, medical supplies, and ammunition for their small arms.

"The interdiction program was a failure," said VADM J. J. Clark, Commander Seventh Fleet. "It did *not* interdict. The Communists got the supplies through; and for the kind of a war they were fighting, they not only kept their battleline supplied, but they had enough surplus to spare so that by the end of the war they could even launch an offensive."[12]

Communist Reaction to the Interdiction Campaign

It must be grudgingly admitted that one of the key reasons why isolation of the battlefield could not be achieved in Korea was the surprising tenacity, determination, and ingenuity displayed by the Communists to keep their rail and highway networks in operation. In spite of incessant daylight attacks and night-time harassment, despite the necessity of working at night, of using old equipment, of having long, exposed, and vulnerable supply lines, the Chinese were able to maintain and even increase the flow of supplies to the battlefront.

In addition to patience and determination, however, the Communists had method and organization for the maintenance and repair of their road and rail networks.

The responsible agency for highway maintenance was the North Korean Department of Military Highway Administration. It was charged with the repair of tunnels, bridges, and roads, and for construction of necessary by-passes. This organization, numbering some 20,000 personnel, was divided into 12 regiments of three or more battalions each. Each battalion (about 500 men) was assigned to a section of North Korea. At important points within each section, platoons of road repair personnel were stationed at two-mile intervals. Their equipment was simple but effective: shovels, sandbags, wicker baskets, picks, axes, and other hand tools. At key bridges and tunnels, in times of emergency, local labor might also be drafted. On such occasions as many as 1,000 laborers, including many women and children, would be used to repair a single bridge or tunnel.

The railroad repair system was equally extensive and equally well organized. The responsible agency was the North Korean Railroad Recovery Bureau, consisting of three brigades and numbering some 26,000 personnel. These brigades were further subdivided into repair teams of 300 people per team. In addition to the simple hand tools mentioned above, each team was equipped with horse and wagon units for the hauling of heavy timbers

---

* The number of rounds of artillery and mortar fire received by the UN forces rose from an average of 150,000 to 200,000 rounds per month in the last six months of 1951 to more than 700,000 rounds in October 1952, the average per month in 1952 being approximately 350,000 rounds per month.

and rails. Moreover, specialized equipment such as welding equipment, surveying equipment, jacks, levers, and cranes were assembled at key repair points. Prefabricated wooden bridges and prefabricated metal spans, as well as timber, rails, cement, and other building materials were also stockpiled, much of it kept in the thousands of caves and tunnels.

The rapidity of the Communist repair effort is indicated by the fact that of one stretch of track near Wonsan, 400 feet were destroyed on 4 April 1952; yet on 5 April the track was repaired and in operation. All along the northeast coast, cuts made in the morning would be repaired by the afternoon.

In the struggle to keep their rail traffic moving, the Reds did two other things to foil our interdiction attacks: (1) they constructed bypasses, and (2) they shuttled rail traffic between breaks.

The construction of a bridge bypass was a simple but effective counter. Most of the rivers in Korea were shallow and fordable. When bridges across such streams were destroyed, with their piers and abutments damaged, the Reds merely laid a temporary bridge across the stream bed itself rather than attempting to repair the nearby bridge. At key locations where the terrain would not permit this simple solution, the Reds would undertake the laborious construction of a lengthy bypass to circumvent the bridge entirely. The bridge at Carlson's Canyon was such an effort.

The Communist response to the hundreds of breaks made in their trackage was the shuttling system. At night, a train would operate as far south on a particular segment of track as possible—12 miles per night was not an unusual average. Its load would then be shifted, usually by truck but often by hand, across the broken bridge or damaged rail bed, to another train. This train would proceed southward as far as possible, hiding in rail tunnels by day, and would again shift its load to another train when it reached an impassable or unrepaired break in the line. While the rate of moving supplies was seriously hampered, a certain amount of supplies went steadily through.

The Reds also invented and exploited every possible method of concealment, deception, and camouflage. Whenever a truck convoy had to be left exposed, it was always covered with straw or foliage, driven beneath the trees, concealed in caves or beneath bridges, or, if in wintertime, covered with white canvas. Along the road between Wonsan and Pyongyang, often referred to by the airmen as "Death Valley," were many well-concealed revetments in which a truck could be hidden quickly. As for locomotives and boxcars, the hundreds of tunnels were excellent hideouts, and there was room inside them for some 8,000 cars—enough room to accommodate every train and locomotive in North Korea. At times, locomotives were deceptively placed in the center of the train rather than in their usual position at the front or back.

Damaged trains and trucks were left in plain view and often painted bright colors to invite attack; operating trucks carried oily rags, which, in the event of an attack, the drivers quickly lit to leave the impression of destruction. Trucks were often concealed near churches, schools, and hospitals, so that an attack on them must also involve danger of striking these buildings as well. Trucks were often concealed in bombed-out buildings. On other occasions, truck hoods were left open and the truck wheels removed, to give the appearance of being "not-serviceable"; but these same vehicles were quickly made serviceable after nightfall.

The use by enemy trucks of our own flags and markings or even the International Red Cross emblem was occasionally reported by our airmen. Trucks moved in convoys, as many as twenty in a column. Spotters were stationed along the roads at every mile to fire their rifles upon approach of one of our planes. Flashing lights along the mountain tops for warning the trains and trucks of an approaching plane were also reported by our observers.

Rail breaks were simulated by strewing debris, mud, and straw across sections of track. Exposed locomotives were covered with foliage or straw, and, in the marshalling yards, supplies were never left uncovered. Wide dispersal and small stockpiles were standard Communist procedure. Around the logistic supply center of Yangdok, for example, were twelve supply storage areas and numerous vehicle parking areas, spread out over an area approximately two and one-half by five miles with the whole area heavily defended by automatic radar-laid guns.

Flak traps were plentiful in North Korea. An open parachute hung on a tree would be visibly exposed to lure an unwary pilot. Dummy trains, trucks, tanks, and even troops (made of straw and cardboard) were exposed at key points to welcome an attack. Tracks suggesting heavy traffic would be made leading to an important looking but empty building. Steel cables were stretched across the narrow valleys into which our planes would sometimes fly. Each of these flak traps was ringed with well-placed and well-concealed guns.

And there were many occasions of the Communists using our radio channels to give pilots false information. This latter trick was usually the least effective, for when the enemy radio was asked to authenticate, he would invariably go off the air.

Perhaps the most effective deception was the Reds' practice of making both bridges and tracks usable by night and unserviceable by day. After the end of a night's work, a crane would lift out a portable span and deposit it in a nearby tunnel until the next day. At those bridges spanning a river, a section of bridge would be floated clear, moored downstream, and camouflaged during the daylight hours. At such bridges, piles of construction material would be left visible to leave the impression of work in progress.

As for the rails, sections of track would be hand-carried into the nearest tunnel and concealed there during the daylight hours, leaving gaps in the lines which, to the pilots, gave the appearance of an unrepaired break.

"Their repair work was simplicity itself," said VADM J. J. Clark. "The minute darkness came, they would lay down the track. They didn't prepare the roadbed; they just laid the cross ties in the mud, and as long as the cars would run, it was all right."

In addition to their organized repair systems and their clever use of concealment and camouflage, the Reds also responded to UN attacks upon interdiction targets with antiaircraft fire. The principal heavy gun was the Soviet 85-mm., a highly mobile and accurate gun mounted on four wheels, firing a 20-pound projectile to an effective altitude of 25,000 feet at the rate of 15 to 20 rounds per minute. The principal automatic weapon was the 37-mm. gun, also a four-wheel mobile unit, firing a 1.6-pound projectile at a rate of 160 rounds per minute.

The number of enemy antiaircraft guns increased steadily in direct ratio to the intensity of our attacks. In May of 1951, the number of heavy guns and automatic weapons in North Korea was estimated to be 925. By March of 1953, the Reds had increased this to 1670 heavy and automatic weapons (37-mm., 76-mm., and 85-mm.) and several thousand of smaller automatic weapons (12.7-mm.). The greatest part of these guns were known to be Soviet, including gun-laying Soviet radar. Some of the latter were mobile radar units which were constantly moved from area to area as the pattern of the UN attacks was varied. In "Death Valley," west of Wonsan, VA-75 reported in August 1952 that during one attack, 350 to 400 bursts could be counted in the air.

The lower pilots carried their attacks (and in many cases only an on-the-deck delivery could insure the needed accuracy), the greater became the danger of flak damage. As in World War II, the majority of flak damage suffered by our airplanes was from small arms. It is interesting to note that while most of the propeller driven AD and F4U pilots (affectionately called "Able Dawgs" and "Hawgs" respectively) never realized the intensity of the small arms fire they were attracting because of engine and propeller noise, the jet pilots in their more silent cockpits were frequently able to hear the intense small arms fire from the ground. This was also confirmed by pilots shot down and later recovered.

To appreciate this growing flak problem, the experience of Air Group

Five in 93 days of operations in 1951 is typical: its aircraft were hit 284 times.

From May until December 1951, the Navy lost 74 aircraft (but only 39 pilots); the Marines lost 39 aircraft (32 pilots) on interdiction missions. The number of aircraft struck by enemy fire was as follows:

DATE	CARRIER	NO. AIRCRAFT STRUCK
Mar. 1951—Oct. 1951	*Boxer*	202
Aug. 1951—Mar. 1952	*Essex*	318
Dec. 1951—June 1952	*Valley Forge*	551
June 1952—Dec. 1952	*Bon Homme Richard*	97

This table indicates the steady rise in the number of aircraft struck by antiaircraft fire from March 1951 until June 1952.

"This heavy build-up of enemy AA batteries," said RADM John Perry, "also tied up many enemy personnel. In the seven months we were on the line, the increase was around 200 per cent—and it continued."[13]

The last figure in the above table shows a sharp falling-off in the number of struck aircraft, due to several reasons. In August of 1952 Rear Admiral Apollo Soucek, CTF 77, ordered that future attacks upon interdiction targets south of Wonsan should not be carried below a minimum altitude of 3,000 feet.

Second, the naval aircraft changed their attack tactics. Wherever there were heavily defended targets (and by mid-1952 all of the key interdiction targets in North Korea were heavily defended), the invariable rule was to attack the guns themselves in conjunction with the interdiction target itself. Flak-suppression became standard procedure. Moreover, larger flights of planes were used, and the number of runs on the targets was reduced. Such countering tactics caused a rapid falling off in the damage being received by our aircraft.

Two conclusions follow from a study of the Communists' reactions to the interdiction campaign. First, the tactics employed by the Reds, and the patience and persistence they displayed, were successful in Korea and may be expected to be seen again. Secondly, the primitiveness of the battle area with regard to its communication network was an advantage to the defenders.

The Weapons of Interdiction Used in Korea

The isolation of a fixed battlefield (using every method short of physical occupation) is a difficult task in any terrain, and under the accepted restrictions in Korea, the attempts at isolation proved to be unprofitable and unsuccessful.

It is appropriate now to determine why interdiction in Korea was unprofitable and did not succeed in "isolation of the battlefield."

First of all, the means available to UN forces for the accomplishment of interdiction were varied and adequate. Three weapons systems were available: the airplane, the naval gun, and the raiding party.

The UN's airplanes ran the gamut from the large B-29 to the Mosquito L-19; the naval gun from the 16-inch to the 20-mm., the bombs from 2,000-pounders to 100-pound delayed-action bombs. Air attacks could be massed and concentrated on key targets or they could be small and widespread among many targets. In addition, UN forces enjoyed the elements of surprise, initiative, and target selection.

In the inventory of UN aircraft, the precision instrument of naval aviation was to prove itself the most effective and versatile weapon of air interdiction. In particular, the AD Skyraider was to be the most successful airplane of the 37-month war. Only the Skyraider could carry and successfully deliver the 2,000-pound bomb with dive-bombing precision against the targets of interdiction: the bridge abutment or span, the tunnel mouth, and the cave entrance. The AD's versatility and weight-lifting capacity (as much as 5,000 pounds on an average carrier mission) made it the war's outstanding performer.

As the war progressed, jet aircraft became capable of carrying bombs, and they too proved to be very effective interdiction weapons, especially as the enemy's antiaircraft efforts intensified. The jets' silent approach, their speed and their steadiness as a weapons platform made them ideal interdiction weapons. Combat losses for the jets were only one-fourth those of the propeller types.

As for the naval gun, the venerable 16-inch gun demonstrated its effectiveness once again. No other size of shell could so effectively blast a coastal interdiction target as the old 16-inch. After such targets as bridge and tunnels had been demolished, the 5-inch guns of the destroyers could usually keep them inactivated; but the smaller naval guns could not profitably effect the initial destruction.

Thus, the means for accomplishing interdiction were obviously adequate. The failure in Korea cannot be laid to a lack of them.

The Target Systems of the Communists

Next, it is necessary to examine the target systems of the Communists' logistic networks.

Broadly speaking, there are three main parts to any logistic system: (1) the sources of raw materials; (2) the points of manufacture; and (3) the distribution system.

During the Korean war, two of these three, and part of the third, could *not* be attacked and destroyed because of the UN's own decision.

Thus, one of the chief reasons for the failure of the interdiction campaign in Korea was the fact that the UN could not attack the most vulnerable parts of a supply system—the sources and the points of manufacture. Only the exposed portions of the supply system *in Korea* could be attacked.

Having been limited to the supply system in Korea, the UN forces had their choice of four types of interdiction targets. First, there were the supply routes themselves: the bridges, tunnels, tracks, roadbeds. Second, there was the rolling stock: locomotives and boxcars, trucks, wagons and carts. Third, there were the personnel who repaired and operated the supply networks; fourth, the stockpiles of materials and supplies in transit or in dumps.

Two of these four target systems were unprofitable for systematic air attack. Obviously, with unlimited manpower available to the Koreans and Chinese, attacking the personnel operating or repairing the supply routes was infeasible. As for attacking the supplies themselves, either in transit or in dumps, this would scarcely have decisive effect for two reasons. First, the *origins* of the supplies were untouchable. Second, the Communists' ability to hide, camouflage, and disperse supplies in the hundreds of caves, tunnels, and huts was acknowledged.

Thus, only two target systems in Korea were left for attack: the rolling stock and the routes themselves. Attacks upon the rolling stock had the disadvantage, once again, of not being able to touch the sources. There was an almost limitless source of trucks and trains in Manchuria; those vehicles and rolling stock destroyed or damaged in Korea need only be replaced. For an interdiction effort to be effective on this target system, the attacks on rolling stock had to inflict damage at a rate exceeding the enemy's capacity for replacement—a highly unlikely performance.

The remaining target system was the route itself. At first glance Korea's looked ideal, choked as it was with bridges, tunnels, and the mountains crowding and twisting the roadbeds and rail lines into devious routes. On the other hand, with the limited number of airplanes available, not every one of the 956 bridges could be demolished, not every one of the 231 tunnels blocked.

Three patterns of attack could be followed: (1) key bridges could be cut, and kept cut; (2) a belt across Korea could be selected and every supply route and target within it destroyed; and (3), widespread damage could be effected upon the roads and rail lines themselves.

This analysis indicates that true isolation of the battlefield, under the UN's self-imposed restrictions, was never achievable in Korea. Of this effort, General Mark Clark wrote: "The Air Force and the Navy carriers may have kept us from losing the war, but they were denied the opportunity of influencing the outcome decisively in our favor. They gained complete mastery of the skies, gave magnificent support to the infantry, destroyed every worthwhile target in North Korea, and took a costly toll of enemy personnel and supplies. But as in Italy, where we learned the same bitter lesson in the same kind of rugged country, our airpower could not keep a steady stream of enemy supplies and reinforcements from reaching the battle line. Air could not isolate the front."[14]

The U. S. Navy can take great pride that it came as close as it did.

Summary

For naval men, interference with an enemy's logistical system has been a traditional occupation throughout history by naval blockade and by direct attacks upon enemy shipping at sea. However, the interference with an enemy's *land* supply in his own territory is a relatively new factor in warfare introduced since the advent of the airplane. Not until World War II did interference with an enemy's logistical system by air reach a significant scale of effort. The ultimate of land logistical interdiction—strategic bombing—was extensively used during World War II in an effort to destroy the opponent's logistical systems in enemy territory.

In modern war, the factor of logistics has come to be an equal partner with strategy and tactics. Strategic bombing, in the broadest sense, is as an interdiction effort—*distant* interdiction to be sure, as opposed to the commonly understood definition of interdiction as meaning isolation of the *immediate* battlefield. But wherever interdiction is applied, near the zone of the battlefield or distantly from it, it is still logistical interference.

The failure of air power, through interdiction, to stop the fighting in Korea follows a historic pattern. Except in a few isolated instances during World War II (such as the Normandy landings), there is much evidence to show that an air effort to interrupt an enemy's supply system *has never been wholly successful*. In World War II, the Luftwaffe failed to starve Britain; the Anglo-American air offensive against the Nazi war-making machinery did not prevent an increase in military production even as late as July 1944. Air interdiction of the battlefront failed in Italy, on a peninsula and in terrain that was prophetic of Korea. There, in the spring of 1944, an intensive air effort had been made to sever the German supply lines and to reduce German supply levels in order to force their retreat. Despite great efforts which achieved limited successes (at times all the Po River bridges were out of commission), the air interdiction campaign in Italy was never decisive upon the conduct of ground operations.* It harassed, it hurt, it impeded the enemy; but it did not have critical results upon the ground fighting.†

In the Pacific, the B-29 bomb and fire-bomb attacks on Japan's industrial cities critically damaged that nation's war-making potential. But there is ample evidence to show that the Japanese were already fast becoming prostrate from the strangulation of the prolonged naval blockade.

Thus, the failure of air power to interdict a battlefield in Korea was not the first time.

On 6 April 1955, almost two years after the truce in Korea, the Red Chinese in a broadcast over the Peking radio, stated that the United Nations "mobilized more than 2,000 military aircraft and still failed to cut off the supply line to tiny North Korea."[15] Regretfully, though their arithmetic was wrong, their conclusion was right.

For many months—from early 1951 through 1952—almost 100 per cent of the offensive effort of the carriers, 60 per cent of the offensive effort of the shore-based Marines' aircraft, 70 per cent of the offensive effort of the Fifth Air Force, and 70 per cent of the blockading efforts of the ships along the east coast was devoted to interdiction. These percentages fluctuated from month to month, and in the last year of the war, as has been recorded, interdiction had less emphasis. Nevertheless, these percentages generally reflect the weight and scale of effort which was made to isolate the Korean battlefield. In the first eighteen months of the interdiction campaign, Task Force 77 flew 20,567 armed reconnaissance and interdiction flights; the Marines ashore flew 25,266 reconnaissance and interdiction flights; the FEAF (Far East Air Force) flew 126,702 reconnaissance and interdiction flights; and Task Force 95 fired 230,000 rounds of ammunition on interdiction missions.

Despite this effort, the enemy was never kept from supplying his needed requirements. At no time—except locally and temporarily—did the enemy limit his combat effort because of supply considerations.

---

* *The Drive on Rome,* Mediterranean Subseries, official U. S. Army History of World War II, by Doctor Sidney Mathews, now in preparation, reaches this same conclusion.

† On page 1010 of the MacArthur hearings, General Bradley testified: ". . . In Italy where we had as good a chance as any I ever heard of of stopping a large hostile army by air, because much of the supplies came through the Brenner Pass, they continued to supply about 25 German divisions even though we bombed the Brenner Pass practically every day."

By every index, in fact, the Communists were able to steadily increase their flow of supplies to the frontlines. Total over-all rail sightings held steadily throughout the war. Antiaircraft fire increased. Vehicular sightings increased from month to month.

All these facts are made more significant when it is appreciated that the enemy forces at the front were supported by long supply lines which were confined to a closely blockaded peninsula, and which were under constant, largely unopposed, attacks by considerable air strength. At the same time, our own supply pipeline was never under attack.

However, because of the limitations imposed which forced airpower to confine interdiction to only a small part of the weakest element of the enemy's logistical system, it does not follow that, having failed in Korea, interdiction must always fail. The full effects of atomic weapons upon an interdiction campaign cannot now be foretold.

In summary, six major reasons are given as to why airpower failed to interdict the Korean battlefield. If these problems are not encountered in a future conflict, or if they are solved, then isolation of a battlefield may yet be effected.

First, interdiction failed because of the ability of the Communists to absorb widespread and heavy punishment, and, through use of unlimited manpower, to keep their highways and rail lines operating.

Second, interdiction failed in Korea because UN forces could not attack the sources and fountainheads of the supply lines.

Third, interdiction failed in Korea because of our inability to find and destroy at night, and in inclement weather, the small individual targets of interdiction which we were able to destroy in daylight.

Fourth, interdiction failed because of the stalemated war. Had the fighting been fluid, the Communists' rate of usage would have increased greatly. Then they would have been forced to use the rails and roads by day. "After my first month on the line with TF-77," said RADM John Perry, "I never believed that complete interdiction was possible with the tools we had available. I did believe—and still do—that in a fluid, as opposed to the existing static campaign, we could cut down enemy supplies to the point where he could not long sustain a major forward move."[16] In the words of General James Van Fleet: "If we had ever put on some pressure and made him fight, we would have given him an insoluble supply problem. Instead, we fought the Communist on his own terms, even though we had the advantages of flexibility, mobility, and firepower. We fought *his* way, which was terrible. We both sat, and dug in, and he was the superior rat. He was small; he could dig holes faster; and if he lost a hundred people in a hole, he'd just go out and find another hundred.

"We might have interdicted the battlefield if we'd attacked, using our advantages and superior weapons. Then we would have made him use up his supplies faster than he could supply himself."[17]

Fifth, interdiction failed because of the very primitive nature of the enemy's exposed supply network.

Sixth, interdiction failed owing to our inability to use the one weapon—the atomic bomb—in our arsenal which might have severed Communist supply lines in Korea.

9.

The Seaborne Artillery

Establishment of Blockade

On 4 July 1950, the following broadcast was made to all shipping in the Pacific Ocean:

> The President of the United States, in keeping with the United Nations Security Council's request for support to the Republic of Korea in repelling the Northern Korean invaders and restoring peace in Korea, has ordered a naval blockade of the Korean coast.

While this broadcast did not mention the limits of the blockade, they were 39°-35′ N on the west coast, and 41°-51′ N on the east coast. These limits were established to keep all sea forces well clear of both Russian and Chinese territory.*

The imposition of a blockade of Korea was not without legal difficulties. The Soviet Union and Communist China both denounced the blockade and refused to acknowledge its existence or legality although both observed it. Early in July 1950, Admiral Joy queried Admiral Sherman: Were Soviet or Chinese merchantmen to be barred from North Korean ports? Admiral Sherman's reply was in strict accord with International Law. All *warships* not under United Nations command, he said, including Russian, would be permitted to enter North Korean ports, except of course, North Korean. All *other* type ships were barred.

As the war opened, the forces for establishing a blockade were meager:

---

* Readers should note that the limit of the blockade on the east coast excluded the port city of Rashin. On p. 2260 and 2276, *Hearings before the House Armed Services Committee and the Senate Foreign Relations Committee, "Military Situation in the Far East,"* Admiral Sherman testified: "The Russians had an arrangement to use Rashin. They did use it at times since the war began." On p. 2097, Lieutenant General Emmett O'Donnell, Jr., testified: ". . . As I remember it, Rashin is a warm-water port. I believe that the Soviet leases that port for its own use and has been doing so for some time. It is possible they have a submarine base there. . . ."

UNITED STATES

USS *Juneau* (CLAA-19)
(CAPT Jesse C. Sowell)
(Until 24 July 1950, flagship of
RADM J. M. Higgins,
ComCruDiv-5)

COMDESDIV 91
(CAPT Halle C. Allan)

USS *Mansfield* (DD-728)
(CDR E. H. Headland)

USS *Swenson* (DD-729)
(CDR Robert A. Schelling)

USS *DeHaven* (DD-727)
(CDR Oscar B. Lundgren)

USS *Collett* (DD-730)
(CDR Robert H. Close)

AUSTRALIAN (5 July)

HMAS *Shoalhaven* (PF)
(CDR Ian H. McDonald, RAN)

BRITISH

HMS *Belfast* (CL)
(CAPT Aubrey St. Clair-Ford, Bt.,
DSO, RN)

HMS *Jamaica* (CL)
(CAPT J. S. C. Salter, DSO, OBE,
RN)

HMS *Cossack* (DD)
(CAPT R. T. White, DSO, until 26
July 50)
(CDR V. C. Begg, after 26 July 50)

HMS *Consort* (DD)
(CDR J. R. Carr)

HMS *Black Swan* (PF)
(CAPT A. D. H. Jay, DSO, DSC)

HMS *Alacrity* (PF)
(CDR H. S. Barber)

HMS *Hart* (PF)
(CDR N. H. H. Mulleneux)

Such as it was, this small force set the blockade.

On 29 June 1950, the first shore bombardment of the war was fired by *Juneau* at Okkye on the east coast. The target was enemy personnel, and four hundred and fifty-nine 5-inch shells were fired at them. Twenty-seven casualties were reported. Okkye was again a target for *Juneau*'s guns on 30 June.

The initial United States naval action of the war took place on Sunday, 2 July, when *Juneau* (in company with *Jamaica* and *Black Swan*) sighted four North Korean torpedo boats in the vicinity of Chumunjin, on Korea's east coast. The four torpedo boats, escorting a small coastal convoy of ten trawlers, were steaming southward when the two groups sighted each other shortly after sunrise.

As the three UN ships turned toward them, the four North Korean torpedo boats made a gallant but futile attack, firing their small guns but failing to launch torpedoes because of VT-fuzed shells exploding around them. The first UN salvo blew up and sank one torpedo boat, halted and burned a second, while the remaining two raced off in opposite directions. One of these two beached itself and was destroyed by gunfire; the other, heading seaward and zigzagging violently, managed to evade the pursuing *Black Swan*. Small-caliber enemy shore guns fired a few rounds at the three UN ships, one shell landing near *Juneau*'s port quarter, but achieved no hits.

The next morning, the *Juneau* discovered the ten trawlers which had taken refuge in Chumunjin, and, according to later reports, sank seven of them.

These two episodes were the opening actions in a blockade and bombardment effort which was to stretch on for more than three years—an effort unique in American naval history. In many respects it was a "crazy, mixed-up" naval blockade, where trains and trucks on land were chased by ships at sea; where Communist troops almost 20 miles from the oceans felt the shock of naval gunfire.

Hereafter, there would be no active surface opposition, no submarine opposition, and practically no enemy air opposition to the blockade. UN naval forces, led by the U. S. Navy, would have complete control of the entire five-hundred-odd miles of the North Korean coastline.

Notwithstanding these facts, the imposition of a blockade of the Korean coast was neither easy nor simple. The geography of the peninsula was a handicap. The western coast, with its 30-foot tides, was a network of embayments, estuaries, and hundreds of off-lying islands, vast mudbanks, numerous shoals, and uncharted rocks. The east coast was precipitous, largely barren, and suitable for mining in many areas. The current on both coasts, and the several Korean rivers emptying into both the Yellow Sea and the Sea of Japan, lent themselves to the use of "drifter" mines. These physical features made the application of a blockade difficult.

Second, the blockade was imposed thousands of miles from the American mainland.

Third, the number of ships for blockading and bombardment purposes was never plentiful.

Fourth, the legal requirement for an effective blockade required that every portion of the blockaded coast had to be under surveillance once every twenty-four hours by ship (not by air).

The enemy was destined to resist the naval blockade and bombardment cunningly and to the limit of his ability. The thirty-six months which followed saw him make great use of mines; he also opposed the blockade and bombardment with coastal and shore defense batteries so well hidden and so deeply tunnelled into the rocky hills of the Korean coast that they were often able to defy the UN's naval strength.

That this naval blockade around Korea was a success, that it hampered, embarrassed, and hurt the enemy, there can be no doubt. The ingenuity, aggressiveness, and persistence displayed by UN naval forces in imposing a resolute blockade at a distance of 5,000 miles from the American continent is worthy of record as well as of tribute.

Minesweepers, frigates, destroyer escorts, destroyers, cruisers, and battleships of the U. S. Navy, and units from seven other navies of the UN, plus the ROK Navy, were destined to fight a bitter, unglamorous, and seemingly futile war along the coastlines of Korea. Many ships were to be hit; an unlucky few were to be sunk. By and large, the headlines of the war would not recognize these surface forces. Their work would largely go untold and un-

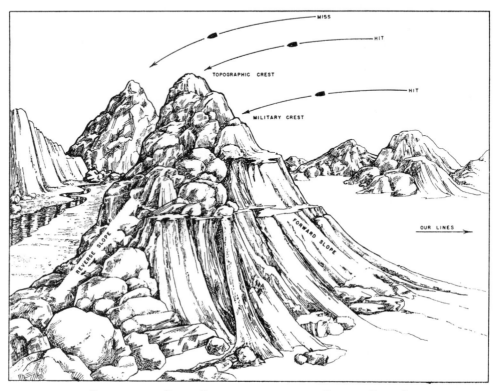

PROBLEMS OF SHORE BOMBARDMENT ON THE KOREAN COAST*

rewarded. VIPs would come and go in a steady parade through the Korean theater—to visit the frontlines, to witness operations aboard carriers and battleships, but only rarely to observe the smaller ships of the blockade and bombardment force in action.

To the "small boys" especially, it was a dreary and often dangerous campaign of constant blockade and bombardment, essential to the war effort and necessary to the support of the fighting ashore.

The First Landing of U. S. Forces in Korea

The USS *Juneau* had the honor of conducting both the first landing and the first raiding party in Korea.

* See also "Deep Naval Gunfire Support for the Marines," page 332.

"When the war began," said CAPT W. B. Porter,[1] *Juneau's* executive officer, "the *Juneau* was anchored in Kagoshima Harbor. We were having an official party—the first one since the end of the war—honoring the local Japanese officials. During the afternoon, we commenced receiving messages announcing an 'incident' in Korea, and telling us to stand by. As unobtrusively as possible, we discontinued the party and sent the Japanese guests ashore.

"The *Juneau's* orders," said Captain Porter, "were to proceed immediately to investigate landings on Kojo-do island. We arrived there the next morning (28 June) shortly before dawn.

"On arrival, the question arose, 'How does one commence an investigation of 'landings' when no amphibious forces (as we know them, but only sampans) were used?' Admiral Higgins decided to send me ashore to investigate.

"I took four Marines with me in the whaleboat. We carried along a large American flag tied to a boat hook. I also had a walkie-talkie radio and one of those 'how to' instruction books for learning Japanese in three weeks. My orders were to investigate, but not to do any shooting except in self-defense.

"We ran into the harbor and went ashore, and after a cautious parade down the muddy village street, sighted a Korean who was marching back and forth with a carbine over his shoulder. At this time the big problem was to distinguish a *South* Korean from a *North* Korean. They all looked alike. However, the villagers soon commenced to bring us tea and hard-boiled eggs. We knew then that they were friendly.

"With hand signals and the aid of the language book, I was able to make it clear to the sentry that I wanted to contact someone of importance. About 11 a.m., we managed to get Pusan on the phone and I talked to the American Consul there. He said that the only landings that he knew of were reported to be at Munsan.

"Whereupon we went back to the whaleboat and back to the *Juneau* which all this time had been covering us with her guns.

"The *Juneau* got under way again, and steamed up to the vicinity of Munsan. This time we had to lie offshore quite a distance, and it took our whaleboat about an hour to get my party ashore.

"Once again, we weren't certain whether or not the spot we were landing was in enemy or friendly hands. We simply walked inland until we came to a road. I posted Marines on each side of the road in the underbrush. Pretty soon, along came a truck. The Marines jumped out onto the road, halted the truck, ordered out the occupants (who seemed to be civilians), and we turned the truck around and drove back into Munsan.

"We went to the police station and contacted the chief of police. He spoke some English and was able to tell us that the only enemy landings he had heard about had taken place near the village of Samchok.

"That was the way we got our information during the first few hours of the war."

The important point for record is that the first Americans ashore after the declaration of war was a group of U. S. Marines led by a naval officer from the USS *Juneau*.

Helping to Hold Pusan

As described in earlier chapters, the period between the commencement of the war on 25 June 1950 and the Inchon landing on 15 September 1950 was one of retreat to a defensible perimeter around Pusan. Four elements of naval support proved vital in the salvation of Pusan:

(1) The amphibious landing at Pohang
(2) The air strikes of naval and marine aircraft
(3) The effective and timely operations of the First Provisional Marine Brigade
(4) The bombardment fire of naval ships along the east coast of South Korea.

In the first three months of the Korean war, with sea forces limited and the ground issue in Korea much in doubt, the task of *blockade* was relegated to secondary importance. Every enemy soldier who could be killed or wounded by naval gunfire, every train or truck that could be stopped, every pound of supplies that could be demolished, would relieve pressure on the endangered Pusan beachhead. The firepower of the Navy's blockading forces was used for the twin tasks of supporting the ground forces with naval gunfire, and the destruction of as much of the enemy's forces and equipment, then enroute to the front, as possible.

Destruction along the enemy's logistic routes was accomplished by the blockade force in two ways: by gunfire and by raiding parties.

Between 29 June and 15 September, inclusive, the ships of the blockade force bombarded strictly military targets along the enemy-held east coast 89 times. Thousands of tons of projectiles destroyed and damaged bridges, warehouses, troops, railroads, tunnels, pillboxes, marshalling yards, factories, oil dumps, and guns. Never again were enemy targets so plentiful. Never again was the enemy's retaliation so light.

For one entire month, until the arrival in the area of the ships of Task

Force Yoke on 21 July, the original ships of the Far East Navy had the Korean coasts exclusively to themselves. *Juneau, Mansfield, De Haven, Swenson,* and *Collett,* like hungry dogs in an unattended butchershop, had more than they could handle.

Rear Admiral Higgins' eastern Korean Support Group made an impressive contribution to the eastern anchor of the endangered and shrinking battleline of the Pusan perimeter in mid-July 1950 near the vicinity of Yongdok. Around this village the Korean mountains halted abruptly and fell precipitously into the sea, and the cliffside roads were compressed against the seashore conveniently exposed to naval gunfire.

At this time in this area, the Third ROK Division was stubbornly retreating before the stabbing attacks of several North Korean divisions. The ROK's only artillery support was that supplied by the ships.

"The situation ashore was still obscure," said British Admiral Andrewes,[2] "the communications with the Army almost nonexistent. So my fleet gunnery officer with an officer from the USS *Juneau* and the Royal Artillery bombardment liaison officer were landed with the object of finding out what was happening. They established communication with an American battalion ashore and arranged a system of wireless communication by giving the Army one Navy wireless set and taking from the Army one Army wireless set for HMS *Belfast* and USS *Juneau*. The party returned on board their ships at about 2130 in a ROK warship of some antiquity."

The evening of 19 July found *Juneau, Higbee, De Haven, Swenson,* and *Mansfield,* with the British cruiser *Belfast,* close ashore to Yongdok. The Korean Military Advisory Group, Lieutenant Colonel Rollins S. Emmerich, USA, senior officer, was attached to the Third ROK Division. Emmerich had earlier radioed instructions for naval targets and would spot the naval ship's fire.

At 1900, the two cruisers and four destroyers opened fire upon the designated targets: troop concentrations, road junctions and artillery emplacements. *Belfast* fired nine-gun salvoes with controlled spots; *Juneau's* fire was deliberate, also using controlled spots. The destroyers joined in, as well as supplying night illumination fire. Two hundred and ninety-seven shells struck the entrenched enemy in Yongdok.

Admiral Higgins reported that the village was destroyed, that large fires were started, and that smoke was still visible to the ships some 12 hours later.[3] Rear Admiral Higgins congratulated Captain St. Clair-Ford's fast-firing *Belfast* crew, saying that her guns had spoken "with authority."

U. S. Army observers on the battleline spotting the fire of the naval ships were effusive. Major V. W. Bennett, U. S. Army, stated that "naval cooperation was of a superior quality." LTCOL Emmerich added ". . . This coordination and use of naval gunfire caused the largest proportions of the Fifth North Korean Division casualties. . . . The naval bombardments were terrific."[4]

Commander Robert A. Schelling of *Swenson* wrote in his war diary for 24 July 1950:

"Report from ashore spotters: 'Fire on enemy personnel in large numbers southeast of Yongdok inflicted heavy casualties. Best day yet.' I interrogated a North Korean prisoner who stated: 'Your artillery is hell. Every time you fire you kill or wound many soldiers. . . .' "

Higgins reported to Joy the results of his east coast gunfire support work in these words:

". . . By directly supporting our hard-pressed forces ashore, the enemy's advance on Pohang was definitely slowed. In the past 24 hours our ships have broken up enemy attacks, silenced enemy batteries, destroyed their observation posts, interdicted their traffic and troop concentrations, and made Yongdok untenable for their forces with heavy personnel losses at Yongdok."

Reinforcements Arrive

By late July, additional ships had sailed into Korean waters in answer to the United Nations' appeal for sea forces: three cruisers (*Helena, Toledo,* HMS *Kenya*), four U. S. destroyers (from DesRon-11), two British destroyers,* one Australian destroyer,† three Canadian destroyers,‡ two New Zealand frigates,§ and one Dutch destroyer.||

Upon arrival of these additional forces, Admiral Joy promulgated a new operation order placing all blockade and support ships in a single task force (96.5) under the command of Commander Cruiser Division Three, Rear Admiral C. C. Hartman.

The task of blockading Korea was divided between east and west coasts. The west coast of Korea was assigned by Admiral Joy to the British forces under Rear Admiral William G. Andrewes, RN (TE 96.53) while the east coast was assigned to U. S. forces in two elements: TG 96.51, under Rear Admiral C. C. Hartman, USN, aboard *Helena* (who, in addition to being

---

* HMS *Cockade* (LCDR H. J. Lee, DSC), HMS *Comus* (LCDR R. A. N. Hennessy).

† HMAS *Bataan* (CDR W. B. M. Marks, RAN).

‡ HMCS *Cayuga* (CAPT J. V. Brock, DSC, RCN); HMCS *Athabaskan* (CDR R. T. Welland, DSC, RCN); HMCS *Sioux* (CDR P. D. Taylor, RCN).

§ HMNZS *Tutira* (LCDR P. J. H. Hoare, RN); HMNZS *Pukaki* (LCDR L. E. Herrick, DSC, RN).

|| Hr. MS. *Evertsen.*

in tactical command of a task group was also in administrative command of the task force), and 96.52 under Rear Admiral John M. Higgins, USN, who had transferred his flag to the USS *Toledo*.

"The main factors contributing to my decision to assign the U. S. Navy to the east coast and the British to the west coast were purely tactical in nature," said Vice Admiral Joy. "For one reason, the east coast with its longer coastline and more numerous accessible targets required more ships for blockade, as well as bombardment and interdiction missions, than the British could muster. Furthermore, since our fast carriers would be operating most of the time in the Sea of Japan it was thought best from the standpoint of coordination to have U. S. ships rather than British operating in the same area as the carriers."

Higbee (DD-806) (CDR Elmer Moore) was the first destroyer from Task Force Yoke to see action. Joining cruisers *Belfast* and *Juneau* on 21 July near Yongdok, *Higbee* squeezed off forty-six 5-inch shells. *Higbee* had the satisfaction of hearing that her fire assisted the ROK troops in briefly recapturing the town.

The cruisers *Toledo* (CAPT Richard F. Stout) and *Helena* (CAPT Harold O. Larson) were the first heavy augmenting ships to arrive. With *Collett* and *Mansfield*, *Toledo* was in action near the now enemy-occupied city of Yongdok on 27 July. Her 79 shells of 8-inch high-capacity fire were directed upon troops and military targets.

Helena fired the first of the thousands of shells she was to expend during the course of the Korean war at the railroad marshalling yards, trains and power plant near Tanchon on 7 August 1950. Altogether, *Helena* fired one hundred and eighty-five 8-inch shells at these targets.

August 8, 1950 saw *Toledo*, *Helena* and *De Haven* get two important east coast bridges.

With exactly 100 rounds, *Toledo* and *De Haven* demolished the bridge at Samchok.

Helena dropped a bridge near Chongjin, but with more difficulty.

"On 8 August, I carried LT R. F. Noble, USMC, as a bombardment spotter," recorded LT Harold W. Swinburne, Jr., *Helena*'s helicopter pilot. "It was the first time a helicopter had ever been used for this sort of work. Our orders were to pick out suitable targets for the main batteries of the USS *Helena*. We selected a railroad bridge. On the first firing run, the ship fired numerous salvos, but only minor damage was done. After coming about to a new firing course, we asked that only one gun be fired for spotting purposes. The first shell was a direct hit and the bridge dropped into the water. The experiment was a success!"[5]

The First Raid

The USS *Juneau* also had the distinction of putting the first raiding and demolition party onto the Korean peninsula.

"On 6 July," said CAPT Porter, "the *Juneau* received a despatch from COMNAVFE addressed to Admiral Higgins saying that if we could disrupt the east coast rail line in the vicinity of Rashin, we could force the Reds to re-route all the rail traffic to the west coast network.

"We got the charts of the area out and chose an appropriate target that looked to be right on the beach. The target was one of the numerous rail tunnels, and it was our plan to rig demolition charges inside and thereby inactivate both the tunnel and the track.

"Before the *Juneau* left Sasebo, I had managed to secure from Fleet activities several Army-type demolition charges, plus detonators, walkie-talkie radios, and the other equipment. I had organized a small commando outfit in a ship which I commanded during World War II, so I was not a complete amateur, although I was far from being a demolition expert. Lieutenant Johnson, the *Juneau's* junior Marine officer, had also had some experience.

"The *Juneau* proceeded to the target area, arriving during the night hours of 11-12 July. We transferred to the destroyer *Mansfield* at 1945, about fifteen miles off the coast, and the latter destroyer took us in to about two miles off the beach. Then we transferred to the *Mansfield* whaleboat.

"Each man in my party[6] was carrying quite a load. I personally had 50 pounds of explosives, a carbine, a box of detonators, a chart, a compass, and a walkie-talkie radio.

"As we approached the beach, it was about 2 a.m. The night was very black and very dark, but the sea was calm. It was difficult in the darkness to estimate distance. A moderate surf was running, and as we neared it (about 30 yards distant, we judged), I asked the coxswain of the whaleboat if he knew how to beach a whaleboat, using a stern anchor. He said no. Just as I commenced explaining to him how to do it, he tossed the anchor over the side.

"We paid out 45 fathoms of line, then attempted to take soundings with paddles, but were unable to touch bottom. We bent on more line to the anchor line, since we still had an estimated 20 yards to go to reach the beach. About this time, the anchor line got fouled in the screw, so we cut it loose and paddled into the beach.

"Just before landing, we heard—and then saw—a locomotive pulling three or four boxcars crossing a cut directly ahead of us. It went into one tunnel, out again, and into a second.

"At any rate, I ordered the landing party out of the boat, and I jumped into the water, carrying my own load. The water was just over my head, and it was a tiring struggle to get ashore. I left two marine guards on the beach, and the rest of us started inland.

"Contrary to our maps, which indicated that the area was flat, the area where we had landed was very hilly and at the beach almost precipitous. It had a 60-degree grade, and was faced with loose rock. This made the upward climb very slow, and there was danger of the party being carried to the bottom under an avalanche of rock. Moreover, there was no rail line near the beach. A collection of fishermen's huts was on our left, about a quarter-mile distant. We trudged inland, leaving our whaleboat crew making repeated dives to clear the fouled propeller.

"For about an hour and a half we worked our way inland over the very hilly and rocky terrain. In the pitchblack darkness I navigated as best I could, using my Army compass and chart.

"Finally, we spotted the lights of a train behind us, and then realized we had gone over the *top* of our target and *past* the rail line. (Later I figured we had gone about three miles inland.)

"We worked laboriously back to the rail line, and found the tunnel. It was about 150 yards long. At the south end of the tunnel there was a large trestle over a deep ravine. I posted one of my two remaining Marines at the north end of the tunnel and the other Marine at the south end of this trestle. The Marine officer, LT Johnson, looked after our security while we worked.

"The four gunner's mates and I started shoveling a trench crosswise beneath the rail line in the middle of the tunnel. We dug a trench about one foot deep and five feet long, planted the charges, and put in several detonators each way along the track. After the charges were rigged, I sent one gunner's mate up to get the Marine at the north end of the tunnel and I proceeded in the darkness down the other direction to notify the other Marine. As I walked along the trestle I lost my footing in the darkness and slipped beneath the ties, dropping the walkie-talkie and my compass. My elbows caught the ties and prevented my fall, but I got skinned up in the process.

"The rest of the mission was without further incident and we walked back to the beach. During our absence the whaleboat crew had succeeded in clearing her screw. We shoved off immediately, and as we neared the *Mansfield,* we heard a train coming from the north. A few seconds later, we saw the flash of our demolition charges as the train tripped them.

"Two days later, the Air Force took pictures of the tunnel area and confirmed the destruction of the train. In the pictures you could still see it sticking out of the tunnel."

On the 6th of August, following this success, a special operations group was established aboard the USS *H. A. Bass* (APD-124) (LCDR Alan Ray, USN) composed of elements of the Marine First Reconnaissance Company (Major Edward P. Dupras, USMC) and Underwater Demolition Team No. One (LCDR David F. Welch, USN). This group would operate under the command of Comtransdiv-111 (CDR S. C. Small, USN) to make a total of six raids (three on each coast) between the 12th and 25th of August, for the purpose of destroying enemy railroads and bridges, and to obtain needed intelligence.

The 14 August attack was typical of the destruction accomplished by these raids. Shortly before midnight, the *H. A. Bass* approached the east coast area at Iwon, 41°-20′ N. The target, code-named "King," was a 200-foot stretch of railroad track between two tunnels. Lying offshore in the darkness, *Bass* lowered her LCPR (Landing Craft, Personnel, Reconnaissance) and put aboard the raiding party. Directed by radio to a point within 500 yards of the beach, the party then disembarked into rubber boats. The Marines paddled through the surf to reconnoiter and secure the objective area; when this was done, the demolition crews were called to come in. The "Utes" rigged charges on both tunnels and on the track itself.

Returning to their boats and paddling clear of the beach, the raiding party was rewarded with the sight of seeing the objective area obliterated as the heavy charges exploded.*

The result of these raids was to retard the advance of the Communists down the coastal road to Pusan.

Doubts Raised of Naval Blockade's Effectiveness

In early August 1950, with the Communists pressing relentlessly toward Pusan, questions were asked as to whether the naval blockade was effective. Air power had taken credit for making the enemy's rail lines inoperable, especially during daylight. All over Korea, roads, bridges, locomotives, and rolling stock had been reported as destroyed. It was axiomatic that an advancing army of 140,000 Communists needed vast quantities of munitions, supplies, personnel, and food, and that all of it could not be hand-carried. How were the Communists supplying themselves?

To some who struggled with this problem, it was an easy jump from an erroneous premise to a false conclusion. If the rail lines were inoperable, obviously the supplies were being moved by sea, perhaps at night. Hadn't aircraft often reported groups of ships, as many as a hundred in a group,

---

* The three units of this special operating group were awarded the Navy Unit Commendation for this series of raids. UDT One was later awarded a second NUC for the period 2 November to 1 December 1950.

all along both coasts? One mission report, typical of others, reported the destruction of a 10,000-ton ship in Inchon harbor. Wasn't this proof of the sea-lifting tactics of the Reds?

"During this period," said Vice Admiral Joy, "I was frequently asked to intensify my naval blockade of Korea. Many felt that the Reds were getting a large proportion of their supplies by water, possibly in small leap-frogging operations at night. The west coast, with its hundreds of islands, made this supposition easy to come by.

"Frequent aircraft reports were received during this period that large numbers of junks or other ships had been sighted, here one day, there another. Immediately it was assumed that these fleets were supply armadas, and I was so informed. I had conferences with my commanders—Rear Admiral Higgins, Rear Admiral Hartman of our east coast blockade forces, and Rear Admiral Andrewes, the British west coast blockade commander.

"All of us agreed that while a small amount of sea traffic might be moving, it was very slight and not significant. Admiral Andrewes offered to employ his aircraft from HMS *Triumph* to photograph every port and inlet on the west coast to corroborate that the supplies were not coming by sea. I accepted his offer."

The admiral also asked the patrol squadrons to check the reports of the "supply armadas." Invariably the reported fleets were investigated and photographed and found to be fishing fleets. The 10,000-ton freighter reported bombed and sunk in Inchon harbor could not be found the following day by Admiral Andrewes' bombardment ships.

"Through our night and day patrols, both radar and visual," said CDR A. F. Farwell, Commanding Officer, Patrol Squadron SIX, "I was able to assure COMNAVFE that the enemy's supplies were *not* coming by sea, even in minute quantities. We then set out to get positive information on how the Reds *were* supplying themselves; we succeeded in getting photographs of camouflaged bypass railroad tracks around the ruined bridges, running over crude log caissons placed in the stream beds. We made photographs of tunnels which showed smoke coming out of trains which were hiding in them, waiting for nightfall.

"Thus, emphasis was shifted back to the railroads. Then when the enemy commenced running trucks at night, the flare-dropping technique was born."[7]

Task Force 95 Established

On 12 September 1950, a change was made in the composition of the blockading and bombardment forces. Rear Admiral Allan E. Smith, USN, broke his flag in USS *Dixie* (AD-14) (CAPT J. M. Cabanillas, USN) at

Sasebo and assumed command of the new Task Force 95.* Henceforth, TF-95 would carry on until the end of the fighting as the "United Nations Blockading and Escort Force."

While this history concerns the U. S. Navy, no record of the blockade and bombardment effort in Korea can be made without recording the valuable contributions of the combatant vessels of nine other nations:

Australia	Great Britain
Canada	Netherlands
Colombia	New Zealand
France	Republic of Korea
Thailand	

Ships of the naval forces of these nations served with credit and effectiveness in the blockade and bombardment effort. This common effort raised many problems: logistic, communication, tactical, operational, and doctrinal. How could a New Zealand destroyer refuel from a U. S. tanker? How could communication and phraseology be standardized? How could recognition signals and signal difficulties be solved? Could olive oil for baking Turkish bread be supplied—or small foul-weather clothing for the men of the Thai frigate?

The solution of these day-by-day problems made significant progress in teaching the naval forces of the free world to work together smoothly and as a team.

So effective was the co-operation and harmony of the forces of the UN Navy that RADM George C. Dyer, the fourth officer to command CTF-95, was prompted to say that "Without any reservations, the association of all these navies together has not only been a very cordial and profitable one on an official basis, and at the highest levels, but on the unofficial and ship's company levels. There has been no major difficulty."

As has been stated, Task Force 95 had the official title "United Nations Blockading and Escort Force." A major part of this force, Task Group 95.1, patrolling Korea's west coast, was commanded throughout the war by a British Rear Admiral. On the east coast, the elements of Task Group 95.2 were frequently commanded by naval officers of the other nations of the UN Navy.

The west coast blockade group, Task Group 95.1, contained three princi-

---

* 95.1 Korean Blockade Group 1: RADM W. G. Andrewes, RN.
  95.2 Korean Blockade Group 2: RADM C. C. Hartman, USN.
  95.5 Escorts ....: CAPT J. H. Unwin, DSC, RN.
  95.6 Minesweepers ....: CAPT R. T. Spofford, USN.
  95.7 ROK Naval Forces ....: CDR M. J. Luosey, USN.

pal elements: the carrier element, the surface blockade and patrol element, and the west coast island defense element.

One United States and one British or Australian carrier furnished the air coverage in Task Element 95.11, relieving each other on a ten-day rotation basis. Flying from the American CVE or CVL was a U. S. Marine squadron. One of the main tasks of TE 95.11 was the harassment of junk traffic in the Taedong River estuary. Task Unit 95.11 also flew interdiction and close air support missions over Eighth Army's left flank.

The patrol and blockade by Task Group 95.1 of Korea's west coast differed from that of the east coast in many respects, principally due to dissimilar hydrographic and geographic conditions. The west coast was a honeycomb of islands; it was an area of high tides, of mud banks, shallows, and difficult channels. Many of the Korean rivers emptied into the Yellow Sea. Nowhere was the water more than 60 fathoms in depth. And within 10 miles of the shore, the depth was less than 20 fathoms. As a consequence, large vessels could not operate as close inshore on the west coast as was often possible on the east coast. The bombardment effort, therefore, was not as great.

In further contrast to the east coast, the more numerous islands made the guerrilla problem on the west coast much more difficult. In the last 18 months of the war, there was a contest with the Communists for control of key islands above the 38th parallel. On some of these captured islands, UN forces had placed radar stations for the control and direction of the UN air forces' aircraft. Some west coast islands served as search and rescue stations for parachuting airmen whose aircraft had suffered damage over "MIG alley." Other west coast islands served well as intelligence outposts. Supporting the west coast islands, therefore, was a much greater part of the over-all task than on the east coast.

The mine menace on the west coast was also different—"better" in the sense that the range of the tides often exposed mines at low water; "worse" in the sense that the enemy could plant mines with greater ease.

Finally, the blockade problem on the west coast was more difficult because of the navigation hazards posed by fast currents, mudbanks, and high tides. Numerous rocks and shoals made a close approach to the mainland hazardous and in many places impossible.

Throughout the blockade of the Korean coasts, the ships of the UN Navy acquitted themselves ably and with distinction. American ships, operating with the carriers, cruisers, destroyers, and frigates of other navies, learned many valuable lessons and techniques from their UN sailing partners that would prove of great value in subsequent years.

Admiral Sir Roderick McGregor, GCB, DSO, RN, following an inspection trip to Korea, had these words of praise for the UN Navy: "I have been much impressed by the way in which the navies of so many nations are co-operating in the Korean War. In spite of differences in language and customs, warships of different navies are operating as one against the common enemy."

Admiral Joy was also laudatory.

"I have only the highest praise for the manner in which our allies contributed to the war effort of the UN Navy," he wrote. "Their co-operation was all that could be desired and they performed every task assigned them, no matter how difficult, with zeal and ability that always evoked my admiration."

Restriction of Fishing by the Blockading Force

One of Rear Admiral Smith's first acts after taking command of TF-95 was to issue an order restricting fishing by North Koreans. Until September 1950, there was no formal interference with fishing activities.

Fish was the main staple of the Korean diet.

In 1939, for example, the Korean fishing industry had ranked third in the world. Along the peninsula's 11,000-mile coastline, where warm and cold water currents joined, were 75 kinds of edible fish, including shrimps, clams, oysters, sardines, crabs, cod and abalones. Other Korean sea food was seaweed, sea slugs and whale meat. In peacetime, approximately 300,000 tons of fish were consumed annually by the Koreans.

Rear Admiral Smith took the attitude that this sea food was legitimate contraband and should be stringently denied the Communists. The restriction of fishing by the UN blockading force would seriously add to the Communists' logistics problems ashore, and force them to import fish from Chinese and Russian sources. The restriction would also be a psychological inducement for the North Koreans to turn against their Commuist masters. Moreover, as the war progressed there was conclusive evidence that many "fishing" boats were really *mining* boats, laying a few or even a single mine nightly in blockaded waters. This mine-laying had to be squelched.

The language of the leaflets distributed to the North Korean fishermen was simple and straight-forward:

> The Communists brought this terrible war down upon you. You cannot fish from your boats until the Communists are killed or thrown out. The United Nations Forces are human and do not desire to harm innocent victims of the war, but if you try to fish again before the Communists are

completely defeated, you must suffer the consequences. A legal blockade has been declared and is enforced by United Nations Forces.

Ships patrolling north of the 38th parallel were ordered to pass out these leaflets, and thereafter to send fishing boats back into port to spread the word. Leaflets were also delivered by airplanes. If the fishermen returned and tried to fish, their boats were to be confiscated or destroyed and the fishermen returned to the beach.

Maddox (DD-731) and *Herbert J. Thomas* (DD-833) delivered a quantity of leaflets to 137 sampans and junks in the week starting 22 September. Delivery was made either by boarding, or calling the vessels alongside. At every interception, the vessels were thoroughly inspected for mines, even to the extent of removing their floor boards.

Because of the order forbidding U. S. naval ships to operate inside the 100-fathom curve on the east coast, unless in swept waters, the largest share of the responsibility for the prevention of fishing by the North Koreans fell upon the small ships of the Republic of Korea Navy who were able to navigate close to the shore where the fishing took place. (Later, in January-June 1952, after the east coast had been swept to the 10-fathom curve as far as Songjin, the destroyers and frigates gave the anti-fishing campaign a high priority.)

The anti-fishing campaign fell into two areas: offshore and inshore. The offshore fishing could be eliminated with comparative ease by the use of patrol ships and patrol aircraft. But squelching the inshore fishing, especially on the west coast with its heavy tides and numerous islands, would be very difficult.

"We started with very limited resources in patrol boats, patrol craft and gunboats," said Rear Admiral George C. Dyer, who was later to command Task Force 95. "Our anti-fishing resources never increased to the desired level.

"Moreover, the complete elimination and control of inshore fishing was an impossibility. Our whaleboats and smaller ships could chase the fishing sampans ashore, and then land a party to blow them up. But blowing up a toughly built sampan wasn't easy. A hand grenade wouldn't do it for long, for the damage could be patched in a few days. Gasoline poured over a sampan would burn it, but unless you stayed and kept pouring gasoline on the sampan until the last piece of timber was burned, the fisherman-owner would put out the fire with sand from the beach.

"The most certain method of controlling the inshore fishing was to confiscate the enemy's fishing boats—and that wasn't simple."

Notwithstanding the hazards and difficulties, the anti-fishing campaign was to prove successful, as will be seen.

The Abortive ROK Landing at Samchok

After dodging several typhoons, the USS *Missouri* (CAPT Irving T. Duke, USN) arrived in Korean waters in the late evening of September 14th after a full-speed run from the east coast of the United States.

"When I was informed that the *Missouri* would join TF-95," wrote RADM Smith, "I planned to use her, the *Helena,* and several destroyers as a diversionary effort on the east coast, on the same day as the initial Marine landings on the west coast at Inchon. By so doing, I hoped to hold back some enemy troops from Inchon and to create an enemy hesitation. I chose Samchok for the diversionary bombardment.

"However, it was difficult to know the exact time of *Missouri's* arrival because of several typhoons which were in her path."

The "Big Mo" celebrated her arrival by firing fifty rounds of 16-inch fire at a bridge near Samchok, using a helicopter spot. The results were excellent.*

Missouri also arrived in time to join a bombardment effort to relieve the stranded ROK *LST-667* at Samchok.

This minor naval amphibious operation had been initiated at Eighth Army Headquarters in Korea, unknown to naval headquarters in Tokyo. The intent of the mission was to land a 700-odd man detachment of ROK troops in the enemy's rear, near Pohang. The detachment's mission was to blow bridges, establish road blocks, and generally hamper the retreat of the North Korean forces as the Eighth Army broke out of the Pusan perimeter.

Since this operation was undertaken without the knowledge of either Admiral Joy or Admiral Smith, the first word that it had aborted came to Admiral C. C. Hartman (ComCruDiv-3) when ROK *LST-667* frantically messaged that she had broached in landing, bashed in her side, and was under heavy enemy fire from mortars and artillery.

Missouri, Helena, Maddox (CDR Preston B. Haines, Jr.), *Herbert J. Thomas* (CDR Sibley L. Ward, Jr.), *Endicott* (CDR John C. Jolly), *Doyle* (CDR Charles H. Morrison, Jr.), and six auxiliary ships were diverted from their primary mission of furnishing naval gunfire at the frontlines in order to rescue the stranded ROK personnel aboard the LST. With much labor,

---

* *Missouri* had to absorb a lot of good-natured ribbing on arrival in Korea. Upon joining the assault forces a few days later at Inchon, *Toledo* wigwagged the question: "Found a mudbank to sit on, Mac?" The "Big Mo" replied: "Go home, small fry, we brought the real guns."

and loss of equipment and precious time, the rescue was finally accomplished on 18 September. Seven hundred and twenty-five South Koreans were rescued, 110 of them wounded, but 81 ROK troops had been killed, captured, or drowned in the process, and a sorely needed LST lost.

Subsequent investigation revealed that the civilian ROK LST skipper had chosen the one rock-ribbed stretch of beach on the otherwise sandy coast. Moreover, he had failed, in three beaching attempts, to cross the surf line properly.

Admiral Joy sent a despatch to Rear Admiral Smith, who had jurisdiction over the ROK Navy, to direct that future ROK amphibious operations, even minor ones, be entrusted to those experienced in such matters.

Missouri Assists the Breakout From the Perimeter

Following the fiasco at Samchok, the *Missouri* continued pounding the east coast positions of the North Korean forces. The Third ROK Division was opposed by the North Korean Fifth Division, the North Korean Seventh Division, and the 101st Security Regiment, all entrenched in the city of Pohang.

The Third ROK Division took up kickoff positions on the south side of Pohang's Hyong-san River. The north side was strongly held by the enemy. Until the ROK troops could cross this stream and gain the coastal road leading north, the UN advance up the east coast was halted.

Missouri answered the KMAG's* request for gunfire support. After the shore fire control party took refuge in a large crater, LTCOL Rollins S. Emmerich, USA, commenced spotting the *Missouri's* fire onto enemy positions across the narrow river a scant 300 yards away. The range from *Missouri* to target was approximately nine miles. The battleship fired 280 high-capacity 16-inch shells which landed with earthquake effect on the northern river bank.

Of this assistance, LTCOL Emmerich recorded: "On the 17th of September we broke the river dike and headed north. The *Missouri's* fire was really demoralizing to those Red troops. We practically waded across that river standing up. The ruins along the river south of Pohang and in the city proper will bear out the effect and accuracy of naval gunfire."[8]

Results of Blockade Forces Against North Korean Forces

The contribution of naval surface forces to the salvation of the Pusan perimeter and defeat of the North Korean army between 25 June and 15 November 1950 is indicated by the following boxscore damage:

* KMAG—Korean Military Advisory Group.

Target	Destroyed	Damaged
Aircraft	1	—
Ammunition dumps	2	1
Artillery positions	44	8
Bridges	14	14
Buildings	—	16
Fuel dumps	2	—
Fuel tanks	—	2
Junks and sampans	62	14
Locomotives	1	—
Mines	323	—
Motor boats	22	5
Observation posts	4	2
PC Boats, YMS	2	4
Pill boxes	3	—
Radio stations	1	1
Radio towers	1	—
RR cars	19	26
RR yards	—	6
Supply dumps	7	5
Tanks	7	—
Transformer stations	1	—
Troop concentrations	—	663
Troops	387	81 POW
Trucks and vehicles	28	15
Tunnels	—	6
Warehouses	12	23

The New War Begins

The period following the successful assault of Inchon and the landing at Wonsan found the blockade and bombardment forces of TF 95 moving farther and farther northward. The enemy coasts were covered as closely as possible while observing the "Stay outside the 100-fathom curve" order. Having denied the Communists the freedom of *advancing* southward by sea, the task was now to prevent them from *retreating* northward by sea.

Aboard the ships off the Korean coasts, few people knew that the original war was ending and that a new war was beginning—a war with Communist China.

On the peninsula in early November, however, it was apparent that the Chinese Communists had intervened. On 24 November their armies com-

COMMUNISTS UNDER THE GUN. *At top,* a group of North Korean prisoners aboard a U. S. warship. *Lower left,* Korean communists in an outclassed vessel surrender to the cruiser *Manchester.* One of the major efforts made by the blockading ships attached to TF 95 was the suppression of fishing. Not only was fish an important staple in Korean diets, but fishing vessels were used in Communist mining activities. *Lower right,* corpses of enemy military dead sprawl grotesquely against background of snow, frozen earth, and stone.

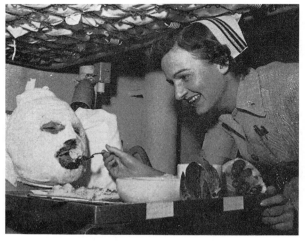

MANY WOUNDED SURVIVED. *At top,* Marine helicopter, with headlight for night operations, picks up injured Marine at Wonsan. *Center,* whirlybird lands aboard Navy Hospital Ship *Consolation. Below,* Marine Pfc. Jack Newman is fed Thanksgiving dinner by Navy Nurse Weece Wood.

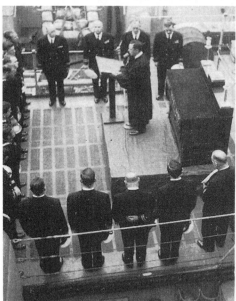

SOME WERE LOST. *At top,* Chaplain reads last rites aboard the cruiser *Toledo* for LTJG David Swenson, killed in action aboard DD *Lyman K. Swenson* at Inchon. *Lower left,* memorial services are held aboard the destroyer escort *Lewis* for seven sailors killed in Korean action. With backs to camera, officer comforts chief petty officer who had had charge of engine room in which sailors were fatally injured. *Lower right,* Marine MAJGEN O. P. Smith visits First Marine Division cemetery at Hamhung.

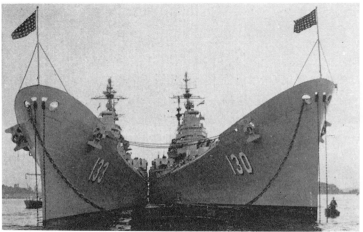

CRUISERS UNDERWAY AND AT ANCHOR. *At top, Rochester* off the east coast of Korea. *Center, Toledo* lies beside *Bremerton* in course of relieving her for another Korean tour. *Below, Los Angeles,* with *Boxer* in background, plies Korean waters.

menced a full-scale attack which succeeded in opening a wedge between the Eighth Army on the west coast and the Tenth Corps on the east coast. Hordes of Chinese poured through the gap. Disaster seemed probable and imminent. All available ships in Japan and several ships already enroute back to the United States were hurriedly recalled and rushed to Korea to stand by to support the evacuation of UN forces. If the onslaught of the Chinese forces could not be contained, it was planned to evacuate the UN forces from Korea via the ports of Inchon, Hungnam, Wonsan, and Pusan. If this proved necessary, every available ship would be required.

On 2 December, the First Marine Division, deep in North Korea, was ordered to withdraw to the area of Hamhung. The surface forces of Task Force 95, operating under the amphibious commander, took up gunfire support stations in Hungnam harbor. (The Hungnam redeployment is fully covered in Chapter 6.)

On the west coast, the ships of the blockade force (TF 95.1) supplied much-needed gunfire and air support to the Eighth Army as it was evacuated from Chinnampo to Inchon.

By mid-January, the UN ground forces had re-established a firm line in South Korea, and the danger of being forced off the peninsula abated.

The original war against the North Korean Communist had now ended. A new war against the Chinese Reds, which would fully occupy Task Force 95 for more than 30 months, had commenced.

Sitzkrieg Blockade

The redeployment of UN forces from North Korea was followed by a period of buildup of personnel, supplies, and equipment in order to resume the offensive.

On 1 January 1951, Rear Admiral William G. Andrewes, Royal Navy, was knighted and promoted to Vice Admiral. For six weeks the British vice admiral continued serving under the American rear admiral.

"This is undoubtedly the first time a vice admiral in the Royal Navy has ever served under a rear admiral in the United States Navy," recorded Admiral Smith.[9] "Both Admiral Brind, Royal Navy, Commander-in-Chief in Hong Kong, and Vice Admiral Andrewes himself stated that they did not desire any change; that he was to remain under my command, even though senior.

"About 12 February 1951, Admiral Joy received a message from Admiral Sherman directing that Vice Admiral Andrewes be made a task force commander. This was due to the fact that Mr. Churchill was demanding a British Commander-in-Chief for the Supreme Atlantic Command. In this situation my objective was to prevent a breakdown in the organization of

Task Force 95 and the *esprit de corps* that both Andrewes and I had worked so hard to gain. I recommended to Joy that I become the deputy and Andrewes the commander of TF 95. This was the accepted solution, and so for the next month and a half Andrewes was Commander Task Force 95. . . ."

Smith resumed command of Task Force 95 on 3 April 1951 after Andrewes' departure from the theater. At this time, also, the operational command of Task Force 95 was shifted from COMNAVFE to Commander Seventh Fleet.*

During this period of change of command and reorganization, Admiral Smith issued a new operation order which determined TF 95's missions in approximate order of priority to be these:

1. Blockade Korea
2. Deliver gunfire support to UN troops on east coast
3. Bombard
4. Conduct anti-mining
5. Escort
6. Conduct anti-submarine warfare
7. Control coastal fishing
8. Obtain intelligence.

The division of Korea into two blockade forces under CTF 95 was continued:

CTG 95.1 (a British Flag Officer)

TE 95.11 Carrier Element 2 CVL, 4 DD
TE 95.12 Surface Blockade & Patrol Element 1 CL, 2 DD, 3 PF, 2 AMS, 1 LST, 1 LSMR, 2 PG, 2 ARS, 2 AMC, 1 PC.
TE 95.15 West coast Island Defence Element—Units of Korean Marine Corps (Islands were Sok-to and Cho-do, off Chinnampo; Paeng-yong-do, Taechong-do, and Yongpyong-do, off Taeju; and Tokchok-to, off Inchon).

CTG 95.2

(A United States Officer† aboard a DD or DE, patrolling independently)

TE 95.21 Wonsan Element 2DD, 2 patrol boats or frigates (Note: The ship types
TE 95.22 Songjin Element 3 DD, 1 DMS, 1 PF   and numbers
TE 95.25 East Island Defense Element—Units of Korean   varied

---

* The reason for doing this was to consolidate the various operating naval task forces so that the Commanding General, Eighth Army, would only have to deal with Com7th-Fleet. In the past he had had to deal with CTF-77, 90, or 95 on an individual basis.

† Usually a destroyer or destroyer escort squadron commander, although the flag officers commanding the cruiser divisions also served.

Marine Corps (Wonsan Islands, Nan-do island near   throughout
Kojo, and Yang-do near Songjin)   the war).
TE 95.24 Hungnam Element 1 DD*
TE 95.28 Bombline Element† 1 DD, I YMS

Also under the CTF 95 was the escort group (TG 95.5), the minesweep group (TG 95.6), and the ROK naval forces (TG 95.7). (In October 1952, a new group, 95.3, was organized as a patrol group in South Korea.)

Smith directed that the east coast blockade commander (CTF 95.2—Rear Admiral Roscoe E. Hillenkoetter, USN) keep at least four ships on patrol, operating in pairs from the 38th parallel to the blockade boundary above Chongjin 41°-50′ N, in order to fulfill the requirements of international law regarding a blockade. The ROK Navy Force (CTG 95.7, Commander Michael J. Luosey) was to establish two check stations on South Korea's east coast for surveillance of coastal traffic. Except in swept waters, it was again specified that ships would remain outside the 100-fathom curve to lessen the danger from mines.

As for the west coast blockade, Task Group 95.1 (RADM A. K. Scott-Moncrieff, RN), the British and American carrier element with their aircraft, would take station near the 39th parallel in order to render close support ashore to the western end of the battleline, as well as to help maintain the blockade. The surface blockade and patrol element (TE 95.12) would maintain a one-ship anti-junk patrol off Chinnampo, and close-in shore patrols near the coast from the northern limit of the blockade to the south.

Smith's shrewd foresightedness and "can-do" attitude are reflected in his war diary of that period. He believed that heavy naval bombardments should be made as soon as possible in the Inchon area. If nothing else, they would deceive and confuse the enemy and force him to divert some of his ground strength to defend the area. Inchon's recapture, of course, would return a valuable port and supply base to the UN forces.

On the east coast, Smith was equally sure that bombardments should take place in the Wonsan area, and, if possible, some of its harbor islands seized. This operation would further confuse the enemy, capitalize on his fear of amphibious assaults, and cause him to wastefully deploy forces in anticipation of another landing at Wonsan. Moreover, the harbor would be a useful point for harassing the main east coast roads and rail lines. (Here, then, was the genesis of the siege of Wonsan.)

Smith believed that by an unremitting naval bombardment of northeast

---

* This Task Element was not created until 27 November 1951. CTE 95.24 was given the mission of bringing the Hungnam area under constant surveillance, of controlling fishing, of preventing mining, and of providing gunfire support to minesweeping ships.
  † On 1 January 1953, the phraseology "element" was altered to "unit".

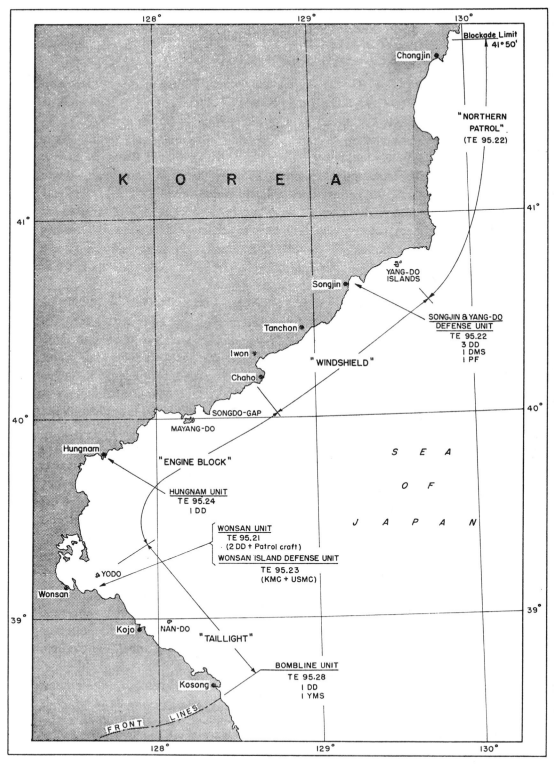

128°   129°   130°

Chongjin
Blockade Limit
41° 50'

"NORTHERN
PATROL"
(TE 95.22)

K O R E A

41°   41°

YANG-DO
ISLANDS

Songjin

SONGJIN & YANG-DO
DEFENSE UNIT
TE 95.22
3 DD
1 DMS
1 PF

Tanchon

Iwon

"WINDSHIELD"

Chaho

SONGDO-GAP

40°   40°

MAYANG-DO

S E A

Hungnam

"ENGINE BLOCK"

O F

HUNGNAM UNIT
TE 95.24
1 DD

J A P A N

WONSAN UNIT
TE 95.21
(2 DD + Patrol craft)
WONSAN ISLAND DEFENSE UNIT
TE 95.23
(KMC + USMC)

YODO

Wonsan

39°   39°

Kojo   NAN-DO

"TAILLIGHT"

BOMBLINE UNIT
TE 95.28
1 DD
1 YMS

Kosong

FRONT LINES

128°   129°   130°

SITZKRIEG BLOCKADE

Korea's exposed transportation complex, day and night, fair weather and foul, ". . . we would get 75 per cent or 80 per cent stoppage of traffic, and certainly a great slowing of traffic."[10]

Smith believed that naval power could not only draw the blockade at sea ever closer (a primary Navy mission) but would also contribute to the interdiction of land communications (a collateral naval mission).

As the UN forces withdrew from Hungnam to re-assemble and resupply themselves for a resumption of the offensive, the Communists were kept guessing how their exposed coastlines would be used against them by the blockading forces of the U. S. Navy.

There were five ways. The first way would be by amphibious feints and demonstrations. From the September 1950 landing at Inchon, the enemy was well aware how decisive and how dangerous an amphibious assault could be. For the remainder of the war he would remain acutely sensitive and apprehensive that another such lightning blow might come at any place and at any moment.

To take advantage of the enemy's sensitivity to amphibious assault, the first of many-to-come amphibious demonstrations was made on 30-31 January 1951 on the east coast near Kansong. RADM Smith, in flagship *Dixie* (AD-14), supervised the feint, which included bombardment and prelanding minesweeping. The USS *Montague* (AKA-98), USS *Seminole* (AKA-105), and several LSTs simulated landing activities.

Ten days later, on 10 February 1951, another fake landing was planned for the Inchon area. The *Missouri* prepared the way with bombardment fire on 8 February, but further operations were cancelled because of the rapid advance of UN ground forces (then engaged in a limited offensive known as "Operation Thunderbolt"), which had outflanked and forced the evacuation of the Inchon area. (In retrospect, it seems certain that the prospect of a second invasion at Inchon made the enemy's evacuation of the area more urgent and rapid).

The second way the enemy would see his exposed coastline used against him was by surprise commando and guerrilla raids such as the one below Chongjin on 7 April 1951. Under the command of Admiral Roscoe E. Hillenkoetter (Commander Cruiser Division One), and covered by the fire of cruiser *Saint Paul* (CA-73, CAPT Chester C. Smith, USN), and destroyers *Wallace L. Lind* (DD-703, CDR Edward B. Carlson, USN), and *Massey* (DD-778, CDR Ed R. King, Jr., USN), 250 men of the 41st Independent Royal Marines landed from the *Fort Marion* (LSD-22) and the *Begor* (APD-127) to destroy the exposed coastal rail line eight miles south of Chongjin. Minesweepers *Incredible, Osprey, Chatterer,* and *Merganser* cleared the nearby beach, with the salvage vessel USS *Grasp* (ARS-24) standing by. There was no enemy opposition. Demolition charges destroyed 100 feet of track, the nearby tunnels, and the railroad embankment to a depth of 15 feet.

Raids similar to these were to harass the enemy for the remainder of the war. (One result of this particular raid was to implant the idea that the ideal way to conduct such raids would be by helicopter).

The third way the exposed enemy coastline would be used against the Communists was by laying siege to his coastal ports.

By mid-February, a night and day siege had begun in Wonsan harbor. (This historic siege is covered in Chapter 12, "The Siege of Wonsan".) Songjin also was to feel the burden of a naval siege, commencing on 8 March, initially set by *Manchester* (CL-83), *Evans* (DD-754), *C. S. Sperry* (DD-697) and Hr.Ms.* *Evertsen* (DD). Still later, on 26 April 1951, the port of Hungnam was placed under siege.

The fourth way the enemy would find his exposed coastlines used against him was at each end of the fighting front. For the rest of the war, American naval guns would fire at enemy troops on each flank of the battleline. In many cases, this fire would be crucially important and locally decisive.

(Each evening, before dusk, UN ground forces would conduct a reconnaissance along the frontlines to observe enemy troop concentrations, armament emplacements, and supply dumps. These infantry patrol reports were assembled and transmitted to the bombline support ships with requests for a certain number of rounds per hour on each selected target).

And finally, the enemy's exposed coastlines were to feel the unremitting sting of bombardment at every point of military value along his coasts. That these bombardments hurt, both physically and psychologically, is demonstrated by the steady rise in the enemy's use of coastal guns to protect himself.

The battleship *New Jersey* (Captain David M. Tyree) returned to war action on 20 May 1951. She was the second of four battleships (*Wisconsin* would be third; *Iowa* would be the fourth) to appear in the Korean theater.

The "Big Jay's" baptism was memorable for her crew. After a bombardment at Kangsong on 20 May, the *New Jersey* moved to Wonsan to participate in the siege. Here on the 22nd, she took one hit and one near miss. The striking shell hit Number One turret, causing little damage, while the near miss killed one man and wounded three who were exposed topside.

The one hundredth day of the sieges of Wonsan, Hungnam, and Songjin came and went, with the enemy fire increasing in accuracy, intensity, and persistence. Early in July frigate *Everett* took a hit which did little material

* Hr. Ms. is a prefix designating ships of the Royal Netherlands Navy.

damage but which killed one man and wounded seven. Cruiser *Helena* reported firing her 10,000th round of the war, *Brinkley Bass* reported firing 3,315 rounds in a single two-week period.

Thus, the application of naval power to the Korean battlefield was steadily increased.

Change of Command and Sit-Down

During the late winter and early spring months of 1951, a series of engagements between UN and Chinese ground forces was taking place. The United Nation forces started their first limited offensive, "Operation Thunderbolt," on 25 January 1951. Naval forces intensified inshore patrolling along the west coast and carried out additional fire missions in support of the advance. During the first few days only light resistance from Chinese Communist outposts was encountered. UN forces advanced 15 to 20 miles to positions north of Suwon, Inchon, and Yoju without serious difficulty. At the beginning of February the enemy made several counterattacks to defend Seoul. The United Nations' advance now developed into a full-scale attack. Carrier-based aircraft subjected the enemy to constant strafing and napalm bombings and established close surveillance of all Han River crossings.

On 10 February, the enemy suddenly vanished from the front. By nightfall of that day Inchon and Kimpo airfields were again in UN hands, as well as the industrial suburb of Seoul, on the southern bank of the Han River.

In the central sector, "Operation Roundup" was launched, again with the objective of inflicting major losses on the enemy. The offensive opened on 5 February, and for the first three days UN troops moved forward without encountering major resistance. A Chinese counterattack developed during the night of 11-12 February which used both mass attack and infiltration tactics. Despite some loss of terrain, the UN forces had now learned to roll with the punch. The main line of resistance was not penetrated, and heavy casualties were inflicted upon the attacking Chinese. By 19 February the enemy's advance in the central sector had come to a standstill.

On 21 February the Eighth Army launched still another limited offensive known as "Operation Killer." As its name implied, the objective was to destroy as many enemy forces as possible. Operation Killer proceeded during the first few days to gain up to ten miles a day as the enemy's rear guard was swept aside by the First Marine Division, which seized the high ground overlooking Hoengsong on 24 February. The Communists fell back along the entire 60-mile front, having suffered serious casualties.

While Operation Killer was eliminating a Chinese salient in the central sector, a limited offensive had been opened early in March in the area east of Seoul. This operation was known as "Operation Ripper," and had the objective of outflanking the enemy and forcing him to abandon the capital city of Seoul. Despite some enemy counterattacks, patrols of the ROK First Division entered Seoul during the early morning hours of 15 March and found it almost empty of enemy troops. Seoul had changed hands four times in the course of nine months.

Toward the end of March, UN forces once more approached the 38th parallel along the entire front. A proposal to the enemy by General Mac-Arthur on 23 March to cease hostilities and negotiate a truce in the field was ignored by the Communist high command.

During the first days of April the Eighth Army gradually pushed closer to the enemy's main supply and assembly area in the "Iron Triangle," between Chorwon, Kumhwa, and Pyongyang. In the central sector a major battle developed for the Hwachon reservoir.* The U. S. Marines entered the town on 18 April.

By mid-April it was apparent that the Communists were preparing another major offensive. For many weeks, reconnaissance aircraft had reported very heavy southbound traffic in enemy rear areas. New enemy units were identified in ever greater numbers within supporting distance of the front. More than 70 Communist divisions were estimated to be south of the Yalu River.

"I arrived in Korea to take command of the Eighth Army only eight days before the Chinese offensive of 22 April," General James Van Fleet told the authors. "Everybody in the Far East was talking about the forthcoming Chinese offensive, some a little fearfully. I even had one plan submitted to me that said when the Reds struck, UN forces should fall back ten miles. I said no, we're not giving up Seoul. I told all my division and corps commanders to get ready to fight, that we were going to mow them down. On the western side of Korea in the Seoul area, the country was open and fairly flat. We knew this terrain. I told my division and corps commanders they'd never find a prettier battlefield for killing Communists.

"I missed an opportunity after the first Red offensive on 22 April. After three or four days I could tell that their attack was fairly shallow and not well supported logistically. The Chinese Army wasn't a mobile Army. I should have assembled reserves and struck. I failed that time.

"But on the next Chinese push, 16 May, I had everything set. After three days I ordered a counterattack toward the 'Iron Triangle', spearheaded by the First Marine Division and Second Infantry.

"I had the First MarDiv and some Korean Marines set for a shore-to-

* See section "The Attack on the Hwachon Dam" in Chapter 8, "The Struggle to Strangle."

shore operation, leapfrogging up the east coast—almost administrative landings. At that time the east coast did not have a big buildup of defensive forces, and we could easily have made landings there. The Navy could have shot us ashore and kept us ashore as we built up. We could have built up faster than the enemy could have managed.

"With those landings, the Chinese couldn't have met it. They're not flexible enough. The Chinese armies had no conception of fast moves; they had no communication system; they had no logistical support.

"In fact, there have been only two armies in the history of the world that have been able to move any direction at any time. That's the American Army and the German Army.

"So in June 1951, we had the Chinese whipped. They were definitely gone. They were in awful shape. During the last week of May we captured more than 10,000 Chinese prisoners.

"It was only a short time later that the Reds asked for a truce.

"Then we were ordered not to advance any further."[11]

In all this intense ground fighting in the spring of 1951, the U. S. Marines' First Division was in the forefront, and often in the van. Despite being separated from the Marine Air Wing and denied its customary close air support, the division won fresh laurels by its aggressiveness and tenacity.

Two events of this period, not directly connected with the naval actions of the Korean war, must be briefly described, for both of them were to have great effect upon the remaining two years of the naval war.

The first of these was the replacement of General Douglas MacArthur.

While the UN forces had undisputed control of both the sea and the air, and while the revitalized UN forces were advancing under the aggressive leadership of Generals Ridgway and Van Fleet, the realization came to most of the military leaders in Korea that under existing conditions a stalemate was approaching. It was obvious that the Chinese could not now achieve their oft-vaunted claim to drive the UN forces into the sea. It was equally clear to the UN command that if the fighting was to be confined solely to the Korean peninsula, and no effort made to destroy the sources of Chinese fighting and logistic power elsewhere, then the UN goal of uniting Korea by force was equally futile.

It is beyond the scope of this book to discuss the circumstances of the relief of General MacArthur. It is sufficient for a naval study of the Korean war to say that MacArthur believed that victory *in* Korea could only be achieved by extending the military conflict *beyond* Korea, as he wrote the authors—"against the nerve center of the Chinese ability to sustain his operations in Korea."

Accordingly, on 11 April 1951, General Matthew B. Ridgway succeeded General Douglas MacArthur as Commander in Chief, United Nations Command.

The second event which was to affect the campaign at sea transpired on 23 June 1951 when the Soviet delegate to the United Nations, Jacob A. Malik, proposed ceasefire discussions between the protagonists. General Ridgway suggested that the meeting take place aboard the Danish hospital ship *Jutlandia*. Eight days later, the Communists accepted the proposal but insisted that the discussions take place in Kaesong between the tenth and fifteenth of July.

Actual armistice discussions commenced on 8 July. The Chief of the UN Delegation was Vice Admiral C. Turner Joy, COMNAVFE. The other U. S. Navy delegate was Rear Admiral Arleigh Burke.

The combination of these two events—MacArthur's dismissal and the commencement of the armistice talks—produced the fighting sit-down which followed. Thereafter, the war on the ground was to become positional, and neither side was to make more than local and limited efforts to change the situation. By mid-June the front had stabilized along the general line between Munsan and Kosong. The flexibility and mobility which naval forces could give to land forces hereafter was not to be used. The firepower and mobility of the UN armies was not to be exploited.

Henceforth, the American Navy would have to content itself with performance of collateral roles for the remaining two years of the war.

The Truce Talks Begin

The first indication that the Communists wanted a truce came on Saturday, 23 June 1951, during a nation-wide broadcast by Mr. Jacob Malik, the Russian delegate to the United Nations, on the United Nations program series entitled, "The Price of Peace."

Malik's talk included the following paragraph:

"The peoples of the Soviet Union believe it possible to defend the cause of peace. The Soviet peoples further believe that the most acute problem of the present day—the problem of the armed conflict in Korea—could also be settled. This would require the readiness of both parties to enter on a path of peaceful settlement of the Korean question. The Soviet peoples believe that as the first step, discussions should be started between the belligerents for a cease fire and an armistice providing for the mutual withdrawal of forces from the 38th parallel. Can such a step be taken? I think it can, provided there is a sincere desire to put an end to the bloody fighting in Korea."

While it is not the purpose of this book to cover the truce talks, a brief discussion of the factors which produced the 24 months of truce talks and a first-hand account of the opening of the talks will be beneficial.[12]

Following Malik's speech, General Ridgway, Commander in Chief, United Nations Command, proposed on 30 June 1951 that a conference for discussing this Soviet armistice proposal be held. Accordingly, a radio broadcast was transmitted to the Commander in Chief of the Communist Forces in Korea. As previously stated, General Ridgway proposed a meeting aboard the Danish hospital ship *Jutlandia,* anchored in Wonsan harbor.

There were many advantages for holding any armistice talks aboard *Jutlandia.* She was a hospital ship, and therefore neutral, and would have ample living accommodations as well as adequate conference, working, and communication facilities. Commodore Kai Hammerich, the Danish commanding officer, was very pleased to offer his ship for this purpose, and was anxious to provide the very best facilities.

On 1 July, however, the North Korean premier, Kim Il Sung, accepted Ridgway's proposal but rejected the *Jutlandia.* Instead, Kim proposed the place of meeting in the city of Kaesong, on the 38th parallel.

The exact reasons why the Communists rejected the hospital ship *Jutlandia* in favor of Kaesong are not known, but it is reasonably certain that the Reds wanted a conference site on the 38th parallel to reinforce their demands in establishing that line as the truce line. Commencing the talks at Kaesong would also allow them to appear as the truce "hosts," and to foster the illusion that the United Nations were asking for an armistice out of military necessity.

Why had the Communists, through the Soviet delegate to the UN, requested a truce? Many times previously, they had rejected overtures to end the fighting. They had done so on 6 December 1950, again on 9 December, on 22 December, on 12 January, and on 18 January 1951. Why were the Chinese now willing to consider a truce? One of the two U. S. Navy delegates to the talks and the Deputy Chief of Staff to COMNAVFE gave the following reasons:

"At the time of the Malik proposal," said Rear Admiral Arleigh A. Burke, "United Nations forces were confident that they could repel any attack launched by the enemy. As a matter of fact, it was hoped that the enemy *would* attack because the enemy's casualties would be much greater and ours much less than if *we* attacked. Also we did not want to advance north any more than necessary to keep contact with the enemy. By advancing north, we shortened the enemy's supply lines and reduced the number of enemy targets, especially transportation targets, for our air and naval power to work on. The farther north we drove the enemy, the less difficulty he would have logistically and the more his relative strength increased.

"Therefore, it was then a question of striking a balance. In June 1951, the United Nations command had reached in its northward movement a line which ran generally northeast from the vicinity of Kaesong towards the northern edge of the now-famous Iron Triangle and reached the east coast in the vicinity of Nam River, about 40 miles north of the 80th parallel. The line was relatively short, was firmly anchored by our Navy at each end, and was highly defensible throughout its length. The UN had adopted the tactic of holding such a line and letting the enemy grind itself down against it, and it had worked very well. After falling into the trap with disastrous results several times in April and May, the Reds decided they had **had** enough.

"From their entry into the war in October 1950, the enemy had boasted that he would drive the United Nations command into the sea. He now knew that this was not going to happen. The enemy was losing men, he was losing equipment, he was losing ground. Time was working against him. Winter was coming on. The trend of military events in Korea was not auspicious for the Communists. In short, they were losing the war.

"It was apparent that if the enemy wanted to retrieve anything from his aggressive venture in Korea, he either would have to do it at the conference table or he would have to get and use all the modern equipment, such as airplanes and tanks, that his allies could spare. This second alternative depended on the scope of outside assistance and could lead to another world war. It would be a matter of starting a big fire in order to call the fire department away from a small fire.

"However, the Communists may have had other reasons for suggesting a truce.

"The Chinese might have come to the conclusion that they had been led down the garden path. They were fighting and losing a war which was not theirs. They must have known from the beginning that the United Nations had never been any threat to them across the Yalu; perhaps the average Chinese 'man in the street' was commencing to realize that fact.

"Another possibility was that they were preparing for a really big push in a couple of months, and a phony armistice conference would serve the double purpose of giving them a breathing spell and lulling the UN forces into lethargy and a false sense of security. During a lull, they could accelerate a build-up of personnel, weapons, and supplies, and strike heavily with more chance of success. They had used these tactics successfully several times before in China, the most notable occasion being in 1946.

"Another possibility was that Communist China wanted to be the sole power in Asia. She could not aspire to this if she continued to pour all of her resources and all of her men into a futile war. She was losing face in Korea, as well as resources and men. Perhaps she thought that it was time to pull out of this ill-considered venture, and concentrate her activities on increasing internal strength and expanding in other more lucrative areas.

"Still another possibility was that much Russian equipment was being lost—equipment which they might prefer to use in other more critical areas. Lost equipment would pay no dividends. Perhaps the Soviet Union told the Chinese and North Koreans that they would get no more equipment after a specified date, and that they should settle their affairs before that date as best they could.

"It was also possible that the Communists realized that they could never dominate all of Korea by military methods, whereas they might achieve domination by other means. If a military armistice were achieved, perhaps they could infiltrate later into the government of the Republic of Korea. Perhaps they felt that their many agents and guerrillas already in South Korea could so dominate elections in the Republic of Korea that the country would eventually go communistic. Perhaps they believed they could sometime in the future contaminate the officials of the Republic of Korea government so that the people would grow tired of that type of government and elect Communists in a period of frustration. In short, perhaps the Communists thought that since they could not gain their ends by military aggression, it would be wiser to try political aggression.

"In any event, not the least likely possibility was the desirability of enticing the western nations to slow down the rearmament that the Soviet Union's aggressive moves had set in motion. A conference to discuss an armistice might cause enough indecision and internal bickering among UN forces to reduce defensive potential and alertness to a low level.

"Still another factor in asking for a truce was the increasing disaffection in the Chinese Communist armies. More and more Chinese wanted to surrender, and desertions mounted.

"Which one of these possibilities instigated the Communists' proposal for armistice on the first anniversary of the Korean War? It will probably never be known. It is more likely that each of them had some influence. The Communists had nothing to lose and everything to gain by suggesting an armistice conference. If the negotiations failed, her propaganda machine could attempt to place the blame on the United Nations for the failure."

In the time interval between the proposal by General Ridgway and the answer by Kim Il Sung, plans were made for the meeting to be held aboard ship under a special task force commanded by Rear Admiral I. N. Kiland. This special task force would be composed of a cruiser, an AGC,* an APA,† and a division of destroyers. It was intended that this special task force could furnish adequate communication facilities, logistic support, and living quarters to the truce delegates, UN officials, reporters, etc.

After Kaesong was designated as the conference site, the opinion was voiced that because the talks would be held ashore instead of aboard ship, the logistics support for the UN truce delegation should be shifted from the Navy to the Eighth Army. There was also considerable discussion as to whether the senior delegate should not be an Army officer. General Ridgway decided that Admiral Joy, already designated, should remain as the senior delegate for two reasons: first, Joy had become acquainted with the problems involved; and secondly, General Ridgway did not desire any of his corps commanders or General Van Fleet to lead the discussions since it might tend to weaken the combat effectiveness of the Eighth Army.

Upon the UN's acceptance of Kaesong, some of the U. S. Navy ships which were originally scheduled to be in Wonsan were ordered to Inchon to render logistic support if that became necessary. It was thought that the correspondents would require additional facilities, both in housing and communications.

The Truce Teams Meet

The first meeting of the main truce delegations was scheduled for 1000 on 10 July 1951. The day dawned cloudy and damp. Helicopters carrying the UN delegation flew north at a few hundred feet altitude above waving white-clad‡ Koreans working in the rice paddies.

"We landed on a level field near the Kaesong Methodist missionary compound," said Admiral Burke. "As we stepped out of the 'copters, we were met by the North Korean liaison officer, a Colonel Chang. Communist photographers and newsmen gathered around. As we got into our United States Army jeeps, which were prominently marked by white flags, the Communists took movies and motion pictures. Armed Chinese troops lined the sides of the landing site. There were also half-a-dozen enemy jeeps on the field, some of them Russian jeeps. Others were captured United States jeeps, still with their United States markings. One of these had two bullet holes in its windshield, which had probably accounted for the ill-fated United States soldier who had painted 'Wilma' on the hood.

---

* AGC—an amphibious command ship.

† APA—an attack transport.

‡ White is the traditional color of mourning in Korea. Since it is worn for 3 years for close relatives, Korean families are in mourning much of the time.

"All of this was a staged act to demonstrate to us their domination of the situation.

"Colonel Chang mounted his jeep and led our convoy on the ten-minute ride to the house assigned to us. Later this house was christened the 'United Nations House'. The short jeep ride did nothing to dispel our forebodings. Along the way, the road was lined with armed guards and photographers. The United Nations house itself was surrounded by armed guards, prominently stationed with burp guns. Going up the steps to the house I found it necessary to push to one side the muzzle of a machinegun held by a young North Korean lad.

"We entered the house. It had been stripped, but the Communists had placed tables and chairs in two rooms so we could use them as conference rooms. After what we had experienced, our trust was not at a high level.

"The staff of our United Nations delegation had earlier proceeded by motor convoy that morning to Kaesong and were already in the United Nations House. LT Horace Underwood, USNR, our Korean interpreter, informed us that the Communists were using a different time than we. In other words, ten o'clock *our* time was nine o'clock *their* time, so we had to wait an hour before the meeting was to start. During the delay, we discussed our communication facilities. We also commented on the large number of Communist newsmen and photographers and the display of armed force with which we had been met.

"About 1050, we proceeded in jeeps to the conference site. As at the UN House, there were many armed guards near the conference house. All the guards were North Koreans. All of them were rather officious in stopping our cars and in directing us where to go.

"We were escorted into a small room of the old one-time splendid house. The center of the room contained a small table on which rested beer, candy, and cigarettes. The five-man enemy delegation was standing. Admiral Joy, followed by the rest of the delegation, proceeded quietly into the tension-filled room. We didn't know the enemy delegates. One of them said, 'I am Nam Il'. Admiral Joy nodded and replied, 'I am Admiral Joy'.

"Before we went to Kaesong, we had been informed that the enemy would have only four delegates; now there were five—three North Koreans and two Chinese. The North Korean delegates were in Russian-type uniforms with good-looking, gray, red-piped blouses with Russian shoulder marks, and very big blue trousers. As is their custom, the Chinese delegates were in woolen khaki uniforms with no insignia of any kind.

"The enemies' uniforms were of two grades: resplendent or very poor. Delegates and a few staff officers were resplendent, the others were very poor.

"Our own delegation and party all wore khaki. It was a meaningful paradox. All the members of the United Nations party—both officers and enlisted men—were clothed alike. This was one more indication of our side practicing the words we preach, while the Communists used the same words but practiced something entirely different. A man could learn much about class distinction by studying the enemy delegation.

"The senior delegate was General Nam Il. He was Chief of Staff, Supreme Headquarters, North Korean Army. Nam was about 38 years old, and in his youth had graduated from a university in Manchuria. Nam was an ardent, clever Communist standing high in Soviet favor; he was Russian-trained and dominated, and spoke Korean with a foreign accent.

"Major General Lee Sang Jo, the next senior North Korean delegate, was Chief of Staff, Front Headquarters, North Korean Army. Lee was about 38 years of age, born in South Korea, but went to China as a boy and was there graduated from the Whampoa Military Academy. Lee became a Communist in 1940 and was instrumental in establishing an underground contact between the Yenam faction and the Kim Il Sung faction of the North Korean Communists for the Korean Independence League in Manchuria.

"The third Korean delegate was Major General Chang Pyong San, North Korean Army, about 35 years old, Chief of Staff of the First North Korean Corps. There were reports that Chang had been an enlisted man in the Soviet Army at one time.

"The senior Chinese delegate was Lieutenant General Tung Hua, deputy commander of the Chinese Communist forces in Korea. He was about 51 years old, an old-line Communist, having been political officer of the First Army in 1930.

"The other Chinese delegate was Major General Hsieh Fang.

"The Communists must have had a difficult time in deciding whether the fifth delegate should be North Korean or Chinese. After a few of our meetings, it was apparent that they had added Chang to the list as a mere nonentity to fill a vacancy. Chang very seldom paid much attention to the proceedings, and still less often contributed anything. Practically all consultations were between the other four delegates.

"As the meetings opened, everyone was nervous and everyone was under a strain. The two delegations looked at each other like circus animals let loose in an arena. At 1105 Admiral Joy suggested that we go to the conference room. The first meeting convened in a rather small room with the delegation facing each other across a green, felt-covered table. Interpreters sat behind their respective delegations. The Communist staff and stenographers were on one side of the room, ours on the other. When the meeting opened, there was a United Nations flag on a small standard in front of Admiral Joy.

"During the first meeting, Communist photographers came streaming into the conference room and took a great number of pictures. We protested, and it was mutually agreed that photographers and newsmen would be excluded from the conference room. This agreement was kept. However, there were large numbers of Communist photographers all around the conference site getting many photographs which would be published in Communist newspapers. In addition, there was an unknown number of Communist newsmen in the area. Our own press was rightly vexed at this one-sided affair.

"Even more important than the indignation of our own press was the obvious result of such an arrangement. All on-the-spot news would be distorted by the Communists, and our own news agencies would have no personal knowledge of the true state of affairs.

"Our delegation finally flatly stated that we would bring 20 members of the press to the conference site. At first, this was agreed to. After Nam Il thought it over, however, he said he could not grant permission for the press at this time unless he received orders from his seniors. He might not have had the authority so we requested him to obtain such permission and notify our liaison officer the next morning. We also informed him that we intended thereafter to receive courteous equitable treatment, and that we would insist upon bringing about 20 newsmen and photographers into the conference site the next morning.

"The next morning, on 12 July, our convoy with 20 newsmen was embarked, but it was not permitted to go on with the newsmen. This was the straw that broke the camel's back.

"The controversy over newsmen and photographers proved to be the first of many. After an exchange of notes between Kim Il Sung and General Ridgway, the matter was finally resolved, and the truce talks got underway.*

"During the subsequent negotiations, crisis followed crisis. In all of them, our UN delegation had two possible courses of action. One was to try to placate the Communists and to take conciliatory measures so the Communists would not break off the conferences. This course of action had been tried in other conferences without much success. The Communists had always taken such an attitude to mean appeasement, and took aggressive action to control the situation because they thought we were weak and

---

* The UN Command delegation succeeded in obtaining Communist agreement to consider press representatives as part of its working personnel with access to the conference area. The Communists also agreed to provisions which would insure neutrality of the conference zone.

impotent and would sacrifice a correct position to gain agreement.

"The other course was the direct, forceful approach. This method had not been overly used in the past. It was early decided by General Ridgway, with the hearty concurrence of the delegation, that this course was the only possible way to obtain equitable terms of a military armistice. *Power* and *strength* were terms the Communist understood, and they were not influenced by much else. Consequently, we always tried to choose a sound, vigorous course of action and state it forcibly. In doing this, special care was taken to insure that these statements were reasonable and could be accepted by reasonable, unbiased men.

"It was reassuring to find that the Joint Chiefs of Staff and other officials at home felt the same way we did about the chosen course of action."

On 15 July, the delegates turned to the question of a truce, starting first with the number one item: the agenda. After much haggling, an agenda was formally adopted on 26 July. The next task would be to fix a military demarcation line. Following that, concrete arrangements were to be made for the cease fire and the armistice. The next item was arrangements relating to the prisoners of war. The fifth item involved recommendations to governments of countries concerned on both sides.

Despite the fact that the Communists had reached a military stage where they were steadily losing—a stage where they could gain virtually nothing on the battlefield, and perhaps lose everything by continuing the war—the Communists came to the truce parley fully expecting United Nations delegates to accept the terms which had been laid down by Malik in his radio speech.

"Such terms," said Admiral Burke, "would have meant the restoration of the situation which existed before the attack by North Korea—just as if there had been no aggression. This solution would have ignored the UN positions in areas north of the 38th and would have meant the resumption of a boundary which could not be defended from the south. It would have meant that the ROKs would be placed in jeopardy again just as soon as the last UN soldier sailed away. It would have paved the way for Communist political conquest of the Republic of Korea—a feat they had been unable to accomplish on the battlefield. But important as were all these factors, there was one even more important factor—it would have shown all Orientals that the Communists had won the victory, and that UN forces were anxious to leave the area they had come to defend; that we would accept terms less than honorable, less than reasonable, in order to get out of more fighting. That would have meant the loss of confidence by other small nations in the strength and stamina of the UN.

"The Communists at the conference table had some reason to believe we would accept those terms, and they insisted that we should accept them.

All logic, all arguments, all reason were of no avail as they sat stiffly and said, 'We are unshakable, your propositions are untenable, you must accept our terms.'

"The Communists, as always, were patient. They had lots of time, and they were not averse to wasting time in the belief that we would become impatient and eventually give in on important points just for the sake of agreement. Only this time, that waiting procedure did not work as successfully for the Communists as it had in the past. Finally, UN *military pressure* convinced them that we had no intention of settling on anything but fair and reasonable terms, and they resumed the conferences.

"They then proposed a solution of the 38th parallel, with a line on a map which looked attractive, if a man did not read the words that went with the picture. It was so foolish that even they were embarrassed by having to support it. Eventually they proposed a line not far from the battleline at that time as the military demarcation line. The military pressure was still on, the battle line was slowly but inexorably moving north against the Communists. Their proposition wasn't good enough. At last they proposed, and we accepted, the current battle line as the military line of demarcation.

"All that took five months. Five months of haranguing, of argument, of ceaseless talking; but mark this well, five months of combat in which our side was winning. That was the reason for their acceptance of the reasonable military line of demarcation. It was *military pressure, not reason,* that persuaded them to be reasonable.

"By accepting that line of demarcation, they relieved themselves of much of the military pressure that had been exerted against them. Again they became recalcitrant as we began to discuss Item 3, the details of the cease fire, and Item 4, prisoners of war."

Thus went the truce talks *ad infinitum.* All the UN delegates grew weary but no less wary as the talking was continued. South Korea's General Paik Sun Yup probably had the most difficult position of all.

Said General Paik: "As a soldier fighting under the UN command I was of course obligated to accept the idea of participating in the truce talks. Yet as a soldier of the Republic of Korea I was also representing a government which did not approve of the parley. However, even though I was in close contact with my government virtually every day, at no time was I advised to do other than to fully cooperate. As a passing suggestion for any such future coordinated parleys, it might be well for the governments concerned to reach full understanding and accord before a joint delegation attempts to present a single policy.

"Translation, I recall, was a very serious obstacle. My government did not like the word 'Chosen,' for example. The North Koreans did not approve of the word 'Hankuk'. It seemed a trivial matter, but it actually was highly important because of the implications inherent in the final selection of the word.*

"We found early that we had to be patient. That was the secret of our somewhat limited success. We wouldn't quarrel. Just be patient. On the outside we would show a smile and look serene. But inside we had to remain firm and unbending. For power is all that the Communists fear and respect.

"I believe that when the truce talks began, the Communists really wanted to have a cease fire. However, even that was difficult to determine accurately. While Nam Il was senior delegate for the Communists and made some minor decisions, for the greater part he had to turn to the Chinese delegate and get his opinion before he would answer a question or make a statement. Of course, behind the Chinese delegate was, and still is, the Kremlin. So it is very difficult to say with any certainty that the Communists did or did not want an armistice. Nobody can know that for sure except the Kremlin.

"Some of the meetings did border on the humorous. I recall one such meeting during which we sat completely silent for 45 minutes, neither side saying a single word until both sides finally got up at the same time and left the tent. Because both delegations merely represented their governments, it was necessary to recess whenever neither delegation had anything new to offer in order to give the respective governments time in which to produce some new proposal with which to try to break the deadlock.

"When the Communists agreed on a demarcation line I was frankly somewhat optimistic and thought that perhaps we might eventually arrive at complete agreement. But now I can see that in too many cases it was the UN delegation which had to give in. The Communist delegation does not give in or arbitrate. Perhaps one of the reasons why this is so, is because the United States was in a very difficult position by virtue of the fact that it was taking such an active leadership in the war itself. Russia, on the other hand, was in a much easier position because it was still supposedly a somewhat disinterested spectator and could exert influence from behind the scenes.

"I suspect that the single event which made me the most angry occurred when one of the North Korean delegates wrote on a small piece of paper the words, 'Imperialist dog is worse than food given to beggars at a funeral home.' However, I realized that such things only pointed up more vividly the wrongness of their cause, their desperation. They had to resort to such

* Korea was called "Chosen" by the Japanese Government of occupation prior to World War II, and subsequently adopted by the North Korean Communist government. The word "Hankuk" was used by South Koreans to mean the Republic of Korea.

personal slander because they did not dare to discuss the issues at stake candidly and truthfully.

"I am convinced that if a truce is finally signed, and the UN troops are withdrawn from Korea, it will be but a short time before we have another and far more disastrous aggression. And the next time the Communists will make complete preparations so that they will not fail. I hope and pray that UN troops will remain in Korea. Not just for the sake of Korea, but for the sake of the free nations of the world. Korea today stands as a symbol of a willingness and a determination to fight aggression wherever and whenever it may appear. For the free nations of the world to back down even once might prove to be disastrous in the extreme."

General Paik Sun Yup's letter to the authors was dated 12 September 1952.

The truce talks were not to end until 27 July 1953, ten months later.

First Year Boxscore for Surface Ships
25 June 1950—30 June 1951

Target	Destroyed	Damaged
Aircraft	2	
Ammunition dumps	11	3
Artillery positions	128	52
Bridges	31	125
Buildings	311	300
Junks and sampans	213	147 (plus 9 captured)
MG and mortar positions	33	15
Mines	700	
Motor boats	22	6
Pillboxes	12	9
PT boats	3	
Land mines	83	
Railroad cars	74	101
Supply dumps	22	16
Tanks	9	3
Troop concentrations	2,150 attacked	
Troop casualties	12,476	
Trucks and other vehicles	134	64
Warehouses	33	46
(Also 537 POWs)		

The Second Year

Rear Admiral George C. Dyer, USN, relieved Rear Admiral Allan E. Smith, USN, as CTF 95 on 20 June 1951. This change of command had nothing at all to do with the fact that in five days the first anniversary of the Korean War would take place. Anniversaries notwithstanding, the Navy's work must go on for 25 more months.

Dyer ruled that this work not only must go on but that it must be intensified. The more the Navy could do from the sea to hurt and embarrass the enemy on land, the better would be our chances in the negotiations at the truce table.

The Combative Spirit

For destroyer skippers especially, the naval war along the Korean coastline was a fertile field for the exercise of initiative and the display of command, and what Rear Admiral George C. Dyer, CTF 95, referred to as "the combative spirit." Especially after the truce talks began, a blockade assignment could either be a monotonous patrol or an action-packed opportunity, depending on the initiative and aggressiveness of the individual commanding officer.

Patrolling ships had specific tasks: the blockade was to be maintained, fishing suppressed, enemy coastal traffic interdicted, mines swept, rescue performed, and the captured islands supported. Those commanding officers who were also element commanders had additional command duties. From them, a nicety of judgment was required to weigh the current situation, balance and apportion the assigned forces, and establish time schedules for replenishment, as well as fight the war. These duties and tasks could be performed routinely, or they could be performed with imaginative aggressiveness.

"Korea was an opportunity to discover and uncover those commanding officers who had a combative spirit," said Rear Admiral George C. Dyer. "An otherwise outstanding naval officer, who might be the best engineer, shiphandler, and administrator in the Service, might also not have that extra quality of combat aggressiveness and pugnacity which is the mark of the victorious naval officer. As a matter of fact, few military leaders have this inner fire and this love of battle which has been traditionally vital to the success of our Navy. The naval war along the Korean coast gave ship skippers the chance to reveal whether or not they had such a combative spirit."

In Admiral Dyer's opinion, many of his ships exhibited a combative spirit, doing more than was expected of them. A typical one of these was the destroyer *Stickell* (DD-888, CDR Jesse B. Gay, Jr.).

The *Stickell* had joined the Northern Patrol (TE 95.22) off Songjin on 16 May 1951. On 24 May, Gay assumed Task Element command.

"I decided that the most effective means of disrupting coastwise rail communications was to knock out a railroad bridge readily observable from sea," said Gay, "and then keep it unusable. I selected for destruction a small bridge between two tunnels south of Songjin. To conserve ammunition and increase gunfire accuracy, the Canadian destroyer *Nootka* (CDR A. B. F. Fraser-Harris), using her whaleboats and a small minesweeping rig, swept a channel inside the 100-fathom curve to within 2,500 yards of the beach. After this, the *Stickell* destroyed the bridge with single gun 'short-range battle practice'."

Thus commenced the "Battle of the Bridge," which would continue until 28 June.

The North Koreans began immediate repairs, using stacked railroad ties for foundations (called "cribbing")—repairs which were discouraged by intermittent air bursts night and day from blockade ships in the vicinity.* At two to three-day intervals, whenever repairs appeared near completion, and after dusting off gun positions in the nearby hills with 40-mm. fire, the *Stickell*, covered by ships of Task Element 95.22, proceeded in the swept channel and destroyed the cribbing.

After *Stickell's* gunfire had demolished the Communist repairs several times, the North Koreans gave up trying to repair the trestle, and, being unable to bypass it due to the terrain, laboriously commenced filling the 30-yard ravine, still harassed by the blockading ships.

On 14 June, *Stickell* landed a group of South Korean soldiers from two small sampans in the area of the besieged bridge. Two prisoners were captured, one of whom was lost when a near miss from a mortar shell capsized one of the two sampans during retirement.

The surviving prisoner stated that he was the boss of a repair gang brought from a town near the Manchurian border to assist in the repair of the bridge. He also revealed that his party had travelled the entire way by train, but that numerous trains were now held up in the tunnels awaiting repairs to the Songjin bridge. The next day the prisoner pointed out various real and fake gun emplacements in the area, and also the police station in a village area south of Songjin, which was taken under fire and destroyed.

For two more weeks, the blockading ships kept the rail line inoperable. Finally, with the bridge gap almost filled with rock and dirt, the *Stickell* chose another bridge a short distance to the north of Songjin and commenced a second "destroy-repair-destroy" cycle.

"The presence of some fifteen South Korean marines and an English-speaking Korean naval lieutenant on board provided excellent opportunities to conduct beach raids," said Gay, "in addition to the routine around-the-clock interdiction and bombardment fire at Chongjin. Great credit is due to the brave Korean marines, who several nights every week

---

* For a similar effort by naval air, see "The Battle of Carlson's Canyon," page 233.

went cheerfully ashore onto hostile beaches. Sometimes they went ashore during a thick fog, guided by radar; on other occasions, they went in during bright moonlight, armed with rifles and Browning semi-automatic rifles and carrying hand grenades and a couple of handbags of clips. Their discovery and progress on the beach could always be followed by the clatter of small arms fire.

"On one occasion, after a reconnaissance in the Chuuron-jang area south of Chongjin, our landing party reported several large sampans on the beach which were being armored with heavy iron plating on the inside. As intelligence reports had also been received of a Communist plan to recapture the islands held by our forces in Wonsan harbor, using armored sampans, we made plans to destroy the reported sampans at our first opportunity.

"Two nights later, the *Stickell* steamed into Kyojo-wan an hour before sunset, ready to destroy the sampans by gunfire. While approaching the desired firing position, a radar target was picked up which was identified as a large motor schooner fleeing to the safety of the Chuuron-jang River. We opened fire at 10,000 yards and hit it at 8,500 yards just as it entered the river. The schooner burst into flames from bow to stern, ran on the beach, and burned for the remainder of the night. Prisoners we captured later revealed that this schooner was manned by North Korean naval personnel and was carrying arms, fuel, and supplies.

"We now returned our attention to the armored sampans.

"On reaching the 100-fathom curve to seaward of them, we discovered that they were protected from our direct fire by large stone masses. I made the decision to land the Korean marines, retiring until after dark and providing gun cover as necessary.

"The ship's motor whaleboat, with Ensign J. B. Farrell, USN, as boat officer and spotter, left the ship about four miles off the beach, towing a sampan filled with the Korean marines. A thousand yards from the selected landing spot, the sampan was cast off to proceed alone, and the spotting party prepared for action.

"As the sampan approached the beach, it was taken under small arms fire from the nearby cliffs, but our call-fire quickly drove off the defenders and the boat landed safely.

"The Koreans located three large armored sampans and destroyed them with hand grenades before being pinned down by mortar fire from a nearby village. Illumination from the *Stickell* permitted the spotter in our whaleboat to locate the enemy mortar and it was promptly silenced, permitting the Korean marines to withdraw without incident under covering fire."

Stickell's landing force performed another type of operation on the night of 14 June when Gay decided to seize one of the Communist-held Yondo

Islands about ten miles northeast of Chongjin. The *Stickell's* Korean marines were disembarked from two sampans at the closest point of the 100-fathom curve. Again, the destroyer's whaleboat was used to tow the sampans close to the beach. The marines landed undetected on the one inhabited island of the group. Local opposition did not develop. Considerable intelligence information was gained from the natives. The natives revealed that an official North Korean delegation was due to visit the islands the following day.

"I ordered our landing party to remain ashore to greet the dignitaries," said Gay.

"Unfortunately, the movements of the *Stickell* in the general vicinity of the Yondo Islands aroused suspicions of the North Koreans that something was amiss, for the scheduled visit failed to materialize."[13]

On the departure of *Stickell* from the theater, on 29 June, the following message was received from Commander Seventh Fleet:

> I have followed *Stickell's* exploits in Songjin during the past two weeks with great interest. The effects of your aggressive spirit and initiative will be remembered by the enemy. Well done. Vice Admiral Martin.

On 29 June 1951, the new ComCruDiv-5, Rear Admiral Arleigh A. Burke, had gone ashore on the east coast near Pohang to witness ROK troop maneuvers as the guest of the Eighth Army Commander, Lieutenant General James Van Fleet. Van Fleet asked Burke to accompany him to a certain area by jeep. Burke suggested it would be easier and quicker to go by helicopter, and that, afterward, Van Fleet could return with him to the cruiser *Los Angeles* for a dish of ice cream.

As the helicopter, piloted by Chief Aviation Pilot C. W. Buss, approached the *Los Angeles* about 1535, the wheels touched the life nets, followed by an RPM loss, and the 'copter crashed on the fantail, dumping both passengers on deck unceremoniously but uninjured.

"With the helicopter out of action," said General Van Fleet "the question arose how I was to get ashore. Burke told me we'd have to make it by boat. We did so without incident, but I didn't know until long after the war that the boat coxswain had not previously had experience in navigating through breakers, and that Burke himself had taken personal charge of the boat and made the landing himself."

On 12 July the *New Jersey* (Captain David M. Tyree, USN) was at the bombline with the destroyer *Leonard F. Mason* (DD-852)(CDR J. B. Ferriter). The battleship's fire that day killed 129 enemy troops. On 18 July, she returned to Wonsan to initiate an intensified bombardment plan known as "Operation Kick-Off." For days and weeks hereafter, ships would fire at known and suspected positions of enemy harbor defense guns in Wonsan with both delayed-burst and air-burst shells.

The no-fishing rule was enforced more rigidly than ever in northeastern Korean waters. The 6th of August saw USS *Carmick* (DMS-32) destroying four fishing sampans near Changjin and taking their 13 occupants into custody. Eight days later, the USS *William Seiverling* (DE-441) (LCDR W. C. Cole) captured nine more poachers off Tanchon. The 19th of August found USS *Thompson* (DMS-38) (LCDR W. H. Barckmann) capturing two fishermen at Tanchon.

The Han River Demonstration

On 26 July 1951, as the truce delegates at Kaesong began what would be a four-month wrangle over the establishment of a military demarcation line, a special naval demonstration was commenced in the Han River.

The reason for this special patrol was to counteract the Communists' immediate claim made at the truce table that the 200 square miles *south* of the 38th parallel and *west* of the Imjin River (including the Ongjin peninsula) were in their hands.

This territory was actually patrolled by UN guerrilla forces. Furthermore, since the city of Seoul was located at the headwaters of the Han River, it was important to insure that any cease fire agreement would provide that the maritime approaches to Seoul were not under Communist control.

It was therefore deemed urgent and prudent to demonstrate visibly to the Communists that this vital area was in UN hands.

On 28 July, accordingly, the USS *Los Angeles* (CA-135, CAPT R. N. McFarlane) entered the swept channel of Haeju-man to commence a shore bombardment of enemy frontline positions, assisted by plane spot. The Communists were caught by surprise; the Reds obviously did not consider that such a large ship could get so far into this shallow and mined sea area and bring guns to bear on the front lines. *Los Angeles* fired forty-four 8-inch rounds and sixty-six 5-inch rounds into frontline positions and received a "well done" for her work.

"The Han River demonstration was a very difficult naval operation," said Rear Admiral George C. Dyer, CTF, who was in charge of its establishment.

"The Han River is a small-sized Yangtze, and its currents run from four to ten knots. The channel shifts rapidly from one side of the river to the other. There are no water-borne navigational aids, and the tides run from twelve to twenty-five feet.

"The first thing we had to do was to survey the channel. This survey work in the Han River was done most capably and energetically by the navigators of the frigates of the British Navy.

"The United States Navy supplied the anchors and buoys and the tugs to handle them.

"The survey work was conducted in power boats which could only work for a period before and after slack water, since at other times their speed of six to eight knots was either just equal or less than the speed of the current.

"The sequence of events was: (1) the small boat survey, (2) the small mine sweepers, (3) the tug with the buoys, and (4) the frigates. Up-river

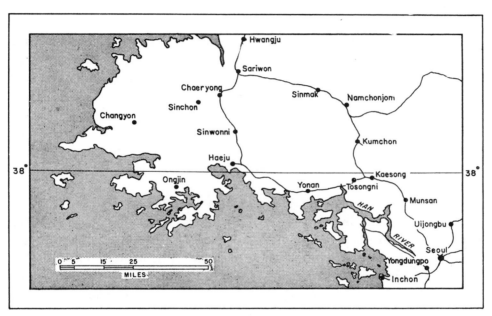

AREA OF THE HAN RIVER DEMONSTRATION

progress was at the rate of about three miles a day until we reached Kyodong Island.

"My hat is off to the British Navy and the Commonwealth Navies for the courage, tenacity, and high degree of seamanship they showed in accomplishing this job.

"When they reached the Kyodong Island area, we established an anchorage there, and commenced taking the enemy under fire.

"The survey then proceeded both westward and eastward. However, the only navigable channel found was one that went westward along the north of Kyodong Island, then turned north at Inson Point and proceeded to the eastward.

"As soon as we showed up north of Kyodong Island, the enemy started constructing batteries at Ayang Point and at the mouth of the Yesong River.

"There was a railroad line that ran from Yenan to Kesong, and a ferry across the Yesong River. There was heavy traffic on this ferry. To shell it regularly, the frigates had to get up to the mouth of the Yesong. The enemy would plant machine guns and mortars in the rice fields at night, and when the frigate came along in the morning, would shell the frigate, and there would be a close fight."

Dyer happened to be on board HMAS *Murchison* (LCDR A. N. Dollard, RAN) for a tour of the estuary during one particularly hot action on 28 September 1951.

"About 1600," recorded LCDR Dollard, "unsuspected batteries of 75-mm. guns, 50-mm. guns, and mortars opened fire on us from the north bank of the Han. We had just reached the Yesong River and had dropped our anchor to let the current turn us around when the first mortar hit."

The Australian frigate picked up her anchor and maneuvered clear, with all guns blazing. The *Murchison's* 4-inch fire scored several hits and silenced all opposition.

This Han River demonstration lasted until 27 November 1951, at which time the negotiators agreed upon a provisional cease fire line.

The disputed territory was recognized as in UN hands.

Naval Gunfire at the Bombline

At the bombline in September, 1951, several naval ships had an opportunity to display their gunnery prowess. *Los Angeles* fired all batteries at enemy troops and gun positions near Kojo on 3-4 September. One hundred and ninety-seven rounds of 8-inch and 123 rounds of 5-inch fire were expended. The shore party controlling her fire was commendatory:

> Many enemy casualties. Explosion observed with considerable smoke and spreading fire. . . . Rounds flushed enemy troops who began fleeing inland. Fire landed among them. In one incident, troops began running back over a small hill, and as they reached the top of the hill, a series of eight-inch air bursts exploded about twenty-five feet above their heads. . . . Your firing destroyed at least three enemy gun positions and caused an untold number of casualties.

The *New Jersey* had a chance to work at the bombline intermittently from 23 September to 3 October 1951.* The naval gunfire liaison party that spotted for her made the following comments:

* *New Jersey's* gunfire was in support of the First Marine Division. Her assistance had been requested by dispatch to Commanding General Tenth Corps, who in turn requested the support from Commanding General Eighth Army, who forwarded the request to Com7thFleet. At this time a request for gunfire support had to be separately submitted for each period that a ship was desired. A specific justification for the request had to be included, and a list of targets to be fired upon had to be furnished.

24 September: ". . . 27 rounds of 16-inch were fired with good effect on Hills 1190 and 951, with many bunkers destroyed, others revealed, and many casualties inflicted on the enemy. . . ."

2 October: ". . . four missions were fired, expending 136 rounds on Hills 802 and 951. Air observers and enemy POWs reported 25 counted enemy bunkers destroyed, 45 estimated destroyed; 200 killed, 400 wounded. . . ."

3 October: ". . . *New Jersey* fired 81 rounds on Hills 796 and 802 with good effect. . . ."

The cruiser *Los Angeles* also was credited with saving the First ROK Corps on the night of 21 November.

"In early November," said VADM J. J. Clark, then Commander Task Force 77, "intelligence sources indicated a strong buildup of enemy forces, with increased artillery and automatic weapons fire in the Kojo area. During the night of 21 November I received an urgent call for assistance to the First ROK Corps, then on the line near Kojo. General Van Fleet's headquarters reported that the enemy was breaking through the Korean lines, and had captured a hill on which an important outpost was located. The First ROKs had run out of ammunition, and the enemy was mauling them very badly. Could we send a ship down there?

"The location of the break-through was beyond the range of destroyer fire. The only heavy ship I had was the heavy cruiser *Los Angeles*.

"I proposed sending her, but my staff called attention to a standing order requiring that one heavy cruiser or battleship be kept with the fast carrier task force at all times to provide AA protection in the event of an air attack. Another reason for this requirement was in case any of those Russian cruisers came out of Vladivostok and ran down into our area during the night.

"These seemed like pretty worthless reasons just then, so I overrode the requirements and ordered the *Los Angeles* to get down there at high speed.

"She arrived off Kojo about 0230 and her 8-inch guns turned the tide of battle. Her 91 rounds of 8-inch fire drove the Communists back and gave the First ROK Corps a breathing spell until morning, when they were able to replenish their ammunition supplies."[14]

The last month of 1951 saw destroyer *Beatty* (DD-756, CDR Means Johnston, Jr.) patrolling the east coast north of Hungnam—"firing at any target worth our ammunition."

During a Sunday patrol southward from Cha-ho, *Beatty* spotted but could not positively identify lines of black dots across all the harbors and inlets along the coast. They appeared to be buoys and were estimated to be supports for anti-landing nets.

Reporting this information to Commander Task Group 95, *Beatty* received the following order: "Put a whaleboat in the water and have a closer look-see."

Beatty complied, selecting the large harbor of Yangwa.

Beatty's whaleboat, manned by a crew of volunteers commanded by Ensign Hugh H. McCreery, USN, was lowered into the water shortly after dawn and proceeded on its mission deep inside the enemy-held harbor. Since the boat crew could not comply with their mission of determining the nature of the objects until there was sufficient light, they remained inside the harbor for over two hours in broad daylight.

When about 1,500 feet off the beach, the whaleboat was suddenly caught in a crossfire from three machine gun nests. Ensign McCreery later estimated more than 100 rounds near the whaleboat, with the bullets walking by as close as five feet.

Over the "walkie-talkie" radio the ship could hear the rat-tat-tat of the machine guns. "I asked Ensign McCreery if he was firing at the enemy or was he being fired upon," said CDR Johnston. His reply was 'Affirmative to both.' Almost simultaneously I asked him if he wanted the *Beatty's* 5-inch guns to commence firing. I ordered my gunnery officer, LT Walter W. Schwartz, USN, to use white phosphorous ammunition which had proved very effective in counterbattery fire."[15]

The whaleboat was directly in the line of fire as the first round was fired. McCreery (also *Beatty's* assistant gunnery officer) radioed spot corrections. The first correction was almost on, and the second resulted in a direct hit on the first machine gun nest. On the third spot, fire was shifted to another nest with another direct hit. Several rounds were fired at the third, which was quickly silenced, although its destruction could not be confirmed. The crew of the whaleboat was simultaneously firing on the enemy with machine guns and even pistols.

The *Beatty's* whaleboat returned unscathed, with a very detailed drawing of the buoy arrangements.

The lines of black dots proved to be anti-landing nets, illustrating the Communists' inbred fear of another amphibious assault.

Tightening the Noose

At the beginning of 1952, the war ashore had assumed all the aspects of a stalemate. Ground action was sporadic, and consisted mainly of probing raids and patrols, varying in size and violence.

Despite the intense and combined efforts of air and naval forces, it was apparent that interdiction of the enemy's supply lines in Korea was not being achieved. The Communists were succeeding in steadily building up their military strength all along the battlefront, and their flow of supplies, while hampered and harassed, was not being interrupted to a critical degree.

The enemy's amazing and rapid capacity for repairing his roads, tunnels, and bridges plus his unlimited manpower, and his protected supply bases north of the Yalu, required greater effort and more efficient interdiction of the blockade forces if the supply networks were to be closed off to an effective degree. The Navy had to draw the blockade and bombardment noose a few notches tighter.*

What more and what else could be done to hurt and harass the Communists?

To Admirals Joy, Martin, and Dyer, there was little new that *could* be done. With the number of ships available, and the political and military restrictions imposed upon the conduct of the war, only an intensification of effort and improvements in technique could increase the Navy's contribution to the war.

In *this* sense, several things *could* be done.

First of all, the surface ships operating with the carrier and blockade forces could be more frequently used for bombardment and interdiction, especially during replenishment and bad weather. As a calculated risk, escort and heavy supporting ships around the carrier task force could be absent from the task force on a one-day-at-a-time basis for gun strikes. The escort of convoys could be reduced.

Secondly, the closer the co-operation between Task Forces 77 and 95, the greater would be the damage inflicted upon the enemy. Commander Task Force 77 was therefore given the task of coordinating the interdiction campaign by air and naval gunfire.

Third, still closer liaison could be established with the U. S. and ROK troops at the bombline, so that naval gunfire at the battlefront might be improved in its effectiveness.

Fourth, the spotting of naval gunfire must be increased; better control would mean greater accuracy and greater damage.

Fifth, additional areas close inshore could be swept clear of mines, and more patrols established to completely eliminate any enemy attempts to short-haul supplies by junk or sampan.

And lastly, a better scheme for the coordination of the air and ground interdiction campaign could be worked out. It was this objective which

---

* In conjunction with the surface interdiction effort described herein, refer to Chapter 8, "The Struggle to Strangle," which describes the naval air interdiction effort.

brought into being the "Package" and "Derail" operations, described on page 349.

Deep Naval Gunfire Support for the Marines

After relieving the First ROK Army Corps, the First Marine Division had taken up positions on the eastern end of the battleline. On their right flank was the First ROK Army, adjacent to the sea. However, the Marine division itself was still within the long-range reach of either cruisers or battleships.

In November 1951, the Marine division requested again that naval ships be made available to support them. Both Tenth Army Corps and COME-USAK approved this request, and a schedule of naval ships to support the division was drawn up.

In the four months which followed, it became standard practice for a new ship, reporting to the Marine Division to perform gunfire support for the first time, to send representatives to a liaison conference. At this meeting the Marines would furnish the necessary maps and overlays of the front-lines and bombline, would explain the terrain topography and targets, and would furnish information regarding voice calls and frequencies. In return the ship's gunnery officer would present information on ammunition availability, times on station, expected periods of replenishment, and other problems. These exchanges always proved invaluable.

During this period on the eastern front, the Marines were facing a deeply entrenched enemy whose main fortifications had been erected on the *reverse* sides of the steep mountains, away from the Marines. (See drawing on page 284.) These positions had proved invulnerable to all but the heaviest ordnance, namely, the naval gunfire of cruisers and battleships.

Major General John T. Selden, USMC, emphasized the importance of naval gunfire in a despatch request for continued gunfire support addressed to Vice Admiral Harold W. Martin, Commander Seventh Fleet.

> Since September the First Marine Division has blasted the majority of enemy's trenches and firing positions on forward slopes. The enemy now mans these with only a sentry force. The majority of his troops remain on the reverse slopes in areas protected from our tank and artillery fire. These down-slope positions are so constructed as to be invulnerable to all but the heaviest ordnance. Artillery ammunition is limited and in general cannot destroy the desired targets. Close air support is not available in quantity. High level bombing rarely hits such targets. Naval gunfire is the only ordnance available which can be effectively employed to destroy these targets, which include regimental command posts and other enemy strongpoints. Request that naval gunfire be continued to hit maximum number these targets.[16]

NAVAL COMMANDERS IN THE SEA WAR IN KOREA. (For commands and dates, see Appendix I.) *At top,* VADM J. J. Clark. *Center,* RADM G. R. Henderson. *Bottom,* RADM G. C. Dyer.

Good Damage Control. When DD *Ernest G. Small* struck a mine off Korea, the bow was loosened by the blast and began to shake itself asunder, endangering the ship. The skipper had the watertight bulkhead aft of the break sealed off and then backed the ship off in an attempt to dislodge the stricken portion.

THE BOW GOES ITS OWN WAY. Here *Small's* forward section is successfully cast adrift and gradually sinks beneath the Korean waters. With the watertight bulkhead holding out the sea, the destroyer limped back to Japan where a temporary bow was fitted for the long trip home.

FAVORITE COMMUNIST TARGETS. *At top,* DMS *Thompson* speeds toward *Iowa* with casualties suffered off Korean east coast. *Below left,* AMS *Osprey,* three times hit by enemy shore batteries. *Below right,* DMS *Endicott,* close-in duellist with the Koreans.

Vice Admiral Martin concurred, ordering that the maximum practical support be given to the Marines by Task Force 77's and 95's cruisers and battleships.

The assigned task for them was not an easy one. The average range to target would be 10 miles for the cruisers, and 16 miles for the battleships. In the very mountainous terrain, with variable and often unpredictable wind conditions, there was lubberly doubt that naval gunfire could be sufficiently accurate to destroy such small targets as artillery pieces, bunkers, and shelters. The naval gunner's were certain they could *hit* the targets, but not so sure that the expenditure of ammunition might not be extravagant.

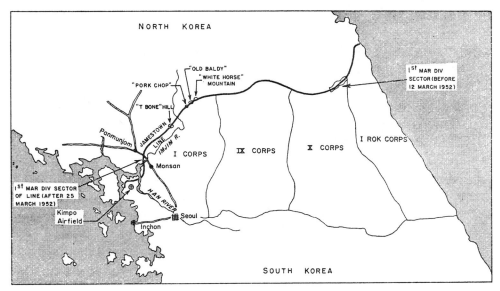

SECTORS FOR DEEP NAVAL GUNFIRE SUPPORT

For two-and-a-half months, the bombline ships fired at the enemy's front-lines. On 7 April 1952, General Selden passed out the report cards to Admiral Martin.

(1) *Wisconsin* had fired 977 rounds of 16-inch caliber projectiles in 43 missions at an average range of approximately 16 miles. This fire had killed an estimated 70 and wounded 359. Three artillery pieces had been destroyed and 7 damaged, 81 bunkers and shelters had been destroyed, and 105 damaged.

(2) *St. Paul* and *Rochester* had fired 1,661 rounds of 8-inch caliber projectiles at an average range of approximately 11 miles. This fire had killed 239 enemy troops and wounded 47. It had destroyed 2 artillery pieces and damaged 3. It had destroyed 116 bunkers and shelters and had damaged 127.

(3) *Manchester* had fired 470 rounds of 6-inch caliber projectiles at an average range of 11 miles. This fire had killed 163 enemy troops and wounded 47. One artillery piece had been destroyed and 8 damaged; 28 bunkers and shelters had been destroyed and 20 damaged.

Was such naval gunfire worth the effort and expense? The answer could only be yes. In General Selden's words, "The support rendered during this period was both effective and justified."

With an average expenditure of between 15 to 23 rounds per mission, naval gunfire was destroying targets for which the expenditure of 50 to 60 rounds of artillery fire was not uncommon. And the deleterious effect on the enemy's morale was immense even if not fully measurable. The Communists had supposed their reverse slope entrenchments impervious to gunfire; consequently, the destruction of their bunkers, command posts, and artillery positions by the flanking and enfilading fire of the cruisers and battleships was totally unexpected.

Reports of the excellent results of naval gunfire came not only from spotters observing the ships' fire but from captured enemy prisoners as well. One prisoner reported that *Wisconsin*'s fire on 25 January had hit his divisional command post, and that half the personnel in it were casualties. Another prisoner confessed that he had been induced to surrender after surviving a heavy naval bombardment, during which his unit had suffered severe casualties. In fact, one shell had landed near his position and had failed to go off. As he looked at the size of the 16-inch shell, he became convinced that it was time to surrender.

Still another prisoner reported that his battalion political officer had explained that the huge craters made by the 16-inch shells were made by atomic artillery.

General Seldon summarized the naval gunfire: "In view of the unusual circumstances confronting the First Marine Division, it is felt that the fire support ships have played a valuable and unique role in applying pressure against enemy military positions and morale."

Communist Resistance to Blockade

Time after time the blockading destroyers would fire at the same coastal targets and provoke no fire in reply. On other occasions, without warning, one or more enemy batteries would open a hot, intense, and accurate fire upon the tormenting ships. In several instances the enemy guns would remain purposely silent in order to entice the patrolling ships closer and closer inshore.

The USS *Thompson* (DMS-38, LCDR W. H. Barckmann) was an early example of how ships were often enticed close ashore by silence.

On 14 June 1951, while searching for lucrative targets in the vicinity of Songjin, the *Thompson* closed the beach to less than 3,000 yards. Suddenly, out of camouflage, four 3-inch mobile batteries commenced a hot and heavy fire on her. The *Thompson* increased speed and headed seaward, while returning the surprise fire. However, before moving clear, she had been struck 13 times, had suffered 6 casualties (3 killed and 3 wounded), and had received extensive damage to her director, radio equipment, and radars. *Thompson* acquitted herself with an equally intense fire on the four guns, forcing them to cease fire.*

The USS *James C. Owens* (DDR-776, CDR Robert B. Erly, USN) was another destroyer to receive a sudden and heavy attack from enemy guns. On 7 May 1952, the *Owens* was interdicting enemy coastal traffic in the vicinity of Songjin and had destroyed two railroad cars and a truck when she received information of activity in the Songjin railroad marshalling yards.

Moving the *Owens* to within 3,000 yards of the target, Erly opened direct fire on the marshalling yards, demolishing a switch engine and eight railroad cars.

At this point, approximately ten enemy guns opened a savage and accurate fire upon the *Owens*. The first salvos straddled immediately. For eleven minutes the enemy's fire was intense and rapid, resulting in six direct hits and much shrapnel from many near misses. Three separate fires broke out in the *Owens* 40-mm. ready-service magazine and two ready-service ammunition racks.

The *Owens* counterbattery fire was equally intense. Two of the enemy guns were seen to explode, and several others silenced.

As the *Owens* left the harbor, she had the satisfaction of continuing the fire several minutes after the enemy guns had quit.

Three *Owens* men had been killed and five wounded. The after officers quarters had been wrecked; cables to the after 40-mm. mounts had been severed. *Owens* made her own repairs, transferred her dead and wounded, and resumed normal operations and was again under fire at Hungnam in less than twenty-four hours.

The USS *Cunningham* (DD-752, CDR A. A. Clark, USN) was likewise to find herself in a hornet's nest of enemy gunfire. After a week of unchal-

---

* One of the Korean war's strange coincidences occurred to *Thompson* (which was struck by enemy gun fire on 3 separate occasions). On 20 August 1952, the same Songjin guns succeeded in hitting her again, striking the flying bridge. Three men were killed, ten injured. *Iowa* rendezvoused with the *Thompson,* sent her doctor aboard, and then took aboard the casualties by highline. Later that evening, *Iowa* bombarded the gun positions which had hit *Thompson.*

lenged inshore patrolling near Tanchon on 19 September 1952, the *Cunningham* had closed to within 3,500 yards of the beach while firing at a repair crew driven into the railroad tunnel.

"At 1430," said Clark,[17] "the enemy batteries opened fire and scored a direct hit with their first salvo. We immediately increased speed, turned to open the range, and started chasing splashes. Within about two minutes we took four more direct hits and about seven to eight air-bursts close aboard. One direct hit ruptured four depth charges, splattering burning TNT over much of the deckhouse aft, the dense smoke making fire control difficult. The leadership and professional skill of the mount captains and after Director Officer were magnificent. The guns which would bear—the after 5-inch mount, and after twin 3-inch/50—countered with 118 rounds of 5-inch/38 and 36 rounds of 3-inch/50 in spite of dense black smoke through mount 51 and air bursts over mount 33.

"Thereafter we weren't hit, although the shore guns kept firing at us all the way out to 16,000 yards, expending an estimated 125 rounds of 75 to 155-mm. The five hits and near misses cost us thirteen casualties (none killed), besides disabling our SG radar and demolishing a forced-draft blower in the forward fireroom."

Clark was fairly certain that the airbursts near *Cunningham* were VT-fuzed, as there were no airbursts away from the ship.

Spotting

Better liaison, better coordination, and *better spotting*—these were the improved techniques which would increase the effectiveness of naval gunfire upon the enemy.

Of the three, perhaps the most important was *spotting,* whether air spot (airplane or helicopter) or the actual observation and control of gunfire by spotters on the ground. However it was done, all hands agreed that the effectiveness of the naval gunnery would be in direct proportion to the amount and quality of the spotting.

The first west coast blockade commander, Rear Admiral W. G. Andrewes, RN, had appraised the value of non-spotted fire in these words: "Unobserved fire is useful for morale purposes, both from the point of view of our own forces and of upsetting the enemy," he said.[18] "Apart from that, it is of little real value, and many thousands of shells must have fallen harmlessly on the barren hills and rocks along the east coast of Korea."

Helicopter spotting was a new gunnery technique, first used in combat by the *Helena* in August of 1950. Opinion was unanimous that a ship using its own helicopter and carrying its own spotting officer possessed one of the best assists to accurate marksmanship that a ship could have.

But helicopter spot had its drawbacks and limitations. In the first place, only certain of the cruisers and battleships had helicopters. Helicopter spot was only rarely available to the destroyers, which expended approximately 90 per cent of the bombardment ammunition fired in the Korean War. Secondly, helicopters were very susceptible to enemy gunfire, even small arms. If there was any enemy opposition, the use of helicopters was extremely hazardous. In Wonsan harbor, for example, helicopters were available, but their primary tasks were minehunting and search and rescue; their use for spotting purposes in that besieged city was highly dangerous because of the heavy enemy antiaircraft fire.

Air spot by regular airplanes had its limitations, too. The first limitation was training. The majority of the spotting pilots, both U. S. Air Force and Navy, were well trained in the technique and doctrine of gunfire spot. In a few instances, however, a lack of training, sometimes humorous, was reflected in the use of non-standard phraseology. The British Admiral in command of Task Force 95.1, Rear Admiral A. K. Scott-Moncrieff, RN, reported in April 1952 that the Dutch ship Hr. Ms. *Piet Hein* (CDR von Freytag Drabbe) became completely bewildered by the use of incorrect procedure by an airborne spotter. "Fortunately," wrote Admiral Moncrieff, "the shoot was prevented from being abortive by the presence of a liaison officer from my staff who was able to translate the vernacular into simple English."

The use of jet aircraft for spotting later in the war revealed the limitations of these aircraft: limited endurance and their need to fly at fairly high altitudes in order to maintain a satisfactory rate of fuel expenditure.

As for propeller-type spotting planes, their value was occasionally diminished by the presence of enemy antiaircraft fire in certain areas such as Wonsan, which forced them to such altitudes as to make their spotting efforts questionable.

Aside from these practical limitations, the use of air and ground spot increased steadily for the remainder of the war. Never was there enough. Requests for spotting assistance always exceeded the capacity for giving it. But the maximum available was hereafter used to increase the effectiveness of naval gunfire on enemy targets.

Whaleboat Operations

As already described, one of the tactics used to advantage by the blockading ships of Task Force 95 was the use of ship's whaleboats for the detection of targets along the coasts or in harbors, as well as for the direction of the ship's gunfire and the capture of enemy sampans and junks.

One outstanding whaleboat operation was conducted by the destroyer

USS *Halsey Powell* (DD-686, CDR Francesco Costagliola, USN) on 18 January 1952, near Hungnam. This operation, to neutralize an enemy supply buildup where a destroyer's gunfire could not reach, came to be known as "Chicken-Stealer."

"Shortly after I arrived in the Hungnam area to be Commander Task Element 95.24," wrote CDR Costagliola,[19] "all ships of the blockade force received a despatch from Admiral Dyer. In essence this despatch pointed out that on many occasions recently, ships had reported *destroying* single junks. Admiral Dyer stated that in his opinion we should show more dash and enterprise in *capturing* junks, which were useful for intelligence purposes, rather than sinking them. This operation had the code name 'Junket'.

"This despatch was received about 13 January 1952. Since I had a shipload of eager lads, we accepted Admiral Dyer's despatch as a direct challenge. We did not think we had much chance of encountering a junk offshore in our area, but in addition to planning for such an eventuality, we thought there was a good possibility there might be some behind such islands as Mayang-do in our area. My executive officer, operations, gunnery, communications, and shore fire control party officers were particularly active in working up a plan to steal a junk. My crew nicknamed our two boats 'Hawk' and 'Falcon'.

"Having received intelligence to the effect that there were many small boats in the harbor of Sam-ho, and since Sam-ho was within enemy gun range from the sea but obscured by a promontory, we requested aircraft spot from CTF 77 for 1000 on the 18th of January. No planes showed up. We decided to try our boats. The spotting boat directed ships' fire on jetties, boats, and a warehouse.

"Upon their return, the boat crew reported the Sam-ho warehouse gutted, jetties damaged, and many of the small boats riddled with shrapnel. The whaleboats had been fired on by a shore battery but escaped damage.

"On 19 January, in the Hungnam area, close scrutiny of the shore line through binoculars revealed a man standing at the entrance to a large cave facing us on the island of Hwa-do. We also observed seven or eight workmen with digging tools enter the cave. The information we had on the island was not clear as to whether or not it was in friendly or enemy hands. Certainly, the cave looked suspicious. Despatches to our immediate superior, ComDesRon-17 (CTG 95.2, CAPT C. E. Crombe) and the local minesweeper commander, confirmed that there were no friendly forces on that island.

"On establishing the fact that the island was enemy, we opened fire on the cave and managed to get one or two rounds into the entrance.

"Following this, a large hand-propelled barge was observed to leave Hungnam harbor and proceed along the shore in the direction of Hwa-do island. This too was taken under fire. At least one casualty was observed among the barge personnel as they worked their way laboriously back into the harbor.

"In the early afternoon, considerable activity could be discerned on the mainland almost directly behind Hwa-do. It appeared that at least a hundred people were loading supplies into small boats, presumably to ferry them to Hwa-do. A few rounds dispersed that activity.

"All this activity on Hwa-do really roused our curiosity. But from our position (which we could not vary very much) we knew something was afoot. The only way to see was to use our whaleboats. On this day, however, the seas were rough and conditions were not considered suitable for launching and loading boats.

"The decision was made therefore to remain in this location until morning, with our anchor 'underfoot' to help keep the ship from drifting.

"Next morning, Sunday, January 20, 1952, the seas were calm. We started putting the boats over at 0630. Although it was only about 8,000 yards from the ship to Hwa-do, the two boats had to travel about twice that far in order to get behind it and do it surreptitiously. Although risky, I decided to keep my ship in the same spot it had been for the last twenty-odd hours, because it was the only one where we could stay close to the island and also observe the section of beach where all the activity had been observed the day before.

"About 0745, the boats were in position, ready to spot our fire. The ship opened fire, one round at a time, as directed by Ensign James Winnefeld, the spotting officer in the first boat. Lieutenant Theodore Curtis, my operations officer in charge of the second boat, kept a few hundred yards away to provide support to the first boat if needed.

"The ship had only two 5-inch mounts manned, as the crew had not quite finished breakfast. Just at eight o'clock we were startled by an explosion about 50 feet off the starboard bow. Water splashed all over the bridge. Within seconds we were backing out of there emergency full. Shells seemed to be falling all around us. Our anchor was still underfoot, but fortunately it did not snag on anything and came along with us.

"At least four guns on Sohojin Point, located about 9,000 yards north-northeast of our position, were shooting at us. Needless to say, we were at General Quarters, shooting back with all our mounts, in very short order. Although we were straddled several times, the ship was not hit and the enemy shells began to fall consistently short, then ceased.

"The boats, meanwhile, were still behind Hwa-do to the west, reconnoitering and encountering no opposition. We returned to a point about 2,000 yards south of our former location, out of range of the enemy battery, and resumed shooting at Hwa-do targets. Unfortunately, a good proportion of possible targets were on a steep reverse slope where the ship could not get at them.

"However, Ensign Winnefeld reported all houses in three small villages had been covered with shrapnel, and four houses completely gutted. Boats along the beach were sprayed with shrapnel. One was destroyed and one was sunk.

"When it became apparent that not much more could be done without the expenditure of a great deal more effort, I recalled the boats. The next couple of days and nights, Hwa-do continued in our plans and operations as a target to receive harassing fire.

"Shortly after this operation, the thought was generated that a bazooka would be a very useful weapon in stepping up the wallop of the whaleboats. On the afternoon of 22 January, the *Halsey Powell* (DD-686) was relieved as TE 95.24, and proceeded to Sasebo for upkeep. There, through Rear Admiral George C. Dyer and the assistance of CMD R. M. Hill (OinC Naval Ordnance Facility, Yokosuka) and the local Army unit, we obtained two 3.5-inch bazookas and a 75-mm. recoilless rifle, with ammunition for both types.

"Upon our return to the Hungnam area on January 30, the weather was bitterly cold and the boats wouldn't start. The engineers worked 'round the clock to get them going. Between rough weather and the severe cold, it wasn't until the afternoon of 6 February that both boats were again running and the sea was calm enough to get them in the water to take a look at the situation on Hwa-do. Finally, at 1430, we got them in the water. One boat had the 75-mm. recoilless mounted on a platform in the bow. The other boat included a 3.5-inch bazooka. Once again, Ensign Winnefeld commanded the 75-mm. boat and Lieutenant Curtis the 3.5-inch.

"The ship went to General Quarters about 1530, ready for any eventuality, and commenced a slow bombardment to keep the enemy occupied.

"About 1545, the boats reported in position and began to direct our fire. As before, however, because of the reverse slope, we were not doing much damage. Permission was requested and granted for the boats to try their luck with the bazooka and recoilless rifle. I gave them permission and the ship ceased fire. The whaleboats took turns, one standing off for support while the other went in to shoot at close range.

"Meanwhile, aboard ship, I nervously looked at the clock. It was 1625. I decided to issue the recall order at 1630. Just then a not very clear communication was received from one of the boats indicating some sort of difficulty. Our first impression was that one of the men had gotten singed on his backside from being too close to the back blast of the recoilless rifle. The next thing we got was a frantic call for fire on a certain area of the island.

"We were a little hesitant to open fire because we couldn't see the boats and were using indirect fire. However, we started pouring out the 5-inch until we heard from the boats again. The boats reported that one man— Donald Flaherty, DC2—was injured and would require the attention of a medical officer. He had been shot in the ankle and the groin. We had no doctor aboard.

"While the boats were making their slow trek back to the ship we radioed our immediate superior in Wonsan, CTG 95.2, Captain C. E. Crombe, for medical assistance. He dispatched the *Twining* (CDR M. C. Osborne) which was also at Wonsan, and which had a medical officer embarked, to meet us.

"It was nearly dark when we finally got the two boats aboard and ran south to rendezvous with *Twining*. We did not have to go very far, however, for she had been steaming at high speed in our direction. Flaherty was soon safely transferred.

"After retrieving the two boats, we got the full story from the boat crews. While shooting at the various targets on the beach, they had spotted a couple of sampans which they thought they could capture (one had fresh fish in it). When the sampans were secured in tow, the two whaleboats started back to the ship, but were taken under small arms fire by the enemy. This was when Flaherty was hit. The radioman in the other boat—William Harrison, RM2—had a bullet graze his head which severed the headband of his earphones. Arthur Talley, BM3, was steering his boat lying on the bottom, using a rifle as a stick to guide the tiller. They still had the sampans in tow when some bigger guns, probably 75-mm., opened up with considerable accuracy and forced them to abandon the prizes.

"Fortunately, the ship's fire managed to stifle the enemy's guns before any more damage was done.

"After Flaherty* was transferred, we returned to the vicinity of Hwa-do Island and Hungnam about 2200. There was a bright, red glow over Hwa-do indicating that fires the boats had set with their shooting in the afternoon were still burning brightly."

Capturing Sampans

On the night of 17 February 1952, minesweeper *Murrelet* (AM-372)

---

* Flaherty recovered but was later discharged from the service with a partial disability. He credits his life in part to a tourniquet which was torn from an American flag carried by the whaleboat.

was steaming independently on blockade and anti-mining patrol between Hungnam and Cha-ho. Near Songdo Gap, radar contact in the direction of the beach was made at a range of 10,000 yards. *Murrelet* changed course to close the range and to get between the target and the beach in order to prevent escape. It was dangerous but exhilarating work.

At a range of 400 yards, *Murrelet* illuminated the target with her 12-inch signal searchlight, and the light disclosed a large two-masted sampan with all sails set. *Murrelet* fired one 20-mm. burst through the rigging, severing and dropping both sails of the sampan. *Murrelet* came alongside, threw over two grappling hooks, and secured the junk. Just as *Murrelet* prepared to put her boarding party aboard, six North Koreans crawled from below decks, raised their hands, and surrendered. The sampan was taken in tow and delivered to the ROK Navy.

"The *Murrelet* got the armed whaleboat idea from Admiral Dyer's 'dashing' and 'aggressive' despatch," said LCDR J. W. O'Neil. "We procured walkie-talkies, built a radar reflector screen for the whaleboat, and then called for volunteers. Almost the entire crew stepped forward. The crew selected was LTJG W. F. Gillen, USNR; ENS Suh In Byuk, ROK Navy; Frank H. Kennon, Jr., BM1; Brown, TN; Cluke, SN; French, SN; Beaugard, QM2; Sherer, RD3; and Chance, FN. A few daylight practice runs proved that we could operate the boat effectively three or four miles from the ship.

"Our method of operation was quite simple. On our night patrols, if a sampan was detected in swept water, the capture would be effected by the ship. If the sampan was detected in unswept water, we would get as close as possible, stop, and put the armed boat in the water. The radar reflector in the boat made a good target and we were able to vector them to any contact very effectively. The whaleboat would approach the sampan and ENS Suh would call on them in Korean to surrender. Then the sampan and occupants would be towed back to the ship.

"This plan met with success the instant it was put in operation. The whaleboat was vectored out on contacts six times and captured six sampans and twenty-six prisoners.

"The seventh time did not work out too well. The whaleboat was vectored about 3.5 miles into Hongwon Roads to a double contact we had picked up. They were successful in making an undetected approach and called upon five North Koreans in each sampan to surrender. The occupants stood up with their hands in the air. The whaleboat took one sampan in tow and started to go alongside the other. So far everything was routine and a carbon copy of the other raids.

"Suddenly one of the Koreans threw a hand grenade into the after compartment of the whaleboat. The explosion killed Kennon, the coxswain, wounded Brown and Cluke, and blew a three-foot hole in the port quarter. Our remaining crew members immediately opened fire with rifles and sub-machine guns, and after a brief but intense fire-fight, killed the occupants of both sampans.

"LTJG Gillen was then faced with the prospect of getting the badly damaged whaleboat back to the ship. The hole was plugged with life jackets, but it was necessary to bail continuously with helmets to stay ahead of the incoming water. Meanwhile, on the *Murrelet*, we listened to the reports of the action via walkie-talkie and were helpless to assist. The ship could not be taken into mined waters. It took the whaleboat about twenty-five minutes to make the return trip. *Murrelet* then ran at top speed to Wonsan and obtained medical attention for the wounded men."

Shore Battery Dueling

One of the most successful ships in dueling with the enemy's coastal guns was the destroyer *Douglas H. Fox* (DD-779, CDR James A. Dare). This ship worked up a procedure especially adapted to the Communist defenses.

"One lesson that I taught my crew which I had learned from World War II," said CDR Dare, "was that if you wanted to make *good* gunners out of *mediocre* gunners, simply take them under enemy fire. Also this procedure seems to have a remarkably good effect on morale.

"In the Korean blockade and bombardment work, every ship had to choose between the evil of long periods at General Quarters, the increasing strain in Condition II; or the relative lack of gunnery coverage in Condition III.

"The *Fox* solved this problem by calling away two sections of Condition III when we were in fairly dangerous territory. This always provided a fore-and-aft 5-inch mount and complete 40-mm. coverage, plus an augmented engineering watch to man the smoke generator and to keep a man in steering aft. Since we could choose the time and duration of these extra stints, it provided fairly easy strain on all concerned.

"The coastal guns of northeast Korea, for the most part, were field artillery pieces. They had no modern control equipment or automatic computers. In my opinion, when the Commies fired at our ships, and ships *opened* the range and ceased counterbattery fire too soon, it gave the Reds confidence and courage. I feel that if the *Fox* had done this, the Communists would have fired on us every time we came in range, probably with more accuracy each time.

"Our system, instead, was to approach a known enemy gun position, probing it with single shot, deliberate fire. When the enemy gun answered, we *closed* the range and commenced a heavy barrage to smother the battery. After we silenced the gun, we shifted to deliberate fire again to destroy it.

"In dangerous areas, I usually kept one 5-inch mount in reserve, one barrel loaded with white phosphorous and the other with VT-fuzed common. A few salvos of this mixture silenced the enemy fire completely (and usually for several days.)"

A typical result of *Fox*'s doctrine was the destruction of an enemy battery on Mayang-do, on 7 May 1952.

At 1155, *Fox* received 12 rounds of fire from the enemy three 76-mm. gun battery. Half of the rounds were white phosphorous. The opening salvo was 20 to 50 yards away, and other straddled within 100 yards. *Fox* closed the range and commenced a rapid, smothering fire, forcing the enemy guns into silence.

Four nights later, in the same area, *Fox* captured eighteen fishermen, of whom nine lived on Mayang-do. The prisoners reported that *Fox's* fire had destroyed both the gun and the housing of one large 105-mm. gun. The gun chief and five gunners were killed, and another gun dismounted.

"The Mayang-do battery never fired on us again," said Dare.

Anti-Fishing Expedition

Destroyer *Douglas H. Fox* was also to have her name recorded very often in action reports during the spring of 1952. In a period of four weeks, *Fox* made the North Korean fishing industry exceedingly unprofitable.

"Our anti-fishing campaign was carefully worked out and centered about our whaleboat raiding party," said CDR Dare. "Since all raiding would be done at night, we put corner reflectors on staffs in the bow and stern of the whaleboat which permitted us to follow it out as far as 14,000 yards on the SG radar.

"In addition to small arms and radio, the whaleboat crew carried hand grenades, demolition charges, hack saws, axes, bolt cutters (for destroying fishing nets), and an engine repair kit in case the whaleboat engine ever failed. Part of the time the whaleboat also carried a 75-mm. recoilless rifle, with about 15 rounds of HC and 15 rounds of white phosphorous. The 'Willie-Peter'* was wonderful for establishing a reference point on the beach from which to direct ship's gunfire.

"The selection of a crew for the whaleboat required careful attention. Not every officer or enlisted man is the right type. My boat cox'n, Shepard, was the kind who could steer by the seat of his pants once he was given a compass course. He was tough and slightly reckless.

---

* "Willie-Peter"—white phosphorous.

"The officer in charge of the boat, LT William R. Doran, was a very good leader, having all the better command virtues. He was also adept with all sorts of small arms; he was the ship's assistant gunnery officer and therefore knew what type of fire support he could get from the ship.

"The ROK naval officer, Ensign Un Soo Koo, was a bright, extrovert type. On many occasions he managed to get information from the captured prisoners in about 30 seconds, which was then transmitted to the ship by radio. One time, he convinced two prisoners, caught 30 minutes earlier, to help spot gunfire on the loading piers and warehouses behind Mayang-do. (I am not certain the prisoners weren't spotting our fire onto their creditors' homes.)

"The other men in the boat crew were the rough and ready 'can-do' type.

"Since I felt rather keenly the risks being taken by my men in the whaleboat raiding party, I always ran the bridge plot of their track and controlled them personally from a portable radio mounted on top of the pilot house. Obviously it was important never to lose track of the whaleboat when sending it 5 to 7 miles away from the ship into the midst of a harbor or into a group of 15 to 20 sampans. In order to intercept the relatively immobile sampans, we usually vectored our whaleboat *inshore* of the targets; the whaleboat would then herd the fishermen to seaward.

"Capturing fishermen required some thoughtful procedures. Invariably, every craft brought alongside was thoroughly searched beforehand. The whaleboat party, therefore, had to do everything to guarantee the ship's safety as well as their own. They did this by going alongside and boarding, searching both sampan and prisoners on the spot, by the light of battle lanterns. After this the sampan would be towed back to the ship *alongside,* rather than astern, so that all guns in the boat could bear. I didn't want an accident like the tragic one which happened to *Murrelet.*

"After capturing sampans, our whaleboat always took care to identify itself on its approach to the ship by pointing a battle lantern toward us until we were quite certain there could be no mistake."

The very successful, one-month anti-fishing campaign which *Douglas H. Fox* conducted while patrolling "Engine Block" and at the bombline is outlined in *Fox*'s war diary. Here, incidentally, the historian's problem is reflected with clarity, for the brief and official words of action reports and war diaries do not contain the colorful and memorable details so important for reader understanding and interest. Accordingly, each entry from *Fox*'s war diary is supplemented by remarks from her commanding officer obtained later by correspondence and interview:

War Diary: 30 April 1952. "... *Fox* raiders in motor whaleboat investigated small radar contacts inshore of rendezvous area at 0217. ..."

Commanding Officer: "The radar contacts proved to be Dan buoys left by the minesweepers, but were not indicated on my charts. As soon as this was ascertained, we sent the boat in to the small rock island which lies in the mouth of Hungnam harbor. The raiding party planted an American flag on the island, plus a sign with surrender instructions printed in Korean, and a white flag on a short staff to wave at us. The raiding crew also painted the *Fox*'s name rather prominently on both sides of this rock."

(Note for history readers): The next day, 1 May, would be the Reds' May Day celebration. When the Communists began their festivities the next morning, they would do so in sight of the *Stars and Stripes.*

War Diary: 6 May 1952: "At 0200, raiders suspended operations after having captured three sampans and 15 North Korean fishermen in the vicinity of Chang-ho ri. *Fox* hoisted two sampans aboard, cut third adrift, and resumed southern patrol . . . at 1148 proceeded to Wonsan to transfer prisoners and sampans to TE 95.23 at Yodo. . . . USS *Ptarmigan* (AM-376) and USS *Toucan* (AM-387) conducted night anti-sampan patrol. At 2315, *Fox* raiders captured 23 North Korean fishermen and one 32-foot sampan in vicinity of Paegan-dan. . . ."

Commanding Officer: "This was the first night the raiders investigated the harbor closure net off Sin 'Chang-ni. They reported it to be a 4-inch hemp cable supported by oil drums, and that the net dropped from it was fairly old and rotten.

"The 23 fishermen off Paegan-dan were nearly their total fishing population. We never again observed more than one or two boats there, and these were very close inshore."

(Note for history readers): Upon being questioned, the fishermen were able to locate a 122-mm. gun at Kajin-ni, which they said was serviced by a company of North Korean soldiers who lived nearby in underground caves. They further reported that the gun was positioned so that only the barrel protruded, and that it had taken four horses to move this gun to its hilltop position. The fishermen also revealed that they had no motorized sampans in their area, that food was scarce, and that soldiers checked them in and out on the hours of 2000 and 0400.

War Diary: 8 May 1952: "*D. H. Fox* raiders cut and destroyed 6,600 feet of fish net and sank 130 main floats of Communist dual-purpose fishing and harbor closure nets off Sin 'Chang-ni."

Commanding Officer: "These nets were formed into interior and exterior traps at both ends. Our Korean ensigns estimated they would provide food for 500 or 600 people. The nets were destroyed by the raiders by first cutting the bolt rope in seven or eight places, towing the sections apart to rip the nets all the way down, and then sinking the whole mess. We doubted that they could be usefully recovered thereafter."

War Diary: 9 May 1952: "*D. H. Fox* raiders conducted close-in search of Hungnam harbor, capturing 12 North Korean fishermen and two junk-type boats with sails. At 0335 completed raiding operations and fired on numerous factories in Hungnam ..."

Commanding Officer: "This was the morning that the officer in charge of the raiding party, LT Doran, made me think back to LT Stephen Decatur. Doran was motoring about in Hungnam harbor in the midst of 30 to 40 sampans. He sized up the two biggest ones, stopped them, searched them, forced them to hoist sail, and escorted them out of the harbor. The sun was almost up as they sailed back into the swept area."

(Note for history readers): The destroyer *Fox's* initiative and aggressiveness during a one-month period resulted in the capture of 120 fishermen and 29 boats, and the destruction of 24,000 lineal feet of fish traps and nets. The captured fishermen also furnished valuable military intelligence.

Air-Gun Strikes

On 4 April 1952, Vice Admiral Joy gave Task Force 77 an additional mission: to coordinate its air strikes with simultaneous gun strikes by the blockade forces. Such a system would increase the damage inflicted, and it would enhance training. Fire from the surface ships would help reduce the enemy antiaircraft fire upon the naval aircraft. In return, the naval aircraft could spot the surface fire of the ships.

These combined strikes were to take place until the end of the war.

The coordination of the fire power of surface ships and the lethal power of a carrier task force's airplanes commenced with the 13 April air-gun strikes on Chongjin.

Philippine Sea (CVA-47, CAPT Willard K. Goodney) and *Boxer* (CVA-11, CAPT John B. Moss) would furnish the air strikes, while the USS *St. Paul* (CA-73, CAPT Roy A. Gano), *Hanson* (DDR-832, CDR W. J. Henning), *T. E. Chandler* (DD-717, CDR T. H. Wells), and British destroyer HMS *Concord* would furnish the gun strikes.

The Chongjin targets were choice ones, especially for the carrier airmen, whose appetites had long been dulled by the steady menu of interdiction targets. Chongjin's Japan Rayon Company and Mitsubishi Iron Works would be primary targets. In addition, the city's numerous warehouses, gun positions, supply buildings, fuel tanks, and barracks would receive attention.

Each carrier launched its entire air group twice during the day; *Boxer's* Air Group Two (CDR A. L. Downing) at 0600 and 1200; *Philippine Sea's*

Air Group Eleven (CDR J. W. Onstott) at 0800 and 1600. Each strike numbered from 52 to 58 planes, and 200 tons of heavy ordnance were pin-pointed on the Chongjin targets.

"My planes flew 132 sorties and dropped 119 tons of ordnance," recorded Commander Downing. "I led the early morning hop, while CDR G. A. Sherwood, the commanding officer of VA-65, led the afternoon flight. Our targets included buildings, large cranes, a loading platform, a drydock, and five fuel tanks, as well as the rayon and iron factories.

"Although it was difficult at the time to assess damage because of the smoke from the fire and explosions, we achieved excellent results, as determined by post-strike photography. We only had one F4U, one AD, and one F9F sustain minor damage because of flak, largely because we sent the Panther jets in ahead on flak-suppression runs and they effectively silenced the AA.

"Fire and explosions shook the city during the attacks," said Downing, "and reports of troop casualties and damage came in from outside sources for days after the strike."[20]

Rear Admiral Apollo Soucek, Commander Task Force 77, had another observation:

"As the air-gun strikes were planned and conducted," he said, "the pilots' enthusiasm was observed to swing upward."

The surface ships were equally pleased with the new system. The coordination of the firing with the bombing improved the accuracy of each while reducing the danger of all.

On 25 April, the USS *Iowa,* accompanied by USS *Duncan* (DDR-874), USS *McCoy Reynolds* (DE-440), and HMAS *Warramunga* (CDR J. H. Ramsay, RAN), was joined by four strikes of 50-odd planes each from Task Force 77 to plaster the industrial targets of Chongjin. It was the second time a battleship had operated so far north.*

"We arrived and fired the first shot at 0530 in the most beautiful dawn you can imagine," recorded Captain W. R. Smedberg, III. "The sea was flat calm—mirror like—and the temperature a balmy 68°. The sun was bright, there was not a cloud in the sky, and a soft breeze was just sufficient to move the dust and smoke away from our targets and our line of fire.

"However, the beautiful dawn didn't remove a feeling of tension. Since Chongjin was the most important industrial and rail transportation center in North Korea, only 48 miles from the Russian border, we had reason to be worried. I couldn't understand how the Reds could sit and watch us wreck that city, with their own planes just across the border. We

---

* *Missouri* had bombarded Chongjin in November 1950.

could see the Russian planes take off on our radars, but they never came closer than 20 miles from us.

"During the day we had grandstand seats for the four hour-long 50-plane carrier strikes that were nicely coordinated with our firing. A total of 200 planes dropped some 230 tons of bombs and napalm. We fired 213 tons from this ship alone. The DDs probably contributed another 25 tons, with approximately 800 rounds of 5-inch.

"Three large steel and iron works, a sprawling rayon factory, three large power and transformer stations, a big roundhouse, two marshalling yards, and a boat repair shop which included eight huge Gantry cranes and one big hammer head or traveling crane were our targets. We had the most fun getting the ship into a spot where we had five of the big cranes enfiladed; we capped the 'T' on them, as it were, and then just started mowing them down. The task force, some 40 or 50 miles away, did a beautiful job of keeping constantly in the area two spotting planes for this ship, so we had a combination of plane and direct spot of the many targets on the water-front, and excellent plane spot with perfect radio communication for the deeper targets.

"At noon, during the bombardment, we intercepted a short range radio broadcast from Peking, which said that American ships were shelling women and children in the densely populated city of Chongjin. At 3 p.m., we heard another broadcast saying that three of the four ships had been sunk."

After this strike, the *Iowa* proceeded south on 27 May to fire at coastal bridges south of Songjin. The battleship fired 98 rounds of 16-inch fire at them and succeeded in damaging all the bridges and closing all the tunnel entrances.

"The remarkable thing about the bombardment work by the battleships in Korea," said Smedberg,[21] "was the most careful supervision of its delivery. Whereas in World War II our BBs fired many nine-gun salvos in bombardment, in Korea we rarely fired anything except single shots. Moreover, most of the battleship fire was spotted. I would also like to emphasize that none of our planes or ships ever shot into villages or residential areas."

"Packages and Derails"

As has been explained in Chapter 8, entitled "The Struggle to Strangle," there was no effort made during the course of the Korean war to coordinate the interdiction campaign in Korea at the theater level. However, within its own area of responsibility (the northeast coast of Korea), the Navy performed its own coordination. On 24 April 1951, Vice Admiral Joy approved the proposal of Rear Admiral Ofstie and directed that the interdiction efforts of surface and air be coordinated. For this purpose Task Force 95 was placed under the operational control of Task Force 77. The senior cruiser division commander (CTG 77.1) henceforth served as CTG 77's representative for the surface gunfire. His duties included the maintenance of an up-to-date list of worthwhile gunfire targets, recommendations for and conduct of the necessary gun strikes, and the periodic evaluation of the program.

In late 1951 Rear Admiral F. Moosbrugger, Commander Cruiser Division Five, summarized the experience of Task Force 95's interdiction efforts by saying that the only effective fire from surface forces was deliberate fire with air- or groundspot. Non-spotted fire might have psychological or harassment effect, he said, but its actual damage to the enemy was limited. A strip of railroad track, or even a bridge, was a very small target, and unless naval gunfire was both accurate and controlled, the ammunition was largely wasted. Admiral Moosbrugger also called attention to the need for better and more complete intelligence on what the blockade and bombardments were accomplishing.

A further step to increase the effectiveness of naval gunfire and to coordinate it with the air strikes of Task Force 77 was instituted on 11 January 1952 by the introduction of two programs known as "Package" and "Derail."

"Package" was a shoreline target suitable both for ships and airplanes. Five points along the main Songjin-Hungnam railroad were carefully chosen (see chart), and given the code name "package," plus a number. At three of the five "packages," the targets included bridges. Radar reflector buoys were planted off each one to assist navigation and gunfire accuracy. At night, ships could get as close to the five targets as 1,500 to 2,000 yards, in most cases.

The "package" targets were also ones which would be difficult for the enemy to repair. And all of them were along the main east coast supply route. If these "packages" could be interdicted, the flow of enemy supplies from the Manchurian sanctuary would be seriously impeded.*

The initial plan called for the cutting of the "packages" by air strikes.

---

* PACKAGE ONE was a small bridge and embankment about 25 feet high and 3,000 feet long. It carried a single-track railroad across a level valley between two tunnels.

PACKAGE TWO was a 220-yard stretch of single-track railroad between two tunnels.

PACKAGE THREE was a stretch of railroad track on an embankment with a small 35-foot two-span bridge crossing a drainage canal.

PACKAGE FOUR was a section of track at the foot of a mountain only 20 feet above the sea coast. There was also a tunnel.

PACKAGE FIVE was a bridge and approach embankment crossing a small steam at the coastline.

Thereafter, air reconnaissance would reveal the enemy's progress in repairing the damage and reopening the rail-line. When the Communist repair effort was about complete, other air strikes would destroy the target again.* However, when the carriers were replenishing, or when bad weather prevented air strikes, the surface forces of Task Force 95 were to take over and keep the "packages" destroyed by gunfire. In addition, patrolling ships were to fire a specified number of rounds (at irregular intervals) every day and every night to hamper and destroy the enemy's repair efforts.

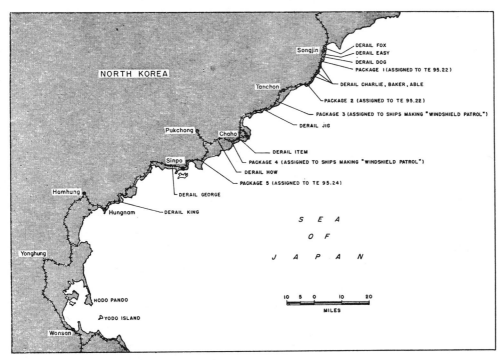

"PACKAGES" AND "DERAILS"

The second program was code-named "derail." The "derail" targets were ones to be kept destroyed solely by naval gunfire. A study of the northeast coast was made, and eleven rail targets chosen.

Like the "packages," the "derail" targets were along the coast, accessible to naval gunfire, and on the main Chongjin to Hungnam railroad. At each "derail," patrolling ships would fire a limited number of shells into them during each 24-hour period.

---

* As the war went on, and the primary work of the carriers of Task Force 77 shifted from interdiction to close air support, "Cherokee" missions and maximum air strikes, the primary responsibility for "Package" became more and more the responsibility of the surface units.

By thus concentrating and coordinating both naval air strikes and naval gun strikes upon the "package" and "derail" targets, it was hoped that the Reds' logistic efforts along the route could be reduced to a trickle—perhaps even brought to a standstill.

Rear Admiral Gingrich Takes Over Task Force 95

The 31st of May 1952 saw the sixth American naval officer take command of Task Force 95. Aboard the USS *Dixie* Rear Admiral John E. Gingrich, USN, relieved Rear Admiral George C. Dyer, USN.

At the time of this change of command, the bombardment and blockade forces of Task Force 95 had been ranging the Korean coasts unchallenged except for coastal gunfire for 23 months. Added to the hundreds of air strikes conducted on the coastal communications by the carriers of Task Force 77 were the hundreds of gun strikes by the surface ships of Task Forces 95 and 77. By now, every worthwhile target within reach of naval gunfire along the enemy-held coast had been repeatedly under siege, and had been hit repeatedly, time and again.

"Reports of destruction, when added together from every source," said Rear Admiral Gingrich,[22] "were such an array of bridges and tunnels, locomotives and trucks, that there was scarcely room in Korea for all of them."

Opportunities for firing at fresh targets were almost non-existent, and there was little reason to waste ammunition on targets that were already untenable or destroyed. In fact, there was some suspicion that the Oriental enemy was purposely planting worthless targets in the oft-shattered areas of northeast Korea simply to invite our ships to waste ammunition on them. Moreover, there was still a great lack of information on precisely what damage our gun strikes were actually achieving.

To Admiral Gingrich, the same conditions which had long existed on the battlefront—stalemate—had now become equally applicable to the war at sea. The war in Korea—in the air, on the ground, and on the seas—was a war of attrition. It seemed to Gingrich that the expenditure of every naval shell had to have some real expectation of damage or it should not be fired. The phase of shooting just to be shooting was over; when targets were ample, it was the only policy an offensive-minded American Navy could follow. Henceforth, thought Gingrich, every bullet and every shell ought to have some Communist's name on it.

"The cost of a 5-inch shell at the end of the Korean pipeline was approximately $200," said Rear Admiral Gingrich. "Unless it did that much damage, we were hurting ourselves more than the enemy."

Moreover, naval gunfire had to be tailored to the target. Five-inch and 3-inch fire was known to be far less effective upon railroad tracks than large caliber fire. The most efficient use of destroyer fire was not to destroy, but to keep the enemy from repairing the track damage. Moreover, rather than shooting in a flat area, it would be better to shoot at the tracks where there were hills and embankments. Any "over" shell which missed the track itself might cause landslides to block the track.

Furthermore, there was little logic in thin-skinned destroyers under the command of "hairy-chested" skippers dueling with enemy coastal batteries simply for the sake of dueling. What gain was there in firing one hundred rounds back at a cavemouth from which a single or half-dozen rounds had been fired? The fire of the Communists was steadily increasing along the coasts in both accuracy and intensity; fuzed projectiles were now being used; some even thought that enemy radar-controlled guns were in evidence. Would the severe damage or even loss of a destroyer be warranted just to silence a single enemy gun manned by perhaps a dozen men?

Gingrich was no less anxious than his predecessors to bring every ounce of his naval strength to bear upon the enemy, but the naval war, he felt, had entered a new phase. If the Korean war was one of attrition, then the UN surface forces must insure that the Communists were more attrited than we.*

The Blockade Pinches

The life of a fisherman in North Korea, even before the war, was a very difficult one. As the farmers had been forced to sell their rice to the Red government at fixed, low prices, so fishermen had to sell their fish at government prices. Quantity quotas were established. If a fisherman met his quota, it was increased. If he did not, his license to fish was revoked. Not long after the war started, the North Korean government enforced a "Fishing Union" which exercised complete control; unless he was a member of the union, a fisherman could not obtain hooks, nets, floats, and other essential equipment.

The northeast coast of Korea was dotted with fishing villages at almost every place where adequate boat shelter could be found. Traditionally, the coastal Koreans rarely bothered with agriculture, and did not maintain rice

---

* By reducing the amount of ammunition fired at night and on harassment missions, and emphasizing ammunition economy, an approximate 50 per cent reduction was made in the amount of ammunition fired:

	July 1952	Oct. 1952
Rounds fired (all sizes):	33,500 (of which	17,069 (of which
Short Tons expended:	2,590.3 32% were	1,451.0 11% were
	unobserved)	unobserved)

The cost of all types ammunition, delivered to the ships in Korea, had been calculated to be $1,940 per short ton. The saving in cost after July 1952 was more than two million dollars per month—and this did not take into account wear and tear on either guns or ships.

paddies. Their dependence upon fish was even more complete than that of the inland Koreans.

The inexorable pressure of the tight naval blockade along the northeast coast made the fisherman's life ever more unbearable. This was evident from the steady stream of escapees and defectors from North Korea. So numerous were the refugees that special UN internee camps had to be established on the islands of Yang-do, near Songjin, and Yo-do, in Wonsan harbor. These two islands became collection points for the hundreds of men, women, and children who left hardships and retaliation by their Communist village overseers, who risked the hazards of the open sea in small boats, who accepted the risk of being mistaken for minelaying personnel while escaping, and who braved these dangers despite the Communists' warning that the Americans automatically killed any North Korean they captured.

The principal reason for so many refugee North Koreans was simply starvation. Fishing had become almost impossible.

Daytime fishing was suicidal because of the carrier and patrol planes and ships patrolling every section of the coast constantly. And at night, when the sampans of a fishing village put out to sea for a catch of pollack or sardines, they could often expect either a warning star shell over their heads, followed by gunfire to drive them ashore, or perhaps an armed whaleboat manned by eager American destroyer or minesweeper sailors, to capture them.

In an effort to break the tight blockade, the Communists organized each coastal village with one or more overseers, who endeavored to prevent the North Koreans from escaping seaward or southward, and who forced the fishermen to fish despite the dangers. The Red procedure was simply to herd the fishermen into their sampans, place guards with machineguns and hand grenades in several of the boats, and at gunpoint, force the fishermen to sea. Any sampan which ventured further than a prescribed distance from the rest of the group was fired upon. On some occasions, entire villages banded together, killed or captured their overseers, and escaped southward by sea en masse.

At some points along the east coast, such as the choice fishing grounds at the island of Mayang-do, the Communists installed radar to warn of the approach of a blockade ship. A system of flashing lights from the radar station would warn the fishermen to return ashore. At other places, warning sirens were installed which howled a warning on the approach of ships. Telephone calls were made from one fishing village to another to warn that a blockade vessel was headed their way.

"The enemy had an excellent alarm system," said Rear Admiral George

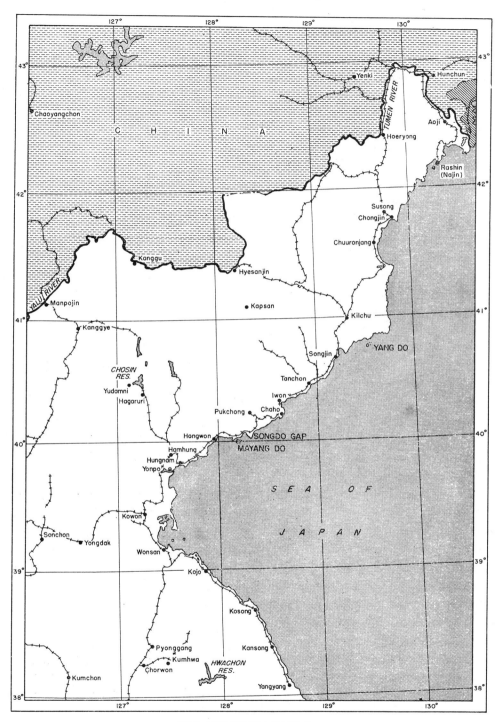

THE TIGHTENING BLOCKADE

C. Dyer. "The east coast of Korea had thousands of Point Lomas and as soon as one of our ships would heave into sight, the word would spread in the vicinity, and the fishermen would head for the beach. Gradually, the enemy built up radar defenses for night alerts against our marauders.

"Rough weather, or weather in which open whaleboats could not operate, limited our operations to about 50 per cent of the days and 35 per cent of the nights.

"It took great intestinal fortitude on the part of our young boat officers and men to engage in this campaign, and it soon separated the men from the boys. The anti-fishing campaign called for the seagoing and small boat talents that were in existence in the earlier days of our Navy."

The flight of civilians from North Korea attested to the success of the anti-fishing campaign. "On 26 September 1952," said CDR A. A. Clark, commanding officer of the USS *Cunningham*, "my ship carried seventy-one refugees south from Yang-do to Yo-do for interview and for further transportation to South Korea.

"Through our ROK naval officers who were aboard for training, we were able to talk to these people, many of whom were women and children—entire families, in fact. These people had been starving, as evidenced by the way they ate the food we prepared on board for them. They also told us that they understood the reason why we had curtailed fishing in North Korea.

"As for my own ship's company, we had lost our feeling of compassion about the hardness of the anti-fishing campaign on the civilian populace when a fishing boat dropped a floating mine for us on 19 September. We sank it with rifle fire."

The blockading ships frequently found small sampans far out at sea, some with only fishermen aboard, some with a single family; and on one occasion, a sampan with a group of young teen-aged boys. Destroyer *Fox* picked up an open boat with three families on 2 May; of the eighteen aboard, nine were women, including five children, aged one to nine. The escapees had planned an escape for three months and had purposely selected the night of the Red May Day celebration to make their way to freedom.

The refugee flow was heaviest during the good weather months. Even so, the hazard of escaping in a small sampan with only six to eight inches of freeboard was great. Whenever refugees were encountered, the blockading vessels took the refugees aboard, hoisted their sampans aboard or took them in tow, and on their next patrol past either Yang-do or Yo-do, sent them ashore to the internee camps for interrogation.

The sailors of the blockade fleet, upon seeing the desperate condition of the refugees, invariably gave them old clothing, food, candy, and money.

Many ships adopted "mascots" and took up collections for the orphanages where some of the younger refugees were taken.

"The internee camp on Yo-do was just to the south of the tiny village of Yodo-ri," said LCDR A. Christopher, intelligence officer of TG 95.2, whose post was on Yo-do island in Wonsan harbor. "It was located on the south side of the air strip, and had the usual barbed wire barricade. The refugees—who averaged 60 to 70 in number—lived in caves which we dug out for them; one cave was a gigantic one which held about 90 people comfortably by Korean standards. These caves were necessary to protect the refugees from the sporadic gunfire which the Communists in Wonsan fired at the air strip.

"Each morning, the KMC* guards ladled out their rations and rice which the refugees cooked themselves. It was my job to interrogate them and to get any useful information they might have. We questioned everybody, including the kids. In fact, one ten-year-old boy told us the location of a mine storage. After interview, the refugees would be transported south to the main camp at Chumunjin.

"From hundreds of interviews of refugees, it was plain that the 'no-fishing' rule had given the Communists extra burdens. The Reds had to try to replace the fish the North Koreans couldn't get with imported fish from Manchuria and China; and because of the battering our planes gave the roads and railroads, this wasn't easy.

"So tight was the naval blockade, in fact, that some of the refugees told me that they had been reduced to eating bark. They couldn't even get fish-hooks. As a consequence, they made fishhooks from the bits of metal they could find. Even so simple an item as cordage was unavailable, and therefore the fishermen had no way to repair their nets. As more and more Koreans escaped, and more and more sampans were demolished by ships' fire, the availability of sampans became acute. One group of fishermen that I interviewed said that the blockade was so tight that they had been reduced to spearing sting-rays to keep from starving."[23]

"Train-Busting"

An elite fraternity of blockade ships was organized in July 1952, called the "Train Busters." To become a member of this exclusive organization, a ship had to receive confirmation of a train's destruction. The first member of the club was the destroyer *Orleck*.

"On July 5th, 1952," wrote CDR E. L. Yates, "my destroyer, the USS *Orleck*, was assigned to the northern patrol—from Yang-do Island to Chong-jin. This run was always made during daylight.

"Our routine instructions required that we provide harassing fire at

* KMC—Korean Marine Corps.

Chongjin, the northern terminus of the patrol. After sending four 6-gun salvos into certain military targets in the town of Chongjin, we headed south to register on and harass some reported shore batteries located on a ridge 13 miles south of Chongjin.

"We opened fire on the batteries while on a southerly course and were turning back north for a second firing run when the batteries opened up on us. Their opening salvo was a straddle at 10,000 yards—amazing accuracy!

"Needless to say, we immediately performed that classic naval maneuver known as 'Getting the Hell out of There'. The enemy guns continued to hold us under fire to an estimated 14,000 yards, but their accuracy diminished rapidly. Inspection of shell fragments, picked up about the decks, indicated that 105- and 155-mm. guns had been used. No damage was sustained and only one man was slightly wounded by a shell fragment. My engineering officer later reported that he was making over 24 knots on two boilers without superheat! This sort of performance in a long-hull destroyer is distinctly frowned on by BuShips.

"Our Patrol Instructions also required that we interdict the 'packages'. The normal procedure was to proceed south from Yang-do, and, on arrival at a 'package,' throw a few rounds in for track damage, then proceed to the next 'package,' and so on to the end of the patrol route; then return to Yang-do.

"In itself, firing at the 'packages' was just another chore. A great many of us had doubts about the value of these bombardments, for we never saw trains in the daytime, nor any lights at night. Yet all the intelligence reports insisted that the rail system was being used at night.

"The 'package' bombardments gave us the idea that by careful planning and preparation, we might catch one of these 'ghost' trains. First of all, we made careful visual inspections of the five 'packages' during daylight from positions as close as safe navigation would permit. We concluded that if we were to trap a train, it could not be done by the rare coincidence of ship and train arriving at the same 'package' at the same time, but rather in the normal manner of catching a train anywhere—just going to the station and waiting for one. And the best time to do so was obviously at night.

"We chose 'Package Two' as our 'station'; the railroad line was within a few hundred feet of the water's edge, and several conspicuous rocks offshore provided excellent radar fixes.

"Setting our train-trap presented a few problems, however. For example, we needed to get as close to the rail-line as possible for both good observation and accurate shooting. But getting closer than 5,000 yards meant that we couldn't use our star shells, because at less than 5,000 yards the parachutes on the illuminating candles were supposed to rip out and drop the flare like a lead balloon. We solved this one by ignoring the BuOrd warning. (It is of interest to note that only about ten per cent of the parachutes failed at 2,500 to 3,000 yards range.)

"Our gunnery problem was solved by designating one 5-inch mount as a destructive mount and the other Condition III 5-inch mount as the illuminating mount. In this manner rapid destructive fire and illumination could be provided with a minimum of flail or warning to enemy observers.

"All methods and techniques having been solved, the *Orleck* on the afternoon of 14 July proceeded from Yang-do on the southern patrol, and arrived at 'Package Two' about sunset. Six or eight registering rounds were fired, and at dusk the *Orleck* continued south into the darkness to return an hour or two later. It was hoped that this feint would lull the track repair crews living in the tunnels into the belief that we wouldn't be back that night.

"On July 15th, the *Orleck* crept in to about 3,000 yards from 'Package Two'. Our topside blowers were secured and the ship was lying quietly to.

"At 0100, the OOD, LT P. H. Klepak, USN, heard the sound of a train approaching from the north. He illuminated immediately and simultaneously opened fire, aiming for the northern tunnel.

"We hit the last car—a caboose—and knocked it athwart the tracks, stopping the train. Further illumination disclosed 15 cars trapped between the tunnels; only the locomotive and tender were able to reach shelter in the southern tunnel.

"The rest of the night was devoted to the systematic and leisurely destruction of this prize: five gondola cars loaded with ten heavy field pieces, a flat car with a tank embarked, and about nine boxcars containing explosives. The exploding of these latter cars made for a completely satisfying night's work.

"Our success that night stirred a competitive spirit between my OOD's— and this competition was 'waiting at the station'—again 'Package Two'—for a train. At 2200, LT Richard P. Carson, USNR, the OOD, spotted a flickering light moving from south to north between the tunnels. He immediately gave orders to illuminate and commence destructive fire. The results were a locomotive, one tender, and one boxcar destroyed. This train was northbound, and the flickering light apparently was from the firebox.

"As a result of these successes we received two very pleasing despatches:

CONGRATULATIONS TO THE DESTROYER ORLECK, TRAIN SMASHER. DESTROYING TWO ENEMY TRAINS IN 12 DAYS IS SUPERB FIGHTING. THE EIGHTH ARMY IS PROUD OF YOU AND YOUR SHIP'S COMPANY. VAN FLEET.

And the second one from Vice Admiral Clark:

CONGRATULATIONS TO THE FIRST OF THE NEW TYPE DE-STROYER TRAIN SMASHER ORLECK. WELL DONE.

"I believe that the destruction of these two trains dispelled any lingering doubts other destroyers may have previously entertained (including ourselves) concerning the nighttime use of the east coast railroad by the Communists. Our own success in this respect was quickly followed by similar successes by other destroyers, and led to the establishment of the 'Trainbusters Club'."*

"The Rails Are Rusty"

Destroyer *Hollister* (DD-788, CDR Hugh W. Howard, USN) was in several scrapes in July 1952, and generally could call herself a lucky ship.

"This was *Hollister*'s second cruise in Korea," wrote Howard,[24] "having been in action from Inchon to Hungnam in 1950-1951. On the first cruise I had had a veteran crew. On the second I had almost a new complement, except the leading petty officers. I also had fourteen new ensigns. However, the entire crew was an eager lot.

"On Thursday, 10 July, we were proceeding along the Hodo Pando-Hungnam-Cha-ho route—we called this area 'The Boulevard'—when we were suddenly taken under accurate enemy gunfire. We responded with counter-battery fire, going to twenty-five knots and making smoke. As we fired, we weaved in towards shore, presenting both a small deflection target and a fast-changing target in range. Then we retired through our smoke, using our after battery in indirect fire. We counted thirty-two splashes around us,

* The "Trainbusters Club" of Task Force 95 was organized in July 1952 by Captain H. E. Baker, CTF-95's operations officer. (Many ships which had destroyed trains before this date were not included.) The following is the list of members of the "Trainbusters Club" and the number of trains credited (not claimed) to each ship as determined by TF 95 records:

1. HMCS *Crusader*	4 trains	11. USS *Trathen*	1
2. USS *Endicott*	3	12. USS *Eversole*	1
3. USS *Orleck*	2	13. USS *Kyes*	1
4. HMCS *Haida*	2	14. USS *Chandler*	1
5. HMCS *Athabaskan*	2	15. USS *McCoy Reynolds*	1
6. USS *Pierce*	2	16. Hr. Ms. *Piet Hein* (LCDR Jonkheer H. de Jonge van El-lemeet)	1
7. HMS *Charity*	2		
8. USS *Porter*	1	17. USS *Carmick*	1
9. USS *Jarvis*	1	18. USS *Maddox*	1
10. USS *Boyd*	1		

   TOTAL: ....28 trains

Each ship whose gunfire had destroyed a train was presented a certificate which read: "For her contribution to the United Nation's cause against Communist aggression by destroying—Communist train(s). In recognition of a job well done CTF-95."

some of them close enough to soak our bridge, but there were no casualties.

"That night we returned and bombarded Mayang-do and Hongwan. During the bombardment we noted an unidentified blip on the radar screen slowly closing us in the vicinity of Mayang-do. We approached cautiously with our depth charge K-guns manned to protect against small craft treachery. Out of the darkness we could make out a sampan, and we closed it. The armed guard on our deck threw grappling irons over, and in moments we had three prisoners.

"The three were only youths about 16 years old. We took them into our head, scrubbed them, put them into dungarees, and then turned them into a temporary 'brig' we had rigged in the boatswain's locker forward. With the aid of our ship's artist, who made sketches of mines, guns, caves, troops, pillboxes, etc., we extracted the information that there were five guns secreted in caves firing at the *Hollister,* and that these guns were fitted onto tracks and could be rolled out for firing, and rolled back into the caves for protection.

"Having this information, and in the spirit of ingenuity and initiative urged by Admiral Gingrich, I asked for volunteers to form a landing party. Following the drawing of straws, the selection was narrowed down to one officer and five men, one of whom was my quartermaster, Buckmaster. The officer was young Ensign J. W. Kline, USNR. Kline had developed a theory during all our interdiction fire at the east coast rail line. If we could only have a *look* at the rails, Kline said, and if they were *rusty,* we could save a lot of ammunition. His theory sounded logical to me.

"They immediately started to get their equipment ready, including a rubber boat, a radar reflector (which they made from a five-gallon milk can), a walkie-talkie radio, and a compass. Using this makeshift equipment, we would be able to vector the rubber boat into the beach.

"At 2000 we were off Hongwan. There was no moon, and as the recon party in the rubber boat departed the *Hollister* and headed into the beach only 1,500 yards away, I told them I would return at 2400 to pick them up in the same spot. We shoved off to do some bombardment farther north, while they headed into the harbor of Hongwan.

"On the dot of 2400, I had the *Hollister* back at the assigned rendezvous, but there was not a pip on our scopes and there was complete quiet ashore. I have never gone through three more agonizing hours as that long wait offshore, lying-to and fearful of dawn, yet not willing to leave my men.

"At about 0230, after what seemed hours, a small pip finally appeared on the radar scope which indicated that a target was closing us from the shore. As the target came closer we challenged it, and to our great relief they answered. I went to the quarterdeck as the party came alongside. With a sickened heart I suddenly realized there were only *four* men in the rubber boat. Kline and my quartermaster were missing.

"Meanwhile, my radar operators reported another pip slowly closing the ship from the north. We immediately locked on this target ready to open fire. As it came closer, we could make out a sampan, from which an apparition rose, calling out not to shoot. It was Ensign Kline and the quartermaster. In the darkness they had become separated from the others, but Kline came back with his answer. 'The rails are rusty,' he proclaimed.

"In addition the raiding party established the location of lines of prepared trenches and pillboxes, spotted a new sampan anchorage, and discovered the existence of an antiboat boom.

"This raid made a crew out of my ship overnight."

Reporting this raid to Commander Task Force 95, Admiral Gingrich informed *Hollister* that such a raid wasn't a normal part of a blockading destroyer's duties.

On the 13th of July, *Hollister* again was taken under fire near Sinch'ant by three guns which made 108 splashes near the destroyer. *Hollister*'s answering fire scored a direct hit on one gun and silenced the other two. As before, the *Hollister* went unscathed.

Two days later, again at Mayang-do, *Hollister* was taken under fire for the fourth time in less than a week. Again the enemy's fire was very close, but again the *Hollister* suffered no hits.

Despite the repeated bracketing by enemy gunfire, the *Hollister* did not qualify for combat pay, as a ship had to be taken under fire *six* times in a period of a month in order to make the grade.

"We joked about our failure to qualify for combat pay," said Howard, "as it appeared that the Communists had read the AlNav and deliberately ceased fire after the fifth day just to thwart us!"

Package One Blocked For Twelve Days

Shortly after midnight on 12 October, 1952, the USS *Walker* (DDE-517, CDR M. C. Walley, USN) patrolling at Package Two, received the following message by voice radio from HMS *Charity* at Package One:

"Have succeeded in stopping train, but need assistance as I am almost out of star shells."

Steaming northward at high speed, the *Walker* joined the British destroyer, which was also experiencing difficulties with her fire control system.

"Since there was only a single track rail line from the Manchurian border to Hungnam," said Walley,[25] "it was apparent that if we could keep this line blocked, nothing could move by rail in either direction. We therefore set about damaging the caboose and engine ends of the train sufficiently to prevent its removal, and attempted, with only minor success, to cut the track ahead and astern of the train. We also maintained harassing fire to prevent repair crews from working.

"After a couple days of this, the *Iowa* (CAPT J. W. Cooper, USN) showed up and we asked that she cut the roadbed for us. This she accomplished quickly and effectively with her 16-inch high-capacity shells. She also hit the locomotive, and dished out a huge hunk of that from the boiler. Returning strikes from Task Force 77, which had unexpended ordnance, were also sent over for our control to assist in maintaining the block.

"During daylight hours the *Walker* lay offshore at a range of 7,000 to 8,000 yards and from time to time lobbed in a shell or two to harass the enemy repair crew as much as possible. In their white clothing they were plainly visible to us.

"One day during this period, my junior officer of the watch, Ensign Dennis O'Connor, got an idea how we might harass the Reds and hold up the work without even firing a shot. O'Connor had noticed that whenever we fired a round, the repair crews would scamper for shelter even before the shell hit. Obviously the Reds had a lookout posted, who, as soon as he saw the flash of our gun, sounded a warning to the repair crew so that in the approximate ten seconds it took for the projectile to reach the tracks and explode, the repair crews had taken cover. So, O'Connor asked my permission to light off our 24-inch searchlight, and I said, 'O.K.'

"We all lined the bridge with binoculars to see what would happen. Sure enough, as O'Connor trained the searchlight in their direction and snapped the shutter open and shut, the repair crews dropped their shovels and ran like hell. Of course, we had a big laugh, and after that it became standard practice for us to use the searchlight every now and then just to save firing a shell. Package One was thus blocked for twelve full days.

"At night the *Walker* moved in to the 100-fathom curve, about 2,500 yards off shore, while another ship would lie-to farther out and furnish illumination fire. This hampered but did not completely stop the Communists' effort to clear the tracks.

"After about a week, apparently realizing that they were not going to roll the cars away, the Communists began doing what we had carefully avoided all this time—one by one the railroad cars were dynamited clear out of the roadbed, and in a few more nights the track was cleared and patched and the 'Red Ball' express was rolling again."

Communist Coastal Defenses

The steady increase in the number of coastal defense guns which the enemy employed in North Korea gave evidence of the effect of the blockade and bombardment effort. If the attacks were *not* wreaking damage and slowing the movement of supplies, why should the Communists bother? The expense of building gun emplacements, the cost of ammunition, the drain of personnel, all added to the enemy's burdens.

More and more often the rocky coasts of North Korea were to see coastal guns installed at points where the roads and rail lines were exposed, or where amphibious attacks might come in. These guns were cleverly placed and almost impervious to gun attack.

Caves were dug in the face of the cliffs either from the front or from the reverse side of the hill. Usually the caves were in groups of three, although single caves were fairly common. The openings were small, only large enough to give the gun a reasonably wide arc of fire, and in no case larger than eight feet square. The entrances of these caves were usually covered with yellow-green cloths, tree limbs, or woven mats—or, in the time of snowfall, by white drop cloths. As a result the entrances were difficult to see, and even more difficult to hit. In fact, the expenditure of ammunition on them rarely succeeded in more than superficial damage.

Most of the guns in these caves were simple field artillery pieces, 75-mm. or 105-mm. On other occasions, tank guns and self-propelled guns were used by the Communists. In a few instances, the wheels would be removed from artillery pieces and the pieces secured on railroad flatcars. The flatcars would then be wheeled into a nearby tunnel until ready for use.

The Third Year

The third year of war, which began 25 June 1952, found the blockade and bombardment operations more standard and routine than ever, but nonetheless arduous and dangerous. Enemy shore-battery fire increased in accuracy as well as amount. The Communists' ability to score hits on our ships at slow speeds and at close range showed steady improvement.

On the ground in Korea, both the Communists and UN forces were digging ever deeper into caves, bunkers, and trenches, laying minefields and stringing barbed wire. Little movement of the frontlines had been seen in over a year, and fighting was largely confined to small-sized but bloody clashes.

At Panmunjom, under a drab circus tent, the UN and Red truce teams remained deadlocked on the thorny problem of prisoner exchange. There was little prospect for a truce; and in fact, the truce talks were recessed in October 1952 for nearly seven months.

Ships of the U. S. Navy were completing their second and third tours of duty in Korean waters, many of them having accumulated eighteen or more

WOODEN BOW AND IRON MEN. The destroyer *Mansfield* also lost her bow to an enemy mine off Wonsan, but safely reached a U. S. port with this jury-rigged wooden substitute. *Below,* the flight deck of a carrier in flames in the crash of a plane. Fire fighters quickly extinguished the blaze, and there were no personnel injuries.

MEMENTOES OF BATTLE. *At top,* RADM James H. Doyle congratulates winners of the Silver Star aboard cruiser *Rochester.* These four had been cox'ns of LCVPs for Inchon. Left to right: Chancey H. Vogt, Seaman; William H. Ragan, Seaman; Richard P. Vinson, Engineman-Fireman; Paul J. Gregory, Seaman Apprentice. *Bottom left,* First Class Metalsmiths W. N. Cox and A. L. Collett measure plugged shell hole in bow of destroyer *Collett,* hit during the Wolmi-do Island attack. *Bottom right,* destroyer *Brush,* first U. S. warship damaged by Korean mine, on fire.

THE ADMIRAL COMES ASHORE. VADM Robert P. Briscoe, commander of Naval Forces Far East, with MAJGEN John T. Selden, USMC, and BGEN Clayton C. Jerome, USMC. *Below*, VADM A. D. Struble and MAJGEN E. L. Almond, USA, at Tenth Corps Headquarters, Korea.

SENIOR NAVAL OFFICERS MEET. *At top,* ADM Forrest P. Sherman, Chief of Naval Operations; ADM Arthur W. Radford, commander in chief, Pacific, VADM Turner Joy, commander, Naval Forces Far East, and CDR Michael J. Luosey, Commander ROK Naval Forces, meet at the Pusan air strip. *Below,* Navy CAPT Morse explains map of Iwon to MAJGEN D. G. Barr, USA, COL Joseph J. Twitty, USA, and LT M. M. Boynton, USN.

months in the theater. An unlucky few ships would spend their fourth Christmas in Korean waters. Personnel aboard ships who had served one previous tour numbered more than seventy-five per cent; and one quarter of the officers and men of the American Navy in Korea had seen *three* full tours in the battle zone. A measure of relief had been introduced as Atlantic Fleet ships appeared for combat service more frequently.

Action reports and war diaries of this period reveal the routine nature of the naval war. Many entries in war diaries simply read, "No Comment," and a few action reports state, "Nothing to report." The feelings of many were summarized by the skipper of *De Haven* (CDR T. C. Siegmund): "We had learned to live with an unsatisfactory situation and still do a good job, no matter how dull it was."

Even the enemy occasionally took a callous and indifferent attitude toward the war. Night-heckling pilots occasionally reported that despite their attacks on truck convoys, the drivers would not extinguish their lights. Ships firing at Wonsan reported the same thing.

The tedium and monotony, however, did not diminish the stringency of the blockade.

The increasing coastal fire from the Communists—which doubled from July 1952 to January 1953—had two immediate results: first, ships increased their patrolling speeds, changed their courses more frequently, and opened their patrolling range to the beach; secondly, ships tried to make sure that every shell fired was a winner. The enemy seemed to have very few radar-controlled *coastal* guns,* which meant that in nighttime, blockading ships could move closer ashore for their intercepting and gunnery efforts, with far less danger from enemy counterbatteries.

The oft-tried tactic of manning a whaleboat with a reconnaissance party, and dispatching it close aboard the designated beach for target observation, still paid dividends from time to time. The whaleboat crews would lie to, waiting, watching, and listening for trains, maintaining communications to the parent ship by walkie-talkie radio.

In many instances they were successful. The effort on 14-15 August 1952 by destroyers *Jarvis* (DD-799) and *Porter* (DD-800) was typical. In this case, in addition to whaleboat parties, the two destroyers were assisted by a ROK torpedo boat. Lying approximately 3,000 yards offshore south of the Songjin area, *Porter* succeeded in damaging two trains while *Jarvis* was getting one.

The sailors of the U. S. Navy, in their ships off Korea, had little to com-

---

* However, the Communists were making increasing use of influence-fuzed shells. It should be noted, moreover, that the enemy was equipped with radar-controlled *AA* guns.

plain about in comparison with their countrymen in the trenches and dugouts of Korea. At sea, at least there were no fleas, no flies, no bunker life. Still, while there was less danger of injury or death than during the Pacific war, and little to be feared from enemy aircraft or submarine torpedoes, the sailormen had an irritating, uncomfortable, and unpleasant existence.

When in range of enemy guns, ships stayed "buttoned up" and personnel were forbidden to expose themselves topside. During the hot summers of Korea, temperatures below decks were stifling, and rest was impossible for the many who found the irregular gunfire too regular for sleeping. The constant jarring of the gunfire caused the glass wool insulation of many ships' overheads to shake loose; no one could sleep in the top bunks from the irritating effect of the glass fibers.

Winters in Korean waters brought the chill and biting Siberian winds, heavy seas, and sub-zero temperatures. Ships' superstructures were frozen beneath tons of ice, locking the forward mounts in azimuth and freezing depth charges in their racks. The icy wind had such a razor's bite that refueling and replenishment often took place on a down-wind course.

But to most of the sailormen, worse than either the blistering summer heat or the biting winter cold was the tedious routine of the war.

The destroyers assigned to Task Force 95 could predict the statistics of a tour in Korean waters with precision: a typical tour would require 110 underway replenishments; the average ship would burn more than 3,000,000 gallons of fuel oil while in the theater. And it would see the expenditure of an average of 2,360 5-inch rounds and 1,341 3-inch rounds.

The endless siege of Wonsan, Hungnam, and Songjin went on and on. Ships patrolled "Taillight," "Engineblock," and "Windshield" day after day after day. Minesweepers in Wonsan made another circuit of "Muffler," and the minesweeps at Songjin went round the harbor once again. The airgun "Cobra" strikes increased.

In this manner, 1953 arrived.

Finale

In January of 1953, a bitterly cold month at sea, six American ships* were taken under fire by Communist batteries, but none was hit. On 27 January one destroyer reported tracking a "skunk" by radar for nearly an hour and a half with plotted speeds as high as twenty-five knots. Did the Communists at last plan to oppose the strangling blockade with torpedo boats?

February 12, 1953 saw the seventh change in Commander Task Force 95

---

* USS *Merganser* (AMS-26); USS *Firecrest* (AMS-10); USS *Pelican* (AMS-32); USS *Colahan* (DD-650); USS *Waxwing* (AM-389); USS *Kidd* (DD-661).

as Rear Admiral Clarence E. Olsen relieved Rear Admiral John E. Gingrich.*

A change was also made in the Task Force 95 organization. Hereafter, the cruiser division commander serving with Task Force 77 as CTG 77.1 would also have additional duty as CTG 95.2, relieving the destroyer squadron commander who had performed this duty.

At the armistice conference table, meanwhile, the peace talks were still suspended. Liaison officers met occasionally, but neither side was willing to alter its position.

At sea, the blockading ships increased their activity as winter relaxed its grip.

On 6 March, the destroyer *Laws* (DD-558), near Hungnam, joined hands with Task Force 77's airplanes to damage several railroad cars despite heavy enemy counterbattery fire. Five days later, *Trathen's* (DD-530) guns damaged several rail cars of a train near Package Four. The Red engineer detached his locomotive from the train and fled into the closest tunnel.

As March passed, and the muddy and slippery roads of Korea dried out, patrolling ships reported increasing numbers of truck convoys along the coastal road. Approximately 500 vehicles were seen on the night of 15-16 March. They were taken under fire, but no estimate of damage could be made.

Along with the enemy's increased coastal defense fire and truck activity, the mine activity increased too. USS *Epperson* (DDE-719) was able to sink five in one day.

The advancing spring saw two ships—one American, one Canadian—clobber trains. HMCS *Crusader* shelled and stopped three trains at Package Three on 15 April. USS *Endicott* (DMS-35) got three out of four on 11 May, also at Package Three.

April saw a sharp upturn in the enemy's counterbattery fire, especially in the vicinity of Wonsan. Four American ships were hit during this month: *Los Angeles, Manchester, Maddox,* and *Kyes.*

For the remainder of the war, destroyer *James E. Kyes* (DD-787, CDR R. A. Thacher) was to receive more than her share of enemy attention. She first reported being shot at near Songjin on 16 March. Ten days later, in the same area, *Kyes* was again taken under fire, this time escaping damage from some fifty rounds of fire. Two days later, accompanying sweeper *Waxbill* near Hungnam, *Kyes* observed ten splashes in their vicinity.

By now the Communists should have learned that American destroyers

---

* The seven CTF 95 commanders in their order of service were (1) RADM C. C. Hartman, (2) RADM A. E. Smith, (3) VADM W. G. Andrewes, R. N., (4) RADM A. E. Smith, (5) RADM G. C. Dyer, (6) RADM J. E. Gingrich, (7) RADM C. E. Olsen.

can be pushed too far. On 1 April, *Kyes* loaded her boat with a reconnaissance party and dispatched them to the area of Cha-ho to watch and listen for trains. Sure enough, one was spotted, but it was in such a position that *Kyes'* guns could not bear. Rather than let the train escape, *Kyes* contacted a night-heckling Fifth Air Force B-26 and vectored him to the area. *Kyes'* initiative was rewarded by hearing the Air Force pilot report "several boxcars destroyed."

April 4 saw *Kyes* under fire again, this time near the island of Mayang-do. *Kyes* got even on the 18th, near Cha-ho, and fired at an enemy train. The enemy's counterbattery fire was rapid and more accurate than usual, and *Kyes* was forced to open range. She would return.

On 17 May, in company with USS *Brush* (DD-745), *Kyes* supported a ROK raiding party above the battleline near Kojo. The ROK troops reported the destruction of two automatic weapons and fourteen sampans.

But *Kyes* did her best night's work on the 19th of May while in company with *Eversole* (DD-789). At Cha-ho, where enemy guns had fired upon her so often and *Kyes* herself had fired at trains several times, *Kyes* and *Eversole* at last succeeded in hitting and stopping a nocturnal train. Illuminating the area with 128 star shells, the two destroyers pumped 418 rounds of 5-inch shells into the doomed train.

This time there could be no doubt of a train's complete destruction.

In late April, at long last, there was a break in the armistice talks, and on the 20th, the exchange of sick and wounded prisoners commenced in "Operation Little Switch."

This break in the negotiations reflected a new atmosphere regarding a truce. To all concerned, it was now apparent that under the imposed political and military limitations, the present two-year stalemate in Korea could not be broken, except at prohibitive cost and the full-fledged extension of the war to the mainland, and perhaps even the use of atomic weapons. Otherwise the war in Korea might continue indefinitely. One GI summarized the conflict in these succinct but bitter words: "The war we can't win, we can't lose, we can't quit."

It was obvious that the Chinese could never win, and it was equally obvious that unless and until the UN changed the framework of its fighting, neither could the UN.

For psychological reasons, however, the Chinese wanted to give the impression that *they* were winning the war during the last few days. The Chinese high command ordered an intensification of the fighting everywhere to create this illusion.

Accordingly, pressure at the frontlines increased, and the Chinese made several herculean efforts to penetrate the UN main line of resistance. At one or two points in the First Marine Division sector, the Communists succeeded in gaining some terrain of little value but at fantastic cost to themselves—16,300 killed or wounded and 81 prisoners taken. Since the objectives themselves were certainly not worth this blood, it was concluded that by these pyrrhic victories the Chinese would claim that the UN was signing an armistice in order to keep them from "winning" the war.

Along the coasts, the enemy's coastal gunfire increased in intensity and accuracy, keeping pace with the activity at the front. Patrolling ships were equally aggressive in matching this enemy fire. The USS *Chandler* (DD-717), assisted by USS *Wiltsie* (DD-716), did her part by destroying one train near Tanchon on 3 June.

At Hungnam, on 12 June, while *Manchester* (CL-83) and the USS *Carpenter* (DDE-825) were bombarding harbor targets, sixteen rounds of enemy fire were observed.

On the 25th of June (the third anniversary of the war), near Tanchon, the USS *Gurke* (DD-783) was taken under fire by heavy enemy guns. Two direct hits and several minor ones were received. Fortunately, no one was killed and only three minor personnel casualties were received.

On the morning of 8 July, ten miles south of Songjin, the USS *Irwin* (DD-794, CDR G. M. Slonim) took a shrapnel explosion in her mainmast from an estimated 80 rounds, which seriously wounded Captain Jack Maginnis (Commander Destroyer Squadron 24) and four other personnel. All electrical and electronic cables on the mast were cut.*

During this final period, the battleship *New Jersey* supported by heavy cruisers *Saint Paul* and *Bremerton* and light cruiser *Manchester,* plus twelve destroyers, stood guard at the east coast bombline. It was the first appearance of a battleship for naval gunfire support at the bombline since *Iowa* in October 1952.

The sixteen ships rotated in three groups (CTU 95.28, 77.1.8, and 77.1.9) at the bombline to give constant support to the eastern anchor of the line. Thirteen thousand rounds of 5-inch, 2,800 rounds of 8-inch, 700 rounds of 6-inch, and 1,774 rounds of 16-inch were poured into enemy positions during the last two months of the war.†

---

* CAPT Maginnis was the senior U. S. naval officer wounded in the Korean War. He was transferred to the *Manchester* and thence to Japan for a series of three operations. He has since returned to active duty.

† After absorbing this punishing naval gunfire for more than three years, the Communists finally developed a tactic which was occasionally and partially successful. First, they discovered and listened in on the ship-shore circuits. As the ships sang out "On the way," the Communist artillerymen would open fire on the UN observation posts in order to keep the spotters' heads down and prevent them from seeing the fall of shells of the ships' fire and thereby correct it.

A large part of the credit for preventing the enemy's frantic efforts to advance along the east coast during the final days of the war was due the naval sharpshooters. When the demarcation line was finally set, there was a definite northward curve on the east coast where the battleline was ahead of the rest of the front.

Vice Admiral Briscoe congratulated the bombarding fleet on 19 June: "Your straight shooting of the past 12 days will not soon be forgotten by the enemy. You knocked him off Anchor Hill, ripped up his frontlines and supply routes, and added another chapter to the lesson that the way of the aggressor is hard."

Thus the longest blockade and bombardment effort ever imposed by the U. S. Navy came to an end.

Significance

The revised "Functions of the Armed Forces and the Joint Chiefs of Staff" assign, as one of the *primary* functions of the Navy, this duty:

> A.1(a) To seek out and destroy enemy naval forces and to suppress enemy sea commerce.

A *collateral* function of the Navy reads as follows:

> B.1. To interdict enemy land and air power and communications through operations at sea.

Any study of the blockading efforts of the United States Navy in Korea must conclude that the naval blockade imposed during the Korean War was both effective and successful. Three of the enemy's five main supply lines were blocked. (1) his deep-water shipping along the east coast; (2) his shallow-water coastal shipping on the west coast; (3) his deep-water shipping routes to the Asiatic seaport cities in China, Manchuria, and North Korea. The enemy was denied the use of the sea for military movements, for the transportation of supplies, and for fishing. In normal times, thousands of junks and numerous steamers moved hundreds of thousands of tons of supplies by sea. The imposed naval blockade of the UN was almost 100 per cent effective. Only an exceedingly small trickle of sea traffic—and that coastal and nocturnal—succeeded in escaping the tight barricade thrown around the peninsula.

This blockade was imposed, however, under very special circumstances, and any conclusions based on the blockading operations in Korea must take into account the almost total absence of enemy air opposition and active enemy naval opposition. Had either or both of these elements been introduced, a totally different blockading operation would have resulted. The siege of the ports of Wonsan, Songjin, and Hungnam might not have been continuous. To have imposed a blockade against vigorous enemy air and submarine opposition would have required many times the numbers of vessels that Task Force 95 was operating. However, even against enemy air and naval opposition, a naval blockade could have been established and made effective, although it doubtlessly would not have been as airtight as was the case, and it would have been infinitely more costly to both Chinese and American forces. Certainly, the pattern and tempo of operations, the weapons used, and the area of operation would have been much different. This blockade had further significance because of the fact that it was the first blockade applied by the U. S. Navy since the Civil War. The British had established a blockade in World War I, and the U. S. Navy had assisted. But this effort was relatively minor and passive. The blockade of the Korean peninsula, therefore, gave the U. S. Navy training and experience for the application of a blockade in other areas.

The effectiveness of the naval blockade, and the enemy's failure to oppose it actively, opened both the Korean coasts for the application of a bombardment and interdiction effort which had known no similar parallel in American naval history. Naval gunfire, designed primarily to attack targets at sea and to support amphibious landings, was given three novel roles: (1) the support of fixed positions at the battlefront (as contrasted with the fluid targets of an amphibious assault); (2), the task of securing both flanks of the UN battleline; (3) the interdiction of rail and road lines along the northeast coast.

The first of these tasks was performed in a highly creditable manner. At every stage of the war, the accuracy and volume of naval gunfire (even at maximum ranges) given to support friendly frontline positions elicited the highest praise from both U. S. Army and the U. S. Marines, and, for the most part, compared most favorably with artillery fire. The devastating effect of the naval seaborne artillery was indicated by the fact that near the coast, the UN frontlines were invariably ahead of the main line of advance.

Generally speaking, the greater the caliber of the naval gun, the greater its effectiveness upon enemy targets at the frontline. If further proof was needed, the 16-inch guns of *Iowa, Missouri, Wisconsin,* and *New Jersey* demonstrated that pound for pound they were the most efficient rifles in the Korean War. While no effective liaison or standard doctrine existed between the Army and the Navy for the use or control of naval gunfire in the first part of the war, these were quickly established, and proved to be effective for the duration. In the words of Rear Admiral Allan E. Smith, the first commander of the "United Nations Blockading and Escort Force," "There were no ready communications between ships and troops in the initial phases because of the prewar attitude that amphibious landings were antiquated and naval gunfire obsolete."[26]

Had the UN forces on the ground been engaged in an offensive war of movement rather than a sit-down war of stalemate, the pattern of naval blockade effort might have been different and the contributions of the blockade forces greater. It was the opinion of Rear Admiral A. K. Scott-Moncrieff, RN, the British west coast blockade commander, that a more aggressive blockade policy, heavily pointed and sustained over 7- to 10-day periods, might have caused the enemy more inconvenience than a steady tempo of operations along both coasts. Admiral Scott-Moncrieff also opined that the UN's failure to make additional amphibious landings had enabled the enemy to build up his defenses all along the coasts, possibly liberating a number of troops.[27] A more offensive blockade policy could not have been taken independently of the ground action, however, but would have been related to offensive action on the ground and in the air as well.

Whether or not naval gunfire could have been as effective or as much used in the face of enemy air and surface opposition must remain a moot question. More active enemy opposition would undoubtedly have expedited the development and use of sea-to-shore missiles fired from distant ranges. The excellent gunfire support supplied by the battleships under the existing artificial conditions in Korea was not sufficient to warrant retention of large rifled guns in the U. S. Navy.

The second task given naval gunfire—security of the flanks—was one of the most important contributions made by the naval blockade forces. "Never in history," said Rear Admiral Allan Smith, "has an Army had its flanks so firmly secured as in the Korean War by our Navy. In March 1951, Admiral Struble and I visited General Ridgway in Taegu. His subordinate generals had kept telling him that the enemy could outflank our western front troop line because of the shallow waters and sometimes dry land. He was assured that our Navy would *not* let this happen; and Ridgway replied that he would give the matter no more concern.

"This mobile artillery and naval air power on both flanks enabled our Army commander to concentrate his strength where such would put the greatest pressure on the enemy. Imagine an Army commander being relieved of concern about his flanks!"[28]

Regarding the third novel task, the collateral one of interdiction, the Navy did *not* succeed in denying either the east coast rail or road systems to the enemy despite the most intense, prolonged, and ingenious efforts to do so. As described in the chapter, "The Struggle to Strangle," neither could the air attacks on the UN's air forces. At no time during the course of the war did either the UN's surface or air interdiction efforts succeed in stopping the flow of enemy supplies from Manchuria to the front to a decisive degree. The gun strikes of the ships of Task Forces 77 and 95 hampered, hurt, and harassed, it is true; but they had neither direct nor decisive effect upon the course of the ground fighting in Korea.

The significance of this failure is to point up the need for balanced forces in the U. S. military establishment. Assuming that the war *had* to be confined to the peninsula, there was only one way to have stopped the steady and constant movement of enemy trains and trucks within North Korea: the physical occupation of the ground, and physical force applied by armed men attacking and holding the routes themselves. Because of the terrain, paucity of suitable targets, and character of the enemy, it is doubted that even the local use of atomic weapons could have isolated the battle-front of Korea.

10.

The PatRons

Introduction

The first-syllable-accented word "patron" is defined in the dictionary as an "upholder" or "supporter." While this word has no direct connection to the naval aviation term "PatRon," (an amalgamation of the two words "Patrol" and "Squadron"), it haply has an indirect relationship in meaning.

Operations by the Navy's patrol squadrons in the Korean War, like those of the submarines and the Service Force, were usually neither glamorous nor newsworthy. Rather, the PatRons were the upholders and supporters of the Korean War. The routine tasks and accomplishments they performed in the Far East were more important and essential in a negative or defensive sense than in a positive or offensive sense. To naval strategists during war, negative information is as vital as positive information. There are *no* enemy ships in the area, there are *no* typhoons or other weather reported which will interfere with the blockade, carrier operations, or an amphibious operation. There is *no* evidence of fishing or mining activities. The enemy is *not* concentrating his shipping forces for an invasion of Formosa.

Such essential information was supplied by the patrol squadrons throughout the Korean War despite weather, night, or the constant danger of enemy fighter opposition.

One of the major duties performed by the patrol squadrons during the Korean War was the careful and constant surveillance they kept over Formosa. In the physical sense, the Seventh Fleet, charged with that island's protection, could not be in two places at once. In the strategic sense, however, it *could* be, thanks to the PatRons. The ceaseless flights of the patrol squadrons droning back and forth through the Formosan Straits made it impossible for the Chinese to attack Formosa so quickly or unexpectedly that the Seventh Fleet could not speed from Korean waters to its defense.

In Korea proper, the flights of the patrol squadrons added to the effective naval blockade. One of the primary missions was the surveillance and photography of merchant shipping. North Korean fishing efforts were constantly under observation by the patrol squadrons. The mere presence of the VP squadrons in the area was a deterrent to the enemy against any use of submarines. Additionally, the weather reconnaissance flights on behalf of the carrier forces, the search for and destruction of mines, and flare-dropping flights were missions whereby the PatRons contributed to the Navy's over-all effort in Korea.

This chapter records the vital part played in the Korean War by the Navy's patrol squadrons, land and sea.

Division of Patrol Squadron Operations

For ease of understanding and explanation, patrol squadron operations during the Korean War are divided into two areas according to the geography of the operating zone in the Far East—Korea and Formosa.

In the Korean area, one Fleet Air Wing staff was assigned to control the three to five squadrons, plus tenders, based in the Japanese-Korean area (usually three land-based squadrons and two seaplane squadrons).

To protect Formosa, another Fleet Air Wing, consisting of one land-based squadron, one seaplane squadron, and one tender, was assigned to control patrol squadron operations in that area.

Fleet Air Wing Six was the patrol squadron command in the Japanese-Korean area, while Fleet Air Wing One was the staff controlling patrol operations in the Formosan Straits.

Korea: Organization of the PatRons

When the war began, there were 8 patrol-type airplanes in the immediate area of Korea: five PBM Mariner seaplanes from Patrol Squadrons 46 (LCDR M. F. Weisner) and 47 (CDR J. H. Arnold) operating from the Naval Air Facility, Yokosuka, supported by a detachment of Fleet Aircraft Service Squadron 119, and 3 additional VP-46 aircraft at Sangley Point, Philippine Islands. There was no Fleet Air Wing staff, no tender, and no land-based aircraft in the immediate area of Korea. VP-46 was in the process of relieving VP-47. During its 6-months' tour in the Far East, VP-47 had also maintained detachments of aircraft at Hong Kong and, occasionally, at Buckner Bay, Okinawa.

On 25 June 1950, Patrol Squadron 47, having completed its normal half-year's tour, was just being relieved. Three of its homeward-bound planes were already at Pearl Harbor, a fourth was at Guam, and a fifth was in the air between Guam and Hawaii. These aircraft were hurriedly recalled and ordered to report to Yokosuka. By 7 July, Arnold's squadron had reassembled and was in action.

One of this squadron's first tasks, commencing 15 July, was the antisubmarine coverage of the convoy travelling from Japan to Pohang to make the amphibious landing of the First Cavalry Division at that point. Another of its early missions was to assist the U. S. Air Force in the rescue of aviators in Korean waters.

Upon the transfer of the Seventh Fleet to General MacArthur's operational control, a detachment of Fleet Air Wing One (based in Guam) was established in Japan. Captain John C. Alderman, Fleet Air Wing One's chief of staff (who happened to be on leave in Japan), was given command of this detachment. This temporary command was known as Fleet Air Wing One Detachment, Japan. Assigned to assist Alderman in the subsequent hectic days of July were CDR D. C. Higgins, CDR D. J. Omeara, LCDR J. L. Burge, LT W. E. Davis, and LT J. B. Black. Alderman's tasks were not only to operate the patrol aircraft assigned to him, but also to take care of all other naval aviation matters of supply and logistics in the Korean area.

By 12 July, thanks to the arrival of Rear Admiral R. W. Ruble, USN, Commander Carrier Division Fifteen, and his staff, it was possible to reorganize and expand the naval air organization. A new command, Naval Air Japan, was established. As best it could, this interim staff dealt with the ever-rapidly increasing demands being made upon naval air for support and coverage.

On the 4th of August 1950, Fleet Air Wing Six was commissioned. This wing would operate and control the patrol squadrons in Korea in lieu of Fleet Air Wing One Detachment, Japan. Fleet Air Wing Six was given control of all American and British patrol squadrons operating in the Japanese-Korean area.

By 9 August 1950, Rear Admiral George R. Henderson, Captain W. E. Gentner, and Captain Joseph Murphy had arrived to form the nucleus of the Fleet Air Japan staff, a naval aviation area command which would function for the remainder of the war.

While these organizational changes were being made, other U. S. Navy patrol squadrons were arriving in the area. VP-6 (CDR A. F. Farwell) flying P2V3 Neptunes,* had arrived in Japan on 7 July and commenced operations initially from Johnson Air Force Base, near Tokyo, and three weeks later from Tachikawa Air Force Base.

The next squadron to arrive was VP-42 (CDR G. F. Smale). This squadron's PBM5 Mariner aircraft landed at Iwakuni, Japan, near Hiroshima, on 21 August 1950.

In addition to these U. S. Navy patrol squadrons, two Royal Air Force

---

* For its outstanding performance in Korea, VP-6 received the Navy Unit Commendation—the only patrol squadron to be so honored during the Korean War.

squadrons operated under the command of Fleet Air Wing One Detachment, Japan, and later under Fleet Air Wing Six. RAF Squadron 88 (Squadron Leader M. Helme) flew from Hong Kong with four Sunderland aircraft, and had begun its patrols on 1 August. A second Royal Air Force squadron, 209 Squadron, commanded by Squadron Leader P. LeCheminant, commenced flight operations (flying four Sunderlands) on 10 September 1950 from Iwakuni.

During the early period of the Korean War, the missions given Fleet Air Wing Six were several: antisubmarine patrol along both coasts of Korea, search and reconnaissance, convoy escort, and weather reconnaissance to assist the operating combat ships. In addition, other missions such as search and rescue, anti-mine, photographic missions and various logistic flights were assigned.

In the first months of the war, the patrol squadrons were able to corroborate the fact that the naval blockade of Korea *was* effective. Numerous, often vague reports were being received in Tokyo that the North Korean Army was being supplied by sea in its advance on Pusan. These reports, often sightings by high-flying bomber aircraft, were proven false by the patrol squadrons whose visual, photographic, and radar surveillance of the coasts showed the "supply" fleets actually to be "fishing" sampan fleets.

Daily patrols were flown along the western shores of Korea in the Yellow Sea and in the Bay of Korea, on the east coast of Korea in the Japanese Sea, as well as in the Tshushima Straits. Whenever the carriers of Task Force 77 were replenishing, an ASW patrol was maintained over them at all times. In addition, a nightly weather reconnaissance mission was flown for the benefit of the carrier task force. The weather information was also beneficial to the shore-based Marines and Air Force aircraft in Korea.

Spotting

In addition to the routine antisubmarine patrols, weather and coastal reconnaissance, there were several unique and unusual missions performed by patrol squadrons during the early period of the Korean War. The first of these was the spotting of naval gunfire.

On 2 August 1950, a VP-6 aircraft conducted a spotting mission for the bombardment of Mokpo by HMS *Cossack* and HMS *Cockade*. So successful was this mission that a second mission was conducted by VP-6 on 6 August, using two P2Vs, when spotting services were furnished to British cruisers *Kenya* (CAPT T. W. Brock) and *Belfast* (CAPT Sir Aubrey St. Clair-Ford, Bt, DSO), the two British destroyers *Cossack* and *Charity,* and the Dutch destroyer *Evertsen* (LCDR D. J. VanDoorninck). The targets were military installations in Inchon. The USS *Sicily* provided four Marine Corsairs from

VMF-323 as escort for the two spotting Neptunes. Heavy antiaircraft fire was expected, but none was seen. The P2Vs were piloted by LT George D. Anderson and LT John W. Stribling; the spotting pilots were Britishers —Royal Artillery Captain Thompson from the fleet combined operations bombardment unit, who spotted for *Ceylon*, and Royal Navy Lieutenant Handley (a Seafire pilot from HMS *Triumph*), who spotted for *Kenya*. The bombardment group fired many salvos into the Inchon railroad station, the Jinson Electrical Works, and the oil storage tanks on the northeast side of the city. The spotters described the results as excellent.

On 7 August, a third spotting mission was conducted by aircraft from Patrol Squadron Six for a bombardment of Tanchon by the USS *Helena* and four destroyers.

Later in the Korean War, a patrol aircraft was called upon for some emergency naval gunfire spotting. On 12 October 1950, while searching for mines in Wonsan harbor, a VP-47 PBM flown by LCDR Randall Boyd was present when the sweepers *Pirate* and *Pledge* were sunk.* Also present was the destroyer minesweeper *Endicott*. The Wonsan batteries opened fire on the sweepers *Pirate* and *Pledge*, and in attempting to dodge the gunfire, *Pirate* struck a mine and sank. Before *Pledge* could move out of range, she suffered the same fate.

Lieutenant Commander Boyd flew over the stricken vessels to give support and to draw the fire from the Wonsan batteries. Air support from the carriers was requested. Meanwhile, the PBM continued to circle the area, spotting the gunfire of DMS *Endicott*. The enemy's surface batteries were effectively silenced.

Interdiction

For the first month after VP-6's arrival, this squadron made many attacks on North Korean targets. The P2V3 Neptunes were capable of carrying a heavy load of either bombs or rockets, in addition to their six bow machine guns. Since VP-6's coastal patrols along the northeast shore of Korea paralleled the rail network, targets along this part of North Korea were frequently seen.

On 29 July 1950, two P2V3s, piloted by LCDR R. L. Ettinger and LT William J. Pressler, were on a coastal reconnaissance patrol near Chongjin. The two Neptunes sighted a railroad train, an appropriate target for their 16 HVAR rockets. The train was quickly destroyed with rockets and 20-mm. fire from the bow guns.

On 13 August, in a flight led by VP-6's executive officer, LCDR E. B. Rogers, two Neptunes attacked several camouflaged power boats and barges

* The sinking of the *Pirate* and *Pledge* is fully covered on page 138.

at Chinnampo which were engaged in minelaying (although this fact was not then recognized). Three of these boats and two barges were sunk in the attack. Rogers' plane took six holes. On the same day, camouflaged Communist ships and patrol craft in the Wonsan area (believed later to have been laying mines) were attacked by other VP-6 aircraft. Two surface craft were damaged in this attack.

A similar attack on 16 August, on the west coast of Korea, on similar surface craft resulted in the loss of the first P2V. The plane, piloted by ENS William F. Goodman, had completed an attack on a small patrol-type enemy vessel in the Chinnampo area when the crew observed fire in the starboard engine. Ensign Goodman made a successful ditching a short distance from the enemy shoreline and the plane's entire crew was later rescued without casualty by the British cruiser *Kenya*.

As a result of the loss of this Neptune, orders were issued that henceforth patrol aircraft squadrons should not be assigned to attack missions. Specifically, the order read: "Aircraft of this force will normally not attack surface or land targets unless specifically directed to do so."

Aerial Mine Spotting and Destruction

One of the most unusual tasks performed by the patrol squadrons during the Korean War was the spotting and destruction of mines. This task commenced in late September 1950 and became increasingly important. After the amphibious assault at Inchon, two PBM aircraft from VP-42 were flown to Inchon harbor and tendered there by the USS *Gardiners Bay*. Their task was to fly low over the approaches to Inchon and Chinnampo, and to spot the anchored mines for the surface sweepers.

The two VP-42 aircraft arrived at Inchon on 2 October and commenced mine search operations the next day. Many minefields were located and reported, as well as numerous drifting and floating mines. A number of these were sunk or destroyed by gunfire by the PBMs.

This initial operation was successful because low tide left the mines exposed or "watching."

In anticipation of the amphibious landing at Wonsan, VP-42 changed its operating locale to Wonsan in early October, joining with the aircraft of VP-47 in the search for mines. In this task, the Mariners teamed with helicopters and surface ships to clear a path through the minefields for the amphibious forces. During this period, VP-42 was credited with the destruction of eight mines.

Mine hunting in a large, slow seaplane was not without its hazards. The Wonsan shore batteries were frequently active. One VP-42 aircraft received two bullet holes from rifle fire north of Wonsan on 28 October. And the destruction of a mine by aircraft machine gun fire required skill and accuracy. The circling pilot had to bring his aircraft close enough to the mine to permit accurate gunfire—but not too close, in order to avoid the subsequent five- to six-hundred-foot geysers of water sent up by the mine's explosion.

An aerial mine search was as tedious and difficult as a search for a periscope feather. Even when a minefield's general location was known, the search demanded excellent and trained eyesight, good surface and water conditions, and, most of all, patience. The surface of the sea could neither be rough nor muddy; the elevation of the sun had to be right. Mine lookouts found that a slightly overcast sky furnished the best type of suffused light for spotting submerged mines.

In regard to mine hunting, the commanding officer of VP-42, Commander G. F. Smale, recorded:

". . . The quality of patience on the part of the plane commander and crew is as important in the search for mines as it is for submarines . . . Lookouts succeed only after many hours of negative results. . . ."[1]

The patrol aircraft of FleetAirWing Six succeeded in destroying 54 mines during the months of September and October—31 of these in the Chinnampo area.*

Logistic Operations by the PatRons

Another of the important collateral tasks performed by the patrol squadrons in the Korean area during the early part of the war was the many logistic and liaison flights flown. Since there were no adequate landplane fields at either of the Fleet bases at Yokosuka and Sasebo, the seaplane patrol squadrons performed a very vital function by linking the naval command in Tokyo and the two major Fleet operating bases.

An outstanding example of this role was the occasion after the Inchon landing when an aircraft of VP-42 carried a cargo of 75 cases of whole blood, weighing 7,000 pounds, from the Naval Air Facility at Yokosuka to the fighting forces at Inchon on 7 October 1950.

Flare Missions

Early in 1951, still another unique mission, code-named "Firefly," was given to the patrol squadrons: flare-dropping missions. This coordinated action of flare and attack aircraft was a distinctly new application of air power in support of ground operations.

---

* For further information regarding the use of aircraft in antimining operations, see Chapter 4, "The Battle of the Mines" et seq.

As has been recorded in Chapter 8, "The Struggle to Strangle," a principal reason for the failure of air power to isolate the battlefield was the limited ability of airplanes to locate and destroy enemy trains and trucks at night. Uncontested air-sea control made it very difficult for the Chinese and North Koreans to move their supplies and munitions by day. By night, and during bad weather, however, the enemy moved his supplies and replenished his needs with little hindrance.

In an effort to hamper and harass the enemy's nocturnal movements, Admiral A. W. Radford, while on an inspection trip to Korea, suggested the use of P4Y2 aircraft as flare planes. Major General Field Harris, Commanding General of the First Marine Air Wing (then operating a night-flying squadron of F4U4N Corsairs and a night-flying squadron of F7F3N Tigercats) formally requested the assignment of appropriate naval aircraft to assist his heckler aircraft by carrying a large number of flares and accompanying them over the roads and rail lines north of the battlefield. Marine All Weather Fighter Squadron 513 had already developed flare tactics using transport-type (R4D) aircraft. However, these planes lacked both self-sealing tanks and armor protection, and the antiaircraft hazard was great.

No specially trained pilots or suitably equipped planes were available for carrying and dropping highly-dangerous magnesium flares. The only possible aircraft that could be modified for the task was a World War II aircraft, the P4Y2 Privateer. (The Air Force used C-47s and C-46s for the flare task.) Two such squadrons were available: VP-772 (CDR D. D. Nittinger) and VP-28 (CDR C. S. Minter, Jr.). It was decided to modify one P4Y2 to carry and drop flares, and to evaluate its performance in Korea.

Accordingly, one P4Y2 aircraft and crew from VP-772 (first reserve patrol squadron in action in Korea) was assigned to the Marine Wing. This aircraft was modified for flare missions by squadron personnel who removed the bomb-bay gasoline tanks and certain electronic equipment so that the aircraft could carry 150 to 250 flares, depending on their size and weight. The squadron also rigged flak curtains around them. On 12 June, this aircraft reported to Pusan, Korea.

The initial evaluation flights proved "excellent," according to Major General Field Harris. The controlling observer, riding in the nose of the P4Y, had good visibility and could make the flare drops more accurately than from a transport. Commencing on 29 June, flare missions were alternated between VP-772 and VP-28, with four aircraft assigned.

"When the P4Ys were first used for the flare dropping operation," said CDR Minter, "the Marine Air Wing was based at K-1, a field near Pusan.

Our operations were normally conducted along the road complex leading south from Wonsan, although the area was frequently changed because of weather or other factors. The flare planes and the Marine intruders* did not depart in company from K-1 since the VP plane cruised at a slower speed than the fighters (though not much slower when the bomb and rocket load was as big as the Marines liked to carry). Rendezvous was accomplished in the target area either by the night fighter picking up the flare plane on radar and homing in, or by the flare plane dropping a flare and having the fighter home on it. A flare mission normally lasted for approximately six hours, one plane having the sunset to midnight session, and a replacement having the midnight to sunrise stint.

"Each plane was scheduled to work with a total of four fighters, which came on the scene individually, spaced approximately one-half hour apart. If a fighter had to abort for some reason, the flare plane frequently was able to work with other planes for illumination purposes for bombing runs or anything else that might be required. The arrangement was obviously quite flexible and was quite interesting for the VP boys, who were accustomed to long, monotonous hours of overwater flying. This seemed almost like legalized flat hatting."[2]

The flare-dropping task called for the patrol aircraft to depart after sunset with a two-ton load of flares and to fly over Korea accompanied by several Marine night-intruder aircraft. (Sometimes as many as seven attack aircraft would utilize the P4Y2's flares for a single flight, although the average was three to four.) Such missions required the most careful and complex teamwork on the part of these planes. First of all, the flare-carrying P4Ys (called "Lamp Lighters") had to make a rendezvous with the night-attack aircraft. When this had been done, a search for enemy truck lights was commenced by the intruder and the flare plane. Upon finding a suitable target, a string of four to seven flares would be dropped to illuminate the target area. The attacking pilot might also ask for the flares to be dropped on a certain heading, and for repeated runs.†

Once the area had been illuminated, the attack pilot searched the ground and attempted to locate targets while the VP plane kept the area illuminated. The Marine intruder pilot had to make his search quickly before the enemy trucks had time to conceal themselves beneath trees or other cover.

* A night fighter aircraft which accompanied the flare-dropping plane and destroyed the illuminated targets with rockets, bombs, or napalm.

† VP-28 reported that one of the squadron navigators became so proficient in flare-dropping by "seaman's eye" that one flare was actually dropped on a moving truck, setting it afire.

These flare-dropping flights proved to be very popular and effective, and were continued by VP-28 and later by VP-871.*

The historical part of Commander McAfee's report reads: "The operation was conducted on a large scale . . . the outstanding fact was that it was one of simplicity and ingenuity. The turning of night into day was realized."

Weather Reconnaissance

One of the most important duties performed by patrol squadrons during the Korean War was the task of weather reconnaissance flights flown each night on behalf of Task Force 77 operating in the Sea of Japan. Weather flights were flown in the Sea of Japan and the Yellow Sea to estimate and evalute the next day's weather for carrier operations.

During the winter months, this service was especially helpful when the bitter Siberian weather with its sudden fogs and lowered visibility conditions might hamper the carrier task force's operations. In July 1951, a similar weather service was inaugurated by the planes of Fleet Air Wing Six for the west coast escort carriers of Task Force 95.2.

Incidents With MIGs

The latter part of the Korean War saw two incidents between patrol aircraft and enemy MIGs. The first occurred on 11 May 1952 when a VP-42 PBM reconnaissance patrol over the Yellow Sea near the Korean coast was attacked by two enemy fighters. One 20-mm. hit in the wing did only minor damage, and the plane returned safely to Iwakuni.

The second attack occurred on 31 July 1952 when a Mariner assigned to VP-731 (CDR W. T. O'Dowd) was attacked by two Chinese MIG aircraft. At the time of this attack the plane was on a reconnaissance mission over the Yellow Sea off the west coast of Korea. Without warning, the two attacking MIGs made a firing run from astern, killing Aviation Machinist's Mate H. G. Goodroad, the tail gunner. The PBM, piloted by LT E. E. Bartlett, Jr., dived to 250 feet and turned toward Japan. The two MIGs made several more firing runs. During the second run, a 37-mm. shell exploded in the PBM's turret hatch, killing Airman Claude Playforth and wounding the starboard waist gunner, Aviation Ordnanceman Third Class R. H. Smith. On the third run, Airman Apprentice H. T. Atkins was injured from exploding 23-mm. projectiles. The Mariner, while seriously damaged, was able to land at the island of Paengnyong-do, off western Korea, for temporary repairs.

* The authors are indebted to LCDR E. R. Hawley, O-in-C VP-28 detachment, for much of the information in this section.

The Formosa PatRons

At the outbreak of the Korean War, there was one Fleet Air Wing in the Pacific, with headquarters at NAS Agaña in Guam. The Fleet Air Wing commander, CAPT Etheridge Grant, was also Commander Fleet Air Guam. On 25 June 1950, CAPT Grant's command consisted of one land-based patrol squadron (VP-28, CDR C. F. Skuzinski—nine P4Y2s) based at Agaña, Guam; and a seaplane squadron (VP-46, LCDR M. F. Weisner—nine PBMs) based at Sangley Point, Philippines. One tender, the AVP *Suisun* (CAPT H. G. Sanchez), was in Tanapag Harbor, Saipan.

Upon the outbreak of the war, Fleet Air Wing One was given the task of preventing any attack upon Formosa. In view of this assignment, Captain Grant was relieved of his duties as ComFairGuam in order to give his full attention to the protection of Formosa.

A daily reconnaissance of the northern sector of the Formosan Straits was begun on 16 July by VP-28, operating from Naha, Okinawa. Patrol Squadron 46 commenced daily reconnaissance patrol of the southern sectors of the Formosan Straits and the China Coast on 17 July, tendered by the USS *Suisun*.

For the remainder of the war, Fleet Air Wing One operated in the Formosa area the land-based patrol squadron at Naha, Okinawa, while the seaplane squadron based in the Pescadores during the summer months shifted its operations to the Philippines during the typhoon season. These two squadrons maintained a continuous 24-hour patrol of the Formosan Straits and the China coast, supported by ready-duty destroyers from the Seventh Fleet maintained in constant readiness in Formosan waters. A round-the-clock coverage of the China coast was maintained with two flights of landplanes of seven to eight hours' duration during the daylight hours and one seaplane patrol during the period of darkness. The area covered was in international waters from south of Swatow to north of Shanghai. The destroyers were occasionally supplemented by cruisers from the Seventh Fleet or the blockade forces operating in Korea.

Operating in the Formosa Area

On 26 July 1950, only a few days after the Formosa reconnaissance patrols had been established, a VP-28 aircraft (CDR C. F. Skuzinski) was attacked in the northern part of the Formosan Straits by F-51 type enemy planes with North Korean markings. The attack did no damage, but it was the first of several such attacks which were to occur.

On 7 December 1950, there was an alert in the Straits. In the early morning darkness, a patrolling VP-46 aircraft, piloted by LTJG R. C. McGuffin, showed an unusual number of targets on its radar scope. McGuffin turned directly toward the blips and passed overhead at 1,000 feet. None of his crew was able to see lights below, but the radar picture showed hundreds of targets in a systematic formation headed eastward toward Formosa. Perhaps this was the first wave of a Chinese assault on Formosa. Perhaps it was only another fishing fleet.

McGuffin turned his Mariner aircraft around and reduced his altitude to 100 feet to make a low-altitude approach across the unknown formation. As McGuffin closed the target, he illuminated it by searchlight. Hundreds of junks in close formation were revealed. They showed no lights and were all headed eastward. The best estimate McGuffin's crew could make was 500 junks.

If this were an invasion attempt, this group would not be alone, certainly. Expanding his search, McGuffin turned northwestward. Approximately 70 miles from the first group, an additional group of approximately 250 junks was contacted. Like the first group, this formation of junks was also on an easterly course.

Could this be an invasion attempt? McGuffin radioed his base and alerted the patrolling destroyers. He then returned to cover and trail the first group.

By this time the ships had reversed course and were sailing westward toward China.

It was never known whether this sighting was a feint, a possible full-fledged attack on Formosa, or merely an incidental meeting of two large formations of fishing vessels.

If either a feint or a full-fledged attack, the Chinese Communists discovered that there was little hope of catching the U. S. Navy off guard.

Attacks by Enemy MIG Aircraft

During mid-1952, several contacts between the aircraft patrolling the Formosan Straits and Communist Chinese MIGs occurred. There were other incidents of surface vessels firing at the patrol airplanes. On 9 September, one of VP-28's planes was fired upon by a Chinese Communist LCI-type vessel. A week later, a similar attack occurred. The next day, a third attack was made; but in all three cases, no damage was received.

On the 20th of September, the first enemy action near Formosa by MIG aircraft occurred. On that day, in the sea near Shanghai, a VP-28 P4Y piloted by LT Harvey R. Britt was attacked by two MIGs. Although five firing passes were made, there was no damage to the P4Y.

On the 22nd of November 1952, a second incident with a MIG occurred.

In the sea off Shanghai, a VP-28 P4Y was attacked by one MIG. The Chinese MIG made eight firing runs during a fifteen-minute period, while the P4Y was at an altitude of 200 feet over the ocean on an easterly course. The weather was good, although there were cumulus clouds at 2,500 feet. The MIG was first identified by the tail gunner, who spotted it coming in astern at a range of five miles. The MIG came under the tail of the P4Y, opened his dive brakes, and flew formation alongside the port wing for approximately ten seconds. Obviously, the Chinese pilot was trying to identify this large blue airplane. As for the MIG, the P4Y pilot and his crew were positive of its identity. A large and a small red star were visible on the side of the fuselage, with Chinese characters alongside.

Satisfied that this was an enemy plane, the MIG peeled off to port, commenced a climb to about 1,000 feet and then began his attack. As he did so, the pilot of the big P4Y turned his plane into the MIG and brought his five turrets into action. For the remaining seven runs, the MIG alternated from side to side, starting his runs about three miles away and pressing them home. His gunnery was atrocious, spoiled by the skillful airmanship of the P4Y pilot and his crew. There was no damage to either plane.

Significance

Of the three elements of naval aviation in Korea—carrier, marine aviation, and patrol—the patrol squadrons had the most routine operations. This does not mean that their operations were without contribution or significance to the war effort. Patrol squadrons increased the effectiveness of the blockade by their reconnaissance flights, the search for and the destruction of mines, and the surveillance of enemy fishing activity. Patrol squadrons furnished up-to-date weather information for the carrier forces which was always helpful and frequently vital. The patrol squadrons performed the unique and unusual mission of providing flare illumination for the Marine night-intruder pilots. They obtained reconnaissance of the coastal areas of Korea, and kept surveillance over merchant shipping in the immediate area of Korea. The seaplane squadrons provided certain logistic and transport functions which could not be supplied by landplane types. The mere presence of highly trained, antisubmarine squadrons in the Korean area discouraged the use of submarines by the enemy. Lastly the patrol squadrons minimized the danger of any invasion of Formosa by the Communists.

In Korea, the land-based patrol airplane proved more efficient than the seaplane. The landplane squadron had greater endurance, greater self-protection and greater operational versatility. For the first time in the history of naval aviation, it saw greater use than did the seaplane. For every nine seaplane sorties, the patrol landplane flew twelve. During World War II, the ratio was reversed.

However, the landplane squadrons required more shore support and provoked sovereignty and basing problems. While seaplane squadrons were more mobile and could operate more flexibly, their operations were not as economical. Seaplane operations in Korea and Formosa highlighted the need for the development of new types of tenders.

To both the seaplane and the landplane, the war in Korea ushered in the **electronics era.**

11.

The Amphibious Threat (1951-1953)

"Korea Is a Peninsula"

The value of amphibious operations was well understood by the United Nations' high command in Korea: MacArthur, Ridgway, Van Fleet, and Clark. This fact is illustrated by the initial remark made by Lieutenant General Van Fleet to Rear Admiral George C. Dyer, soon after the latter had reported for duty in Korea as Commander Task Force 95.

Van Fleet and Dyer had first become acquainted during the Greek Civil War in 1947 when Van Fleet was in charge of the U. S. Military Mission to that country. At the time Dyer was Commander Cruiser Division Ten.

"At our meeting in Greece in 1947," said Dyer, "I stressed the fact that Greece was a peninsula. Its geography made the application of naval power particularly appropriate. Her coastlines were vulnerable both to amphibious assault and naval bombardment."

Admiral Dyer further pointed out to General Van Fleet that Greece had a small but first-rate Navy, and it was his belief that these naval units could be very helpful against the Communists. Van Fleet never forgot the discussion.

Four years passed before Van Fleet and Dyer met again in Seoul, Korea, in June 1951. There, as Dyer was being ushered into Van Fleet's office, the three-star general rose from his chair, threw his arms skyward, and exclaimed, "Korea is a peninsula!"

Generals Ridgway and Clark also knew the value of amphibious attack and took advantage of every opportunity to keep the UN amphibious threat alive to the enemy. They ordered amphibious training exercises conducted both in Japan and Korea. Marines of the First Division performed landing exercises in Hwachon Reservoir in plain view of Communist observation posts.

Communist Vulnerability to Amphibious Attack

The complete control of the air by UN air forces over the battleline forced the Communists to burrow ever deeper into the ground. As a result, their frontline defenses became increasingly immobile and vulnerable to amphibious attack. By the fall of 1951, in fact, fighting on the Korean peninsula had degenerated into trench warfare reminiscent of the Civil War siege of Richmond, or Flanders in World War I. Conventional weapons—artillery, close air support—were at best only partially effective.

By the summer of 1952, the Communists had taken advantage of the stalemate to build as strong a defense line as military history had ever seen. General Maxwell D. Taylor, who had helped to crack Germany's Siegfried Line during World War II, considered the Chinese defenses along the 150-mile Korean front even more formidable than the Siegfried Line.

Essentially, the Communist defense was a honeycomb of underground tunnels stretching from one coast of Korea to the other. A single tunnel might extend for miles. Many of the tunnels and fortifications were so deep and strongly built that they were impervious to bombs and artillery fire. Not only had the Communists reverted to trench warfare, they had been forced to glorify it—largely because of the threat of UN firepower from air, land, and sea.

As soon as the Reds retreated to a new hill, the hole-boring began. First, they dug on the protected side near the top; then they gophered their way around to the side facing the UN lines. Gradually, transections were dug linking all the tunnels together in a spiderweb of passages, bunkers, observation posts, and gun positions. To U. S. Marines who had fought at Tarawa, Iwo Jima, and Okinawa during World War II, the defensive trench system in Korea was more elaborate, although not as formidable.

At the same time the enemy was rat-holing at the front, he was also strengthening his coastal defenses.* The Communists had been caught napping at Inchon and they were already too much committed on the stalemated battleline to be caught flatfooted a second time. With Pohang, Inchon, Wonsan, Iwon, and Hungnam as constant reminders, the Communists knew and feared the United States amphibious capability.

General Mark Clark aptly described the Communists' fear of amphibious assault: ". . . The enemy had an overwhelming preoccupation with the defense of his coastline. He had tasted the whip of our amphibious techniques at Inchon and was afraid of it. He did everything he could, particularly on the beaches around Wonsan on the east coast, to prepare for a possible new assault from the sea by our amphibious infantry units. And

* See Chapter 9, "The Seaborne Artillery."

he knew that every one of our American divisions had been, or could easily be, trained to wage amphibious warfare.

"Hundreds of thousands of North Koreans built and manned the beach defenses along every stretch of coastline that conceivably could be used for an amphibious invasion. Behind them were Chinese Communist forces in reserve positions from which they could move quickly to bolster the defenses at any beach under attack.

"The defense system along the beaches, like the defense system at the front, was very deep and depended in large measure on underground installations for its effectiveness. But in addition to the underground works there were lines of open trenches spreading back from the beaches so that any troops attacking from the sea would be forced to attack one line of trenches after another, once they attained their foothold on dry land. Barbed wire was strung along the water's edge. Minefields were plentiful. Large areas of rice paddy land were flooded to make them giant tank traps which would mire our equipment in mud. Preparations were made to flood other areas during an invasion so that flood waters themselves could be used as a defensive weapon."[1]

UN Amphibious Planning

For the final two years of the war, United Nations commanders continuously considered the feasibility of amphibious attack against both the east and west coasts of Korea. For example, it was once proposed by Vice Admiral Clark to make an amphibious assault north of Wonsan, just above the Hodo Pando peninsula. The idea was not to permanently hold Hodo, but to seize the land long enough to locate and spike the vexatious guns of that area. Other full-scale assaults were proposed and considered at various times.

"On the west coast, the Haeju peninsula looked the most promising," said Vice Admiral Robert P. Briscoe, who was then COMNAVFE. "Tentative plans were made for a corps landing in that area in the event the truce negotiations fell apart.

"We gathered all the advance intelligence that was needed, estimated the size of forces required, and defined the major problems that would most likely be encountered.

"It developed that the major problem of an amphibious assault at Haeju was not the assault itself, but how we would get our heavy equipment across the rice paddies to high ground, once we were ashore. The Haeju problem was further complicated by the lack of reserve troops in the area. To make a landing in Corps strength, we would have needed two Army divisions and one Marine division from the United States."

On the east coast, the most promising site for an amphibious operation was the Kojo peninsula just south of Wonsan; from there, UN forces could move down the valley to the southwest and cut off communications between the North Korean and Chinese armies.

"Neither of these amphibious assaults was ever conducted," said Briscoe, "because we simply did not have the troops available in the Far East. We had sufficient shipping, we had the necessary gunfire and air support for a landing, but we simply did not have the troops. After the stalemate developed, we never had more than two reserve divisions in the Far East area at any given time. One of these was kept in Japan, and the other was held in reserve in Korea."

Had General Van Fleet been permitted to do so, he would have broken the stalemate with an amphibious landing.

The Kojo Feint

A plan to land at Kojo was first proposed in mid-1951 by Rear Admiral T. B. Hill while Chief of Staff to Commander in Chief, Pacific Fleet. Hill envisioned an amphibious end-around landing on Korea's eastern coast, in the vicinity of Kojo. Once ashore, the troops would drive southwestward to link up with the Eighth Army and thereby cut off the North Korean Army from its source of Chinese supply.

"This plan was known as 'Wrangler'," said Vice Admiral Clark, "and it appeared to have excellent chance of success.

"It had the approval of the Commander in Chief Far East, General Ridgway, and also General Van Fleet, Eighth Army. But very soon after I arrived in October 1951, General Omar Bradley, Chairman of the Joint Chiefs of Staff, visited the Eighth Army headquarters in Korea and disapproved the plan, stating: 'We want no more of the enemy's real estate.'

"For more than a year I heard no more about Kojo," Clark continued, "until October 1952, when I was Commander Seventh Fleet. At that time Admiral Radford arrived, in company with Vice Admiral Briscoe, to inspect the Seventh Fleet. Radford remained overnight in the flagship, and visited Task Force 77 the next day. Briscoe had proposed feinting an amphibious demonstration in the Kojo area in an attempt to draw enemy troops from their underground frontline positions. It was never intended to land any of our troops, but it was hoped that the enemy would react to the demonstration by sending his troops to the defense of Kojo, and that the Navy and Air Force could then destroy the enemy as they moved. General Mark Clark approved the idea, and designated me as Commander Joint Amphibious Task Force Seven, placing under my command various amphibious forces, including units from the Sixteenth Corps, the First Cavalry

Division, and 118th Regimental Combat Team. Major General Anthony Trudeau was in command of the troops, and Rear Admiral Francis X. McInerney commanded the amphibious group."

The Kojo operation, known as "Operation Decoy," had the following concept in the operation plan of Commander Joint Amphibious Task Force Seven:

> This force, supported by coordinated joint action, will seize by amphibious assault, occupy and defend a beachhead in the Kojo area with the Eighth Cavalry Regimental Combat Team in order to:
> a. Create an enemy psychological reaction favorable to the United Nations.
> b. Draw enemy reinforcements to defense of the objective area
> c. Fully exploit the enemy's physical and psychological reaction.[2]

A noteworthy feature of the Kojo plan was that it made no mention that the operation was to be only a demonstration landing.

"For deception purposes," said Admiral Clark, "knowledge of the demonstration aspect was confined to only the highest echelons of command."

The subordinate commands, including the carrier and the minesweeper commanders, were unaware that the operation would be a feint.

October 15th was tentatively chosen for D-day. In accordance with Clark's orders, Joint Amphibious Task Force Seven prepared and distributed plans on 25 September both for a Corps landing and for a Regimental landing. On 4 October, General Clark authorized execution of the Regimental landing plan.

The existence of two plans caused little inconvenience at the Army Corps and Division and the naval task force levels; but on the lower levels, where movements actually had to be made, ships' capacities determined, boat assignment tables* developed, and command relationships and liaison established, there was considerable difficulty in separating the two operations.[3]

Commander Seventh Fleet agreed that the requirement for the development of two plans did cause some confusion, but the most complicating factor was the short planning time. Admiral Clark considered it remarkable, in view of this disadvantage, that the plan was resolved so satisfactorily.[4]

Ship movements for the Kojo operation began on 1 October. Troop-loading operations commenced 6 October at Muroran, Otaru, and Hokkaido, where the Eighth Regimental Combat Team was located. Troop transports —Task Group 76.4 (ComTransDiv-14) in the *Bayfield* (APA-33)—began

---

* A boat assignment table is a table for determining what boats are available, and how and when they will be used in the ship-to-shore movement.

departing Hokkaido for the rehearsal area at Kangung, Korea, on 9 October.

Rehearsal operations were conducted on D-minus-three day, 12 October, under most adverse weather conditions. Winds in excess of 25 knots caused a two-hour delay in the H-hour rehearsal time. Four LCVPs broached during landing operations and were lost. Another was lost as it was being lowered into the water. Because of the dangerous surf conditions, the ship-to-shore movement was discontinued after the fifth wave. High winds and heavy seas prohibited the planned minesweeping for that day.

"At sunrise on the morning of the 14th," said Admiral Clark, "my flagship, the USS *Iowa,* joined the other ships in a bombardment of Kojo in a realistic softening-up process preparatory to the mock landing—but the Communists still did not know it was to be a mock landing. Every effort was made to give them the impression that another invasion such as the one at Inchon was impending."

The *Iowa,* the cruisers, and the destroyers continued shelling the beaches all night, until H-hour the next morning. The only ships to receive heavy counterbattery fire were the minesweepers, which were operating within visual range of enemy gunners.

"The transports held reveille at three A.M. the morning of D-day," said Commander Paul J. Hidding,[5] executive officer of the U. S. transport *Mountrail* (APA-213, CAPT William H. Farmer). "As dawn broke, the clouds were so heavy and visibility so poor that the enemy could not possibly have seen us. Therefore, he could not have been fooled into thinking we were really going to land.

"As a consequence, the announcement of H-hour was postponed until about 1130, at which time we were told that H-hour would be at 1400.

"Our transport, which was 23,000 yards offshore, immediately started lowering boats and loading troops. The troops were re-embarked aboard ship, however, before the boats departed for the beach. At this time the weather was fairly calm. But in the 45 minutes it took them to reach the turnaway line, 5,000 yards from the beach, the wind whipped up to 35 or 40 knots. The enemy also lobbed a few shells at the incoming boat waves without causing damage. By the time the boats got back to the ship, the wind had intensified to 55 knots. Ours was the only transport to send all its boats ashore. With the winds at gale force, we had quite a time picking up 26 boats, particularly the LCMs. One of the transports—*Okanogan* (APA-220)—had four boats completely destroyed during recovery. Thanks to excellent seamanship, all of the other boats were recovered without serious casualty by 1630. The transport group then departed for Pohang-dong to disembark the Eighth Regimental Combat Team."

"Naval air and gun bombardment continued throughout D-day in spite of high winds and heavy seas," wrote Captain P. W. Watson, commanding officer of *Bon Homme Richard.*[6] "Both props and jets smashed at the beaches and their approaches in anticipation of a landing. In addition to pummeling strong points, the flyers destroyed 12 buildings, blew up an ammunition dump, and caused a large secondary explosion in a fortified area. Meanwhile, the landing craft headed for the beach, but on reaching a point 5,000 yards out, they reversed course and returned to the ships. Shortly thereafter, the operation was officially termed an exercise. One Skyraider received a direct hit in the wing from medium flak but was able to ditch safely. The pilot, LTJG Walter Alt, was picked up in good condition by the helicopter of the USS *Iowa.*

"Having no indication whatsoever that the projected 'landing' was not genuine, the *Bon Homme Richard* and Air Group Seven spared no effort to make the Kojo operation a success. Consequently, when the real nature of the operation was disclosed, many of those concerned felt let down."

Air and naval bombardment continued throughout D-plus-one day, 16 October. At 1900 Joint Amphibious Force Seven was dissolved and all naval units returned to their routine assignments.

Significance

Except for the manning and activation of formerly unoccupied gun positions at Kojo, after D-minus-three day, there was actually little evidence of enemy reaction to the Kojo feint.

A U. S. intelligence agent who landed at Kojo on the night of 13 October reported enemy beach defenses had been evacuated, and that only a small number of troops were seen in the objective area. The intensified shore-battery fire later encountered by our minesweepers and the fire support ships indicated that these guns were manned, possibly by troops already in the immediate areas.

On D-minus-three day, pilots from Task Force 77 reported sighting approximately 1,000 enemy troops passing through the objective area. The cause of this troop movement was never determined.

In his action report,[7] Commander Task Force 77 reported that only ten enemy troops were killed by air attack in the period from 12 to 18 October. If the Kojo demonstration had brought any large number of enemy troops into the open, it was only at night.

Intelligence reports disclosed, however, that in the three months following the Kojo feint, the enemy relocated both North Korean and Chinese Communist reserve divisions from interior positions to coastal areas around Wonsan and Kojo. Although there is no indication that such a plan was afoot before the demonstration, it cannot be concluded that this change resulted from the demonstration. "The actual effect of the Kojo amphibious demonstration is difficult to determine," said Vice Admiral Briscoe, "except that the immobility of the Communist forces was strongly indicated."

As far as damage inflicted on the enemy during the aerial and surface bombardment, Commander Seventh Fleet drew the following conclusions:[8]

Aircraft Operations. It is impossible to draw a direct comparison of damage between the two periods, due to the diversified nature of the targets; however, it will be noted that the destruction achieved by aircraft in the 1-5 October period was, in general, slightly greater than that achieved in the 12-16 October period, with slightly less tonnage of bombs and considerably fewer sorties. This is attributed to the fact that the former period was devoted primarily to prebriefed and coordinated heavy strikes, while by contrast the amphibious operation required a much greater percentage of non-attack missions. . . . It is concluded that less damage was done by aircraft, with a greater expenditure of effort, during the Kojo demonstration than during a normal operating period.

Ship Bombardment. It appears that considerably more damage was done by naval gunfire during the period of the Kojo demonstration than during the earlier period. This opinion is reinforced by the fact that a greater percentage of unobserved and unevaluated fire occurred during the operation than during normal periods of deliberate gunfire. Considering these factors, it is estimated that approximately three times as much damage was done by naval gunfire during the Kojo demonstration as during a normal 5-day period; however, the expenditure of ammunition was about five times the normal.

Another factor to be considered in arriving at a cost analysis of this operation is the interruptions of upkeep schedules of ships which were mobilized for the operation. This is particularly applicable in the case of destroyers, which are in short supply, as always. The operation required 128 destroyer days which would otherwise have gone into much-needed upkeep.

The foregoing is not intended to belittle the value of the demonstration as a training maneuver. Such training is invaluable, and cannot be measured in the light of cost. However, it is considered that the concept of drawing the enemy into the open in order to inflict severe losses on him was not realized and, in retrospect, had very little possibility of succeeding under the existing conditions of stalemate and limited United Nations resources.

Perhaps the most serious deficiency encountered in the Kojo demonstration was the lack of a means for early and positive identification of aircraft. Numerous instances occurred when unidentified aircraft appeared over Wonsan and in the objective area during the actual operation. Although no enemy air attacks were made on either ships or aircraft, lack of early warning and positive identification was a source of much worry.

In his action report, Admiral Clark stated, "Air defense was the greatest weakness of advance force operation, due to the difficulty of locating and identifying bogies. The ships' radars experienced considerable interference due to proximity to land so that blind alley of approach existed. . . . A contributing factor also was the presence of numerous Air Force aircraft and their reluctance to respond to calls for identification."[9]

Subordinate commanders, particularly the carriers and minesweepers, commented adversely on not knowing the true nature of the Kojo operation. Until the night before D-Day, only the highest echelons knew that the landing was to be a fake. Some of the lower echelon commands considered the risks taken and the casualties sustained were not justified.

"On the other hand, if Kojo was to fool anybody, we had to make it look real," said Admiral Briscoe. "Then, too, there was the possibility the landing would actually be made, and it was not decided until after the troops were loaded that it would be a feint."

In summary, the Kojo operation was designed to bring the enemy out into the open, to expose him to attack, and to throw him off balance in the belief that a major amphibious assault was in progress. It did not achieve all that was hoped for. However, the operation did prove that the United Nations forces would have been able to land at Kojo against very little opposition and with few casualties. Communist prisoners of war stated later that the Communists had planned to wait until our troops had landed at Kojo before making any countermoves.

Regarding the probable result of any major amphibious assault in enemy territory, the principal Navy and Army commanders were emphatic.

"An amphibious assault behind enemy lines would have broken the back of the Chinese Communist forces at any time," said Vice Admiral Briscoe, "due to the concentration of Communist forces near the battleline. An attack against their rear would have cut their line of supply and brought them out into the open where our superior firepower would have been decisive.

"But an amphibious assault would have required more troops—and we did not have the troops."

General Van Fleet believed an amphibious assault might have been decisive, but that the war could have been won without one.

"The Navy could have shot us ashore," said Van Fleet, "and kept us ashore as we built up. We could have built up faster than the Chinese could have met our attack.

"In fact, the Chinese could not have met us at all. He was not flexible enough. He had no method of movement or control. He had no concept of fast moves, he had no communication systems, he had no mobility, he had no logistics support system to maintain his momentum, as we have.

Senior Officers in Korea. *At top,* ADM Robert B. Carney, GEN Maxwell D. Taylor, USA, VADM Robert P. Briscoe and VADM James L. Holloway are pictured from left at Eighth Army Headquarters, Seoul. *Below,* CAPT Raymond R. Waller, Captain of the *Philippine Sea,* confers with RADM Walter F. Boone, Commander, Carrier Division Five.

BATTLE OF CARLSON'S CANYON. *At top,* this key North Korean railroad bridge, near Kil-chu, was discovered on 2 March 1951 by LCDR Clement M. Craig. It was an ideal bridge for interdiction, since it was both long and high (600′ by 60′); it was located between tunnels (2 at each end); and it would be difficult to bypass. *Below,* one span has been knocked out and three others damaged in first raid on 3 March, led by LCDR Harold G. Carlson. So pleased was RADM Ofstie, CTF 77, with the successful attack, that the bridge was named "Carlson's Canyon."

COMMIES DESPERATELY REBUILD. Within eleven days, the enemy had reconstructed the bridge, using interlocking wooden piers to replace smashed spans. *Below*, further air strikes knocked the spans out faster than the Communists could rebuild them. But the desperate need for the rail connection kept them trying.

THE CONTEST CONTINUES. *Above,* bridge supports have been buttressed or replaced and only track laying is required to make the span operational, but . . . . *Below,* air strikes five and six finish the job off, downing all rebuilt spans and piers. Originally 600 feet long and 60 feet high, the bridge is useless.

"This was the Chinese Communist Army's greatest weakness. He could not sustain an offensive—nor could he long hold out against a sustained offensive. The enemy didn't have the means of logistic support, he didn't have the 'know how,' he didn't have the schooling. It takes a long time to learn about supporting a moving army.

"If UN forces had opened up an offensive all along the front and continued to push" said General Van Fleet, "we would have put such a strain on his logistic supply line, forcing him to work in the daytime as well as night, that he would have been given an insoluble logistic problem. In short, if United Nations forces had utilized their inherent advantages of mobility, flexibility, and firepower, we could not have been stopped. We could have won the war at any time. Instead of doing that, we fought the war on the enemy's terms and according to his rules. The war was never stalemated. It was a sit-down on our part.

"Winning the war was not our job. Our job was to sit on the battleline and let air drop in and punish him in the hope it would subdue him enough to sign on the dotted line. It was a sit-down by order of the United Nations. It was a self-imposed loss, because we could and should have won it."

12.

The Siege of Wonsan

Conception of Siege*

The American naval siege in Wonsan harbor, which grew to be the longest in modern American naval history, was begun on 16 February 1951.†

On the day the operation began, there was no plan to lay an indefinite or constant siege to Wonsan. The "siege of Wonsan" was progressive, originally conceived by Rear Admiral Allan E. Smith, during the period of the Hungnam evacuation as part of a plan for capturing certain islands on both coasts, including at least one in Wonsan harbor.

At the time Smith proposed his plan, UN forces were in retreat from the initial onslaught of the Chinese Communist armies. During the confusing days of December 1950, UN forces faced not only the prospect of being forced off the Korean peninsula, but also the possibility that World War III was beginning.

Smith's immediate evaluation was that his blockade and bombardment forces had to get back on the offensive; that if they had something tangible to accomplish, they could contribute to the stabilization of the land fighting.

"My evaluation," Admiral Smith recorded,[1] "showed that it would be good naval warfare to hold certain strategically-placed islands. The first one I chose was Cho-do, in the entrance of Chinnampo. The next one was Paengnyong-do, just south of Changsangot Peninsula. The third one was Tokchok-to, at the entrance to Inchon. The fourth one was off Kunsan

---

* "Siege is the surrounding and investing of an enemy locally by an armed force (land or sea), cutting off those inside from all communications for the purpose of starving them into surrender, for the purpose of attacking the invested locality and taking it by assault." From *International Law (Chiefly as Interpreted by the United States)*, by Charles Cheney Hyde.

† Because of its strategic location, Wonsan received the greatest attention. However, the east coast ports of Songjin and Hungnam were also besieged, although not as closely as Wonsan. The former two ports were besieged from their *outer* harbors as contrasted to Wonsan's *inner* harbor.

(not needed as the frontline held to north of it). And the fifth was the island group in Wonsan harbor.

Smith's plan was to put on these islands 150 or 200 South Korean Marines. This he did, equipping them only with rifles, though later they were issued a few burp guns and hand grenades. Thus when the Eighth Army came north again, these positions would have been retained, and we would not have to recapture all those hundreds of islands on the west coast.

Smith proposed this plan to COMNAVFE and it was approved.

It is thus clear that the "siege of Wonsan" was originally only a plan to seize one or more of the dozen-odd islands in the harbor until the UN forces again fought their way northward to capture North Korea, including Wonsan itself. The prospect that the war would stalemate in a few months across the narrow waist of Korea *south* of that port was not then a matter for consideration.

Harbor of Refuge

To appreciate the extraordinary nature and the importance of the 861-day naval siege of Wonsan, a description of that city and the geography and hydrography of its harbor are needed for the reader's understanding and interest.

The city of Wonsan, strategically located on Korea's east coast in the relatively tideless Sea of Japan, was the principal seaport of North Korea. The harbor was large—three hundred square miles—and naturally protected from storms. In a part of the world often plagued with typhoons, the Japanese had named the port the "Harbor of Refuge" because it was rarely in a storm's track.

Unlike other ports to the north, Wonsan was ice-free in winter. Its anchorage had a mud bottom over good holding ground in six to eight fathoms of water.

These were the features which, in 1880, caused the Japanese (who had just been granted use of the harbor) to begin its maritime development. In that year Wonsan was only a small, sleepy, and isolated village.

In 1950, the city of Wonsan had grown to be a thriving and modern seaport by Oriental standards. It was a strategic rail center, a naval base, a road transportation hub, and an industrial complex. The city's estimated population was 100,000.

Wonsan was the terminus of the cross-peninsular rail and road line to the North Korean capital of Pyongyang. It was also a pivotal location for the north-south rail line, and for highways in both directions.

The principal industry centered around its huge petroleum refinery—a plant covering 4,000,000 square feet, with an annual capacity of almost

2,000,000 barrels. Before the Korean War commenced, it was believed that the Wonsan refinery was supplied by ships from the Russian wells on Sakhalin, the long and rugged island adjoining Siberia.*

In addition to the refining industry in Wonsan, several other industries were located in or near the city. The Korean Railroad Company maintained a modern plant in Wonsan for the construction, repair, and maintenance of locomotives and rolling stock. A lead smelting company, a steel pipe company, a coke plant, a flour mill, a shipyard, a fishing cannery, and a "sake" brewery were also numbered among the Wonsan industries. Wonsan was also the center of great fishing activity.

Wonsan's seaport had excellent facilities. A 900-foot concrete wharf in the inner harbor was equipped with warehouses and railroad sidings. A large 40-ton travelling crane was reported in use on this wharf. At either end of the wharf were several quays and piers for small vessels. The oil refinery had its own pier several hundred feet in length.

These features and industries, therefore, as well as the importance of the harbor, were the factors underlying the establishment of the naval siege.

The physical features of Wonsan made it a location of great beauty. The islands dotting the harbor, the mountains which rose up within and behind the city and to the north on the peninsula called Hodo Pando, and the picturesque curve of the bay, had made Wonsan a summer resort center.

This was the city which would see the longest siege in modern naval warfare.

Difficulties and Advantages of Siege

To besiege Wonsan's inner harbor actively and at close range involved risks and dangers. First, the harbor was landlocked, and enemy gunfire from all sides could be expected. Second, much of the old minefield was still present, and it was safe to assume that the Communists had refreshed the swept areas since December 1950, and would try to re-mine the harbor at every opportunity. This could be, and was, done surreptitiously at night from the small, ubiquitous fishing sampans. Third, the siege of Wonsan would be hazardous because of the restricted navigation. In addition to mines, the numerous islands and shoals in the harbor would complicate navigation and gunnery.

On the other hand, there were many advantages in besieging Wonsan, in holding its harbor and capturing its islands. First, the enemy would be forced to divert large numbers of troops to protect himself against a second invasion—troops which might otherwise be in or supporting the battlefront.

---

* See "The Wonsan Oil Refinery Strike," in Chapter 2, "Retreat to Pusan."

Second, by holding and clearing the Wonsan minefields, UN forces would be able to invade whenever it suited their purposes. Any movement of UN ground forces north of Wonsan would demand the opening of an additional port for logistic support of the armies. Third, as has been stated, the city of Wonsan was an important Communist transportation center, lying astride the main rail and road arteries between northeast Korea and the frontlines. It was also the terminus of the only east-west railroad in North Korea. Naval gunfire could bring these important transportation routes under fire. Fourth, by holding the harbor, the best port in North Korea would be securely closed; fishing activity therein could be controlled by establishing a checkpoint on one of the nearby harbor islands. Fifth, the harbor could be an effective base from which to obtain enemy intelligence and conduct guerrilla operations. Sixth (although this reason was not initially apparent), Wonsan harbor could be an important search and rescue point for our aviators and aircraft.

And last, to be able to lay siege to the main port in North Korea, to hold its islands, and to bring gunfire to bear on its military targets, would have demoralizing effect upon the Communists, and be of great psychological value to the United Nations.

These were the reasons why it was essential to lay siege to Wonsan.

Initial Operations

After a path through the minefield had again been swept by MinRon Three commencing 12 February, the initial siege operations in Wonsan were begun by the destroyers USS *Wallace L. Lind* (DD-703, CDR E. B. Carlson) and USS *Ozbourn* (DD-846, CDR C. O. Akers) on 16 February 1951.* Rear Admiral Smith, the blockade commander, was on hand, embarked in the cruiser *Manchester*.

The two destroyers bombarded the harbor's military installations, but the swept area was so small and navigation so difficult that the two destroyers fired the bombardment at anchor.

Two days later, again at anchor, and at the conclusion of a snowstorm, *Ozbourn* received from Sin-do Island, the first Wonsan counterbattery fire, which wounded two men. Dragging her bottomed anchor, *Ozbourn* got underway toward the outer harbor. Her Mark 56 director was damaged, her after deckhouse holed, her starboard searchlight demolished. She was the first U. S. siege ship to be struck in Wonsan.

It was obvious that if a siege was to be effective, Wonsan's harbor islands had to be captured or neutralized.

* ComDesDiv 112, CAPT B. F. Roeder.

The Harbor Islands (1951)

Of the numerous islands in the Bay of Wonsan, UN forces eventually occupied and used seven: Yo-do, Mo-do, Sa-do, Sin-do, Tae-do, Ung-do, and Hwangto-do.

The first island captured was Sin-do. Enemy troops as well as enemy guns had been reported on Sin-do. To prepare the island for capture, therefore, two destroyers and two frigates, under the command of Commander De-

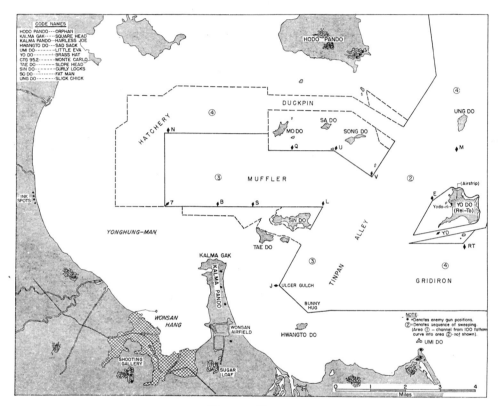

WONSAN HARBOR

stroyer Division 112 (CAPT B. F. Roeder), commenced a two-hour bombardment at 0700 on the morning of 24 February, with spotting furnished by *Manchester's* helicopter. Three hundred fifty-eight 5-inch and two hundred and fifty-nine 3-inch shells blasted the island at 0900. Following this bombardment, a detachment of 210 Korean marines went ashore. The landing was unopposed and the island was reported secure at 1018. Sin-do, lying only 4,000 yards from Kalma Gak, would provide a fine observation post for spotting naval gunfire and for observing the train and truck traffic in Wonsan city.

The next island occupied was Yo-do, the largest island. There was no opposition or interference, and the occupation by 210 Korean marines was without incident.

Yo-do was approximately 2,500 yards long and 1,500 yards wide, with an elevation of 377 feet. One cove and beach, suitable for landing, were located on the western side of the island. Nearby was the tiny fishing village of Yodo-ri, with a population of some 70 men, women, and children. The town consisted of several huts and one school. The size, location, and topography of Yo-do made it an ideal base for implementing the siege.

In mid-March, the Communists made an attempt to make a sampan landing on Tae-do, but were driven off by gunfire from the destroyers.

Three days after this attempt, 24 March 1951, the U. S. destroyer *English* (DD-696) (CDR R. J. Toner) landed a shore fire control party on Tae-do. Except for a leper colony of one hundred fifty people, Tae-do was not occupied. The island was also the site of a former Japanese fort, and lay even closer to Wonsan. On the following day, the cruiser *Saint Paul* and four destroyers, including the *English*, fired on targets in Wonsan with good results, their gunfire being corrected by the spotters on Tae-do.

Operating from Yo-do, the Korean marines gradually expanded control over several other islands in the bay: Mo-do, So-do and Hwangto-do. The latter island was the best spotting and observation post of all.

The first naval officer assigned to the Wonsan harbor islands was LT James S. Lampe, Jr., an intelligence officer from the staff of Commander Task Force 95. Lampe, the son of Presbyterian missionary parents, spoke fluent Korean, having been born in Korea and having lived there for eighteen years.

"I landed on the island of Yo-do on 13 June 1951, with orders to report to CTG 95.2," said Lampe. "At this time, we held and were using five of the harbor islands: Yo-do, Hwangto-do, Sa-do, Mo-do, and Sin-do. By far, the most important were Yo-do, our base island, and Hwangto-do, our naval gunfire spotting island.

"I lived on Yo-do. It was the best island for a base and was far enough out in the harbor to be reasonably safe from enemy guns, and in a good position where our ships could support us in case of a counterinvasion.

"Before I arrived, the Korean marines, in March or April 1951, had installed a large 4-foot searchlight on the top of the hill on the north side of Yo-do, just above the village. Power for the light was furnished by a gas engine, and it was manned by a crew of Korean marines. In case of invasion, this light was to be used to illuminate the beach in front of the village; otherwise we used the searchlight at night to give our planes a checkpoint. (Incidentally, this searchlight drew a great deal of fire from the Wonsan batteries—almost every day after a night's use. However, no direct hits were ever received up till the time I left (August 1952), although there were near misses several times.)*

"For several months, I lived in a tent near the small village of Yodo-ri. On 14 July 1951, the island of Yo-do became the headquarters for units of the 41st Royal Independent Commandos, commanded by LTCOL D. P. Drysdale, MBE, Royal Marines. The next day, the U. S. Marine who was to command the Wonsan islands, LTCOL Richard G. Warga, established his new command on Yo-do (CTE 95.23).

"There were several tents in our 95.23 camp—four for living quarters, one for a messhall, and one for an outhouse. They were placed on a little slope near the village and in the trees. During my fourteen months on Yo-do, I tried unsuccessfully to get a toilet seat from one of the destroyers for our outhouse; we did our best to sand and whittle the seat to make it more comfortable, but it never was.

"Our group of tents made a nice target. Many times when the Hodo Pando batteries fired at the ships near Yo-do, a few rounds would strike near our tents. Although there were many close hits and fragments, luckily, no casualties were suffered from this fire."

Shore Fire Control Parties on Hwangto-do

Perhaps the most useful of the Wonsan harbor islands for the siege ships was the island of Hwangto-do, one of three islands used for the spotting of ships' gunfire. The barren and rocky island, without a single tree, had an elevation of 160 feet, and was only 3,000 yards from the shore, and therefore closest to enemy guns and mortars. Hwangto-do was also closest to the city of Wonsan, to the much-battered Wonsan airfield, and to the important road running southward to the front through the Anbyon Valley. This road was the enemy's main supply route in the eastern sector. From the observation post atop Hwangto-do, spotters could look directly upon Wonsan, the Anbyon Valley road, and several important bridges along this railroad and highway.

Until June 1951, Hwangto-do could only be approached in sampans because of the mine danger. Sampans were not endangered because the mines were anchored six to ten feet beneath the sea surface and below their keels. Because of the island's proximity to enemy gunfire, all movement to and from this island was at night. A Korean Marine Corps LCVP was used to carry food and other supplies to the other "friendly" islands but had not been used to supply Hwangto-do.

* According to RADM Dyer, the original 4-foot searchlight was replaced in the early fall of 1951 with a battleship searchlight. "Getting it ashore was quite a problem," the Admiral wrote.

"In July," said LT Lampe, "we were told by a prisoner that the mine-fields protecting the eastern beach of Kalma Gak were in two rows, and that a boat could go safely from the middle of Tae-do to the western tip of Hwangto-do without crossing a mine line. Since the garrison platoon on Hwangto-do had been asking for food, ammunition and additional men, the situation warranted trying to take the LCVP to the island. That particular day, a strong westerly wind made it impractical to try to send the usual sampans. It would have been necessary to scull all the way from Yo-do, a trip that would have taken all night.

"Therefore I loaded the LCVP with all the things Hwangto-do needed, and I headed for the island following the route recommended by the POW. The trip was without mishap and turned out to be the first of many. There-after, I took all the supplies into Hwangto-do by LCVP, always at night.

"In early July 1951, Captain W. L. Anderson, USN, was CTG 95.2, em-barked in USS *Blue* (DD-744). While discussing the effectiveness of the ships' gunfire with the captains of the *Blue* (CDR R. S. Burdick) and the USS *Frank E. Evans* (DD-754, CDR G. L. Christie), it was brought out that the fire might be more effective with a Shore Fire Control Party stationed close in to the targets. I assured them that the island of Hwangto-do could be used for this purpose and would be an ideal location.

"We made out a list of the things the party should take with them. In-cluded was all the food they would use, the kind of clothing and bedding, the kinds and numbers of weapons, and the amount of ammunition and the radio gear most suitable. A volunteer party was picked, and a night chosen to go in. Volunteers were requested because the party could expect to be under close, accurate enemy artillery and mortar fire, and, of course, there was the ever-present threat of an enemy landing. Raiding sampans coming out from the south couldn't be detected by radar from the siege ships, and the ships would be unable to take them under fire when they were close to the island. Even so, everyone wanted to volunteer.

"On the night of 5-6 July 1951, I took them in to Hwangto-do in one of the destroyer's whaleboats and got them 'squared away'. The whaleboat carried a radar reflecting screen, and the ships kept a close watch on our progress. We landed on the only beach on the island. This beach was on the west side of the island and was very exposed to enemy fire. The rest of the island coast was rough rock and couldn't be approached because of under-water rocks. Nearby was a cluster of ten fishing huts.

"The shore fire control party holed up in one of the fishing huts. The Korean Marine Corps garrison platoon was most happy to have them on the island.

"The results achieved by the *Evans* and the *Blue,* using this shore fire control party, were extremely good. As I recall, they fired at a torpedo station and supply buildings in Wonsan. The team stayed on the island for three or four days and I brought them out. From time to time, other ships' teams took their place. The ships' interdiction and bombardment fire was materially improved."

This employment became more frequent with many other siege ships landing their own SFCPs on Hwangto-do. A small party of U. S. Marines was posted to Hwangto-do on 19 July 1951, and remained there for the rest of the siege, the personnel being rotated every four months.*

Siege Procedure

As has been stated, one of the main purposes of laying siege to Wonsan, in addition to being able to bombard the enemy's main road and rail lines leading to the front, was to clear the enemy minefields still remaining in Wonsan, and to prevent the enemy from planting others. This was no easy task. Minesweeping had to be continuous. In a single day the Communists could re-mine the swept areas, using a few of the always-plentiful sampans. Even a small sampan could carry as many as four mines.

"During my period in Korea as CTF 95," said Rear Admiral George C. Dyer, "most new mines were laid during periods of rainfall, snowfall, or winds strong enough to raise the waves in Wonsan to the 'high chop level'. During such periods, with the radars in our ships it was impracticable to detect sampans laying mines. None were laid during actual typhoons because the winds and sea currents caused the enemy to know that the mines would probably be wasted, and they had none to waste."

To clear the minefields, four or five minesweepers were assigned to the Wonsan task group, two of them operating every day sweeping the harbor and its approaches. Since these small vessels lacked the means of fully defending themselves from Wonsan's shore batteries, it was the duty of two (sometimes three) assigned destroyer types patrolling Wonsan to suppress enemy fire upon them.

By the end of April the sweepers had sunk or exploded 29 mines in the harbor of Wonsan. March 30th was the big day when *Thompson, Pelican, Chatterer* and *Merganser* had swept and destroyed 15 mines.

At this early stage of the siege, a typical day's routine can be described as follows:

The minesweepers, supported by destroyers, would make a daily sweep in

* The island of Hwangto-do was successfully raided by Communist sampans on the night of 28-29 November 1951. All of the ten houses were burned by the raiders, seven Korean Marines and one civilian killed, and five civilians captured.

an assigned area. If the sweeps were fired upon, the destroyers would retaliate. During a day's patrol, the destroyers would also have certain bombardment missions. And whenever lucrative targets were spotted in Wonsan (either by ship spotters, naval gunfire parties on the islands, or aircraft) they would be taken under fire by the destroyers.

At night, alone or in conjunction with night-heckling and reconnaissance aircraft from the carriers or the Fifth Air Force in Korea, the destroyers would fire at assigned or observed targets, in most cases with the spotting assistance of the shore fire control parties stationed on the "friendly" islands.

From time to time, the siege would be augmented by the rocket attacks of the LSMR division,* by the air strikes from Task Force 77, and by heavy gun strikes. During mid-March 1951, the first of many cruiser and battleship bombardments to strike Wonsan during the siege was conducted. *Manchester* (CL-83, CAPT Lewis S. Parks) accompanied by *Lind* (DD-703, CDR Edward B. Carlson) made a surprise raid on enemy troop barracks in Wonsan on 17 March. Intelligence reports later stated that more than 6,000 casualties had been inflicted. On 19 March, the first battleship to participate in the siege, the USS *Missouri*, blasted enemy gun positions with her 16-inch fire.

Wonsan Bombardments by Night

In early April 1951, an interesting experiment was initiated between the bombarding ships of Task Force 95 and the aircraft of the Twelfth Reconnaissance Squadron, Fifth Air Force. Already, as the result of both air and gun strikes on their supply lines, the Communists had suspended efforts to move supplies by day. All resupply through the Wonsan transportation complex was done at night. Reconnaissance aircraft of the Air Force had the mission of photographing the road and rail lines of North Korea every flyable night so that a check could be kept on the number and amount of supplies getting through to the enemy frontlines. Other night-flying aircraft of the First Marine Air Wing (F7F Tigercats and F4U Corsairs) and Fifth Air Force (largely B-26s) were out upon every occasion to damage and destroy as much of this night supply work as possible. In this effort, the attacking Navy, Marine, and U. S. Air Force aircraft were ably assisted by flare-dropping P4Y2 Privateers from Fleet Air Wing Six.†

At Wonsan, the night-heckler and night-attack aircraft found the siege

* The LSMR division fired twelve thousand nine hundred and twenty-four 5-inch rockets at Wonsan from June through September 1951. Their first and biggest day in Wonsan was the night of 20-21 May, when "Operation Fireball" was completed. Two LSMRSs—*401* and *403*—fired a total of 4,903 rockets at Wonsan targets in a 35-minute period.

† See Chapter 10, "The PatRons."

ships willing teammates. Star shells fired by the destroyers enabled the attack aircraft to locate targets more easily and make attacks upon them. The aircraft, in return, spotted the bombardment fire of the destroyers and increased its effectiveness.

The work of DesRon One ships *Floyd B. Parks* (DD-884), *Agerholm* (DD-826), and *John R. Craig* (DD-885) on the night of 5 May 1951 was typical of this work.

"This was the *Parks'* first of two 30-day periods in Wonsan," recorded CDR H. G. Claudius, USN.[2] "Two of my officers, LT Harold A. Bres, USN, and LTJG Urban G. Whitaker, Jr., USNR, worked out an excellent procedure for working with our own Task Force 77 planes during the day and with Air Force planes at night. Many Air Force planes checked in with us at night looking for targets. We gave targets to these planes, and in addition to vectoring them in, we assisted them to locate the target area with star shells. On their arrival in the area we would illuminate the target for them to make their runs and drop their ordnance. We continued illumination to assist them in evaluating their attack.

"After unloading their bombs, the planes usually had thirty to forty minutes they could remain in the area, and they were generally glad to use this time to spot for us. During this night bombardment work, the planes kept clear of our fire but remained in a position where they could spot our fall of shot, using illumination provided by star shells fired from another mount. The spotting ability of these pilots varied but was generally considered good, and in the case of some Air Force pilots who had had some Navy spotting indoctrination was excellent. Nearly all the pilots we worked with were most enthusiastic, with the result that the Reds in Wonsan got little rest or freedom of movement day or night."

With the *Agerholm* illuminating, the B-26 spotting plane directed the fire of *Parks* and *Craig* on a Wonsan bridge. The two destroyers fired ten rounds and made two direct hits. After demolishing a new supply building, the attention of the spotting plane was called to a truck convoy moving through Wonsan. While the destroyers furnished illumination, the B-26 attacked and destroyed several of the trucks.

Later the same night by the light of the destroyer's star shells, a second B-26 damaged a chemical factory and demolished four storage tanks.

Brinkley Bass Suffers First Casualty

On the 95th day of the Wonsan siege, 22 May 1951, an enemy shore battery succeeded in bringing death aboard one of the blockading ships.

"When we arrived for our first two-week tour in Wonsan," wrote CDR A. F. Beyer, Commanding Officer, USS *Brinkley Bass*,[3] "everything appeared to be quiet. Enemy shore batteries were relatively inactive, and our ships would anchor during daylight as well as at night, providing a sitting-duck situation for the enemy but a simplified fire control problem for us. Shortly after arrival we were fired upon and lost our anchor in the hurry to maneuver clear. We quickly learned to provide a moving target during good visibility, but we continued to anchor at night. We also learned other important survival techniques, such as keeping men clear topside, wearing as much protective clothing as possible (we would have welcomed some of those flak suits used later on during the war), wearing Kapok life jackets, etc.

"On 20 May 1951 we were left alone in Wonsan. The other ships were on other assignments or were receiving logistic support. At one time during the day we were at our battle stations and close enough to the enemy beaches at Umi-do so that we could spray the area with 40-mm. fire. . . . Not many hours later we were on the receiving end of their shells. Rapid maneuvering and heavy counterbattery fire kept us from receiving any direct hits; however, we were finally sprayed with shrapnel as a result of a 120-mm. near miss to starboard. This resulted in ten personnel casualties (we were at General Quarters and manning our 40-mm. guns) and superficial structural damage. Three of the casualties were serious, and one man, Fireman Apprentice John D. Bryan, died later. After that day we decided not to man our machine guns but to keep the personnel involved below decks. Later the same afternoon, the *Manchester* and several destroyers returned. We transferred our wounded to the *Manchester* and continued firing on assigned targets.

"Every day thereafter we could expect some enemy action, especially late in the afternoon, because the setting sun favored the shore batteries due west of the swept areas. Knowing this, the situation was never dull and all hands kept themselves ready to come to General Quarters on a moment's notice. It was almost a relief when we returned fire in an effort to destroy the enemy's gun emplacements. At least we lost some of the tense feeling.

"Moreover, there was enough humor aboard to keep us on an even keel. For example, we continued to show movies in the messhall and in the wardroom. One picture was a World War II battle action story. At the exact moment when General Quarters was sounded in the movie, our own G.Q. announced the fact that we were again under fire. For a brief second there was some confusion, but not for long."

Two days before the *Bass* suffered her casualty, the battleship *New Jersey*, while bombarding Wonsan targets, took a hit atop Number One turret. This shell did little damage, but a subsequent near miss killed one man and wounded three.

On 24 May, cruiser *Manchester* and destroyer *Brinkley Bass* detected targets south of Hodo Pando islands and opened fire. A Communist sampan formation was broken up and four sampans captured, each of them reinforced for carrying four mines.

Results of First 100 Days of Siege

At the completion of the first 100 days of the Wonsan siege, 27 May 1951, Admiral Smith reported that it had cost the enemy the following:

> 107 trucks destroyed; 238 damaged
> 8,195 troop casualties
> 149 buildings destroyed; 466 damaged
> 34 bridges destroyed; 83 damaged
> 63 railroad cars destroyed
> 3 tunnels damaged
> 11 locomotives damaged
> 54 small boats destroyed; 238 damaged.

Despite flurries of enemy gunfire and a few hits, the cost of wreaking this damage upon the Chinese and North Korean enemy had been small.

As on the railroads in North Korea, the Communists in Wonsan had been forced to organize a repair effort for the city's road and rail lines as a result of the destructive attacks of UN ships and aircraft.

On several occasions during this period, the enemy's fire had suddenly picked up as the Communists made determined efforts to drive the siege ships out of the harbor. Following a heavy Task Force 77 strike of 270 sorties on 6 July, the Reds retaliated with an especially heavy bombardment on 17 July 1951; more than 500 splashes were counted in the water around *O'Brien* (DD-725, CDR C. W. Nimitz, Jr.), *Blue* (DD-744, CDR R. S. Burdick), and *Cunningham* (DD-752, CDR L. P. Spear). In return, the three destroyers pumped out 2,336 rounds of 5-inch fire, in a four-and-a-half hour exchange. The Communist bombardment was continuous and well coordinated from three areas—Umi-do, Kalma Gak, and Hodo Pando—but inflicted no more serious damage than spraying two LSTs near Yo-do with fragments.

"This exchange was known as 'The Battle of the Buzz Saw'," said RADM Dyer. "After this date I made it compulsory that at all times in daylight, and for all bombardments, either night or day, ships should be underway."

The Enemy Defenses of Wonsan

As the siege of Wonsan was laid, there were few enemy batteries around the bay of Wonsan. As the siege lengthened, however, the number of guns defending the harbor rose steadily.

Likewise, the enemy shore defense system in Wonsan, which in the beginning was limited, was steadily strengthened. As UN minesweeps swept "Broadway" and "Lower Broadway" ever closer to the shore, the enemy's entrenchments were expanded to include the beaches nearest the swept areas. Shore entrenchments were also positioned at other places where the Communists thought the UN forces might land—the beaches near Wonsan city and on the south coast of the bay and, later, in the western portions of the bay.

The Communists' shore batteries were placed so as to cover both the ship operating areas and to sweep the potential landing sites: heavy machine guns and mortars were positioned near the probable landing beaches, and 76-mm. batteries in the nearby hills. The harbor's heavy guns (122-mm. and 155-mm.) were located farther back from the shoreline and positioned to take the ship operating area under fire.

In the early months of the siege, the enemy's batteries were located as follows:

All harbor guns were of the field artillery type, as distinguished from naval or regular fixed shore defense guns. With few exceptions, these guns were hidden in caves or tunnels, cleverly camouflaged, and were rolled out for firing and rolled back inside for protection, for the Communists soon learned that an exposed gun was certain to be destroyed.

In the early months of the war a great many empty gun emplacements, caves, and tunnels were in evidence. Two reasons are likely. First, in case one position became too hot, a gun could be moved to a new position. Second, empty gun positions often attracted fire from planes and ships. By the end of the second year of the siege, however, there were few empty gun positions, as more guns were brought into the area.

"Most of the low, near-to-the-water gun positions in the Wonsan area had a single entrance," said LT James S. Lampe, the intelligence officer assigned to Yo-do. "This entrance was for the gun itself, and it was always as small as possible. Only a few of the gun caves—usually the big ones—had a personnel entrance. These came in from the back side of the hills, permitting the crews to man their guns without being exposed to our fire.

"Most of the heavy gun positions had large rooms for ammunition storage as well as crew's quarters. The Communists did not seem concerned about having their ammunition and gun crews in the same hole.

"In addition to the field artillery pieces, there were two other types of guns used against our siege ships: tanks and rail-mounted guns.

"Tanks were positioned at several points around the bay, but were most prominent at certain positions on 'Sugar Loaf', a small hill on Kalma Gak, plus other tanks on Kalma Gak proper. Two of these tank positions were set up so that the tank could fire through 'gunports' located at the very base of the hill. The tank itself was never exposed, but was moved forward until the gun barrel protruded from the port. Another tank often came around the north end of 'Sugar Loaf' to fire, but beat a hasty retreat whenever it was taken under fire.

"In the latter part of 1951, four rail-mounted guns appeared in the bay. Three of these were north of the city, not far from the beach. These, too, were retractable into caves.

"As far as I could determine from the refugees who fled to the islands from Wonsan, all of the harbor defense guns were North Korean manned. It is doubtful that the Chinese manned any of the guns. North Korean Army units manned most of the harbor guns except the Hodo Pando batteries, which were manned by a North Korean Navy unit.

"In regard to their control procedures, they zeroed-in certain positions where they were most apt to catch a ship with little maneuvering room. In many of the firing positions, the Communists hacked a circular groove in the hard-packed ground, into which the wheels of the gun carriage fitted snugly. Around this circular track various points were marked to zero-in selected points with rapidity. The Red gun crews learned to work as teams, and even developed a definite plan of coordination between the widely-spaced batteries. Spotting stations equipped with plotting boards were established and splash information was passed by telephone to a fire control station. The fire control station would calculate corrections and phone them to the batteries. The Reds had no automatic machines or computers, but nonetheless they became fast and accurate. They also reported ships sunk from time to time. One destroyer was reported sunk three times, and when it appeared the fourth time in the bay, they claimed we had changed the numbers on a new ship.

"The presence of our siege ships and minesweepers inside the harbor was definitely a severe irritant and worry for the Communists. During the first year of the siege of Wonsan, there were four occasions when the Reds believed a landing was imminent. These scares usually followed a maximum air strike by Task Force 77 or a heavy bombardment by a battleship, or a combination of the two. They were kept continually on their toes and never dared to leave the harbor lightly defended."

The increase of enemy gunfire resulted in six ships being hit in July: *Everett* (PF-8); *LSMR-409; LSMR-525; O'Brien* (DD-725); *LSMR-412;* and *Helena* (CA-75). In August, the siege ships were untouched. In September, two were hit: *William Seiverling* (DE-441); and *Heron* (AMS-18).

"The limited area available to the ships in Wonsan made it extremely difficult for our ships to maintain their positions when subjected to fire from the shore batteries," wrote RADM George D. Dyer, the blockade commander. "In order to provide them with more advantageous positions, the sweeping of additional areas between the islands and the providing of so-called escape routes from the inner harbor were undertaken in mid-June 1951. This extremely hazardous operation was pressed in the 'Lower Broadway' area with vigor. Upon completion of the initial sweeping in late August 1951, sweeping was started on 2 September in the new 'Muffler' area. This latter area permitted a much closer approach to the city."

If the enemy hoped to lift the siege with increased gunfire, however, and provide himself an opportunity for re-mining the swept areas and recapturing the harbor islands, he failed.

Doubts Raised Regarding Continuance of Siege

While none of the ships of the UN Navy had yet been lost or even seriously hit, there began to be some doubt as to whether the siege was worthwhile. In the first 180 days of the siege, approximately 50,000 naval shells had been pumped into the city's targets. The doubts were expressed largely because there was no accurate way of determining precisely *what* the bombardment was doing to the enemy's over-all capability and to his morale.

Outwardly, a little speculation was in order. It was evident, after six months of the siege, that neither the bombs from aircraft nor the gunfire from ships, even in combination, had succeeded in halting the steady flow of material through Wonsan at night. The daytime flow had been effectively dammed, however, and a great deal of damage had been done in six months:

Target	*Destroyed*	*Damaged*
Guns	262	230
Trucks—Vehicles	178	348
Junks—Sampans	89	299
Bridges	36	100
Tunnels	—	15
Railroad cars	66	80

But at night, as the observers on the friendly islands could plainly see, the enemy trains and trucks rolled steadily southward despite the gunfire and harassment. In view of this heavy nocturnal traffic, was the known and estimated damage sufficient to justify the risks being taken? The risk to the destroyers and minesweepers in the harbor was already great and was still growing. It was easy to imagine the tragedy which might occur if a lucky hit in a steering mechanism should veer a speeding ship into the minefield or aground on one of the numerous islands.

Risk to the siege ships was accepted. Damage to the enemy, however, was only one criterion of the value of the siege. The very fact that enemy resistance was on the increase was evidence that the siege was hurting. Also, it was known that large numbers of enemy troops were bivouacked near Wonsan to defend the area from an amphibious assault. One intelligence report said that 79,200 troops were stationed in the vicinity of Wonsan to counter an invasion. Several American aviators—Air Force, Navy, and Marine—had already been rescued from the harbor where they might have been captured or lost. And by what yardstick could the psychological value of this thorn-in-the-side siege be measured?

"The question of the desirability of continuing the Wonsan siege was raised at least twice during my tenure as CTF 95," said Admiral Dyer. "The best brains in the Army and Navy—Forrest Sherman, MacArthur, Ridgway —were all convinced of the necessity of the siege."

The siege was therefore continued and accelerated.

A heavy gunstrike by surface forces (*New Jersey* and *Toledo*) pounded Wonsan targets on 2 July 1951. On 18 September 1951, the first coordinated air-gun strike by Task Force 95 was conducted in Wonsan commanded by Rear Admiral George C. Dyer aboard USS *Toledo* (CAPT Hunter Wood). Other ships included HMS *Glory*, USS *Parks*, USS *John R. Craig*, USS *Orleck*, and USS *Samuel N. Moore*. The same ships repeated the bombardment next day, joined by the three rocket ships, *LSMR-409, 412,* and *525*.

The air-gun bombardment was repeated on 10 October. For this strike, a British task force, under the command of Rear Admiral A. K. Scott-Moncrieff, participated, led by the Australian light aircraft carrier *Sydney*[*] (CAPT D. H. Harries, RAN) and supported by cruiser HMS *Belfast* and destroyers HMS *Concord,* USS *Colahan,* HMCS *Cayuga,* HMS *Comus,* and USS *Shields*. A large enemy troop center had been located in Wonsan, and heavy damage was done to this concentration.

A third heavy bombardment, led by *Wisconsin,* struck military targets in the besieged city on 20 December.

The Helicopter Ship (LST-799) in Wonsan

The value of holding the harbor of Wonsan for rescue purposes is revealed by the fact that *LST-799* (the first ship of the U. S. Navy to serve as a helicopter carrier in wartime) rescued twenty-four aviators between March

---

[*] *Sydney* created a record for this time by flying 89 sorties in one day, and 147 sorties in two days.

1951 and November 1952, most of them while operating in or near the Bay of Wonsan.

"After the Hungnam evacuation," said LT T. E. Houston, skipper of the *LST-799*, "we returned to Yokosuka for a conversion which was designed to make us into a helicopter base for minespotting helicopters and a tender and supply ship for minesweeping boats and ships. We had space and facilities topside to handle three helicopters, although we frequently had but two aboard, and more often only one.

"The planned use for our helicopters was originally that of minespotting, not rescue; but as time went on, our 'copters got more and more into the role of rescue."

After conversion, *LST-799* arrived in Wonsan on 20 March 1951 to serve as a harbor headquarters for ComMinRon Three (Captain Richard C. Williams, USN) and a floating helicopter and minesweeping boat base.

"On our arrival in Wonsan," said Houston, "we anchored on the leeward side of Yo-do. At this state of the siege, we weren't concerned about shore-battery fire; and our helicopter pilots in March and April of 1951 had quite a lark. They used to fly around the city of Wonsan quite freely and unharmed. The North Koreans and Chinese would wave at them and seemed not to care.

"By mid-summer, however, the honeymoon was over, and the Reds were no longer hospitable to sight-seeing helicopters. I was told that this unfriendliness on their part was attributable to the practice of some helicopter pilots' dropping hand grenades in the general vicinity of the North Koreans while they were enjoying their toilet."[4]

LST-799 effected its first rescue in Wonsan on 5 April. The rescued pilot was Ensign M. S. Tuthill.

"It was a beautiful spring afternoon," recalled Houston, "and we had just finished an emergency rescue drill. The alarm sounded, and the boatswain passed the word, 'Away the rescue party, away!' Our rescues were usually performed by helicopter, but we also kept an LCVP ready.

"Dashing out on deck, I joined the rest of my crew topside watching a parachuting figure whose plane was just crashing into the ocean,

"The LCVP was away first, and the helicopter soon after. But the 'copter reached the downed pilot first, and as it often happened, the helicopter crewman had to jump into the water and assist the downed pilot into the hoisting sling. While the helicopter returned the pilot, the LCVP picked up the crewman. Except for a chill, both were in good shape. This was Ensign Tuthill's second dunking and helicopter rescue; he understandably had a high regard for the whirley-birds.

"The majority of our rescues were performed while underway," continued Houston, "and most of them were over land. If a rescue call came in while the 'copter was flying a mine spot mission, the 'copter would return, refuel, assemble all the information, and take off again. I would head the LST to the nearest safe spot to landward to close the distance as much as possible.

"The rescue missions themselves were carried out independently by the helicopter unit. They did the job as they saw fit."

One of the most tragic helicopter rescue attempts took place on 3 July 1951 from Wonsan harbor. *LST-799* temporarily left the harbor, and the MinRon-3 helicopter unit was based aboard the relief helicopter ship, the *LST Q-009.*

The helicopter pilot was LTJG John Kelvin Koelsch, who had recently completed a full tour of combat rescue duty flying from the USS *Princeton.* Upon the return of *Princeton* to the United States in late May 1951, Koelsch volunteered for an additional combat tour, and was assigned to ComMinRon-3 in early June.

Koelsch had given an outstanding account of himself aboard *Princeton,* rescuing at least two of his shipmates. He had also developed a type of floating sling that came to be adopted by others, and he had personally engineered and developed several safety devices for the operation of helicopters in cold weather.

"Koelsch was based on *LST-799* for just a few weeks," said LT Houston, "and he impressed me as being a very quiet, reserved person who was always ready for any rescue mission, no matter how dangerous, and he let this be known. If anything happened, he wanted to be a part of it. While on board, he rescued Ensign M. D. Nelson, near Yo-do, on 22 June."

On the late afternoon of 3 July, about an hour before darkness, a "Mayday" call was received aboard *LST Q-009* saying that a Marine pilot had been shot down twelve miles west of Kosong, a small town thirty-five miles south of Wonsan. Despite the late hour, and the worsening weather, LTJG Koelsch and his crewman, George M. Neal, AM3, volunteered to make the pickup.

Covered by a flight of four Corsairs, Koelsch proceeded to the rescue area, but because of a nearly solid overcast of low clouds, was forced to leave his protective escort. Koelsch was last seen descending through a break in the low overcast about 1810.

Koelsch first located a parachute, then proceeded to search the surrounding area in the gathering darkness. This area, the Anbyon Valley, was the enemy's main supply road leading to the battlefront from Wonsan. Accordingly, this road was infested with AA guns and automatic weapons.

A few moments later, the circling pilots heard Koelsch's radio message that he had found the downed pilot and was heading for the pickup.

This was the last word of Koelsch, Neal, and the Marine pilot (CAPT James V. Wilkins, USMC) until the end of the war. In December 1954, as a result of an award recommendation by Captain Wilkins, the subsequent events of the rescue and the captivity of Koelsch were laboriously pieced together.

Despite intense ground fire which had struck his helicopter in one place, Koelsch had pressed on to make the pickup. Of this fire, Captain Wilkins later said: "He found me, after two passes into the most intense small-arms fire I've ever witnessed."

As Captain Wilkins secured himself in the hoisting sling, a burst of AA fire struck the helicopter, and it crashed against the mountainside. Of the three, the only one who suffered injuries was Captain Wilkins, who was seriously burned on the legs.

For nine days the three men avoided capture. Captain Wilkins was unable to walk, and Koelsch and Neal made a crude pallet and were attempting to carry him to the coast.

On 12 July, having reached the beach, the three were captured while Koelsch was attempting to obtain food and water from a village. Koelsch's subsequent conduct and example in prison camp elicited the highest praise from his fellow prisoners.

A few months later, LTJG Koelsch died of starvation and dysentery. For his gallantry and heroism during the rescue attempt and his subsequent captivity, he was posthumously awarded the Congressional Medal of Honor on 3 August 1955.

Air-Surface Teamwork

By mid-summer 1951, the siege ships assigned to Task Group 95.2 in Wonsan harbor for thirty-day periods had learned to whet air-surface teamwork and coordination to a razor sharpness. Task Force 77 periodically assigned aircraft to the bombarding vessels for spotting duty in order to increase the effectiveness of the naval gunfire. The ships themselves sent shore fire control parties to Hwangto-do, Mo-do or Tae-do islands to assist the naval gunfire liaison parties spot the ships' gunfire.

The alacrity and effectiveness of the teamwork developed between naval ships, shore fire control parties, and planes is illustrated by an event recorded by CDR H. G. Claudius, commanding officer of the USS *Floyd B. Parks,* during September 1951:

"We had a shore fire control party from the ship on Hwangto-do, who spotted for us during the day and sometimes at night. One afternoon we had two Task Force 77 planes spotting our bombardment on Kalma Gak.

At the same time, two of our AMS-type minesweeps in formation were sweeping just off the south beach of the harbor. We received a hurry-up call from our shore fire control party on Hwangto-do that they could see the Reds were working two guns out from caves to open up on the minesweeps, who were probably only about 4,000 yards from the gun positions. We immediately vectored the two TF 77 planes, who still had rockets, to the enemy guns. All in a couple of minutes, and before the enemy guns could get off a shot at the minesweepers or return to the cover of their caves, the planes had been vectored in to where they could see the guns and plaster them with a full load of rockets. Through the alertness and instant action of the shore fire control party, the ship's CIC and gunnery team, and the TF 77 pilots, our minesweepers were probably saved from casualties and damage and two enemy guns were damaged or destroyed."[5]

The Second Year

The first anniversary of the Wonsan siege—16 February 1952—found the destroyers *Rowan* (DD-782), *Twining* (DD-547), and *Gregory* (DD-802) pounding the Wonsan targets with the usual harassing and interdiction fire.

The mineswept areas of the harbor had been gradually increased to the west and southwest, enabling the ships to get closer and closer to targets ashore. The swept areas were marked with yellow buoys to delineate the edge of the minefields. Near these buoys, and in the close-ashore portions of the swept areas, the siege ships soon learned to be especially alert and mobile, for the Communist gunners had carefully "zeroed-in" the marker buoys, and used them for spot correction of their gunfire.

While sweeping mines in "Ulcer Gulch" on 5 March 1952, USS *Pelican* (AMS-32) and USS *Curlew* (AM-8) were taken under fire by the Kalma Gak batteries. Both ships lit off their smoke generators and escaped being hit. The use of smoke to cover the retirement of the sweepers always proved helpful and became standard practice.

The enemy guns continued active in March. *Manchester* (CL-83), *Kyes* (DD-787), *McGinty* (DE-365) and *Douglas H. Fox* (DD-779) were on the receiving end of a heavy and accurate outburst on 13 March, but aided by a Task Force 77 strike, succeeded in silencing the enemy guns. On 20 March *Wiltsie* (DD-716) and *Brinkley Bass* (DD-887) came under fire. *Osprey* (AMS-28) was the next day's target; while on the 22nd of March, *Brinkley Bass* (DD-887) and *Stickell* (DD-888) were under fire.

On 24 March, the enemy guns achieved a direct hit on *Brinkley Bass* amidships, just aft of the torpedo tubes, which seriously wounded one man and caused injuries to four others.

On 28 March, the frigate *Burlington* (PF-51) was straddled.

April 1952 was to see even greater efforts made by the enemy to cripple or sink a ship. On 18 occasions the patrolling minesweepers, destroyers, and ships of the Wonsan element were fired upon. Only three were hit, however—destroyer *Leonard F. Mason* on the 2nd of May (no casualties) and *Cabildo* (LSD-16) on the 25th of May (two personnel casualties).

During April and May, the fire of the bombarding ships took a steady toll of guns, junks, trucks, tanks, bridges, and buildings in Wonsan harbor. On the last day of April *Maddox* (DD-731) and *Laffey* (DD-724) damaged ten boxcars of a nocturnal train.

This period saw *Maddox* (CDR H. A. Hanna) and *Laffey* (CDR H. J. Conger) on the receiving end of one of Wonsan's longest and heaviest bombardments. The two destroyers were supporting two sweepers, one working in "Tin Pan Alley" with *Laffey*, the other in "Muffler" with *Maddox*. Shortly afterwards, the Hodo Pando guns opened the duel. *Maddox* and *Laffey* increased speed to 25 knots, opened fire, commenced the "war dance"* and turned to make a fast changing target in deflection.

"We were intermittently under fire from Hodo Pando, Kalma Gak and the Umi-do area," said CDR Conger. "I personally saw about 200 splashes around us, although some thought they counted as many as 300. One hit close enough to throw a handful of shrapnel on our bridge, one chunk knocking out one of the bridge windshields."

For six hours, the two destroyers made figure eights between Ung-do and "Ulcer Gulch."

"I feel certain our counterbattery fire did a lot of damage to the Hodo Pando batteries," said Conger. "This duel took place on the second day of our thirty-day tour in the harbor, and those particular guns never fired on us again."

The "Mayor" of Wonsan

The siege of Wonsan during this period can be illustrated by the typical experiences of one of those who held the title "Mayor of Wonsan."† A non-political office, this honorific title was conferred, beginning in May 1952, upon those who held the command of Task Unit 95.2.1. The evidence of the title was a large, gilded wooden key.

The creator of the title "Mayor of Wonsan" is unknown to the authors despite considerable research.‡ However, the symbolic "Key to the City

---

* The "War Dance" can be defined as high speed evasive maneuvering to avoid enemy gunfire.

† In addition to the title "Mayor of Wonsan," RADM Allan E. Smith held the title "Duke of Wonsan."

‡ Refer Commander Blockade and Escort Force letter P15, serial 573 dated 20 April 1954. RADM T. C. Ragan herein states: "At the time the idea of the 'Mayor of Wonsan'

of Wonsan" was originated in May 1952 by CDR R. J. Ovrom, then Commander Escort Squadron Nine.

Commander Ovrom had the gilded key made at Ship Repair Facilities, Yokosuka, Japan, by a Japanese craftsman; on one side was the inscription, "Welcome to Wonsan"; on the other, "The Bay of Eternal Prosperity." This key was passed from one CTU 95.2.1 to another until the end of the war, when the key was sent to the U. S. Naval Academy museum for safekeeping.

Captain R. D. Fusselman, as Commander Escort Destroyer Division Thirteen, aboard the USS *Jenkins*, held the title during the period of 16 September to 6 Ooctober 1952.

"Being the 'Mayor of Wonsan'," said Captain Fusselman,[6] "gave me the task of running the activities within the harbor itself; to supervise the minesweepers working in the western end of 'Muffler' and in the southern end of 'Tin Pan Alley'; to furnish covering destroyers and destroyer escorts; to work closely with our naval personnel, Marines, and the Koreans on the friendly islands; to coordinate and work with the ships of the outer harbor blockade; and of course, to keep CTF-95 (Admiral Gingrich) informed.

"By the time I assumed the job, the Communists had added shore defense guns all around Wonsan harbor, so that it was necessary for the patrolling ships to maintain a good speed, about fifteen knots, and never to stay on one course too long. By this time, also, the enemy gunfire had gotten so accurate that we no longer anchored at night.

"The enemy guns, for the most part, were practically invisible. Most of them were dug into caves in the hillsides and could be retracted for protection. Others were on the reverse slopes and couldn't be seen. Still others were mobile, and the Communists changed their locations every so often. The only way you could spot them was by the flashes and smoke of their fire. Sometimes, you couldn't see the flashes because of the sun, and many of their guns didn't put out a lot of smoke.

"It was a common chuckle among our ships that the Communists had a gunnery school right in Wonsan city, and that one of our primary jobs was to serve as suitable targets for the training of artillerymen.

"At any rate the enemy's gunnery improved constantly and kept us on our toes. Personally, I think my ships were lucky not to be hit. The only

---

award was conceived, this staff expended considerable effort searching the records to establish the time of origin of the 'Key to the City' and of the title 'Mayor of Wonsan.' The best information indicated that it started in May 1952. From that date on, the relieving of duties as Commander Task Unit 95.2.1 by Destroyer Squadron commanders had an additional ceremony included. The incoming commander was presented the wooden 'Key to the City' and given the title 'Mayor of Wonsan.' "

reason they weren't was because of our evasive tactics. Whenever the enemy guns opened up on us, our ships cranked on speed, started the 'war dance', and made themselves a rapidly moving target.

"The minesweepers had the toughest job, having to work close to the beach and in constant danger of gunfire. The sailors on the destroyers realized this and often contributed their ice cream ration to those fellows.

"Over-all, I believe that the siege of Wonsan was very worthwhile. We did a lot of damage on the MSR* and to military installations in Wonsan. Also, with the harbor kept free of mines, our Navy posed a constant threat of invasion.

"But more important, perhaps, was the excellent training our ships and people received. Wonsan taught us not to forget basic gunnery doctrines and techniques; it taught us the value of knowing how to use optical control and of having a good director setup, and not to depend entirely on our electronic equipment.

"The 30-day duty in Wonsan gave all hands a boost in morale, pep, enthusiasm, and efficiency. There was a noticeable buildup in unit pride, and a visible determination not to have a machinery breakdown that would force a ship off the firing line.

"Most of all, the duty at Wonsan gave all hands a feeling of mutual interest and interdependence. To those who served there, Wonsan pointed up the need for balanced forces *within* our Navy—forces which intimately know each other's capabilities and limitations."

"MAYORS OF WONSAN"

Name		Term
CAPT Warren E. Gladding	COMCORTDESRON 1	5-29-52 to 6- 7-52
CAPT Allan A. Ovrom	COMDESDIV 52	6- 7-52 to 6-22-52
CDR Robert M. Hinckley, Jr.	COMCORTDIV 92	6-22-52 to 6-24-52 7- 3-52 to 7- 9-52
CDR Nels C. Johnson	COMDESDIV 262	6-24-52 to 7- 3-52 8- 3-52 to 8-13-52
CAPT James B. Grady	COMDESDIV 112	7- 9-52 to 7-17-52
CAPT Milton T. Dayton	COMDESDIV 11	7-17-52 to 7-29-52 10-19-52 to 11- 2-52
CDR Louis Lefelar	COMDESDIV 132	7-29-52 to 8- 3-52
CAPT Richard B. Levin	COMDESRON 2	8-13-52 to 8-23-52
CAPT Selby K. Santmyers	COMDESDIV 12	8-23-52 to 8-25-52
CDR Frederick M. Stiesberg	COMCORTDIV 92	8-25-52 to 9-17-52 10- 6-52 to 10-15-52

* Main Supply Route.

Name		Term
CAPT Raymond D. Fussel-man	COMCORTDESDIV 13	9-17-52 to 10- 6-52
CAPT Walter E. Linaweaver	COMDESRON 15	10-15-52 to 10-19-52
CDR Antoine W. Venne, Jr.	COMCORTDIV 92	11- 2-52 to 11-11-52
CDR Colin J. MacKenzie	COMCORTDESDIV 13	11-11-52 to 11-18-52
CDR Robert J. Ovrom	COMCORTRON 9	11-18-52 to 12-16-52
		1-23-53 to 2-23-53
CAPT Albert L. Shepherd	COMDESDIV 202	12-16-52 to 1-10-53
CAPT Carl E. Bull	COMDESDIV 172	1-10-53 to 1-23-53
CAPT Lester C. Conwell	COMDESDIV 72	2-23-53 to 3-21-53
CAPT Dale Mayberry	COMDESDIV 282	3-21-53 to 4- 3-53
CAPT Harold G. Bowen, Jr.	COMDESDIV 92	4- 3-53 to 4-16-53
CDR Stephen W. Carpenter	CO USS SHELTON	4-16-53 to 4-20-53
CAPT John C. Woelfel	COMDESRON 3	4-20-53 to 4-21-53
CDR Edward J. Foote	CO USS GURKE	4-21-53 to 4-23-53
CDR Donald F. Quigley	CO USS BRUSH	5- 9-53 to 5-15-53
CDR Albert L. Gebelin	COMDESDIV 52	5-18-53 to 5-21-53
CAPT Richard E. Myers	COMDESRON 7	5-31-53 to 6-15-53
		7- 1-53 to 7-22-53
CAPT Jack Maginnis	COMDESRON 24	6-15-53 to 7- 1-53
CAPT Carl M. Dalton	COMDESRON 11	7-22-53 to end of hostilities

(Note: The above list does not include the names of many officers who were temporarily in command at Wonsan while CTU 95.2.1 was absent for replenishment, refuelling, etc.)

The "Bald Eagle" of the Essex

The naval aviator of the Korean War most rescued from the harbor of Wonsan was Commander Paul N. Gray, commanding officer of VF-54, a Skyraider squadron aboard the *Essex*. To him especially, and to the dozens of other pilots who ditched and parachuted to safety there, the occupation of Wonsan harbor was justified as a collecting point for disabled airmen and aircraft.

"My first misfortune" wrote Gray,[7] "occurred on 7 September 1951, while dive bombing a bridge at a place called Majon-ni. I was hit in the engine and I had a tense flight of about 50 miles as the oil ran out. I watched the pressure drop to zero about five miles short of Wonsan but was able to glide to the harbor, where a South Korean patrol boat picked me up.

"The second misfortune, and probably the closest of all, happened while strafing a train in the railyard at Wonsan. I sustained a direct hit by heavy enemy antiaircraft fire. A later count showed 57 separate holes in my plane. I landed at an emergency strip in South Korea, and after plugging the most essential hydraulic lines, took off again and flew the plane back to the *Essex*, where it was used as a source of spare parts. The date was 28 October 1951.

"From this time until January 1952, I avoided further emergency landings mainly because the AA fire missed the vital parts of my plane. However, on 22 January, my luck changed and I was hit again by a 37-mm. shell directly in the engine. At the time I was leading a bombing hop on the rail line north of Wonsan, about 25 miles from the harbor. The plane immediately caught fire and the engine quit. Apparently three or more cylinders had been blown off by the explosion. Largely because of my loud prayers, the engine caught again and ran intermittently until I got to the water just off the beach at Wonsan. The USS *Gregory* fished me out of the very cold water more frozen than I ever care to be again.

"Later, on 30 January 1952, while bombing a rail line south of Kowan, I was again presented with another 37-mm. hit in the engine. This one blew off a blade of the propeller, and before I could cut the mixture, the engine almost vibrated itself off the airplane. By alternately opening and closing the mixture control, I again nursed the plane just off the beach at Wonsan, and was picked up by the USS *Twining*.

"Upon returning to the *Essex*, RADM John Perry told me that the Navy could take no more chances on my getting 'smoked', and restricted me thereafter to flying antisubmarine patrol missions in the vicinity of the task force."

During these episodes, the pilots of VF-54 posted a sign in the squadron ready room in honor of their bald-headed skipper: "Use caution when ditching damaged airplanes in Wonsan harbor. Don't hit CDR Gray."

The Emergency Airstrip on Yo-do

As the air interdiction campaign to cut the Communists' rail and road supply lines in 1951 and 1952 intensified, there was a rise in the damage and loss of naval aircraft.* Many damaged planes had ditched alongside the siege ships in Wonsan harbor in similar fashion to Commander Gray, although not as frequently. This fact highlighted the need of an emergency airstrip on one of Wonsan's captured islands.

To illustrate this fact, the helicopter ship, *LST-799*, had rescued 24 aviators—U. S. Navy, South African, U. S. Marine, and British—the ma-

---

* See Chapter 8, "The Struggle to Strangle."

jority of them in the vicinity of Wonsan. The following are summaries of most of these rescues:

15 May 51 at Chinnampo. Rescued LT J. A. Winterbotham, attached HMS *Glory*.

30 September 51 at Hungnam, rescued CAPT J. W. Tuttle, USMC, pilot delivered to LSD—5. (Helicopter flown by LT J. M. Farwell and J. E. Kincaid, AD1.)

3 October 51, rescued 2nd LT A. M. Muller attached Second Squadron *Bon Homme Richard*, delivered to LSD 5. Intense small arms fire in the pickup area. As helicopter ascended, several riflemen popped up from underbrush and opened fire. (Helicopter flown by Chief Aviation Pilot C. W. Buss and R. O. Sherrill, AD3.)

3 October 51, rescued 2nd LT A. M. Muller attached Second Squadron South African Air Force, 55 miles west of Wonsan. Heavy small arms fire encountered. Pilot delivered to LSD 5. (Helicopter flown by LT J. M. Farwell and crewman W. H. Williams, AD2.)

6 October 51, rescued ENS W. C. Bailey, USN, 507924, attached VA-923, *Bon Homme Richard*, effected from Wonsan. Downed pilot fifteen miles northeast Hungnam. (Helicopter flown by Chief Aviation Pilot C. W. Buss and S. W. Manning, AT3.)

22 October 51 at Wonsan, rescued CAPT Edward N. Lefarvie, 30579, USMC, from behind enemy lines 40 miles southwest of Wonsan. Antiaircraft and small arms fire encountered throughout the mission. (Helicopter flown by LT JG G. Hamilton and crewman D. J. Cowser, AD3.)

29 January 52 at Wonsan, rescued LT S. B. Murphy, 428338, USN.*

3 February 52 at Wonsan, rescued LT Robert J. Geffel of VF-653.

3 February 52, LTJG N. J. Johnson of VF-794 rescued south of Hamhung by LT J. W. Ross, returned to *LST-799* where treated for shock and exposure.

20 March 52 at Wonsan, rescued ENS E. B. Bernard, 506693, USN, attached to VF-653 USS *Philippine Sea*. (Helicopter flown by LT C. R. Severns and crewman T. C. Roche, AD2.)

30 March 52 at Wonsan, rescued ENS H. E. Sterrett, 538313, USNR. (Helicopter piloted by LT C. R. Severns and crewman T. C. Roche, AD2.)

12 May 52 at Wonsan, rescued LT J. Newendyke, 471388, USNR. (Helicopter piloted by ADC(AP) W. L. Dunn and crewman C. H. Cooley, ADC.)

29 May 52 rescued ENS Glen M. Wicker, USN, 507908, attached to USS *Philippine Sea*. (Helicopter piloted by ADC(AP) W. L. Dunn and crewman E. Stewart, AD2.)

9 June 52 at Wonsan, rescued ENS F. Lofton, USN, 507764, attached to USS *Princeton*. (Helicopter piloted by LT B. F. McMullen and crewman T. C. Roche, AD1.)

* Murphy, a night attack pilot, had been shot down in the Hungnam area. When the rescue helicopter (piloted by LTJG J. T. Stultz and R. L. Martin, ADAN), reached the scene, Murphy was seen running across the snow-covered rice paddies pursued by enemy soldiers. When he stopped momentarily to light a flare, a bullet creased his neck. Stultz landed and picked up Murphy, who said he had been running for thirty minutes.

10 June 52 at Wonsan, rescued ENS R. N. Hensen, from USS *Princeton*. (Helicopter flown by LT C. R. Severns and crewman T. C. Roche, AD1.)

10 June 52 rescued LCDR Cook Cleland, 99640, USNR, attached VF-653 from USS *Valley Forge*. (Rescued by LT B. E. McMullen and W. R. Moore, AL2.)

13 June 52 rescued LCDR Leonard Robinson, commanding officer VF-64, USS *Boxer*.

13 June 52 rescued LTJG W. F. Moore, USN, 508222, attached VF-193, USS *Princeton*.

13 June 52 rescued LTJG C. K. Alford, 460904, USNR, VF-193, USS *Princeton*.

16 June 52 rescued LTJG W. A. Buttlar, 494638, USN. (Helicopter flown by LT B. E. McMullen, crewman R. A. McDaniel, AD3.)

18 June 52 rescued LTJG A. Zimmerly 507754, USN, VF-63, USS *Boxer*. (Rescued by LT B. E. McMullen and crewman Decker.)

"The *799's* total pilot recovery score," said LT Paul D. Drummond (who had relieved LT Houston as its skipper in November 1951), "was twenty-four, two of which were by boat and twenty-two by helicopter. Our big rescue day was 13 June 1952.

"At about 1300 we received a 'Mayday'. Lieutenant Birton E. McMullen, the helicopter pilot, took off with his crewman, R. A. MacDaniels, AD3, in the direction of Hodo Pando. Information received via radio indicated that there was a pilot down about ten miles inland and that a CAP* was orbiting him.

"McMullen proceeded to the scene and located the downed pilot. Because of ground fire and rough terrain, the pickup had to be made by hoist on the run.

"The CAP did a good job of strafing during the pickup, with some of the pilots making dry runs because they were out of ammunition. The downed pilot, who turned out to be LTJG C. K. Alford, was in good shape, with only slight burns on one hand and one on the side of his face.

"Alford's plane had caught fire, and he had bailed out. During his descent, he was fired upon, and returned the fire with his own pistol. Upon reaching the ground, he discarded his parachute. Three armed soldiers approached his hiding place. When they were within fifteen feet, Alford opened fire, dropped two, and the third soldier fled.

"During the course of the return trip," continued Drummond, "one of the escort airplanes spotted a dye marker. This pilot was LTJG W. F. Moore, who had been hit by AA fire and had ditched just east of Hodo Pando. LT McMullen located Moore and picked him up. This made four people in a 'copter designed to carry only three.

* Combat Air Patrol.

"For this reason we on the ship were concerned lest the helicopter's heavy load make landing aboard hazardous.

"However, McMullen reported that since he was almost out of gas, his load wasn't excessive.

"When the 'copter got close enough for us to see, it looked like four people were riding in the front seat of a Model T Ford. I doubt if a helicopter ever brought back a more satisfying load."[8]

Two famous aviators—one Navy and one Marine—were rescued by *LST-799* from Wonsan. On the 10th of June 1952, LCDR Cook Cleland was rescued. Cleland was skipper of reserve squadron VF-643 from *Valley Forge*. He was the aviator who had won the Thompson Trophy race at the National Air Races in Cleveland, Ohio, in 1948.

The famous Marine aviator whose life was saved by a helicopter from *LST-799* was Colonel Robert E. Galer, USMC, a Congressional Medal of Honor winner of World War II.

"The 'May Day' came in about 1700," said LT Drummond. "The report stated there was a pilot down about sixty miles in a straight line southwest of Wonsan, and about all of this distance inland. This 120-mile round trip was just about maximum for a rescue helicopter. It was also very late in the afternoon, and there was doubt that enough daylight remained to effect a rescue. Flight after sunset was extremely difficult because the horizon was often not visible. Moreover, the flight had to be made over a circuitous route to skirt known gun positions. And to make the rescue even more ticklish, the rescue would be made at a height near the helicopter's ceiling.

"It was decided to give it a try, however. The helicopter pilot was LT E. J. McCutcheon, who had been aboard only a few days, and who, except for one or two mine reconnaissance missions, had had little time to acquaint himself with the area. McCutcheon took off and headed for the coast where the CAP of two Corsairs were waiting to lead him in.

" 'Mac' was fortunate in that the weather was clear, and after sunset he had a beautiful full moon, which permitted him to see the horizon.

"The helicopter arrived at the pickup position while there was still light enough for him to find LTCOL Galer, and he commenced making the pickup. This had to be done 'on the run' to retain enough 'lift' to keep from crashing the helicopter on the hillside. As it turned out, the 'copter did slide off and dragged LTCOL Galer through the underbrush before 'Mac' lifted him clear of the ground. Control was recovered before anything more serious occurred, and the 'copter cleared the area for the trip home.

"As soon as we heard he was on the way home, we made a beeline for the point where he was expected to cross the coastline. By this time it was dark, and McCutcheon's fighter escort was low on fuel. There was a 'Dumbo' (amphibian) in the air to relieve his escort in the vicinity of the coastline and to assist in guiding the 'copter back to the ship. We lighted ship, lining the edges of the main deck with battle lanterns laid on their backs, turned both signal search lights vertically, and fired flares every few seconds.

"The 'Dumbo' contacted 'Mac' and got him headed in our direction. Just about the time McCutcheon was starting to throw gear overboard to lighten his load, he spotted us. He arrived on deck about 2030 with approximately ten gallons of gas and a great sense of relief. Other than bruises and one or two possible cracked ribs, COL Galer was in good condition."

There was little doubt that the siege of Wonsan proved worthwhile for the rescue of UN aviators.

To the Naval and Marine officers who were living on Yo-do during this period, the value of having an emergency airstrip was easy to recognize.

The naval officer assigned to Yo-do, LT James S. Lampe, Jr., also a naval aviator, has recorded how the idea of an airstrip on Yo-do originated.

"The credit for proposing an airstrip on Yo-do belongs to LTCOL Richard G. Warga, USMC, the Commander East Coast Defense Element (CTE 95.23)," said Lampe. "He and I were billeted together in our tent camp on Yo-do when the idea was broached. We had seen several planes ditch in the general area of Wonsan during the summer of 1951 and we had talked to most of the pilots. Winter was approaching, and ditching planes in that frigid water would make survival even more difficult.

"One morning in August, LTCOL Warga was hunkered over our Coleman burner on the floor of our tent, frying the eggs I had scrounged from a destroyer the previous day. Warga asked me, as an aviator, if it wouldn't be possible to crash land a plane on one of the Yo-do beaches, rather than ditch it in the harbor. I told him no, it wouldn't, because no beach of the island was long enough and the curvature of the beaches wasn't right. We then got to wondering if a plane could crash land in the 'valley' portion of Yo-do.

"As far as I know that was how the idea to build an airstrip on Yo-do germinated. After breakfast, COL Warga and I walked from one end of the 'valley' to the other several times, estimating its usable length, how much leveling would have to be done, and how much equipment would have to be moved ashore. We estimated that two bulldozers could make a 'crash' strip in a couple of weeks, and, with additional time, a short landing strip. The possibility looked good to us.

"COL Warga sent a dispatch to CTF 95 recommending the project—not without misgivings, however. We both knew how close the airstrip would be to enemy artillery fire."

Of the several friendly islands of Wonsan, Yo-do was the only one suitable for an airstrip. Even so, the strip would be short and would accommodate only propeller-type planes—no jets. By running the emergency field completely across the island in the "valley" from northeast to southwest, a runway length of some 2,400 feet could be obtained.

But many obstacles to building an airstrip on Yo-do were evident. Could it be kept operational in such close proximity to the Wonsan shore batteries? The Kalma Gak batteries were 13,500 yards distant. The batteries on Hodo Pando were 10,000 yards distant. And the batteries behind Umi-do were closest of all—only 8,000 yards. Building a strip under the muzzles of these guns might be difficult. And after it was built, could it be operated? Perhaps the enemy guns could keep the strip so pocked with holes that it would be useless for landing aircraft.

There was also some opposition to building a field on an island above the stagnant battlefront which, if a truce were ever signed, would have to be evacuated. Why build an airfield and later have to donate it to the enemy?

Finally, there was the consideration that the island of Yo-do might be recaptured. In Wonsan itself, the memory of the 28-29 November 1951 raid on Hwangto-do was still fresh. On the west coast of Korea, the Communists succeeded in recapturing one of the ROK-held islands in the Yalu Gulf (the island of Taehwa-do). On the east coast near Songjin an enemy raid had been carried out on the Yang-do islands, a tiny three-island group about five acres in area, on 19 February 1952. Thirty sampans had attacked the little island of Kil-chu at 0130. Destroyer *Shelton* (DD-790, CDR Stephen W. Carpenter), the New Zealand frigate *Taupo* (LCDR K. A. Cradock-Hartoff, MBE, RN), and the USS *Endicott* (DMS-35, LCDR L. W. Barnard) helped break up the attack. Two waves of enemy troops succeeded in getting ashore, but a stout defense by the defending 83rd ROK Marine Corps Company (led by former all-American halfback First Lieutenant Joseph Bartos, USMC) killed or captured the attackers. Of the 86 enemy raiders who had landed, 80 were killed and 6 were wounded. A simultaneous raid on the nearby island of Myongchon by 15 sampans was broken up, the ships sinking 10 sampans and inflicting heavy casualties in the remaining five. A near miss punctured *Taupo's* engine room and *Shelton* suffered 15 casualties from three shore battery hits.

Building an airstrip on Yo-do might invite its capture.

The Seventh Fleet Commander, Vice Admiral Robert P. Briscoe, took

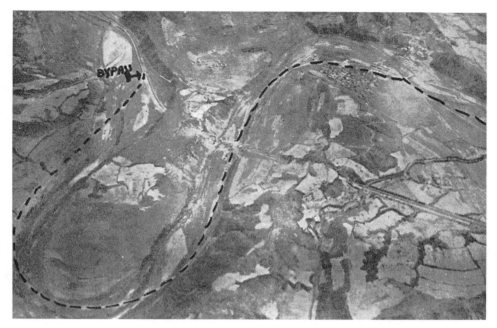

THEY TRY SOMETHING ELSE. With the bridge out for good, the Communists tried a four-mile by-pass, but by the time that was ready another key bridge to the south was drawing the attention of naval aviation. *Below,* RADM Thomas S. Combs presents the Distinguished Flying Cross and Air Medal with three gold stars to CDR Carlson for outstanding services.

More Bridge Busting. *At top,* one of six major Yalu River highway bridges linking Korea (left bank) and Manchuria. Carrier plane has just dropped a thousand-pound bomb on Korean side. *Below,* the Koko-do Bridge at Pohang collapses after receiving direct hit by gunfire from the *Rochester*.

NAVY FLIERS SCORE A BULLSEYE. *Top*, Han River span at Seoul is closed until further notice after direct hit by naval aircraft bombing runs. *Below*, the Navy's only use of aerial torpedoes in Korea smashed Hwachon Dam, foiling Communist use of the entrapped waters prior to an offensive.

WORKED-OVER RAILROAD. *At top,* Task Force 77 aircraft effectively knock out the railroad of the main line system north of Wonsan. *Below,* a rail sector south of Kowon after a concentrated attack by aircraft also from Task Force 77.

all these factors into consideration, but when considered in the light of how many Seventh Fleet aircraft might have been saved and might be saved in the future, the dangers and obstacles were readily accepted. In fact, the salvage of a single plane would be worth the effort. The mental comfort such a field would give to Task Force 77 pilots was yet another factor in favor of the airstrip.

"We made an effort to talk to each pilot who ditched in Wonsan," said Lampe, "and without exception every one said that such a strip would be a great help and a great comfort when they were striking in the Wonsan area."

The Seabees of ACB-1 (Naval Beach Group One, Officer in Charge, CDR Wm. C. Bowers, CEC) were confident that if the Marines could *hold* it and the Navy *operate* it, they could *build* it.

With typical enthusiasm and zest, the Seabees (3 officers and 75 men) sailed from Japan aboard *LST-692* on 3 June 1952, debarking on Yo-do and commencing work on the airstrip on 9 June.

"The LST arrived at Yo-do with a long pontoon strapped to each side," said LT Lampe. "Each of these pontoons ran almost her entire length. Because of this, and because our only beach had a very shallow gradient, I anticipated some trouble in getting her close enough to the beach to offload equipment.

"However, the Seabees had it all worked out. Before beaching, the pontoons were dropped in the water, strapped together, and then pushed onto the beach with the bow of the LST. The Seabees were offloading their heavy equipment in jig time."

Engineers had estimated that 45 days would be required to construct a 120 × 2,400 foot strip. Despite annoying gunfire on two days (13 and 21 June), the Seabees finished the job in one-third the estimated time, reporting the runway operational on 25 June. By removing rock from one end of the field, the Seabees managed to widen the strip to 200 feet, and improved one end of the runway by adding ramps to the water's edge in order to facilitate the removal of dud aircraft by barge.

The strip was first used on 15 July 1952 when seven Corsairs of VF-193 *(Princeton)*, ran low on fuel after an afternoon's fruitless search for their downed comrade, LTJG Harold A. Riedl, who had been shot down 30 miles northwest of Hungnam. Three of the searching Corsairs refueled on Yo-do and returned to *Princeton*. The other four spent the night, and returned safely to their carrier the next day.*

---

* Riedl was rescued the next morning by *Iowa's* helicopter (flown by LT Robert L. Dolton and crewman Willis A. Meyers, AM1) after a wet, sleepless, and insect-ridden night during which time Red soldiers had come within ten feet of his hiding place.

Although the Communists tried many times to neutralize the field with gunfire, they never succeeded.

In honor of the officer who had ordered it built, Vice Admiral R. P. Briscoe, now COMNAVFE, the airstrip was named Briscoe Field.

Briscoe Field was to prove of immense value the final year of the war, as it became the rescue point for many pilots and aircraft.

Patrolling "Muffler" and "Tin-Pan Alley"

To the destroyer-minesweeper teams besieging Wonsan's harbor day after day, the duty was routine but never monotonous. Even in the swept areas of "Muffler" and "Tin-Pan Alley," there was constant danger not only from enemy gunfire on three sides, but from drifting mines and surreptitiously planted moored mines as well.

"The Chinese needed only a few hours and they could have re-mined Wonsan," said Rear Admiral Gingrich, CTF 95. "Our intelligence revealed how the Communists would tie mines to logs and float them down the Namdae Chon River into the harbor to try and drive us out.

"First they used plain logs and timed their passage from the launching points out into the swept areas of 'Muffler' and 'Tin-Pan Alley', watching them with binoculars. After they had established the time pattern, they would lash contact mines to other logs, using a pelican hook with a soluble washer. This soluble washer was timed to dissolve and deposit the mine in the swept area."[9]

The accuracy of the enemy guns steadily improved, and they were able to achieve hits with fewer and fewer rounds. USS *Lewis* (DE-535, LCDR G. B. Hawkins) was struck twice on 21 October 1952. The first shell struck the forward fireroom and disabled the number one boiler, but fortunately it was a dud. The second shell struck *Lewis'* fantail, doing minor damage. *Lewis'* casualties were seven dead and one wounded.

"Nowhere was the primitiveness of the Korean War more evident than in Wonsan harbor," said Commander Sheldon H. Kinney, commanding officer of the USS *Taylor* (DDE-468). "We only had to worry about mines and shore guns; not aerial, naval, or submarine opposition. Even so, these two were enough to keep us on our toes.

"There were several thumb rules which were pretty generally accepted by the destroyers that worked in Wonsan. One was that if you got close to the corners of the swept areas, especially those close inshore, your chances of being fired upon were increased, because these positions had

---

During the rescue of Riedl, the airplane of Ensign Robert E. Roberts of VF-193 was struck by antiaircraft fire, punching a 3-inch hole in the wing, and smashing the canopy. Roberts suffered cuts and lacerations but landed safely aboard *Princeton*.

been zeroed-in. Second, if two or more ships were operating in the same area close together, the probability of receiving enemy fire was greater. The Communists fired often because the swept areas were fairly small and in maneuvering the ships to stay clear of their gunfire, the danger of collision or running into the minefields was greater. Third, the Communists usually fired late in the afternoon when the sun was in position to make *us* excellent targets and to make it very difficult to locate the offending battery. Somebody even coined a phrase for this, 'the Wonsan cocktail hour.'

"During the entire period my destroyer was in Wonsan harbor, we followed the usual procedure of being in a modified Condition III. At no time did we ever sound General Quarters. We kept one mount of our 3-inch and two 5-inch mounts manned with control and plotting crews on station. A senior gunnery department officer on watch was free to conduct indirect call fire from CIC or direct fire from the MK 37 director. This arrangement permitted prompt fire when required. Below decks, we set Condition Able continuously.

"Our most interesting and busy day in Wonsan," continued CDR Kinney, "occurred on 18 September. On this particular day, *Taylor* was 'riding shotgun'* on the USS *Heron* (AMS-18) (LTJG Dixon Lademan), which was conducting a routine minesweeping operation in 'Tin-Pan Alley.'

"About 1130 that morning, both ships commenced to receive very accurate and heavy enemy fire estimated to be 155-mm. in size. The first salvo bracketed both ships. We checked the surrounding land areas but were unable to see where this fire was coming from. The *Heron* immediately cut loose her heavy magnetic minesweeping gear and commenced a retirement in a northeasterly direction towards Yo-do island.

"I rang up 22 knots and commenced making a smoke screen with both fog generator and fireroom smoke, laying it in between the *Heron* and the firing batteries. This smoke proved very effective in screening *Heron,* and *Taylor* then doubled back to enjoy the immunity from observation. The enemy fire ceased.

"A spotter on one of the friendly-held islands reported to us that the probable location of the guns was in the hills to the south of the city, and that their range was too far from us to permit reaching them with our 5-inch fire. Not being able to return the enemy fire irked us.

"Several days later, however, we got even. On the 26th of September the visibility was particularly excellent. At this time the island spotters were

---

* "Riding shotgun," a term adopted from the Old West, meant acting as guard and protector of another ship exposed to enemy action and unable to protect itself, or, in minesweeping, the mine-destroying vessel itself.

able to make a very good count of visible gun positions in the surrounding hills. They counted about thirty guns. We fired at several things during the day—sampans in the harbor; boxcars and flatcars in the marshalling yards, using air spot from Air Force Mustang aircraft; and enemy gun batteries.

"Early in the afternoon, the crew of the main battery director detected smoke from an enemy battery on a hill behind the city. The range was 16,600 yards. We plotted the guns in and determined that these were the same guns that had fired on us but a few days before. We closed in to the very edge of the southwest corner of 'Muffler' in order to come within range. Then we opened fire. 'Fire for effect' was followed by a direct hit which sent a billowing cloud of white smoke towering into the sky. The gun was silenced, and it was later verified by the island spotters that a large supply of ammunition had been detonated."[10]

The Harbor Islands

By the fall of 1952, seven islands in Wonsan harbor were in UN hands —Yo-do, Mo-do, Sa-do, Tae-do, Sin-do, Ung-do and Hwangto-do. The rest of the numerous small islands had been rendered untenable by the raids of the Korean Marine Corps. After the leper colony from Tae-do had been evacuated by UN forces to an island off South Korea, that island was used as a gunfire spotting post. Ung-do had been garrisoned to prevent its capture and use by the Communists.

The largest island, Yo-do, continued to serve as harbor headquarters for CTE 95.23, commanded by a colonel or lieutenant colonel, U. S. Marines, with 12 U. S. Marines. Also, the island was headquarters of the Seventh KMC battalion, approximately 700 marines, who had the mission, under CTE 95.23, of protecting all the "friendly" Wonsan harbor islands. Atop Yo-do, 377 feet high, was an observation post which commanded a good general view of the entire harbor.

Three of the friendly islands were utilized as spotting posts for ANGLICO* shore fire control parties: Mo-do, Tae-do and Hwangto-do.

The island of Mo-do was closest to the Hodo Pando batteries, approximately 6,000 yards distant. Although many of the 40-odd Hodo Pando guns were on reverse slopes, the flash of their fire could be seen from Mo-do, and bearings taken. Simultaneous bearings on the Hodo Pando guns were also taken from Yo-do, to accurately position the location of these batteries.

With an elevation of 236 feet, Mo-do also commanded a good view of the enemy batteries which had the nickname "Ink Spots" (see chart). These guns were heavy batteries (155-mm.) and could reach all the harbor islands,

* ANGLICO means "Air Naval Gunfire Liaison Company."

including Yo-do. The "Ink Spots" were also in a position to defilade the entire swept channel of "Muffler," and were a constant irritation to the sweepers working in that area.

Mo-do was the usual post of one naval officer and three men of the ANGLICO, whose duties, in addition to spotting naval gunfire, were to maintain a plot of worthwhile targets, of the Hodo Pando batteries and the "Ink Spots," and to maintain a nightly count of truck traffic moving south. Whenever the siege ships were firing into Mo-do's area, the naval gunfire spotting team would correct the ships' fire.

The island of Tae-do was closest to the Kalma Gak batteries, and was the duty post of one naval officer and three men of the ANGLICO.

Still the most important and hazardous island was Hwangto-do. Assigned to this island was a U. S. Marine Officer and three spotters, plus a contingent of Korean Marines to protect the island from nocturnal sampan raids. As at Mo-do and Tae-do, the duty was four months in duration.

Life on Hwangto-do was a cave existence of C-rations, noise, and darkness. The occupants could come outside only at night. A light or a fire at night drew heavy mortar fire. Daylight meant constant danger from mortar and machine gun as well as artillery fire. The shore fire control parties dug bunkers on the north side of the island, where they lived, and a lookout bunker at the top of the island for observation purposes. The island was without water, except for one small well. Additional water, food, ammunition, and supplies had to be brought in at night across a small landing beach which faced Wonsan.

On clear nights, the enemy truck traffic moving south from Wonsan was visible from the Hwangto-do observation post. The number of trucks whose headlights could be counted averaged 300. On occasions, the southward-moving truck count rose as high as 700. For every truck in convoy whose headlights could be seen, three or four without headlights could not be seen. Whenever the truck count out of Wonsan was above normal, increased activity along the battlefront could be expected a few days later.

The senior naval officer ashore on the harbor islands was the intelligence officer of Commander Task Group 95.2, a destroyer or destroyer escort squadron commander, who was afloat.

"I arrived on Yo-do on 16 July 1952 as the relief of LT James S. Lampe, Jr.," said LCDR A. Christopher, "remaining on Yo-do until March 1953. Lampe met me at the just-finished airstrip in a jeep, and we started up to the camp. We hadn't gone fifty feet when a 155-mm. shell exploded about 250 yards away. Before we got to the camp near the top of the hill, three or four more lit around the road. That was quite a greeting!

"The campsite was protected by a forty-yard-wide land minefield which surrounded the site. Only the road and one guarded path passed through the minefield. The land mines were a mixture of trip-wire mines and regular mines. We also had a few machine gun posts around the site.

"All of the Americans on Yo-do lived in this tent camp. Later, we dug ourselves more comfortable bunkers. The camp had been well placed on a reverse slope so that the enemy's artillery fire couldn't reach us too well. Once in a while, however, we took some tree bursts on the ridge behind us that shook us up. Below our camp was a bluff, which fell some 100 feet almost vertically to the sea.

"Near our tents were slit trenches where we retired whenever the Reds were shooting at us; also available was a communal privy.

"My companions numbered three other intelligence officers: LT Joseph B. McNeill, Jr., USN; an Air Force officer, 1st LT John Intorcia; and my South Korean assistant and interpreter, LT Chiang Jung Taek.

"Our worst night, I suppose, was during Typhoon Karen, which passed just south of Wonsan on 18 August 1952. It blew like hell, and during the night our tents took off. Every few minutes a tree would fall down, or a limb would be torn off and fall into the land mines, causing them to explode. From one explosion, a few fragments of shrapnel went through my tent.

"The rest of the night we were wet, cold, and miserable. But the thing which really set our nerves a-jangle was to have an enemy mine break its moorings, hit the rocky beach below us, and explode.*

"Mostly we ate canned food, although the destroyers and heavy ships were always generous about giving us fresh food whenever we went aboard. Later on, we established a better messing system. All water had to be chlorinated.

"I had several duties on Yo-do. Among other things, I served as intelligence officer for CTG 95.2 and kept a situation plot for the island defense element commander. I also did all the interrogations of the North Korean refugees and prisoners of war.

"Each morning I assembled all the information from the shore fire control parties who were assigned to Mo-do, Tae-do and Hwangto-do—truck counts, target information, active gun positions and the like.

"Whenever I received word that one of our cruisers or battleships was coming in for a bombardment of Wonsan, I would make a trip to the

---

* For one month after this typhoon, the Seventh Fleet sighted and sank more than forty mines which had broken their moorings and drifted out to sea. It was one of these mines which caused the loss of *Sarsi,* a tug, and damage to destroyer *Barton.* Also, it was Typhoon Karen which caused the siege ships to temporarily leave the harbor for the safety of deeper water. This was the only lapse in the siege of Wonsan.

other islands where we had shore fire control parties, getting the best and latest target information.

"When the 'heavy' came in, I would meet her in the outer channel, go aboard, and give her the target information. Once aboard, my first job was to get the 'heavy's' secondary battery all lined up on the Hodo Pando guns, so that they could be taken under fire as the ship entered the inner harbor. I assisted optical control in spotting the exact caves in which the guns were located.

"After orienting the secondary battery, I commenced briefing the main battery plot on their targets.

"I think the Wonsan bombardments which were set up in this fashion did a lot of damage. Our shore fire control parties on Mo-do, Tae-do, and Hwangto-do were sharp and experienced. When they gave a 50-yard spot correction, it *was* fifty yards.

"One excellent bombardment took place on 23 September 1952, when the *Iowa* had General Mark Clark, Admiral Briscoe, and Vice Admiral J. J. Clark aboard. We had late target information on some of the Hodo Pando guns, and when the 'Big Mo' opened up on them she got a magnificent secondary explosion from an ammunition storage for that battery. The smoke went several thousand feet in the air. These particular guns were permanently silenced.

"In my opinion, the siege of Wonsan was very worthwhile for a number of reasons. It was valuable as an intelligence outpost. It was valuable as a rescue point for aviators and airplanes. And it was a thorn in the side to the Communists, who could never be sure we wouldn't make a landing some place in the area."[11]

Third Year of Siege

The start of the final year of the siege saw destroyers *De Haven* and *Samuel N. Moore* on guard in Wonsan. For the remaining five months there was little change of pattern, although there was a constant increase in Communist effort to drive the American Navy out of the harbor. The Communist gunners seemed determined to sink at least one American ship to compensate for the 861-day long siege.* The enemy's ammunition, which from time to time had been rationed, was used liberally as a truce ap-

---

* By photo interpretation, it was estimated that slightly more than 1,000 guns (75-mm. and larger), artillery emplacements, mortars (81-mm. or larger), and machine guns were positioned in the Wonsan area. Percentagewise, this number constituted approximately fifty-five per cent of the air and coastal defenses of North Korea. The majority of these were antiaircraft guns; approximately 160 of the enemy guns were able to shoot at the siege ships.

proached. April, May, and June witnessed the heaviest volume of enemy fire as the Communists fired approximately sixteen hundred, thirteen hundred, and eleven hundred rounds respectively—more than half of them at the siege vessels.

The "friendly" islands, too, received a steady increase in the enemy fire, particularly the island of Yo-do.

"I lived on Yo-do for the last four and one-half months of the war," said LCDR William L. Thede,[13] assigned to COMNAVFE Special Support Group, TG 96.8. "I lived in a bunker near the airstrip, and from time to time helped to control the fire of the siege ships.

"Commencing in February 1953, we noted increased fire from the Wonsan batteries, both on the islands and at the siege ships. One of these batteries was on Hodo Pando, and we believed it to be a battery of Russian Naval 107-mm. guns. We dug up several duds from one of the Yo-do rice paddies from this battery. The shells were new, definitely of that odd size, and Russian. However, I have no reason to think the guns were manned by other than North Koreans.

"But the worst and most frequent fire on Yo-do was 90-mm. fire which came from the Umi-do area (we called this area 'Little Eva') and from the hills behind Wonsan city (an area we called the 'Shooting Gallery'). We also took a lot of fire from Kalma Gak and other areas of the bay.

"On many days, as the end of the war approached, we received as many as two or three hundred bursts in the Yo-do area in a single day.

"The purpose of this fire, in my opinion, was to neutralize Briscoe airfield, although they never did it. Occasionally, the guns seemed to be shooting for the FS-type* ship which occasionally anchored off Yodo-ri, bringing our supplies. The Wonsan guns rarely fired at night, although I do remember one occasion when the 'Little Eva' battery kept firing until 2130, 'walking' shells up and down the strip. That day we had several planes—four or five—land on the strip, and apparently they were trying to hit them. After they completed firing at the strip, we would destroy the duds, and the Seabee Detachment would repair all strip damage during the hours of darkness. The strip was never inoperable as a result of enemy fire.

"With all their fire on Yo-do, the Communists never made a direct hit on any planes while I was there, although several were hit with shrapnel while on the strip. The Air Force C-47s from Seoul which landed on the Yo-do strip bringing our supplies never stayed long. They would taxi up to the seaward end of the strip, unload as quickly as possible, keeping their engines running, and then take off immediately.

* Small cargo ship.

"As for our carrier planes, we rarely had more than two or three on the field at any one time. We had three revetments on the seaward end of the strip, and these positions gave pretty good protection to any planes parked there.

"The worst damage that Yo-do took from the Wonsan guns happened in May 1953. At this particular time we were in the process of moving into a new area, and were building an ammunition bunker; temporarily, we had stored a batch of 30- and 50-caliber machine gun ammunition, some land mines, C-3 explosive, and hand grenades in a pit at the far end of the airstrip. Just before lunch a lucky round made a direct hit on this storage, and for 45 minutes, we had quite a noisy, smoky mess on our hands. No one was hurt, however.

"As for the ships, the fire on them increased steadily, and the ability of the Reds to get hits with fewer and fewer rounds improved. Also, the Reds made much greater use of air burst shells in the last months of the siege. In my opinion, the Reds were using a 'barrage' or area type of fire, where they would 'zero-in' a particular area, or spot, and then fire a barrage at that general spot with a certain number of rounds whenever a ship was close to it. Maneuvering ships, instead of receiving a steady volume of fire, went through *areas* of gunfire. We drew two lines on our charts toward the 'Little Eva' batteries. Outside these lines ships would not be taken under fire; but if they crossed them, they would almost invariably be taken under fire by the 'Little Eva' batteries.

"In my opinion, the siege of Wonsan was well worthwhile. At one time, in 1951, as many as 60,000 troops were reported in the Wonsan area to guard against an amphibious landing. By holding the harbor we forced the Chinese to defend it with guns and troops which otherwise could have been used at the front, or elsewhere."

Five times in each of the months of April, May, and June, the Wonsan batteries succeeded in hitting an American ship. The cruiser *Los Angeles* was lightly damaged twice in a week—the last time on 2 April.

Most of the other hits were on the patrolling destroyers, causing only superficial damage to the ships, but not always so in personnel casualties. *Maddox* had three casualties from a direct hit on the main deck on 16 April. *Kyes* had nine casualties from a fantail hit on 19 April.

"The opening salvo was so far off we weren't even sure they were firing at us," said Commander R. A. Thacher, *Kyes'* commanding officer, "but they quickly spotted on. They must have estimated our speed correctly at 25 knots, which was the speed most destroyers went to for counter-battery fire. Since we couldn't go faster with two boilers, we slowed to 15 knots, and most of the following salvoes were over's. I believe firmly that if we hadn't slowed, we would have been hit several times around the bridge area."[12]

Accompanied by cruiser *Bremerton*, and destroyers *Twining* and *Colahan*, the battleship *New Jersey* fired 115 rounds into Wonsan on 5 May. Her first salvo destroyed a main observation post. Sixteen-inch shells also struck and exploded a concrete ammunition bunker. The "Big Jay" also fired at an enemy battery at Hodo Pando, collapsing the cave mouths and obliterating the firing tracks. For almost three weeks this battery was silent. Again on 11-12 July, the "Big Jay" plastered the Hodo Pando guns. These 164 rounds silenced the battery for the rest of the war.

USS *Brush* had nine casualties on 15 May; USS *Wiltsie* took a single hit on 11 June as the result of 45 rounds of 105-mm. fire; on 14 June the heavy cruiser *Bremerton* counted four rounds in the seas around her. On 15 June, USS *Lofberg* (DD-759), USS *John A. Bole* (DD-755) and USS *Current* (ARS-22) were on the receiving end of more than 100 rounds of large caliber fire, but none of the three was hit. On 17 June, *Henderson* (DD-785) received superficial damage from 80 rounds from the Wonsan batteries.

On the 18th of June, a bad day for the siege ships, cruiser *Saint Paul* was under fire. USS *Irwin* (DD-794) took a main deck hit which caused five casualties. The hardest hit was *Rowan* (DD-782). Forty-five rounds of shellfire bracketed her, five striking. One shell, thought to be a 155-mm., punched a two-foot hole on her starboard side at frame 209, a scant eight inches above the waterline. Another shell demolished the Mark 34 radar. Several other holes were visible in her side. Nine people were wounded, two of them seriously.

Gurke had three casualties on 25 June. The daylight patrol movements of the ships were somewhat restricted during June and July, but there was no intention of abandoning the siege, even for an instant.

Minesweeper *Symbol* (AM-123) and destroyer *Wiltsie* (DD-716) drew fire on 7 July. The same day *Lofberg* (DD-759), *John W. Thomason* (DD-760) and *Hamner* (DD-718) received 300 rounds, *Thomason* being slightly damaged by straddling air bursts. On 11 July, cruiser *Saint Paul* was hit by one 105-mm. shell at her 3-inch/50 gun mount, but no personnel were injured, as these guns were not manned. On the 23rd, she was again under attack, some of the shells falling as close as ten yards; but this time, there was no damage.

The Red gunners in Wonsan were to succeed in neither of their missions: they could neither sink a ship nor could they drive the American Navy out of the harbor.

The Siege Ends

On the last day of the war, 27 July 1953, amidst preparation to abandon the harbor in accordance with the truce, the siege ended as it had begun, with minesweepers sweeping and the destroyers patrolling, taking the Wonsan targets and guns under fire. Destroyers *Wiltsie* and *Porter,* and cruiser *Bremerton* fired salvoes at Wonsan targets until a minute before the 2200 deadline.

The smaller harbor islands were abandoned on the day of the truce. Yo-do, with its more extensive installations, took longer to evacuate; equipment had to be removed, storage dumps emptied, fortifications destroyed.

The last two ships to leave the harbor—the cruiser *Bremerton* and destroyer *Cunningham*—did so on the late afternoon of 1 August, after a day of pleasant swimming in the harbor which had felt the fury and stricture of a full-scale siege.

The siege of Wonsan had demonstrated the courage and tenacity of the American Navy. The important rail and highway center, with its many industries, once a city of 100,000 and now half that size, was a mass of cluttered ruins. So important had this city been as a transportation hub that the Communists had been forced to great effort to repair and rebuild the almost daily damage. Hardly an undamaged building was visible. Many industries had gone underground.

In a land-locked harbor which had been heavily mined and which the enemy had sought constantly to re-mine, where shallow, shoal-filled waters abounded, and despite the most intense enemy opposition, a siege of 861 days had been imposed with skill, determination, and success by a tireless and efficient team of American sailormen.

13.

On the Line

Introduction

Only rarely during the height of the interdiction campaign (on such occasions as the Hwachon Reservoir attack in May 1951 and the raid on Rashin in August) was the mission of Task Force 77 varied. Commencing with the air-gun strike on Chongjin on 13 April 1952, however, and definitely after June, the missions given the carrier airmen of Task Force 77 turned more and more toward strikes on industrial, military, and frontline targets, and less and less to interdiction and armed reconnaissance flights. As was described earlier, there was plentiful evidence that the interdiction campaign was a failure. For the next six months of the final year of the war, the carriers' efforts would strike primarily industrial targets in North Korea. For the last six months of the war, Task Force 77 would give the bulk of its support to frontline troops.

This shift of emphasis and employment was heartening and pleasing to all hands, planners and pilots alike. To the carrier division commanders and their staffs, such attacks were more in keeping with the inherent ability of a carrier task force to employ surprise and concentration. To the pilots, such attacks were happy respite from the dangerous and dreary interdiction and armed reconnaissance missions. As to accomplishments, the sudden onslaught of combined carrier strikes upon an oil refinery, a manufacturing installation, or a supply concentration point meant greater destruction and damage, with less risk of damage or loss to our own forces.

Such employment also kept the enemy off balance. The initial strikes in June 1952, on the enemy's hydroelectric plants, for example, brought on little antiaircraft fire; the same attack a few weeks later provoked AA fire of greater intensity and accuracy. The intervening time had allowed the enemy, anticipating repeated attacks, to rush guns to that location for its protection. A few months after the Suiho attack, for example, photo analysis revealed that the number of heavy and automatic guns surrounding the dam had increased from 71 to 167. Meanwhile, the carriers had shifted their offensive power to other targets.

By thus avoiding a rigid and unchanging routine, the naval aviators were able to inflict heavier damage at lesser cost. Too often in the Korean War, the conflict became rigidly set in fixed patterns: the enemy could be fairly certain that our night flyers would appear over the coast a few minutes after sunset or three hours before daylight; he could be certain, if he saw a colored-smoke rocket or our troops laying down their colored frontline panels, that a close air support strike was enroute; from previous attacks he could often anticipate what the direction of dive-bombing approach would be, and thus better emplace his AA defense weapons in preparation.

The final year of the Korean War saw a definite trend toward more flexible employment of the carriers. While the interdiction effort continued until the end of the war (the plan was to strike the rail lines and bridges at least once every three weeks), it received less emphasis. Bridge and track-busting strikes were employed only to keep the enemy's AA dispersed and his repair organization tied down.

In the final twelve months of the war, the carriers attacked a variety of targets, from hydroelectric plants to zinc mills, more than forty times, and developed a new type deep support air mission (termed the "Cherokee" strike).

The Attack on Suiho (23 June 1952)

The ceaseless and unspectacular attacks upon interdiction targets during months on end had a welcome climax on 23 June 1952, when, as an explosive finale to the first two years of war, the Navy, Marines, and Fifth Air Force in Korea began a two-day series of attacks upon the thirteen major electric power plants in North Korea.

For twenty-four months, these hydroelectric power plants had been ordered spared from destruction.* In the early months of the Korean War, this had been done partly in hope that the war would be won, North Korea occupied, and a costly and needless destruction avoided. After the Inchon landing, the hydroelectric power system had not been molested lest it give the Chinese Communists an excuse for entering the war. Later, after the

---

* The hydroelectric plants had been placed out of bounds early in the war: "Joint Chiefs of Staff in view of alarming situation which CINCFE has reported, authorized him (MacArthur) to undertake the planned bombing in Korea near the frontier including target at Sinuiju, the Korean end of the Yalu bridges, provided CINCFE at the time of receipt of message still considered such action to be necessary to the safety of his forces. *He was not authorized, however, to bomb any powerplants on the Yalu River . . .";* JCS despatch 7 November 1950 to CINCFE (summarized by General Collins to a Congressional subcommittee).

Chinese Communists' entrance, there was some thought that attacking the power plants might prejudice the course of the armistice negotiations.

By June 1952, however, after nearly a year of wrangling at the truce table, it was clear that there was little immediate hope either of negotiating a cease-fire or of capturing all of Korea by force. Continuing to spare any legitimate military target in North Korea for fear of prejudicing the armistice talks no longer was justified.

The truce talks, in fact, were destined to drag on for another year. Key military leaders in the Far East had consistently held that the North Korean hydroelectric power plants were legitimate military targets, that their continued operation directly contributed to the enemy's war effort. These power plants furnished the Communist radar network with electrical power; they operated the MIG-15 air complex near Antung. It was known that many small, isolated and underground factories making war material in North Korea used this electric power. Moreover, a large portion of the system's electrical capacity was transmitted to Manchuria for such arsenals as the Anshan steel industry, the Antung aluminum plant, and the Fushun coal mines.

"The spark to attack the North Korean hydroelectric power plants was struck by the Navy," said LCDR Nello D. S. Andrews, USNR, intelligence officer, Staff, Commander Task Force 95.[1] "In April 1952 I had briefed Admiral Dyer on the report of an interrogation of a North Korean Brigadier General of Artillery by the name of Lee Il, who had escaped to the Wonsan harbor island of Tae-do on 21 February 1952. He told us that the Communists were aware that UN forces had a policy not to hit their power installations. According to him, this policy was a source of great comfort to the Reds, for the electrical power provided heat for their buildings and power for their underground factories.

"Upon hearing this, Admiral Dyer immediately requested by despatch to CINCFE that the ban be lifted. A few days later CINCFE advised us that the matter was under study.

"Approximately a month later, during the turnover period when Admiral Gingrich was relieving Admiral Dyer, it seemed appropriate to bring up the matter again. That morning, I had just received a Task Force 77 press release concerning the preceding day's operations, which included mention of damage to an electrical transformer in the Wonsan area. I explained to Admiral Gingrich the long-standing prohibition against bombing or bombarding the hydroelectric system, part of which was exposed along the east coast in our area of responsibility. Admiral Dyer asked me to leave the briefing and get copies of our exchange of despatches recommending that we lift this restriction.

"Immediately after the briefing, Admiral Gingrich and Admiral Dyer helicoptered from our cruiser to the *Missouri* to have lunch with Vice Admiral J. J. Clark, who had recently relieved Vice Admiral Briscoe as Commander Seventh Fleet.

"Admiral Clark gave the proposal his enthusiastic approval, I was told, and personally took the matter up with Admiral Briscoe (COMNAVFE) and General Mark Clark (CINCFE), who in turn referred the matter to the Joint Chiefs of Staff."

General Mark Clark has described before a Congressional subcommittee how the authority to strike the North Korean power complexes was obtained:

". . . When I went to the Far East, I looked around to see what can I do on my own responsibility within my sphere of authority, what can I do in Korea over here to make the Communists realize that we are still fighting. . . . These hydroelectric plants which were turning out the power for Manchuria, for their industry, it seemed to me, should be destroyed. I was denied the right to hit the Suiho, the big one, so I sent a message to the Joint Chiefs of Staff just telling them that I was going to attack the following places, and I told them how I was going to attack them, with what kind of planes, with what kind of bombs, and gave them a certain number of hours notice that if they wanted to stop me, they would have time.

"I did not ask for permission. Much to my surprise, that came back approved and saying 'We delegate to you the authority to bomb the Suiho dam . . .' ."[2]

The Navy's part in the raid was laid on personally by Vice Admiral J. J. Clark.[3]

"I was aware," said VADM Clark, "that General Clark had informed the JCS that he was going to bomb the hydroelectric plants. It happened that I was on a visit to Tokyo and sitting in the office of Rear Admiral McMahon (Chief of Staff, COMNAVFE) when the JCS's approval despatch came in.

"I told McMahon that bombing the big Suiho dam was a job for the Navy, and he commented that the Air Force would probably be glad to have us. I told him to offer them 36 ADs, each of them loaded with 5,000 pounds of bombs, and he wrote up a message to FAFIK to that effect.

"On my way back to the operating area aboard the *Philippine Sea* two days later, I decided to go directly over to Seoul and discuss the Suiho mission in person with LTGEN Glenn O. Barcus, Commanding General, FAFIK. In the interval, there had been a flurry of despatches between General Barcus and Admiral Soucek, and the Navy's contribution had been reduced to only 20 divebombers.

"Later, I learned that the Suiho hop was almost cancelled at this stage because of the serious MIG interference potential near the Suiho dam. In fact, General Barcus had a despatch all written up ready to send to FEAF and to General Clark recommending cancellation of the strikes on Suiho.

"It was at this moment that Barcus got my departure report saying I was headed for Seoul to see him. When he received it, he told his staff to

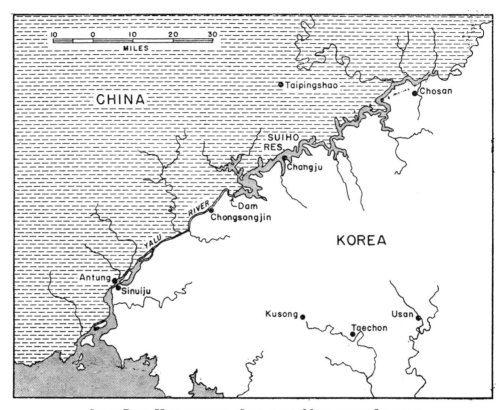

SUIHO DAM, HYDROELECTRIC SOURCE FOR MANCHURIAN INDUSTRY

hold up the Suiho cancellation despatch until I got there, for he had guessed why I was coming.

"After going over the problem with General Barcus, I told them I didn't see any reason we couldn't hit Suiho. I said that we could get in and out of there without too much trouble. I noted that the strike plans called for only 20 Navy divebombers; I said that 20 weren't enough, that we ought to send as heavy a strike in there as possible and really clobber that dam. I offered him 36 divebombers, and he accepted that."

Like the 1950 attacks upon the Yalu bridges, an attack upon the Suiho installation would be difficult. The fourth largest power plant in the world (about 400,000 KW, the same as U. S.'s Bonneville), the power plant lay on the North Korean side of the Yalu River within sight of the untouchable Manchurian territory, only 35 miles from the Antung air complex loaded with more than 250 MIGs. Because of the importance of this installation any strike in that vicinity would probably arouse intense Communist fighter opposition. The site was heavily defended—28 heavy antiaircraft guns and 43 automatic guns, some of them radar-controlled—and many of them on the Manchurian side of the river. Moreover, the Chinese had taken advantage of our "holy land" restrictions against over-flying Manchuria and had emplaced their batteries to better cover the only directions of attack. From long experience in "MIG Alley" above Suiho, it was known that the fire from these guns was intense and accurate.

The location of the hydroelectric plant at the western mouth of the Yalu River meant that an attack upon it by the Seventh Fleet's aircraft would require a long, cross-Korea flight. Unless skillfully planned and executed, this would give the enemy's antiaircraft and fighter defenses an ample alert period. And like the Yalu bridge attacks, the necessity of avoiding Manchurian territory predetermined the choice of attack courses. (This strike would be the first time that naval aircraft had operated in "MIG Alley" since the attacks on the Yalu bridges in the fall of 1950.)

The active planning, which had begun at the JOC at Seoul two days before the strike, included general target assignments and allocated attack forces, not only for Suiho, but for the twelve other hydroelectric dams in North Korea. Early in the planning, it had been decided not to use B-29s for the Suiho attacks. The "Superfort" bombers were not considered suitable because of the necessity for surprise, the heavily-defended nature of the target, and the need for pinpoint bombing (concentrating on the powerhouse, transformer yards, and penstocks on the North Korean side of the river, and *not* the dam itself). B-29s had proven too vulnerable to MIGs in daylight attacks, and there was no assurance that they could make the strike without violating the Manchurian sanctuary in their bombing runs, or without having some of the bombs released at high altitude fall on the wrong side of the river. Instead, the fighter-bombers of the Navy, Marines, and Air Force were selected to strike Suiho, although there was some doubt whether, since the B-29s had been unable to penetrate the alert MIG defenses, the Skyraiders of the Navy could do so. The carrier aircraft of the west coast carrier, under Commander Task Force 95, who would join the attacks, had to be carefully coordinated with the others.

H-hour of 0930 June 23 was chosen for the attack.

The day before the attack, Admiral Apollo Soucek's staff and the flight leaders, supervised by the strike leader, CDR A. L. Downing, USN, worked 'round the clock preparing the details of the strike: the ordnance loadings, the fuzing, the flight schedules. Intelligence materials were assembled and distributed, and pilot briefings held. Strike leaders busily worked out the details of navigation, rendezvous, fuel consumption, order of attack, direction of attack, and direction and route of recovery.

"The strike planning was done aboard the *Boxer* under CDR A. L. Downing's supervision," said CDR Neil MacKinnon, Commanding Officer, VA-195.[4] "Although we had to anticipate that the hop into that heavily defended area of 'MIG Alley' would be rough, we still welcomed a change of pace from bombing the railroads."

"Our attack plan was very tight," said CDR Downing. "We had a plus or minus one minute to get on target and three minutes to attack and clear the target. Arrival too soon and killing time over the target would not be popular, nor would a melee with the F84s that were to follow us be a pleasant exercise."

Early in the morning of the 23rd, H-hour was postponed on account of weather, the Fifth Air Force saying that a 48-hour delay might be needed. Shortly before lunch, however, another message flashed into the *Boxer*, flagship of Admiral Soucek, then Commander Task Force 77. The weather outlook over the target was improving. Attack on Suiho was re-scheduled for 1600.

"When H-hour was being kicked around that morning," said Downing, "me and my plotting board were in a sweat trying to figure out the new launch times so we could all arrive at the proper time over the target."

During the morning, while this rash of despatches concerning the possible cancellation of the strike was being exchanged, *Bon Homme Richard* and *Philippine Sea* joined with *Boxer* and *Princeton*. For the first time in 18 months, a full carrier task force of four carriers would be operating together. The attack from their decks was to be the biggest to date of the entire Korean War.

At 1400, with the Fleet into the wind, launching for the Suiho attack commenced. Thirty-five AD Skyraiders rendezvoused from VA-65 (CDR G. A. Sherwood, USS *Boxer*), VA-195 (CDR Neil MacKinnon, USS *Princeton*), and VA-115 (CDR C. H. Carr, USS *Philippine Sea*). Thirty-one of these Skyraiders carried two 2,000-pound bombs and one 1,000-pounder each; the remaining four, in addition to two 2,000-pounders, carried a survival bomb* for dropping to anyone unfortunate enough to be shot down.

Shortly after the 35 Skyraiders passed the North Korean coast, the jet fighters joined up. These 35 planes were flown from VF-24 (LCDR William

---

* Package containing survival gear.

A. Jernigan, Jr., USS *Boxer*), VF-191 (CDR John Sweeny, USS *Princeton*), and VF-112 (CDR James V. Rowney, USS *Philippine Sea*). Twenty-four of the F9Fs were each carrying two 250-pound general purpose bombs, and all carried full trays of ammunition for their guns. (The jets not carrying bombs were the target combat air patrol planes, which required extra fuel.)

The weather over Korea was improving to the naval airman's advantage. The route and the vicinity of the target still were reported clouded, but the area near the Suiho dam was reported clear. This meant that the pilots could use cloud cover for surprise *before* and concealment *after* the raid.

The attack group skimmed among the clouds and past the highest mountain tops of North Korea, then commenced a slow let-down to remain below radar detection height. The route chosen across Korea was over isolated territory in order to minimize the possibility of ground spotters detecting and reporting the group.

Already circling the Yalu in "MIG Alley" were eighty-four F86s whose task it was to provide continuous cover for the naval group. Eight minutes before the scheduled time of attack, the Sabre pilots reported to CDR Downing that more than 200 swept-wing MIGs were visible, parked on the airfields in the Antung complex.

When would they come up?

At 1555, only five minutes from the target, the attack group from Task Force 77 commenced a high-power climb to reach dive-bombing altitude. If surprise had not been achieved, the MIGs from Antung and the guns surrounding Suiho would soon be working them over; but as the group came in sight of the huge dam, it was obvious that surprise had been achieved.

Commander Downing ordered the attack to begin. The Panthers commenced their flak-suppression dives. The ADs, meanwhile, reversed their course and commenced their runs. Downing led the *Boxer* dive-bombing planes in; on his tail was MacKinnon with the *Princeton* divebombers; and following him, Carr led the *Philippine Sea's* ADs.

"Our target was not the dam itself but the Suiho powerhouse," said CDR MacKinnon, "and it was an excellent aiming point. It was a building 80 feet by 500 feet housing the generators, transformers, and switching equipment. There was a fair crosswind blowing north to south which complicated our bombing, but which cleared the target of the smoke and dust of the exploding bombs. I saw a few puffs of AA fire as we were in our attack, but it was not enough to hinder us."

Other targets were the transformer yard and the penstocks. Each Skyraider salvoed its bombs at 3,000 feet, simultaneously firing its machine guns to keep enemy heads down, and levelling from its run by 1,500 feet altitude.

The antiaircraft fire was now coming up, and pilots later reported it as "intense machine gun fire, plus moderate, continuous predicted fire from heavy weapons and automatic antiaircraft fire." Bursts were accurate at all levels up to 10,000 feet. As expected, most of the fire was "out of bounds" from across the river in Manchuria.

As the last Skyraider entered its dive, the final flights of flak-suppression F9Fs dove on the defending guns on the North Korean side of the river. Of their work, LT T. G. Dreis later said: "The flak suppression was terrific. The AA looked rough when the jets first went in. After they made their runs, there was nothing to it. They really did a job."

In less than 180 seconds, the entire Navy attack, having dumped ninety tons of bombs on Suiho's installations, was up and away, streaking to the southeast.

"The majority of the bombs were on target," said Vice Admiral Clark, "and post-strike photography showed no misses."

Two or three secondary explosions were observed to follow from inside the powerhouse, and all of the pilots could see dense smoke and dust roiling from the powerhouse, thousands of feet high. Of the attack CDR Downing said: "The bombing was excellent; the powerhouse looked like a volcano erupting."

Despite the large number of enemy guns surrounding the dam, only five of the Navy's planes were hit by antiaircraft fire. One Skyraider from VA-115, flown by LTJG M. K. Lake, was seriously hit and set on fire in the starboard wheel well; but with his wingman, Lake was able to reach Seoul's Kimpo airfield, where a successful wheels-up landing was made. Considering the concentrations of guns protecting Suiho, the flak-suppression efforts of the jets had been highly effective.

"It was obvious that we had caught them flatfooted," said CDR Mac-Kinnon. "I attribute our success to the excellent planning and leading by CDR Downing, to our mountain-top approach, and to the sudden, last-minute climb to bombing altitude. The strike, which we had anticipated would be a rough one, turned out to be a textbook hop. The timing was perfect, we hit every checkpoint on schedule, and the bombing was excellent."

"Although we only had one briefing with the strike leaders," said CDR Downing, "the entire exercise went off as though we had been doing it for years. By my own timing, the last man was out of his dive and on retirement course in two minutes flat from the first flak-suppression pass—a real tribute to the superb work of the flight leaders of the following elements."[5]

As the naval aircraft concluded their runs, the U. S. Air Force's attacking F84 Thunderjets—124 of them—appeared in a well-coordinated second strike. Interservice teamwork was excellent. If any reprisal was to come from the MIGS across the Yalu, surely the moment had come; but by now, the high-circling Sabres could see less than 80 airplanes instead of the more than 200 observed a few minutes earlier.

Where were the MIGs? Had they assumed that industrial targets in Manchuria were to be hit and flown off to cover them? Or was an attack on the Antung air base complex itself expected and the planes hastily flown clear? Or were the Red pilots simply without orders, unready or unwilling to interfere?

Whatever their reasons, the expected stiff aerial opposition never materialized, and the remainder of the U. S. Air Force attack blasted the Suiho plant opposed only by the defending guns. Concurrent with the Suiho attack, twelve other power complexes in North Korea received similar treatment.

The next day, the Suiho plant was still smoking, and North Korea's electric power was seriously reduced. The capital of Pyongyang was without power; factories on both sides of the Yalu were paralyzed, and lights all over Korea and Manchuria were going out.

The attack on the North Korean power plants had done several things, not the least of which was to rekindle enthusiasm among the naval airmen, sated by the monotonous routine of interdiction. The strike had shown the Navy's flexibility to surprise and accurately hit a heavily-defended target. It had also shown the harmony of effort and precision which the U. S. Navy and U. S. Air Force could effect, which prompted General Barcus to say "My hat's off to the Navy for a terrific job. We must get together again sometime."

The Chief of Naval Operations, Admiral William Fechteler, congratulated the Seventh Fleet Commander and the pilots of Task Force 77:

> It is with great pride that I read the despatch and news reports of the magnificent accomplishment of your forces in the superb attacks upon the North Korean power installations. The excellent performance of duty and high combat effectiveness demonstrated by your forces and particularly the pilots involved in the actual combat are deserving of the highest praise and inspiration of your own people and a warning to the enemy of his inevitable defeat. Well Done.

The surprise assault certainly caused extensive damage* to the electric

---

* It must be recalled that Suiho was only one of 13 power plants struck on 23 and 24 June. For these two days of attacks, the Navy flew 546 sorties; the U.S. Marines, 139. The U. S. Air Force communique of 2 July 1952 summarized the Suiho damage:
"The Suiho hydroelectric plant is unserviceable. Overall damage at Suiho installation

system of North Korea and Manchuria. The strikes forced the relocation of enemy AA guns all over Korea. Rear Admiral H. E. Regan, Commander Carrier Division One, only a month later was able to report the successful destruction of several bridges which, prior to the hydroelectric power raids, had been too well defended to attack.

Finally, the Communists were left in doubt as to the future targets and locations which might be attacked.*

The Strike on Pyongyang (11 July 1952)

The highly satisfactory results achieved by the carrier strike on 23-24 June not only inflicted severe damage to the hydroelectric system of North Korea, but the attacks were also visible demonstration to the Communists that a new corner in the Korean War had been turned. The psychological effect was pronounced, both at the Panmunjom armistice table and in the North Korean capital. The Pyongyang radio denounced the missions as "sneak attacks," adding that "anyone with common sense knows that a hydroelectric power station is a project of peaceful construction devoid of all military significance."

But even more impressive strikes were now being scheduled. A plan was developed at Far Eastern Air Force headquarters in Tokyo to attack military targets in the North Korean capital city of Pyongyang. Its 40-odd military targets—warehouses, bridges, troop barracks, factories, and Army headquarters—had been spared for months for the sake of the armistice talks. But now there was even less reason to withhold attacks upon the capital city's military targets than there had been for withholding attacks on the hydroelectric plants.

Attacking Pyongyang's military installations, however, would be a difficult and demanding task. Many planes had been lost over Pyongyang, and pilots generally considered the city one of the worst "flak-traps" in North Korea. Photographic interpretation showed 48 heavy antiaircraft guns and more than 100 smaller automatic guns ringing the North Korean capital. The enemy's antiaircraft opposition was certain to be both intense and accurate. Moreover, there were prisoner-of-war camps in the environs of the city, and these had to be avoided in the bombings.

---

was severe, although the dam itself was purposely left intact. The target lay on the North Korean side of the river and was attacked without any overflight of Manchurian territory. Serious damage to the Suiho generator and control house was caused by direct bomb hits. Several buildings were destroyed and others damaged near the plant. Other bomb bursts caused major damage in the transformer yard."

* In a congratulatory message to the Naval and Air Force pilots participating in the attacks, Lieutenant General O. P. Weyland, Commanding General, FEAF, said that the raids constituted a fitting climax to two years of coordinated and applied air power and "may be taken as a gentle hint of more to come if the Commies want it that way. . . ."

Two carriers were scheduled to make a full-scale, full-day contribution: *Princeton* and the *Bon Homme Richard,* the latter recently arrived in Korean waters for her second tour, with Air Group Seven aboard.

"This was the first time in our six months' tour that my Air Group joined with another one for a combined strike," said CDR G. B. Brown, Commander Carrier Air Group Seven.[6]

"The strike on Pyongyang was scheduled for 11 July. Since our ship was carrying Admiral H. E. Regan, then CTF 77, and his staff, the *Princeton* air group commander, CDR William Denton (CVG-19), flew over to our ship a couple of days prior to the attack, bringing some of his squadron commanders, and we laid our plans for the strike.

"Our plans followed the now-standard strike procedure: the jets being launched some time after the props, joining us a few miles from the target, and preceding us down in our dives in order to knock out the enemy guns. The props, both Corsairs and Skyraiders, would follow them, and after their recovery, the jets would again cover our retirement."

The launch began at 0831 on 11 July with a single mishap. Ensign E. B. Conrad, a VF-72 pilot flying an F9F-2, lost power after the catapult shot and ditched. Conrad was unhurt, and was quickly rescued by the *Princeton* helicopter.

Bon Homme Richard launched 45 aircraft; *Princeton,* 46. The combined strike group, led by Commander Denton, CVG-19, rendezvoused over the island of Yo-do in Wonsan harbor. Brown, leading the *Bon Homme Richard* aircraft, and flying an AD himself, joined above and behind the *Princeton* strike group.

"The weather at the time of launching was pretty good," said Brown, "although there was only a very small spread between the wet and the dry temperatures.

"Our course to the target took us directly over the enemy town of Yongdok, a supply storage site which had been on the receiving end of dozens of naval air attacks. On this occasion, even though we were flying along at approximately 18,000 feet, the Yongdok guns opened upon us, and shrapnel from one burst hit one of my Corsairs—not seriously, however, and it was able to continue. But it was a prelude of what was to come."

The carrier aircraft had been chosen to make the initial attacks and to strike several targets in Pyongyang on the southeast side of the city, the ones nearest the POW camps: an ammunition storage area, a vehicle camp, a headquarters and troop billeting area, a factory, a railroad locomotive repair shop, and a railroad roundhouse. Other target areas had been assigned to aircraft of the U. S. Fifth Air Force, the U. S. Marines, the Australian Air Force, and aircraft from HMS *Ocean* (CAPT G. L. G. Evans, RN), the

British carrier operating under Commander Task Force 95. These elements of the UN air force were scheduled to relieve each other in an all-day, all-out attack on the city's military targets.

As the carrier aircraft sped toward the target, the Sabres of the Fifth Air Force were taking off from their South Korean bases to form a barrier patrol in "MIG Alley," and thereby prevent MIGs from interfering with the attacks on Pyongyang.

"The weather over Pyongyang was good," said Brown. "Exactly on schedule, our flak-suppression jets from the task force joined up and took high cover; we picked up speed during the run-in. Each one of my ADs was carrying three 1,000-pound bombs; the Corsairs, one each.

"As we neared the city, which was very prominent because of its location in a big bend of the Taedong River, the AA commenced. It started at Sonchon and followed us all the way in. It was as heavy and accurate as anything I saw during World War II; moreover, much of this stuff came from *radar*-controlled mounts, something we hadn't worried about during the Pacific war.

"The flak-suppression dives of the jets were effective and timely. Later, we gave them credit for destroying five guns and silencing two more. Despite their good work, however, some of my boys were hit. LT E. P. Cummings and his observer, L. L. Tooker, AT1, took a direct hit which blew off part of the AD's tail surface. We saw their plane go straight in and crash about a mile from the target.

"Two other *Richard* aircraft were hit prior to the commencement of our bombing runs. One Corsair, flown by LTJG G. G. Jeffries, took a direct hit by heavy AA in the leading edge of his port wing, but the shell passed on through without exploding; even so, Jeffries pressed home his attack despite the damage.

"The *Bon Homme Richard's* targets were the railroad roundhouse, the locomotive repair yard, and the ammunition storage area. LCDR F. H. Ervin, LCDR W. M. Harnish, LTJG J. A. Ryes and ENS P. G. Merchant made direct hits on the large rail repair shop. LCDR W. E. Teufer and LT W. L. Harris made direct hits on the roundhouse. As for the ammo' storage area, all bombs fell within the assigned area, and it looked well battered."

The bombing by the *Princeton* strike group was equally effective. During the dive LCDR L. F. Dutemple, flying an AD from VA-195, was hit and lost to AA fire, and his aircraft was seen to crash nearby. Two Corsairs from VF-193 were also hit, but landed at friendly bases in South Korea.

Photographs taken after the strike showed that the roundhouse was 60 per cent destroyed, including two locomotives therein, while the railroad repair shop was 50 per cent destroyed.

"This mission was one of the most accurate attacks that my air group made," said Brown. "The antiaircraft fire we encountered from Pyongyang's radar-controlled heavy guns, and the fire from their medium and automatic weapons was the heaviest and most accurate we encountered during our entire tour."

The *Princeton* pilots agreed.

"It was the heaviest flak we saw," recorded LCDR N. W. Boe, commanding officer of VF-193. "It was so thick we could have dropped our wheels and landed on the stuff."[7]

As the naval aircraft recovered from their attacks and headed homeward, the high-flying jets soon picked up radio reports from the Fleet. The weather in the Sea of Japan and along the east coast of Korea had suddenly worsened, fog had formed, and ceilings were down to 200-300 feet, with visibility reduced to less than 500 yards.

"The jets in our strike group, on hearing this, decided to land at Suwon and Kanghong," said Brown. "The rest of us—all props—kept heading homeward. We vectored into the Fleet by YE,* and let down through a 5,000-foot overcast division by division, at two-minute intervals. Upon breaking out of the stuff at about 300 feet, and being vectored in to the carrier, we couldn't see across the task force. However, with the aid of our 'hooker' control atop the *Bon Homme Richard* bridge, we all got aboard without further incident."

The remainder of the carrier strikes against Pyongyang had to be cancelled because of the weather.

The strikes on the capital city, less Task Force 77 aircraft, continued the rest of the day. A total of 1,400 tons of bombs and 23,000 gallons of napalm were delivered upon Pyongyang's targets during an 11-hour period by 1,254 aircraft.

For two days the Pyongyang radio was off the air. When a weak signal was again emitted, the North Koreans called the day's strikes "brutal," adding that they had been ordered as retaliation for the failure of the armistice talks.

The Pyongyang radio also stated that 1,500 buildings had been destroyed and 900 damaged. One bomb had made a direct hit on a large air raid shelter, causing large casualties among high Communist party members.†

* A radio homing device.

† Pyongyang was again heavily attacked by Task Force 77 five weeks later, on 29 August 1952, in an operation named "All United Nations Air Effort." This second raid was even larger (1403 sorties) than the one on 11 July. Two hundred and sixteen sorties

The Sindok Mine Strike (27 July 1952) and Kilchu Magnesite
Plant Strike (28 July 1952)

The success of the raids on Suiho and Pyongyang, which had cost the enemy so much and the Allied air forces relatively little, was accepted as good evidence of the wisdom of de-emphasizing the interdiction program.

True, there were only a few targets in all of North Korea like the hydro-electric plants and the military concentrations in Pyongyang worthy of massed air attacks. But this more flexible pattern of air attack meant greater damage inflicted in proportion to losses sustained.

From June until the end of 1952, naval air conducted a series of attacks which took the formidable title "coordinated maximum effort air strikes." On twelve days of July 1952, Task Force 77 aircraft struck a variety of industrial targets, ending with an attack on the Sindok lead and zinc mill and the Kilchu magnesite plant on 27 and 28 July.

The zinc mill had been processing and shipping 3,000 tons of zinc and lead to Russia via China every month. Destroying it would certainly cost the Communists more than another hundred breaks in the rail lines.

In the now well-established pattern, the jets struck the antiaircraft guns first and last, allowing the propellered ADs and F4Us to saturate the area with 500-pound, 1,000-pound and 2,000-pound bombs.

> *Bon Homme Richard* 27 July; Sindok: ". . . Flak suppression was effective, accurate bombing and strafing runs taking its toll in Communist gun positions. The ADs dropped all their bombs in the target area, destroying or badly damaging the main plant and heavily damaging the transformers and other buildings in the vicinity. . . ."

> *Princeton* 28 July; Kilchu Magnesite Plant: ". . . A total of thirty-eight aircraft (25 F4Us and 13 ADs) in two strike groups dropped forty tons of bombs and rockets resulting in 60 per cent destruction of the magnesite plant; complete destruction of a thermo-electric plant which furnished power to the magnesite plant; major damage to a barracks area; also three to five cuts in the main railroad bridge leading south from Kilchu."

All planes but one returned safely from the strikes. LTJG E. M. Crow of VF-193 bailed out and was rescued by *Helena's* helicopter during the Kilchu strike.

The Raid on Changpyong-ni (20 August 1952)

The year 1952 saw the "air task group" concept tested in the Korean War. Two such groups, Air Task Group One* (CDR C. H. Crabill, Jr., aboard

---

from *Boxer* (CVG-2) and *Essex* (ATG-2) struck warehouses, gun positions, railroad cars, a rubber factory, and oil tanks. Seven *Boxer* aircraft were hit by the AA fire, but no pilots were lost. All targets were well covered.

* ATG-1 had a second tour in the Korean theater aboard *Boxer,* commencing 12 May 1953.

Valley Forge) and Air Task Group Two (CDR J. G. Daniels, III, aboard *Essex*) saw action and both groups performed excellently.

The air task group concept had arisen during the early days of the Korean War, during the time when the largest single attack group launched from the carriers rarely exceeded 12 to 16 planes. Only on the most infrequent occasions had the carrier air group commanders functioned in their designed role of tactical airborne coordinator. During the first 18 months of the war, even squadron commanders found few missions for leading their entire squadrons at one time. Squadrons had as many as four or five officers who were qualified and experienced to lead the usual four to twelve planes launched on close air support, interdiction, or armed reconnaissance missions.

With this pattern, obviously, the airborne duties of the air group commander in the Korean War bore little resemblance to similar duties in World War II.

However, there were other reasons for the air task group idea. The principal advantage was that a carrier's complement of aircraft could be tailored to suit the mission at hand. If the mission was attack, the aircraft could be predominantly attack types. If air defense was the mission, all fighters could be carried. And for such hostilities as those in Korea, a balanced group could be placed aboard.

Whatever the carrier's airplane complement, a senior naval aviator of the rank of commander, supported by a small staff, would be assigned as Air Task Group Commander. There would be no administrative organization; the designated squadrons would simply report to the Air Task Commander for *operational* control.

"There were some misgivings about the air task group concept at first," said Commander Daniels ATG-2 commander. "The principal reservation was that such a grouping of squadrons might lack the traditional sense of pride, unity, and loyalty that comes with belonging to any organization. However, in actual practice in Korea I believe there was as much fierce pride among my pilots for belonging to Air Task Group Two as there was in any air group.

"Actually the air task group is analogous to an air group except that the air task group commander doesn't have to contend with the petty administrative details of the chain of command. He simply has an air group without paper work. His primary job is to get the group in fighting shape.

"In my opinion, the tours of ATG-1 and ATG-2 in Korea certainly proved the merit of the air task group concept."

Typical of the performance of Air Task Group Two was the 20 August 1952 attack on Namyang-ni, a large supply area located south of the Yalu River, on the west coast of Korea.

"This was another of the several mass attacks of this period," said Daniels, "similar to the ones on the hydroelectric power plants and the two attacks on Pyongyang in July and August. This particular mission was at extreme range for the jets, and it demanded the most careful timing and integration, not only among the planes of the *Essex* but between the various other elements of the UN air forces."

Since the target was only a few miles from the Yalu River, and almost directly beneath "MIG Alley," it was expected that fighter opposition would be heavy.

"Our flight was made up of 43 planes from the *Essex* and 62 from the *Princeton*," said Daniels. "The weather over Korea was good, with only a few scattered clouds over the mountains.

"I was leading the *Essex* Panther jets, so we took off quite a bit later than the props. We joined them on schedule northwest of Wonsan.

"As we neared the target, we could see the Yalu River. I had good voice communications with the Air Force F86s who had set up the usual barrier patrol in 'MIG Alley'.

"We arrived at the push-over point exactly on time, and went in just ahead of the props. The Air Force had given us the intelligence on the location and number of the enemy AA guns, and I must say that their information was excellent. On an attack such as this, its success depends on accurate knowledge about the guns; if their *exact* locations are known, the flak-suppression aircraft can really do a job on them. Otherwise, if you are not sure of their whereabouts, all you can do is strafe the general area, and that's not too effective."

The flak-suppression runs of the *Essex* and *Princeton* aircraft were precise, and the Corsair and Skyraider pilots later reported the flak as light and inaccurate.

"None of the *Essex* planes were hit," said Daniels, "and our entire attack was completed in less than two minutes. As we cleared the targets, a strike of Fifth Air Force F84 fighter bombers came right in behind us. It was beautiful coordination.

"As we climbed for altitude, I got a jolt. The Sabre jets patrolling above us near the Yalu River said that twelve MIGs had broken through and were heading our way.

"We climbed as rapidly as possible for altitude to protect the props. We had gotten back up to about 12,000 when my section leader, LT Hal Crumbo, tally-hoed four MIGs.

"Their pass was simply one quick 'whoosh' high above us, with no one exchanging a shot. I don't think they spotted the prop planes below us."

Flying high cover at 16,000 feet with 12 *Princeton* Panther jets, Commander John Sweeny (Commanding Officer, VF-191) had also spotted the MIGs.

"We had radio contact both with the Air Force radar station on Cho-do island, and with the Sabres above us," said Sweeny, "so we had ample warning that they were coming.

"My three divisions were in step-up formation, with my team on top and staggered to the north. There was about 1,000 feet between divisions.

"I first spotted two MIGs jumping us from abeam. We immediately went to 100 per cent power, and at the right time turned into them, when they broke off and climbed away. Immediately after, three MIGs came up on our tail, so we reversed course to take them head-on. At this, they pushed over to pass beneath us. I got my sights on the lead plane, but he was so far below me that there was no reason to waste the ammunition. As we reversed to base course, two more MIGs started a run from the other beam, but again broke off when we turned into them. They simply put on full power and left us. The speed and rate of climb of those MIGs impressed all of us. They were painted green and brown, and their red stars were plainly visible. But I certainly wasn't impressed with either their formation flying or their flight discipline.

"At no time did they come close enough for us to get a shot, yet all the while they were shooting wildly at nothing.

"All considered, it wasn't much of an engagement, but it was the only time in my tour that we got close to MIGs. However, that small episode gave my pilots a lift, for it was quite apparent that the airmanship and teamwork of the MIG pilots were as bad as their gunnery.

"After this hop we kept hoping to get back into MIG territory and suck them down to low altitude where we could turn inside them. But it never happened."[8]

The homeward flight of the strike group was uneventful.

"Of the nineteen buildings in the supply area," said Daniels,[9] "photo reconnaissance showed ten of the buildings completely destroyed, while the other nine had up to 70 per cent damage.

"The significance of this strike was its split-second timing and coordination, the beautiful teamwork that was achieved with the other Air Force and Marine planes attacking the same target, and the effective flak suppression which permitted almost casual bombing with excellent accuracy by the Skyraiders and Corsairs."

The *Boxer* Drones (28 August 1952)

On 28 August 1952, the Navy began a series of guided missile operations by Guided Missile Unit 90 aboard the USS *Boxer*. Pilotless radio-controlled

World War II "Hellcats" (F6F5) converted to guided missiles, equipped with a television guidance system, and loaded with high explosives, were conducted to the target by control planes.

Between 28 August and 2 September, six guided missile attacks were launched against selected bridges.

This marked the first use of the guided missile in combat from carriers. Several missiles found their targets, and only one was abortive due to faulty control.

The Destruction of the Aoji Oil Refinery (1 September 1952)

One of the few targets in northeast Korea suitable for a massed carrier air strike was the oil refinery at Aoji, a synthetic oil producing center in the far northeast corner of Korea, only eight miles from Russian territory and four miles from the Manchurian border.

Here was a target that *only* the Navy could strike under the accepted ground rules which specified "no flying" over the Manchurian arsenal-sanctuary. This tip of northeast Korea was beyond the effective reach of land-based fighters; and it could not be touched by B-29s without their overflying one or both of the borders. But from the mobile air bases of the Navy, the target was only a skip and a jump.

"Aoji was one of the main sources of gasoline for the Communists in Korea," said VADM J. J. Clark, Commander of the Seventh Fleet.[10] "This huge petroleum center had been long spared because of its location. I knew that naval air could knock it out.

"I went to General Mark Clark, the Commander in Chief of the United Nations Command, and asked authority to strike it.

"After referring the problem to the JCS, General Clark gave me the go-ahead."

Three carriers—*Essex, Princeton,* and *Boxer*—furnished two large co-ordinated strikes to smash the Aoji refinery on 1 September 1952. *Essex* launched 29 planes from ATG-2, *Princeton* launched 63 planes from CVG-19, and *Boxer* launched 52 planes from CVG-2.

Simultaneous naval air strikes were also directed upon an iron works near Munsan and the thermoelectric plants, transformers, warehouses, and supply buildings in Chongjin.

The strike on the Aoji refinery was routine and almost leisurely. No antiaircraft fire or MIG opposition was encountered, permitting repeated runs on the target.

The destruction of the refinery was complete, as indicated in these excerpts from the reports of the strike:

Princeton: ". . . extensive damage to the refinery with smoke and flames visible to a great distance. . . ."

Essex: ". . . completely successful with 100 per cent coverage and damage on all targets assigned. . . ."

Boxer: ". . . No opposition was offered and *Boxer* planes inflicted heavy damage. . . ."

The total absence of antiaircraft fire from Aoji proved conclusively that the Communists had taken advantage of this "restricted" area's nearness to Manchuria and Russia. By building industrial plants in this northeast corner, the Communists believed them to be inviolate.

This largest all-Navy air attack of the Korean War proved them wrong.

The Raid on Kowon (8 October 1952)

The second instance of the Navy's escorting B-29s during the Korean War occurred on 8 October 1952 (the first had been the raid on Rashin in August 1951).

"One of the worst flak traps in northeast Korea was the rail center at Kowon," said Captain Ray M. Pitts, USN, operations officer of Commander Seventh Fleet.[11] "Every time we sent a strike in there, we ran into trouble, and dozens of pilots had been lost or suffered damage from the intense antiaircraft fire which surrounded Kowon.

"It occurred to our Seventh Fleet staff that a joint raid could be worked up by the Air Force and the Navy for hitting Kowon. On one of my trips to Tokyo, I went over to FEAF headquarters and told them about the Navy's plan.

"Our idea was to send an escorted group of B-29s over Kowon. The Superforts would be loaded with 500-lb. VT-fuzed bombs.[12] Their bombing targets would be the antiaircraft guns around Kowon. Immediately after their attack, while the Reds were all torn up by the effect of this bombing, the Navy would send in a low-level strike right behind the Superforts. The Navy's targets would be the marshalling yard and the supply and storage areas of Kowon. I offered to furnish Navy fighter escort for the B-29s."

The plan was accepted. On 8 October 1952, a combined Air Force-Navy strike walloped Kowon.

Twelve F2H2 Banshees, led by Commander Denny P. Phillips, Commanding Officer, VF-11, from the USS *Kearsarge*, rendezvoused with ten Superforts over South Korea. The B-29s' base altitude was 21,000 feet, with the three levels of Banshee cover at 25,000, 30,000, and 35,000 feet.

The Superfort attack was without incident, except for one brief moment during the approach to Kowon when a group of fighters was tally-hoed in the distance. Prompt recognition of the planes by LT Jack O'Donnell as F-86 Sabres, not MIGs, settled the pilots' nerves.

The marksmanship of the ten B-29s was precise, and CDR Phillips recorded his squadron's praise: "The Air Force was to be commended, both for perfection in carrying out the scheduled rendezvous and the excellence of their bomb drop."

Four minutes after the B-29 attack, a large strike group from Air Groups 19 and 101, and Air Task Group 2, numbering 89 aircraft in all, bombed and rocketed Kowon. The rail, communication, troop, and supply facilities were successfully bombed and rocketed, with much reduced interference from the Kowon gun.

The Navy's opinion of the attack system was high. Rear Admiral R. F. Hickey reported that the joint attack "opened the door to future coordination highly desirable in certain areas of enemy territory."

The strike on Kowon, however, proved to be the last instance during the Korean War of the Navy escorting B-29s.

"The Kowon coordination was a great success," said Captain Pitts, "but unfortunately, we were not able to do it again.

"It was my understanding that at this time our Air Force bombers were shifting to a 'jet-stream' type of single-plane, night-time bombing attack; they told me that putting any large groups of B-29s over Korea for a daylight attack wasn't possible."

The successful attack on Kowon and the teamwork between Air Force and Navy was summed up by a VF-11 historical report:

The raid was highly successful and all aircraft returned safely.

The Cherokee Strikes (9 October 1952 to July 1953)

As the interdiction campaign dwindled, and the carrier strikes such as those just described blasted the few industrial targets in Korea, it was appreciated that a more fruitful employment for naval air power ought to be found. Under the self-imposed ground rules, it was obvious that the war might continue indefinitely unless some new way could be found to make the enemy return to and be more amenable at the truce table. October 1952 had seen an indefinite suspension of the truce talks, a recess which would last for 199 days (until 26 April 1953).

But a new target system or even a worthwhile *old* one for naval air power was hard to find. "Strategic" type targets had never been plentiful in North Korea, even in peacetime. The few that had existed had been hit repeatedly. After two years of war, new or worthwhile strategic targets did not exist. "Maximum air effort" targets, such as Chongjin, Aoji, Wonsan, Suiho, and

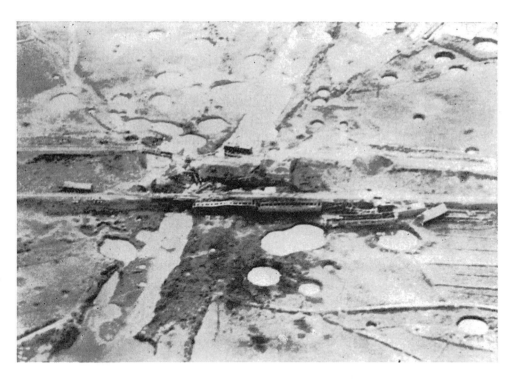

BLASTED ROLLING STOCK. *At top,* after the train stopped burning, the enemy pushed it off the tracks and began repair work. *Below,* membership certificate in Task Force 95's Train Busters Club, organized in 1952 by CAPT Harold G. Baker. Ultimately 13 U. S. warships and several from other nations won certificates.

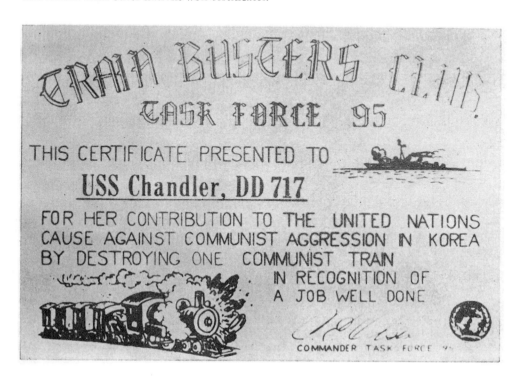

Naval Commanders in the Sea War in Korea. (For commands and dates, see Appendix I.) Reading left to right, *top,* VADM H. M. Martin, RADM W. G. Tomlinson. *Center,* RADM R. A. Ofstie, RADM F. W. MacMahon. *Bottom,* RADM John Perry, RADM A. Soucek.

NAVAL COMMANDERS IN THE SEA WAR IN KOREA. (For commands and dates, see Appendix I.) Left to right, *top,* RADM J. M. Hoskins, RADM E. C. Ewen. *Center,* RADM H. E. Regan, RADM R. F. Hickey. *Bottom,* RADM W. D. Johnson, RADM R. E. Blick.

NAVY AIR BLASTS NORTH KOREAN MILITARY TARGETS in "maximum air effort" program. *At top,* the second carrier plane attack within five weeks against Pyongyang featured more than 1,400 sorties against 40-odd targets. *Below,* the attack continued next day, laying waste Communist warehouses, oil tanks and ordnance.

Pyongyang, were few and had been frequently hit. The transportation networks, in the waning interdiction campaign, had been demonstrated to be unproductive target systems. Standard close air support missions (which had been resumed on 13 July 1952) were often disappointing along the stalemated and stagnant battleline. The Communists were so deeply and solidly entrenched that strafing attacks and the delivery of light bombs and rockets had little effect.

What, then, could the carriers do?

The answer was found by Vice Admiral J. J. "Jocko" Clark, the Seventh Fleet's commander.

"In May 1952, shortly after I had taken command of the Seventh Fleet," said VADM Clark, "I visited Korea at the invitation of General Van Fleet, and remained with him at his headquarters for several days. He arranged trips for me to visit the battlefield. On 30 May I visited Major General J. T. Selden, commanding the First Marine Division, at his headquarters south of Panmunjom. General Selden flew me up and down the frontlines in his helicopter and then took me to individual command posts in the frontlines by jeep.

"While flying behind our frontlines, I noticed many concentrations of our own forces that were not underground. These included supply concentrations, personnel housing, medical centers, truck parks, and ammunition dumps. As I flew over these areas, it occurred to me that if the enemy had the same air power and air supremacy that *we* enjoyed at the battleline, it would be impossible to have so much of our material freely exposed and in the open. I then reasoned that the enemy could not fight a kind of war he was fighting and still have *all* his forces, supplies, and equipment underground. *Some* of his stocks of supplies had to be above ground, out of sight and out of range of our artillery.

"On returning to the Seventh Fleet on 31 May, therefore, I asked Rear Admiral John Perry, Commander Carrier Division One, to obtain aerial photographs of the territory behind the enemy's frontlines which was out of reach of artillery.

"Later, after the photos had been assessed, Perry reported a multitude of worthwhile targets all along the front.

"In the pictures, many underground tunnels were visible, and in some cases the enemy had even dug tunnels all the way through the mountains. Of course these fortifications and the stagnant condition of the frontlines made regular close air support strikes ineffective. But even though he might have a lot of his war supplies buried in the hills, a lot of it was exposed which would make excellent targets for the concentrated, surprise and pinpoint attacks of naval aircraft."[13]

This was the origin of what came to be known as the "Cherokee Strikes," named in Clark's honor because of his Cherokee ancestry.

"The decision to call the new system 'Cherokee' may have sounded whimsical to some," said Captain Ray M. Pitts, "but there was a definite reason for choosing it. We thought first of giving the system a name that would have tactical significance—like 'carrier tactical strike.' But we decided against that for we wanted a name that would mean something totally different from 'close air support.' You can't hang an argument on a word like 'Cherokee.'

"After Admiral Clark germinated the idea, the rest of the staff set to work to translate it into action.

"I made a trip through the lines in Korea to see if the general concept was workable. First, I checked with the key officers of our First Marine Division. I also made a swing around several battalion command posts discussing the proposed 'Cherokee' system with them.

"Next I went to Seoul to the JOC to clear the concept with the Fifth Air Force on the working level. There was nothing in writing.

"Then I went to Tenth Corps headquarters and talked to them.

"Everybody was enthusiastic and thought the 'Cherokee' plan would work and that it deserved a try.

"My own opinion was that the *best* place for our naval air power to destroy enemy supplies was at the front, not somewhere back in North Korea. At the front, every bullet, every round of artillery, every pound of supplies was twice as expensive to the Reds as it was crossing the Yalu. In my opinion, we could do more harm in a stalemated war by destroying the enemy's logistics at the battleline.

"Upon my return, Vice Admiral Clark and I went over to Rear Admiral Hickey's flagship. His operations officer (CDR Louis Hurd) and air intelligence officer (CDR R. P. Fuller) took a look at all the maps and photos I had brought back and they agreed we had found a worthwhile new target system.

"That was how the 'Cherokee' system got underway."[14]

The first Cherokee strikes were flown on 9 October 1952. Three strikes, totalling 91 aircraft, were launched from *Kearsarge*, *Princeton* and *Essex* on troop and supply areas beyond the range of Tenth Corps artillery.

To the carrier aviators, the first Cherokee strike was simply "one more hop," and there is little in either ship or squadron records to distinguish the day of 9 October. VF-821's report mentions the day in one brief sentence: "Flak-suppression hop of eight F9Fs led by CDR D. W. Cooper." Another *Essex* squadron history, VF-871 says simply, "eight planes hit troop bunkers." CDR L. W. Chick's squadron, VA-55, records the results of two missions that day without embellishment: "Twelve ADs destroyed eight mortars, three 37-mm. gun positions, 400 feet of trench, eight bunkers, and started two fires;" and "eight ADs destroyed two artillery positions and three bunkers while covering 90 per cent of the target area." *Kearsarge's* Skyraider squadron, VA-702, recorded that "eleven aircraft hit a supply area twenty miles north of the Punchbowl."

"By mid-October," continued Vice Admiral Clark, "Task Force 77 had gradually shifted a large proportion of its strike effort to the Cherokee program until about 50 per cent of its air attack potential was being devoted to this type mission. General Van Fleet enthusiastically approved the program and authorized the division commanders to move their bomblines temporarily to include worthwhile targets for the duration of the strike."

Especially happy was the foot soldier in the line. To him, the various concepts of close support, its mechanics, and its methods of control, were meaningless. To him, also, the sight of a large number of planes, from whatever source, demolishing enemy targets with heavy bombs was an exhilarating tonic.

After the first few Cherokee strikes, however, there was confusion at the JOC and concern at Air Force headquarters. The Fifth Air Force in Korea looked on the new missions as regular close air support, while the Far East Air Force headquarters was concerned lest the new system jeopardize Air Force control of air power over the frontlines.

Lieutenant General Otto P. Weyland, FEAF, informed Vice Admiral Clark that he did not believe that the FAFIK controllers were capable of handling large numbers of strike aircraft loaded with large bombs on missions so close to friendly lines. He added that in recent months, there had been seven cases of unidentified but friendly aircraft inadvertently dropping bombs on the friendly side of the front. None of these was definitely attributable to the Navy, he said, but such accidents did emphasize the need for proper liaison and control.

"The initial confusion," said Vice Admiral Clark, "was one of simple misunderstanding. My only objective in originating and planning the Cherokee hops was to utilize the striking power of the Seventh Fleet for the infliction of the greatest possible damage upon the enemy with the least cost to our own forces.

"The misunderstanding was due to two things: first, the basic difference between a 'Cherokee' type strike and a regular close air support mission; and second, the method of controlling them."

The Cherokee strikes were different from close air support strikes in several respects. In the case of close air support, missions were not pre-briefed, the planes carried a standard bomb loading, and only eight planes could be handled over any particular target at one time. No flak-suppression planes accompanied the close air support aircraft. Moreover, the close air support aircraft were required to remain on call for considerable periods of time. The flights checked in with the frontline control parties and were often controlled by the light Mosquito aircraft who spotted their targets and directed their attacks. Finally, close air support targets were those limited to the area between the main line of resistance and the bombline. Good visibility was required to identify targets and deliver close air support.

The Cherokee strikes, on the other hand, were heavy air power missions outside of the bombline. They were pre-briefed, pre-arranged strikes, carrying weapons specially selected for the target. The number of planes over the target was unlimited because no individual control was needed. The target was selected from intelligence or photographic interpretation, and at the pre-briefing all pertinent information available was given to the pilot. The Cherokee strike aircraft used jet aircraft loaded with antipersonnel bombs for flak-suppression. Artillery, when available, was also used to augment the flak-suppression. The Cherokee strikes proceeded to the target as an organized unit, and the timing of the attacks called for delivery immediately upon arrival, with a minimum of time on station.

The misunderstandings of Cherokee were satisfactorily resolved on 17 November at a conference between Eighth Army, Commander Seventh Fleet, and Fifth Air Force. It was agreed that close air support missions would continue as before, that the Cherokee strikes *were* different, and would not interfere with them. However, the Cherokee strikes henceforth would be coordinated through FAFIK, would check in and out with the TACP* of the Army Corps in the area, and would use Mosquito type aircraft to mark the targets. Eighth Army also agreed to move the bombline position closer to the frontlines on specific occasions in order to permit the naval aircraft to strike. In some cases the bombline was moved as close to friendly troops as 300 yards—a rare tribute to the accuracy of the naval airmen.

The use of the Cherokee strikes at the battleline reached its peak in November and December, with the Air Force joining the Cherokee campaign.

The opinions of the pilots of Task Force 77 with regard to the Cherokee program ran to each end of the enthusiasm-apathy scale. Those who were fortunate enough to see tangible evidence of their attacks could appreciate why the "ground-pounders" in the frontlines were enthusiastic. Those who saw or heard no results of their work—and pilots often saw little because of the smoke and dust—were unimpressed. VA-702 recorded this opinion: "Much enemy flak was encountered on these missions, and pilots usually considered a Cherokee strike as 'hot'. The strikes are very effective in knocking out enemy artillery pieces."

On 22 November, the *Essex* and *Kearsarge* teamed up for two coordinated Cherokee missions in the Kumwha sector of the front witnessed by a dis-

* Tactical Air Control Party.

tinguished group of observers: General Hoyt Vandenberg, Commanding General U. S. Air Force; Lieutenant General O. P. Weyland, Commanding General Far Eastern Air Force; Lieutenant General Glen O. Barcus, Commanding General FAFIK; and Lieutenant General James Van Fleet. This enemy sector had come to have the name "Artillery Valley" because of the intense AA fire which was frequently poured into UN lines. Lieutenant General R. H. Jenkins, Ninth Corps Commander, moved the bombline south about 5,000 yards to permit the Task Force 77 aircraft to strike.

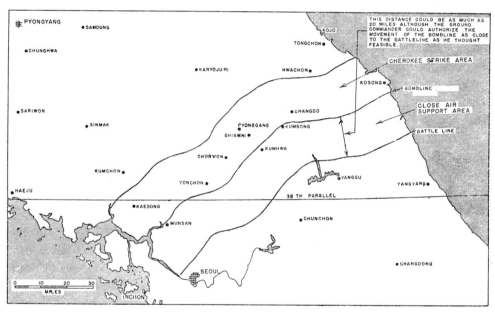

CHEROKEE STRIKES CUT ENEMY GUN POTENTIAL NEAR
KUMWHA BY NINETY PER CENT

The first strike on "Artillery Valley" was credited with destroying three artillery pieces and five enemy bunkers, and damaging four artillery pieces and five enemy bunkers. The second strike destroyed twenty-five personnel shelters and damaged ten more. The frontline controllers reported that ninety per cent of the Navy planes' 1,000-pound bombs were on target.

"It was impressive to see those divebombers and fighters dive so steeply," said General Van Fleet. "The heavy bombs they carried (2,000 lbs.) were really mountain busters, and even from our distance the whole earth shook."

After watching the strikes, General Van Fleet radioed the Fleet:

I witnessed two magnificent strikes totalling thirty-six aircraft at approximately 1500 today. Present were Generals Vandenberg, Weyland, and Barcus. Congratulations on the accurate and breathtaking performance. Hope all pilots and planes returned safely. Van Fleet.

"By a combination of Navy and Air Force Cherokee strikes and Army artillery efforts," said Vice Admiral Clark, "the enemy's gun potential in the Kumwha area was reduced to about 10 per cent of what it had been."

The new strike program steadily grew in proportion until more than half the naval air effort—approximately 2,500 sorties per month—was being applied along the frontlines—either as close air support missions (nicknamed "Call Shot") or as pre-briefed strikes (nicknamed "Cherokee"). The period from 2 November to 25 November was typical: 522 Cherokee missions, and 212 Call-Shot sorties.

"On several occasions," said Captain Ray M. Pitts, "the Cherokee program was credited with disrupting several major buildups and attacks by the Communists north of the bombline in the fall of 1952.

"On one occasion, I was attending a briefing at First Marine Division headquarters. During the briefing, it was revealed that there was an enemy buildup in their area, and they had reports of a limited Communist push.

"This enemy concentration seemed an ideal target for a Cherokee, so I copied down the coordinates of the area and fired a priority despatch to Commander Seventh Fleet for information of Commander Task Force 77.

"Admiral Clark verified the mission to CTF 77 by voice radio. Next morning at first light, a Navy jet photo plane took pictures of the area.

"The developed pictures corroborated the buildup; by 1030 that same morning, a heavy Cherokee strike was on its way.

"Later, our forces captured some prisoners who told us that this raid had taken a heavy toll; that the Chinese were burying their dead the rest of the night, including their general."[15]

The table of total damage by the Task Force 77 aircraft for this period was as follows:

Target	Destroyed	Damaged
Supply Areas	5	3
Bunkers	56	102
Trenches	680 yards	435 yards
Mortars	40	15
Artillery	34	31
Personnel Shelters	34	7
Troop Casualties	59	—
Caves	1	5
Buildings	6	—
Rail Cuts	6	—
Railroad Cars	1	4

Usually, only estimates of damage to the enemy fortifications could be given, except on the occasions when a hill or a section of the enemy line was captured. The Communist entrenchments were well constructed and deeply tunneled into the rocky Korean hills. As many as six openings led from bunkers. The bunkers were strongly built, usually fifteen feet in diameter.

On such deeply-dug entrenchments, only the heaviest bombs proved effective. Light bombs, even napalm, did little damage to the tunnels, bunkers, and dugouts. The 1,000- and 2,000-pounders carried by the Corsairs and Skyraiders, however, often collapsed the tunnels and bunkers, burying alive the Communist soldiers therein. On other occasions the terrific blast of these bombs was sufficient to kill. Dead Communist soldiers were sometimes found with their brains oozing from their ears as a result of the heavy blasts.

The Cherokee strike pilots also dropped heavy bombs fuzed for delays of up to twelve hours in order to harass and hamper the enemy for long periods during the nights.

"On one day in early December in the 'Iron Triangle' area," said CDR R. P. Fuller, Air Intelligence Officer of Carrier Division Five, "TF-77 planes had twenty-seven secondary explosions from Cherokee strikes. One ammo storage blew so high that the smoke rose up to 2500 feet."[16]

As the year 1953 commenced, the Cherokee program hit a snag.

"The danger of bombing friendly troops in the Cherokee program was always recognized," said Vice Admiral Clark, "and every reasonable precaution was taken to prevent it. Target location and identification was very difficult because of the similarity of terrain, the profusion of ridges, ravines, canyons and streams along the battlefront. This problem was intensified by the snows and fog of wintertime."

During January to September 1952, there had been no less than 63 instances of bombs having been dropped behind friendly lines. Of the 63, the Fifth Air Force was responsible for 39 and the Marines 18, and the Navy was thought accountable for the six unidentified flights.

"In December and January," continued Admiral Clark, "bombs were dropped on four occasions inside friendly lines. Newspaper correspondents happened to be on the scene and published detailed accounts of the mishaps. One of them occurred on 21 December, when a CTF 77 airplane accidentally released a bomb on Republic of Korea troops. One man was killed and four injured. Again on 17 January, two bombs were dropped by early morning night-hecklers which killed three ROK Army soldiers and wounded eight others.

"In view of the publicity, General Clark activated an inter-Service board to investigate the incidents and to assign Service responsibility.

"Since the Fifth Air Force in Korea was charged with the sole responsibility for the prevention of friendly bombings," said Admiral Clark, "a campaign was immediately instituted by them to prevent recurrence. The Fifth Air Force instituted a policy that any air group commander whose planes were involved would be relieved, and the pilots involved recommended for court-martial. As a result, Fifth Air Force's participation and interest in the Cherokee strikes dwindled, and to some extent the Navy's did also. This was unfortunate, because it slowed down the use of Cherokee strikes at the battleline for several weeks."

By March 1953, however, control procedures, careful briefings, and improving weather permitted a return to heavier emphasis on Cherokee support to the frontlines. Planes with missions at or near the frontlines were controlled by radar until they were definitely north of the bombline.

Cherokee targets were selected jointly by the Commander Task Force 77 planning officer and Headquarters Eighth Army in a new attempt at closer liaison and control.

On 1-10 March, Admiral Hickey and his staff toured the frontline areas to obtain the Army reactions to the Task Force 77 attacks.

The general Army opinion of the heavy Cherokee strikes continued to be excellent. The strikes, they said, usually demolished the targets. While the results were not always visible or measurable, the program was undoubtedly hurting the enemy and reducing his attack potential. In fact, several of the Cherokee missions had blunted and even prevented enemy attacks.

"I was on this frontline inspection trip," said CDR R. P. Fuller, "and every single Army man and Marine we spoke to, from private to general, praised the Cherokee strikes. 'Can you imagine', they would tell us, 'what *our* reaction would be if the Reds had *their* airpower striking us here in the frontlines?'

"The best evidence that the Cherokee program was hurting the enemy was his AA reaction," continued Fuller. "The Communists never wasted ammunition, yet they often exhausted their local stores of ammo trying to counteract the Cherokees."[17]

The Army suggested that naval flight leaders, in addition to bringing their own jet fighters for flak suppression, might want to request friendly artillery fire to keep the Communists' heads down. The *Philippine Sea's* pilots were quick to recognize that the antiaircraft suppression effect of artillery fire, when it could reach a Cherokee target, often was superior to that of the jet fighters.

Lieutenant General James Van Fleet, Eighth Army's commander, had an excellent opinion of the effectiveness of the Cherokee program. Indeed, the General visualized it as having a potential for something more than defensive strikes in defense of a static front.

"The Cherokee strikes really clobbered the enemy," said General Van Fleet, "and would have been better if we had just put on a ground attack with them. The Cherokee program was a system which, properly used, could have broken the sit-down; they were heavy strikes of concentrated effort delivered over a short period. If followed up by ground action, they might have caused a break-through or caused the enemy to react violently to restore his lines, consuming his reserves of manpower and ammunition until he was exhausted over a period of a week to ten days. Then the ground armies could have been released to produce a war of movement instead of a war of digging in."

The Cherokee strike program continued for the remainder of the war.

Panthers Tangle with Russian MIGs

One of the most dramatic incidents of the Korean War happened on 18 November 1952, when U. S. Navy pilots encountered Russian MIGs.

On this day, Task Force 77 (under the command of Rear Admiral R. F. Hickey) was operating in far northern Korean waters, engaged in a two-day "maximum air" strike effort on targets in North Korea, principally against industrial targets in Chongjin, Kilchu, and Hoeryong, a city on the Yalu River. On the previous day, Task Force 77 had launched five co-ordinated air strikes on Chongjin, and the coastal city had also been bombarded by the battleship *Missouri* and the heavy cruiser *Helena*.

On the 18th of November, as on the day before, the task force was operating southeast of Chongjin (approximately 90 miles from Vladivostok), striking Hoeryong. The task force was in the same sea area that it had used on many previous occasions.

Cruising at 13,000 feet above the task force, centered around the carriers *Oriskany*, *Essex*, and *Kearsarge*, was a team of four F9F5 Panther aircraft* from *Oriskany's* VF-781 Pacemaker squadron (LCDR S. R. Holm).

The Panther pilots were:

> LT Claire R. Elwood—Team Leader
> LTJG John D. Middleton—Wingman
> LT Elmer R. Williams—Section Leader
> LTJG David M. Rowlands—Wingman

Because of a fuel boost pump failure in LT Elwood's plane, the four Panther aircraft had descended from normal combat air patrol altitude to the 13,000-foot level.

---

* This was the F9F5's first appearance in the Korean War.

Shortly after noon, various groups of unidentified aircraft crossing ahead of the task force from northwest to northeast were detected by the task force on radar at distances of from 40 to 100 miles.

At 1335, however, a group of unidentified aircraft, estimated at eight, was plotted on a direct approach toward the task force.

The *Oriskany's* air controller alerted the CAP and ordered a vector and climb toward the unknown aircraft.

Because of his malfunctioning engine which forced him to remain at a lower altitude, Elwood detached his second section (LT Williams and LTJG Rowlands) to make the contact. Williams and Rowlands continued the climbing vector. At approximately 1350, upon reaching 15,000 feet, Williams tally-hoed seven condensation trails high above him. The aircraft were MIGs. At the time of contact the planes were approximately north of the task force, 45 miles away. The fight which followed lasted a furious and confused eight minutes.

In a loose, abreast formation, the seven silver-colored MIGs passed high above the two Panther pilots, made a descending turn, and split into two groups—one four-plane group and one three-plane group—in an attempt to box in the two Navy planes.

"At this point," said LT Williams,[18] "we lost sight of the MIGs because their contrails had stopped. However, we continued our climb to 26,000, and upon levelling off I spotted four MIGs making a flatside attack on us from the ten o'clock position.

"As the four came toward us and reached firing range, I turned hard left into them, spoiling the effectiveness of their run, even though neither Rowlands nor I was able to bring our own guns to bear.

"The four MIGs recovered to our right, in a sort of strung-out formation, with the fourth MIG especially far back.

"I continued my wrapped-up turn, and came on around for a tail shot at this last MIG. I commenced firing from 15° off his tail.

"My first burst sent him into an uncontrolled spiral. Dave Rowlands followed this crippled MIG down to 8,000 feet, where he left it smoking in a deep graveyard spiral. Later, gun camera film confirmed the kill of this MIG.

"Meanwhile, the other three MIGs pulled up and away from me, and split into a pair and a single in an attempt to get on each side of me.

"The pair of MIGs then made an attack. I rolled into a sharp turn, and got a head-on burst at the second one.

"I kept turning into subsequent attacks," continued Williams, "and on several passes, I was able to reverse my turn in time to get a shot at an overshooting MIG. In one such counter I scored some hits, for in the gun camera film which was later developed, parts could be seen flying off. Either by my gunfire or this pilot's deliberate action, the MIG ran out his dive brakes and decelerated so rapidly that I had to pull away sharply. I only missed a collision with him by a narrow margin."

As Rowlands rejoined the fight from below, a MIG promptly made a head-on attack on him. The dogfight became a melee. At some unknown time during the dogfight, the three other MIGs joined the battle.

"This MIG started firing at me from 'way out," said Rowlands,[19] "and then broke off his attack in a steep-climbing turn. By now, there seemed to be MIGs all around me.

"I countered each attack as best as I could. On one of them, I succeeded in getting a MIG in my sights and fired a long burst. He started smoking, but a split second later my attention was diverted by another MIG making an attack on me. He and I wound up in a tight circle across from each other, and neither of us able to get on the other's tail. Finally, the MIG simply leveled his wings and climbed very rapidly away from me."

Until now, despite all the flying bullets, the two naval aircraft had not suffered a hit. Both Williams and Rowlands were operating their engines at 100 per cent power.

"At this point," continued Williams, "I succeeded in getting another MIG burning. I stayed on his tail, trying to finish him off, when I spotted another MIG coming up *my* tail. As I rolled into a hard right turn, I felt my plane shake."

A high explosive shell had struck Williams' plane, severing the rudder control and knocking out the aileron boost. With the MIG still on his tail, Williams dived his crippled plane for the clouds, 10,000 feet below.

"The MIG stayed right behind me in a tight trail position," said Williams, "and continued to fire at me even as we went into the clouds. My only evasive maneuver was a series of zooms—applying hard forward and back pressure on the stick control."

Meanwhile, a third Navy Panther was climbing to join the fracas. At his request, LTJG Middleton was detached from his leader, LT Elwood, and climbed to join the scrap involving his two squadron friends.

Upon reaching the fight, a MIG made a head-on run at Middleton. Simultaneously, Middleton saw Williams, a MIG, and Rowlands diving for the clouds. Rowlands, out of ammunition, had fallen in alongside the MIG, flying a loose wing position on it in an effort to draw him away from Williams.

"The most unbelievable part of the incident," said Middleton, "was the sight of Rowlands sitting so close on a MIG's tail with the MIG firing away like mad at Williams."

While Middleton dove toward his teammates to render aid, a second MIG attacked him, but his shots missed.

Following this attack, the MIG reversed its course and the pilot either lost Middleton in the sun or became engrossed in getting ready to make an attack on Rowlands. In either case, Middleton was now in position for a full-deflection shot at his attacker. He commenced firing from far out, and continued firing as the MIG's superior speed left his Panther tailing behind. Middleton saw the enemy pilot bail out, and the MIG crashed into the sea.

"After watching the enemy pilot land in the water," said Middleton, "I orbited around him with my emergency IFF on, as I was convinced he would be of more benefit to us alive than dead."*

"I am convinced that Middleton saved my life," said Rowlands, "as the MIG he shot down was making a run on me."

After reaching the safety of the clouds, the three Panthers were given a radar steer to return to the task force. All three pilots landed aboard *Oriskany* without further difficulty.

As the task force retired toward the south at the conclusion of the two-day effort, all ships in Task Force 77 were a buzz of activity and talk. Radar plots and logs were exchanged; Williams, Rowlands, and Middleton were pumped for observations, opinions, and comments.

That the MIGs were Russian ones from the Vladivostok complex there seemed little doubt.

"Every time we had taken the task force up that far north before, or even just a battleship, we got some kind of reaction in the form of airplanes rising up from the vicinity of Vladivostok," said VADM J. J. Clark, Commander Seventh Fleet aboard *Missouri*. "This was plain from many radar plots. Usually, they seemed to be just flying some sort of barrier patrol as protection for their own area.

"On this occasion, however, there were about 60 or more images on the radar scope at various times during the afternoon. The bunch which tangled with our planes were headed straight for the Fleet, and only 35 to 40 miles away when the initial contact was made. I can only surmise that they had orders to attack."[20]

Said the Air Intelligence Officer of ComCarDiv-FIVE, CDR R. P. Fuller, "At the time of this melee, there was one division of F9F2s and one division of F2H2s from the *Kearsarge* Air Group airborne and less than two minutes away. Why *they* were not vectored into the scrap, I'll never know."

---

* The fate of the pilot of this MIG is unknown. "Due to faulty plotting," said VADM Clark, "the ships closest to this area regrettably failed to make a search for the MIG pilot. We didn't pick him up."

Both Williams and Middleton were convinced that the MIG pilots had not used the superior points of their aircraft to advantage.

"The poor showing of the MIGs was not wholly due to inexperience," said Williams, "although that was a factor. They seemed to use good offensive tactics, but their gunnery was not good. Part of their failure to shoot us down was no doubt wild shooting. But I believe another reason for their poor marksmanship was the inferior gunsight with which the MIG was equipped."

Rowlands was in agreement with his team leader.

"The pilots of VF-781 concluded that we were very fortunate to have come back with our whole skins," said Rowlands. "The MIG pilots were inexperienced and sacrificed their aircraft's advantages without hesitation. As for their gunnery, theirs was about like mine—wild. All of them fired too far out for accuracy."

The Navy-MIG incident was still a conversation piece during the visit of the newly-elected U. S. President, Dwight D. Eisenhower, to Korea in early December, three weeks later.

"On 3 December," said Vice Admiral Clark, "I was invited by General Van Fleet to his headquarters in Seoul to meet the President-elect, Dwight D. Eisenhower. At the suggestion of Admiral Briscoe, I took along in my plane the three *Oriskany* pilots—Lieutenants Williams, Middleton, and Rowlands—who had fought the Russian MIGs so that they would be available in case Mr. Eisenhower might wish to see them. As it happened, he did.

"When we arrived in Seoul at the Eighth Army Headquarters I told General Van Fleet I had brought them along, and he said he'd tell 'Ike' they were present. The President came out, shook hands, and invited them into his private suite. Present were the Secretary-designate of Defense, Mr. Charles E. Wilson, Admiral Radford, Admiral Briscoe, General Van Fleet, and myself.

"While the three officers were telling their story to the President, in walked General Weyland, commanding the Far East Air Force, and Lieutenant General Barcus, commanding the Fifth Air Force. It was at once realized by everybody present that the Navy had stolen the show."

The naval pilots were impressed by the knowledge of air warfare that the President displayed, and his desire to know what the pilots wanted in their combatant aircraft.

"President Eisenhower congratulated us," said Rowlands, "and was quite interested in just where the fight started and who had started it. He also wanted a firsthand account of the fight."

"The President's reaction to our story was one of elation," said Williams, "but what impressed me most was his desire to get our opinion and evaluation of our present aircraft and what we pilots wanted in performance of future aircraft."

Later that evening, Vice Admiral Clark took LT Williams and his wingmates to Admiral Radford's quarters for a further interview.

"Admiral Radford was critical of our pilots becoming separated during the dogfight," said Vice Admiral Clark, "because, according to accepted combat doctrine, it is basic that fighter planes stick close together for mutual protection. I had to agree with Admiral Radford, except for the final score; *that* was in our favor."

Minor though it was, this encounter had several results and repercussions. It had demonstrated the definite superiority of the MIG over the most advanced Navy fighter then operational in the Fleet: the F9F5. Only the superior training and better marksmanship of the naval pilots had evened the score. Official records credit Williams and Middleton with the destruction of one plane each, Rowlands with one damaged. This is undoubtedly conservative. Later compilations of radar plots and pilot interviews indicated a strong possibility that only one or possibly two of the original seven MIGs returned to base. Five or perhaps even six were either shot down directly, damaged so severely as to crash, or ran out of fuel on the way home.

Another result of the incident was to re-emphasize the basic purpose of the fighter: air-to-air combat. The peculiar nature of the Korean War and the usual employment of Navy fighters had unconsciously subordinated their primary function to bombing, rocketing, and flak-suppression.

Also, the scrap had partly counterbalanced two recent Task Force 77 losses to enemy MIGs. On 4 October 1952, LT Eugene F. Johnson, a VF-884 Corsair pilot aboard *Kearsarge,* had been shot down by a MIG near Wonsan. Johnson's was one of seven F4Us attacking Yongpo. While in a dive, he had been attacked by four MIGs, and his plane was seen to crash.

Three days later, a second Navy pilot had been lost to MIGs. On 7 October 1952, near Hungnam, a *Princeton* F4U pilot, ENS John R. Shaughnessy, VF-193, had been set afire and shot down by a MIG. Shaughnessy had succeeded in parachuting clear of his burning Corsair, and been picked up by the USS *Boyd* (DD-544). While in the water, Shaughnessy had become entangled in his parachute shroud lines and been nearly drowned when rescued. He expired on board the *Boyd.*

"These MIG attacks followed no special pattern," said VADM Clark. "Each time they appeared, the Task Force would send our jet combat air patrol out to catch them, but when our jets were on station, the MIGs failed to appear. Indications pointed to the fact that the Communists were using radar control for these MIGs. As a result of these attacks, Task Force 77 began a program of destroying these enemy radar stations which continued through the rest of the war as the opportunity afforded."

To many of the naval airmen, the destruction of the MIGs on the 18th of November had partially evened the score.

Finally, the battle had tested the air defense capability of a carrier task force.

In the official report of Commander Carrier Division Five, Rear Admiral R. F. Hickey reported that the task force communications and radar performance had been "excellent" and the "coordination between ships' CIC's (Combat Information Centers) highly efficient."

The "Bedcheck Charlies"

During the last several months of the Korean war, the Communist enemy adopted a tactic which long went uncountered—the use of "Bedcheck Charlies."*

The Bedcheck Charlies were antique aircraft of two types—YAK-18 Soviet-built training planes (a low-wing, single-engine aircraft with a cruising speed of 100 knots and a cruising radius of approximately 200 miles); or PO-2s (a Russian-built wood and fabric bi-plane with a top speed of 110 mph). Each of these aircraft was capable of carrying one or two small bombs.

At odd intervals on dark nights, singles or small groups of YAK-18 or PO-2 aircraft would fly from grass fields in North Korea over the battleline or to the Seoul area, flying as low as possible to reduce the possibility of radar detection. Their wood and fabric construction made radar detection difficult. Buzzing low over the city in the darkness, these raids succeeded in arousing the sleeping city. Air raid alarms would be sounded; in most cases searchlights would be lit off; and during the course of these nocturnal maraudings, the Bedcheck Charlie would drop one or two small bombs. The damage was usually trivial and often nonexistent. But the harassment and nuisance value was far from insignificant.

In May and June, the Reds became increasingly bold and succeeded in doing some damage.

On 3 May, a group of Bedcheck Charlies dropped nine bombs in the X Corps and I ROK Corps areas along the battleline, but no casualties were reported. Shortly after midnight, 26-27 May, a group of Bedcheck Charlies (estimated at six PO-2s) succeeded in dropping four small 100-pound general purpose bombs and eight 50-pound artillery shells on K-14 airfield near Inchon, puncturing the gasoline pipeline. On the night of 2 June

* Russian trainer aircraft, nicknamed "Sewing Machines," had been similarly used against the Germans in World War II.

a group of Bedcheck Charlies was reported over K-6 airfield (near Pyong-taek, 30 miles south of Inchon), obviously feeling for the neat lines of parked airplanes. This was the greatest danger of these raids—the possibility that the Bedcheck Charlies might locate and inflict severe damage to aircraft parked on the South Korean airfields, some of which had little or no suitable AA defenses for low, slow-flying, wooden training planes.

The night of 8 June saw a nine-plane raid on Seoul which, according to newspaper reports, killed two persons and injured eight. The first bomb hit only 1,000 feet away from President Syngman Rhee's residence, while a second hit a school building 400 yards away. Another bomb struck in front of the Seoul press billets, and flying glass slightly injured a *Life* magazine photographer.[21] Many thought the attack on Rhee's residence was an attempt to make the ROK President more amenable to the impending truce.

On the night of 16 June, a 15-plane Bedcheck Charlie raid succeeded in bombing a petroleum, oil, and lubrication dump near Inchon, torching 52,000 gallons of petroleum products. The raid commenced at 10:30 P.M. and continued for two hours, as searchlights and AA fire criss-crossed the skies. Smoke and flames from the burning 40-acre area were visible the next day for 40 miles. It was the Seoul area's fifth raid in nine nights.[22]

To combat these raids, there were not available either to the Fifth Air Force in Korea or the First Marine Air Wing planes which were slow enough to destroy these trainers and which were also equipped with the necessary night-fighter electronic equipment to detect them. The jet-type night fighters employed (FAFIK was flying F-94s; the Marines, F3D Sky-knights) could not slow down sufficiently to engage the Bedcheck Charlies. On a few occasions a team of flare-dropping aircraft and a T-6 "Texan" trainer had been launched while a Bedcheck Charlie raid was in progress, with the hope that they could illuminate and destroy the pestiferous planes; but the system never worked.

"When I learned about these enemy night raids," said VADM J. J. Clark, Commander Seventh Fleet, "I asked my staff if there wasn't something the Navy could do to lend the Air Force a helping hand.

"The operations officer for CarDivOne, CDR John P. Conn, suggested that we send Corsair F4U5N night fighters ashore to assist in combating these nuisance raids. Since our planes were Corsairs, and the Marines had an airfield at K-8 from where they operated Corsairs, the F4U5Ns could be based at that airfield, which was 35 miles south of Seoul.

"Without further ado, and not waiting for him to accept, I sent a message to Lieutenant General S. E. Anderson, commanding the Fifth Air Force, advising him that a detachment of Corsairs from the Fleet was on its way

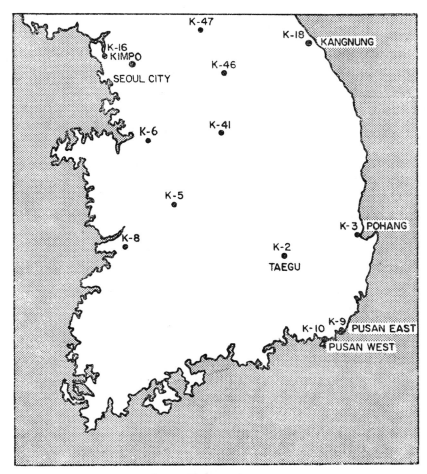

SOUTH KOREAN AIRFIELDS

to report to him in an effort to knock out these Bedcheck Charlies. Two F4U5Ns were sent in from each carrier.

"The Navy night pilots (all from VC-3) received a week's familiarization. On the night of 29 June, LT Guy P. Bordelon, attached to *Princeton,* shot down two of the Bedcheck Charlies.

"Admiral Briscoe told me about this when I arrived in the office on the 30th for a routine visit," said VADM Clark. "I immediately decided to award LT Bordelon a Silver Star Medal for his feat, and since I was scheduled to fly back to Korea that night, I decided to go to K-6 to witness the operations of our night fighters and to lend encouragement to their efforts.

"As we approached the field at about 2230 that night, we were ordered to land at K-3 because of an air raid. We turned around and flew to K-3, but that field was blanketed by heavy fog. We finally landed at 0130 next day at Taegu.

"Afterwards we learned that the reason for the alert at K-6 had been another enemy raid. LT Bordelon had shot down two more night fighters. Then and there, I decided to present him with a gold star in lieu of a second Silver Star.

"Accordingly, I flew to General Anderson's headquarters in Seoul. Both the feats of LT Bordelon had been confirmed by the radar track kept by the Air Force, although no wreckage of the downed planes was ever found. I then flew to K-6 where luncheon was given in honor of LT Bordelon by Major General McGee, USMC, under whose immediate jurisdiction the feats had been accomplished, and who had flown over for the occasion from K-3. Bordelon told us that when he had made contact with the enemy planes, each of them began to take violent evasive action.

"In a traditional ceremony I presented Bordelon with both awards at the same time, promising him, or anyone else who shot down five planes at night, a Navy Cross.

"On the night of July 17th, Bordelon succeeded in bagging his fifth enemy plane. Since his operations were conducted under General Anderson, commanding the Fifth Air Force, after obtaining authority from the Secretary of the Navy, I asked the General to make the presentation of the Navy Cross at once. This he did at an appropriate ceremony at Fifth Air Force headquarters.

"LT Bordelon had attained for himself the distinction of being the first and only night ace in the U. S. Navy. As a result of his effort, enemy night raids on Seoul ceased, and the city was able to sleep once more."

The Truce Talks Resumed

During the winter months of 1952-1953, the stalemated war dragged on in the same monotonous pattern, with little change in the battleline, with little ground action other than patrol activity, and with little hope for an end to the bleak and bitter war.

January at Panmunjom saw occasional meetings between liaison officers, at which the Communists made false charges about overflights and bombardments of the neutral zone. The fighting along the front consisted only of harassing probes and limited objective offensives. By Presidential order, the island of Formosa was de-neutralized.

February saw little change, with continued limited activity along the front. Late in the month, there was a pickup in close air support by Seventh Fleet aircraft. Typical of this work was a mission on 21 February 1953. Six *Valley Forge* VF-54 ADs, led by their skipper, CDR Henry J. Suerstedt,

Jr., were diverted from a routine close air support mission and put to work on a hill in Ninth Corps area where UN troops were attempting to regain control of the crest. Communist troops were dug in on the defilade side of the crest and artillery could not reach them. Suerstedt's ADs made runs parallel to the front of the UN troops, dropping 500- and 1,000-pound bombs on the Communist side of the ridge at distances reported by the "Mosquito" as only 75 yards from the UN troops. Following these runs, three of the ADs strafed. The ridge was reported as taken. The "Mosquito" reported 100 per cent accuracy and ordnance effectiveness: sixteen bunkers destroyed or severely damaged, and two caves destroyed, along with many enemy troops.

March saw a die-hard Communist riot in the POW compounds at Yongcho and Koje Islands, and several hard attacks by the Reds, but with no exchange of real estate, however.

April and springtime, however, brought new developments.

The major event was a resumption of the deadlocked truce talks. To a UN invitation to exchange seriously sick and wounded prisoners in accordance with the Geneva Convention, the Communists surprised the world by saying "Yes." On 6 April, therefore, talks were commenced at Panmunjom which led to agreement on 11 April. "Operation Little Switch" commenced on 20 April. Six thousand six hundred and seventy Communist personnel and 684 UN prisoners (149 of them U. S.) were exchanged.

Spurred by this speedy agreement, steps were taken to reopen the main truce talks.

On 26 April, following the exchange of sick and wounded, the 199-day recess of the armistice negotiations was ended. Prospects that an end to the stalemated conflict might be imminent suddenly became brighter.

At sea, April Fool's Day began with Task Force 77 repeating the oft-repeated tasks once again. The rail lines from Kilchu to Tanchon were hit. Close air support was given to U. S. IX Corps. Naval gunfire spot was furnished for still another bombardment of Songjin. Targets in Wonsan, including the harbor guns, were struck. One F9F5 from VF-51 (flown by LT E. J. Thabet) was hit by flak. Thabet parachuted to safety over Wonsan, being rescued by LST helicopter.

On 13 April, the beleaguered city of Chongjin was battered in another maximum air-gun strike. One hundred and nineteen sorties from *Philippine Sea's* Carrier Air Group Nine and *Oriskany's* Carrier Air Group Twelve hit the city's transportation network and its mining and ordnance areas. Pilots reported the destruction of a communications center in a harmless-looking bank building.

April 21st was "Boy-San Day," when the pilots of *Princeton* and

Oriskany struck targets of their own preference. Two hundred and twenty-three sorties were flown. Even so, the targets were much the same—the supply and industrial areas of northeast Korea, the Hodo Pando guns of Wonsan, a jet sweep past Pukchong, and naval gunfire support and Cherokee missions. The best result, perhaps, was the fact that no pilots were lost.

The Big Push

As the main armistice talks were reopened, there was only one major obstacle to a truce: what to do with the 114,500 Chinese and 34,000 North Korean prisoners who refused to return to their homeland. The Communists insisted they had to be returned—using force if necessary. The UN's position was that no prisoner who refused repatriation should be returned to Communist control against his will. The government of the United States refused to compromise on this cardinal principle. ". . . The principle that force shall not be used to compel resisting prisoners to go home excludes every form of coercion. We cannot, consistently with that principle, create a situation where such persons are offered no alternative to repatriation other than indefinite captivity or custody."

For weeks, the truce talks pivoted on this thorny issue. At the resumption of the plenary sessions the Communist negotiators made a proposal that all prisoners not directly repatriated be sent to an agreed neutral state where, for the succeeding six months, representatives of the states to which they belonged would "explain" to them matters related to their return. The disposition of any remaining nonrepatriates after the six months had passed would be referred to the political conference called for under the draft Armistice Agreement. Subsequent negotiations centered upon three matters: the choice of a suitable neutral state; the question whether the prisoners who did not accept repatriation should be turned over to the neutral state outside Korea, which the United Nations Command considered a difficult and unnecessary operation; and the length of time the nonrepatriates should remain in neutral custody, after which the UN Command insisted they must be released to civilian status.

On May 7 the Communist representative submitted a revised proposal providing for establishment of a neutral commission, to be called the Neutral Nations Repatriation Commission and to be composed of the four states already agreed upon as members of the Neutral Nations Supervisory Commission—Czechoslovakia, Poland, Sweden, and Switzerland—plus India. This proposal provided that the Commission would take custody of the prisoners in Korea. It further provided that the nonrepatriates would remain in neutral custody for four months, and that thereafter the disposition of any remaining prisoners would be referred to the political conference.

On May 13 the United Nations Command presented a counterproposal providing for the release of all Korean nonrepatriates immediately after the armistice, sending only the Chinese nonrepatriates into neutral custody where India alone would provide the necessary military forces for their control, and shortening to two months the period during which the nonrepatriates would remain in neutral custody.

This proposal was immediately rejected by the Communists.

Optimism plummeted once again.

To further complicate the truce negotiations, President Syngman Rhee announced on 25 May that his Republic of Korea government would not accept any armistice that would leave Korea divided; his government further threatened to withdraw all ROK divisions from the UN command and use them independently to continue the war if a truce was signed. On the same date the UN team issued a counterplan, which provided for the transfer of all nonrepatriates to neutral custody for 90 days. However, the guarantee that no prisoner would be forced home against his will remained. This was followed by a ten-day recess.

On 4 June, the much-recessed armistice talks were resumed, and another attempt was made to settle the repatriation issue. Rhee ordered his ROK truce team member to boycott further meetings. The Communists agreed to accept an "explanation" period after the armistice, during which time, under the Five Power Commission's supervision, they could interview each Chinese and Korean prisoner who refused repatriation and try to induce him to return to Communist homeland.

With this stumbling block removed, the single issue obstructing a truce was the readjustment of the military demarcation line on which the armistice was to be based.

As before, whenever the truce prospects brightened, the enemy increased his efforts to gain ground along the MLR (Main Line of Resistance). Several outposts changed hands repeatedly, but no major change had yet occurred in the location of the frontlines.

"The pattern of enemy offensive activity intensified early in June," said VADM J. J. Clark. "The UN command received reports of troop movements toward the front, and many concentrations of Communists armies in the forward area were noted. Attacks along the line increased, ranging from company to division size. The heaviest concentration was in the eastern sector.

"All this activity on the part of the Communists was simply a question of 'face', which is all-important to the Oriental mind. At the time of the armistice, the Reds wanted to appear in an offensive role. They seemed determined to seize enough ground for propaganda purposes so they could say that UN forces were signing an armistice to avoid a military defeat."

On the eastern sector, after a bitter struggle, Anchor Hill and Hill 812 passed into enemy hands in late May and early June. This was followed by heavy action in the central sector, where the Communists attacked the Ninth U. S. and Second ROK Corps in division strength. Heavy concentrations of enemy artillery and mortar fire preceded all attacks. In the Second ROK Corps sector, Communist forces succeeded in pushing back the main line of resistance, capturing Capitol Hill, Finger Ridge, Outpost 'Texas', and portions of Christmas Hill.

"Noting this heavy enemy activity," continued VADM Clark, "I visited General Taylor's Eighth Army headquarters. On 6 June, I ordered Task Force 77 and Task Group 95.11 to exert maximum carrier air effort in support of the United Nations troops at the battleline."

During this final period of the war, Task Force 77 saw a new burst of activity. Four carriers operated on the line almost continuously, despite poor weather. Many operating records were smashed: total sorties flown, tonnages of armament delivered, total days at sea. Underway replenishment at night—of a magnitude never before known (27 times in 49 days) —became routine.

The following are excerpts from reports of the period:

Boxer: (CAPT Marshall B. Gurney; Air Task Group One, CDR L. A. Whitney)

11 June 1953: 130 sorties. The ADs proved exceptionally effective in a close air support mission on the central front. The Mosquito controller reported 500 yards of trenches destroyed, 15 mortar positions destroyed, and 12 secondary explosions. . . .

14 June 1953. 131 sorties. Jet Cherokee strikes hit supply buildings near the eastern frontline near Anchor Hill. ADs and jets were both used in close air support on eastern and central MLR. 1625 yards of trench, 8 mortar positions, and 9 gun emplacements were destroyed by close air support missions. . . .

15 June 1953: 147 sorties. Today's strikes were part of the maximum effort put out by Task Force 77 in support of a counteroffensive by UN forces to retake ground lost the previous week in the vicinity of "Anchor Hill". In the effort, 650 yards of trench, 3 machine gun positions, 7 mortar positions, and 73 buildings were destroyed. "Well Done's" were received from CG 8th Army, ComSeventhFlt, CTF 77, CincPacFlt, and ComNavFe. . . .

Lake Champlain: (CAPT George T. Mundorff, USN; CVG-4, CDR John Sweeny)

15 June 1953: Props again rendered close air support to United Nations troops, and jet strikes were directed to billeting and supply targets in the Cherokee area. One hundred forty-seven sorties were flown, dropping 103

tons of ordnance. The *Lake Champlain* (which had commenced combat operations two days earlier) received the following from CTF 77: "You amateurs turned in a veteran performance today X We are proud of you X."

Philippine Sea: (CAPT Paul H. Ramsey; Carrier Air Group Nine, CDR T. D. Harris)

15 June 1953: The heaviest naval air blow of the conflict was struck today. . . Today was an all-Navy show for strikes in support of the ground forces to regain "Anchor Hill." At the end of the day's operation, "Anchor Hill" was referred to by Air Group pilots as "Anchor Valley." The hill was regained by friendly ground forces and the operation was praised by General Lee of the ROKs and General Taylor of the Eighth Army. . . .

Princeton: (CAPT O. C. Gregg; Carrier Air Group Fifteen, CDR John E. Parks)

15 June 1953: The combat sortie record for aircraft carriers is believed to have been broken when 172 and 184 sorties were launched during 2 single-day operations (14 and 15 June).

On 14 and 15 June, Task Force 77 had delivered 300 and 403 frontline missions respectively. Admiral Clark described the Seventh Fleet's contribution to the Anchor Hill operation.

"After conferences with Lieutenant General H. K. Lee, who commanded the First ROK Corps, I ordered a concentrated surface gunfire and carrier air strike to support the recapture of Anchor Hill and its surrounding terrain. My flagship, the *New Jersey,* and the cruiser *St. Paul* would join the shoot.

"Carrier planes, assisted by the *New Jersey,* and the *St. Paul,* began an intense bombardment and bombing of the area on the 14th which continued throughout the morning of the 15th.

"Accompanied by Rear Admiral Harry Sanders (Commander Cruiser Division One) and Captain Herschel A. House of my staff, I flew by helicopter to an outpost near the scene of action. There I witnessed the attempt to re-occupy the lost territory.

"Supported beautifully by Seventh Fleet's planes, General Lee's troops had no difficulty in recapturing two of the hills, but on the main peak of Anchor Hill the enemy held out stubbornly until after four o'clock in the afternoon."

The battleship *New Jersey* laid down one of the heaviest bombardments of the war to assist in the capture of Anchor Hill. (This was the first use of a battleship at the bombline since *Iowa* had been so employed in October 1952.) The "Big Jay" reported 44 bunkers destroyed, 20 heavily damaged, 2 caves closed, 610 yards of trench torn up, 13 gun positions destroyed, and 13 others damaged.

"I have never seen a greater display of courage than that of the ROK troops in climbing the mountainous terrain of Anchor Hill," said Clark. "The ROKs would climb a few steps, only to be picked off by machine gun and artillery fire which was deadly accurate. Other ROKs would take the place of their fallen comrades. There was a large bomb crater about half-way up the hill in which several men had taken shelter from the blistering barrage. As I watched with binoculars, the enemy dropped a mortar shell into the crater, and men could be seen rolling part way down the steep slope until they stopped and lay still. They were dead. Again, farther up the hill, other ROK soldiers reached rocky terrain which offered some protection for a time, but the enemy again waited until twenty or thirty troops were concentrated among the rocks, then he delivered a heavy artillery barrage in their midst.

"Despite the enemy's intense opposition, the ROK Fifth Division troops reached the summit about four o'clock, supported by Seventh Fleet planes and ships. The entire complex was captured. The Communist enemy had suffered more than 3,000 casualties, while the First ROK Corps casualties were only 200 killed and 300 wounded. Lieutenant General Lee credited the carrier aircraft and the naval gunfire support for making it possible for his forces to seize Anchor Hill.

"Unfortunately," said VADM Clark, "the enemy regained the main peak later that night due to faulty leadership and supply arrangements. The enemy offensive on the eastern front was crushed, however, and fighting in that area subsided."

Congratulatory dispatches for the naval support came from many commands. General Taylor said in his despatch:

> Today has been a costly one for our enemies. The frontline troops of Army Eight were in praise of the magnificent report they received from the planes of the Seventh Fleet and the gunfire of the ships at sea. . . .

Lieutenant General Lee radioed:

> Please accept my deepest thanks and appreciation for the magnificent effort of your naval air and surface forces in support of the Corps' operation. I have never seen a better performance. . . .

For 700 days, Communist intransigence had opposed the truce. Ironically, on 16 June, as a truce agreement was finalized at Panmunjom, a sudden and unexpected action on the part of President Syngman Rhee came close to ending the truce talks once and for all.

At lunch that day, Lieutenant General William K. Harrison, Jr., the senior UN negotiator, had confided to Vice Admiral Clark that the last remaining adjustment of the demarcation line was about to be made and that he expected an armistice within three or four days. At four o'clock in the afternoon, in fact, Harrison telephoned Clark to say that all remaining points of discussion had been agreed upon and that it was only necessary to translate the terms into the various languages before the armistice would be signed. In four days, Harrison told Clark, the actual signing could take place.

It was at this stage of the negotiations that President Syngman Rhee dramatically released the 27,000-odd anti-Communist prisoners in his custody. Rhee also declared martial law throughout the Republic of Korea and recalled his army officers stationed in the United States, saying that the armistice meant suicide for South Korea, and that if the United States signed the armistice, it would be an act of betrayal and appeasement.

At Panmunjom, the Communists hotly denounced the action of Rhee, accusing him of freeing the prisoners so they could be enlisted in the ROK Army, and further accused the United States of complicity in the release. The Communist negotiators demanded that the released POWs be recaptured—a manifestly impossible task.

For several anxious days there was deep concern in UN circles, particularly among the Allies who had contributed forces to the UN command, lest the unilateral action by Rhee break up the truce negotiations, re-kindle the war, and perhaps even expand its scope.

In late June, the President of the United States, Dwight D. Eisenhower, sent Mr. Walter S. Robertson, the Assistant Secretary of State for Far Eastern Affairs, to Korea to confer with Mr. Rhee.

Upon Robertson's arrival, 26 June, a series of demonstrations took place throughout South Korea. President Rhee repeated that it was South Korea's desire not to sign an armistice, but to fight on to the bitter end. On 25 June, speaking to 300,000 Seoul citizens on the occasion of the third anniversary of the Korean War, President Rhee asked that his country ". . . be allowed to decide our own fate."

The Communist response to these demonstrations and announcements was one of the heaviest attacks of the war. The Chinese attack was directed at the Second ROK Corps, commanded by General Chung Il Kwon, in what many considered to be a punishment attack to belittle the ROK Army and to persuade President Rhee to agree to a truce.

The Reds struck in force on the night of 13 June. Six enemy divisions, numbering 13,000 men, assaulted the Second ROK Army Corps sector of the battleline. When their administrative allotment of artillery ammunition had been expended, the Second ROK Corps withdrew in good order to a distance of six to eight miles, fighting a delaying action. On the right flank the ROK Capitol Division, commanded by General "Tiger" Song, gave ground slowly and successively, withdrawing its artillery safely, and bloodily punishing the enemy.

For the next six days the carriers of Task Force 77 stood by the endangered sector. Vice Admiral Clark directed on 14 July that until further notice, all Task Force 77 air effort would support the battlefront.

Lake Champlain (CAPT L. B. Southerland; CVG-4, CDR J. R. Sweeney)

15 July 1953: . . . inclement weather limited flight operations to 23 sorties . . . concentrated on close and deep support of hard-pressed UN troops along the east central front. The Tactical Air Controller of one of the Cherokee missions reported that their drop on an ammunition dump, which resulted in five secondary explosions, was "the best run in weeks."

Boxer (CAPT M. B. Gurney; ATG-1, CDR L. A. Whitney)

16 July 1953: 111 sorties were flown, almost all in the bulge area of the front near Kumwha. . . . Two Cherokee strikes . . . destroyed 35 personnel shelters, 20 bunkers, 400 yards of trenches and an artillery position. Three secondary explosions resulted. Other Panther flights of the day destroyed eight trucks, cut five bridges, and damaged storage and staging areas.

To quell the attack, Eighth Army also requested that armed reconnaissance flights along the enemy's main supply routes be increased. To advance, any Chinese offensive must be supported logistically, and by daylight.

By chance, one *Lake Champlain* squadron commander had driven over the same roads and across the same bridges in June that he would be bombing in July.

"To the novice in Korea, a particularly good way to distinguish North Korea from South Korea was by the quality of roads and bridges," said CDR W. W. Kelly, commanding officer of VF-62. "In South Korea, the roads looked like clean white ribbons from the air. The bridges were wide, white, and conspicuous-looking. In contrast, the North Korea roads and bridges were small, damaged, and unused-looking.

"On 16 July, I was leading an armed recco hop when the main controller called on the radio, diverted my flight, and ordered us to bomb all the bridges in a certain area.

"We quickly plotted the coordinates and found that the targets were in friendly territory. I could identify this particular area personally because, a few days before, I had been on a board of investigation and had driven over it in a jeep.

"I immediately thought this might be a fake enemy transmission since the sender was diverting my flight and asking us to bomb our own territory. After he authenticated, however, he told us that the Chinese forces had broken through in this area, and we were to knock the bridges out to slow them down.

"Unfortunately, we were not armed for bridge-busting. We did our best with our 250-pound bombs, and I think it kept the enemy slowed down. Just as we were leaving the target, my air group commander came along with eight *Lake Champlain* Skyraiders. They had 2,000-lb. bombs, and I personally saw CDR Sweeney's bomb blow a section of bridge high in the air."[23]

For the remaining two weeks of the war, the four carriers pounded the enemy forces, setting new records for sorties flown on three successive days—24 July, 598; 25 July, 608; 26 July, 649. Seven thousand five hundred and seventy-one offensive sorties, half of them at the bombline, were delivered in an all-out effort to stabilize the front.

"As it turned out," said Admiral Clark, "the Chinese Communist Army was not prepared for a general offensive. Most of the Communist soldiers had only two or three days' rations in their pockets, and they couldn't move fast enough.

"By the 19th of July, the full weight of the enemy onslaught had subsided and friendly counterattacks gradually reduced the extent of his frontal penetration.

"This release of prisoners by President Rhee had prolonged the war about five weeks, during which time United Nations troops, including South Koreans, sustained 46,000 casualties while the Communists had suffered an estimated 75,000 casualties."[24]

Vice Admiral R. P. Briscoe, Commander Naval Forces Far East, despatched his congratulations:

Please pass to all units of your Fleet my congratulations upon the superb effort they have put out during the past few weeks. In spite of almost impossible operating weather, they have prevented the enemy from capitalizing on his advantage and have added immeasurably to the destruction of his resources. A hearty well-done to all of you.

The Last Day

The last day of the war began like the ones before. Task Force 77 aircraft destroyed and damaged 23 railroad cars, 11 railroad bridges, one railroad tunnel, 69 buildings, 100 yards of trench and 9 highway bridges. Forty rail and three highway cuts were made.

Philippine Sea:

The day had a fast start with 49 sorties launched before the truce. . .

Boxer:

On 27 July, 77 sorties were flown. Missions consisted of strikes, armed reconnaissance, and interdiction. At 1000, the cease-fire agreement was signed at Panmunjom which became effective twelve hours later. At 2200, all hostilities ceased, but until that time F9Fs hit airfields at Yonpo, Koeman, and Hamhung West.

Lake Champlain:

On 27 July, in conjunction with the signing of the truce, a leaflet drop was conducted on major cities along the east coast of Korea. Simultaneously, strikes were made to render all airfields in North Korea non-operational at the time of the signing of the truce. Close air support missions were carried out by the props before the truce was signed—124 sorties flown, 61 tons dropped.

To some pilots of Task Force 77 the last day was unusual only in the sense that targets were plentiful but couldn't be hit. To others it was a last chance to qualify for an Air Medal.

"My flight was assigned the airfield at Hyesanjin," said CDR W. W. Kelly. "Our orders, which we had acknowledged receipt of in writing, were to hit *only* the airfield, and if for any reason we couldn't do it, we were to jettison our loads at sea.

"Our flight of eight Banshees hit the coast at Kilchu, staying under a low overcast as we headed up the valley. Here, in the same places we had often looked in vain for fruitful targets, and where if we found a train or a truck we'd fight among ourselves to see who would get a shot at it, we suddenly saw large piles of material—one large pile of what looked like telephone poles; larger crates of material, lumber, etc.

"Then to complete our sense of frustration, we saw a train chugging down the valley very conspicuously. We couldn't and we didn't shoot it up, but went on to our target at Hyesanjin."[25]

At sea, the blockade and bombardment work went on as before. The cruiser *Saint Paul* (CAPT C. W. Parker, USN) fired the last round of the war at sea at 2159.

On the harbor islands of Wonsan the day was no different either, although the tempo was less. At the designated time of cease fire—2200—the east coast islands' defense forces commenced the destruction of the islands' fortifications.

Ashore, the front was generally quiet, although a few rounds of enemy mortar and artillery fire were received in the First Marine Division's area until 2153, when five rounds of 82-mm. mortar landed in the First Korean Marine Corps Regimental Combat Team's area.

Some U. S. Marines reported Chinese policing their front a full thirty minutes before the agreed-upon hour of 2200. Chinese troops could be seen looking for souvenirs. Some of the enemy troops waved lighted candles, flashlights, and banners in celebration.

On "T-Bone Hill", the Communists erected an arch of tree limbs and called out for UN troops to "come on over and we will walk through the arch as brothers."

On "Old Baldy," North Korean girls could be seen singing and dancing, while the Red soldiers waved large papier-mâché Picasso peace doves as the hillside microphones blared out an invitation to "come on over and talk."

On "Arsenal Hill" a man's voice invited the UN soldiers to join him in the song, "My Old Kentucky Home." Other Chinese soldiers danced and sang, banged pans together, and erected huge signs proclaiming the signing of the Armistice.

One group of Chinese soldiers approached a Marine listening post, asked for water, and tried to carry on a conversation. Still others hung up gift bags and shouted, "How are you? Come on over and let's have a party!"

It was a strange ending to the strangest war the United States Navy had ever fought.

14.

Conclusion

At 2200, on the night of 27 July 1953, an uneasy truce settled along the battleline in Korea. The 37-month-and-2-days war had ended. It had cost the United States 142,091 casualties* and almost twenty billion dollars.

What had been gained by this expenditure of blood, time, and treasure? Had the United Nations and the United States won or lost the Korean War?

A single, simple answer to that question cannot be given as this book goes to print, for there still are two diametrically opposed views, which cause continued and bitter argument. One view, although not wholly accepted in political and diplomatic circles, is that the Korean war represented a victory for the West since the Free World was able to demonstrate the real value of collective security; and furthermore, it was able to accomplish what it set out to do: to localize and punish aggression, to drive the invader back to his lair, and to notify him that future forays would be met with even greater force.

This viewpoint is summarized by a 12 February 1956 editorial in the Washington *Post*.

> President Truman, for the United Nations, fought the war for a limited objective, and this he achieved. He achieved a successful result, moreover, without damaging our dominion in world strategy. Actually, that dominion was improved, and in the process Mr. Truman kept the Russian intervention limited with his atomic deterrent.

This point of view also holds that any expansion of the Korean War, inside or outside Korea, might have brought Russia into the conflict; and since neither the Free World nor the United States was then militarily prepared for a larger conflict, the risk of involving the Soviets was not to be taken.

The other view, generally prominent in military circles, is that the

* Department of Defense press release 1088-54. These figures are described as "tentative final."

490

Korean War was a loss, militarily as well as psychologically. Even though the means for defeating the enemy were available, they were not used; and our failure to defeat the aggressor was an invitation to future aggression and truculence.

These views were reflected in such statements as General Mark Clark's, "We lacked the determination to win the war"; and by Admiral J. J. Clark's remark to the authors: "You shouldn't be in a war if you don't want to win it"; or in General Van Fleet's answer to the authors' question, "Under the accepted conditions of war, could the Korean War have been won without too great a cost?" General Van Fleet's reply was that the Chinese Communists were beaten in June 1951 when a truce was first requested, and they could have been beaten "any time" in succeeding months. These views were certainly held by General MacArthur. When asked by the authors, "With forces available in the Far Eastern theater, what strategy should have been followed after Chinese entry?", General MacArthur replied: "It was fundamental that the only strategy to be followed in such a situation was to apply maximum power of our naval and air arm in support of our hardpressed ground forces. This means: to have directed our attack against the nerve center of the Chinese ability to sustain his operations in Korea."

This point of view holds that Russia would never have dared to intervene in Korea.

To the question, "Did the United States win or lose the Korean War?" therefore, no answer can now be given. For if the United Nations (or the United States) had taken military action to defeat the Red Chinese either under the MacArthur formula (blockade China, bomb across the Yalu, use Chiang's troops)—or the Van Fleet plan (decisively defeat the Chinese on the Korean peninsula itself)—or the "Jocko" Clark format (drop just one A-bomb anywhere in North Korea)—no one can say now whether the Soviets might have intervened. As Admiral Clark said, "The only man who can say if such actions would have expanded the war or not is Stalin— and he's dead."

Leaving this question to future historians to answer, one thing nevertheless remains plain. Without command of the seas between the Free World and Korea, and in the waters adjacent to that beleaguered peninsula, the Korean War, as fought, most certainly would have been *lost* both militarily and politically with a finality that would now be plain to every American. Operations by ground and air forces were completely dependent on a steady flow of personnel and supplies, the bulk of which came across the vast Pacific ocean.

This conclusion is substantiated by these factors:

a. Six of every seven people who went to Korea went by sea.

b. Fifty-four million tons of dry cargo, 22 million tons of petroleum products went to Korea by ship.

c. Every soldier landed in Korea was accompanied by five tons of equipment, and it took 64 pounds every day to keep him there.

d. For every ton of trans-Pacific air freight, there were 270 tons of trans-Pacific sea freight. For every ton of air freight, four tons of gasoline for the airplanes had to be delivered across the Pacific by ship.

No war involving the United States exemplified the value of sea power better than the Korean War. The need of a strong, balanced, and adequate U. S. Navy for controlling the oceans for our purposes and for denying them to an enemy was made elementarily clear.

General Van Fleet's opinion of the Navy's work in Korea was direct and to the point: "We could not have existed in Korea without the Navy," he told the authors. "The sea blockade was so complete that it was taken for granted. And at the same time the enemy could not supply himself by water. Naval gunfire on both east and west coasts added to his burden; and had the Eighth Army wished to go on the offensive, naval gunfire on the flanks would have made it much easier. Freedom from enemy air and naval attack left us free to operate in the open."

Without seapower, certainly, the United States could never have gotten her soldiers and their equipment, her airmen and their aircraft, to the scene of conflict, nor supplied them once there. Nor could the weight of this nation's strength have been applied upon the enemy without the American Navy.

One principal result of the Korean War was to validate the naval concepts about future war which had been revealed in the B-36 Hearings before Congress in the fall of 1950: that the United States must have flexibility, mobility, and balance not only in its military planning but in its military machinery. The "modern" military school of thought that had thrived between 1945 and 1950—that a Navy's use in any future war would only be that of convoy and patrol—was proved fallacious.

Concerning what Korea had proved about the future of the Navy and the Marine Corps, two leading Generals of the U. S. Army were emphatic. General Van Fleet, asked if a Navy was necessary in the atomic age, said abruptly, "The need of a Navy is a self-evident fact." General MacArthur was equally certain: "Naval supremacy," he wrote, "is essential to the conduct of any insular campaign." Regarding the need and use of the U. S. Marine Corps in the event of future Korean type conflicts, General MacArthur said: "Any campaign of this type at once calls for the employment of amphibious maneuver for which, by virtue of its training and integration

ENEMY FLAK WAS HEAVY. *At top,* despite antiaircraft fire, some of it radar controlled, Aoji oil refinery was destroyed by 144 planes from CVs *Boxer, Essex,* and *Princeton.* Only four miles from Manchuria, this main source of Communist gasoline was beyond range of U N land-based aircraft. *Below, Kearsarge* fighters destroyed a village apparently civilian but known to conceal troops and supplies.

SHIP ACTIONS: *Top,* battleship *New Jersey* pounds coastal installations near the 38th parallel with her three sixteen-inch turrets. *Center,* exploding phosphorous shell from *New Jersey* leaves a fiery trail over targets. *Bottom,* seaplane tender *Floyds Bay* typifies the less heavily armed ships that performed vital support missions during the Korean conflict.

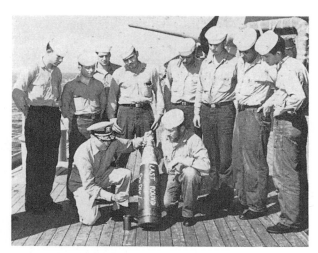

THE LAST ROUND. *At top,* RADM Harry Sanders aboard flagship *St. Paul* autographs last shell fired in war. *Center,* the round hurtled into enemy gun emplacement at 2157 on 27 July 1953. *Below,* RADM Clarence E. Olsen presents new CPO hat to Chief Edward L. Smith on release from Communist prison on 30 August.

NAVY FULFILLS DIPLOMATIC MISSION. *Upper,* RADM Arleigh Burke and VADM Turner Joy, chief U N delegates to Kaesong cease-fire conference. *Center,* the armistice building, Panmunjon. *Below,* GEN Mark W. Clark, USA, signs the armistice agreement, with VADM Briscoe and CDR James E. Shew looking on.

with sea-borne operations, the Marine Corps is far better adapted than any other military unit."

Vice Admiral C. T. Joy, the naval theater commander for the first two years of the war and the chief of the UN Command Truce Delegation Team, made the following cogent summary upon his departure from the Far East:

"The Korean War may not go down in history as a major war or as a war that appreciably changed the maps of the world. But it nevertheless is a war of deep significance. It has been a war to prevent a larger war by serving notice on a ruthless enemy that he can go so far and no farther. From the standpoint of national preparedness we have been awakened to the danger that surrounds us. Let us hope that we remain awake. From the standpoint of battle effectiveness, the Korean War has re-emphasized lessons which were almost lost sight of in the years that closely followed World War II. We know now that there is no quick, easy, cheap way to win a war. Sole reliance for our security cannot be placed in any one weapon or in any one branch of the Services. We cannot expect the enemy to oblige by planning his wars to suit our weapons. We must plan our weapons to fight war where, when, and how the enemy chooses. The choice of time, place, and circumstances rests with him.

"We need balance between the Services and balance within the Services. In the Navy, for example, we have learned that we cannot ever again neglect our minesweeping force. We cannot neglect our air arm. Inchon and Hungnam have again forcibly emphasized the vital need for our amphibious force. We cannot write off the naval gun as obsolete; the Korean War has again proved its worth. We have found a pressing need and full use for all of our naval weapons. And while the Navy's role in the war has gone unpublicized for the most part, it is sufficient to know that but for the Navy the war in Korea would come to a sudden halt. The job of getting the troops there and keeping them supplied is just as essential as it ever was, whether it makes interesting reading or not.

"During the last ten months of my tour in the Far East I was fortunate, or unfortunate, enough to face our common enemy across the conference table. If there are still those in the Free World who believe that the enemy can be moved by logic, or that he is susceptible to moral appeal, or that he is willing to act in good faith, those remaining few should immediately disabuse themselves of that notion. It was a mistake to assume, or even hope, that the enemy was capable of acting in good faith. Future textbooks can set down the maxim that the speed with which agreement is reached with the Communists varies directly as the military pressure applied, and

that the worth of any agreement is in proportion to the military strength
you are able and willing to apply to enforce it.

"As for the future, it should be clear that there is nothing inevitable
about the onward and upward progress of the United States or the United
Nations. In fact there is nothing inevitable about our survival. History
is littered with the graves of civilizations that assumed all is well. All is
not well. We will survive and progress to the extent that we are aware of
the enemy who threatens us, and to the extent that we stay strong enough
to meet him in the arena of his choosing. Nothing can erase the tragedy
that is Korea. But if Korea has taught us that in unity lies the strength that
will preserve our freedom, then Korea has not been in vain. . . ."

Appendices

APPENDIX I

Naval Commanders During Korean War

COMMANDER NAVAL FORCES FAR EAST

VADM C. T. JOY	26 Aug 49–4 June 1952
VADM R. P. BRISCOE	4 June 52–27 July 1953

COMMANDER SEVENTH FLEET (*TF-70*)

VADM A. D. STRUBLE	6 May 50–28 March 1951
VADM H. M. MARTIN	28 March 51–3 March 1952
VADM R. P. BRISCOE	3 March–20 May 1952
VADM J. J. CLARK	20 May 52–27 July 1953

COMMANDER TASK FORCE 77

(In order of appearance)

Officer	Command	Ship	Periods
RADM J. M. HOSKINS	CCD 3	*Valley Forge*	OTC TF-77 during period 25 June–25 Aug 1950
		Valley Forge	22 Oct–5 Nov 1950
RADM E. C. EWEN	CCD 1	*Phil. Sea*	25 Aug–22 Oct 1950 (OTC)
		"	5 Nov–25 Dec 1950
		"	9 Jan–19 Jan 1951
		"	12 Feb–26 Feb 1951
RADM R. A. OFSTIE	CCD 5	*Princeton*	25 Dec 50–9 Jan 1951
		"	19 Jan–12 Feb 1951
		"	26 Feb–4 Apr 1951
		"	19 Apr–6 May 1951
RADM W. G. TOMLINSON	CCD 3	*Boxer*	4 Apr–19 Apr 1951
		"	17 May–18 May 1951
		"	19 May–2 June 1951
		"	1 July–14 July 1951
		"	10 Aug–22 Aug 1951
		"	19 Sep–3 Oct 1951
RADM G. R. HENDERSON	CCD 5	*Princeton*	6 May–17 May 1951
		"	18 May–19 May 1951
		"	2 June–30 June 1951
		"	14 July–10 Aug 1951
RADM JOHN PERRY	CCD 1	*Essex*	22 Aug–19 Sep 1951
		"	3 Oct–7 Oct 1951
		"	17 Oct–31 Oct 1951
		"	29 Nov–12 Dec 1951
		"	28 Dec 51–1 Feb 52
		"	20 Feb–5 Mar 52
		Valley Forge	23 Apr–14 May 52
		"	26 May–11 June 52
RADM J. J. CLARK	CCD 3	*B. H. Richard*	19 Sep–3 Oct 1951
		"	7 Oct–17 Oct 1951
		"	31 Oct–29 Nov 1951
RADM F. W. McMAHON	CCD 5	*Valley Forge*	12 Dec–28 Dec 1951
		"	1 Feb–20 Feb 1952
		"	5 Mar–2 Apr 1952
		"	16 Apr–23 Apr 1952

RADM A. SOUCEK	CCD 3	Phil. Sea	2 Apr–16 Apr 1952
		Boxer	14 May–26 May 1952
		"	11 June–6 July 1952
		"	4 Aug–4 Sep 1952
		Valley Forge	4 Jan–22 Jan 1953
		"	11 Feb–15 Mar 1953
		"	29 Mar–11 Apr 1953
		"	22 Apr–15 May 1953
RADM H. E. REGAN	CCD 1	B. H. Richard	6 July–4 Aug 1952
		"	4 Sep–21 Sep 1952
		"	18 Oct–1 Nov 1952
RADM R. F. HICKEY	CCD 5	Kearsarge	21 Sep–18 Oct 1952
		"	1 Nov–25 Nov 1952
		"	18 Dec 52–4 Jan 53
		"	22 Jan–11 Feb 1953
		"	15 Mar–29 Mar 1953
		"	11 Apr–22 Apr 1953
RADM W. D. JOHNSON	CCD 1	B. H. Richard	25 Nov–18 Dec 1952
		Boxer	15 May–4 June 1953
		Lake Champ.	14 June–27 June 53
		"	14 July–27 July 53
RADM R. E. BLICK	CCD 3	Princeton	4 June–14 June 1953
		"	27 June–14 July 1953

(NOTE: The above represents 56 changes of command among 13 Rear Admirals during 37 months of combat.)

AMPHIBIOUS FORCE FAR EAST (TF-90)

RADM J. H. DOYLE	25 June–27 Sep 1950
RADM L. A. THACKREY	27 Sep–11 Oct 1950
RADM J. H. DOYLE	11 Oct 50–24 Jan 1951
RADM I. N. KILAND	24 Jan–3 Sep 1951
RADM T. B. HILL	3 Sep–8 Oct 1951
RADM C. F. ESPE	8 Oct 51–5 June 1952
RADM F. X. McINERNEY	5 June–21 Nov 1952

FIRST MARINE AIR WING (TF-91)

MGEN F. HARRIS	25 June 50–29 May 1951
BGEN T. J. CUSHMAN	29 May–26 July 1951
MGEN C. F. SCHILT	27 July 51–11 Apr 1952
MGEN C. C. JEROME	11 Apr 52–8 Jan 1953
MGEN V. E. MEGEE	8 Jan 53–27 July 53

BLOCKADE AND ESCORT FORCE (TF-95)*

RADM J. M. HIGGINS	25 June–25 July 1950**
RADM C. C. HARTMAN	25 July–12 Sep 1950
RADM A. E. SMITH	12 Sep 50–19 Feb 1951
VADM W. ANDREWES, RN	19 Feb–3 Apr 1951
RADM A. E. SMITH	3 Apr–20 June 1951
RADM G. C. DYER	20 June 51–31 May 1952
RADM J. E. GINGRICH	31 May 1952–12 Feb. 53
RADM C. E. OLSEN	12 Feb 53–27 July 53

* On 3 April 1951, Task Force 95 was placed under 7th Fleet for direct operational control in Korean operations.

** Then "Japan-Korea Support Group." UN Blockade and Escort Force was first organized on 12 September 1950.

FIRST MARINE DIVISION

BGEN E. A. CRAIG	7 July 1950*–3 Sept 50
MGEN O. P. SMITH	25 July 50–25 Feb 1951
	5 Mar–26 Apr 1951
BGEN L. B. PULLER, Acting**	25 Feb–5 Mar 1951
MGEN G. C. THOMAS	26 Apr 51–10 Jan 1952
MGEN J. T. SELDEN	11 Jan 1952–Beyond 30 June 1952

* 1st Provisional Marine Brigade, date on which its formation was directed, began unloading at Pusan, 2 August 1950.

** While MGEN O. P. SMITH commanded IX Corps.

LOGISTIC SUPPORT FORCE (TF-92)*

CAPT J. M. P. WRIGHT	3 Apr 51–29 Feb 52
RADM B. B. BIGGS	29 Feb 1952–21 Nov 52
RADM F. X. McINERNEY	21 Nov 52–13 Feb 53
RADM M. E. MURPHY	13 Feb 53–27 Jul 53

* Activated 3 April 1951 and placed under operational control of Com7thFleet for Korean operations. Its formation combined into one force all ships of ComServRon 3 and ComServDiv 31 previously operating under Com7thFleet as TG-70.7 and TF-79, and under ComNavJap at TG-96.4.

FLEET AIR WINGS

KOREA

FLEET AIR WING ONE DETACHMENT JAPAN

(25 June to 4 Aug 1950)	CAPT Etheridge Grant

FLEET AIR WING SIX (Commissioned 4 August 1950)

CAPT J. C. Alderman, Acting	4–29 August 1950
CAPT J. M. Carson	29 August–9 October 1950
CAPT R. C. Bauer, Acting	9 October–8 November 1950
CAPT H. J. Dyson	8 November 1950–10 Nov 1951
CAPT J. D. Greer	10 November 1951–(16 Oct 52)[1]
CAPT A. D. Schwarz	(22 Apr 53)[2]–27 July 1953

FLEET AIR WING FOURTEEN

CAPT J. B. Paschal	(16 Oct 52)[1]–(22 Apr 1953)[2]

[1] On 16 October 1952, FAW 14 relieved FAW 6.
[2] On 22 April 1953, FAW 6 relieved FAW 14.

Sources for information on all four wings were: Historical Reports, PacFlt Evaluation Group Reports, and BuPers Awards directives.

FORMOSA

FLEET AIR WING ONE

CAPT E. Grant	1 July 1950–2 March 1951
CAPT F. R. Jones, Acting	2–9 March 1951
CAPT L. T. Morse, Acting	9 March–4 April 1951
CAPT J. F. Greenslade	4 April 1951–16 June 1952
RADM T. B. Williamson (with addtl dy as Com FAW-2, assumed 12 June)	16 June 1952–(8 Sep 1952)[1]
CAPT T. O. Dahl	(7 Mar 1953)[2]–5 June 1953
RADM T. B. Williamson	5 June 1953–15 July 1953
RADM T. J. Hedding	15 July–27 July 1953

FLEET AIR WING TWO

RADM T. B. Williamson	(8 Sep 1952)[1]–7 March 1953

[1] On 8 September 1952, FAW-2 relieved FAW-1.
[2] On 7 March 1953, FAW-1 relieved FAW-2.

APPENDIX II

Air Groups in Task Force-77

Air Group	Ship	Sqdns	A/C	Dates in Theater
FIVE CDR H. P. Lanham	*Valley Forge* (CVA 45) CAPT L. K. Rice	VF-51 VF-52 VF-53 VF-54 VA-55	F9F F9F F4U F4U AD	25 June 1950 to 23 Nov 50
ELEVEN CDR R. W. Vogel (KIA) CDR Ralph Weymouth	*Philippine Sea* (CVA 47) CAPT W. K. Goodney *Valley Forge* (CVA 45) CAPT J. M. Carson	VF-111 VF-112 VF-113 VF-114 VA-115	F9F F9F F4U F4U AD	1 Aug 50 to 28 Mar 51 28–30 Mar 51 (for return to USA)
THREE CDR W. F. Madden	*Leyte* (CVA-32) CAPT T. U. Sisson (LantFlt CVA)	VF-31 VF-32 VF-33 VF-34 VA-35	F9F F9F F4U F4U AD	9 Oct 1950 to 19 Jan 1951
TWO CDR D. M. White	*Boxer* (CVA 21) CAPT Cameron Briggs (Note 1)—VA-65	VF-21 VF-22 VF-63 VF-64 VA-65	F4U F4U F4U F4U AD	15 Sep 1950 to 22 Oct 1950
TWO CDR R. W. Rynd	*Valley Forge* (CVA 45) CAPT J. M. Carson *Philippine Sea* (CVA 47) CAPT Ira Hobbs	VF-64 VA-65 VF-24 VF-63	F4U AD F4U F4U	16 Dec 50 to 28 Mar 51 28 Mar 51 to 2 June 51
NINETEEN CDR Richard C. Merrick (KIA) (MIA) CDR Charles R. Stapler (19 May–10 June, shot down)	*Princeton* (CVA 37) CAPT W. O. Gallery	VF-191 VF-192 VF-193 VA-195	F9F2 F4U F4U AD	5 Dec 1950 to 29 May 1951
NINETEEN "X RAY" CDR Charles R. Stapler (MIA) CDR A. L. Maltby (Acting)	*Princeton* (CVA 37) CAPT W. O. Gallery	VF-23 VF-821* VF-871* VF-34	F9F F4U F4U F4U	2 June 1951 to 10 Aug 1951

* Reserve Squadron.

Note 1—The operation of five squadrons on an Essex carrier proved too cumbersome. After this, only four squadrons were used.

Air Group	Ship	Sqdns	A/C	Dates in Korean Th.
101 CDR Wm. W. Brehm	*Boxer* (CVA 21) CAPT Dennis J. Sullivan	VF-721* VF-884* VF-791* VA-702*	F9F F4U F4U AD	27 Mar 1951 to 3 Oct 1951
102 CDR H. W. Fink	*Bon Homme Richard* (CVA 31) CAPT C. B. Gill	VF-781* VF-783* VF-874* VA-923*	F9F F4U F4U AD	30 May 1951 to 30 Nov 1951
FIVE CDR M. U. Beebe	*Essex* (CVA 9) CAPT A. W. Wheelock	VF-172 VF-51 VF-53 VF-54	F2H† F9F F4U AD	22 Aug 1951 to 5 Mar 1952
FIFTEEN CDR R. F. Farrington	*Antietam* (CVA 36) CAPT G. J. Dufek	VF-831* VF-837* VF-713* VA-728*	F9F F9F F4U AD	15 Oct. 1951 to 22 Mar 1952
Air Task Group 1 CDR C. H. Crabill, Jr.	*Valley Forge* (CVA 45) CAPT Oscar Pederson	VF-52 VF-111 VF-653* VF-194	F9F F9F F4U AD	12 Dec 1951 to 13 June 1952
ELEVEN CDR J. W. Onstott	*Philippine Sea* (CVA 47) CAPT Allen Smith, Jr.	VF-112 VF-113 VF-114 VA-115	F9F F9F F4U AD	30 Jan 1952 to 8 July 1952
TWO CDR A. L. Downing	*Boxer* (CVA 21) CAPT Dennis J. Sullivan	VF-24 VF-63 VF-64 VA-65	F9F F4U F4U AD	10 Mar 1952 to 6 Sept 1952
NINETEEN CDR William Denton, Jr.	*Princeton* (CVA 37) CAPT Paul D. Stroop (until 31 Aug) CAPT W. R. Hollings- worth	VF-191 VF-192 VF-193 VA-195	F9F 4FU 4FU AD	14 Apr 1952 to 18 Oct 1952
SEVEN CDR G. B. Brown	*Bon Homme Richard* (CVA 31) CAPT P. W. Watson	VF-71 VF-72 VF-74 VA-75	F9F F9F F4U AD	21 June 1952 to 18 Dec 1952
Air Task Group 2 CDR J. G. Daniel	*Essex* (CVA 9) CAPT W. F. Rodee	VF-23 VF-821 VF-871 VA-55	F9F F9F 4FU AD	18 July 1952 to 13 Jan 1953

* Reserve Squadron.
† First appearance in theater.

Air Group	Ship	Sqdns	A/C	Dates in Korean Th.
101 (Redesignated Air Group 14)	*Kearsarge* (CVA 33) (LantFlt CVA) CAPT T. E. Clark	VF-11 VF-721* VF-884* VA-702*	F2H F9F F4U AD	14 Sept 1952 to 22 Feb 1953
102 (Redesignated Air Group 12)	*Oriskany* (CVA 34) CAPT Paul H. Ramsey	VF-781* VF-783* VF-874* VA-923*	F9F5 F9F5† F4U AD	28 Oct 1952 to 2 May 53
FIVE CDR. C. V. Johnson	*Valley Forge* (CVA 45) CAPT R. E. Dixon	VF-51 VF-52 VF-92 VF-54	F9F5 F9F5 F4U AD	30 Dec 1952 to 10 June 1953
NINE CDR T. D. Harris	*Philippine Sea* (CVA 47) CAPT Paul H. Ramsey	VF-91 VF-93 VF-94 VA-95	F9F2 F9F2 F4U AD	29 Jan 1953 to 27 July 53
FIFTEEN CDR John E. Parks	*Princeton* (CVA 37) CAPT W. R. Hollings-worth (until 17 May 53) CAPT O. C. Gregg	VF-152 VF-153 VF-154 VA-155	F4U F9F F9F AD	13 Mar 1953 to 27 July 1953
Air Task Group 1 CDR A. L. Whitney	*Boxer* (CVA 21) CAPT M. B. Gurney	VF-52 VF-111‡ VF-151 VF-194	F9F5 F9F5 F9F5 AD	12 May 1953 to 27 July 1953
FOUR CDR John Sweeney	*Lake Champlain* (CVA 39) CAPT G. T. Mundorff (LantFlt CVA)	VF-22 VF-62 VF-44‡ VA-45	F2H2 F2H2 F4U AD	10 June 1953 to 27 July 1953

* Reserve squadrons.

† First appearance in theater.

‡ On 30 June 1953, these two squadrons interchanged ships in order to leave aboard *Boxer* only two jet squadrons instead of the original three.

APPENDIX III

Task Organizations for Pohang, Inchon, Wonsan, and Hungnam

POHANG LANDING—18 JULY 1950

90 Attack Force, RADM J. H. Doyle, USN.
- (a) 91.0 Landing Force, MAJGEN Hobart Gay, USA
- (b) 90.1 Tactical Air Control Group, CDR Elmer Moore, USN.
- (c) 90.2 Transport Group, CAPT V. R. Roane, USN.

Mount McKinley (FF)	1 AGC
Cavalier (F)	1 APA
Union	
Titania	
Oglethorpe	3 AKA

- (d) 90.3 Tractor Group, CAPT Norman W. Sears, USN.

611 (F)	1 LST
Other LST as assigned	15 LST
Lipan	1 ATF
Conserver	1 ARS
5 LSU	5 LSU
Cree (temporary)	1 ATF

- (e) 96.5 Gunfire Support Group, RADM J. M. Higgins, USN.

Juneau	1 CLAA
Kyes	
Higbee	
Collett	
HMAS *Bataan*	

- (f) 90.4 Protective Group, LCDR D'Arcy V. Shouldice, USN.

90.41	COMINRON 3, LCDR D'Arcy V. Shouldice, USN.	
	Pledge	1 AM
	Kite (AMS-22)	
	Chatterer (AMS-40)	
	Redhead (AMS-34)	3 AMS
90.42	COMINDIV 31	
	Partridge (AMS-31)	
	Mockingbird (AMS-27)	
	Osprey (AMS-28)	3 AMS
90.43	*Higbee*	
	Kyes	2DD
	As screen for movement of objective only—then under CTG 96.5	

- (g) 90.5 Close Air Support Group
  Aircraft as assigned from Seventh Fleet
- (h) 90.6 Deep Air Support Group
  Aircraft as assigned from FEAF
- (i) 90.7 Reconnaissance Group, LCDR J. R. Wilson, USN.

Diachenko	1 APD
UDT 3 (Det.)	1 UDT (Det.)

- (j) 90.8 Control Group, LCDR Clyde Allmon, USN.

Diachenko	1 APD
Lipan	1 ATF

- (k) 90.9 Beach Group, LCDR Jack Lowentrout, USN.
  Beachmaster Unit One (Det.)
  UDT 3 (Det.)

(l) 90.20 Administrative Element, CO, *Conserver*
     Conserver   1 ARS
     Lipan   1 ATF
     HMS *Main* (At Sasebo)   1 AH
(m) 90.0 Follow-up Shipping Group, CAPT D. J. Sweeney, USN.
     USNS *Ainsworth*
     USNS *Shanks*   2 AP
     7 LST   7 LST
     Other vessels as assigned
(n) 96.2 Patrol Aircraft Group, CAPT Richard W. Ruble, USN.
     Aircraft as assigned.

INCHON INVASION—15 SEPTEMBER 1950

JOINT TASK FORCE SEVEN	VADM Arthur D. Struble
Task Force 90—Attack Force	RADM James H. Doyle
92.1 Landing Force 1st Marine Division (Reinforced)	MAJGEN Oliver P. Smith
90.00 Flagship Element	
Mount McKinley AGC	CAPT Carter A. Printup
Eldorado (RADM Lyman K. Thackrey embarked) AGC	CAPT Joseph B. Stefanac
90.01 Tactical Air Control Element	CDR Theophilus H. Moore
Tactical Air Squadron 1	
90.02 Naval Beach Group Element	CAPT Watson T. Singer
90.02.1 Headquarters Unit	
90.02.2 Beachmaster Unit	LCDR Martin C. Sibitzky
90.02.3 Boat Unit 1	LCDR Herman E. Hock
90.02.4 Amphibious Construction Battalion	LCDR M. Ted Jacobs, Jr.
90.02.5 Underwater Demolition Team Unit	LCDR David F. Welch
90.03 Control Element	LCDR Clyde Allmon
Diachenko APD	LCDR James R. Wilson
90.03.1 Control Unit Red	LCDR Ralph H. Schneeloch, Jr.
Horace A. Bass APD	LCDR Alan Ray
90.03.2 Control Unit Green	LT Reuben W. Berry
PCEC 896 PCEC	LT Reuben W. Berry
90.03.3 Control Unit Blue	LT Theodore B. Clark
Wantuck APD	LCDR John B. Thro
90.04 Administrative Element	CAPT Virginius R. Roane
90.04.1 Service Unit	
Consolation 1 AH	CAPT Charles M. Ryan
12 LSU (plus additional LSUS on arrival) 12–20 LSU	
90.04.2 Repair and Salvage Unit	CDR Emmanuel T. Goyette
Lipan	LCDR Howard K. Smith
Cree	LT George E. Poore
Arikara 3 ATF	LCDR Kenneth A. Mundy
Conserver 1 ARS	LT James L. Thompson
Askari 1 ARL	LCDR Robert J. Siegelman
YTB 405	

	Gunston Hall		CDR Charles W. Musgrave
	Fort Marion		CDR Noah Adair, Jr.
	Comstock	3 LSD	CDR Emmanuel T. Goyette
90.1	Advance Attack Group		CAPT Norman W. Sears
	92.12.3 Advance Landing Force		
	3rd Battalion (RCT) 5th		
	Marines)		
	90.11 Transport element		CAPT Norman W. Sears
	Fort Marion (F)		CDR Noah Adair, Jr.
	3 LSU embarked		
	90.11.1 Transport Unit		CDR Selden C. Small
	Horace A. Bass		LCDR Alan Ray
	Diachenko		LCDR James R. Wilson
	Wantuck		LCDR John B. Thro
90.2	Transport Group		CAPT Virginius R. Roane
	George Clymer (F)		CAPT Raymond S. Lamb
	Cavalier		CAPT Daniel J. Sweeney
	Pickaway		CAPT Samuel H. Crittenden, Jr.
	Henrico		CAPT John E. Fradd
	Noble	5 APA	CAPT Michael F. D. Flaherty
	Union		CAPT Gerald D. Zurmuehlen
	Alshain		CAPT Robert N. S. Clark
	Achernar		CAPT Crutchfield Adair
	Oglethorpe		CAPT Paul F. Heerbrandt
	Seminole		CAPT Henry Farrow
	Thuban		CDR Erle V. Dennett
	Whiteside		CAPT Eugene L. Lugibihl
	Washburn	8 AKA	CAPT James A. Prichard
	President Jackson	1 AP	CAPT Charles A. Ferriter
	Gunston Hall#		CDR Charles W. Musgrave
	Comstock#	2 LSD	CDR Emmanuel T. Goyette
	#3 LSU embarked		
90.3	Tractor Group		CAPT Robert C. Peden
	LST 611		LT Delmar E. Blevins
	LST 715		LT Willie J. Gros
	LST 742		LT Robert B. Leonnig
	LST 802		LT Vladimir Fedorowicz
	LST 845		LT John F. Butler
	LST 1048		LT Rayburn M. Quinn
	LST 1123		LT Charles L. Wall
	LST 1134		LT William B. Faris
	LST 1138		LT Mike Stapleton
	LST 857		LT Dick Weidemeyer
	LST 859		LT Leland Tinsley
	LST 898		LT Robert M. Beckley
	LST 914		LT Ralph L. Holzhaus
	LST 973		LT Robert I. Trapp
	LST 799		LT Trumond E. Houston
	LST 883		LT Charles M. Miller
	LST 975	17 LST	LT Arnold W. Harre
	SCAJAP LST	30 LST	
	LSM 419	1 LSM	LT John R. Bradley

90.4	Transport Division 14 7th RCT U.S. Marines and MAG 33		CAPT Samuel G. Kelly
	Bayfield (F)		CAPT William E. Ferrall
	Okanogan		CAPT Timothy F. Donohue
	Bexar		CAPT Clarence E. Coffin, Jr.
	Thomas Jefferson	4 APA	CAPT Tyrrell D. Jacobs
	Algol		CAPT John A. Edwards
	Winston		CAPT Jack Maginnis
	Montague	3 AKA	CAPT Henry P. Wright, Jr.
	Catamount		CDR Kenneth Loveland
	Colonial	2 LSD	CDR Thomas J. Breene
90.5	Air Support Group		RADM Richard W. Ruble
	90.51 CVE Element		RADM Richard W. Ruble
	Badoeng Strait		CAPT Arnold W. McKechnie
	Sicily	2 CVE	CAPT John S. Thach
	90.52 CVE Screen		CDR Byron L. Gurnette
	Hanson	1 DDR	CDR Cecil R. Welte
	Taussig		CDR William C. Meyer
	George K. Mackenzie		CDR William R. Laird, Jr.
	Ernest G. Small	3 DD	CDR Franklin C. Snow
90.6	Gunfire Support Group		RADM John M. Higgins
90.61	Cruiser Element		RADM John M. Higgins
	90.6.1 Fire Support Unit 1		RADM John M. Higgins
	Toledo (F)		CAPT Richard F. Stout
	Rochester	2 CA	CAPT Edward L. Woodyard
	HMS Kenya		CAPT P. W. Brock, RN
	HMS Jamaica	2 CL	CAPT J. S. C. Salter D.S.O., O.B.E. RN
90.62	Destroyer Element		CAPT Halle C. Allan, Jr.
	90.6.2 Fire Support Unit 1		CAPT Halle C. Allan ,Jr.
	Mansfield		CDR Edwin H. Headland
	De Haven		CDR Oscar B. Lundgren
	Lyman K. Swenson	3 DD	CDR Robert A. Schelling
	90.6.3 Fire Support Unit 3		CDR Robert H. Close
	Collett		CDR Robert H. Close
	Gurke		CDR Frederick M. Radel
	Henderson	3 DD	CDR William S. Stewart
90.63	LSMR Element		CDR Clarence T. Doss, Jr.
	90.6.4 Fire Support Unit 4		CDR Clarence T. Doss, Jr.
	LSMR 401		LCDR Melvin E. Bustard, Jr.
	LSMR 403		LT Frank G. Schettino
	LSMR 404	3 LSMR	LT George M. Wrocklage
90.7	Screening and Protective Group		CAPT Richard T. Spofford
	Rowan	DD	CDR Alan R. Josephson
	Southerland	DDR	CDR Homer E. Conrad
	Bayonne		LCDR Harry A. Clark
	Newport		LCDR Percy A. Lilly, Jr.
	Evansville		LCDR Elliot V. Converse, Jr.
	HMS Mounts Bay		CAPT J. H. Unwin, D.S.C., RN
	HMS Whitesand Bay		LCDR J. V. Brothers, RN
	HMNZS Tutira		LCDR P. J. H. Hoare, RNZN
	HMNZS Pukaki	7 PF	LCDR L. E. Herrick, D.S.C., RNZN

	RFS *La Grandiere*	8 PF	CDR Urbain E. Cabanie
	Pledge (F)	AM	LT Richard Young
	Partridge		LTJG Robert C. Fuller, Jr.
	Mocking Bird		LTJG Stanley P. Gary
	Kite		LTJG Nicholas Grkovic
	Osprey		LTJG Philip Levin
	Redhead		LTJG "T. R." Howard
	Chatterer	6 AMS	LTJG James P. McMahon
90.8	Second Echelon Movement Group		CAPT Louis D. Sharp, Jr.
	92.2 7th Infantry Division (Reinforced)		
	USS *General G. M. Randall*		CAPT Alexander C. Thorington
	USS *General J. C. Breckinridge*		CAPT Fremont B. Eggers
	USS *General H. W. Butner*	3 AP	CAPT Dale E. Collins
	USNS *Fred C. Ainsworth*		
	USNS *General Leroy Eltinge*		
	USNS *Aiken Victory*		
	USNS *Private Sadao S. Munemori*	4T-AP	
	SS *African Rainbow*		
	SS *African Pilot*		
	SS *Robin Kirk*		
	SS *Helen Lykes*		
	SS *Meredith Victory*		
	SS *Empire Marshall*		
	SS *Mormacport*		
	SS *Lawrence Victory*		
	SS *Southwind*		
	SS *Beaver Victory*		
	SS *Robin Goodfellow*		
	SS *California Bear*		
90.9	Third Echelon Movement Group		CAPT Albert E. Jarrell
	X Corps troops		
	USS *General William A. Mann*	AP	CAPT Charles H. Walker
	USNS *General William Weigel*		
	USNS *Marine Phoenix*	2T-AP	
	SS *Robin Trent*		
	SS *Dolly Turman*		
	SS *Charles Lykes*		
	SS *Twin Falls Victory*		
	SS *American Veteran*		
	SS *American Attorney*		
	SS *Empire Wallace*		
	SS *Greenbay Victory*		
	SS *P. & T. Navigator*		
	SS *Luxembourg Victory*		
	SS *Belgium Victory*		
	SS *Bessemer Victory*		
	SS *Cotton State*		
91	Blockade and Covering Force		RADM Sir William G. Andrewes, K.B.E., C.B., D.S.O.
	HMS *Triumph*	CVL	CAPT A. D. Torlesse, D.S.O., RN
	HMS *Ceylon*	CL	CAPT C. F. J. L. Davies, D.S.C., RN
	HMS *Cockade*		LCDR H. J. Lee, D.S.C., RN

HMS *Charity*		LCDR P. R. G. Worth, D.S.C., RN
HMCS *Cayuga*		CAPT Jeffry V. Brock, D.S.C., RCN
HMCS *Sioux*		CDR P. D. Taylor, RCN
HMCS *Athabaskan*		CDR R. T. Welland, D.S.C., RCN
HMAS *Bataan*		CDR W. B. M. Marks, RAN
HMAS *Warramunga*		CDR O. H. Becher, D.S.C., RAN
HNethMS *Evertsen*	8 DD	LCDR D. J. van Doorninck
ROK Naval Forces		CDR Michael J. Lousey, USN
Paik Doo San (PC 701)		CDR Chai Yong Nam
Kum Kang San (PC 702)		CDR Lee Hi Jong
Sam Kak San (PC 703)		CDR Lee Sung Ho
Chi Ri San (PC 704)	4 PC	LCDR Hyun Sihak
YMS 302		
YMS 303		
YMS 306		
YMS 307		
YMS 501		
YMS 502		
YMS 503		
YMS 510		
YMS 512		
YMS 515		
YMS 518	11 YMS	
Task Force 77—Fast Carrier Group		RADM Edward C. Ewen (in *Philippine Sea*)
Carrier Division 1		RADM Edward C. Ewen
Philippine Sea	1 CV	CAPT Willard K. Goodney
Carrier Division 3		RADM John M. Hoskins
Valley Forge	1 CV	CAPT Lester K. Rice
Carrier Division 5		
Boxer	1 CV	CAPT Cameron Briggs
77.1 Support Group		CAPT Harry H. Henderson
Worcester		CAPT Harry H. Henderson
Manchester	2 CL	CAPT Lewis S. Parks
77.2 Screen Group		CAPT Charles W. Parker
DesDiv 31		CAPT Charles W. Parker
Shelton (FFF)		CDR Charles B. Jackson, Jr.
James E. Kyes		CDR Fran M. Christiansen
Eversole	3 DD	CDR Charles E. Phillips
Higbee	1 DDR	CDR Elmer Moore
DesDiv 111		CAPT Jeane R. Clark
Wiltsie (FF)		CDR Carrol W. Brigham
Theodore E. Chandler		CDR William J. Collum, Jr.
Hamner	3 DD	CDR Jack J. Hughes
Chevalier	1 DDR	CDR Blake B. Booth
DesDiv 112		CAPT Bernard F. Roeder
Ozbourn		CDR Charles O. Akers
McKean		CDR Harry L. Reiter, Jr.
Hollister	3 DD	CDR Hugh W. Howard
Frank Knox	1 DDR	CDR Sam J. Caldwell, Jr.
CortRon 1		
Fletcher		CDR W. M. Lowry
Radford	2 DDE	CDR Elvin C. Ogle

Task Force 79—Commander Service Squadron 3		CAPT Bernard L. Austin
79.1 Mobile Logistic Service Group		CAPT John G. McClaughry
Cacapon (Initially)(F)		CAPT John G. McClaughry
Passumpsic (Initially)	2 AO	CAPT Frank I. Winant, Jr.
Mount Katmai	1 AE	CAPT Albert S. Carter
Graffias	1 AF	CAPT William W. Fitts
79.2 Objective Area Logistic Group		CAPT Philip H. Ross
Navasota (Initially)	1 AO	CAPT Robert O. Strange
Virgo (F)	1 AKA	CAPT Philip H. Ross
Grainger	1 AK	CDR Horace C. Laird, Jr.
Hewell		LT Stanley Jaworski
Ryer		LT Gurley P. Chatelain
Estero	3 AKL	LT Tom Watson
79.3 Logistic Support Group		CAPT Bernard L. Austin
Piedmont		CAPT James R. Topper
Dixie	2 AD	CAPT Jose M. Cabanillas
Kermit Roosevelt	1 ARG	CDR Lester C. Conwell
Jason	1 ARH	CAPT William B. Epps
Cimarron	1 AO	CAPT Stanley G. Nichols
Warrick		CAPT George Fritschmann
Uvalde	2 AKA	CAPT Louis F. Teuscher
Nemasket	1 AOG	LT Harry F. Dixon
Karin	1 AF	LCDR Berley L. Maddox
79.4 Salvage and Maintenance Group		
Mataco	1 ATF	LT Frank P. Wilson
Bolster	1 ARS	LT Billis L. Whitworth
Task Force 99—Patrol and Reconnaissance Force		RADM George R. Henderson
USS *Curtiss*	AV	CAPT Anson C. Perkins
USS *Gardiners Bay*	AVP	CAPT Frank G. Raysbrook
USS *Salisbury Sound*	AV	CAPT Francis R. Jones
99.1 Search and Reconnaissance Group		CAPT Joseph M. Carson
99.11 Patrol Squadron 6		CDR Arthur F. Farwell, Jr.
99.12 88th Squadron RAF		Squadron Leader P. Helme
99.13 209th Squadron RAF		Squadron Leader P. Le Cheminant
99.2 Patrol and Escort Group		CAPT Joseph M. Carson
99.21 Patrol Squadron 42		CDR Gordon F. Smale
99.22 Patrol Squadron 47		CDR Joe H. Arnold

WONSAN—25 JUNE TO 15 NOVEMBER 1950

Joint Task Force Seven (VICE ADMIRAL A. D. Struble, USN)
90　Attack Force (RADM J. H. Doyle, USN)

(a) 92.1　Landing Force (MAJGEN O. P. Smith)
　　　　　First Marine Division (Reinforced)

(b) 90.00　Flagship Element (CAPT C. A. Printup)

Mount McKinley (FF)	1 AGC

(c) 90.01　Tactical Air Control Element (CDR T. H. Moore, USN)

90.01.1　TacRon 1	
90.01.2　TacRon 3	2 TacRon

(d) 90.02 Naval Beach Group Element (CAPT W. T. Singer, USN)
        90.02.1   Headquarters Unit
        90.02.2   Beachmaster Unit (LCDR M. C. Sibitzky, U)
        90.02.3   Boat Unit One (LCDR H. E. Hock, USN)
        90.02.4   Amphibious Construction Battalion
                 (LCDR M. T. Jacobs, Jr., USN)
        90.02.5   UDT Unit (LCDR Wm. R. McKinney, USN)

(e) Administrative Group (RADM L. A. Thackery) (Relieved by RADM J. H. Doyle for Iwon operation).

90.10	Flagship Element (CAPT J. B. Stefanac)	
	Eldorado (Assigned later for Iwon)	1 AGC
90.1.1	Medical Unit	
	Consolation	
	LST 898 (H)*	
	LST 975 (H)*	2 LST(H)
90.1.2	Repair and Salvage Unit	
	(CAPT P. W. Mothersill, USN)	
	Lipan	
	Cree	
	Arikara	3 ATF
	Conserver	1 ARS
	Askari	1 ARL
	Gunston Hall	
	Fort Marion	
	Comstock	
	Catamount	
	Colonial	5 LSD
	Plus other units as assigned.	
90.1.3	Service Unit (LCDR Johnston, USN)	
	LSU	15 LSU

(f) 90.2 Transport Group (CAPT V. R. Roane, USN)

90.21	Transport Division Able (CAPT S. G. Kelly)	
	Bayfield (F)	
	Noble	
	Cavalier	
	Okanogan	4 APA
	Washburn	
	Seminole	
	Titania	
	Oglethorpe	
	Achernar	5 AKA
	Marine Phoenix	1 TAP
90.22	Transport Division Baker (CAPT A. E. Jarrell, USN)	
	Henrico (F)	
	George Clymer (GF)	
	Pickaway	
	Bexar	
	Union	
	Algol	
	Alshain	

* When directed by CTG 90.3.

			Winston	
			Montague	5 AKA
			USNS *Aiken Victory*	1 TAP
			SS *Robin Goodfellow*	1 AK
(g)	90.3		Tractor Group (CAPT R. C. Peden, USN)	
			LST 1123 (F), 715, 742, 799, 802, 845, 883, 898, 914,	
			973, 975, 1048, 1138 (Assigned later for Iwon)	13 LST
			SCAJAP LST	23 LST
			LSM 419	1 LSM
			*Gunston Hall**	
			*Fort Marion**	
			*Comstock**	
			*Catamount**	
			*Colonial** (Assigned later for Iwon)	5 LSD
			*3 LSU embarked	15 LSU
(h)	90.4		Control Group (LCDR Clyde Allmon, USN)	
			PCEC 896 (Central Control Vessel)	1 PCEC
		90.4.1	Control Unit Blue (LT S. C. Pinksen, USN)	
			Wantuck	1 APD
		90.4.2	Control Unit Yellow (LT A. C. Ansorge, USN)	
			H. A. Bass	1 APD
(i)	90.6		Reconnaissance Group (CDR S. C. Small, USN)	
			H. A. Bass	
			Wantuck	2 APD
			UDT One and Three	
(j)	95.2		Gunfire Support Group (RADM C. C. Hartman, USN)	
			Helena	
			Rochester	
			Toledo	3 CA
			HMS *Ceylon*	1 CL
			DESRON Nine (3 DD)	
			HMS *Cockade*	
			HMCS *Athabaskan*	
			HMAS *Warramunga*	6 DD
			LSR Div-11*	
			LSMR-401	
			LSMR-403	
			LSMR-404	
			Plus other units assigned	
(k)	95.6		Minesweeping and Protective Group	
			(CAPT R. T. Spofford, USN)	
			Collett	1 DD
			Diachenko	1 APD
			Doyle	
			Endicott	2 DMS
			Pledge	
			Incredible	2 AM
			Kite	

* Report to CTG 95.2 upon arrival objective area. Report to CTF 90 when released by CTG 95.2.

		Merganser	
		Mocking Bird	
		Osprey	
		Partridge (Assigned later for Iwon)	
		Redhead	
		Chatterer	7 AMS
		HMS *Mounts Bay*	
		HMSNZ *Pukaki*	
		HMSNZ *Putira*	
		FS *La Grandiere*	4 PF
		8 Japanese Minesweepers	
		4 Japanese Mine Destruction and danning vessels	
		1 ROK FS	
		Plus other units assigned	
(l)	96.2	Patrol and Reconnaissance Group	
		(RADM H. H. Henderson, USN)	
		Curtiss (AV-4)	1 AV
		Gardiners Bay (AVP-39)	1 AVP
		PATRON SIX	9 P2V
		VP-42	9 PBM-5
		VP-47	8 PBM-5
		88th Sunderland Squadron	3–4 Sunderlands
(m)	96.8	Escort Carrier Group	
		(RADM R. W. Ruble, USN)	
		Badoeng Strait	
		Sicily	2 CVE
		Taussig	
		Hanson	
		George K. Mackenzie	
		Ernest G. Small	
		Southerland	
		Rowan	6 DD
(n)	70.1	Flagship Group (CAPT I. T. DUKE, USN)	
		Missouri (BB-63)	1 BB
(o)	77	Fast Carrier Force	
		(RADM E. C. Ewen, USN)	
		Boxer	
		Leyte	
		Valley Forge	
		Philippine Sea	
		Manchester	
		DESRON-11, DESDIV-31,	
		Fletcher	
		Gurke	
		Henderson	11 DD, 2 DDE, 3 DDR
		DESDIV 92 less *Brush*	
		(reports from TF 95 about 14 Oct)	2 DD, 1 DDR
(p)	79	Logistics Support Force	
		(CAPT B. L. Austin, USN)	
		Units assigned Service	
		Squadron THREE and Service Division 31	

HUNGNAM REDEPLOYMENT

Task Force 90—Commander Amphibious Group 1		RADM James H. Doyle
90.00 Flagship Element		
Mount McKinley (FF)		CAPT Carter A. Printup
Mobile Surgical Team No. 1 embarked	1 AGC	
90.01 Tactical Air Control Element		CDR Ralph . WArndt
Tactical Squadron 1		CDR Ralph W. Arndt
90.02 Repair and Salvage Unit		CDR Lester C. Conwell
Kermit Roosevelt	1 ARG	CDR Lester C. Conwell
Askari	1 ARL	LT Gerhardt W. Rueber
Bolster		LT Billis L. Whitworth
Conserver	2 ARS	LT James L. Thompson
Tawakoni	1 ATF	LT Lewis B. Scribner
90.03 Control Element		LCDR Clyde Allmon
Diachenko		LCDR James R. Wilson
Begor	2 APD	LCDR William A. Walker III
PCEC-882	1 PCEC	LT Patrick H. Sullivan
90.2 Transport Group		CAPT Samuel G. Kelly
90.2.1 Control Unit		LT Theodore B. Clark
Diachenko	1 APD	LCDR James R. Wilson
90.21 Transport Element		CAPT Albert E. Jarrell
Bayfield		CAPT William E. Ferrall
Henrico (F)		CAPT John E. Fradd
Noble	3 APA	CAPT Michael F. D. Flaherty
Winston		CAPT Jack Maginnis
Seminole		CAPT Henry Farrow
Montague	3 AKA	CAPT Henry P. Wright Jr.
USS *General J. C. Breckenridge*		CAPT Fremont B. Eggers
USS *General G. M. Randall*		CAPT Alexander C. Thorington
USS *General W. M. Mitchell*	3 AP	CAPT Philip S. Creasor
USNS *Fred C. Ainsworth*		
USNS *General A. W. Brewster*		
USNS *General D. I. Sultan*		
USNS *General E. T. Collins*		
USNS *General H. B. Freeman*		
USNS *General S. Heintzelman*	6 T-AP	
USNS *Sergeant Andrew Miller*	1 T-AK	
SS *Alamo Victory*		
SS *Argovan* (Canadian registry)		
SS *Bedford Victory*		
SS *Belgium Victory*		
SS *Bel Jeanne* (Norwegian registry)		
SS *Bel Ocean* (Norwegian registry)		
SS *California*		
SS *Canada Mail*		
SS *Carleton Victory*		
SS *Choctaw*		
SS *Citrus Packer*		
SS *Clarksburg Victory*		

SS *Cornell Victory*
SS *Del Alba*
SS *Denise*
SS *Elly*
SS *Empire Marshall* (British registry)
SS *Empire Wallace* (British registry)
SS *Enid Victory*
SS *Exmouth Victory*
SS *Gainesville Victory*
SS *Green Valley*
SS *Groton Trails*
SS *Helen Lykes*
SS *Hunter Victory*
SS *John Hanson*
SS *John Lyras* (British registry)
SS *Kelso Victory*
SS *Kenyon Victory*
SS *Lafayette Victory*
SS *Lane Victory*
SS *Letitia Lykes*
SS *Madaket*
SS *Manderson Victory*
SS *Meredith Victory*
SS *Morgantown Victory*
SS *Mormacmoon*
SS *Nathaniel Palmer*
SS *New Zealand Victory*
SS *Norcuba*
SS *Paducah Victory*
SS *Provo Victory*
SS *Rider Victory*
SS *Robin Gray*
SS *Robin Hood*
SS *Robin Kirk*
SS *Sea Splendor*
SS *Sea Wind*
SS *Southwind*
SS *St. Augustine Victory*
SS *Taineron*
SS *Towanda Victory*
SS *Twin Falls Victory*
SS *Union Victory*
SS *Virginia City Victory*
SS *Wacosta*
SS *Wesleyan Victory*   57 Time Charter Vessels
Fentriss
Malay Maru #2
Senzan Maru
Shinano Maru
Tobato Maru
Yone Yama Maru
USNS AKL 18   7 SCAJAP Charter Vessels
27 SCAJAP LSTs

	3 ROK LSTs		
	Fort Marion#		CAPT Philip W. Mothersill
	Colonial#		CDR Thomas J. Greene
	Catamount#	3 LSD	CDR Kenneth Loveland
	# 3 LSU embarked		
	LST 715		LT Willie J. Gros
	LST 742		LT Robert B. Leonnig
	LST 799		LT Trumond E. Houston
	LST 802		LT Vladimir Fedorowicz
	LST 845		LT John F. Butler
	LST 883		LT Charles M. Miller
	LST 898		LTJG Raul B. Perez
	LST 914		LT Ralph L. Holzhaus
	LST 973		LT Robert I. Trapp
	LST 975		LT Arnold W. Harer
	LST 1048		LT Rayburn M. Quinn
	LST 1134	12 LST	LT William B. Faris
	LSM 419	1 LSM	LT John R. Bradley
90.8	Gunfire Support Group		RADM Roscoe H. Hillenkoetter
	Saint Paul (F)		CAPT Chester C. Smith
	(CTG 90.8 embarked)		
	Rochester	2 CA	CAPT Edward L. Woodyard
	Destroyer Suqadron 16		CAPT Claude A. Dillavou
	Destroyer Division 162		CAPT James D. Whitfield
	Zellars		CDR Fred D. Michael
	Charles S. Sperry		CDR Robert M. Brownlie
	Massey		CDR Ed R. King, Jr.
	Forrest Royal	4 DD	CDR Orvill O. Liebschner
	LSMR *Division 11*		CDR Clarence T. Doss, Jr.
	LSMR 401		LCDR Melvin E. Bustard, Jr.
	LSMR 403		LT Frank G. Schettino
	LSMR 404	3 LSMR	LT George M. Wrocklage
	Destroyer Division 161		
	English		CDR Raymond J. Toner
	Hank		CDR Albert R. Olsen
	Wallace L. Lind		CDR Edward B. Carlson
	Borie	4 DD	CDR Merle F. Bowman
95.2	Blockade, Escort and Mine-sweeping Group		RADM John M. Higgins
	Rochester (F)		
	(CTG 95.2 embarked)	1 CA	CAPT Edward L. Woodyard
	Destroyer Division 161		
	English		CDR Raymond J. Toner
	Hank		CDR Albert R. Olsen
	Wallace L. Lind		CDR Edward B. Carlson
	Borie	4 DD	CDR Merle F. Bowman
	Escort Squadron 5		CAPT William M. Searles
	Sausalito		LCDR Francis W. Deily
	Hoquiam		LCDR Edward A. Lane
	Gallup		LCDR William W. Boyd
	Gloucester		LCDR Thomas C. Clay
	Bisbee		LCDR William F. Gadberry
	Glendale	6 PF	LCDR John C. Taylor, Jr.

95.6	Minesweeping units		CAPT Richard T. Spofford
	Endicott (F)		CAPT John C. Jolly
	Doyle	2 DMS	CDR Charles H. Morrison, Jr.
	Incredible	1 AM	LT Edward P. Flynn, Jr.
	Curlew		LTJG George S. Grove
	Heron	2 AMS	LTJG Dixon Lademan
	Under TG 90 for Operational Control		
	Missouri	1 BB	CAPT Irving T. Duke
	Duncan	1 DDR	CDR Everett G. Sanderson
	Consolation	1 AH	CAPT Charles M. Ryan
	Foss	1 DE	LCDR Henry J. Ereckson
96.8	Escort Carrier Group		RADM Richard W. Ruble
96.81	Carrier Element 1		CAPT John C. Alderman
	Badoeng Strait (FF)	1 CVE	CAPT John C. Alderman
	VMF 323		MAJ Arnold A. Lund, USMC
	Destroyer Division 71		CAPT Russell S. Smith
	Lofberg		CDR Robert W. McElrath
	John A. Bole	2 DD	CDR Marion H. Buaas
	Hanson	1 DDR	CDR Cecil R. Welte
96.82	Carrier Element 2		CAPT John S. Thach
	Sicily	1 CVE	CAPT John S. Thach
	VMF 214		MAJ William M. Lundin, USMC
	Destroyer Division 72		CAPT Byron L. Gurnette
	Mackenzie		CDR William R. Laird, Jr.
	Taussig		CDR William C. Meyer
	Ernest G. Small	3 DD	CDR Franklin C. Snow
96.83	Carrier Element 3		CAPT Edgar T. Neale
	Bataan (USS)	1 CVL	CAPT Edgar T. Neale
	VMF 212		LCOL Richard W. Wyczawski, USMC
	Brinkley Bass		CDR Aaron F. Beyer, Jr.
	Arnold J. Isbell	2 DD	CDR Fletcher Hale, Jr.
96.84	Screen Element		CAPT Russell S. Smith
	Destroyer Squadron 7		CAPT Russell S. Smith
	Lofberg		CDR Robert W. McElrath
	John A. Bole		CDR Marion H. Buaas
	Mackenzie		CDR William R. Laird, Jr.
	Taussig		CDR William C. Meyer
	Ernest G. Small	5 DD	CDR Franklin C. Snow
	Hanson	1 DDR	CDR Cecil R. Welte
	Destroyer Division 52		CAPT David A. Harris
	Brinkley Bass		CDR Aaron F. Beyer, Jr.
	Arnold J. Isbell	2 DD	CDR Fletcher Hale, Jr.
	Task Force 77—Fast Carrier Force		RADM Edward C. Ewen
77.1	Support Group		CAPT Irving T. Duke
	Missouri (F) (Vice Adm. Arthur D. Struble, Commander SEVENTH Fleet embarked)	1 BB	CAPT Irving T. Duke
	Manchester	1 CL	CAPT Lewis S. Parks
	Juneau	1 CL (AA)	CAPT William T. Kenny
77.2	Screen Group		CAPT Jeane R. Clark
	Destroyer Squadron 11		CAPT Jeane R. Clark

Destroyer Division 111		
Wiltsie (FF)		CDR Carrol W. Brigham
(COMDESRON 11 embarked)		
Theodore E. Chandler		CDR William J. Collum, Jr.
Hamner	3 DD	CDR Jack J. Hughes
Chevalier	1 DDR	CDR Blake B. Booth
Destroyer Division 112		CAPT Bernard F. Roeder
Ozbourn (F)		CDR Charles O. Akers
McKean		CDR Harry L. Reiter, Jr.
Hollister	3 DD	CDR Hugh W. Howard
Frank Knox	1 DDR	CDR Sam J. Caldwell, Jr.
Destroyer Squadron 3		CAPT Charles W. Parker
Destroyer Division 31		CAPT Charles W. Parker
Shelton		CDR George D. Roullard
James E. Kyes		CDR Fran M. Christiansen
Eversole	3 DD	CDR Charles E. Phillips
Higbee	1 DDR	CDR Elmer Moore
Destroyer Squadron 5		CAPT Ulysses S. G. Sharp
Destroyer Division 51		CAPT Ulysses S. G. Sharp
Rowan (FF)		CDR Alan R. Josephson
Gurke		CDR Frederic M. Radel
Henderson	3 DD	CDR William S. Stewart
Southerland	1 DDR	CDR Homer E. Conrad
Destroyer Division 52		CAPT David A. Harris
Arnold J. Isbell (F)		CDR Fletcher Hale, Jr.
Stickell		CDR Jesse B. Gay, Jr.
Brinkley Bass	3 DD	CDR Aaron F. Beyer, Jr.
Duncan	1 DDR	CDR Everett G. Sanderson
Destroyer Squadron 7		CAPT Russell S. Smith
Destroyer Division 71		
John A. Bole		CDR Marion H. Buaas
Lofberg	2 DD	CDR Robert W. McElrath
Destroyer Division 72		
Taussig		CDR William C. Meyer
Ernest G. Small	2 DD	CDR Franklin C. Snow
Destroyer Division 92		CDR William C. Norvell
Maddox		CDR Preston B. Haines, Jr.
Brush		CDR Fletcher L. Scheffield, Jr.
Samuel N. Moore	3 DD	CDR Robert H. Wanless
Herbert J. Thomas	1 DDR	CDR Sibley L. Ward, Jr.
Escort Destroyer Division 61		CAPT William L. Messmer
Fred T. Berry (FF)		CDR Victor H. Wildt
Norris		CDR James L. P. McCallum
Keppler		CDR Thomas D. Cunningham
McCaffery	4 DDE	CDR Ellis H. McDowell
77.3 Carrier Group		RADM John M. Hoskins
Leyte		CAPT Thomas U. Sisson
Carrier Division 3		RADM John M. Hoskins
Valley Forge (FF)	2 CV	CAPT Joseph M. Carson
77.4 Carrier Group		RADM Edward C. Ewen
Carrier Division 1		RADM Edward C. Ewen
Philippine Sea (F)		CAPT Willard K. Goodney
Leyte	2 CV	CAPT Thomas U. Sisson

Carrier Division 5		RADM Ralph A. Oftsie
Princeton (F)	1 CV	CAPT William O. Gallery
Air Group 19 embarked		CDR Richard C. Merrick
79.2 Hungnam Logistic Support Group		CAPT Bernard L. Austin
Dixie	1 AD	CAPT Joseph R. Hamley
Mount Katmai		CAPT Albert S. Carter
Paricutin	2 AE	CAPT Myron W. Graybill
Graffias		CDR John S. Reese
Merapi	2 AF	LCDR Carlton S. Livingston
Chara		CAPT George G. Palmer
Diphda		CDR Charles Truxall
Uvalde	3 AKA	CAPT Louis F. Teuscher
Deal		LCDR Paul V. Evans
Hewell		LT Stanley Jaworski
Ryer	3 AKL	LT Gurley P. Chatelain
Pollux	1 AKS	CAPT Harry B. Dodge
Ashtabula		CAPT John A. Williams
Cacapon		CAPT John G. McClaughry
Cimarron		CAPT Stanley G. Nichols
Kaskaskia		CAPT Thompson F. Fowler
Mispillion		CAPT Carl F. Stillman
Passumpsic	6 AO	CAPT Frank I. Winant, Jr.
Kishwaukee	1 AOG	LCDR Richard L. Kenedy
Jason	1 ARH	CAPT William B. Epps

APPENDIX IV

COMMANDS RECEIVING PRESIDENTIAL UNIT CITATIONS AND NAVY UNIT COMMENDATIONS FOR KOREAN WAR

The following commands received the Presidential Unit Citation during the Korean War:

Ship or Squadron	Date
Helicopter Squadron ONE	3 July 50–27 July 53
Marine Fighting Squadron 214	3–6 Aug 50; 8–14 Sep 50; 12 Oct–26 Nov 50; 15 Dec 50–1 Aug 51
Marine Fighting Squadron 323	3–6 Aug 50; 8–14 Sep. 50; 12 Oct–26 Nov 50; 15 Dec 50–1 Aug 51
USS *Chatterer* (AMS 40)	10–24 Oct 50
USS *Incredible* (AM 249)	10–24 Oct 50
*USS *Kite* (AMS 22)	10–24 Oct 50
USS *Merganser* (AMS 26)	11–24 Oct 50
USS *Mocking Bird* (AMS 27) (including ComMinDiv 31 and staff)	10–24 Oct 50
*USS *Osprey* (AMS 28)	10–24 Oct 50
USS *Partridge* (AMS 31)	10–24 Oct 50
USS *Pirate* (AM 275) (including ComMinDiv 32 and staff)	11–12 Oct 50
USS *Pledge* (AM 277)	10–12 Oct 50
*USS *Redhead* (AMS 34)	11–24 Oct 50
Marine Observation Squadron SIX	2 Aug 50–27 July 53

The following commands received the Navy Unit Commendation during the Korean War:

Ship or Squadron	Date
Patrol Squadron SIX	30 July 51–16 Jan 52
USS *Cacapon* (AO 52)	8 Aug–27 Dec 50
USS *Graffias* (AF 29)	23 Sep–30 Dec 50; 23 June 52–9 Mar 53
USS *Grasp* (ARS 24)	1 Feb–15 Oct 51
USS *Henrico* (APA 45)	15 Sep–25 Dec 50
*USS *Kite* (AMS 22)	18–29 July 52; 15–26 Nov 52
Minesweeping Boat Division ONE	7–20 Apr 52; 7 Aug–2 Sep 52; 12–15 Oct 52
USS *Mount Katmai* (AE 16)	18 Aug–28 Dec 50
USS *Murrelet* (AM 372)	10–31 May 52
USS *Noble* (APA 218)	15 Sep–25 Dec 50
*USS *Osprey* (AMS 28)	16 Apr–19 May 52; 12 Oct–15 Oct 52
*USS *Redhead* (AMS 34)	7 May–5 June 52; 12 Aug–8 Sep 52; 12 Oct–15 Oct 52
T.E. 90.32 (LSTs 799, 857, 859, 883, 898, 914, 973 and 975)	15–16 Sep 50

Ship	Air Group	Date
USS *Badoeng Strait* (CVE 116)		3 Aug 50–1 Aug 51
USS *Bon Homme Richard* (CVA 31)	CVG 7	22 June–18 Dec 52
USS *Essex*	CVG 5	21 Aug 51–5 Mar 52
USS *Leyte* (CVA 32)	CVG 3	9 Oct 50–19 Jan 51

* Note that the *Kite*, *Osprey* and *Redhead* received both the PUC and the NUC.

USS *Philippine Sea*	CVG 11	4 Aug 50–30 Mar 51
	CVG 2	31 Mar 51–31 May 51
	CVG 9	31 Jan–27 July 53
USS *Princeton* (CVA 37)	CVG 19	5 Dec 50–10 Aug 51
	CVG 19	15 Apr–18 Oct 52
	CVG 15	13 Mar–15 May 53
	CVG 15	11 June–27 July 53
USS *Sicily*		3 Aug 50–1 Aug 51
USS *Valley Forge*	CVG 5	3 July–18 Nov 51
	CVG 5	1 Jan–5 June 53
	ATG 1	11 Dec 51–11 June 52

APPENDIX V

Patrol Squadrons Serving in Korean War

Squadron	Commanding Officer	Type A/C	Attached to	Dates in Theater	Base
VP-46 Sea	(1) CDR M. F. Weisner	9PBM5	FAW-1	15 July 50–5 Feb 51	Pescadores Sangley Hong Kong
	(2) CDR R. L. Donley	9PBM5		30 Sept 51–4 Apr 52	Iwakuni
	(3) CDR R. S. Dail	12PBM5		24 Feb 53–27 July 53	Sangley Buckner Bay Pescadores Subic Bay
VP-28 Land	(1) CDR C. F. Skuzinski	9P4Y-2	FAW-1	14 July 50–7 Aug 50	Naha
	(2) CDR C. S. Minter	9P4Y-2	FAW-6	5 Apr 51–9 Oct 51	Itami
VP28* (Det A)	(3) LCDR E. R. Hawley	4P4Y-2	FAW-6	1 Oct 51–14 Dec 51	Atsugi K-1, Korea
	(4) CDR C. B. McAfee	9P4Y2S	FAW-1 & 2	30 May 52–30 Nov 52	Naha
VP-1 Land	(1) CDR J. B. Honan	9P2V3	FAW-1	7 Aug 50–14 Nov 50	Naha
	(2) CDR W. M. Ringness	9P2V3	FAW-1	2 May 51–1 Sept 51	Naha
	(3) CDR W. M. Ringness CDR J. D. Quillin	9P2V5	FAW-6 & 14	28 Mar 52–1 Oct 52	Atsugi
	(4) CDR J. D. Quillin	9P2V5	FAW-1 & 2	30 May 53–27 July 53	Kadena
VP-6 Land	(1) CDR A. F. Farwell	9P2V3	FAW-6	7 July 50–11 Feb. 51	Johnson AFB To Tachikawa 6 Aug To Atsugi 5 Jan
	(2) CDR G. Howard	9P2V3	FAW-6	30 July 51–15 Jan 52	Atsugi

* Det A was supplemented in its flare-dropping task by two crews from VP-871

520

Squadron	Commanding Officer	Type A/C	Attached to	Dates in Theater	Base
VP-22 Land	(1) CDR R. J. Davis	9P2V3	FAW-1	14 Nov 50–2 May 51	Naha
	(2) CDR W. Godwin	9P2V4	FAW-1	1 Dec 51–31 May 52	Naha
	(3) CDR W. P. Tanner	9P2V5	FAW-1 & 2	30 Nov 52–30 May 53	Naha Kadena
VP-731* Sea	(1) CDR H. S. Wilson	9PBM5	FAW-1	5 Feb 51–13 Aug 51	Buckner Bay Sangley Point Hong Kong Pescadores
	(2) CDR W. T. O'Dowd	9PBM	FAW-6 & 14	1 June 52–8 Dec 52	Iwakuni
VP-47 Sea	(1) CDR J. H. Arnold	9PBM5	FAW-6	25 June† 50–28 Dec 50	Yokosuka Iwakuni
	(2) CDR W. T. Hardaker	9PBM5	FAW-1	13 Aug 51–5 Mar 52	Pescadores Sangley Buckner Bay Hong Kong
	(3) CDR H. E. Thayer	12PBM5	FAW-6 & 14	29 Nov 52–1 June 53	Iwakuni
VP-2 Land	(1) CDR R. Turner, Jr. CDR M. J. Berg	9P2V4	FAW-1	1 Sept 51–1 Dec 51	Naha
VP-772*	(1) CDR D. D. Nittinger	9P4Y-2	FAW-6	11 Feb 51–7 Aug 51	Atsugi
(VP-17) Land	(2) CDR R. L. Dahllof	10P4Y2	FAW-6 & 14	29 Dec 52–30 June 53	Iwakuni
VP-892* Sea	(1) LCDR E. R. Swanson	9PBM5	FAW-6	1 May 51–9 June 51	Iwakuni
(later VP-50)	(2) CDR W. H. Chester	9PBM5	FAW-1 & 2	5 Mar 52–1 Sept 52	Buckner Bay Sangley Hong Kong Pescadores

* Reserve squadron.
† VP-47 was in area when war started.

Squadron	Commanding Officer	Type A/C	Attached to	Dates in Theater	Base
VP-40 Sea	(1) CDR V. Utgoff	9PBM5	FAW-6	1 June 51– 15 Dec 51	Iwakuni
	(2) CDR M. S. Whitener	12PBM5	FAW-1 & 2	3 Sept 52– 24 Feb 53	Sangley Point Buckner Bay Pescadores
VP-42 Sea	(1) CDR G. F. Smale	9PBM5	FAW-6	21 Aug 50– 10 Apr 51	Yokosuka To Iwakuni 19 Aug 50
	(2) CDR J. L. Skinner	9PBM5	FAW-6	8 Dec 51– 2 June 52	Iwakuni
VP-871* (Det A) Land	(1) CDR F. H. Holt	9P4Y-2	FAW-6	10 Dec 51– 4 July 52	Atsugi K-1 Korea Atsugi
VP-9 Land	CDR J. B. Filson	9P4Y-2	FAW-6	29 June 52– 5 Jan 53	Iwakuni
VP-29 Land	CDR L. B. Smith	9P2V5	FAW-6 & 14	27 Sept 52– 5 Apr 53	Atsugi
VP-48 Sea	CDR F. G. Bessel	12PBM5	FAW-1 & 2	26 July 53– 27 July 53	Sangley Point
VP-57 Land	CDR V. J. Coley	9P2V5	FAW-6 & 14	29 Mar 53– 27 July 53	Atsugi
VP-7‡ Land	CDR R. L. Milner	9P2V5	FAW-6 & 14	30 June 53– 27 July 53	Iwakuni
VP-50 Sea	LCDR N. D. McClure	12PBM5	FAW-6	5 June 53– 27 July 53	Iwakuni

* Reserve squadron.
‡ An Atlantic Fleet patrol squadron.

TASK FORCE 77 SORTIES FOR KOREAN WAR

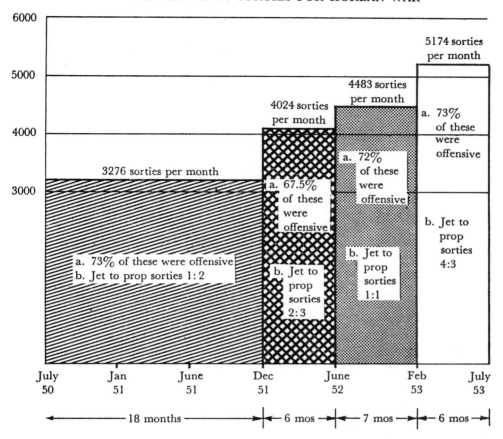

APPENDIX VI

Glossary of Technical Terms and Abbreviations

AD	Skyraider-Douglas Divebomber
AD	Destroyer Tender
AE	Ammunition Ship
AF	Store Ship
AGC	Amphibious Force Flagship
AH	Hospital Ship
AK	Cargo Ship
AKA	Assault Cargo Ship
AKL	Cargo Ship—Light
AKS	Stores Issue Ship
AM	Minesweeper
AMS	Auxiliary Motor Minesweeper
ANGLICO	Air and Naval Gunfire Liaison Company
AO	Oiler
AOG	Gasoline Tanker
AP	Transport
APA	Assault Transport
APD	High Speed Transport
ARG	Repair Ship—Internal Combustion Engines
ARH	Repair Ship—Heavy Hull Damage
ARL	Repair Ship—Landing craft
ATF	Ocean Tug—Fleet
AV	Seaplane Tender
AVP	Seaplane Tender, Small
CA	Heavy Cruiser
CinCFE	Commander in Chief, Far East
CinCPacFlt	Commander in Chief, Pacific Fleet
CL	Light Cruiser
CMC	Commandant of the Marine Corps
CNO	Chief of Naval Operations
ComCarDiv	Commander Carrier Division
CO	Commanding Officer
COMNAVFE—Commander Navy Far East	
COMPHIBGRUONE—Commander Amphibious Group One	
CTF	Commander Task Force
CVA	Aircraft carrier—Attack
CVE	Aircraft Carrier—Escort
CVL	Aircraft Carrier—Small
DD	Destroyer
DDE	Escort Destroyer
DDR	Radar Picket Destroyer
DMS	Destroyer Minesweeper
EUSAK	Eighth United States Army in Korea
FAFIK	Fifth Air Force in Korea
FEAF	Far East Air Force
FECOM	Far East Command

F2H2	McDonnell "Banshee" Jet Fighter
F4U	Vought "Corsair" Fighter
FMF	Fleet Marine Force (Pac—Pacific; Lant—Atlantic)
F7F-3	Grumman "Tigercat" Night Fighter
F9F-2, 3, 5	Grumman "Panther" Jet Fighter
GCI	Ground Control Intercept
GHQ	General Headquarters
HO3S-1	Sikorsky Helicopter
JCS	Joint Chiefs of Staff
JOC	Joint Operations Center
JSPOG	Joint Strategic Planning and Operations Group
JTF	Joint Task Force
KMAG	Korean Military Advisory Group
LANT	Atlantic
LCM	Landing Craft, Mechanized
LCPR	Landing Craft, Personnel, Reconnaissance
LCVP	Landing Craft, Vehicle and Personnel
LSD	Landing Ship, Dock
LSM	Landing Ship, Medium
LSMR	Landing Ship, Medium Rocket
LST	Landing Ship, Tank
LSU	Landing Ship, Utility
LVT	Landing Vehicle, Tracked
LVT(A)	Landing Vehicle, Tracked (Armored)
MAG	Marine Air Group
MAW	Marine Air Wing
NGF	Naval Gunfire
NK	North Korea
NKPA	North Korean Peoples Army
OY	Consolidated-Vultee light observation plane
PAC	Pacific
PC	Submarine Chaser
PCEC	Escort Amphibious Control Vessel
PF	Frigate
PhibGru	Amphibious Group
PhibTraPac	Training Command, Amphibious Forces, Pacific Fleet
POL	Petroleum, Oil, Lubricants
POW	Prisoner of War
RCT	Regimental Combat Team
ROK	Republic of Korea
SCAJAP	Supreme Commander Allied Powers, Japan
TAC	Tactical Air Coordinator
TADC	Tactical Air Direction Center
TG	Task Group
TF	Task Force
UN	United Nations
UDT	Underwater Demolition Team

UNC	United Nations Command
USA	United States Army
USAF	United States Air Force
USMC	United States Marine Corps
USN	United States Navy

VMF	Marine fighter type aircraft squadron
VMF(N)	Marine night fighter type aircraft, all-weather squadron
VMO	Marine observation type aircraft squadron
VMR	Marine transport type aircraft squadron

WP	White phosphorous

YMS	Motor Minesweeper
YTB	Harbor Tug, Big
YW	District Barge, Water (self-propelled)

APPENDIX VII

Enemy Aircraft Destroyed by Navy Pilots in Korean War

3 July 50	ENS E. W. Brown (VF 51, F9F2 USS *Valley Forge*)	1 YAK-9
3 July 50	LTJG L. H. Plog (VF 51, F9F2 USS *Valley Forge*)	1 YAK-9
9 Nov 50	LCDR W. T. Amen (VF 111, F9F2 USS *Philippine Sea*)	1 MIG-15
18 Nov 50	LCDR W. E. Lamb (VF 52, F9F3	1 MIG-15
	LT R. E. Parker USS *Valley Forge*)	
18 Nov 50	ENS F. C. Weber (VF 31, F9F2 USS *Leyte*)	1 MIG-15
1 June 51	LT Simpson Evans (Exchange Duty with the 5th Air Force)	1 MIG-15
23 Oct 51	LT Walter Schirra (Exchange Duty with the 5th Air Force)	1 MIG-15
6 Dec 51	LCDR Paul Pugh (Exchange Duty with the 5th Air Force)	1 MIG-15
22 Dec 51		1 MIG-15
18 Nov 52	LTJG J. D. Middleton (VF 781 F9F5 USS *Oriskany*)	1 MIG-15
	LT E. R. Williams (VF 781 F9F5 USS *Oriskany*)	1 MIG-15
30 June 53	LT G. B. Bordelon (VC-3, F4U5N USS *Princeton* on TAD with	2 YAK 18s
5 July 53	5th Air Force)	2 PO 2s
16 July 53		1 PO 2

Enemy Aircraft Destroyed by Marine Corps Pilots in Korean War

21 Apr 51	LT H. Daigh (VMF 312, F4U4 USS *Bataan*)	1 YAK
21 Apr 51	CAPT P. C. DeLong (VMF 312, F4U4 USS *Bataan*)	2 YAKs
1 July 51*	CAPT E. B. Long (VMF(N) 513, F7F3N)	1 PO 2
12 July 51	CAPT D. L. Fenton (VMF(N) 513, F4U5NL)	1 PO 2
23 Sep 51	MAJ E. A. Van Gundy (VMF(N) 513, F7F3N)	1 PO 2
4 Nov 51	MAJ W. F. Guss (Exchange Duty with the 5th Air Force)	1 MIG
Feb 52	LTCOL J. Payne (Exchange Duty with the 5th Air Force)	1 MIG
5 Mar 52	CAPT V. J. Marzello (Exchange Duty with the 5th Air Force)	1 MIG
7 June 52	LT J. W. Andre (VMF(N) 513, F4U5NL)	1 YAK-9
12 July 52		1 MIG
19 July 52	MAJ J. H. Glenn (Exchange Duty with the 5th Air Force)	1 MIG
22 July 52		1 MIG
Aug–Oct 52†	MAJ A. J. Gillis (Exchange Duty with the 5th Air Force)	3 MIGs
10 Sep 52	CAPT J. G. Folmar (VMA 312, F4U USS *Sicily*)	1 MIG
3 Nov 52‡	MAJ W. Stratton (VMF(N) 513, F3D2)	1 YAK-15

* The first night kill by a United Nations aircraft.

† Kills were in this period; exact dates not in historical record.

‡ First enemy jet destroyed by an airborne intercept radar equipped fighter.

8 Nov 52	CAPT O. R. Davis (VMF(N) 513, F3D2)	1 MIG
Nov 52	CAPT R. Wade (Exchange Duty with the 5th Air Force)	1 MIG
10 Dec 52	LT J. A. Corvi (VMF(N) 513, F3D2)	1 PO 2
12 Jan 53	MAJ E. P. Dunn (VMF(N) 513, F3D2)	1 MIG
28 Jan 53	CAPT J. R. Weaver (VMF(N) 513, F3D2)	1 MIG
31 Jan 53	LTCOL R. F. Conley (VMF(N) 513, F3D2)	1 MIG
7 Apr 53 ⎱ 12 Apr 53 ⎰	MAJ R. L. Reed (Exchange Duty with the 5th Air Force)	1 MIG 1 MIG
18 May 53	CAPT H. L. Jensen (Exchange Duty with the 5th Air Force)	1 MIG
11 July 53§	MAJ J. F. Volt (Exchange Duty with the 5th Air Force)	6 MIGs
20 July 53	MAJ T. M. Sellers (Exchange Duty with the 5th Air Force)	2 MIGs

§ Date of 5th and 6th kills; dates of first four not in historical records.

APPENDIX VIII

*U. S. Navy Casualties in Korean War**

DEATHS

a. Killed in action		279
b. Died of Wounds		23
c. Missing in action and known or presumed dead		156
		458 TOTAL
Wounded in action		1,576
Missing in Action (Of this number, 35 were returned to naval control after prisoner exchange)		9†

TOTAL CASUALTIES 2,043

* From DOD Press Release #1088—54 dtd 5 November 1954.

† Of these nine, six are possibly alive although the Reds deny they hold them. " . . . there are reports that they were paraded through the streets of Swatow, China after their plane was shot down by the Chinese in January 1953. The other three Navy "missing" are believed to be dead but sufficient evidence for a finding of presumptive death has not been found as of September 30th." (1954)—Quoted from Defense Department press release, mentioned above.

APPENDIX IX

U. S. Ships Lost or Damaged

LOST—5

Name	*Date & Cause*	*Place*	*Remarks*
USS *Magpie* (AMS-25)	29 Sep 50 Mined	36-20N 129-28E	Blew up, 21 MIA 12 survivors
USS *Pirate* (AM-275)	12 Oct 50 Mined	Wonsan	Sunk
USS *Pledge* (AM-277)	12 Oct 50 Mined	Wonsan	Sunk

Ext.D.—Extensive damage	Sup.D.—Superficial damage
Sev.D.—Severe damage	Neg.D.—Negative damage
Ma.D.—Major damage	Cons.D.—Considerable damage
Mi.D.—Minor damage	cas.—casualties
Sl.D.—Slight damage	KIA—Killed in action
Lt.D.—Light damage	WIA—Wounded in action
Mo.D.—Moderate damage	MIA—Missing in action

Name	Date & Cause	Place	Remarks
USS *Partridge* (AMS-31)	2 Feb 51 Mined	38-20N 128-38E	Sunk
USS *Sarsi* (ATF-111)	27 Aug 52 Mined	Hungnam	Sunk 7 cas., 92 rescued

DAMAGED—87

Name	Date & Cause	Place	Remarks
USS *Brush* (DD-745)	26 Sep 50 Mined	Tanchon	10 WIA, 9 KIA
USS *Mansfield* (DD-728)	30 Sep 50 Mined	38-45N 128-15E	Damaged, 5 MIA, 48 WIA
USS *C. S. Sperry* (DD-697)	23 Dec 50 Shore Battery	Songjin	3 hits.
USS *Ozborn* (DD 846)	Shore Battery	Wonsan	2 casualties
USS *Walke* (DD-723)	12 Jun 51 Mined	East coast	ExtD. 61 cas.
USS *Thompson*[1] (DMS-38)	14 Jun 51 Shore battery	Songjin	Ext.D. 3 KIA, 4 WIA
USS *Hoquiam* (PF-5)	7 May 51 Shore battery	Songjin	Sl.D. 1 cas.
USS *New Jersey* (BB-62)	20 May 51 Shore battery	Wonsan	Sl.D. 4 cas.
USS *Brinkley Bass* (DD-887)	22 May 51 Shore battery	Wonsan	Mi.D. 8 cas.
USS *F. E. Evans* (DD-754)	18 Jun 51 Shore battery	Wonsan	Sl.D. 4 cas.
USS *Tucker* (DDR-875)	28 Jun 51 Shore battery	Wonsan	Sup.D. 1 hit.
USS *Everett* (PF-8)	3 Jul 51 Shore battery	Wonsan	Mi.D. 8 cas.
USS *Helena* (CA-75)	31 Jul 51 Shore battery	Wonsan	Mi.D. 2 cas.
USS *Dextrous* (AM-341)	11 Aug 51 Shore battery	Wonsan	Sup.D. 1 KIA, 3 WIA
USS *William Seiverling* (DE-441)	8 Sep 51 Shore battery	Wonsan	Fireroom flooded. No. cas.
USS *Redstart* (AM-378)	10 Sep 51 Shore battery	Wonsan	Mi.D. No cas.
USS *Heron* (AMS-18)	10 Sep 51 Shore battery	Wonsan	Sup.D. No cas.
USS *Firecrest* (AMS-10)	5 Oct 51 Shore battery	Hungnam	Sl.D. No cas.
USS *Ernest G. Small* (DDR-838)	7 Oct 51 Mined	East coast	Ext.D. 27 cas.
USS *Renshaw* (DDE-499)	11 Oct 51 Shore battery	Songjin	Sl.D. 1 cas.
USS *Samuel N. Moore* (DD-747)	17 Oct 51 Shore battery	Hungnam	Mo.D. 3 cas.
USS *Helena* (CA-75)	23 Oct 51 Shore battery	Hungnam	Sl.D. 4 cas.
USS *Osprey* (AMS-28)	29 Oct 51 Shore battery	Wonsan	Cons.D. 1 cas.

Name	*Date & Cause*	*Place*	*Remarks*
USS *Gloucester* (PF-22)	11 Nov 51 Shore battery	Hongwon	Li.D. 12 cas.
USS *Hyman* (DD-732)	23 Nov 51 Shore battery	Wonsan	Mi.D. no cas.
LST 611	22 Dec 51 Shore battery		Sup.D. No cas.
USS *Dextrous* (AM-341)	11 Jan 52 Shore battery	Wonsan	Mi.D. 3 cas.
USS *Porterfield* (DD-682)	3 Feb 52 Shore battery	Sokto	Mi.D. No cas.
USS *Endicott* (DMS-35)	4 Feb 52 Shore battery	Songjin	Mi.D. No cas. 2 hits
USS *Shelton* (DD-790)	22 Feb 52 Shore battery	Songjin	Mo.D. 15 cas. 3 hits
USS *Henderson* (DD-785)	23 Feb 52 Shore battery	Hungnam	Mi.D. No cas.
USS *Rowan* (DD-782)	22 Feb 52 Shore battery	Wonsan	Mi.D. No cas. 1 hit.
USS *Wisconsin* (BB-64)	16 Mar 52 Shore battery	Songjin	Neg.D. 3 cas. 1 hit.
USS *Brinkley Bass* (DD-887)	24 Mar 52 Shore battery	Wonsan	Mo.D. 5 cas. 1 hit.
USS *Endicott* (DMS-35)	7 Apr 52 Shore battery	Chongjin	Neg.D. No cas.
USS *Endicott* (DMS-35)	19 Apr 52 Shore battery	Songjin	Mi.D. No cas. 1 hit.
USS *Osprey* (AMS-28)	24 Apr 52 Shore battery	Songjin	Mi.D. no cas. 1 hit.
USS *Cabildo* (LSD-16)	26 Apr 52 Shore battery	Wonsan	Mi.D. 2 cas. 1 hit.
USS *Maddox* (DD-731)	30 Apr 52 Shore battery	Wonsan	Sup.D. No cas.
USS *Laffey* (DD-724)	30 Apr 52 Shore battery	Wonsan	Sup.D. No cas.
USS *Leonard F. Mason* (DD-852)	Shore battery 2 May 52	Wonsan	Sup.D. No cas.
USS *James C. Owens* (DD-776)	7 May 52 Shore battery	Songjin	Cons.D. 10 cas. 6 hits.
USS *H. J. Thomas* (DDR-833)	12 May 52 Shore battery	Wonsan	Sup.D. No cas. 1 hit.
USS *D. H. Fox* (DD-779)	14 May 52 Shore battery	Hungnam	Mi.D. 2 cas. 1 hit.
USS *Cabildo* (LSD-16)	25 May 52 Shore battery	Wonsan	Sup.D. 2 cas.
USS *Murrelet* (AM-372)	26 May 52 Shore battery	Songjin	Sl.D. No cas. 2 hits.
USS *Swallow* (AMS-36)	25 May 52 Shore battery	Songjin	Sl.D. No cas. 3 hits.
USS *Firecrest* (AMS-10)	30 May 52 MachGunMts.		Mi.D. No cas.
USS *Buck* (DD-761)	13 Jun 52 Shore battery	Kojo	Motor launch damage. 2 cas.

Name	Date & Cause	Place	Remarks
USS *Orleck* (DD-886)	19 Jul 52 Shore battery	Songjin	Mi. D. 4 cas. 1 hit recd 50 rds 75 mm
USS *John R. Pierce* (DD-753)	6 Aug 52 Shore battery	Tanchon	Mo.D. 10 cas. 7 hits
USS *Barton* (DD-722)	10 Aug 52 Shore battery	Wonsan	Mi.D. 2 cas. 1 hit
USS *Grapple* (ARS-7)	12 Aug 52 Shore battery	Wonsan	Mi.D. below waterline 1 hit, **no cas.**
USS *Thompson* (DMS-38)	20 Aug 52 Shore battery	Songjin	Mi.D. 13 cas. air burst vic bridge near misses
USS *McDermut* (DD-677)	27 Aug 52 Shore battery	Pkg 4–5	Sup.D. No cas. 60 rds 3700 yds.
USS *Competent* (AM-316)	27 Aug 52 Shore battery	Pkg 4–5	Sup.D. No cas. Lost sweep **gear**, shrapnel near miss
USS *Agerholm* (DD-826)	1 Sep 52 Shore battery	Kangsong area bombline	Sup.D. 1 cas.
USS *Frank E. Evans* (DD-754)	8 Sep 52 Shore battery	Tanchon	Sl.D. No cas. near misses recd 69 rds.
USS *Barton* (DD-722)	16 Sep 52 Mined	90 mi. east of Wonsan	Ma.D. 11 cas.
USS *A. A. Cunningham* (DD-752)	19 Sept 52 Shore battery	Songjin	Mo.D. 8 cas. 5 hits, 7 air bursts, recd 150 rds 105 mm 3 guns, 1st rd direct hit initial range 3500 yards
USS *Perkins* (DDR-887)	13 Oct 52 Shore battery	Kojo	Sup.D. 18 cas., straddled 5 rds 5000 yds, 2 near misses sprayed with shrapnel.
USS *Osprey* (AMS-28)	14 Oct 52 Shore battery	Kojo	Mi.D. 4 cas.
USS *Lewis* (DE-535)	21 Oct 52 Shore battery	Wonsan	Mo.D. 8 cas. 2 hits, 50 rds 4–6 guns.
USS *Mansfield* (DD-728)	28 Oct 52 Shore battery	Wonsan	Mi. shrapnel damage. No cas. recd 40 rds 4 guns cont. straddles 4300–8000 yds, suspected radar controlled.
USS *Uhlmann* (DD-687)	3 Nov 52 Shore battery	Lat 40-10 Long 128-34.	Mi.D. 13 cas. 3 hits, recd 160 rds.
USS *Kite* (AMS-22)	19 Nov 52 Shore battery	Wonsan	1 small boat destroyed, 5 cas.
USS *Thompson*[3] (DMS-38)	20 Nov 52 Shore battery	Wonsan	Mi.D. 1 cas. 1 hit recd 89 rds.
USS *Hanna* (DE-449)	24 Nov 52 Shore battery	Songjin	Mo.D. 1 cas. 1 hit recd 60 rds.
USS *Halsey Powell* (DD-686)	6 Feb 53 Shore battery	Hwa-do	Whaleboat damaged, 2 cas.
USS *Gull* (AMS-16)	16 Mar 53 Shore battery	Pkg 2	Mi.D. 2 cas. 1 hit, recd 60 rds 5400–9000 yds
USS *Taussig* (DD-746)	17 Mar 53 Shore battery	Pkg 1	Sl.D. 1 cas. 1 hit, recd 45 rds 6400–10,000 yds
USS *Los Angeles* (CA-135)	27 Mar 53 Shore battery	Wonsan	Sl.D. No. cas. 1 hit, recd 40 rds 105 mm.
USS *Los Angeles* (CA-135)	2 Apr 53 Shore battery	Wonsan	Mi.D. 13 cas. 1 hit

Name	*Date & Cause*	*Place*	*Remarks*
USS *Maddox* (DD-731)	16 Apr 53 Shore battery	Wonsan	Sl.D. 3 cas. recd 209 rds heavy fire 1–76 mm hit.
USS *James E. Kyes* (DD-787)	19 Apr 53 Shore battery	Wonsan	Sl.D. 9 cas. 1 hit recd 60 rds 155 mm 8–12,000 yds.
USS *Maddox* (DD-731)	2 May 53 Shore battery	Wonsan	Mo.D. No cas. 1 hit recd 186 rds 105 mm 4–6 guns Hodo Pando, several near misses.
USS *Owen* (DD-536)	2 May 53 Shore battery	Wonsan	Mi.D. No cas. 1 hit recd 100 rds 105 mm 4 guns Hodo Pando 1 near miss several straddles.
USS *Bremerton* (CA-130)	5 May 53 Shore battery	Wonsan	Sup.D. 2 cas. recd 18 rds 76–135 mm 1 near miss.
USS *S. N. Moore* (DD-747)	8 May 53 Shore battery	Wonsan	Sup.D. No cas. 1 hit recd 60 rds 90 mm
USS *Brush* (DD-745)	15 May 53 Shore battery	Wonsan	Mi.D. 9 cas. 1 hit recd 20 rds 76 mm.
USS *Swift* (AM-122)	29 May 53 Shore battery	Yang-do	Sup.D. 1 cas. 1 hit recd 30 rds 76 mm.
USS *LSMR 409*	4 Jun 53 Shore battery	Walsa-ri	Mi.D. 5 cas. 2 hits recd 30 rds 76 mm.
USS *Wiltsie* (DD-716)	11 Jun 53 Shore battery	Wonsan	Sup.D. No cas. 1 hit recd 35 rds 76 mm several air bursts.
USS *Henderson* (DD-785)	17 Jun 53 Shore battery	Wonsan	Superficial damage
USS *Irwin* (DD-794)	18 Jun 53 Shore battery	Wonsan	Mi.D. 5 cas. 1 hit recd 90 rds.
USS *Rowan* (DD-782)	18 Jun 53 Shore battery	Wonsan	Mo.D. 9 cas. 5 hits recd 45 rds 76–155 mm at 7500 yds.
USS *Gurke* (DD-783)	25 Jun 53 Shore battery	Songjin	Sl.D. 3 cas. 2 hits recd 150 rds 76–90 mm 6–11,000 yds shrapnel from 5 near misses.
USS *Manchester* (CL-83)	30 June 53 Shore battery	Wonsan	Sup.D. No cas. 30 min. gun duel, near misses.
USS *John W. Thomason* (DD-760)	7 Jul 53 Shore battery	Wonsan	Mi. shrapnel damage, recd 150 rds 107 mm from Hodo Pando, near misses.
USS *Irwin* (DD-794)	8 Jul 53 Shore battery	Pkg 2	Mi.D. 5 cas. recd 80 rds 76 mm air bursts close abd.
USS *Saint Paul* (CA-73)	11 Jul 53 Shore battery	Wonsan	Sev. under water damage. No cas. 1 hit, 76–90 mm.

APPENDIX X

Statistics on U. S. Naval Operations in Korea

A. *Naval Air Combat Operations*

1. Combat sorties flown by Navy/Marine Aircraft: 275,912. (25 June 1950–27 July 1953) (Of this total, 204,995 were offensive sorties; 44,160 defensive and 26,757 reconnaissance. The total figure does *not* include non-combat flights.)

2. Ordnance Expenditures by Navy/Marine aircraft:
   (a) Bombs (tons):   163,062(178,399)*
   (b) Rockets (number):   267,217(274,189)*
   (c) Ammunition (thousands of rounds):   68,608(71,804)*
3. Damage inflicted on enemy (25 June 50–8 June 53)
   (a) Troops killed   86,265
   (b) Buildings destroyed   44,828
   (c) Locomotives destroyed   391
   (d) Railroad cars destroyed   5,896
   (e) Vehicles destroyed   7,437
   (f) Bridges (rail and road destroyed)   2,005
   (g) Tanks destroyed   249
   (h) Bunkers destroyed   20,854
   (i) Power plants destroyed   33
   (j) Supply dumps, shelters, stacks destroyed   1,900
   (k) Enemy vessels destroyed   2,464
4. Enemy aircraft destroyed by Navy/Marine Corps (25 June–31 May 53)
   (a) Aerial combat   23
   (b) Destroyed on ground   74
5. Navy Marine aircraft lost to enemy action (25 June 50–27 July 53)
   (a) Aerial combat   5
   (b) Anti-aircraft fire   559

B. *Naval Surface Operations:* (25 June 1950–31 May 53)

1. Shipboard ammunition fired
   (rounds—16″ to small arms)   4,069,626
2. Damage inflicted on enemy:† June 50–June 52
   (a) Buildings destroyed   3,334
   (b) Vessels and small craft destroyed   824
   (c) Locomotives destroyed   14
   (d) Trucks destroyed   214
   (e) Tanks destroyed   15
   (f) Bridges destroyed   108
   (g) Supply dumps destroyed   93
   (h) Mines destroyed   1,535
   (i) Troops (Casualties)   28,566
3. U.S. Navy Ship Casualties:
   (a) Ships damaged   73
   (b) Ships sunk (4 minesweepers, 1 tug)   5

C. *Military Sea Transportation Service*‡ (June 50 to June 53)

1. Cargo (Measurement tons)   52,111,299
2. Passengers   4,918,919
3. Petroleum (Long tons)   21,828,879

* Figures in parentheses are estimates for period ending 27 July 53. Other figures are through 31 May 1953 only.

† Latest figures available. Figures when used in text are projected on basis of past operational reports. In all cases projections are conservative.

‡ Figures to, from and within the Far East.

Notes

Chapter 1

[1] Defense treaty signed 1 January 1948 by Belgium, Netherlands, and Luxembourg.

[2] The Brussels Treaty was signed 17 March 1948 by the Benelux countries, plus England and France. It was another regional collective defense arrangement within the framework of the United Nations and modeled to a considerable extent after the Rio Treaty. (*A Decade of American Foreign Policy 1941-49*, Department of State, p. 1333.)

[3] Soviet forces first entered Korea on 12 August 1945, and proceeded with immediate occupation.

[4] *Background Information on Korea. Report from the House of Representatives, the Committee on Foreign Affairs, Report No. 2495, July 11, 1950,* p. 3.

[5] *Ibid,* p. 10.

[6] *Unification and Strategy. A Report of the Investigation by the Committee on Armed Services, House of Representatives, March 1, 1950,* p. 1.

[7] *Ibid,* p. 42.

[8] *Ibid,* p. 2

[9] *Ibid,* p. 9.

[10] During the *"National Defense Program—Unification and Strategy"* hearings which followed, Chairman Vinson stated as follows: ". . . The rumors became so prevalent and it was floating around to such an extent in Congress that it was necessary for me, speaking on behalf of the Committee, to see the Secretary of Defense and get a statement to the effect that he wasn't going to transfer the Marines to the Army and he wasn't going to transfer Marine aviation to the Air Force." p. 386.

[11] From copy of Secretary of Defense Louis Johnson's letter to Mr. Carl Vinson, reprinted in a *Report of Investigation by the Committee on Armed Services, House of Representatives, on Unification and Strategy, March 1, 1950,* p. 6.

[12] *Ibid,* p. 7.

[13] *"The National Defense Program—Unification and Strategy." Hearings before the Committee on Armed Services, House of Representatives, 81st Congress, First Session, October 6, 7, 8, 10, 11, 12, 13, 17, 18, 19, 20, and 21, 1949,* p. 63.

[14] *Ibid,* p. 64; also 402-3.

[15] *Ibid,* p. 401.

[16] *Ibid,* pp. 471-473.

[17] *Ibid,* p. 52; also p. 525.

[18] *Ibid, Testimony of General Omar Bradley,* pp. 515-541.

[19] *Ibid,* p. 41.

[20] *Ibid,* p. 41.

[21] *Ibid,* p. 57.

[22] *Ibid,* Testimony of Admiral (then Captain) Arleigh A. Burke, who was to become Chief of Naval Operations on 17 August 1955. p. 255.

[23] *Ibid,* Testimony of Admiral Louis E. Denfeld, Chief of Naval Operations. p. 349, *et al.* Admiral Denfeld was to be subsequently relieved as CNO on the recommendation of the Secretary of the Navy, Francis P. Matthews.

[24] *Ibid,* p. 302-3.

[25] *Ibid,* p. 257.

[26] *Unification and Strategy. A Report of Investigation, Committee on Armed Services, House of Representatives, March 1, 1950,* p. 15.

[27] *Hearings before the Committee on Armed Services, House of Representatives, 81st Congress, October 6-21, 1949,* p. 536.

[28] *Ibid,* p. 466.

[29] *Ibid,* p. 559.

[30] On page 1740, *Hearings before the House Armed Services Committee and the Senate Foreign Relations Committee on "Military Situation in the Far East,"* Secretary Acheson explained how Korea came to be excluded from the U. S.'s defensive perimeter: ". . . The United States had certain points which were a defensive perimeter. At those points (Okinawa, Philippines) United States troops were stationed; there they would stay and there they would fight.

"In regard to other areas, I said nobody can guarantee that; but what we can say is that if people will stand up and fight for their own independence, their own country, the guaranties under the United Nations have never proved a weak reed before, and they won't in the future. I think that is a fairly accurate statement of what has happened. . . . . .

"What I said here (in the Press Club Speech of 12 Jan. 1950) is almost exactly what Mr. Dulles was saying in Korea in June 1950."

[31] See pages 1990-2, *Hearings before House Armed Services Committee.* Regarding these intelligence reports, Secretary of State Dean Acheson said: "I do not believe there was a failure of intelligence. . . . . . Intelligence was available to the Department prior to the 25th of June, made available by the Far East Command, the CIA, the Department of the Army, and by the State Department representatives here and overseas, and shows that all agencies were in agreement that the possibility for an attack on the Korean Republic existed at that time, but they were all in agreement that its launching in the summer of 1950 did not appear imminent.

"The view was generally held that since the Communists had far from exhausted the potentialities for obtaining their objectives through guerilla and psychological warfare, political pressure and intimidation, such means would continue to be used rather than overt military aggression."

[32] Dispatches quoted from *MacArthur 1941-1951* by C. A. Willoughby, p. 352.

[33] All paraphrased excerpts.

[34] *Background Information on Korea, House Committee on Foreign Affairs, Report No. 2495, 11 July 1950,* p. 48.

[35] *Ibid,* p. 53.

Chapter 2

[1] Interview, October 1950.

[2] *State NR 260405Z, June 1950* (paraphrased excerpt).

[3] Summarized *Report of Proceedings No. 1, 25 June 1950— 9 July 1950, Flag Officer Second in Command Far East Stations,* F02F2/2960/24 of 4 NOV 1950.

[4] For a complete list of Navy kills in Korea, see Chapter XIII, entitled "On The Line," and Appendix VII.

[5] The forces which carried the 24th Division to Korea as designated by COMNAVFE OpOrder 7-50 were the following:

TF 90:   *Mount McKinley* (Captain Carter A. Printup)
          Cavalier   (Captain Daniel J. Sweeney)
          Union   (Captain G. D. Zurmuehlen)
          LST 611
          14 SCAJAP LSTs

TG 96.6 *Juneau*
          HMS *Jamaica*
          Mansfield
          De Haven
          Swenson

Collett
HMS *Black Swan*
HMS *Alacrity*
HMS *Shoalhaven*
HMS *Hart*
Arikara

[6] Personal interview, 30 January 1956.

[7] Commander Pollock was killed in an air accident in the United States on 6 November 1952.

[8] Interview, *Valley Forge*, November 1950.

[9] *EUSAK 231025K July 1950* (paraphrased excerpt).

[10] *Dictionary of U. S. Military Terms for Joint Usage (1st Revision).*

[11] *Crusade in Europe,* General D. D. Eisenhower, p. 46

[12] Thus, in 1943, the Army Air Force in the War Department publication FM 100-20, (*Command and Employment of Air Power,* July 1943, p. 12, para 16) stated its opinion of close air support: "In the zone of contact, missions against hostile units are most difficult to control, are most expensive, and are, in general, least effective. Targets are small, well-dispersed, and difficult to locate. In addition, there is always a considerable chance of striking friendly forces. . . . ."

[13] During the Hearings before the House Armed Services Committee in October 1949, Brigadier General Vernon E. Megee, USMC, made a statement about close air support that read like prophesy in July 1950: ". . . If war should come tomorrow, the Tactical Air Squadrons of the Navy and Marine Corps would have to provide the major part of the troop air support, even as they did in the beginning of the last war. What we have is able to move on short notice—would that it were more." (Page 197, *National Defense Program—Unification & Strategy*).

[14] Captain Walter Karig, USNR, CDR Malcolm W. Cagle, USN, and LCDR Frank A. Manson, USN, from official sources, *Battle Report VI, The War in Korea* (New York, 1954), pp. 103-4.

[15] *COMNAVFE dispatch 230736Z July 1950* (excerpt paraphrased).

[16] *COMNAVFE dispatch 270732Z July* (paraphrased excerpt). Between 26 August and 4 September, Captain Charles E. Crew, USMC, of the ANGLICO trained a total of nine TACPs, all Air Force personnel. These TACPs were trained at Camp McGill, near Tokyo, and later served with the Army's 7th Division. Of the nine officers in charge of these parties, four were pilots who had done close support in Korea. Eight of the nine thought the Navy system of close air support superior.

[17] Personal interview on 6 April 1955.

[18] Letter to authors, 9 February 1956.

[19] *COMCARDIVONE dispatch 901003Z Aug* (paraphrased excerpt).

[20] *COMNAVFE 190046Z Aug 50* (excerpt paraphrased).

[21] *COMNAVFE 220945Z Aug 50* (excerpt paraphrased).

[22] *COMSEVENTHFLT 010344Z Sept 50* (paraphrased).

[23] *USS Valley Forge Preliminary Action Report, 1 September 1950.*

[24] *USS Philippine Sea ltr 080, 1 September 1950.*

[25] CVG-5 ltr 073-50 of 30 October 1950.

[26] For a complete account of these Marine battles, see *U. S. Marine Operations in Korea; the Pusan Perimeter,* by CAPT Nicholas A. Canzona, USMC, and Lynn Montross.

[27] *Battle Report, op. cit.,* pp. 170-171.

[28] Sec. VII, SecDef memo dtd 21 April 1948. Incidentally, this same definition remains in Naval Warfare Informative Publication (NWIP) 22-3.

[29] In a Far East Air Force Mission Summary dated 16 Nov 1950, missions as far distant as twenty miles in advance of friendly forces were listed as "close air support."

[30] In the period between 26 July and 3 Sept 1950, almost *half* of the Navy's close air support sorties were delivered *outside* the bombline.

[31] Army Air Support Center letter ATASC-D 373.21 of 1 December 1950, Encl 1, Sect 2, para 12.

[32] *PacFlt Interim Evaluation Report No. 1,* Vol. 1, p. 8.

Chapter 3

[1] "Perhaps there never has been so much opposition to any MacArthur operational plans as there was to his proposal that Inchon should be the location for the undertaking. Members of his staff in whom he had the greatest confidence doubted that Inchon was the right place. Opinion in military circles in Washington, where decisions were made, also was divided. But Louis Johnson, then Secretary of Defense, left MacArthur free to choose Inchon, or any other place. . . ." "MacArthur's Greatest Battle" by Bascom N. Timmons, *Collier's,* Dec. 16, 1950, p. 14.

"General Collins had initially opposed him in the Inchon venture, and only the backing of Louis A. Johnson, the then Secretary of Defense, had given him the chance to put it over. . . ." *The Untold Story of General MacArthur,* by Frazier Hunt (page 466).

[2] Testimony of General J. Lawton Collins, *Hearings before House Armed Services and Senate Relations Committee on Military Situation in Far East,* page 1295: Collins said he went over to Tokyo "to find out exactly what the plans were. Frankly, we were somewhat in the dark, and as it was a matter of great concern, we went out to discuss it with General MacArthur. We suggested certain alternative possibilities and places. . . . ."

[3] Letter to authors dated 19 March 1956.

[4] *Battle Report, op. cit.,* p. 167.

[5] *Ibid,* p. 169, and personal correspondence with authors.

[6] *Ibid,* p. 2618.

[7] *Ibid,* p. 168.

[8] *The New Breed,* Geer, p. 113.

[9] *Roosevelt and Hopkins,* by Robert E. Sherwood, p. 591.

[10] Interview with author, June 1951 and April 1956.

[11] Interview, December 1950.

[12] *Battle Report, op. cit.,* p. 199.

[13] For details of this bombardment, see Chapter X, "The PatRons".

[14] Task Element 90.62 (USS *Mansfield* (DD-728); USS *De Haven* (DD-727); USS *Henderson* (DD-785); USS *Gurke* (DD-783); USS *Lyman K. Swenson* (DD-729); and USS *Collett* (DD-730)) received the Navy Unit Citation for the Wolmi attack.

[15] APDs—*H. A. Bass, Diachenko, Wantuck.*
LSD—*Fort Marion* (3LSU embarked).

[16] CG, FMF, PAC ltr serial 0657/913 G131 of 23 September 1950.

[17] Volume V, *Pacific Fleet Interim Evaluation Report,* 25 June—15 November 1950, p. 727.

[18] The eight LSTs (Task Element 90.32) who made this landing were *799* (LT T. E. Houston), *857* (LT D. Weidemeyer), *859* (LT L. Tinsley), *883* (LT C. M. Miller), *914* (LT R. L. Holzhaus), *973* (LT R. I. Trapp), *898* (LT Robert M. Beckley) and *975* (LT A. W. Harer). All of them were awarded the Navy Unit Commendation for their excellent performance at Inchon.

[19] Paraphrased from Com7thFlt dispatch 270144Z of Sept. 1950.

Chapter 4

[1] *Report by the Joint Strategic Survey Committee to the Joint Chiefs of Staff on Record of the Actions taken by the JCS relative to the United Nations Operations in Korea, Number 43.* Hereafter referred to as *"JSSC".*

[2] *JSSC Report 49.*

[3] Chief of Staff, FECOM memo to JSPOG, 26 September 1950.

[4] Letter to authors, 19 March 1956.

[5] Tenth Corps OpOrder No. 3, dtd 2 October 1950.

[6] JCS 92801, 27 September 1950.

[7] JCS 92985, 29 Sept. 1950.

[8] CINCFE dispatch to JCS C-64805, 28 Sept 1950.

[9] JCS dispatch 93709, 9 Oct 1950.

[10] EUSAK War Diary, 1 October 1950.

[11] Message from the U. S. Ambassador to England to Secretary of State, 3 October 1950.

[12] Personal interview, 25 October 1950.

[13] General MacArthur's letter to authors, dated 19 March 1956.

[14] Notes to authors from Captain N. B. Atkins dated 24 April 1956.

[15] Personal interview, October 1955.

[16] See Chapter III, "The Magnificent Gamble".

[17] Dispatch from CTG 95.7 to CTF 95 on 1 Oct stated that ROK *PC-703* went alongside *YMS-504* to assist with controlling the damage and the flooding.

[18] Note from LCDR C. E. McMullen, dated 24 April 1956.

[19] Others with mine warfare experience flown to the Far Eastern theatre included CDR George C. Ellerton, Mr. James M. Martin, and CDR D. N. Clay from Admiral Radford's staff at Pearl Harbor.

[20] "Now Russia Threatens Our Seapower," *Collier's,* Sept 4, 1951.

[21] Interview with authors, October 1950.

[22] Dispatch from CTE 95.67 to CNO, 17 October 1950.

[23] Interview with CDR H. W. McElwain, Intelligence Officer, TF90, 3 May 1956.

[24] See "The Nootka Incident," p. 204.

Chapter 5

[1] Letter to authors dated 24 January 1956.

[2] Lecture to the Naval War College on the subject "Mine Countermeasures Based on Experiences in Korea, 1950," by Captain S. M. Archer, USN.

[3] Interview with author, September 1951.

[4] *Battle Report, op. cit.,* pp. 360-61.

[5] Letter to authors 7 June 1956.

[6] *Time,* 30 October 1950, p. 35.

Chapter 6

[1] See Chapter VIII, "The Struggle to Strangle", for an account of the Yalu River bridge strikes.

[2] Interview with authors, 1951.

[3] *Battle Report, op. cit.,* p. 399.

[4] Interview with authors, 1951.

[5] By Lynn Montross and Captain Nicholas A. Canzona, USMC.

[6] FAFIK 302350 Nov 50 (excerpt paraphrased).

[7] First Marine Division special action report for period 8 October to 15 December 1950.

[8] Letter from Commanding General Seventh Division dated 10 January 1951.

[9] Interview with authors, April 1956.

[10] ComPhibGruThree war diary, December 1950.

[11] ComPhibGruThree war diary, January 1951.

[12] *Battle Report, op. cit.,* pp. 429-30.

[13] CTF 90's action report, *Hungnam Redeployment,* serial 005 of 21 Jan 1951.

[14] Interview, 28 Oct 1955.

[15] *The Hungnam Evacuation,* by Lynn Montross, December 1951.

[16] *Ibid.*

[17] *Action Report, Commander Seventh Fleet,* 1 Nov-26 Dec 1950.

Chapter 7

[1] Letter to authors, dated 1 February 1956.

[2] Notes of LCDR C. W. Coe, Commanding Officer, USS *Redstart* (AM-378), March 1956.

[3] LCDR I. M. Laird's letter to authors, dated 20 April 1956.

[4] Letter from CoMinRon-3 to CNO, dated 31 May 1951.

[5] CINCPAC Interim Evaluation Report No. 5, dated 1 July 1952 to 31 January 1953.

[6] CINCFE INTSUM 3040, 5 Jan 1951; CINCFE INTSUM 3097, 3 Mar 1951; CINCFE INTSUM 3103, 9 Mar 1951; CINCFE INTSUM 3125, 31 Mar 1951; CINCFE INTSUM 3128, 3 Apr 1951; CINCFE INTSUM 3144, 19 Apr 1951.

[7] Letter from CTE 95.24 to Intelligence Officer CTG 95.2, dated 2 May 1952.

[8] Letter from CTE 95.24 to Intelligence Officer CTG 95.2, dated 6 May 1952.

[9] Interview with authors, 19 March 1956.

[10] Operations Report by ROK Navy headquarters, Vol. VI, from October 1, 1951 to December 31, 1951 (translated by Captain Chung Kyu Sup, ROK Naval Attache to United States, March 1956).

[11] *Ibid.*

[12] Interview with authors, 12 March 1956.

[13] *Zeal* (AM-131) *Action Report,* September 1952.

[14] War Diary, USS *Douglas H. Fox* (DD-779) covering period from 29 April to 14 May 1952.

[15] Interview, 31 January 1956.

[16] Notes supplied authors by LCDR C. W. Coe, Commanding Officer of the USS *Redstart.*

[17] "Men of the Minesweepers," *Collier's,* 10 November 1951.

Chapter 8

[1] JCS dispatch to CINCFE 7 November 1950: "In view of alarming situation which CINCFE has reported, CINCFE is authorized to undertake the planned bombing in Korea near the fronts, including . . . the Korean end of the Yalu bridges. . . ." (Paraphrased excerpt).

[2] Personal letter to authors, 14 December 1950.

[3] Personal interview, December 1955.

[4] Com7thFlt 230542Z, January 1951 (paraphrased excerpt).

[5] COMNAVFE 201440Z, February 1951 (paraphrased excerpt).

[6] Personal interview, 14 July 1955.

[7] Personal interview, 9 August 1955.

[8] Personal interview, 6 August 1955.

[9] COMNAVFE Press Release, dated 5 January 1952.

[10] Personal letter, 31 January 1956.

[11] CG FEAF 070735Z, July (paraphrased excerpt).

[12] Interview, 1 February 1956.

[13] Personal letter, 3 February 1956.

[14] General Mark W. Clark, *From the Danube to the Yalu,* p. 2-3.

[15] Walter Kerr, New York *Herald Tribune,* April 6, 1955.

[16] Personal letter, 3 February 1956.

[17] Personal interview, 30 January 1956.

Chapter 9

[1] Interview with authors, November 1955.

[2] *Summarized Report of Proceedings* No. 2, of 9 July 1950-29 July 1950, FO2FE/2960/24 of 22 November 1950, paragraph 44.

[3] ComCruDiv-5, War Diary, 19 July 1950.

[4] Personal correspondence with authors, dated 15 December 1950.

[5] Letter to authors, dated 8 January 1951.

[6] List of party: CDR W. B. Porter, USN; 2nd LT R. M. Johnson, USMC; Myron K. Lovejoy, GMC; Junior E. Wilson, GM3; Howard C. Scheunemann, GM3; Paul A. Keane, BM2; Willard L. Crider, PFC, USMC; Robert E. Dugan, PFC, USMC; Wm. J. Ghrist, PFC, USMC; and Jack L. Pope, PFC, USMC.

[7] Personal letter to authors, 28 March 1956. For a complete description of the interdiction campaign, see Chapter 8, "The Struggle to Strangle".

[8] *Battle Report, op. cit.,* p. 255.
[9] Letter to authors, dated 20 August 1952.
[10] Letter to authors, dated 24 January 1956.
[11] Interview, 28 February 1956.
[12] Those who wish to explore the Korean truce talks more fully should read, *How Communists Negotiate,* by Admiral C. Turner Joy, USN (Ret.).
[13] Letter to authors, 1 May 1956.
[14] Interview, 1 February 1956.
[15] Interview, 18 March 1956.
[16] Commanding General First Marine Division dispatch 150109Z, January 1952.
[17] Interview with authors, July 1955.
[18] *Summarized Report of Proceedings* No 2, 9 July 1950-29 July 1950, FO2FE/2960/24 of 22 November, 1950, paragraph 55.
[19] Personal letter to authors, 8 September 1955.
[20] CVG-2 Action Report, page 5, for 13 April 1952.
[21] Interview, 30 January 1956.
[22] Personal interview, 22 August 1955.
[23] Interview, 27 February 1956.
[24] Letter to authors, dated 23 September 1955.
[25] Interview, July 1955.
[26] Personal letter to authors, 24 January 1956.
[27] CTG 95.1 report, dated 25 May 1952.
[28] Personal letter from Rear Admiral Smith, 24 January 1956.

Chapter 10

[1] VP-42 historical report.
[2] Letter to authors, 3 April 1956.

Chapter 11

[1] General Mark W. Clark, *From the Danube to the Yalu.*
[2] Commander Joint Amphibious Task Force Seven OpPlan 22A-52.
[3] CTF 90 action report for Kojo operations, 18 October 1952.
[4] Com7thFlt endorsement on CTF 90 action report, 10 December 1952.
[5] Interview with authors, 13 April 1956.
[6] *Bon Homme Richard's* action report, dated 15 October 1952.
[7] ComCarDiv-5 (CTF77) serial 099, dated 31 October 1952.
[8] Com7thFlt report of Kojo operation, 25 January 1953.
[9] Com7thFlt action report, dated 25 January 1953.

Chapter 12

[1] Personal letter to authors, dated 20 August 1952.
[2] Personal letter to authors, dated 10 August 1955.
[3] Personal letter to authors, dated 15 August 1955.
[4] Personal interview and letter, 1 February 1956.
[5] Personal letter to authors, dated 10 August 1955.
[6] Interview, July 1955.
[7] Personal letter, dated 2 September 1955.
[8] Personal letter, 9 February 1956.
[9] Interview, 22 August 1955.
[10] Interview, 10 December 1955.
[11] Interview, 27 February 1956.
[12] Personal letter to authors, 10 September 1955.
[13] Interview, 21 March 1956.

Chapter 13

[1] Interview, 7 January 1956.

[2] *Interlocking Subversion in Government Departments.* Hearing before the Subcommittee on the Judiciary, U. S. Senate, 83rd Congress, Second Session, Testimony of General Mark W. Clark, August 10, 1954, p. 1697. Also refer to General Clark's book, *From the Danube to the Yalu,* pages 70-73.

[3] Interview, 1 February 1956.

[4] Interview, 13 February 1956.

[5] Personal letter, 23 February 1956.

[6] Interview, 30 August 1955.

[7] VF-193 Historical Report.

[8] Interview, 7 September 1955.

[9] Interview, October 1955.

[10] Interview, 1 February 1956.

[11] Interview, 15 February 1956.

[12] A VT-fuzed bomb is one which bursts into hundreds of fragments close to the ground. It is a particularly good weapon for anti-personnel work.

[13] Personal interview, 30 January 1956.

[14] Interview, 15 February 1956.

[15] Interview, 14 February 1956.

[16] Interview, 17 July 1956.

[17] Interview, 17 July 1956.

[18] Personal letter, dated 11 October 1955.

[19] Personal letter, dated 26 September 1955.

[20] Interview, 1 February 1956.

[21] *The New York Times,* June 9, 1953.

[22] *The Sun,* Baltimore, June 17, 1953.

[23] Interview, 14 February 1956.

[24] Interview, 30 January 1956.

[25] Interview, 14 February 1956.

Index

The Naval Institute Press is the book-publishing arm of the U.S. Naval Institute, a private, nonprofit, membership society for sea service professionals and others who share an interest in naval and maritime affairs. Established in 1873 at the U.S. Naval Academy in Annapolis, Maryland, where its offices remain today, the Naval Institute has members worldwide.

Members of the Naval Institute support the education programs of the society and receive the influential monthly magazine *Proceedings* and discounts on fine nautical prints and on ship and aircraft photos. They also have access to the transcripts of the Institute's Oral History Program and get discounted admission to any of the Institute-sponsored seminars offered around the country.

The Naval Institute also publishes *Naval History* magazine. This colorful bimonthly is filled with entertaining and thought-provoking articles, first-person reminiscences, and dramatic art and photography. Members receive a discount on *Naval History* subscriptions.

The Naval Institute's book-publishing program, begun in 1898 with basic guides to naval practices, has broadened its scope in recent years to include books of more general interest. Now the Naval Institute Press publishes about one hundred titles each year, ranging from how-to books on boating and navigation to battle histories, biographies, ship and aircraft guides, and novels. Institute members receive discounts of 20 to 50 percent on the Press's more than eight hundred books in print.

Full-time students are eligible for special half-price membership rates. Life memberships are also available.

For a free catalog describing Naval Institute Press books currently available, and for further information about subscribing to *Naval History* magazine or about joining the U.S. Naval Institute, please write to:

Membership Department
U.S. Naval Institute
291 Wood Road
Annapolis, MD 21402-5034
Telephone: (800) 233-8764
Fax: (410) 269-7940
Web address: www.usni.org